JAAatpl
JOINT AVIATION AUTHORITIES

Theoretical Training Manuals

Revised Edition

PRINCIPLES OF FLIGHT

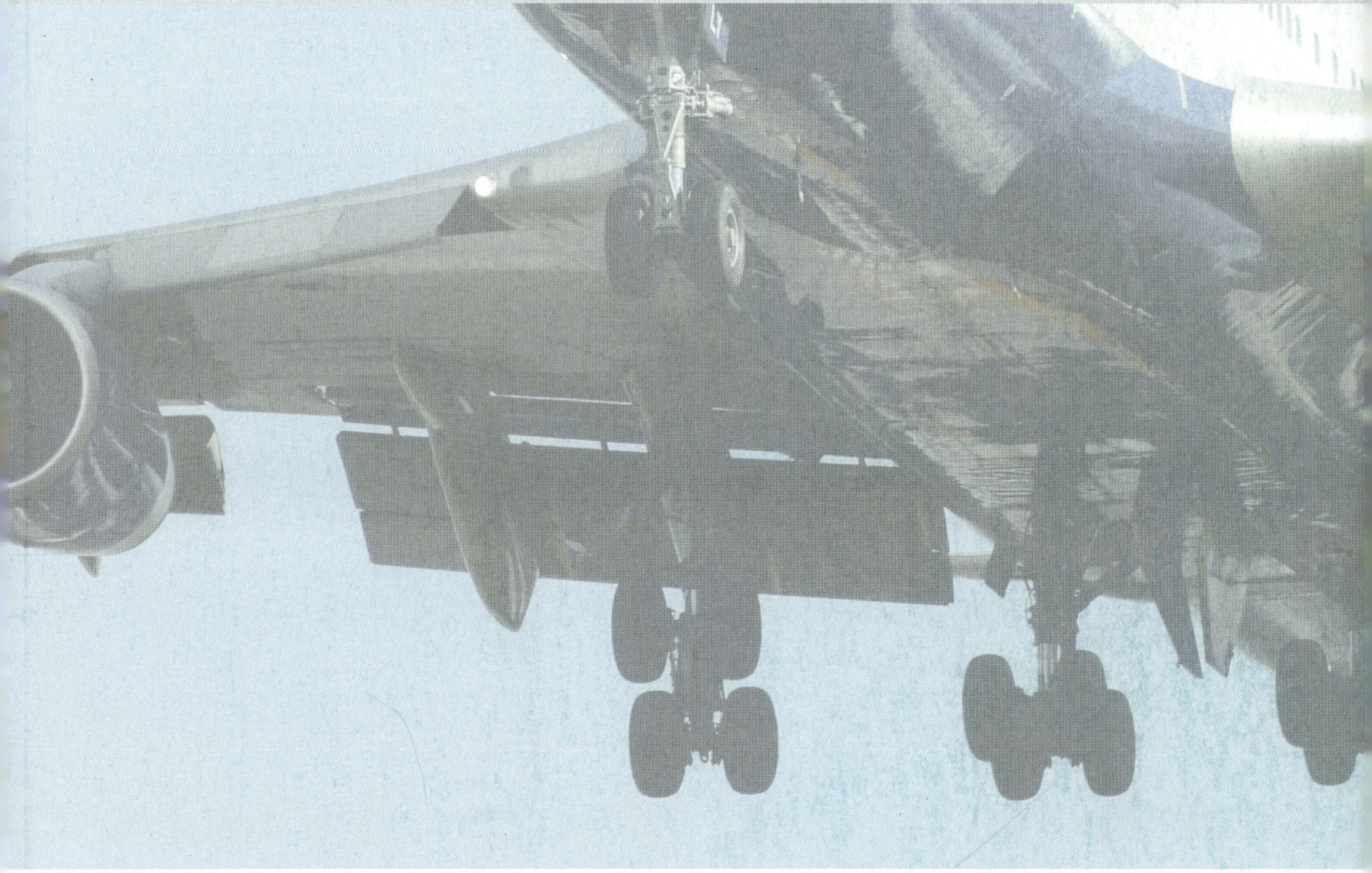

This learning material has been approved as JAA compliant by the United Kingdom Civil Aviation Authority

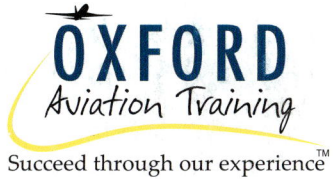
Succeed through our experience

© Oxford Aviation Services Limited 2005
All Rights Reserved

This text book is to be used only for the purpose of private study by individuals and may not be reproduced in any form or medium, copied, stored in a retrieval system, lent, hired, rented, transmitted or adapted in whole or in part without the prior written consent of Oxford Aviation Services Limited.

Copyright in all documents and materials bound within these covers or attached hereto, excluding that material which is reproduced by the kind permission of third parties and acknowledged as such, belongs exclusively to Oxford Aviation Services Limited.

Certain copyright material is reproduced with the permission of the International Civil Aviation Organisation, the United Kingdom Civil Aviation Authority and the Joint Aviation Authorities (JAA).

This text book has been written and published as a reference work to assist students enrolled on an approved JAA Air Transport Pilot Licence (ATPL) course to prepare themselves for the JAA ATPL theoretical knowledge examinations. Nothing in the content of this book is to be interpreted as constituting instruction or advice relating to practical flying.

Whilst every effort has been made to ensure the accuracy of the information contained within this book, neither Oxford Aviation Services Limited nor the publisher gives any warranty as to its accuracy or otherwise. Students preparing for the JAA ATPL theoretical knowledge examinations should not regard this book as a substitute for the JAA ATPL theoretical knowledge training syllabus published in the current edition of 'JAR-FCL 1 Flight Crew Licensing (Aeroplanes)' (the Syllabus). The Syllabus constitutes the sole authoritative definition of the subject matter to be studied in a JAA ATPL theoretical knowledge training programme. No student should prepare for, or is currently entitled to enter himself/herself for the JAA ATPL theoretical knowledge examinations without first being enrolled in a training school which has been granted approval by a JAA-authorised national aviation authority to deliver JAA ATPL training.

Oxford Aviation Services Limited excludes all liability for any loss or damage incurred or suffered as a result of any reliance on all or part of this book except for any liability for death or personal injury resulting from Oxford Aviation Services Limited's negligence or any other liability which may not legally be excluded.

Cover photo by Derek Pedley: www.airteamimages.com

First published by Jeppesen GmbH, Frankfurt, Germany: 2001
Second edition: Jeppesen GmbH, Frankfurt, Germany: 2002

This edition published by Transair (UK) Ltd, Shoreham, England: 2005
Printed in Singapore by KHL Printing Co. Pte Ltd

Contact Details:

Ground Training Department
Oxford Aviation Services Ltd
Oxford Airport
Kidlington
Oxford OX5 1RA
England

Tel: +44 (0)1865 844299
E-mail: ddd@oxfordaviation.net

Transair Pilot Shop
Transair (UK) Limited
Shoreham Airport
Shoreham-by-Sea
West Sussex BN43 5PA
England

Tel: +44 (0)1273 466000
E-mail: info@transair.co.uk

For further information on products and services from Oxford Aviation Training and Transair visit our websites at: www.oxfordaviation.net and www.transair.co.uk

FOREWORD

Joint Aviation Authorities (JAA) pilot licences were first introduced in 1999, and have now been adopted by nearly all member states. A steadily increasing number of non-European countries have also expressed the intention of aligning their training with JAA requirements, and some have already begun this process. The syllabi and the regulations governing the award and the renewal of licences are currently defined by the JAA's licensing agency, known as "Joint Aviation Requirements-Flight Crew Licensing", or JAR-FCL. Over the next few years, JAA responsibilities, including licensing, will gradually be transferred to the new European Aviation Safety Agency (EASA).

The JAR-FCL ATPL theoretical training requirements and associated ground examinations, although possibly similar in scope to those previously used by many national authorities, are inevitably different in a number of respects from the syllabi and examinations previously used under national schemes. Consequently, students who wish to train for the JAA ATPL licence need access to study material which has been specifically designed to meet the requirements of the new licensing system. This series of text books, prepared by Oxford Aviation Training (OAT) and published exclusively by Transair Pilot Shop, covers all JAR-FCL requirements and is specifically designed to help student pilots prepare for the ATPL theoretical knowledge examinations.

OAT is one of the world's leading professional pilot schools. Established for 40 years, Oxford has trained more than 14,000 professional pilots for over 80 airlines, world-wide. OAT was the first pilot school in the United Kingdom to be granted approval to train for the JAA ATPL and has been the leading contributor within Europe to the process of defining and improving the training syllabus. OAT led and coordinated the joint-European effort to produce the ATPL Learning Objectives which are now published by the JAA as the definitive guide to the theoretical knowledge requirements of ATPL training.

Since JAA ATPL training started in 1999, OAT has achieved an unsurpassed success rate in the JAA ATPL examinations. At the start of this year, OAT students had successfully passed more than 25,000 individual JAR-FCL examinations and currently more than 300 students a year graduate from Oxford's theoretical training programmes. The text books, together with an increasing range of Computer Based Training (CBT) products, are also now used by other Flight Training Organizations both in Europe and increasingly, throughout the world. Recognized by leading National Aviation Authorities as being fully compliant with JAR-FCL training requirements, the series has now effectively become the de-facto standard for JAR-FCL ATPL theoretical training. This achievement is the result of OAT's continued commitment to the development of the JAA licensing system. OAT's unrivalled experience and expertise make these books the best learning material available to any student who aspires to hold a JAA ATPL. The series is continually updated, with this year's edition incorporating specimen examination papers and "feedback" information, all specifically intended to help candidates prepare fully for their ATPL theoretical examinations

For those aspirant airline pilots who are not yet able to begin training but hope to do so in the future, these text books provide high-quality study material to help them prepare thoroughly for their formal training. The books also make excellent reading for general aviation pilots or for aviation enthusiasts who simply wish to further their knowledge of aeronautical subjects. We trust that your study of these books will not only be enjoyable but, for those of you currently undergoing ATPL training, will also lead to success in the JAA ATPL ground examinations.

Whatever your aviation ambitions, we wish you every success and above all, happy landings.

Mike Langley
Commercial Director

Oxford Aviation Training
March 2005

Textbook Series

Book	Title	JAR Ref. No.	Subject
1	010 Air Law	010	
2	020 Aircraft General Knowledge 1	021 01	Airframes & Systems
		021 01 01/04	Fuselage, Wings & Stabilising Surfaces
		021 01 07	Hydraulics
		021 01 05	Landing Gear
		021 01 06	Flight Controls
		021 01 08/09	Air Systems & Air Conditioning
		021 01 09/10	Anti-icing & De-icing
		021 04 00	Emergency Equipment
		021 01 11	Fuel Systems
3	020 Aircraft General Knowledge 2	021 02	Electrics – Electronics
		021 02 01	Direct Current
		021 02 02	Alternating Current
		021 02 05	Basic Radio Propagation.
4	020 Aircraft General Knowledge 3	021 00	Powerplant
		021 03 01	Piston Engines
		021 03 02	Gas Turbines
5	020 Aircraft General Knowledge 4	022	Instrumentation
		022 01	Flight Instruments
		022 03	Warning & Recording
		022 02	Automatic Flight Control
		022 04	Power Plant & System Monitoring Instruments
6	030 Flight Performance & Planning 1	031	Mass & Balance
		032	Performance
7	030 Flight Performance & Planning 2	033	Flight Planning & Monitoring
8	040 Human Performance & Limitations	040	
9	050 Meteorology	050	
10	060 Navigation 1	061	General Navigation
11	060 Navigation 2	062	Radio Navigation
12	070 Operational Procedures	070	
13	080 Principles of Flight	080	
14	090 Communications	091	VFR Communications
		092	IFR Communications
15	Reference Material		CAP 696, CAP 697, CAP 698
			Aerodrome Information
			JAR FCL 1 Subpart J

PRINCIPLES OF FLIGHT

TABLE OF CONTENTS

Chapter 1	Overview and Definitions
Chapter 2	The Atmosphere
Chapter 3	Basic Aerodynamic Theory
Chapter 4	Subsonic Airflow
Chapter 5	Lift
Chapter 6	Drag
Chapter 7	Stalling
Chapter 8	High Lift Devices
Chapter 9	Airframe Contamination
Chapter 10	Stability and Control
Chapter 11	Controls
Chapter 12	Flight Mechanics
Chapter 13	High Speed Flight
Chapter 14	Limitations
Chapter 15	Windshear
Chapter 16	Propellers
Chapter 17	Specimen Questions

CHAPTER 1 - OVERVIEW AND DEFINITIONS

Contents

	Page
OVERVIEW	1 - 1
GENERAL DEFINITIONS	
MASS	1 - 5
FORCE	
WEIGHT	
CENTRE OF GRAVITY	
WORK	1 - 6
POWER	
ENERGY	
KINETIC ENERGY	
NEWTON'S FIRST LAW OF MOTION	1 - 7
INERTIA	
NEWTON'S SECOND LAW OF MOTION	
VELOCITY	
ACCELERATION	
MOMENTUM	1 - 8
NEWTON'S THIRD LAW OF MOTION	
GLOSSARY	1 - 9
LIST OF SYMBOLS	1 - 14
SELF ASSESSMENT QUESTIONS	1 - 15

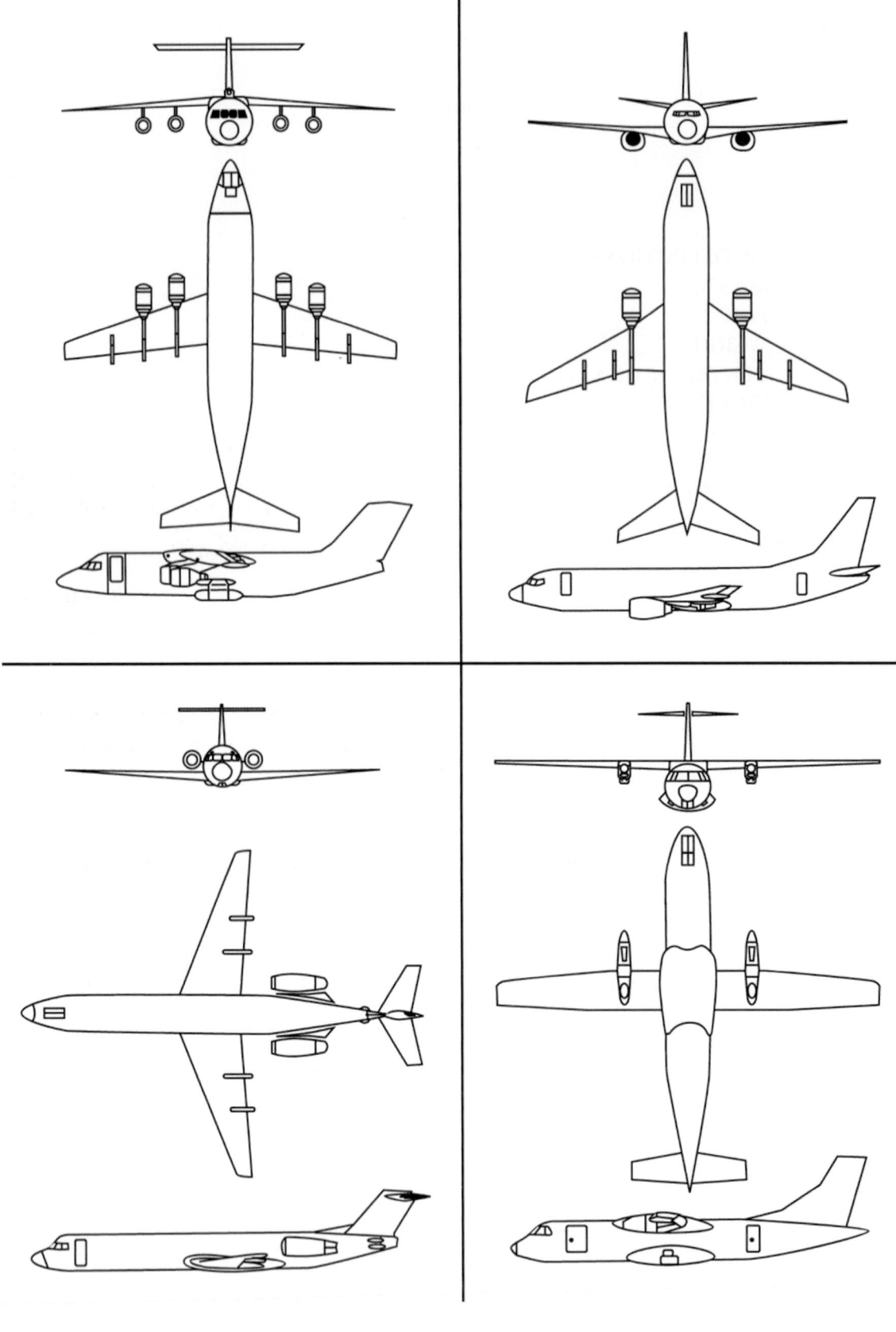

PRINCIPLES OF FLIGHT   **OVERVIEW AND DEFINITIONS**

1.1 OVERVIEW

The primary requirements of an aircraft are as follows:

(a) A wing to generate a lift force.

(b) A fuselage to house the payload.

(c) Tail surfaces to add stability.

(d) Control surfaces to change the direction of flight and,

(e) Engines to make it go forward.

The process of lift generation is fairly straightforward and easy to understand. Over the years aircraft designers, aerodynamicists and structural engineers have refined the basics and by subtle changes of shape and configuration have made maximum use of the current understanding of the physical properties of air to produce aircraft best suited to a particular role.

Aircraft come in different shapes and sizes, usually, each designed for a specific task. All aircraft share certain features, but to obtain the performance required by the operator the designer will configure each type of aeroplane in a specific way.

As can be seen from the illustrations on the facing page, the position of the features shared by all types of aircraft - i.e. wings, fuselage, tail surfaces and engines varies from type to type.

Why are wing plan shapes different?

Why are wings mounted sometimes on top of the fuselage instead of the bottom?

Why are wings mounted in that position and at that angle?

Why is the horizontal stabiliser mounted sometimes high on top of the fin rather than on either side of the rear fuselage?

Every feature has a purpose and is never included merely for reasons of style.

An aeroplane, like all bodies, has mass. With the aircraft stationary on the ground it has only the force due to the acceleration of gravity acting upon it. This force, its WEIGHT, acts vertically downward at all times.

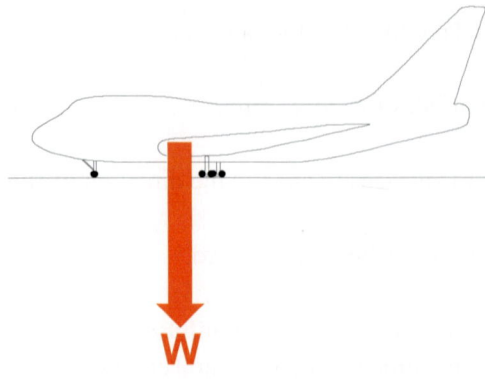

Figure 1.1 The Force of Weight

Before an aeroplane can leave the ground and fly the force of weight must be balanced by a force which acts upwards. This force is called LIFT. The lift force must be increased until it is the same as the aeroplane's weight.

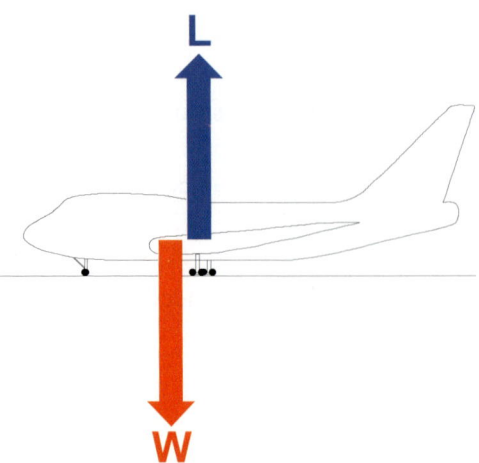

Figure 1.2 The Forces of Weight and Lift

PRINCIPLES OF FLIGHT — OVERVIEW AND DEFINITIONS

To generate a lift force the aeroplane must be propelled forward through the air by a force called THRUST, provided by the engine(s).

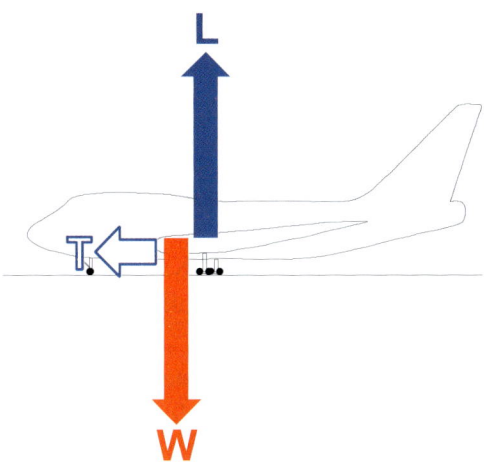

Figure 1.3 The Forces of Weight, Lift and Thrust

From the very moment the aeroplane begins to move, air resists its forward motion with a force called DRAG.

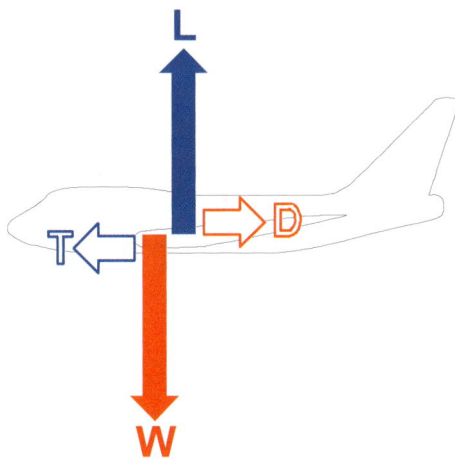

Figure 1.4 The Forces of Weight, Lift, Thrust and Drag

PRINCIPLES OF FLIGHT   **OVERVIEW AND DEFINITIONS**

When an aeroplane is moving there are four main forces acting upon it:-

> WEIGHT, LIFT, THRUST and DRAG.

These are all closely interrelated. i.e.:-

> The greater the weight - the greater the lift requirement.
>
> The greater the lift - the greater the drag.
>
> The greater the drag - the greater the thrust required, and so on...

Air has properties which change with altitude. Knowledge of these variables, together with their effect on an aeroplane, is a prerequisite for a full understanding of the principles of flight.

The structural and aerodynamic design of an aeroplane is a masterpiece of compromise. An improvement in one area frequently leads to a loss of efficiency in another.

An aeroplane does not 'grip' the air as a car does the road. An aeroplane is often not pointing in the same direction in which it is moving.

PRINCIPLES OF FLIGHT OVERVIEW AND DEFINITIONS

1.2 GENERAL DEFINITIONS

Mass

Unit - Kilogram (kg) - 'The quantity of matter in a body.' The mass of a body is a measure of how difficult it is to start or stop. ("a body", in this context, means a substance. Any substance; a gas, a liquid or a solid).

e.g. (a) The larger the mass, the greater the FORCE required to start or stop it in the same distance.

(b) Mass has a big influence on the time and/or distance required to change the direction of a body.

Force

Unit - Newton (N) - 'A push or a pull'. That which causes or tends to cause a change in motion of a body.

There are four forces acting on an aircraft in flight - pushing or pulling in different directions.

Weight

Unit - Newton (N) - 'The force due to gravity'. ($F = m \times g$)
Where (m) is the mass of the object and (g) is the acceleration due to the gravity constant, which has the value of $9 \cdot 81$ m/s^2. (A 1 kg mass "weighs" $9 \cdot 81$ newtons)

e.g. If the mass of a B737 is 60,000 kg
and $F = m \times g$
it is necessary to generate: [60,000 kg x 9.81 m/s^2]
588,600 N of lift force.

Centre of Gravity (CG)

The point through which the weight of an aircraft acts.

(a) An aircraft in flight is said to rotate around its CG.

(b) The CG of an aircraft must remain within certain forward and aft limits, for reasons of both stability and control.

Work

Unit - Joule (J) - A force is said to do work on a body when it moves the body in the direction in which the force is acting. The amount of work done on a body is the product of the force applied to the body and the distance moved by that force in the direction in which it is acting. If a force is exerted and no movement takes place, no work has been done.

e.g. (a) Work = Force x Distance (through which the force is applied)

(b) If a force of 10 Newton's moves a body 2 metres along its line of action it does 20 Newton metres (Nm) of work. [10 N x 2 m = 20 Nm]

(c) A Newton metre, the unit of work, is called a joule (J).

Power   *Rate*

Unit - Watt (W) - Power is simply the rate of doing work. (the time taken to do work)

e.g. (a) $$\text{Power (W)} = \frac{\text{Force (N) x Distance (m)}}{\text{Time (s)}}$$

(b) If a force of 10 N moves a mass 2 metres in 5 seconds, then the power is 4 Joules per second. A Joule per second (J/s) is called a Watt (W), the unit of power. So the power used in this example is 4 Watts.

Energy

Unit - Joule (J) - Mass has energy if it has the ability to do work. The amount of energy a body possesses is measured by the amount of work it can do. The unit of energy will therefore be the same as those of work, joules.

Kinetic Energy

Unit - Joule (J) - 'The energy possessed by mass because of its motion'. 'A mass that is moving can do work in coming to rest'.

$$KE = \tfrac{1}{2} m V^2 \text{ joules}$$

The kinetic energy of a 1 kg mass of air moving at 52 m/s (100 knots) is 1352 joules; it possesses 1352 joules of kinetic energy. [0.5 x 1 x 52 x 52 = 1352 J]
From the above example it can be seen that doubling the velocity will have a greater impact on the kinetic energy than doubling the mass. (velocity is squared).

Newton's First Law of Motion

'A body will remain at rest or in uniform motion in a straight line unless acted on by an external force'.

To move a stationary object or to make a moving object change its direction a force must be applied.

Inertia

'The opposition which a body offers to a change in motion'. A property of all bodies. Inertia is a quality, but measured in terms of mass, which is a quantity.

e.g. (a) The larger the mass, the greater the force required for the same result.

(b) A large mass has a lot of inertia.

(c) Inertia refers to both stationary and moving masses.

Newton's Second Law of Motion

'The **acceleration** of a body from a state of rest, or uniform motion in a straight line, is proportional to the applied force and inversely proportional to the mass'.

Velocity

Unit - Metres per second (m/s). - 'Rate of change of displacement'

Acceleration

Unit - Metres per second per second (m/s^2) - 'Rate of change of velocity'.
A force of 1 newton acting on a mass of 1 kg will produce an acceleration of 1 m/s^2

$$\text{Acceleration} = \frac{\text{Force}}{\text{Mass}}$$

e.g. (a) For the same mass; the bigger the force, the greater the acceleration.

(b) For the same force; the larger the mass, the slower the acceleration.

Momentum

Unit - Mass x Velocity (kg-m/s) - 'The quantity of motion possessed by a body'. The tendency of a body to continue in motion after being placed in motion.

e.g. (a) A body of 10 kg mass moving at 2 m/s has 20 kg-m/s of momentum.

(b) At the same velocity, a large mass has more momentum than a small mass.

Newton's Third Law

'Every action has an equal and opposite reaction'

e.g. (a) If a force accelerates a mass in one direction, the body supplying the force will be subject to the same force in the opposite direction.

1.3 GLOSSARY

Aerofoil - A body so shaped as to produce aerodynamic reaction normal to the direction of its motion through the air without excessive drag.

Aft - To the rear, back or tail of the aircraft.

Air brake - Any device primarily used to increase drag of an aircraft at will.

Ambient - Surrounding or pertaining to the immediate environment.

Amplitude - Largeness; abundance; width; range; extent of repetitive movement (from extreme to extreme).

Attitude - The nose-up or nose-down orientation of an aircraft relative to the horizon.

Boundary Layer - The thin layer of air adjacent to a surface, in which the viscous forces are dominant.

Buffeting - An irregular oscillation of any part of an aircraft produced and maintained directly by an eddying flow.

Cantilever (wing) - A wing whose only attachment to the fuselage is by fittings at the wing root, has no external struts or bracing. The attachments are faired-in to preserve the streamline shape

Control lock (Gust lock) - A mechanical device designed to safeguard, by positive lock, the control surfaces and flying control system against damage in high winds or gusts when the aircraft is parked.

Control Reversal - At high speed: the displacement of a control surface producing a moment on the aircraft in a reverse sense because of excessive structural distortion. At low speed: the displacement of an aileron increasing the angle of attack of one wing to or beyond the critical angle, causing a roll in the direction opposite to that required.

Convergent - Tend towards or meet in one point or value.

Critical Mach number (M_{CRIT}) - The free stream Mach number at which the peak velocity on the surface of a body first becomes equal to the local speed of sound.

Damping - To slow down the rate; to diminish the amplitude of vibrations or cycles.

Geometric Dihedral - The angle between the horizontal datum of an aeroplane and the plane of a wing or horizontal stabiliser semi-span.

Divergent - To incline or turn apart. **Divergence** - A disturbance which increases continually with time.

Eddy - An element of air having intense vorticity.

Effective Angle of Attack (α_e) - The angle between the chord line and the mean direction of a non-uniform disturbed airstream.

Equilibrium - A condition that exists when the sum of all moments acting on a body is zero AND the sum of all forces acting on a body is zero.

Fairing - A secondary structure added to any part to reduce its drag.

Feel - The sensations of force and displacement experienced by the pilot from the aerodynamic forces on the control surfaces.

Fence - A projection from the surface of the wing and extending chordwise to modify the wing surface pressure distribution.

Fillet - A fairing at the junction of two surfaces to improve the airflow.

Flightpath - The path of the Centre of Gravity (CG) of an aircraft.

Fluid - A substance, either gaseous or liquid, that will conform to the shape of the container that holds it.

Free stream velocity - The velocity of the undisturbed air relative to the aircraft.

Gradient (Pressure) - Rate of change in pressure with distance.

Gust - A rapid variation, with time or distance, in the speed or direction of air.

Gust lock - See control lock.

Instability - The quality whereby any disturbance from steady motion tends to increase.

Laminar Flow - Flow in which there is no mixing between adjacent layers.

Load Factor - The ratio of the weight of an aircraft to the load imposed by lift. The correct symbol for load factor is (n), but is colloquially known as (g).

$$\text{Load Factor} = \frac{\text{Lift}}{\text{Weight}}$$

Mach Number (M) - The ratio of the True Air Speed to the speed of sound under prevailing atmospheric conditions.

$$M = \frac{TAS}{\text{Local Speed of Sound (a)}}$$

Magnitude - Largeness; size; importance.

Moment (N-m) - The moment of a force about a point is the product of the force and the distance through which it acts. The distance in the moment is merely a leverage and no movement is involved, so moments cannot be measured in joules.

Nacelle - A streamlined structure on a wing for housing engines (usually).

Normal - Perpendicular; at 90°.

Oscillation - Swinging to and fro like a pendulum; a vibration; variation between certain limits; fluctuation.

Parallel - Lines which run in the same direction and which will never meet or cross.

Pitot tube - A tube, with an open end facing up-stream, wherein at speeds less than about four tenths the speed of sound the pressure is equal to the total pressure. For practical purposes, total pressure may be regarded as equal to pitot pressure at this stage.

Pod - A nacelle supported externally from a fuselage or wing.

Propagate - To pass on; to transmit; to spread from one to another.

Relative Airflow, (Relative Wind), (Free Stream Flow) - The direction of airflow produced by the aircraft moving through the air. The relative airflow flows in a direction parallel and opposite to the direction of flight. Therefore, the actual flight path of the aircraft determines the direction of the relative airflow. Also, air in a region where pressure, temperature and relative velocity are unaffected by the passage of the aircraft through it.

Scale - If a 1/10th scale model is considered, all the linear dimensions are 1/10th of the real aircraft, but the areas are 1/100th; and if the model is constructed of the same materials, the mass is 1/1000th of the real aircraft. So the model is to scale in some respects, but not others.

Schematic - A diagrammatic outline or synopsis; an image of the thing; representing something by a diagram.

Separation - Detachment of the airflow from a surface with which it has been in contact.

Shockwave - A narrow region, crossing the streamlines, through which there occur abrupt increases in pressure, density, and temperature, and an abrupt decrease in velocity. The normal component of velocity relative to the shock wave is supersonic upstream and subsonic downstream.

Side-slip - Motion of an aircraft, relative to the relative airflow, which has a component of velocity along the lateral axis.

Slat - An auxiliary, cambered aerofoil positioned forward of the main aerofoil so as to form a slot.

Spar - A principal spanwise structural member of a wing, tailplane, fin or control surface.

Speed - Metres per second (m/s) is used in most formulae, but nautical miles per hour or knots (kt) are commonly used to measure the speed of an aircraft. There are 6080 ft in 1 nautical mile and 3.28 ft in 1 metre.

Speed of Sound (a) - Sound is pressure waves which propagate spherically through the atmosphere from their source. The speed of propagation varies ONLY with the temperature of the air. The lower the temperature, the lower the speed of propagation. On a 'standard' day at sea level the speed of sound is approximately 340 m/s (660 kt TAS).

Stability - The quality whereby any disturbance of steady motion tends to decrease.

Stagnation point - A point where streamlines are divided by a body and where the fluid speed is zero, relative to the surface.

Static vent - A small aperture in a plate fixed to form part of the fuselage and located appropriately for measuring the ambient static pressure.

Throat - A section of minimum area in a duct.

True Air Speed (TAS) or (V) - The speed at which the aircraft is travelling through the air.

Turbulent Flow - Flow in which irregular fluctuations with time are superimposed on a mean flow.

Velocity - The same as speed, but with direction specified as well.

Viscosity - The resistance of fluid particles to flow over each other. All fluids have the property of viscosity. A fluid with high viscosity would not flow very easily. The viscosity of air is low in comparison to something like syrup, but the viscosity that air does have is a very important consideration when studying aerodynamics.

Vortex - A region of fluid in circulatory motion, having a core of intense vorticity, the strength of the vortex being given by its circulation.

PRINCIPLES OF FLIGHT

OVERVIEW AND DEFINITIONS

Vortex generator - A device, often a small vane attached to a surface, to produce one or more discrete vortices which trail downstream adjacent to the surface, promote mixing in the boundary layer and delay boundary layer separation. (Increases the kinetic energy of the boundary layer).

Vorticity - Generally, rotational motion in a fluid, defined, at any point in the fluid, as twice the mean angular velocity of a small element of fluid surrounding the point.

Wake - The region of air behind an aircraft in which the total pressure has been changed by the presence of the aircraft.

Wash-out - Decrease in angle of incidence towards the tip of a wing or other aerofoil.

Wing Loading - Ratio of aircraft weight to wing area.

$$\text{Wing Loading} = \frac{\text{Aircraft Weight}}{\text{Wing Area}}$$

Zoom - Using kinetic energy to gain height.

1.4 LIST OF SYMBOLS

The following symbols are used throughout these notes. However, no universal defining standard for their use exists. Other books on the subject may use some of these symbols with different definitions. Every effort has been made to employ symbols that are widely accepted and that conform to the JAA Learning Objectives.

a	speed of sound	m	mass
AC	aerodynamic centre	n	load factor
AR	aspect ratio	p	pressure
b	span	Q or q	dynamic pressure
C	Centigrade	S	area; wing area
c	chord length	T	temperature
C_D	drag coefficient	t/c	thickness-chord ratio
CG	centre of gravity	V	free stream speed (TAS)
CP	centre of pressure	Vs	stall speed
C_L	lift coefficient	W	weight
Cm	pitching moment coefficient		
D	drag		
Di	induced drag		
F	force		
g	acceleration due to gravity also used for load factor		
K	Kelvin		
L	lift		
L/D	lift to drag ratio		
M	Mach number		

GREEK SYMBOLS

α	(alpha) angle of attack
β	(beta) sideslip angle
γ	(gamma) angle of climb or descent
Δ	(delta) increment in
μ	(mu) Mach angle
ρ	(rho) density
σ	(sigma) relative density
φ	(phi) angle of bank

OTHERS

∝	proportional to
≑	is approximately equal to

NB. The Greek symbol γ (gamma) has been used in these notes to denote angle of climb and descent. The JAA Learning Objectives use θ (theta). Evidence exists that a question in the exam uses γ (gamma) for angle of climb and descent. The notes have been amended to use γ, but consider either γ or θ to indicate angle of climb and descent. (15th Sept 2000).

PRINCIPLES OF FLIGHT **OVERVIEW AND DEFINITIONS**

SELF ASSESSMENT QUESTIONS

Aircraft (1)
Mass: 2,000 kilograms (kg)
Engine thrust: 4,000 Newtons (N)
V_1 speed: 65 knots (kt)
Take-off run to reach V_1: 750 metres (m)
Time taken to reach V_1: 30 seconds (s)

Aircraft (2)
Mass: 2,000 kilograms (kg)
Engine thrust: 8,000 Newtons (N)
V_1 speed: 130 knots (kt)
Take-off run to reach V_1: 1,500 metres (m)
Time taken to reach V_1: 40 seconds (s)

where, 1 nautical mile = 6080 ft and 1 metre = 3.28 ft

At V_1 both aircraft experience an engine failure and take-off is abandoned.

a) How much work was done to aircraft (1) getting to V_1

b) How much power was used to get aircraft (1) to V_1

c) How much work was done to aircraft (2) getting to V_1

d) How much power was used to get aircraft (2) to V_1

e) How much momentum does aircraft (1) possess at V_1

f) How much momentum does aircraft (2) possess at V_1

g) How many times greater is the momentum of aircraft (2)

h) How much kinetic energy does aircraft (1) possess at V_1

i) How much kinetic energy does aircraft (2) possess at V_1

j) How many times greater is the kinetic energy of aircraft (2)

k) State the mass and velocity relationship of both aircraft and compare to their momentum and kinetic energy

l) Which has the greater effect on kinetic energy, mass or velocity

m) What must be done with the kinetic energy so the aircraft can be brought to a stop

1. An aircraft's mass is a result of:

    a) Its weight
    b) How big it is
    c) How much matter it contains
    d) Its volume

2. The unit of mass is the:

    a) Joule
    b) Watt
    c) Newton
    d) Kilogram

3. The definition of a force is:

    a) That which causes a reaction to take place
    b) Thrust and drag only
    c) A push or a pull
    d) The result of an applied input

4. The unit of force is the:

    a) Mass-kilogram
    b) Newton-metre
    c) Joule
    d) Newton

5. The unit of weight is the:

    a) Kilogram
    b) Newton
    c) Watt
    d) Kilowatt

6. Weight is the result of:

    a) The force on mass due to gravity
    b) The action of a falling mass
    c) How much matter the object contains
    d) The rate of mass per unit area

7. About which point does an aircraft rotate:

   a) The wings
   b) The main undercarriage
   c) The centre of gravity
   d) The rudder

8. If a force is applied to a mass and the mass does not move:

   a) Work is done even though there is no movement of the mass
   b) Work is done only if the mass moves a long way
   c) Power is exerted, but no work is done
   d) No work is done

9. The unit of work is called the:

   a) Pascal
   b) Joule
   c) Watt
   d) Kilogram

10. The unit of power is called the:

    a) Joule
    b) Newton-metre
    c) Watt
    d) Metre per second

11. If a force of 20 Newton's moves a mass 5 metres:

    1 - the work done is 100 Nm
    2 - the work done is 100 Joules
    3 - the work done is 4 Joules
    4 - the work done is 0.25 Joules

    The correct statements are:

    a) 1 only
    b) 1 and 3
    c) 1 and 2
    d) 2 only

12. If a force of 50 Newton's is applied to a 10 kg mass and the mass moves 10 metres and a force of 50 Newton's is applied to a 100 kg mass which moves 10 metres:

    a) The work done is the same in both cases
    b) Less work is done to the 10 kg mass
    c) More work is done to the 10 kg mass
    d) More work is done to the 100 kg mass

13. The definition of power is:

    a) The rate of force applied
    b) The rate of movement per second
    c) The rate of doing work
    d) The rate of applied force

14. If a force of 500 Newton's moves a mass 1000 metres in 2 mins, the power used is:

    a) 4167 Watts
    b) 250 Kilowatts
    c) 1 Megawatt
    d) 4 Watts

15. Kinetic energy is:

    a) The energy a mass possesses due to its position in space
    b) The energy a mass possesses when a force has been applied
    c) The energy a mass possesses due to the force of gravity
    d) The energy a mass possesses because of its motion

16. The unit of kinetic energy is the:

    a) Joule
    b) Metre per second
    c) Watt
    d) Newton-metre per second

PRINCIPLES OF FLIGHT   OVERVIEW AND DEFINITIONS

17. When considering kinetic energy:

   1 - a moving mass can apply a force by being brought to rest
   2 - kinetic energy is the energy possessed by a body because of its motion
   3 - if a body's kinetic energy is increased, a force must have been applied
   4 - kinetic energy = ½ m V² joules

   The combination of correct statements is:

   a)   1 and 2
   b)   1, 2, 3 and 4
   c)   4 only
   d)   2 and 4

18. The property of inertia is said to be:

   a)   The energy possessed by a body because of its motion
   b)   The opposition which a body offers to a change in motion
   c)   That every action has an equal and opposite reaction
   d)   The quantity of motion possessed by a body

19. Considering Newton's first law of motion:

   1 - a body is said to have energy if it has the ability to do work
   2 - the amount of energy a body possesses is measured by the amount of work it can do
   3 - a body will tend to remain at rest, or in uniform motion in a straight line, unless acted upon by an external force
   4 - to move a stationary object or to make a moving object change its direction, a force must be applied

   The combination with the correct statements is:

   a)   3 and 4
   b)   3 only
   c)   1 and 2
   d)   1, 2, 3 and 4

PRINCIPLES OF FLIGHT   **OVERVIEW AND DEFINITIONS**

20. Considering Newton's second law of motion:

    1 - every action has an equal and opposite reaction
    2 - if the same force is applied, the larger the mass the slower the acceleration
    3 - if two forces are applied to the same mass, the bigger the force the greater the acceleration
    4 - the acceleration of a body from a state of rest, or uniform motion in a straight line, is proportional to the applied force and inversely proportional to the mass

    The combination of true statements is:

    a) 1 only
    b) 1, 2, 3 and 4
    c) 2, 3, and 4
    d) 3 and 4

21. Newton's third law of motion states:

    a) The energy possessed by a mass is inversely proportional to its velocity
    b) Every force has an equal and opposite inertia
    c) For every force there is an action
    d) Every action has an equal and opposite reaction

22. The definition of velocity is the:

    a) Rate of change of acceleration
    b) Rate of change of displacement
    c) The quantity of motion possessed by a body
    d) The acceleration of a body in direct proportion to its mass

23. When considering acceleration:

    1 - acceleration is the rate of change of velocity
    2 - the units of acceleration are metres per second
    3 - the units of acceleration are kilogram-metres per second
    4 - the units of acceleration are seconds per metre per metre

    The combination of correct statements is:

    a) 4 only
    b) 1 and 4
    c) 1 only
    d) 1 and 2

24. The definition of momentum is:

    a) The quantity of mass possessed by a body
    b) The quantity of inertia possessed by a body
    c) The quantity of motion possessed by a body
    d) The opposition which a body offers to a change in velocity

25. A force of 24 Newton's moves a 10 kg mass 60 metres in 1 minute, the power used is:

    1 - 24 Watts
    2 - 240 Watts
    3 - Force times distance moved in one second
    4 - Force times the distance the mass is moved in one second

    Which of the preceding statements are correct

    a) 1 and 3
    b) 1, 3 and 4
    c) 2 and 4
    d) 4 only

26. When considering momentum:

    1 - Momentum is the quantity of motion possessed by a body
    2 - Momentum is the tendency of a body to continue in motion after being placed in motion
    3 - A mass of 2000 kg moving at 55 m/s has 110,000 kg-m/s of momentum
    4 - A large mass moving at 50 m/s will have less momentum than a small mass moving at 50 m/s

    The correct combination of statements is:

    a) 1 and 3
    b) 1, 2, 3 and 4
    c) 1, 2 and 3
    d) 2, 3 and 4

INTENTIONALLY

LEFT

BLANK

ANSWERS

Aircraft number (1) V1 speed of 65 knots = 33.5 m/s

Aircraft number (2) V1 speed of 130 knots = 67 m/s

- a) 3,000,000 joules
- b) 100,000 watts
- c) 12,000,000 joules
- d) 300,000 watts
- e) 67,000 kg-m/s
- f) 134,000 kg-m/s
- g) Twice
- h) 1,122,250 joules
- i) 4,489,000 joules
- j) Four times greater
- k) Same mass, speed doubled, momentum doubled, but kinetic energy four times greater.
- l) Velocity has a greater effect on kinetic energy than mass.
- m) It must be dissipated by the braking systems.

No	A	B	C	D	REF	No	A	B	C	D	REF
1			C			14	A				
2				D		15				D	
3			C			16	A				
4				D		17		B			
5		B				18		B			
6	A					19	A				
7			C			20			C		
8				D		21				D	
9		B				22		B			
10			C			23			C		
11			C			24			C		
12	A					25		B			
13			C			26			C		

CHAPTER 2 - THE ATMOSPHERE

Contents

Page

INTRODUCTION . . . . 2 - 1
THE PHYSICAL PROPERTIES OF AIR
    STATIC PRESSURE
        TEMPERATURE . . . . 2 - 2
    AIR DENSITY
    INTERNATIONAL STANDARD ATMOSPHERE . . . . 2 - 3
DYNAMIC PRESSURE . . . . 2 - 4
    MEASURING DYNAMIC PRESSURE . . . . 2 - 6
RELATIONSHIPS BETWEEN AIR SPEEDS . . . . 2 - 7
    INDICATED AIR SPEED
    CALIBRATED AIR SPEED
    EQUIVALENT AIR SPEED
    TRUE AIR SPEED
    SPEED OF SOUND . . . . 2 - 8
    MACH NUMBER
    CRITICAL MACH NUMBER
AIRSPEED
    ERRORS AND CORRECTIONS . . . . 2 - 9
        INSTRUMENT ERROR
        POSITION ERROR (PRESSURE ERROR)
        COMPRESSIBILITY ERROR
    'V' SPEEDS
SUMMARY . . . . 2 - 10
SELF ASSESSMENT QUESTIONS . . . . 2 - 11
    ANSWERS . . . . 2 - 17

PRINCIPLES OF FLIGHT   THE ATMOSPHERE

2.1 INTRODUCTION

The atmosphere is the medium in which an aircraft operates. It is the properties of the atmosphere, changed by the shape of the wing, that generate the required Lift force.

The most important property is air density (the "thickness" of air)

> KEY FACT: If air density decreases, the mass of air flowing over the aircraft in a given time will decrease. Not usually considered during the study of Principles of Flight, keeping the idea of Mass flow (Kg/s) in the 'back of your mind' can aid general understanding.
>
> A given mass flow will generate the required Lift force, but a decrease in air density will reduce the mass flow.
>
> To maintain the required Lift force if density is decreased, the speed of the aircraft through the air must be increased. The increased speed of airflow over the wing will restore the mass flow and Lift force to its previous value.

2.2 THE PHYSICAL PROPERTIES OF AIR

Air has substance! Air has mass; not very much if compared to other matter, but nevertheless a significant amount. A mass of moving air has considerable kinetic energy, e.g. when moving at 100 knots the kinetic energy of air can inflict severe damage to man-made structures.

Air is a compressible fluid and is able to flow or change its shape when subjected to even minute pressure differences. (Air will flow in the direction of the lower pressure). The viscosity of air is so low that very small forces are able to move the molecules in relation to each other.

When considering the portion of atmosphere in which most aircraft operate (up to 40,000ft); with increasing altitude the characteristics of air undergo a gradual transition from those at sea level. Since air is compressible, the lower layers contain much the greater part of the whole mass of the atmosphere. Pressure falls steadily with increasing altitude, but temperature falls steadily only to about 36,000 ft, where it then remains constant through the stratosphere.

2.2.1 STATIC PRESSURE

The unit for static pressure is N/m^2, the symbol is lower case 'p'.

a) Static pressure is the result of the weight of the atmosphere pressing down on the air beneath.

b) Static pressure will exert the same force per square metre on all surfaces of an aeroplane. The lower the altitude the greater the force per square metre.

PRINCIPLES OF FLIGHT — THE ATMOSPHERE

c) It is called static pressure because of the air's stationary or **static** presence.

d) An aircraft always has Static pressure acting upon it.

Newtons per square metre is the SI unit for pressure. 1 N/m^2 is called a Pascal and is quite a small unit. In aviation the hectoPascal (hPa) is used. ('hecto' means 100 and 1 hectoPascal is the same as 1 millibar).

Static pressure at a particular altitude will vary from day to day, and is about 1000 hPa at sea level. In those countries that measure static pressure in inches of mercury (ins Hg), sea level static pressure is about 30 ins Hg.

2.2.2 TEMPERATURE

The unit for temperature is °C, or K. Degrees Celsius (or centigrade) when measured relative to the freezing point of water, or Kelvin when measured relative to **absolute** zero. (0°C is equivalent to 273 K).

Temperature decreases with increasing altitude, up to about 36,000ft and then remains constant.

2.2.3 AIR DENSITY

The unit for density is kg/m^3 and the symbol is the Greek letter ρ [rho].

a) Density is 'Mass per unit volume' (The "number" of air particles in a given space).

b) Density varies with static pressure, temperature and humidity.

   (i) Density decreases if static pressure decreases.

   (ii) Density decreases if temperature increases.

   (iii) Density decreases if humidity increases. (This will be discussed later).

Air Density is proportional to pressure and inversely proportional to temperature. This is shown in the ideal gas law formula below.

$$\frac{p}{T\rho} = \text{constant}, \quad \text{more usefully it can be said that} \quad \rho \propto \frac{p}{T}$$

where, p = pressure; T = temperature and ρ = density

Density decreases with increasing altitude because of decreasing static pressure. However, with increasing altitude temperature also decreases, which would tend to increase density, but the effect of decreasing static pressure is dominant.

2.2.4 INTERNATIONAL STANDARD ATMOSPHERE (ISA)

The values of temperature, pressure and density are never constant in any given layer of the atmosphere. To enable accurate comparison of aircraft performance and the calibration of pressure instruments, a 'standard' atmosphere has been adopted. The standard atmosphere represents the mean or average properties of the atmosphere.

Europe uses the standard atmosphere defined by the International Civil Aviation Organisation (ICAO).

The ICAO standard atmosphere assumes the following mean sea level values:

Temperature   15°C
Pressure   1013·25 hPa
Density   1·225 kg/m^3

The temperature lapse rate is assumed to be uniform at a rate of 2°C per 1,000 ft (1·98°C) from mean sea level up to a height of 36,090 ft (11,000 m) above which the lapse rate becomes zero and the temperature remains constant at −56·5°C.

ICAO Standard Atmosphere

Altitude (ft)	Temperature (°C)	Pressure (hPa) (p)	Density (kg/m^3) (ρ)	Relative Density (σ)
0	*15*	*1013·25*	*1·225*	*1·0*
5,000	5·1	843·1	1·056	0·86
10,000	−4·8	696·8	0·905	0·74
15,000	−14·7	571·8	0·771	0·63
20,000	−24·6	465·6	0·653	0·53
25,000	−34·5	376·0	0·549	0·45
30,000	−44·4	300·9	0·458	0·37
35,000	−54·3	238·4	0·386	0·31
40,000	*−56·5*	*187·6*	*0·302*	*0·25*
45,000	−56·5	147·5	0·237	0·19
50,000	−56·5	116·0	0·186	0·15

NOTE: The air density at 40,000 ft is only ¼ of the sea-level value.

2.3 DYNAMIC PRESSURE

The unit for dynamic pressure is N/m² and the symbol is lower case 'q' or upper case 'Q'.

a) Because air has mass, air in motion must possess **kinetic energy**, and will exert a force per square metre on any object in its path. (KE = 1/2 m V^2)

b) It is called DYNAMIC pressure because the air is moving in relation to the object being considered, in this case an aircraft.

c) Dynamic pressure is proportional to the density of the air and the square of the speed of the air flowing over the aircraft.

An aircraft immersed in moving airflow will therefore experience both Static **AND** Dynamic pressure. (Remember, static pressure is always present).

The kinetic energy of **one cubic metre** of air moving at a stated speed is given by the formula:

$$\text{Kinetic Energy} = \tfrac{1}{2} \rho V^2 \text{ joules}$$

where ρ is the local air density in kg/m³ and V is the speed in m/s

If this cubic metre of moving air is completely trapped and brought to rest by means of an open-ended tube **the total energy will remain constant,** but by being brought **completely to rest** the kinetic energy will become pressure energy which, for all practical purposes, is equal to:

$$\text{Dynamic Pressure} = \tfrac{1}{2} \rho V^2 \text{ N/m}^2$$

Consider air flowing at 52 m/s (100 kt) with a density of 1·225 kg/m³

(100 kt x 6080ft = 608000ft/hour ÷ 3·28 = 185366metres/hour ÷ 60 ÷ 60 = 52m/s)

Dynamic pressure = 0·5 x 1·225 x 52 x 52 = 1656 N/m² (16·56 hPa)

If speed is doubled, dynamic pressure will be four times greater

0·5 x 1·225 x 104 x 104 = 6625 N/m² (66·25 hPa)

PRINCIPLES OF FLIGHT   **THE ATMOSPHERE**

If the area of the tube is $1m^2$ a **force** of $\frac{1}{2} \rho V^2$ Newtons will be generated. (Force = Pressure x Area)

Dynamic pressure ($\frac{1}{2} \rho V^2$) is common to **ALL** aerodynamic forces and determines the air loads imposed on an aeroplane moving through the air.

The symbol for dynamic pressure ($\frac{1}{2} \rho V^2$) is **q** or **Q**

$$Q = \frac{1}{2} \rho V^2$$

KEY FACTS

1. A pilot needs to know how much dynamic pressure is available, but dynamic pressure cannot be measured on its own because static pressure will always be present. The sum of Static and Dynamic pressure, in this context, is known as "Total" Pressure. (Dynamic + Static pressure can also be referred to as Stagnation or Pitot Pressure).

    Total Pressure = Static Pressure + Dynamic Pressure

    This can be re-arranged to show that:

    Total Pressure − Static Pressure = Dynamic Pressure

2. The significance of dynamic pressure to the understanding of Principles of Flight cannot be over-emphasised.

    Because dynamic pressure is dependent upon air density and the speed of the aircraft through the air, it is necessary for students to fully appreciate the factors which affect air density.

    a) **Temperature** - increasing temperature decreases air density. Changes in air density due to air temperature are significant during all phases of flight.

    b) **Static pressure** - decreasing static pressure decreases air density. Changes in air density due to static pressure are significant during all phases of flight.

    c) **Humidity** - increasing humidity decreases air density. (The reason increasing humidity decreases air density is that the density of water vapour is about 5/8 that of dry air). Humidity is most significant during take-off and landing.

    Increasing altitude will decrease air density because the effect of decreasing static pressure is more dominant than decreasing temperature.

PRINCIPLES OF FLIGHT   **THE ATMOSPHERE**

2.3.1 MEASURING DYNAMIC PRESSURE

All aerodynamic forces acting on an aircraft are determined by dynamic pressure, so it is essential to have some means of measuring dynamic pressure and presenting that information to the pilot.

A sealed tube, open at the forward end, is located where it will collect air when the aircraft is moving. The pressure in the tube (Pitot tube) is Dynamic + Static and, in this context, is called "Pitot" Pressure. (Because the air is inside the Pitot tube).

Some way of 'removing' the static pressure from the pitot pressure must be found. A hole (vent) in a surface parallel to the airflow will sense static pressure. Referring to Fig 2.1, if the pressure from the pitot tube is fed to one side of a diaphragm mounted in a sealed case, and static pressure is fed to the other side, the two static pressures will cancel each other and the diaphragm movement will be influenced only by changes in dynamic pressure.

Movement of the diaphragm moves a pointer over a scale so that changes in dynamic pressure can be observed by the flight crew. But the instrument is **calibrated at ISA sea level density**, so the instrument will only give a 'true' indication of the speed of the aircraft through the air when the air density is $1 \cdot 225$ kg/m^3.

This is not a problem because the pilot needs an indication of dynamic pressure, and this is what the instrument provides. The instrument is made in such a way that it indicates the square root of the dynamic pressure in nautical miles per hour (knots) or statute miles per hour (MPH). So, if this **"Indicated Air Speed"** is doubled, the speed of the aircraft through the air will also be doubled.

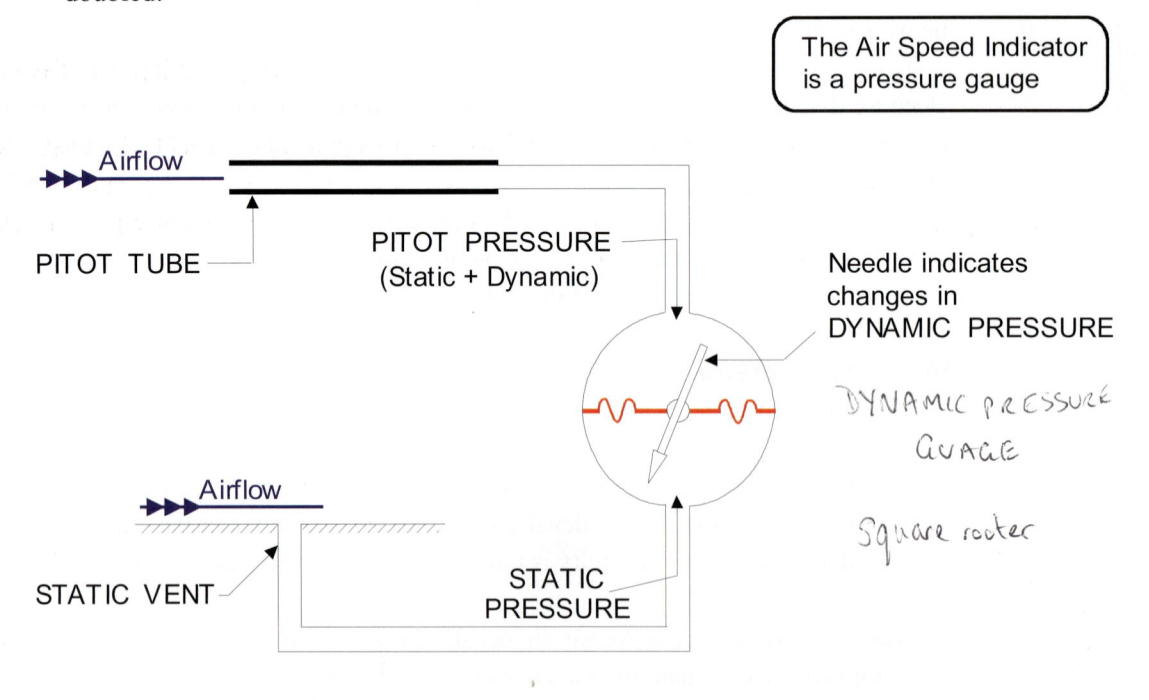

Figure 2.1 Schematic of Air Speed Indicator (ASI)

PRINCIPLES OF FLIGHT — THE ATMOSPHERE

2.4 RELATIONSHIPS BETWEEN AIR SPEEDS

Indicated Air Speed: (IAS). The speed registered on the Air Speed Indicator.

Calibrated Air Speed: (CAS). An accurate measure of dynamic pressure when the aircraft is flying slowly. The position of the pitot tube(s) and static vent(s), together with the aircraft's configuration (Flaps, landing gear etc.) and attitude to the airflow (Angle of attack and sideslip) will affect the pressures sensed; **particularly the pressures sensed at the static vent(s)**.

V speeds

Under the influence of the above conditions a false dynamic pressure (IAS) will be displayed. When IAS is corrected for this 'position' or 'pressure' error, as it's called, the resultant is Calibrated Air Speed. (The airspeed corrections to be applied may be displayed on a placard on the flight-deck, or in the Flight Manual, and will include any instrument error).

Equivalent Air Speed: (EAS). An accurate measure of dynamic pressure when the aircraft is flying fast. Air entering the pitot tube(s) is compressed, which gives a false dynamic pressure (IAS) reading, but only becomes significant at higher speeds.

At a given air density, the amount of compression depends on the speed of the aircraft through the air. When the IAS is corrected for 'position' **AND** 'compressibility' error, the resultant is Equivalent Air Speed.

True Air Speed: (TAS) or (V). The speed of the aircraft through the air. THE ONLY SPEED THERE IS - All the other, so called, speeds are pressures.

$$TAS = \frac{EAS}{\sqrt{\sigma}}$$

Where, σ is Relative Density

The Air Speed Indicator is calibrated for 'standard' sea level density, so it will only read TAS if the density of the air through which the aircraft is flying is $1\cdot225$ kg/m^3. Thus at 40,000 ft where the 'standard' density is one quarter of the sea-level value, **to maintain the same EAS the aircraft will have to move through the air twice as fast!**

The Air speed relative to the relative airflow, free stream flow, relative wind.

Temperature is the only thing factor that effects the speed of sound.

relative airflow: close to but unaffected by the presence of the AC. magnitude relative to the — TAS parallel to and in the opposite direction to the aircraft flight path.

PRINCIPLES OF FLIGHT — THE ATMOSPHERE

The Speed of Sound: (a). Sound is 'weak' pressure waves which propagate spherically through the atmosphere from their source. **The speed at which pressure waves propagate is proportional to the square root of the absolute temperature of the air.** The lower the temperature, the lower the speed of propagation. On a 'standard' day at sea level the speed of sound is approximately 340 m/s (660 kt TAS).

At higher aircraft True Air Speeds (TAS) and/or higher altitudes, it is essential to know the speed of the aircraft in relation to the local speed of sound. This speed relationship is known as the **Mach Number (M).**

$$M = \frac{TAS}{a}$$

where (a) is the local speed of sound

i.e. If the True Air Speed of the aircraft is four tenths the speed at which pressure waves propagate through the air mass surrounding the aircraft, the Mach meter will register 0·4 M

Critical Mach Number: (M_{CRIT}) The critical Mach number is the Mach number of the **aircraft** when the speed of the airflow over some part of the aircraft (usually the point of maximum thickness on the aerofoil) first reaches the speed of sound.

2.5 AIRSPEED

This information is to reinforce that contained in the preceding paragraphs.

The airspeed indicator is really a pressure gauge, the 'needle' of which responds to changes in dynamic pressure ($1/2 \, \rho \, V^2$).

> The Air Speed Indicator is a pressure gauge

Calibration of the airspeed indicator is based on standard sea level density (1·225 kg/m³). The "airspeed" recorded will be different from the actual speed of the aircraft through the air unless operating under standard sea-level conditions (unlikely). The actual speed of the aircraft relative to the free stream is called true airspeed (TAS), and denoted by (V). The "speed" recorded by the airspeed indicator calibrated as above, if there are no other errors, is called equivalent airspeed (EAS).

It may seem to be a drawback that the instrument records equivalent rather than true airspeed. But the true airspeed may always be determined from it. Also, many of the handling characteristics of an aircraft depend mainly on the dynamic pressure, i.e. on the equivalent airspeed, so it is often more useful to have a direct reading of EAS than TAS.

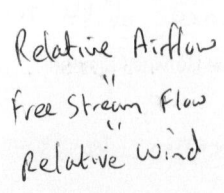

PRINCIPLES OF FLIGHT THE ATMOSPHERE

2.5.1 ERRORS AND CORRECTIONS

An airspeed indicator is, however, also subject to errors other than that due to the difference between the density of the air through which it is flying and standard sea level density.

a) **Instrument Error:** This error may arise from the imperfections in the design and manufacture of the instrument, and varies from one instrument to another. Nowadays this type of error is usually very small and for all practical purposes can be disregarded. Where any instrument error does exist, it is incorporated in the calibrated airspeed correction chart for the particular aeroplane.

b) **Position Error (Pressure Error):** This error is of two kinds, one relating to the static pressure measurement, the other to the pitot (total) pressure measurement. The pitot tube(s) and static port(s) may be mounted in a position on the aircraft where the flow is affected by the presence of the aircraft, changes in configuration (flaps and maybe gear) and proximity to the ground (ground effect). If so, the static pressure recorded will be the local and not the free stream value. The pitot pressure may be under-recorded because of incorrect alignment - the tube(s) may be inclined to the airstream instead of facing directly into it (changes in angle of attack, particularly at low speeds). The magnitude of the consequent errors will generally depend on the angle of attack, and hence the speed of the aircraft.

c) **Compressibility Error:** At high speeds, the dynamic pressure is not simply $1/2 \rho V^2$, but exceeds it by a factor determined by Mach number. Thus the airspeed indicator will over-read.

Because of the errors listed, the "speed" recorded on the airspeed indicator is generally not the equivalent airspeed. It is called instead the indicated airspeed. Corrections to rectify the instrument and position errors are determined experimentally. In flight, using special instruments, measurements are taken over the whole range of speeds and configurations, from which a calibration curve is obtained which gives the corrections appropriate to each indicated airspeed. The compressibility error correction may be obtained by calculation.

The indicated airspeed, after correction for instrument, position (pressure) and compressibility errors, gives the equivalent airspeed $1/2 \rho V^2$.

2.5.2 'V' SPEEDS

These include: V_S, V_1, V_R, V_2, V_{MD}, V_{MC}, V_{YSE} and many others - these are all Calibrated Air Speeds because they relate to aircraft operations at low speed. However, the appropriate corrections are made and these speeds are supplied to the pilot in the Flight Manual as IAS.

V_{MO} - The maximum operating IAS is however an EAS because it is a high speed, but again is supplied to the pilot in the Flight Manual as an IAS.

PRINCIPLES OF FLIGHT **THE ATMOSPHERE**

2.6 SUMMARY

1. Dynamic pressure (Q) is affected by changes in air density.

$$Q = \tfrac{1}{2} \rho V^2$$

    a) air density decreases if atmospheric pressure decreases,

    b) air density decreases if air temperature increases,

    c) air density decreases if humidity increases.

        (i) With the aircraft on the ground:

        Taking-off from an airfield with low atmospheric pressure and/or high air temperature and/or high humidity, will require a higher TAS to achieve the same dynamic pressure (IAS).

    For the purpose of general understanding:

    A constant IAS will give constant dynamic pressure.

    d) increasing altitude decreases air density because of decreasing static pressure.

        (i) With the aircraft airborne:

        As altitude increases, a higher TAS is required to maintain a constant dynamic pressure. Maintaining a constant IAS will compensate for changes in air density.

2. There is only one speed, the speed of the aircraft through the air, the TAS. All the other, so called, speeds are pressures.

The Air Speed Indicator is a pressure gauge.

3. Aircraft 'V' speeds are CAS, except V_{MO} which is an EAS, but all are presented to the pilot in the Flight Manual as IAS.

PRINCIPLES OF FLIGHT   **THE ATMOSPHERE**

SELF ASSESSMENT QUESTIONS

1. When considering air:

    1 - Air has mass
    2 - Air is not compressible
    3 - Air is able to flow or change its shape when subject to even small pressures
    4 - The viscosity of air is very high
    5 - Moving air has kinetic energy

    The correct combination of all true statements is:

    a) 1, 2, 3 and 5
    b) 2, 3 and 4
    c) 1 and 4
    d) 1, 3, and 5

2. Why do the lower layers contain the greater proportion of the whole mass of the atmosphere:

    a) Because air is very viscous
    b) Because air is compressible
    c) Because of greater levels of humidity at low altitude
    d) Because air has very little mass

3. With increasing altitude, up to about 40,000 ft, the characteristics of air change:

    1 - Temperature decreases continuously with altitude
    2 - Pressure falls steadily to an altitude of about 36,000 ft, where it then remains constant
    3 - Density decreases steadily with increasing altitude
    4 - Pressure falls steadily with increasing altitude

    The combination of true statements is:

    a) 3 and 4
    b) 1, 2 and 3
    c) 2 and 4
    d) 1 and 4

4. When considering static pressure:

   1 - In aviation, static pressure can be measured in hectopascal's
   2 - The SI units for static pressure is N/m^2
   3 - Static pressure is the product of the mass of air pressing down on the air beneath
   4 - Referred to as static pressure because of the air's stationary or static presence
   5 - The lower the altitude, the greater the static pressure

   The correct statements are:

   a) 2, 4 and 5
   b) 1, 2, 3, 4 and 5
   c) 1, 3 and 5
   d) 1 and 5

5. When considering air density:

   1 - Density is measured in millibar's
   2 - Density increases with increasing altitude
   3 - If temperature increases the density will increase
   4 - As altitude increases, density will decrease
   5 - Temperature decreases with increasing altitude, this will cause air density to increase

   The combination of correct statements is:

   a) 4 only
   b) 4 and 5
   c) 5 only
   d) 2, 3 and 5

6. Air density is:

   a) Mass per unit volume
   b) Proportional to temperature and inversely proportional to pressure
   c) Independent of both temperature and pressure
   d) Dependent only on decreasing pressure with increasing altitude

7. When considering the ICAO International Standard Atmosphere and comparing it with the actual atmosphere, which of the following statements is correct:

    1 - Temperature, pressure and density are constantly changing in any given layer of the actual atmosphere
    2 - A requirement exists for a hypothetical 'standard' atmosphere
    3 - The values given in the International Standard Atmosphere exist at a the same altitudes in the actual atmosphere
    4 - The International Standard Atmosphere was designed for the calibration of pressure instruments and the comparison of aircraft performance calculations

    a) 1, 2 and 3
    b) 2, 3 and 4
    c) 1, 2, 3 and 4
    d) 1, 2 and 4

8. When considering the ICAO International Standard Atmosphere, which of the following statements is correct:

    1 - The temperature lapse rate is assumed to be uniform at 2°C per 1,000 ft (1.98°C) up to a height of 11,000 ft
    2 - Sea level temperature is assumed to be 15°C
    3 - Sea level static pressure is assumed to be 1.225 kg/m^3
    4 - Sea level density is assumed to be 1013.25 hPa

    a) 1, 2, 3 and 4
    b) No statements are correct
    c) 1, 3 and 4
    d) 2 only

9. A moving mass of air possesses kinetic energy. An object placed in the path of such a moving mass of air will be subject to which of the following:

    a) Dynamic pressure
    b) Static Pressure
    c) Static pressure and dynamic pressure
    d) Dynamic pressure minus static pressure

PRINCIPLES OF FLIGHT   **THE ATMOSPHERE**

10. Dynamic pressure is:

    a) The total pressure at a point where a moving airflow is brought completely to rest
    b) The amount by which the pressure rises at a point where a moving airflow is brought completely to rest
    c) The pressure due to the mass of air pressing down on the air beneath
    d) The pressure change caused by heating when a moving airflow is brought completely to rest

11. Dynamic pressure is equal to:

    a) Density times speed squared
    b) Half the density times the indicated airspeed squared
    c) Half the true airspeed times the density squared
    d) Half the density times the true airspeed squared

12. A tube facing into an airflow will experience a pressure in the tube equal to:

    a) Static pressure
    b) Dynamic pressure
    c) Static pressure plus dynamic pressure
    d) The difference between total pressure and static pressure

13. A static pressure vent must be positioned:

    a) On a part of the aircraft structure where the airflow is undisturbed, in a surface at right angles to the airflow direction
    b) On a part of the structure where the airflow is undisturbed, in a surface parallel to the airflow direction
    c) At the stagnation point
    d) At the point on the surface where the airflow reaches the highest speed

14. The inputs to an Air Speed Indicator are from:

    a) A static source
    b) Pitot pressure
    c) A pitot and a static source
    d) Pitot, static and density

PRINCIPLES OF FLIGHT   THE ATMOSPHERE

15. The deflection of the pointer of the Air Speed Indicator is proportional to:

    a) Dynamic pressure
    b) Static pressure
    c) The difference between static and dynamic pressure
    d) Static pressure plus dynamic pressure

16. Calibration of the Air Speed Indicator is based upon the density:

    a) At the altitude at which the aircraft is flying
    b) At sea level ICAO International Standard Atmosphere temperature
    c) At sea level
    d) At sea level ICAO International Standard Atmosphere +15°C temperature

17. When considering the relationship between different types of air speed:

    1 - True Air Speed (TAS) is read directly from the Air Speed Indicator
    2 - Equivalent Air Speed is Indicated Air Speed corrected for position error
    3 - Indicated Air Speed is not a speed at all, it's a pressure
    4 - True Air Speed is the speed of the aircraft through the air

    Which of the above statements are true:

    a) 1 only
    b) 2 and 3
    c) 3 and 4
    d) 1 and 4

18. When considering the relationship between different types of air speed:

    1 - Calibrated Air Speed is Indicated Air Speed corrected for position error
    2 - Equivalent Air Speed is Indicated Air Speed corrected for position error and compressibility
    3 - Position error, which causes false Indicated Air Speed readings, is due to variations in the pressures sensed at the pitot and static ports
    4 - The Air Speed Indicator is calibrated to read True Air Speed when the ambient density is that of the ICAO International Standard Atmosphere at sea level

    The combination of correct statements is:

    a) Non of the statements are correct
    b) 1, 2 and 4
    c) 2 and 3
    d) 1, 2, 3 and 4

PRINCIPLES OF FLIGHT   **THE ATMOSPHERE**

19. The speed of sound:

    a) Is dependent upon the True Air Speed and the Mach number of the aircraft
    b) Is inversely proportional to the absolute temperature
    c) Is proportional to the square root of the absolute temperature of the air
    d) Is directly proportional to the True Air Speed of the aircraft

20. Mach number is:

    a) The aircraft True Air Speed divided by the local speed of sound
    b) The speed of sound in the ambient conditions in which the aircraft is flying
    c) The True Air Speed of the aircraft at which the relative airflow somewhere on the aircraft first reaches the local speed of sound
    d) The Indicated Air Speed divided by the local speed of sound sea level

21. An aircraft's critical Mach number is;

    (a) The speed of the airflow when the aircraft first becomes supersonic
    (b) The speed of the aircraft when the airflow somewhere reaches the speed of sound
    (c) The Indicated Airspeed when the aircraft first becomes supersonic
    (d) The aircraft's Mach number when airflow over it first reaches the local speed of sound

ANSWERS

No	A	B	C	D	REF
1				D	
2		B			
3	A				
4		B			
5	A				
6	A				
7				D	
8				D	
9			C		
10		B			
11				D	
12			C		
13		B			
14			C		
15	A				
16		B			
17			C		
18				D	
19			C		
20	A				
21				D	

CHAPTER 3 - BASIC AERODYNAMIC THEORY

Contents

                                                                                                         Page

THE PRINCIPLE OF CONTINUITY .... 3 - 1
BERNOULLI'S THEOREM .... 3 - 2
STREAMLINES AND THE STREAMTUBE .... 3 - 3
SUMMARY .... 3 - 4
SELF ASSESSMENT QUESTIONS .... 3 - 5

PRINCIPLES OF FLIGHT • BASIC AERODYNAMIC THEORY

3.1 THE PRINCIPLE OF CONTINUITY

One of the fundamental laws of the universe is **"ENERGY and MASS can neither be created nor destroyed"**, only changed from one form to another. To demonstrate the effect this basic 'Principle of Continuity' has on aerodynamic theory, it is instructive to consider a streamline flow of air through a tube which has a reduced cross sectional area in the middle.

The air mass flow, or mass per unit time, through the tube will be the product of the cross-sectional-area (A), the airflow velocity (V) and the air density (ρ). Mass flow will remain a constant value at all points along the tube. The **Equation of Continuity** is:

$$A \times V \times \rho = \text{Constant}$$

Because air is a compressible fluid, any pressure change in the flow will affect the air density. However, at low subsonic speeds (< 0·4 M) density changes will be insignificant and can be disregarded. The equation of continuity can now be simplified to: $A \times V$ = constant, or:

$$\text{Velocity (V)} = \frac{\text{constant}}{\text{Area (A)}}$$

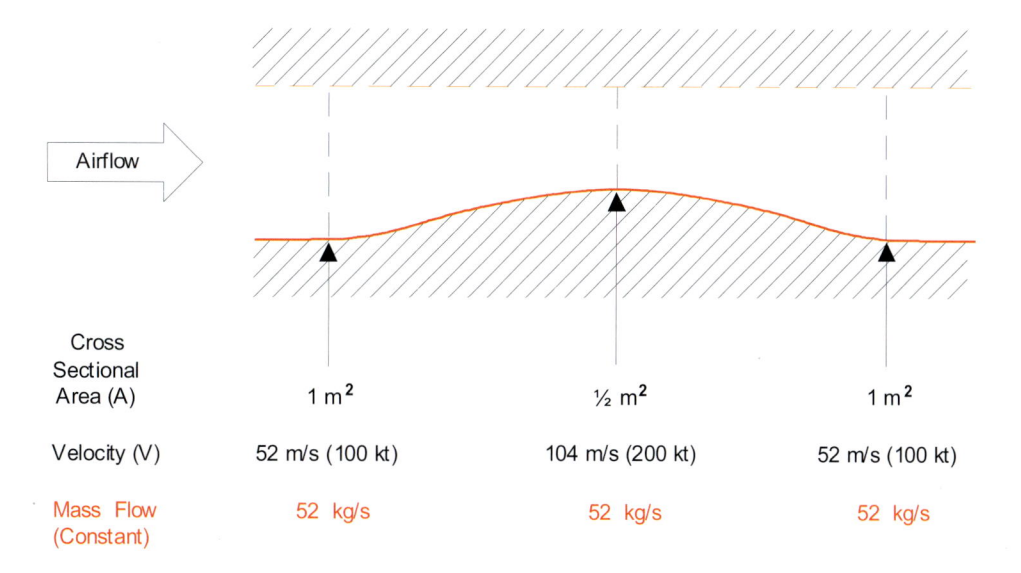

Cross Sectional Area (A)	1 m²	½ m²	1 m²
Velocity (V)	52 m/s (100 kt)	104 m/s (200 kt)	52 m/s (100 kt)
Mass Flow (Constant)	52 kg/s	52 kg/s	52 kg/s

Figure 3.1 The Principle of Continuity

Because the mass flow **must** remain constant, it can be seen from the equation of continuity that the reduction in the tube's cross-sectional area results in an increase in velocity and, vice versa.

The equation of continuity enables the velocity changes of airflow around a given shape to be predicted mathematically, (< 0·4 M).

PRINCIPLES OF FLIGHT   BASIC AERODYNAMIC THEORY

3.2 BERNOULLI'S THEOREM

"In the steady flow of an **ideal** fluid the sum of the pressure and kinetic energy per unit volume remains constant".
(NB: An ideal fluid is both incompressible and has no viscosity).

This statement can be expressed as: **Pressure + Kinetic energy = Constant** or:

$$p + \tfrac{1}{2} \rho V^2 = \text{constant}$$

Consider a mass of air: Static Pressure 101325 N/m², Density 1.225 kg/m³ and Velocity 52 m/s, its dynamic pressure will be: 1656 N/m². [Q = ½ x 1.225 x 52 x 52]

Pressure (101325 N/m²) + Kinetic energy (1656 N/m²) = Constant (102981 N/m²)

	(100 kt) 52 m/s	(200 kt) 104 m/s	(100 kt) 52 m/s
Dynamic Pressure	1656 N/m²	6624 N/m²	1656 N/m²
Static Pressure	101325 N/m²	96357 N/m²	101325 N/m²
TOTAL PRESSURE	102981 N/m²	102981 N/m²	102981 N/m²

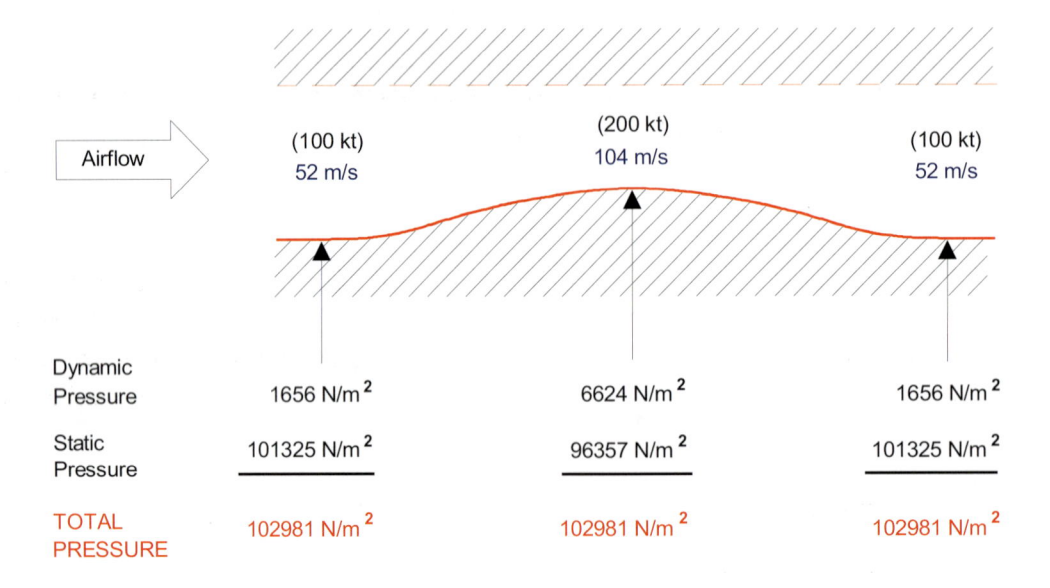

Figure 3.2 Bernoulli's Theorem

Because the velocity of air at the throat has doubled, its dynamic pressure has risen by a value of four, and the static pressure has decreased. The significant point is that:
Static Pressure + Dynamic Pressure is a constant. This constant can be referred to either as:

TOTAL PRESSURE, STAGNATION PRESSURE or PITOT PRESSURE.

It can be seen that flow velocity is dependent on the shape of the object over which it flows. And, from Bernoulli's theorem it is evident that an increase in velocity will cause a decrease in static pressure, and vice versa.

PRINCIPLES OF FLIGHT | BASIC AERODYNAMIC THEORY

The tube illustrated in Figures 3.1 and 3.2 is used only to demonstrate the Principle of Continuity and Bernoulli's Theorem and is of no practical use in making an aeroplane fly.

But, an aerodynamic force to oppose the weight of an aircraft can be generated by using a specially shaped body called an aerofoil.

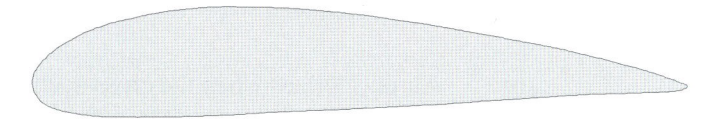

Figure 3.3 "Typical" Aerofoil Section

The airflow velocity over the top surface of a lifting aerofoil will be greater than that beneath, so the pressure differential that results will produce a force per unit area acting upwards. The larger the surface area, the bigger the force that can be generated.

In the next section we see that the flow over the top of the aerofoil looks very like the tube in Fig. 3.2 and the principle of continuity and Bernoulli's theorem still apply.

3.3 STREAMLINES AND THE STREAMTUBE

A streamline is the path traced by a particle of air in a steady airflow, and streamlines cannot cross. When streamlines are shown close together it illustrates increased velocity and vice versa. Diverging streamlines illustrate a decelerating airflow and resultant increasing pressure and converging streamlines illustrate an accelerating airflow, with resultant decreasing pressure.

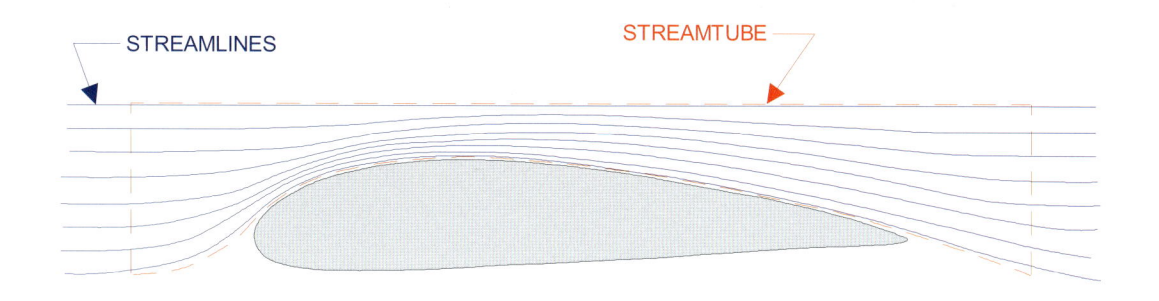

Figure 3.4 Streamlines and a Streamtube

A streamtube is an imaginary tube made of streamlines. There is no flow into or out of the streamtube through the "walls", only a flow along the tube. With this concept it is possible to visualise the airflow around an aerofoil being within a tube made-up of streamlines.

3.4 SUMMARY

(1) At flow speeds of less than about 0·4 M, pressure changes will not affect air density.

(2) Continuity:
    (a) Air accelerates when the cross-sectional-area of a streamline flow is reduced

    (b) Air decelerates when the cross-sectional-area increases again.

(3) Bernoulli:
    (a) If a streamline flow of air accelerates, its kinetic energy will increase and its static pressure will decrease.

    (b) When air decelerates, the kinetic energy will decrease and the static pressure will increase again.

(4) By harnessing the Principle of Continuity and Bernoulli's Theorem an aerodynamic force can be generated.

PRINCIPLES OF FLIGHT BASIC AERODYNAMIC THEORY

SELF ASSESSMENT QUESTIONS

1. If the cross sectional area of an airflow is mechanically reduced:

    a) The velocity of the airflow remains constant and the kinetic energy increases
    b) The velocity of the airflow remains constant and the mass flow increases
    c) The mass flow remains constant and the static pressure increases
    d) The mass flow remains constant and the velocity of the airflow increases

2. The statement, "Pressure plus Kinetic energy is constant", refers to:

    a) Bernoulli's theorem
    b) The principle of continuity
    c) Newton's second law of motion
    d) The Magnus effect

3. If the velocity of an air mass is increased:

    a) The dynamic pressure will decrease and the static pressure will increase
    b) The static pressure will remain constant and the kinetic energy will increase
    c) The kinetic energy will increase, the dynamic pressure will increase and the static pressure will decrease
    d) The mass flow will stay constant, the dynamic pressure will decrease and the static pressure will increase

4. When considering a streamlined airflow, which of the following statements is correct:

    1 - A resultant decrease in static pressure is indicated by streamlines shown close together
    2 - An increase in velocity is indicated by streamlines shown close together
    3 - Accelerating airflow with a resultant decreasing static pressure is indicated by converging streamlines
    4 - Diverging streamlines indicate decelerating airflow with a resultant increasing static pressure

    a) 2 and 4
    b) 1, 3 and 4
    c) 2, 3 and 4
    d) 1, 2, 3 and 4

5. If the pressure on one side of a surface is lower than on the other side:

    a) A force per unit area will exist, acting in the direction of the lower pressure
    b) No force will be generated, other than drag
    c) A force will be generated, acting in the direction of the higher pressure
    d) The pressure will leak around the sides of the surface, cancelling-out any pressure differential

6. When considering a streamtube, which of the following statements is correct:

    1 - Different sizes of streamtube are manufactured to match the wing span of the aircraft to which they will be fitted
    2 - A streamtube is a concept to aid understanding of aerodynamic force generation
    3 - There is no flow into or out of the streamtube through the "walls", only flow along the tube
    4 - A streamtube is an imaginary tube made-up of streamlines

    a) 1 only
    b) 1 and 3
    c) 2, 3 and 4
    d) 1, 2 and 3

7. At flow speeds less than four tenths the speed of sound, the following will be insignificant:

    a) Changes in static pressure due to temperature
    b) Changes in density due to static pressure
    c) Changes in density due to dynamic pressure
    d) Changes in static pressure due to kinetic energy

8. In accordance with the principle of continuity:

    1 - Air accelerates when the cross-sectional area of a streamline flow is reduced
    2 - When air accelerates the density of air in a streamline flow is increased
    3 - Air decelerates when the cross-sectional area of a streamline flow is increased
    4 - Changes in cross-sectional area of a streamline flow will affect the air velocity

    Which of the preceding statements are true:

    (a) 1, 2, 3 and 4
    (b) 1 and 4
    (c) 3 and 4
    (d) 1, 3 and 4

9. In accordance with Bernoulli's theorem:

1 - If a streamline flow of air decelerates, its kinetic energy will decrease and the static pressure will increase
2 - If a streamline flow of air accelerates, its kinetic energy will increase and the static pressure will decrease
3 - If a streamline flow of air is accelerated, the dynamic pressure will increase and the static pressure will increase
4 - If a streamline flow of air is decelerated, its dynamic pressure will decrease and the static pressure will increase

the combination of correct statements is:

a) 1, 2, 3 and 4
b) 3 only
c) 1, 2 and 4
d) 3 and 4

10. The statement, "Energy and mass can neither be created nor destroyed, only changed from one form to another", refers to:

a) Bernoulli's theorem
b) The equation of kinetic energy
c) The principle of continuity
d) Bernoulli's principle of continuity

INTENTIONALLY

LEFT

BLANK

No	A	B	C	D	REF
1				D	
2	A				
3			C		
4				D	
5	A				
6			C		
7			C		
8				D	
9			C		
28			C		

CHAPTER 4 - SUBSONIC AIRFLOW

Contents

	Page
AEROFOIL TERMINOLOGY	4 - 2
BASICS ABOUT AIRFLOW	4 - 4
TWO DIMENSIONAL AIRFLOW	4 - 4
INFLUENCE OF DYNAMIC PRESSURE	4 - 5
INFLUENCE OF ANGLE OF ATTACK	4 - 6
CENTRE OF PRESSURE	4 - 8
MOVEMENT OF THE CENTRE OF PRESSURE	
AERODYNAMIC FORCE COEFFICIENT	
DEVELOPMENT OF AERODYNAMIC PITCHING MOMENTS	4 - 10
AERODYNAMIC CENTRE	
PITCHING MOMENTS OF A SYMMETRICAL AEROFOIL	4 - 11
SUMMARY	4 - 12
SELF ASSESSMENT QUESTIONS	4 - 13

PRINCIPLES OF FLIGHT — SUBSONIC AIRFLOW

Ratio 80:20

LIFT FORCE

DRAG FORCE

FLOW DECELERATING (DECREASING KINETIC ENERGY) DUE TO ADVERSE PRESSURE GRADIENT (PRESSURE INCREASING FROM MINIMUM STATIC PRESSURE BACK TO FREE STREAM)

(−)

(+)

80

20

(HIGHER THAN STATIC)

Stagnation Pressure

"SUCTION" PEAK DUE TO ACCELERATED FLOW AROUND LEADING EDGE PROFILE (INCREASING KINETIC ENERGY AND DECREASING STATIC PRESSURE)

UPWASH IN FRONT OF AEROFOIL BECAUSE OF LOWER PRESSURE ON TOP SURFACE

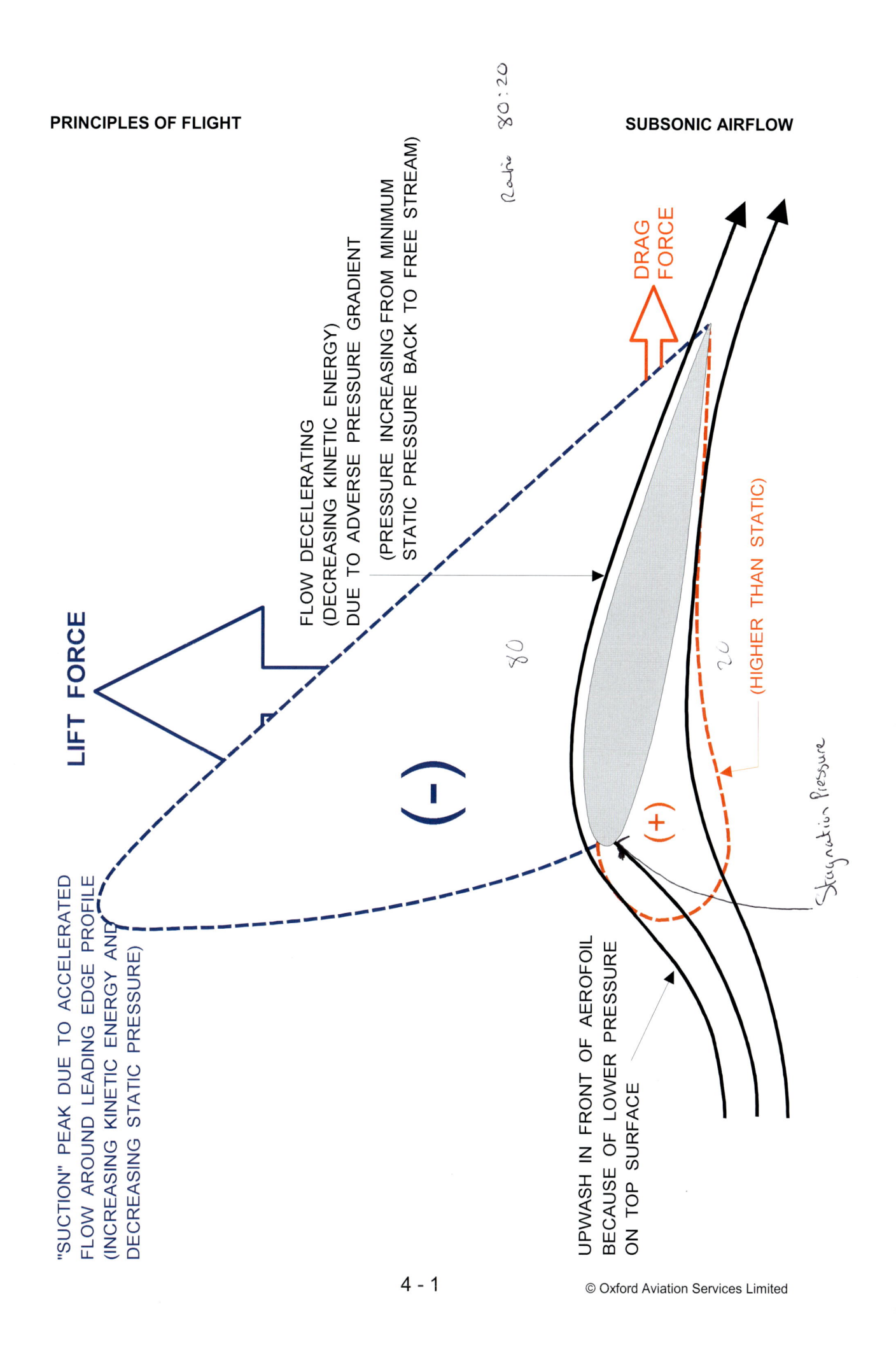

PRINCIPLES OF FLIGHT SUBSONIC AIRFLOW

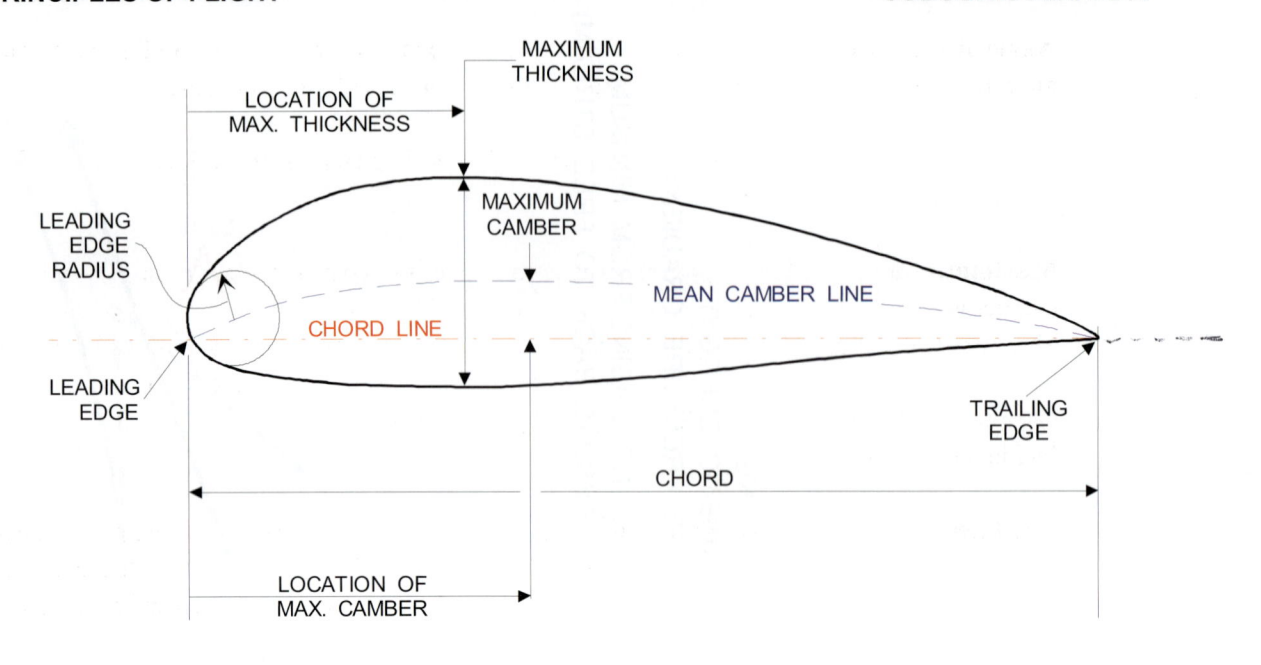

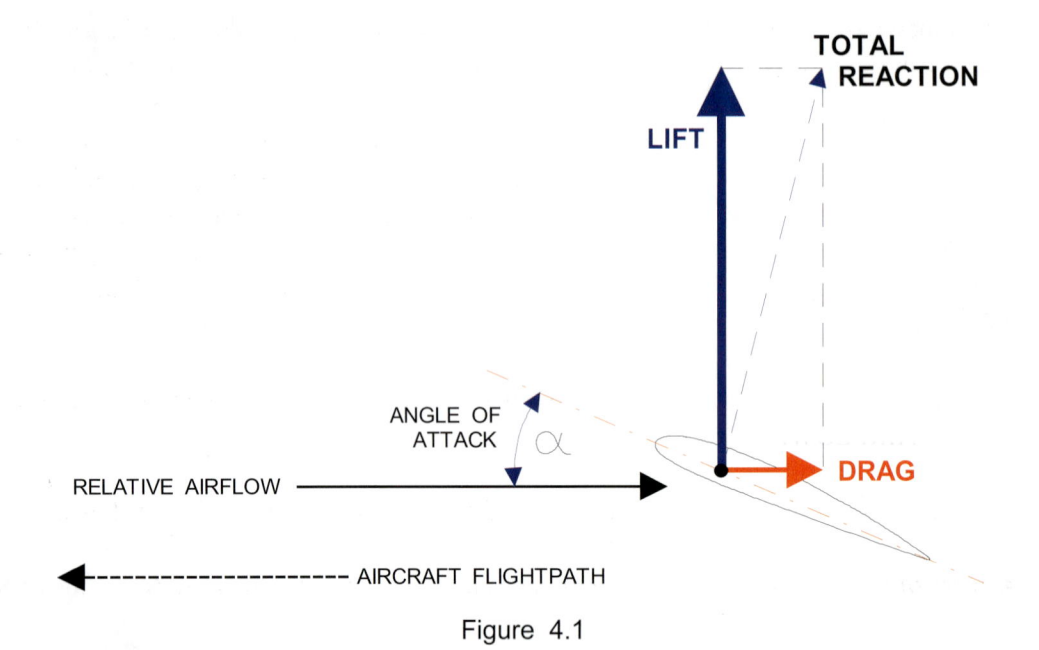

Figure 4.1

4.1 AEROFOIL TERMINOLOGY

Aerofoil: A shape capable of producing lift with relatively high efficiency.

Chord Line: A straight line joining the centres of curvature of the leading and trailing edges of an aerofoil.

Chord: The distance between the leading and trailing edges measured along the chord line.

When a line joining together the centre of included circles is curved the aerofoil is considered cambered.

PRINCIPLES OF FLIGHT   **SUBSONIC AIRFLOW**

Angle of Incidence: The angle between the wing root chord line and the longitudinal axis of the aircraft. (This angle is fixed for the wing, but may be variable for the tailplane).

Mean Line or Camber Line: A line joining the leading and trailing edges of an aerofoil, equidistant from the upper and lower surfaces.

Maximum Camber: The maximum distance of the mean line from the chord line. Maximum camber is expressed as a percentage of the chord, with its location as a percentages of the chord aft of the leading edge. When the camber line lies above the chord line the aerofoil is said to have positive camber, and if the camber line is below the chord line it is said to have negative camber. **A symmetrical aerofoil has no camber** because the chord line and camber line are co-incidental. *Otherwise Asymmetric.*

Thickness/Chord ratio: The maximum thickness or depth of an aerofoil section expressed as a percentage of the chord, with its location as a percentages of the chord aft of the leading edge. The thickness and thickness distribution of the aerofoil section have a great influence on its airflow characteristics.

Leading edge radius: The radius of curvature of the leading edge. The size of the leading edge radius can significantly effect the initial airflow characteristics of the aerofoil section.

Relative Air Flow (Relative Wind or Free Stream Flow): Relative Air Flow has three qualities.
(1) DIRECTION - air parallel to, and in the opposite direction to the flight path of the aircraft, in fact the path of the CG; the direction in which the aircraft is pointing is irrelevant.
(2) CONDITION - air close to, but unaffected by the presence of the aircraft; its pressure, temperature and velocity are not affected by the passage of the aircraft through it.
(3) MAGNITUDE - The magnitude of the Relative Air Flow is the TAS.

    If air flow does not possess all three of these qualities, it is referred to as EFFECTIVE AIRFLOW.

Total Reaction: The resultant of all the aerodynamic forces acting on the aerofoil section.

Centre of Pressure (CP): The point on the chord line, through which Lift is considered to act.

Lift: The aerodynamic force which acts at 90° to the Relative Air Flow.

Drag: The aerodynamic force which acts parallel to and in the same direction as the Relative Air Flow (or opposite to the aircraft flight path).

Angle of Attack (α or alpha) (can also be referred to as Aerodynamic Incidence) The angle between the chord line and the Relative Air Flow.

    The angle between the chord line and the effective airflow is referred to as the EFFECTIVE ANGLE OF ATTACK.

PRINCIPLES OF FLIGHT   SUBSONIC AIRFLOW

4.2 BASICS ABOUT AIRFLOW

When considering airflow velocity, it makes no difference to the pressure pattern if the aircraft is moving through the air or the air is flowing over the aircraft: it is the **relative velocity** which is the important factor. To promote a full understanding, references will be made to both wind-tunnel experiments, where air is flowing over a stationary aircraft, and aircraft in flight moving through 'stationary' air.

Three dimensional airflow: Three dimensional flow is the true airflow over an aircraft and consists of a hypothetical two dimensional flow modified by various pressure differentials. Three dimensional airflow will be examined later.

Two dimensional airflow: Assumes a wing with the same aerofoil section along the entire span with no spanwise pressure differential or flow.

4.3 TWO DIMENSIONAL AIRFLOW

This **CONCEPT,** figures 4.2 and 4.3, is used to illustrate the basic principles of aerodynamic force generation.

As air flows towards an aerofoil it will be turned towards the lower pressure at the upper surface; this is termed **upwash.** After passing over the aerofoil the airflow returns to its original position and state; this is termed **downwash.**

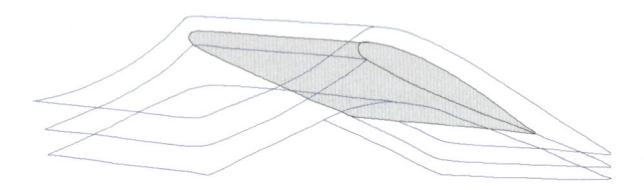

Figure 4.2

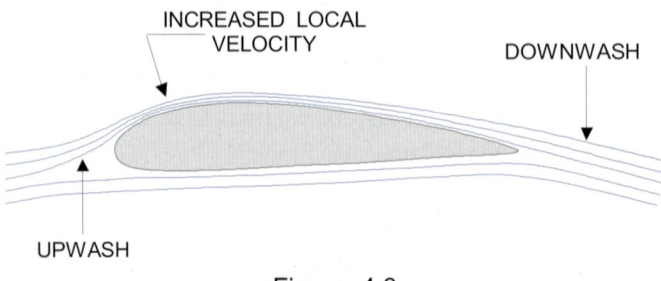

Figure 4.3

PRINCIPLES OF FLIGHT

SUBSONIC AIRFLOW

Influence of Dynamic Pressure: Fig. 4.4 shows an aerofoil section at a representative angle of attack subject to a given dynamic pressure (IAS). "If the static pressure on one side of a body is reduced more than on the other side, a pressure differential will exist".

Fig. 4.5 shows the same aerofoil section at the same angle of attack, but subject to a higher dynamic pressure (IAS). "If the dynamic pressure (IAS) is increased, the pressure differential will increase".

REPRESENTATIVE ANGLE OF ATTACK
AND A GIVEN DYNAMIC PRESSURE

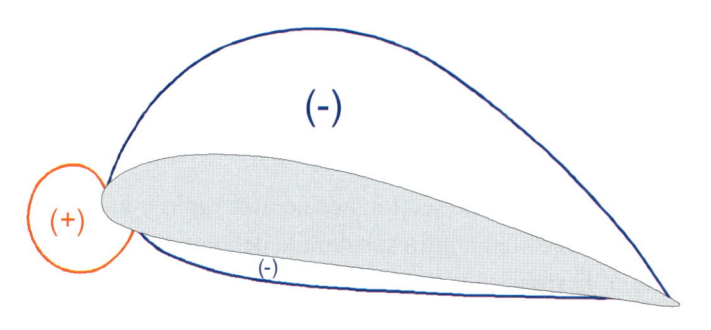

Figure 4.4

SAME ANGLE OF ATTACK
INCREASED DYNAMIC PRESSURE

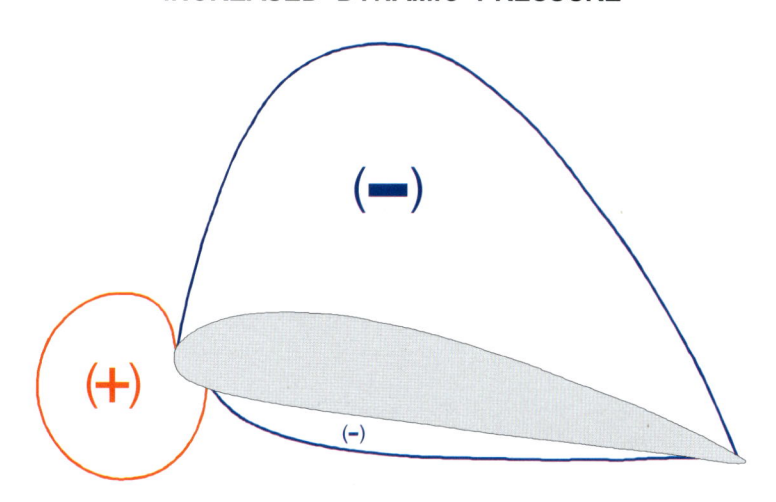

Figure 4.5

The pressure differential acting on the surface area will produce an upward acting force. "If the dynamic pressure (IAS) is increased, the upward force will increase".

PRINCIPLES OF FLIGHT SUBSONIC AIRFLOW

Influence of Angle of Attack: At a constant dynamic pressure (IAS), increasing the angle of attack (up to about 16°) will likewise increase the pressure differential, but will also change the pattern of pressure distribution.

The aerofoil profile presented to the airflow will determine the distribution of velocity and hence the distribution of pressure on the surface. This profile is determined by the aerofoil geometry, i.e. thickness and distribution (fixed), camber and distribution (assumed to be fixed for now) and by the angle of attack (variable).

The greatest positive pressure occurs at the stagnation point where the relative flow velocity is zero. This stagnation point is located somewhere near the leading edge. As the angle of attack increases from $-4°$ the leading edge stagnation point moves from the upper surface around the leading edge to the lower surface. It is at the front stagnation point where the flow divides to pass over and under the section. The pressure at the stagnation point is Static + Dynamic.

The flow over the top of the section accelerates rapidly around the nose and over the leading portion of the surface - inducing a substantial decrease in static pressure in those areas. The rate of acceleration increases with increase in angle of attack, up to about 16°. (Anything which changes the accurately manufactured profile of the leading portion of the surface can seriously disrupt airflow acceleration in this critical area. e.g. ice, snow, frost, dirt or dents). The pressure reduces continuously from the stagnation value through the free stream value to a position on the top surface where a peak negative value is reached. From there onwards the flow continuously slows down again and the pressure increases back to the free stream value in the region of the trailing edge.

At angles of attack less than 8° the flow under the section is accelerated much less, reducing the pressure to a small negative value, also with subsequent deceleration and increase in pressure back to the free stream value in the region of the trailing edge.

The pressure differential between the leading edge stagnation point and the lower pressure at the trailing edge creates a force acting backward which is called 'form (pressure) drag'. (This will be discussed in more detail later).

Angle of Attack ($-4°$) - The decrease in pressure above and below the section are equal and no differential exists. There will, thus, be no lift force. (Fig. 4.6). This can be called the "zero lift angle of attack".

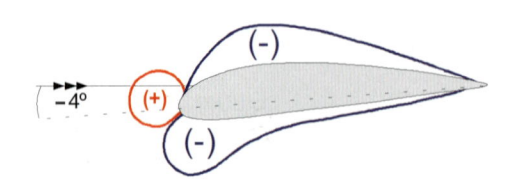

Figure 4.6

PRINCIPLES OF FLIGHT

SUBSONIC AIRFLOW

Angles of Attack (0° to 8°) - Compared to free stream static pressure, there is a pressure decrease over the upper surface and a lesser decrease over most of the lower surface. For a cambered aerofoil there will be a small amount of lift even at small negative angles (-4° to 0°).

Angles of attack (0° to 16°) - Increasing the angle of attack increases the lift force because the acceleration of the airflow over the top surface is increased by the reduction in effective cross-sectional area of the local streamtube.

The reduced pressure 'peak' moves forward as the angle of attack increases.

The greatest contribution to overall lift comes from the upper surface.

Pressure Gradient: Is a change in air pressure over distance. The greater the difference in pressure between two points, the steeper the gradient. A favourable gradient is when air pressure is falling in the direction of airflow. An adverse pressure gradient is when air pressure is rising in the direction of airflow, such as between the point of minimum pressure on the top surface and the trailing edge. The higher the angle of attack, the steeper the pressure gradient. At **angles of attack higher than approximately 16°**, the extremely steep adverse pressure gradient prevents air that is flowing over the top surface from following the aerofoil contour and the previously smooth streamline flow will separate from the surface, causing the low pressure area on the top of the section to suddenly collapse. Any pressure differential remaining is due to the pressure increase on the lower surface only. This condition is known as the stall and will be described in detail in Chapter 7.

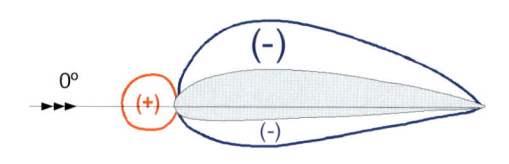

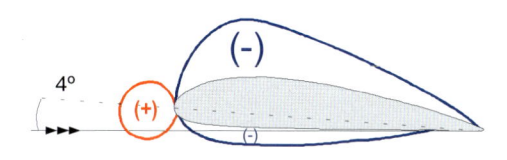

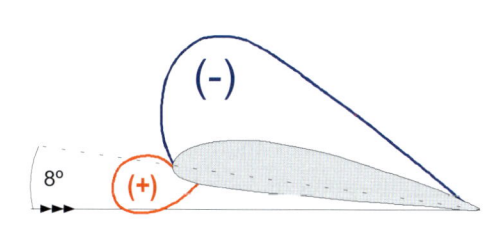

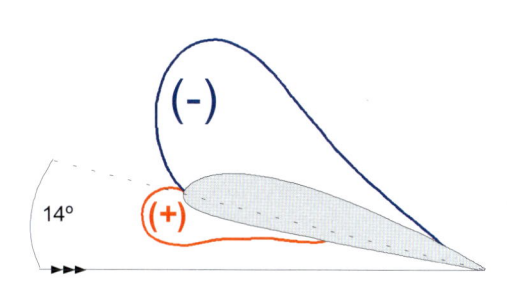

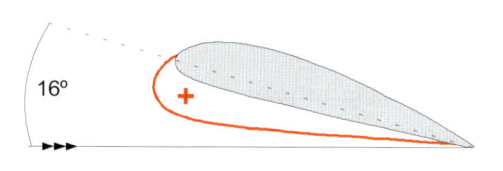

Figure 4.7

Centre of Pressure (CP): The whole surface of the aerofoil contributes to lift, but the point along the chord where the distributed lift is **effectively** concentrated is termed the Centre of Pressure (Fig. 4.8). The location of the CP is a function of camber and section lift coefficient. i.e. angle of attack.

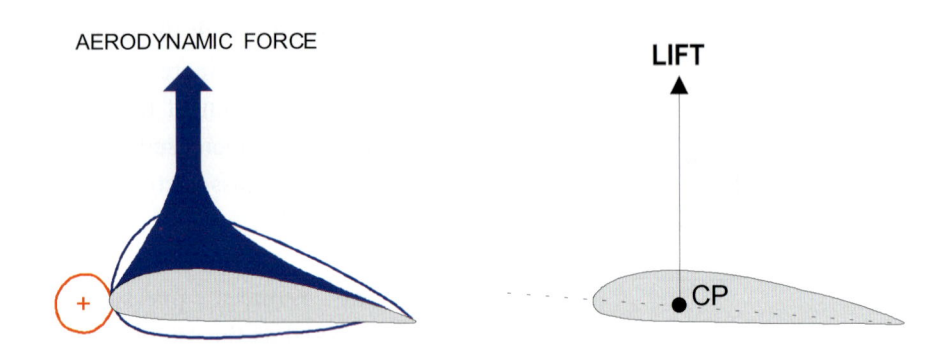

Figure 4.8

Movement of the Centre of Pressure: As the angle of attack increases from 0° to 16° the upper 'suction' peak moves forward (Fig. 4.7) so the point at which the lift is effectively concentrated, the CP, will move forward. The CP moves forward and the magnitude of the lift force increases with increase in angle of attack until the stall is reached when the lift force decreases abruptly and the CP generally moves back along the chord (Fig. 4.9). **Note that the CP is at its most forward location just before the stall ($C_{L\ MAX}$)**

Aerodynamic Force Coefficient: A coefficient is a dimensionless number expressing degree of magnitude. An aerodynamic force coefficient is a common denominator for all A/C of whatever weight, size and speed. An aerodynamic force coefficient is a dimensionless ratio between the average aerodynamic pressure and the airstream dynamic pressure.

By this definition a lift coefficient (C_L) is the ratio between lift divided by the wing planform area and dynamic pressure and a drag coefficient (C_D) is the ratio between drag divided by the wing planform area and dynamic pressure.

The use of the coefficient of an aerodynamic force is necessary since the force coefficient is:

a) An index of the aerodynamic force independent of area, density and velocity. It is derived from the relative pressure and velocity distribution.

b) Influenced only by the shape of the surface and angle of attack since these factors determine the pressure distribution.

PRINCIPLES OF FLIGHT **SUBSONIC AIRFLOW**

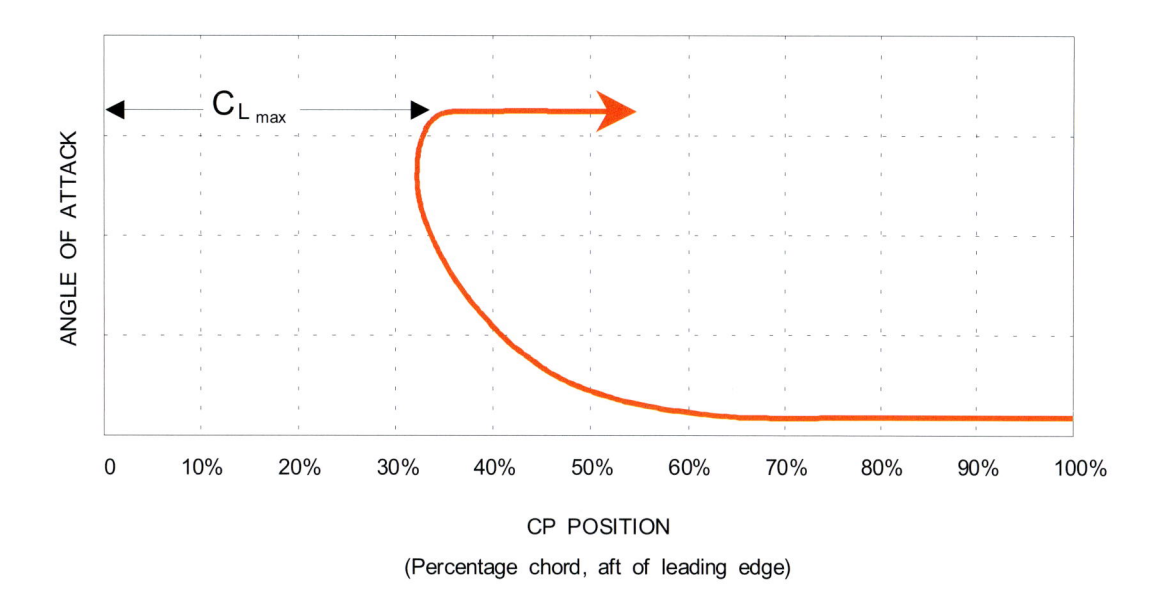

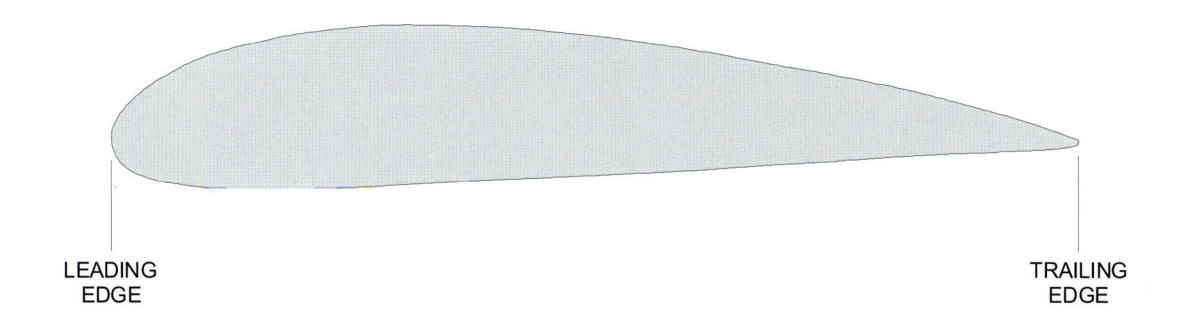

Figure 4.9 CP Movement with Angle of Attack

$$C_L = \frac{\text{Lift Pressure}}{\text{Dynamic Pressure}}$$

$$C_D = \frac{\text{Drag Pressure}}{\text{Dynamic Pressure}}$$

PRINCIPLES OF FLIGHT   SUBSONIC AIRFLOW

Development of Aerodynamic Pitching Moments: The distribution of pressure over a surface is the source of aerodynamic moments as well as forces. There are two ways to consider the effects of changing angle of attack on the pitching moment of an aerofoil.

a) Changes in the magnitude of lift acting through a **moving CP**, or more simply:

b) Changes in the magnitude of lift always acting through an Aerodynamic Centre, which is fixed.

Aerodynamic Centre (AC): The AC is a 'fixed' point on the chord line and is defined as: 'The point where all changes in the magnitude of the lift force effectively take place', AND: 'The point about which the pitching moment will remain constant at 'normal' angles of attack'. **A nose-down pitching moment exists about the AC** which is the product of a force (lift at the CP) and an arm (distance from the CP to the AC). Since an increase in angle of attack will increase the lift force, but also move the CP towards the AC (shortening the lever arm), the moment about the AC remains the same at any angle of attack within the "normal" range.

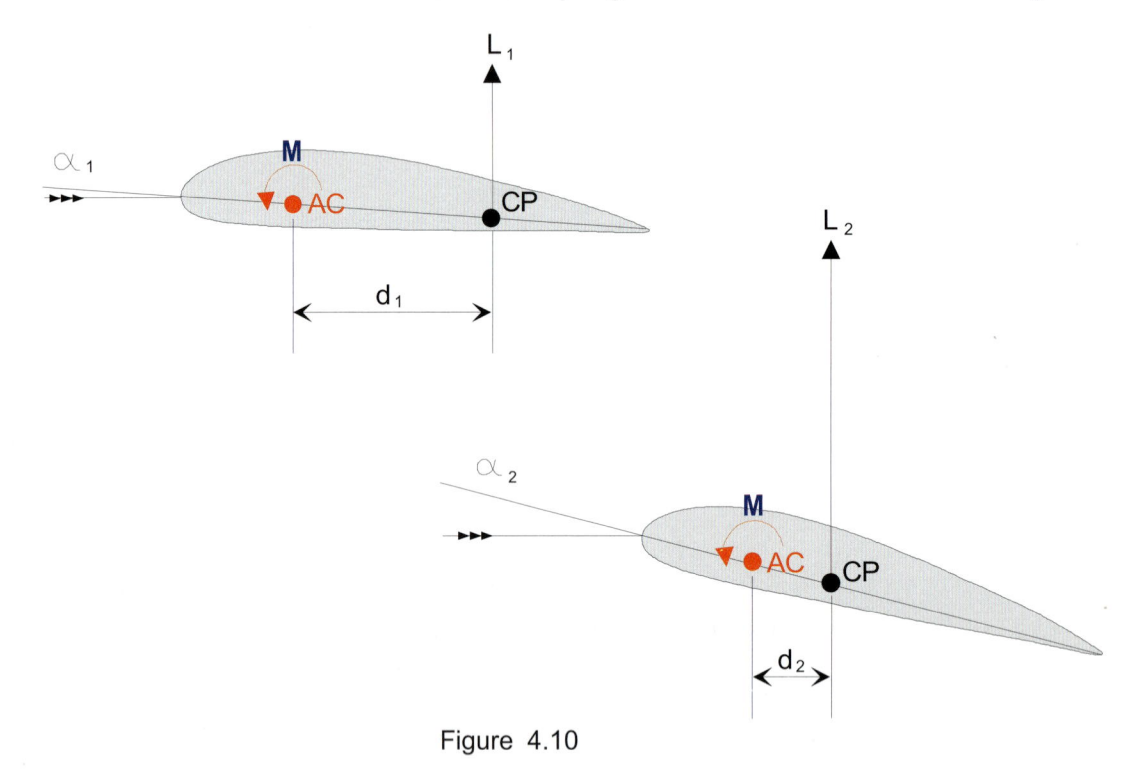

Figure 4.10

MOMENT (M) REMAINS THE SAME AT 'NORMAL' ANGLES OF ATTACK BECAUSE

$L_1 \times d_1$ at α_1 = $L_2 \times d_2$ at α_2

When considering subsonic airflows of less than M0·4, the AC is located at the 25 % chord point for any aerofoil regardless of camber, thickness and angle of attack.

The aerodynamic centre (AC) is an aerodynamic reference point. The most direct application being to the longitudinal stability of an aircraft, which will be discussed in Chapter 10.

PRINCIPLES OF FLIGHT

SUBSONIC AIRFLOW

Pitching Moment for a Symmetrical Aerofoil: Note the change in pressure distribution with angle of attack for the symmetrical aerofoil in Fig 4.11. When at zero angle of attack, the upper and lower surface forces are equal and located at the same point. With an increase in angle of attack, the upper surface force increases while the lower surface force decreases. A change in the magnitude of lift has taken place with no change in the CP position - a characteristic of symmetrical aerofoils. Thus, the pitching moment about the AC for a symmetrical aerofoil will be zero at 'normal' angles of attack - one of the big advantages of symmetrical aerofoils.

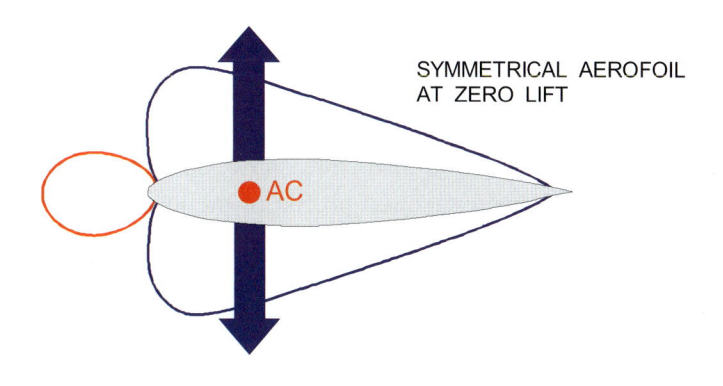

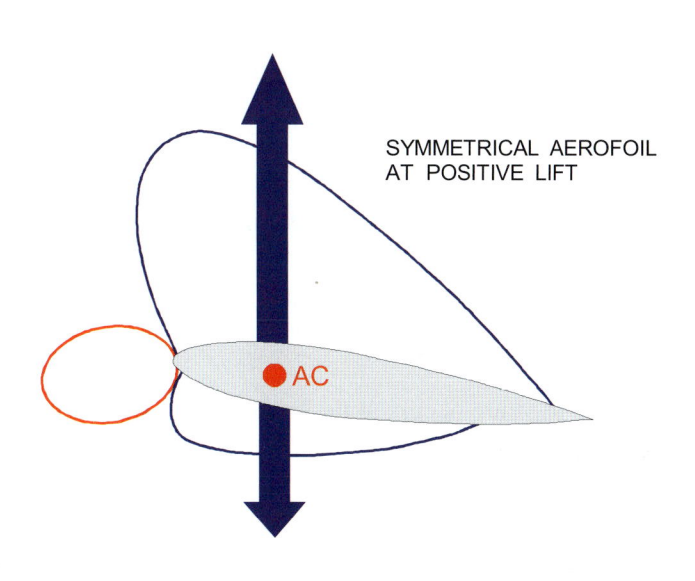

Figure 4.11

PRINCIPLES OF FLIGHT   **SUBSONIC AIRFLOW**

4.4 SUMMARY

Airflow pattern, and ultimately lift and drag, will depend upon:

a) Angle of attack - **airflow cross-sectional area change**

b) Aerofoil shape (thickness & camber). - **airflow cross-sectional area change**

c) Air density - **mass flow of air** (decreases with increased altitude)

d) Velocity - **mass flow of air** (changes with aircraft TAS)

The Lift force is the result of the pressure differential between the top and bottom surfaces of an aerofoil; the greatest contribution to overall lift comes from the top surface.

Anything (Ice in particular, but also frost, snow, dirt, dents and even water droplets) which changes the accurately manufactured profile of the leading portion of the upper surface can seriously disrupt airflow acceleration in that area, and hence the magnitude of the lift force.

An increase in dynamic pressure (IAS) will increase the lift force, and vice versa.

An increase in angle of attack will increase the lift force, and vice versa, (0° to 16°)

The centre of pressure (CP) of a cambered aerofoil moves forward as the angle of attack increases. The (CP) of a symmetrical aerofoil does not move under the influence of angle of attack. (within the confines of 'normal range').

Throughout the normal range of angles of attack the aerofoil nose down pitching moment about the aerodynamic centre (AC) will remain constant. The AC is located at the quarter chord position for subsonic flow of less than M0·4.

The coefficient of lift (C_L) is the ratio between lift per unit wing area and dynamic pressure.

As the angle of attack increases from −4° the leading edge stagnation point moves from the upper surface around the leading edge to the lower surface.

The greatest positive pressure occurs at the leading edge stagnation point, where the relative flow velocity is zero.

Form (pressure) drag is the result of the pressure differential between the leading edge and trailing edge of the aerofoil.

An increase in dynamic pressure (IAS) will increase form drag, and vice versa.

The coefficient of drag (C_D) is the ratio between drag per unit wing area and dynamic pressure.

PRINCIPLES OF FLIGHT **SUBSONIC AIRFLOW**

SELF ASSESSMENT QUESTIONS

1. With reference to aerofoil section terminology, which of the following statements is true:

   1 - The chord line is a line joining the centre of curvature of the leading edge to the centre of the trailing edge, equidistant from the top and bottom surface of the aerofoil.
   2 - The angle of incidence is the angle between the chord line and the horizontal datum of the aircraft.
   3 - The angle between the chord line and the relative airflow is called the aerodynamic incidence or angle of attack.
   4 - The thickness/chord ratio is the maximum thickness of the aerofoil as a percentage of the chord; the location of maximum thickness is measured as a percentage of the chord aft of the leading edge.

   a) 1, 2, 3 and 4
   b) 1, 2 and 4
   c) 2, 3 and 4
   d) 2 and 4

2. The definition of lift is:

   a) the aerodynamic force which acts perpendicular to the chord line of the aerofoil
   b) the aerodynamic force that results from the pressure differentials about an aerofoil
   c) the aerodynamic force which acts perpendicular to the upper surface of the aerofoil
   d) the aerodynamic force which acts at 90° to the relative airflow

3. An aerofoil section is designed to produce lift resulting from a difference in the:

   a) negative air pressure below and a vacuum above the surface.
   b) vacuum below the surface and greater air pressure above the surface.
   c) higher air pressure below the surface and lower air pressure above the surface.
   d) higher air pressure at the leading edge than at the trailing edge.

4. On an aerofoil section, the force of lift acts perpendicular to, and the force of drag acts parallel to the:

   a) flightpath.
   b) longitudinal axis.
   c) chord line.
   d) aerofoil section upper surface.

5. When the angle of attack of a symmetrical aerofoil is increased, the centre of pressure will:

   a) have very limited movement.
   b) move aft along the aerofoil surface.
   c) remain unaffected.
   d) move forward to the leading edge.

6. Why does increasing speed also increase lift?

   a) The increased impact of the relative wind on an aerofoil's lower surface creates a greater amount of air being deflected downward.
   b) The increased speed of the air passing over an aerofoil's upper surface decreases the static pressure, thus creating a greater pressure differential between the upper and lower surface.
   c) The increased velocity of the relative wind overcomes the increased drag.
   d) Increasing speed decreases drag.

7. The point on an aerofoil section through which lift acts is the:

   a) midpoint of the chord.
   b) centre of gravity.
   c) centre of pressure.
   d) aerodynamic centre.

8. The angle between the chord line of the aerofoil section and the longitudinal axis of the aircraft is known as:

   a) the angle of attack.
   b) the angle of incidence.
   c) dihedral.
   d) sweep back.

9. The angle between the chord line of an aerofoil section and the relative wind is known as the angle of:

   a) incidence.
   b) lift.
   c) attack.
   d) sweepback

10. A line drawn from the leading edge to the trailing edge of an aerofoil section and equidistant at all points from the upper and lower contours is called the:

    a) chord line.
    b) camber.
    c) mean camber line.
    d) longitudinal axis.

11. At zero angle of attack, the pressure along the upper surface of a symmetrical aerofoil section would be:

    a) greater than atmospheric pressure.
    b) equal to atmospheric pressure.
    c) less than atmospheric pressure.
    d) non existent.

12. The angle of attack of an aerofoil section directly controls:

    a) amount of airflow above and below the section.
    b) angle of incidence of the section.
    c) distribution of positive and negative pressure acting on the section.
    d) the angle relative to the horizontal datum

13. When the angle of attack of a positively cambered aerofoil is increased, the centre of pressure will:

    a) have very little movement.
    b) move forward along the chord line.
    c) remain unaffected.
    d) move back along the chord

14. The term "angle of attack" is defined as the angle:

    a) formed by the longitudinal axis of the aeroplane and the chord line of the section.
    b) between the section chord line and the relative wind.
    c) between the aeroplane's climb angle and the horizon.
    d) formed by the leading edge of the section and the relative airflow.

PRINCIPLES OF FLIGHT   **SUBSONIC AIRFLOW**

15. Which of the following statements is true:

    1 - Relative airflow, free stream flow, relative wind and aircraft flightpath are parallel.
    2 - Aircraft flightpath, relative airflow, relative wind and free stream flow are parallel, but the aircraft flightpath is opposite in direction.
    3 - The pressure, temperature and relative velocity of the free stream flow are unaffected by the presence of the aircraft.
    4 - The relative wind is produced by the aircraft moving through the air.
    5 - The direction of flight is parallel with and opposite to the relative airflow.

    a)   5 only
    b)   3, 4 and 5
    c)   1 and 2
    d)   1, 2, 3, 4 and 5

16. Which of the following statements is correct:

    1 - Maximum camber is the maximum distance between the top and bottom surface of an aerofoil section.
    2 - The thickness/chord ratio is expressed as a percentage of the chord.
    3 - It is easier for air to flow over a well rounded leading edge radius than a sharp leading edge.
    4 - Two dimensional airflow assumes a wing with the same aerofoil section along its entire span, with no spanwise pressure differential.
    5 - Air flowing towards the lower pressure of the upper surface is called upwash.

    a)   1, 2, 3, 4 and 5
    b)   2, 3 and 4
    c)   2, 3, 4 and 5
    d)   1 and 5

17. When considering an aerofoil section at a constant angle of attack, which of the following statements is true:

    a)   If the static pressure on one side is reduced more than on the other side, a pressure differential will exist.
    b)   If dynamic pressure is increased, the pressure differential will decrease.
    c)   The pressure differential will increase if the dynamic pressure is decreased
    d)   Dynamic pressure and pressure differential are not related.

18. Considering an aerofoil section subject to a constant dynamic pressure, which of the following statements is correct:

    a) If the angle of attack is increased from 4° to 14° the pressure differential will not change but lift will be greater due to increased dynamic pressure acting on the lower surface.
    b) Up to about 16°, increasing the angle of attack will increase the pressure differential between the top and bottom surface of the aerofoil.
    c) Changing the angle of attack does not affect the pressure differential, only changes in dynamic pressure affect the pressure differential.
    d) Up to about 16°, increasing the angle of attack decreases the pressure differential between the top and bottom surface of the aerofoil section.

19. When considering the effect of changing angle of attack on the pitching moment of an aerofoil, which of the following statements is correct:

    1 - At 'normal' angles of attack the pitching moment is nose up.
    2 - The pitching moment about the aerodynamic centre (AC) is constant at 'normal' angles of attack.
    3 - The aerodynamic centre (AC) is located approximately at the 25% chord point.
    4 - The moment about the aerodynamic centre (AC) is a product of the distance between the aerodynamic centre (AC) and the centre of pressure (CP) and the magnitude of the lift force.

    a) 1, 2, 3 and 4
    b) 4 only
    c) 3 and 4
    d) 2, 3 and 4

20. Ice contamination of the leading portion of the aerofoil has which of the following consequences:

    1 - The profile of the leading portion of the surface can be changed, preventing normal acceleration of the airflow and substantially reducing the magnitude of the lift force.
    2 - Form (pressure) drag will be increased because of the increased frontal area of the aerofoil section.
    3 - Loss of lift will have a greater effect than an increase in form (pressure) drag.
    4 - At 'normal' angles of attack lift can be lost entirely if enough ice accumulates.

    a) 1, 2, 3 and 4
    b) 1, 3 and 4
    c) 1, 2 and 3
    d) 3 and 4

INTENTIONALLY

LEFT

BLANK

PRINCIPLES OF FLIGHT — SUBSONIC AIRFLOW

No	A	B	C	D	REF	No	A	B	C	D	REF
1			C			11			C		
2				D		12			C		
3			C			13		B			
4	A					14		B			
5			C			15				D	
6		B				16			C		
7			C			17	A				
8		B				18		B			
9			C			19				D	
10			C			20	A				

PRINCIPLES OF FLIGHT **SUBSONIC AIRFLOW**

CHAPTER 5 - LIFT

Contents

	Page
AERODYNAMIC FORCE COEFFICIENT	5 - 1
THE BASIC LIFT EQUATION	5 - 2
INTERPRETATION OF THE BASIC LIFT EQUATION	
THE LIFT CURVE	5 - 6
INTERPRETATION OF THE LIFT CURVE	
VELOCITY - DYNAMIC PRESSURE RELATIONSHIP	5 - 8
DENSITY ALTITUDE	5 - 9
AEROFOIL SECTION LIFT CHARACTERISTICS	
MINIMUM FLIGHT SPEEDS	
INTRODUCTION TO DRAG CHARACTERISTICS	5 - 10
LIFT/DRAG RATIO	
EFFECT OF WEIGHT ON MINIMUM FLIGHT SPEED	5 - 12
CONDITION OF THE SURFACE	
FLIGHT AT HIGH LIFT CONDITIONS	
EFFECTS OF HIGH LIFT DEVICES	
THREE DIMENSIONAL AIRFLOW	5 - 15
WING TERMINOLOGY	
WING AREA	
WING SPAN	
AVERAGE CHORD	
ASPECT RATIO	
ROOT CHORD	
TIP CHORD	
TAPER RATIO	
SWEEP ANGLE	
MEAN AERODYNAMIC CHORD	
WING TIP VORTICES	5 - 16
INDUCED DOWNWASH	
WAKE TURBULENCE	5 - 18
WAKE VORTEX CHARACTERISTICS	
DISTRIBUTION OF TRAILING VORTICES	5 - 19
VORTEX MOVEMENT NEAR THE GROUND	5 - 20
THE DECAY PROCESS OF TRAILING VORTICES	5 - 21
PROBABILITY OF WAKE TURBULENCE ENCOUNTER	
WAKE TURBULENCE AVOIDANCE	

GROUND EFFECT	5 - 22
THE IMPACT OF GROUND EFFECT	
HIGH AND LOW TAIL CHARACTERISTICS	5 - 23
INFLUENCE OF TAILPLANE CAMBER ON PITCHING MOMENT	5 - 24
TAILPLANE ANGLE OF ATTACK	5 - 25
ENTERING GROUND EFFECT	5 - 26
LEAVING GROUND EFFECT	5 - 27
SUMMARY	5 - 28
ANSWERS FROM PAGE 5 - 7	5 - 29
ANSWERS FROM PAGE 5 - 8	5 - 30
SELF ASSESSMENT QUESTIONS	5 - 31

PRINCIPLES OF FLIGHT — LIFT

5.1 AERODYNAMIC FORCE COEFFICIENT

The aerodynamic forces of both lift and drag depend on the combined effect of many variables. The important factors being:

- a) Airstream velocity (V) ⎫ **Dynamic Pressure** ($\frac{1}{2} \rho V^2$)
- b) Air density (ρ) ⎭
- c) Shape or profile of the surface ⎫ **Pressure Distribution** (C_L or C_D)
- d) Angle of attack ⎭
- e) **Surface area** (S)
- f) Condition of the surface
- g) Compressibility effects (to be considered in later chapters)

Dynamic Pressure: The dynamic pressure ($\frac{1}{2} \rho V^2$) of the airflow is a common denominator of aerodynamic forces and is a major factor since the magnitude of a pressure distribution depends on the energy given to the airflow (KE = $\frac{1}{2} m V^2$).

Pressure Distribution: Another major factor is the relative pressure distribution existing on the surface. The distribution of velocities, with resulting pressure distribution, is determined by the shape or profile of the surface and the angle of attack (C_L or C_D).

Surface Area: Since aerodynamic forces are the result of various pressures distributed on a surface, the surface area (S) is the remaining major factor - the larger the surface area for a given pressure differential, the greater the force generated.

Thus, any aerodynamic force can be represented as the product of three major factors:

1. The dynamic pressure of the airflow ($\frac{1}{2} \rho V^2$)
2. The coefficient of force determined by the relative pressure distribution (C_L or C_D), and
3. The surface area of the object (S)

The relationship of these three factors is expressed by the following equation:

$$F = Q \; C_F \; S$$

where, F = aerodynamic force (Lift or Drag)

Q = dynamic pressure ($\frac{1}{2} \rho V^2$)

C_F = coefficient of aerodynamic force (C_L or C_D)

S = surface area (S)

PRINCIPLES OF FLIGHT — LIFT

5.2 THE BASIC LIFT EQUATION

Lift is defined as the net force generated normal (at 90°) to the relative airflow or flight path of the aircraft.

Lift Constant at any given moment.

The aerodynamic force of lift results from the pressure differential between the top and bottom surfaces of the wing. This lift force can be defined by the following equation:

$$L = \tfrac{1}{2}\rho\, V^2\, C_L\, S$$

Correct interpretation of the Lift formula is a key element in the complete understanding of Principles of Flight.

$$\underset{\text{TO BALANCE WEIGHT}}{\longrightarrow} L = \tfrac{1}{2}\underset{\text{AIR DENSITY}}{\rho}\, \underset{\text{TAS}}{V^2}\, \underset{\text{ANGLE OF ATTACK}}{C_L}\, \underset{\text{FIXED WING AREA}}{S}$$

(Circled: $\tfrac{1}{2}\rho V^2$ — DYNAMIC PRESSURE (IAS))

NB. For the sake of clarity; during this initial examination of the lift formula it is stated that C_L is determined by angle of attack. This is true, but C_L is also influenced by the shape or profile of the surface and other factors which will be amplified in later sections.

- An aircraft spends most of its time in straight and level flight.

- How much lift is required?
  The same as the weight.

- Consider that at any moment in time weight is constant, so lift must be constant.

- While generating the required lift force the less drag the better, because drag has to be balanced by thrust and thrust costs money.

- The value of lift divided by drag is a measure of aerodynamic efficiency. This has a maximum value at one particular angle of attack. For a modern wing this is about 4°. If this "optimum" angle of attack is maintained, maximum aerodynamic efficiency will be achieved. Note: Maximum C_L and minimum C_D are not obtained at best L/D.

PRINCIPLES OF FLIGHT   **LIFT**

- Lift is generated by a pressure differential between the top and bottom surface of the wing. Pressure is reduced by the air accelerating over the top surface of the wing. The wing area must be big enough to generate the required lift force.

- Air gets thinner as altitude increases. If the speed of the aircraft through the air is kept constant as altitude is increased, the amount of air flowing over the wing in a given time would decrease - and lift would decrease.

- For a constant Lift force as altitude is increased, a constant mass flow must be maintained. As air density decreases with altitude the speed of the wing through the air must be increased; the true airspeed (TAS).

If you refer to the ICAO Standard Atmosphere chart on page 2 - 2, the air density at 40,000 ft is only one quarter of the sea level value. We can use this as an example to illustrate the relationship between the changes in TAS that are required as air density changes with altitude.

TO KEEP LIFT CONSTANT AT 40,000 ft, TAS MUST BE DOUBLED

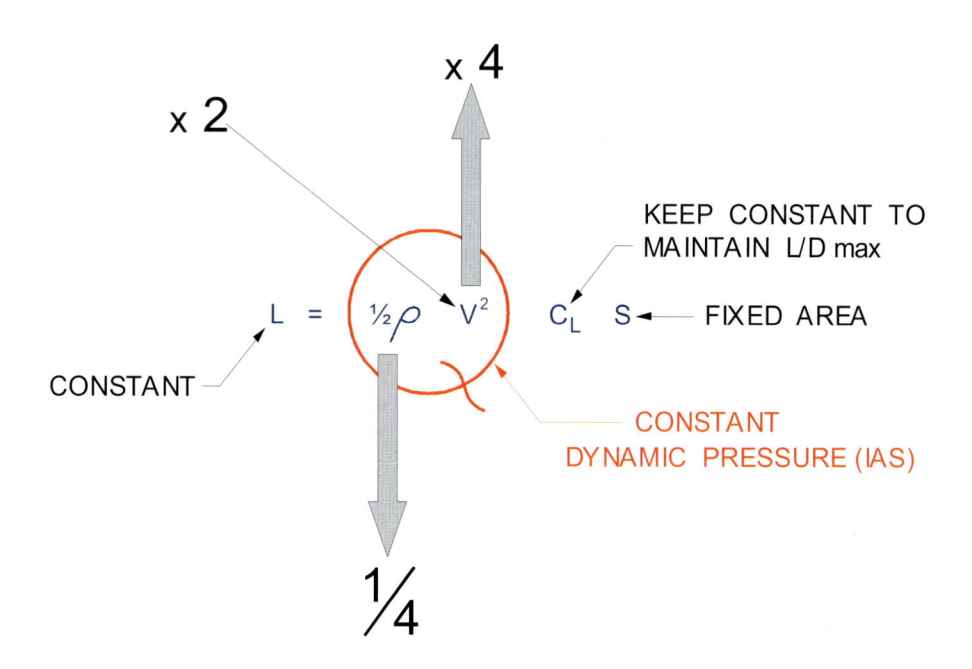

$$L = \tfrac{1}{2}\rho V^2 \, C_L \, S$$

- L = CONSTANT
- $\tfrac{1}{2}\rho V^2$ = CONSTANT DYNAMIC PRESSURE (IAS)
- ρ × $\tfrac{1}{4}$
- V^2 × 4, V × 2
- C_L — KEEP CONSTANT TO MAINTAIN L/D max
- S — FIXED AREA

For this example we will assume the optimum angle of attack of 4° is maintained for aerodynamic efficiency and that the wing area is constant.

At 40,000 ft the air density is $\tfrac{1}{4}$ of the sea level value, so the speed of the aircraft through the air must be doubled to maintain dynamic pressure (hence lift) constant. TAS is squared because essentially we are considering the kinetic energy of the airflow (KE = $\tfrac{1}{2}$ m V^2).

PRINCIPLES OF FLIGHT — LIFT

The lift formula can also be used to consider the relationship between speed and angle of attack at a constant altitude (air density).

IF SPEED IS DOUBLED, C_L MUST BE REDUCED TO ¼ OF ITS PREVIOUS VALUE

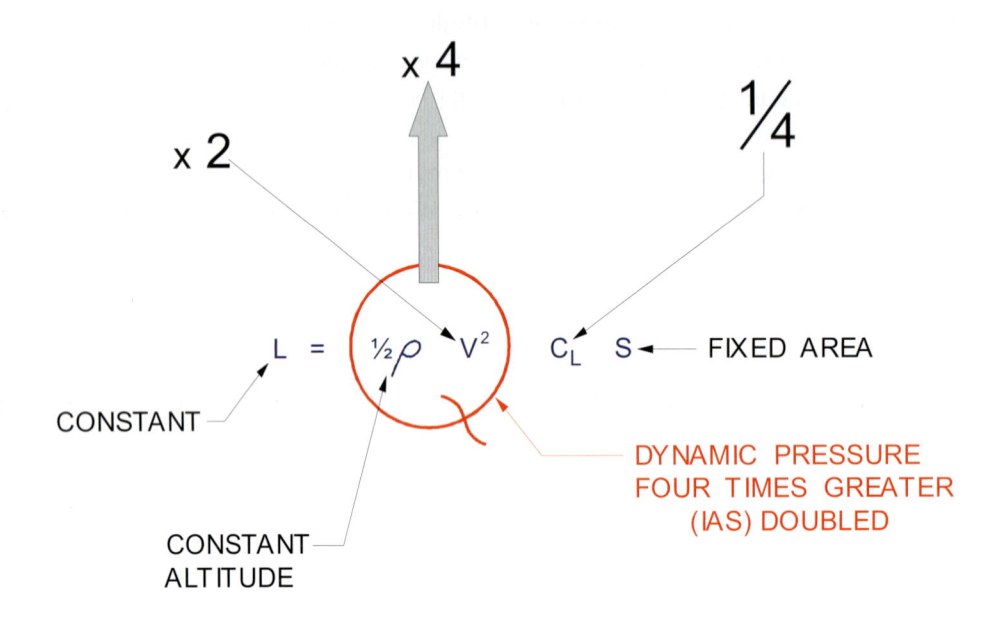

$$L = \tfrac{1}{2}\rho V^2 \; C_L \; S$$

- L = CONSTANT
- ½ρ — CONSTANT ALTITUDE
- V² — ×2 (speed), ×4 (dynamic pressure)
- DYNAMIC PRESSURE FOUR TIMES GREATER (IAS) DOUBLED
- C_L — ¼
- S — FIXED AREA

As speed is changed, angle of attack must be adjusted to keep lift constant.

As an example: if IAS is doubled, TAS will double, and the square function would increase dynamic pressure (hence lift) by a factor of four. As the aircraft is accelerated, the angle of attack must be decreased so that the C_L reduces to one quarter of its previous value to maintain a constant lift force.

It is stated on page 2 - 4 that IAS will vary approximately as the square root of the dynamic pressure. The proportionality between IAS and dynamic pressure is:

$$IAS \propto \sqrt{Q}$$

For the sake of simplicity and to promote a general understanding of this basic principle (though no longer true when considering speeds above 0.4 M), it can be said that TAS will change in proportion to IAS, at constant altitude, (double one, double the other etc).

The lift formula can be transposed to calculate many variables which are of interest to a professional pilot. For example: if speed is increased in level flight by 30% from the minimum level flight speed, we can calculate the new C_L as a percentage of $C_{L\,MAX}$:

PRINCIPLES OF FLIGHT — LIFT

$$L = \tfrac{1}{2}\rho V^2 C_L S \qquad \text{transposed becomes:} \qquad C_L = \frac{L}{\tfrac{1}{2}\rho V^2 S}$$

as density, lift and wing area are constant, this can be written: $C_L \propto \dfrac{1}{V^2}$

30% above minimum level flight speed can be written as 1.3

$\dfrac{1}{V^2}$ now becomes $\dfrac{1}{(1.3)^2} = \dfrac{1}{1.69} = 0.59 \times \dfrac{100}{1} = 59\%$

While maintaining level flight at a speed 30% above minimum level flight speed, the C_L would be 59% of $C_{L\,MAX}$

REVIEW: Lift must balance weight in straight and level flight so at any moment in time, weight and the lift required is constant.

a) to maintain constant lift if density varies because of altitude change, the TAS must be changed.

   (i) if altitude is increased, density decreases, so TAS must be increased.

   (ii) if altitude is decreased, density increases, so TAS must be decreased.

Maintaining a constant IAS will compensate for density changes.

b) to maintain constant lift if speed is changed at a constant altitude (density), the angle of attack must be adjusted.

   (i) if speed is increased, angle of attack must be decreased, (if speed is doubled, angle of attack must be decreased to make C_L one quarter of its previous value).

   (ii) if speed is decreased, angle of attack must be increased, (if speed is halved, angle of attack must be increased to make C_L four times its previous value).

c) generally, a cruise speed is chosen so the aircraft operates at its optimum angle of attack (L/D max - approximately 4°).

PRINCIPLES OF FLIGHT LIFT

5.3 THE LIFT CURVE

Fig. 5.1 shows the lift curve of an aerofoil section, with lift coefficient (C_L) plotted against angle of attack. It is evident that the section is symmetrical because no lift is produced at zero angle of attack.

The lift curve is a convenient way to illustrate the properties of various configurations and will be used extensively throughout these notes.

Lift coefficient increases with angle of attack up to a maximum ($C_{L\,MAX}$), which corresponds to the 'Critical' angle of attack. Continuing to increase the angle of attack beyond this point makes it impossible for the airflow to maintain its previous smooth flow over the contour of the upper surface, and lift will reduce. This phenomena, stall, will be discussed in detail later.

5.3.1 INTERPRETATION OF THE LIFT CURVE

a) To generate a constant lift force, any adjustment in dynamic pressure must be accompanied by a change in angle of attack. (At C_L less than $C_{L\,MAX}$).

b) For a constant lift force, each dynamic pressure requires a specific angle of attack.

c) Minimum dynamic pressure is determined by the maximum lift coefficient ($C_{L\,MAX}$), which occurs at a specific angle of attack (approximately 16°).

d) The angle of attack for $C_{L\,MAX}$ is constant. (This is true for a given configuration).

e) If more lift is required due to greater operating weight, a greater dynamic pressure is required to maintain a given angle of attack.

f) The greater the operating weight, the higher the minimum dynamic pressure.

To use the lift formula with specific values, it is necessary to convert each item to SI units.

The mass of the aircraft is 60,000 kg, to convert to a weight the mass must be multiplied by the acceleration of gravity (9·81 m/s²). The wing area is 105 m². Density is the ICAO Standard Atmosphere sea level value of 1·225 kg/m³.

The speed resulting from the calculation will be in m/s. There are 6080 ft in one nautical mile and 3·28 ft in one metre.

The lift formula: $L = \tfrac{1}{2} \rho V^2 C_L S$

when transposed to calculate speed becomes: $V = \sqrt{\dfrac{L}{\tfrac{1}{2} \rho C_L S}}$

PRINCIPLES OF FLIGHT LIFT

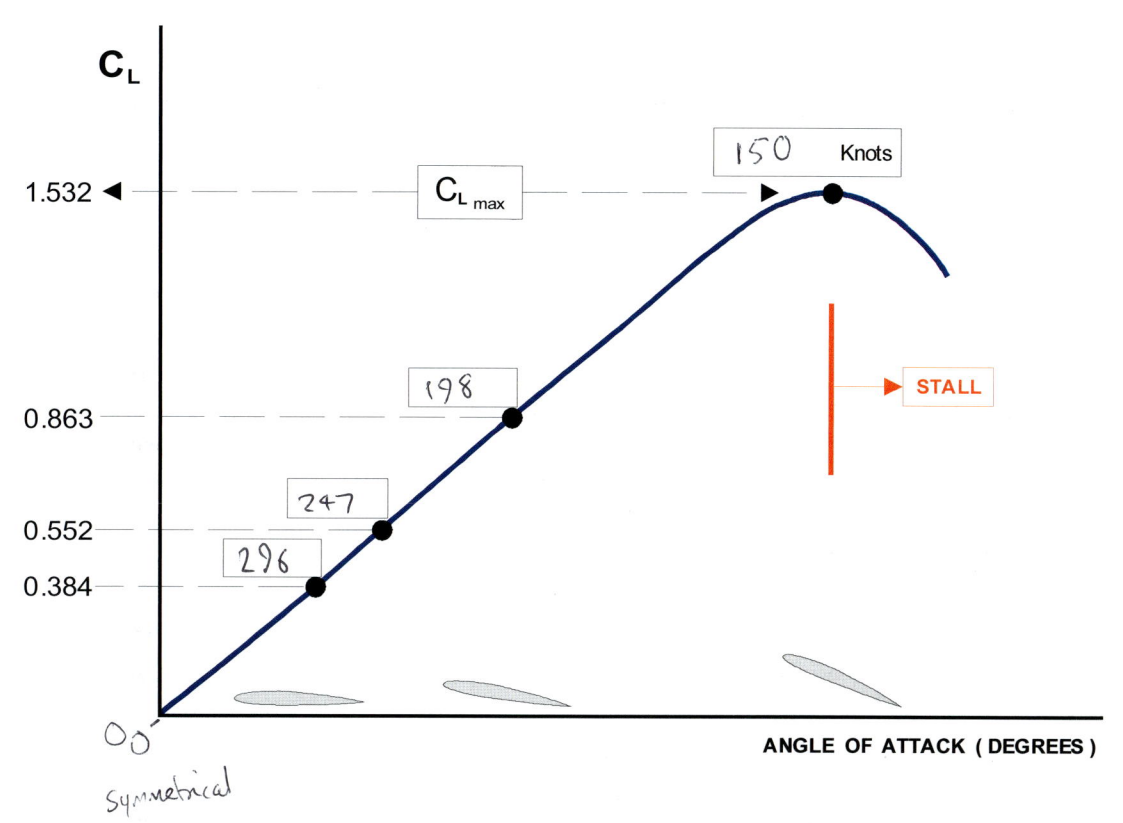

Figure 5.1 Typical Lift Curve

(Annotations visible on figure: C_L values 1.532, 0.863, 0.552, 0.384 with handwritten airspeeds 150 Knots, 198, 247, 296; 0° marked "symmetrical"; $C_{L\,max}$ and STALL labelled.)

Please answer the following questions: ("Answers" are provided on Page 5 - 29)

a) How many Newtons of lift are required for straight and level flight?

b) Calculate the airspeed in knots for each highlighted coefficient of lift.

c) What is the lowest speed at which the aircraft can be flown in level flight?

d) What coefficient of lift must be used to fly as slowly as possible in level flight?

e) Does each angle of attack require a particular speed?

f) As speed is increased what must be done to the angle of attack to maintain level flight?

g) At higher altitude air density will be lower, what must be done to maintain the required lift force if the angle of attack is kept constant?

h) At a constant altitude, if speed is halved, what must be done to the angle of attack to maintain level flight?

PRINCIPLES OF FLIGHT   **LIFT**

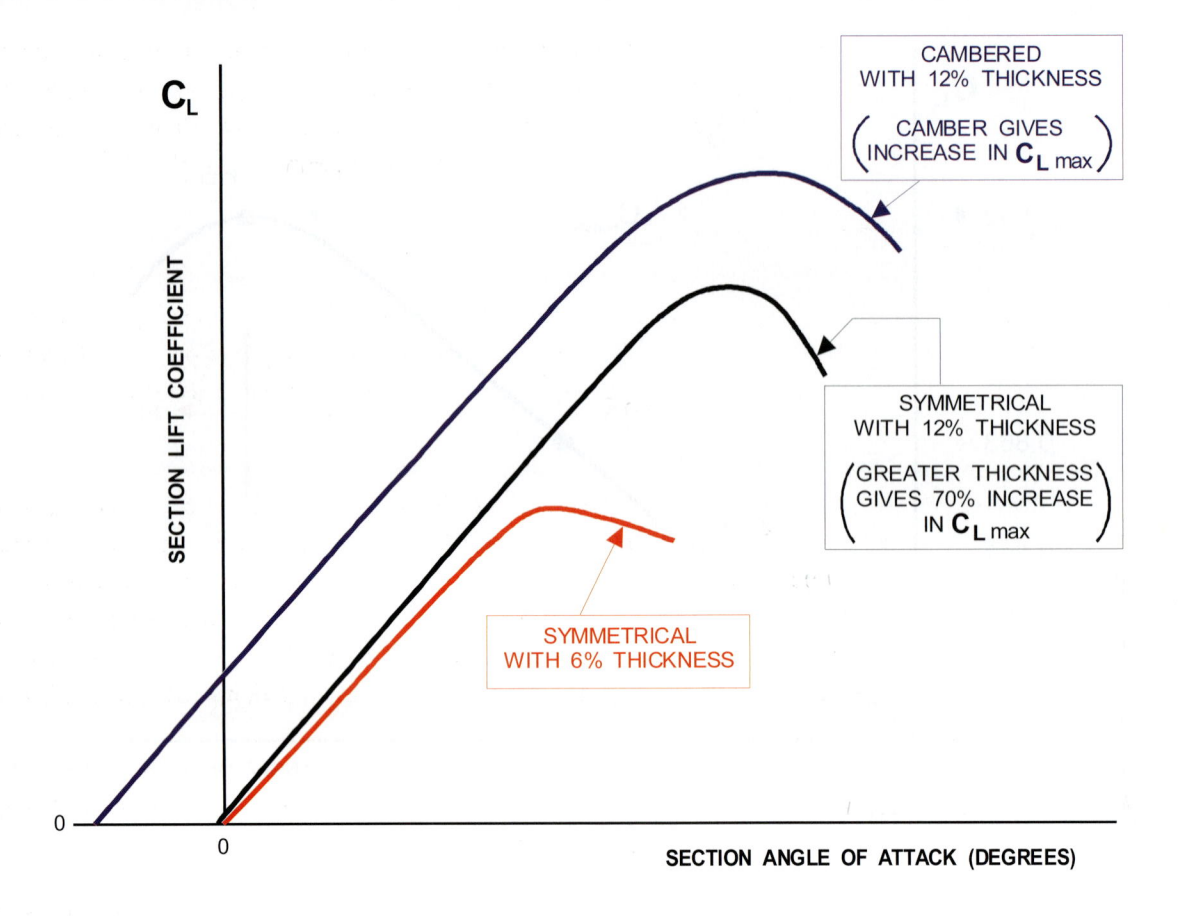

Figure 5.2

Using the above graph, please answer the following questions: ("Answers" on Page 5 - 30)

a) Why does the cambered aerofoil section have a significantly higher $C_{L\,MAX}$?

b) For the same angle of attack, why do the symmetrical aerofoil sections generate less lift than the cambered aerofoil section?

c) Why does the cambered aerofoil section of 12% thickness generate a small amount of lift at slightly negative angles of attack?

d) For a given angle of attack, the symmetrical aerofoil section of 6% thickness generates the smallest amount of lift. In what way can this be a favourable characteristic?

e) What are the disadvantages of the symmetrical aerofoil section of 6% thickness?

5.4 VELOCITY - DYNAMIC PRESSURE RELATIONSHIP

It is very important to understand the relationship between the velocity used in the force equations and dynamic pressure. The velocity in the force equation is the speed of the aircraft relative to the air through which it is moving - the True Air Speed (TAS).

PRINCIPLES OF FLIGHT — LIFT

At a given angle of attack: "For a constant lift force a constant dynamic pressure must be maintained". When an aircraft is flying at an altitude where the air density is other than sea level ISA, the TAS must be varied in proportion to the air density change. With increasing altitude; the TAS must be increased to maintain the same dynamic pressure ($Q = ½ \rho V^2$).

5.4.1 DENSITY ALTITUDE

Air density at the time of take-off and landing can significantly affect aircraft performance. If air density is low, a longer take-off run will be needed. Air density is a product of pressure, temperature and humidity. Humidity reduces air density because the density of water vapour is about 5/8 that of dry air.

On an airfield at sea level with standard pressure, 1013 hPa set in the window will cause the altimeter to read zero. This is the 'Pressure Altitude', which can be very misleading because dynamic pressure depends on the TAS and air density, not just air pressure. If the temperature is above standard, the density of the air will be less, perhaps a lot less, with no direct indication of this fact visible to the pilot. If the temperature is 25°C it would be 10°C above standard (25 - 15 = 10). The air density would be that which would exist at a higher altitude and is given the name, 'high density altitude'.

In practical terms, this means that the aircraft will need a higher TAS for a given dynamic pressure, hence a longer take-off run to achieve the required IAS.

To remember what 'high density altitude' means, think of it as 'HIGH density ALTITUDE'.

5.4.2 AEROFOIL SECTION LIFT CHARACTERISTICS

Fig. 5.2 shows aerofoil sections with different thickness and camber combinations producing specific C_L against α plots.

a) An increase in the thickness of a symmetrical aerofoil gives a higher $C_{L\,MAX}$.

b) The introduction of camber also has a beneficial effect on $C_{L\,MAX}$.

The importance of maximum lift coefficient is obvious: The greater the $C_{L\,MAX}$, the lower the minimum flight speed (stall speed). However, thickness and camber necessary for a high $C_{L\,MAX}$ will produce increased form drag and large twisting moments at high speed. So a high $C_{L\,MAX}$ is just **one** of the requirements for an aerofoil section. The major point is that a high $C_{L\,MAX}$ will give a low minimum flight speed (IAS).

If an aerofoil section of greater camber is used to give a lower minimum flight speed, the efficient cruise speed will be lower due the generation of excessive drag. It is better to use an aerofoil section that is efficient at high cruise speed, with the ability to temporarily increase the camber of the wing when it is necessary to fly slowly. This can be achieved by the use of adjustable hinged sections of the wing leading and trailing edges **(Flaps).**

PRINCIPLES OF FLIGHT — LIFT

5.5 INTRODUCTION TO DRAG CHARACTERISTICS

Drag is the aerodynamic force parallel to the relative airflow and opposite in direction to the flight path. **(Drag, as a complete subject, will be discussed in detail later)**. As with other aerodynamic forces, drag forces may be expressed in the form of a coefficient which is independent of dynamic pressure and surface area.

$$D = Q \, C_D \, S$$

Drag is the product of dynamic pressure, drag coefficient and surface area. C_D is the ratio of drag per unit wing area to dynamic pressure. If the C_D of a representative wing were plotted against angle of attack, the result typically would be a graph similar to that shown in Fig. 5.3. At low angles of attack C_D is low and small changes in angle of attack create only small changes in C_D. But at higher angles of attack, the rate of change in C_D per degree of angle of attack increases; C_D change with angle of attack is exponential. Beyond the stalling angle of attack ($C_{L\,MAX}$), a further large increase in C_D takes place.

5.5.1 LIFT/DRAG RATIO

An appreciation of the efficiency of lift production is gained from studying the ratio between lift and drag; a high L/D ratio being more efficient.

The proportions of C_L and C_D can be calculated for each angle of attack. Fig. 5.4 shows that the L/D ratio increases with angle of attack up to a maximum at about 4°; this is called the 'optimum' angle of attack. The L/D ratio then decreases with increasing angle of attack until $C_{L\,MAX}$ is reached.

NB: The plot of lift, the plot of drag and the plot of L/D ratio shown in Fig. 5.4 are all at different scales and no conclusions should be drawn from the intersection of plots.

The maximum lift/drag ratio (L/D_{MAX}) of a given aerofoil section will occur at one specific angle of attack. If the aircraft is operated in steady level flight at the optimum angle of attack, drag will be least while generating the required lift force. Any angle of attack lower or higher than that for L/D_{MAX} reduces the L/D ratio and consequently increases drag for the required lift.

Assume the L/D_{MAX} of Fig. 5.4. is 12·5. In steady flight at a weight of 588,600N and IAS to give the required lift at 4° angle of attack, the drag would be 47,088N (588,600 ÷ 12·5). Any higher or lower speed would require a different angle of attack to generate the required lift force. Any angle of attack other than 4° will generate more drag than 47,088 N. Of course, this same 'aircraft' could be operated at a different weight and the same L/D_{MAX} of 12·5 could be obtained at the same angle of attack. But a change in weight requires a change in IAS to support the new weight at the same angle of attack. The lower the weight, the lower IAS required to stay at the L/D_{MAX} angle of attack, and vice versa.

For a given configuration (Flaps, gear, spoilers and airframe contamination) and at speeds less than M0·4, changes in weight will not change L/D_{MAX}.

PRINCIPLES OF FLIGHT — LIFT

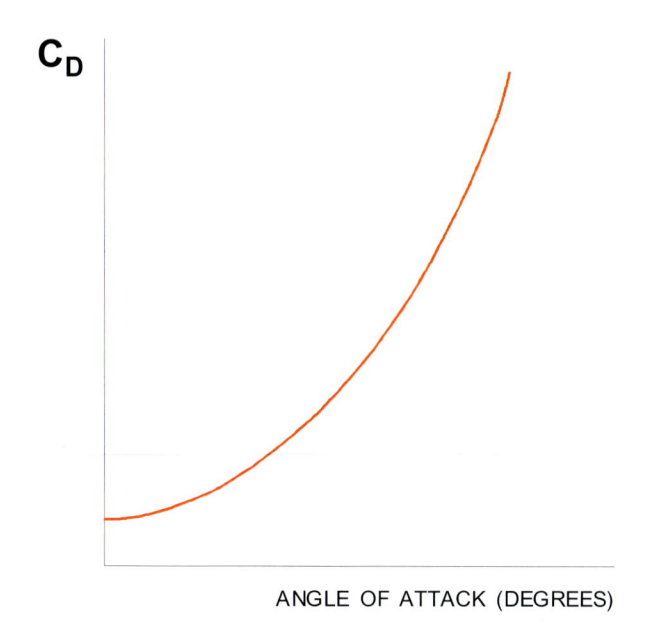

Figure 5.3

required lift, min drag.

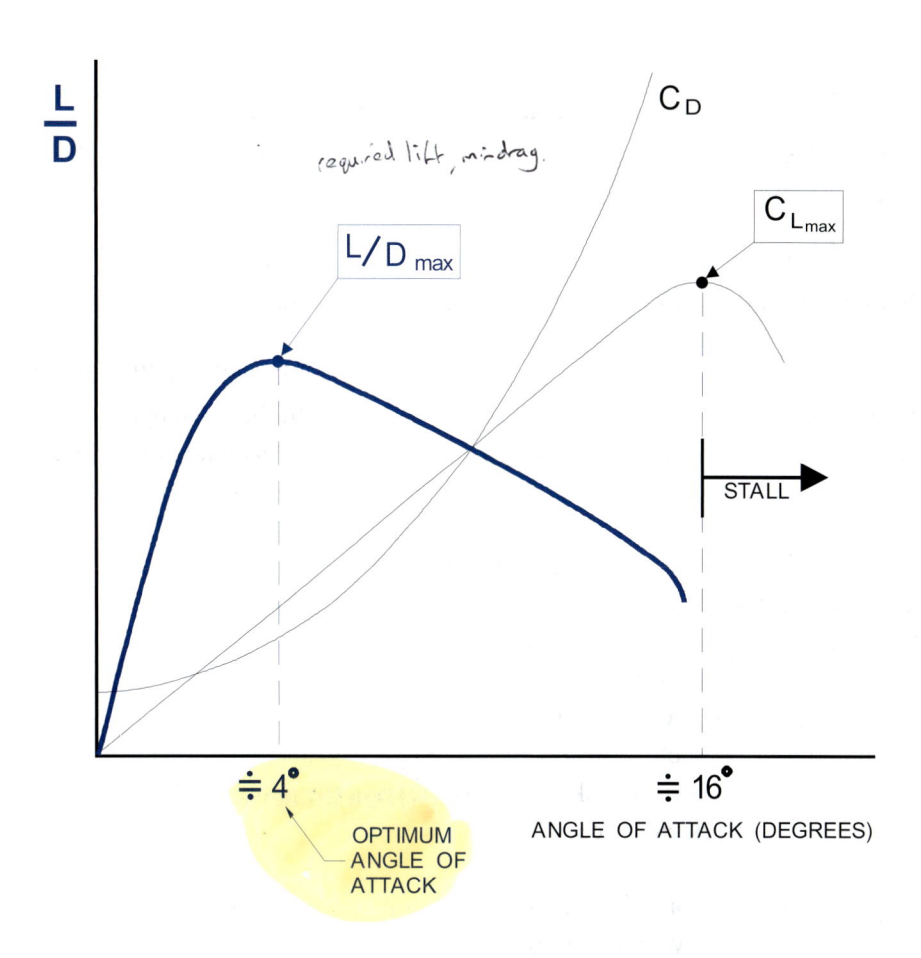

Figure 5.4

The design of an aircraft has a great effect on the L/D ratio. Typical values are listed below for various types.

Aircraft Type	L/D_{MAX}
High performance sailplane	from 25 to 60
Modern jet transport	from 12 to 20
Propeller powered trainer	from 10 to 15

5.6 EFFECT OF AIRCRAFT WEIGHT ON MINIMUM FLIGHT SPEED

A given aerofoil section will always stall at the same angle of attack, but aircraft weight will influence the IAS at which this occurs. Modern large jet transport aircraft may have just over half their maximum gross take-off weight made-up of fuel. So stall speed can vary considerably throughout the flight.

5.7 CONDITION OF THE SURFACE

Surface irregularities, especially near the leading edge, have a considerable effect on the characteristics of aerofoil sections. C_{LMAX} in particular, is sensitive to leading edge roughness. Fig. 5.5 illustrates the effect of a rough leading edge compared to a smooth surface. In general, C_{LMAX} decreases progressively with increasing roughness of the leading edge. Roughness further downstream than about 20 percent of the chord from the leading edge has little effect on C_{LMAX} or the lift-curve slope. Frost, snow and even rainwater can significantly increase surface roughness. Dirt or slush picked-up from contaminated parking areas, taxiways and runways can also have a serious affect. In-flight icing usually accumulates at the leading edge of aerofoils and will severely increase surface roughness causing a significant decrease in C_{LMAX}.

5.8 FLIGHT AT HIGH LIFT CONDITIONS

The aerodynamic lift characteristics of an aircraft are shown by the curve of lift coefficient versus angle of attack in Fig. 5.6, for a specific aircraft in the clean and flap down configurations. A given aerodynamic configuration experiences increases in lift coefficient with increases in angle of attack until the maximum lift coefficient is obtained. A further increase in angle of attack produces stall and the lift coefficient then decreases.

Effect of High Lift Devices: The primary purpose of high lift devices (flaps, slots, slats, etc) is to reduce take-off and landing distance by increasing the C_{LMAX} of the aerofoil section and so reduce the minimum speed. The effect of a "typical" high lift device is shown by the lift curves of Fig. 5.6. The principal effect of the extension of flaps is to increase C_{LMAX} and reduce the angle of attack for any given lift coefficient. The increase in C_{LMAX} afforded by flap deflection reduces the stall speed in a certain proportion. **(High lift devices will be fully covered later)**.

PRINCIPLES OF FLIGHT — LIFT

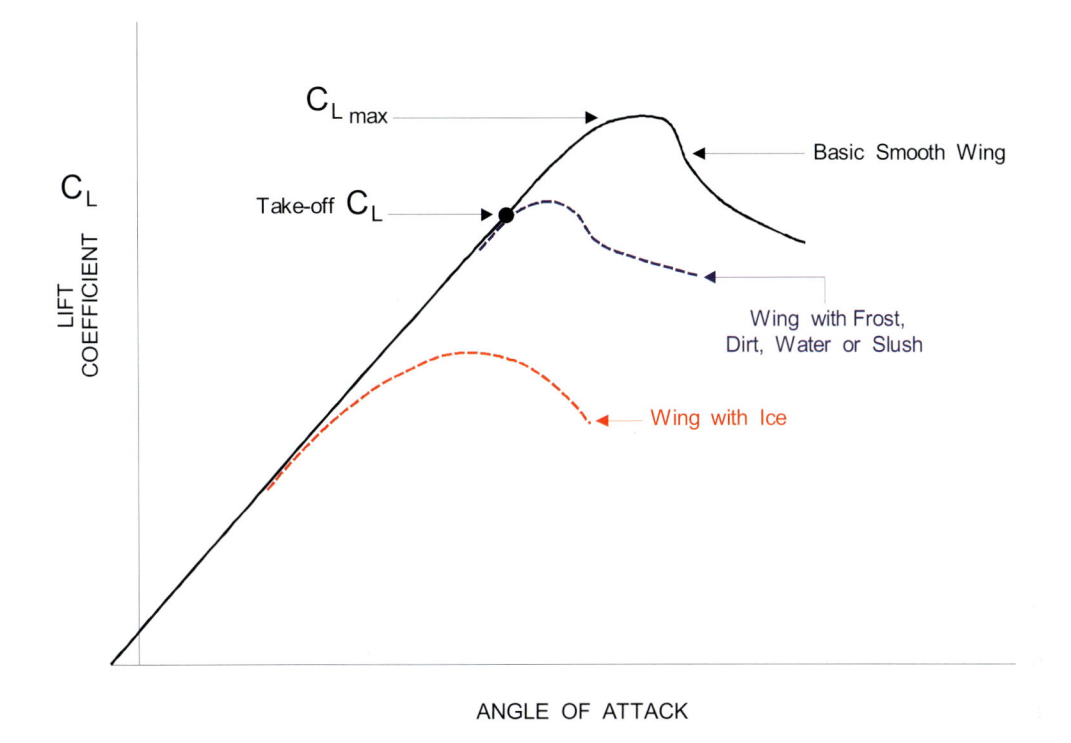

Figure 5.5

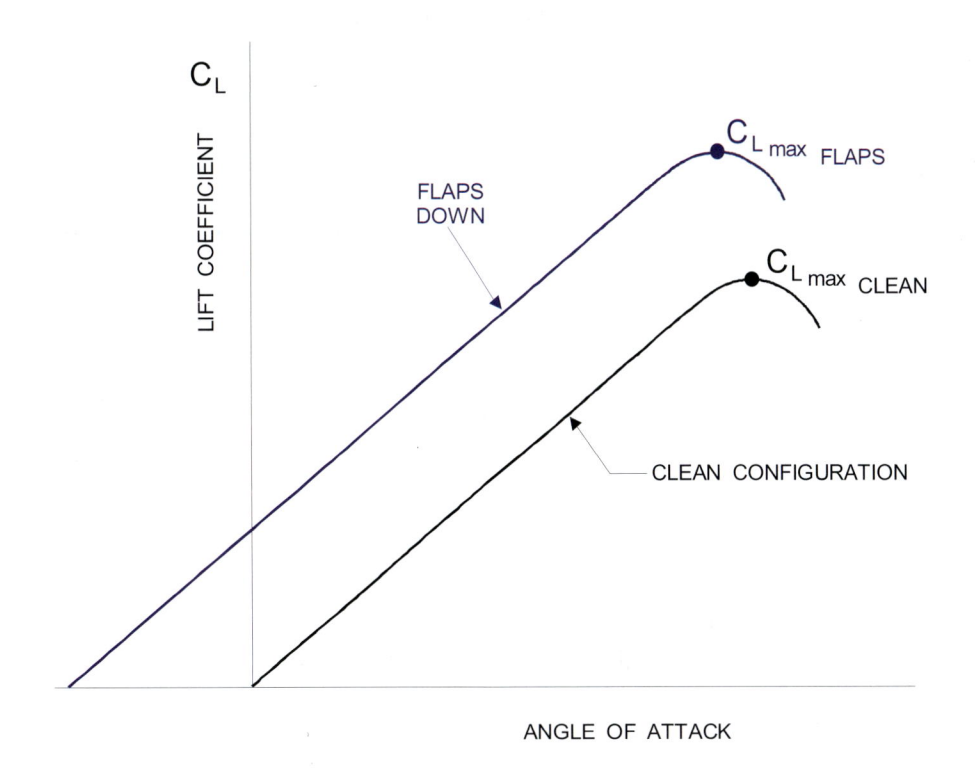

Figure 5.6

PRINCIPLES OF FLIGHT   **LIFT**

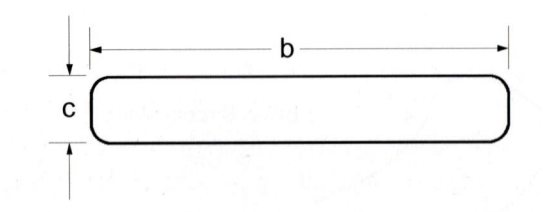

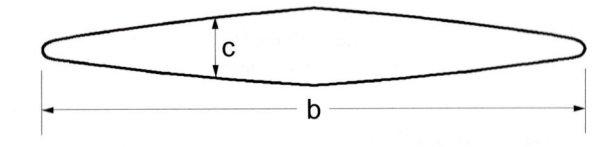

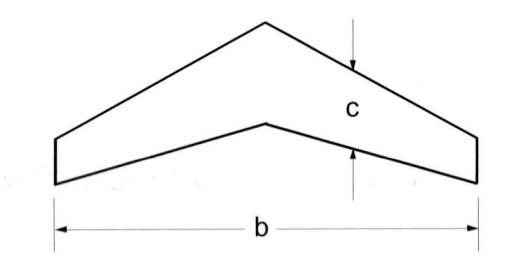

S = WING AREA, sq. m (b x c)

b = SPAN, m

c = AVERAGE CHORD, m

AR = ASPECT RATIO

AR = b/c

AR = b^2/S

C_R = ROOT CHORD, m

C_T = TIP CHORD, m

C_T/C_R = TAPER RATIO

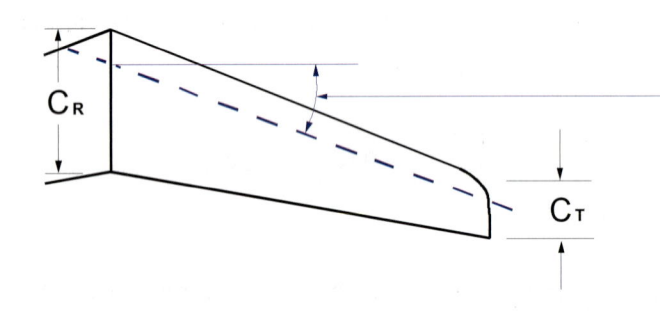

SWEEP ANGLE, degrees

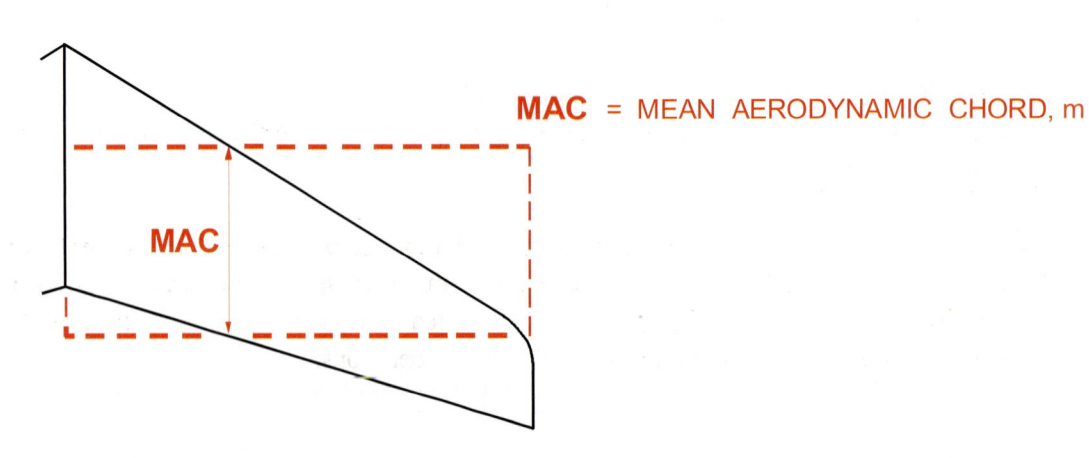

MAC = MEAN AERODYNAMIC CHORD, m

Figure 5.7 Wing Terminology

PRINCIPLES OF FLIGHT

5.9 THREE DIMENSIONAL AIRFLOW

So far we have considered only two dimensional airflow. This has been a foundation for an appreciation of the actual pattern of airflow over an aircraft. Even minute pressure differences will modify airflow direction by inducing air to flow towards any region of lower pressure. Three dimensional airflow modifies the **effective** angle of attack, increases drag, alters stalling characteristics and can influence the control and stability of the aircraft. From now on, instead of just an aerofoil section, the entire wing will be considered.

5.10 WING TERMINOLOGY

Wing Area (S): The plan surface area of the wing. Although a portion of the area may be covered by fuselage or engine nacelles, the pressure carryover on these surfaces allows legitimate consideration of the entire plan area.

Wing Span (b): The distance from tip to tip.

Average Chord (c): The geometric average. The product of the span and the average chord is the wing area (b x c = S).

Aspect Ratio (AR): The proportion of the span and the average chord (AR = b/c). If the planform has curvature and the average chord is not easily determined, an alternative expression is (b^2/S). The aspect ratio of the wing determines the aerodynamic characteristics and structural weight. Typical aspect ratios vary from 35 for a high performance sailplane to 3 for a jet fighter. The aspect ratio of a modern high speed jet transport is about 12.

Root Chord (C_R): The chord length at the wing centreline.

Tip Chord (C_T): The chord length at the wing tip

Taper Ratio (C_T / C_R): The ratio of the tip chord to the root chord. The taper ratio affects the lift distribution and the structural weight of the wing. A rectangular wing has a taper ratio of 1.0 while the pointed tip delta wing has a taper ratio of 0.0

Sweep Angle: Usually measured as the angle between the line of 25% chords and a perpendicular to the root chord. The sweep of a wing causes definite changes in compressibility, maximum lift, and stall characteristics.

Mean Aerodynamic Chord (MAC): The chord drawn through the geographic centre of the plan area. A rectangular wing of this chord and the same span would have broadly similar pitching moment characteristics. The MAC is located on the reference axis of the aircraft and is a primary reference for longitudinal stability considerations.

PRINCIPLES OF FLIGHT   LIFT

5.11 WING TIP VORTICES

Air flowing over the top surface of a wing is at a lower pressure than that beneath. The trailing edge and the wing tips are where the airflows interact. The pressure differential modifies the directions of flow, inducing a span-wise vector towards the root on the upper surface and generally, towards the tip on the lower surface, Fig. 5.8. "Conventionally", an aircraft is viewed from the rear. An anti-clockwise vortex will be induced at the right wing-tip and a clock-wise vortex at the left wing-tip, Figs. 5.9, 5.10 & 5.11.

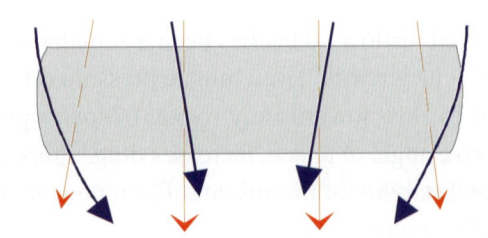

Figure 5.8

Figure 5.9

[Handwritten note: Wing Tip Vortices will only effect the airflow over the wing for 1½ chord lengths in from the trailing edge.]

At higher angles of attack (Lower IAS) the decreased chordwise vector will increase the effect of the resultant spanwise flow, making the vortices stronger.

Induced Downwash: (Fig. 5.12) Trailing vortices create certain vertical velocity components in the airflow in the vicinity of the wing, both in front of and behind it. These vertical velocities cause a downwash over the wing resulting in a reduction in the effective angle of attack. The stronger the vortices, the greater the reduction in effective angle of attack. Because of this local reduction in effective angle of attack, the overall lift generated by a wing will be below the value that would be generated if there were no spanwise pressure differential. It is the production of lift itself which reduces the magnitude of the lift force being generated. To replace the lift lost by the increased downwash, the aircraft must be flown at a higher angle of attack. This increases drag. This extra drag is called **induced drag.** The stronger the vortices, the greater the induced drag.

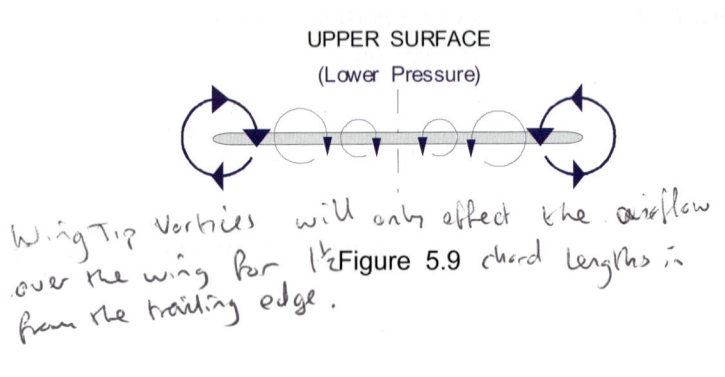

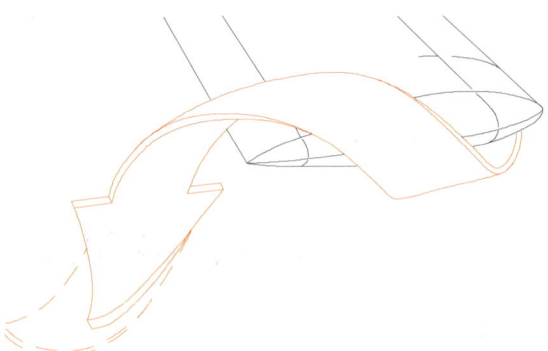

Figure 5.10

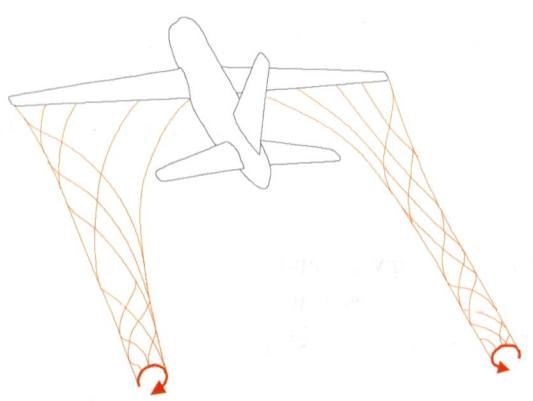

Figure 5.11

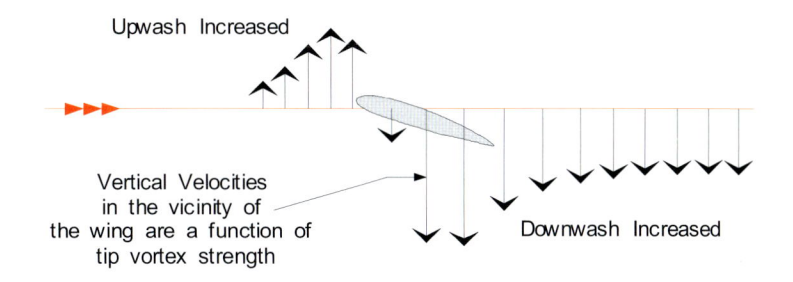

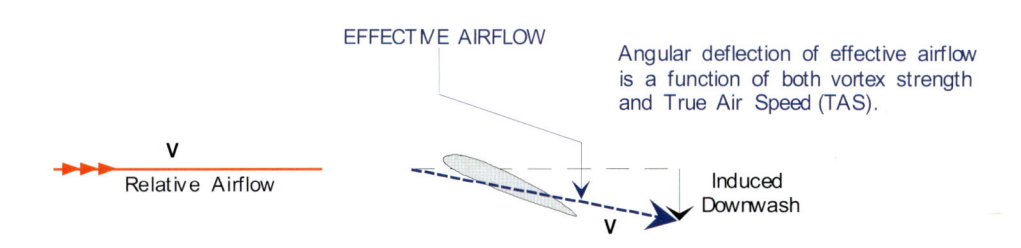

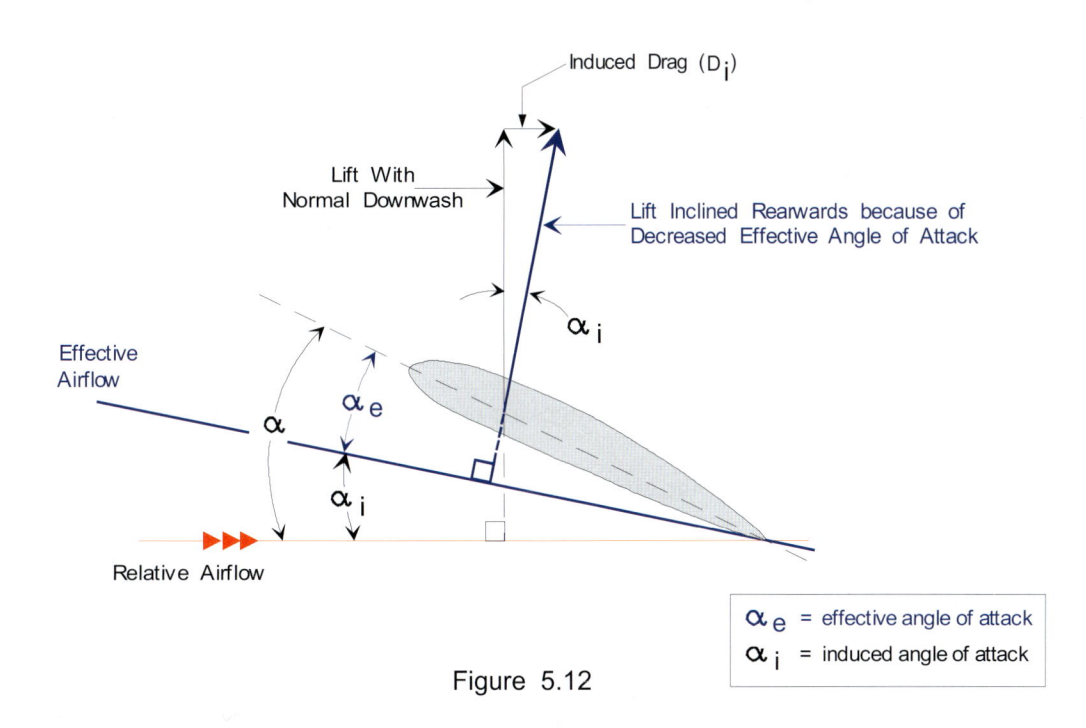

PRINCIPLES OF FLIGHT

LIFT

Upwash Increased

Vertical Velocities in the vicinity of the wing are a function of tip vortex strength

Downwash Increased

EFFECTIVE AIRFLOW

Angular deflection of effective airflow is a function of both vortex strength and True Air Speed (TAS).

V
Relative Airflow

Induced Downwash

Induced Drag (D_i)

Lift With Normal Downwash

Lift Inclined Rearwards because of Decreased Effective Angle of Attack

α_i

Effective Airflow

α α_e

α_i

Relative Airflow

α_e = effective angle of attack
α_i = induced angle of attack

Figure 5.12

Wing tip vortices, in particular their influence on upwash and downwash, have a significant effect on several important areas of aircraft aerodynamics, stability and control. Some of these effects will be examined now and throughout the remaining chapters.

PRINCIPLES OF FLIGHT   LIFT

5.12   WAKE TURBULENCE: (Ref: AIC 17/1999)

Trailing wingtip vortices extend behind aircraft for a considerable distance and can present an **extreme hazard** to any aircraft unfortunate enough to encounter them. Maximum tangential airspeed in the vortex system may be as high as 90 m/s (300 ft/sec) immediately behind a large aircraft. Wake turbulence cannot be detected, so it is important for pilots to be aware of the potential distribution and duration of trailing vortices, plus modifications made to the "classic" vortex system by surface wind speed and direction.

Aircraft Wake Vortex Characteristics: Wake vortex generation begins when the nosewheel lifts off the runway on take-off and continues until the nosewheel touches down on landing. Wake vortices exist behind every aircraft, **including helicopters**, when in flight, but are most severe when generated by heavy aircraft. They present the greatest danger during the take-off, initial climb, final approach and landing phases of flight - in other words, at low altitude where large numbers of aircraft congregate. A wake turbulence encounter is a hazard due to potential loss of control and possible structural damage, and if the experience takes place near the ground there may be insufficient time and/or altitude to recover from an upset.

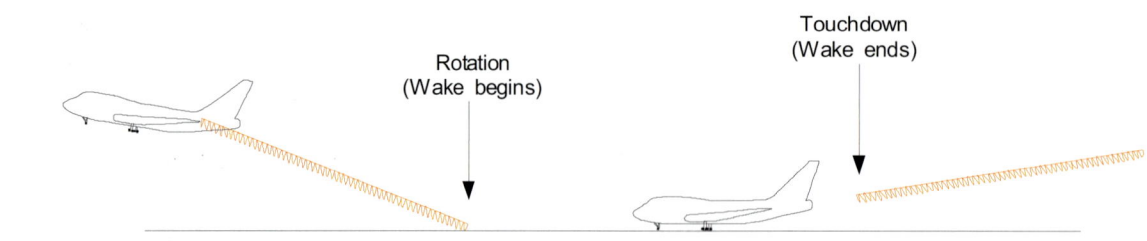

Figure 5.13

The characteristics of trailing vortices are determined by the "generating" aircraft's:

(a)   Gross weight - the higher the weight, the stronger the vortices.

(b)   Wingspan - has an influence upon the proximity of the two trailing vortices.

(c)   Airspeed - the lower the speed, the stronger the vortices.

(d)   Configuration - vortex strength is greatest with aircraft in a "clean" configuration (for a given speed and weight).

(e)   Attitude - the higher the angle of attack, the stronger the vortices.

PRINCIPLES OF FLIGHT LIFT

As a general rule, the larger the "generating" aircraft relative to the aircraft encountering the wake turbulence, the greater the hazard. There is also evidence that for a given weight and speed a helicopter produces a stronger vortex than a fixed-wing aircraft.

Distribution of Trailing Vortices: Typically the two trailing vortices remain separated by about three quarters of the aircraft's wingspan and in still air they tend to drift slowly downwards and level off, usually between 500 and 1000 ft below the flight path of the aircraft. Behind a large aircraft the trailing vortices can extend as much as nine nautical miles.

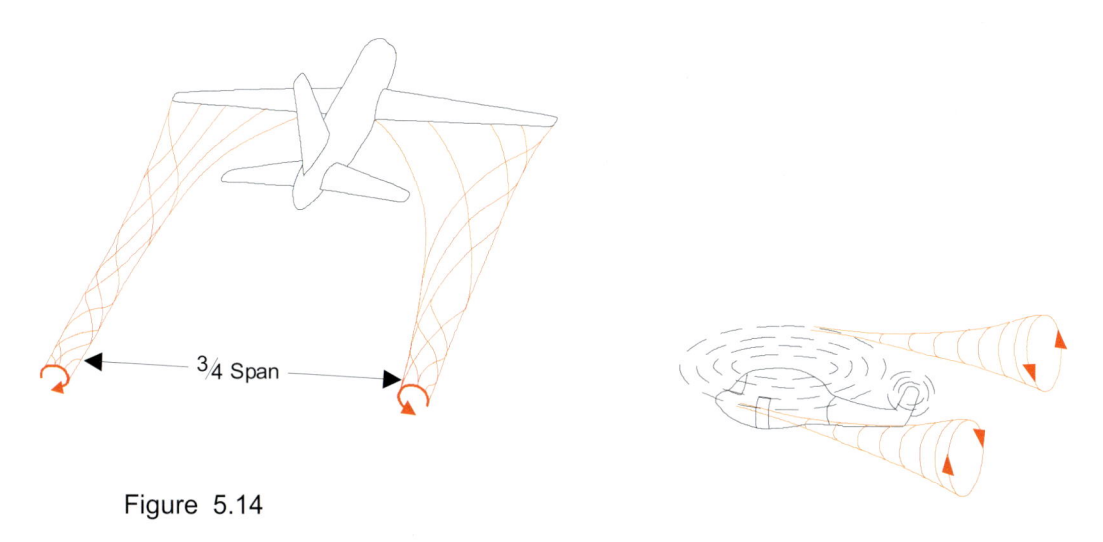

Figure 5.14

Figure 5.15

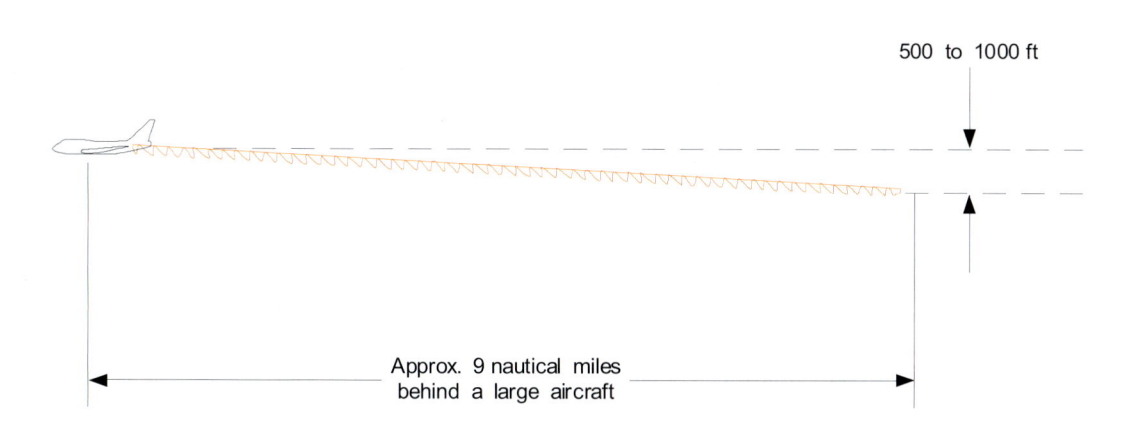

Figure 5.16

PRINCIPLES OF FLIGHT

Vortex Movement near the Ground: Fig. 5.17 shows that if the generating aircraft is within 1000 ft of the ground, the two vortices will "touch-down" and move outwards at about 5 kts from the track of the generating aircraft at a height approximately equal to ½ the aircraft's wingspan.

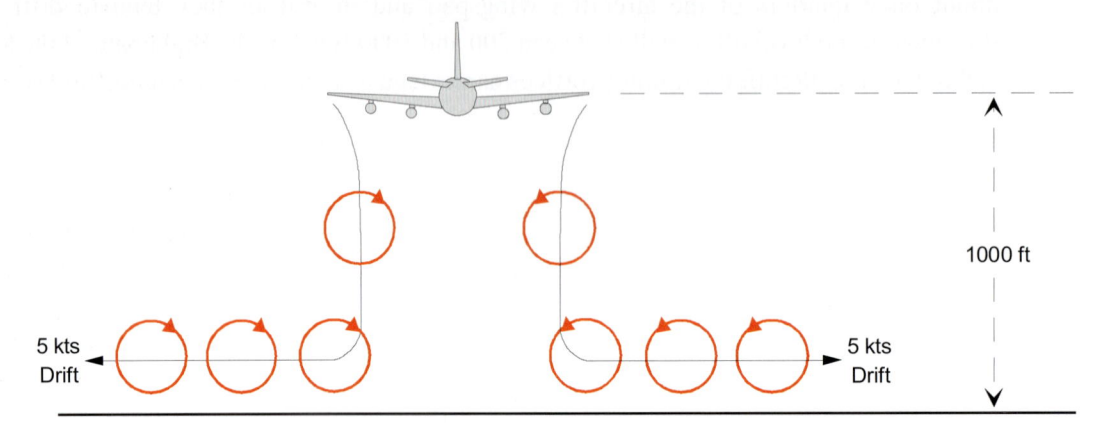

STILL AIR - (viewed from the rear)

Figure 5.17

In a crosswind, if the surface wind is light and steady, the wake vortex system "in contact" with the ground will drift with the wind. Fig. 5.18 shows the possible effect of a crosswind on the motion of a vortex close to the ground. With parallel runways, wake turbulence from an aircraft operating on one runway can be a potential hazard to aircraft operating from the other.

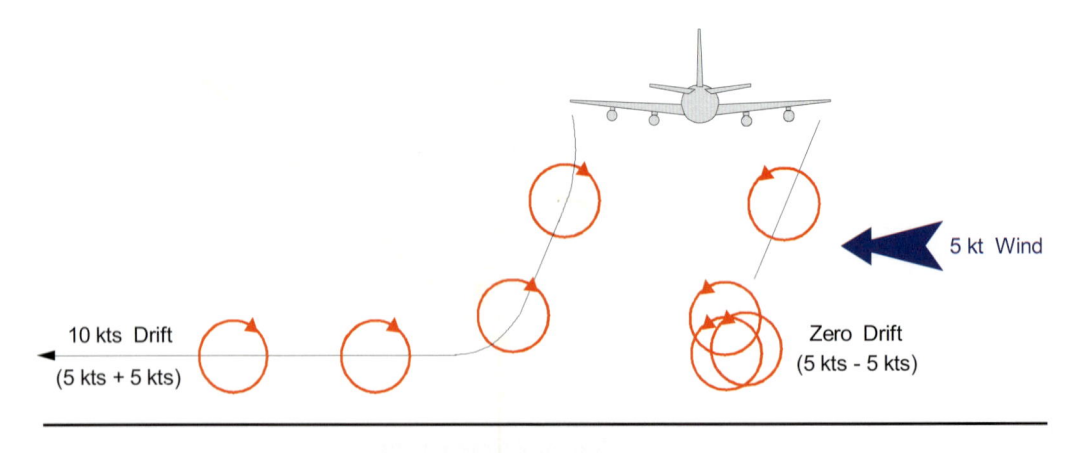

5 kt CROSSWIND - (Viewed from the rear)

Figure 5.18

PRINCIPLES OF FLIGHT — LIFT

The Decay Process of Trailing vortices: Atmospheric turbulence has the greatest influence on the decay of wake vortices; the stronger the wind, the quicker the decay.

Probability of Wake Turbulence Encounter: Certain separation minima are applied by Air Traffic Control (ATC), but **this does not guarantee avoidance.** ATC applied separation merely reduces the probability of an encounter to a lower level, and may minimise the magnitude of the upset if an encounter does occur. Particular care should be exercised when following any substantially heavier aircraft, especially in conditions of light wind. The majority of serious incidents, close to the ground, occur when winds are light.

Wake Turbulence Avoidance: If the location of wake vortices behind a preceding or crossing aircraft are visualised, appropriate flight path control will minimise the probability of a wake turbulence encounter. Staying above and/or upwind of a preceding or crossing aircraft will usually keep your aircraft out of the generating aircraft's wake vortex. Unfortunately, deviating from published approach and departure requirements in order to stay above/upwind of the flight path of a preceding aircraft may not be advisable. Maintaining proper separation remains the best advice for avoiding a wake turbulence encounter.

Rolling

Increased Wing Tip Vortices

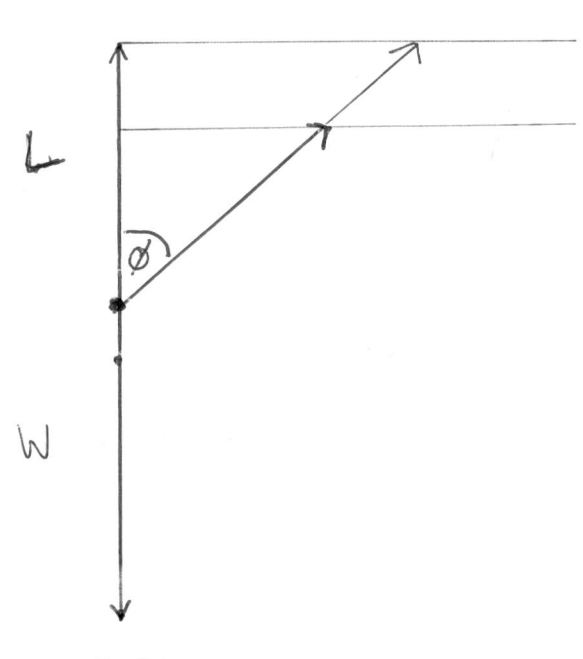

PRINCIPLES OF FLIGHT LIFT

5.13 GROUND EFFECT

When landing and taking off, the closeness of the wing to the ground prevents full development of the trailing vortices, Fig. 5.19, making them much weaker. Upwash and downwash are reduced, causing the effective angle of attack of the wing to increase, (ref: Fig. 5.12). Therefore, when an aircraft is **"in ground effect"** lift will generally be increased and induced drag (C_{Di}) will be decreased. In addition, the reduced downwash will effect both longitudinal stability because of CP movement, and the pitching moment because of changes to the effective angle of attack of the tailplane, (Ref: Fig. 5.21).

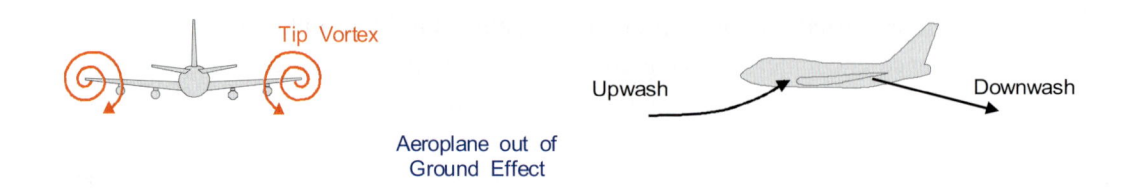

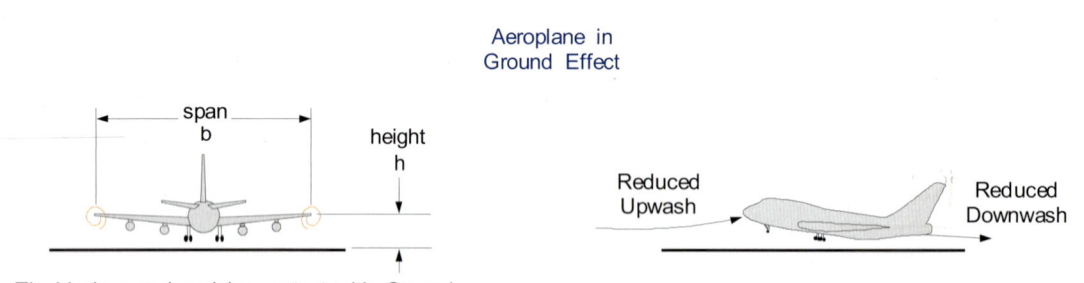

Figure 5.19

The Impact of Ground Effect: The influence of ground effect depends on the distance of the wing above the ground. A large reduction in C_{Di} will take place only when the wing is **very close** to the ground, (within half the wingspan).

For a representative aircraft with a 40m span, (Ref. Fig. 5.20):

(a) At a height of 40m, the reduction in C_{Di} is only 1.4%.

(b) At a height of 10m, the reduction in C_{Di} is 23.5%, but

(c) At a height of 4m, the reduction in C_{Di} is 47.6%

PRINCIPLES OF FLIGHT
LIFT

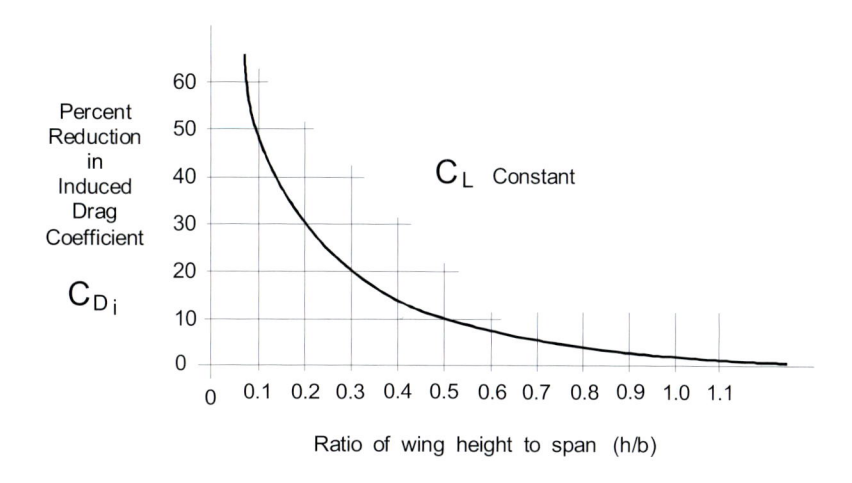

Figure 5.20

The height of the wing above the ground when the aircraft is in the landing attitude is influenced by its mounting position on the fuselage. From the graph in Fig. 5.20 it can be seen that the last few metres makes a big difference to the reduction of C_{Di}. In general, it can be said that a low wing aircraft will experience a greater degree of ground effect than an aircraft with a high mounted wing.

High and Low Tail Characteristics: While ground effect may possibly change the aerodynamic characteristics of the tailplane in its own right, a low mounted tailplane will have its effective angle of attack modified by the changing downwash angle behind the wing. A high mounted tailplane **may** be outside the influence of the changing downwash angle and not suffer the same disadvantages.

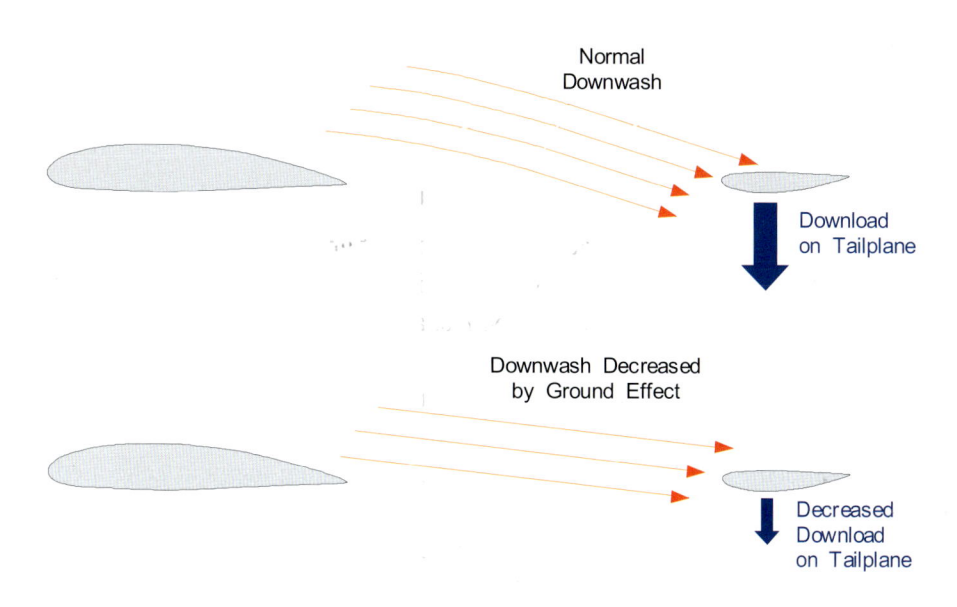

Figure 5.21

PRINCIPLES OF FLIGHT

LIFT

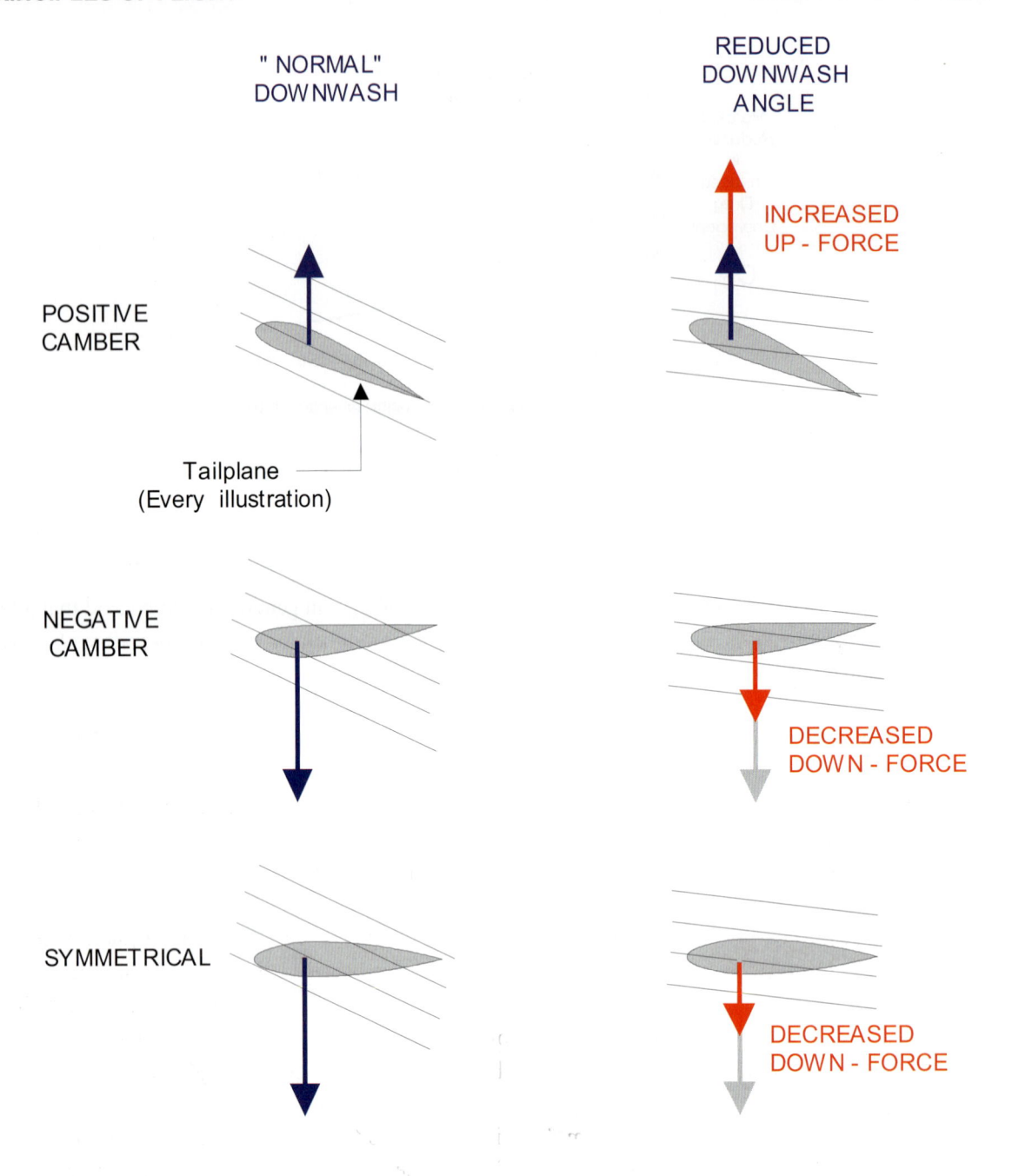

Figure 5.22   Influence of Camber on Effect of downwash on pitching moment

Influence of Tailplane Camber on Pitching Moment: It can be seen from Fig. 5.22 that the type of tailplane camber does not influence the pitching moment generated when downwash from the wing changes. Decreased downwash will always result in an aircraft nose down pitching moment. The opposite will be true of increased downwash.

Downwash will change not only because of ground effect, but also when flaps are operated and when a shockwave forms on the wing at speeds higher than M_{CRIT}, so appreciation of this phenomena is a key element towards a full understanding of Principles of Flight.

PRINCIPLES OF FLIGHT   LIFT

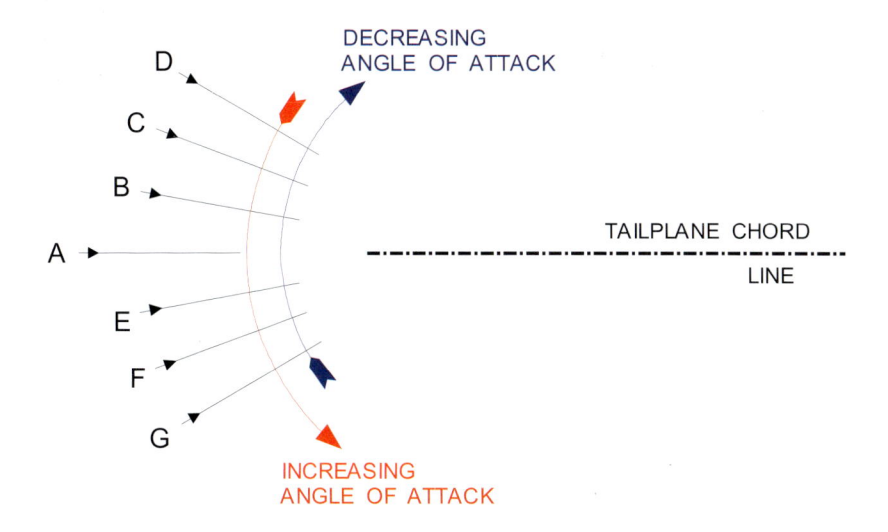

Figure 5.23 Influence of Downwash on Tailplane Angle of Attack

Tailplane Angle of Attack: Angle of Attack is the angle between the chord line and the Relative Airflow. The Relative Airflow has three characteristics:

1. Magnitude - the speed of the aircraft through the air; the True Air Speed (TAS)

2. Direction - parallel to and in the opposite direction to the aircraft flight path, and

3. Condition - unaffected by the presence of the aircraft.

Air flowing off the wing trailing edge (downwash) cannot be defined as relative airflow because it does not conform to the definitions. Neither is it possible to think strictly of a tailplane angle of attack. Airflow which has been influenced by the presence of the aircraft (direction of flow and dynamic pressure) must be thought of as **Effective Airflow**. And the angle between the chord line and the effective airflow must be thought of as **Effective Angle of Attack**.

Consider Fig. 5.23. Airflow from direction (A) gives the tailplane zero (effective) angle of attack. Airflow from direction (E, F or G) would be an increase in (effective) angle of attack. If airflow from direction (G) is now considered, flow from (F, E, A, B, C or D) would be a decrease in (effective) angle of attack. **The term "negative angle of attack" is not used**.

CONCLUSION
Increasing downwash (G to D) gives a decrease in tailplane (effective) angle of attack and decreasing downwash (D to G) gives an increase in tailplane (effective) angle of attack.

It is necessary to understand the effect of changing downwash on tailplane angle of attack, but it is vital to understand the influence of downwash on aircraft pitching moment.

PRINCIPLES OF FLIGHT — LIFT

Entering Ground Effect: Consider an aircraft entering ground effect, assuming that a constant C_L and IAS is maintained. As the aircraft descends into ground effect the following changes will take place:

(a) The decreased downwash will give an increase in the **effective** angle of attack, requiring a smaller wing angle of attack to produce the same lift coefficient. If a constant pitch attitude is maintained as ground effect is encountered, a "floating" sensation may be experienced due to the increase in C_L and the decrease in C_{Di} (thrust requirement), Fig's. 5.12 & 5.24. The decrease of induced drag will cause a reduction in deceleration, and any excess speed may lead to a considerable "float" distance. The reduction in thrust required might also give the aircraft a tendency to climb above the desired glide path, "balloon", if a reduced throttle setting is not used.

(b) If airspeed is allowed to decay significantly during short finals and the resulting sink-rate arrested by increasing the angle of attack, upon entering ground effect the wing could stall, resulting in a heavy landing.

(c) The pilot may need to increase pitch input (more elevator back-pressure) to maintain the desired landing attitude. This is due to the decreased downwash increasing the effective angle of attack of the tailplane, Fig. 5.21. The download on the tail is reduced, producing a nose down pitching moment.

(d) Due to the changes in the flowfield around the aircraft there will be a change in position error which may cause the ASI to misread. In the majority of cases, local pressure at the static port will increase and cause the ASI and altimeter to under read.

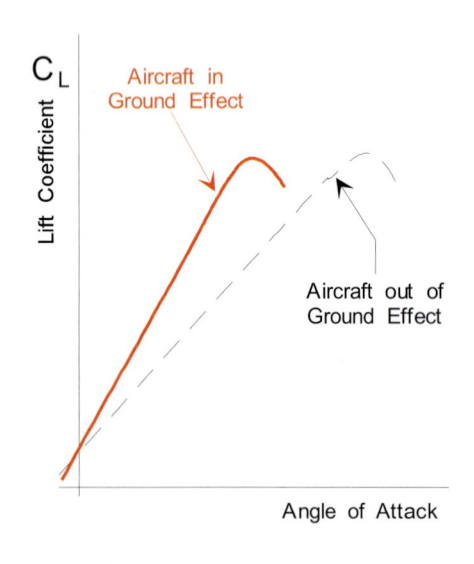

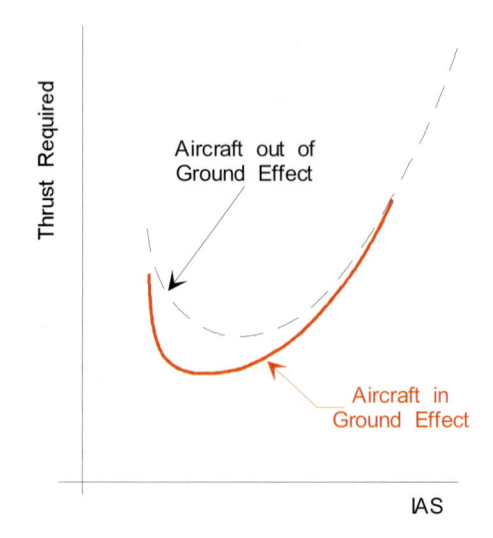

Figure 5.24

PRINCIPLES OF FLIGHT — LIFT

Leaving Ground Effect: The effects of climbing out of ground effect will generally be the opposite to those of entering. Consider an aircraft climbing out of ground effect while maintaining a constant C_L and IAS. As the aircraft climbs out of ground effect the following changes will take place:

(a) The C_L will reduce and the $C_{D\,i}$ (thrust requirement) will increase. The aircraft will require an increase in angle of attack to maintain the same C_L.

(b) The increase in downwash will generally produce a nose up pitching moment. The pitch input from the pilot may need to be reduced (less elevator back-pressure).

(c) Position error changes may cause the ASI to misread. In the majority of cases, local pressure at the static port will decrease and cause the ASI and altimeter to over read.

(d) It is possible to become airborne in ground effect at an airspeed and angle of attack which would, after leaving ground effect, cause the aircraft to settle-back on to the runway It is therefore vitally important that correct speeds are used for take-off.

(e) The nose up pitching moment may induce an inadvertent over rotation and tail strike.

5.14 SUMMARY

Three major factors influence production of the required lift force:

(a) Dynamic Pressure (IAS)

(b) Pressure Distribution (Section profile & Angle of attack)

(c) Wing Area (S)

To provide a constant lift force, each IAS corresponds to a particular angle of attack.

The angle of attack at $C_{L\,MAX}$ is constant.

A higher aircraft weight requires a lift force to balance it; an increased IAS is needed to provide the greater lift at the same angle of attack.

As altitude increases a constant IAS will supply the same lift force at a given angle of attack.

A thinner wing will generate less lift at a given angle of attack, and have a higher minimum speed.

A thinner wing can fly faster before shock wave formation increases drag.

A thinner wing requires high lift devices to have an acceptably low minimum speed.

The Lift/Drag ratio is a measure of aerodynamic efficiency.

Contamination of the wing surface, particularly the front 20% of the chord, will seriously decrease aerodynamic performance.

Wing tip vortices:

(a) Decrease overall lift production.

(b) Increase drag.

(c) Modify the downwash which changes the effective angle of attack of the tailplane.

(d) Generate trailing vortices which pose a serious hazard to aircraft that encounter them.

(e) Affect the stall characteristics of the wing

(f) Change the lift distribution.

The sudden full effects of vortices or their absence must be anticipated during take-off and landing.

PRINCIPLES OF FLIGHT   **LIFT**

ANSWERS FROM PAGE 5 - 7

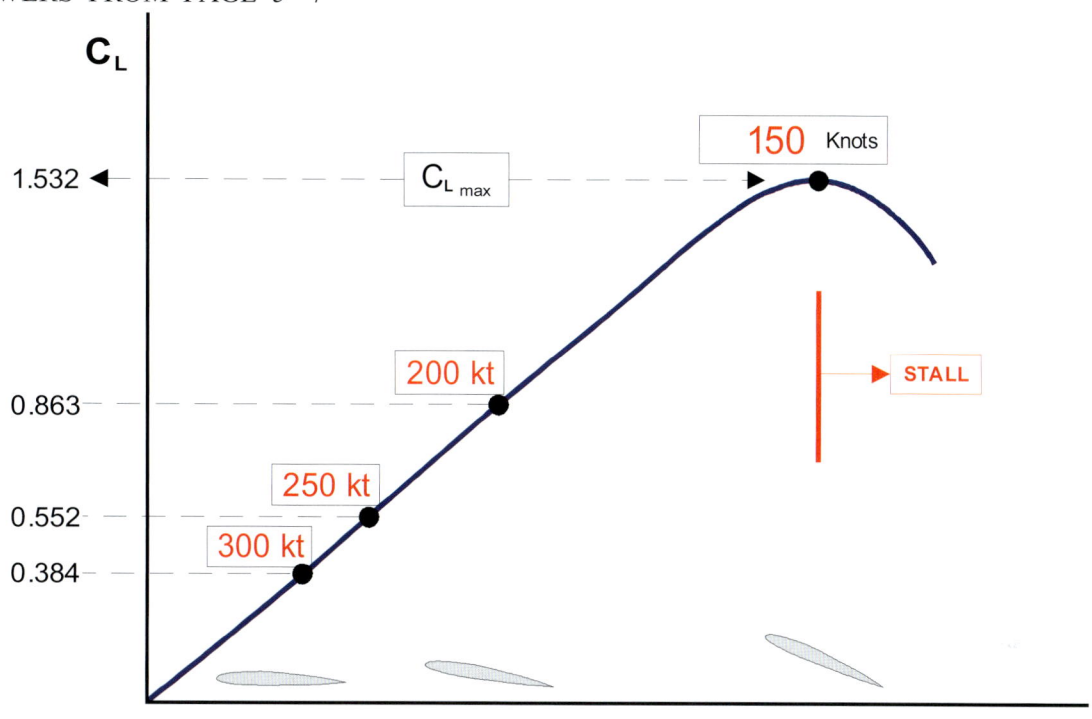

[Graph: C_L vs Angle of Attack (degrees), showing points at:
- 1.532 — $C_{L\,max}$ — 150 Knots (STALL)
- 0.863 — 200 kt
- 0.552 — 250 kt
- 0.384 — 300 kt]

a) How many Newtons of lift are required for straight and level flight? **588,600 N**.

b) Calculate the airspeed in knots for each highlighted coefficient of lift. **As above**.

c) What is the lowest speed at which the aircraft can be flown in level flight? **150 kt**.

d) What coefficient of lift must be used to fly as slowly as possible in level flight? $\mathbf{C_{L\,MAX}}$

e) Does each angle of attack require a particular speed? **Yes**.

f) As speed is increased what must be done to the angle of attack to maintain level flight? **Angle of attack must be decreased**.

g) At higher altitude air density will be lower, what must be done to maintain the required lift force? **Increase the True Airspeed (TAS)**.

h) At a constant altitude, if speed is halved, what must be done to the angle of attack to maintain level flight? **Increased so that C_L is four times greater**.

PRINCIPLES OF FLIGHT — LIFT

ANSWERS FROM PAGE 5 - 8

[Graph: Section Lift Coefficient (C_L) vs Section Angle of Attack (degrees), showing three curves:
- CAMBERED WITH 12% THICKNESS (CAMBER GIVES INCREASE IN $C_{L\,max}$)
- SYMMETRICAL WITH 12% THICKNESS (GREATER THICKNESS GIVES 70% INCREASE IN $C_{L\,max}$)
- SYMMETRICAL WITH 6% THICKNESS]

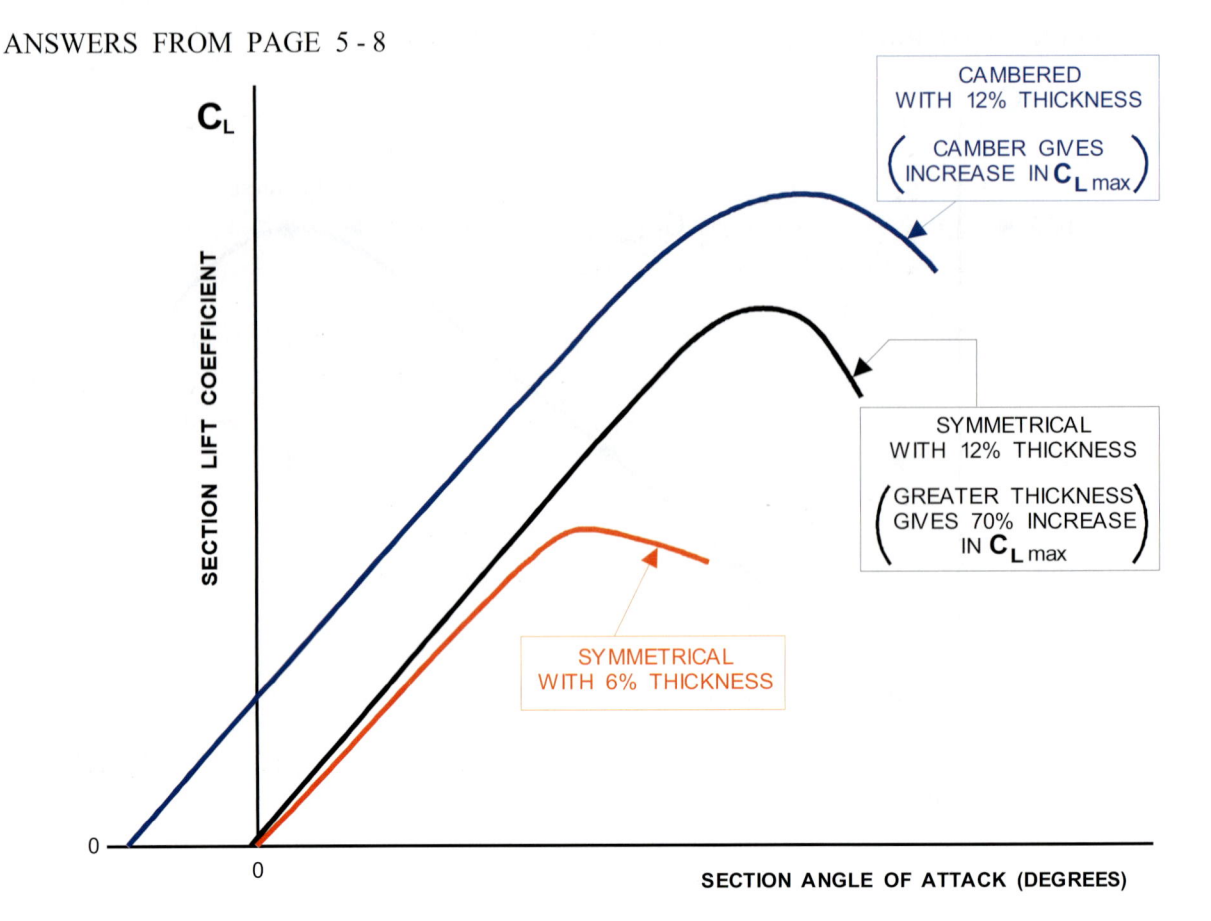

(a) Why does the cambered aerofoil section have a significantly higher $C_{L\,MAX}$? **When compared to a symmetrical section of the same thickness: at approximately the same stall angle, the cross sectional area of the "streamtube" over the top surface is smaller with a more gradual section change. This allows greater acceleration of the air over the top surface, and a bigger pressure differential.**

(b) For the same angle of attack, why do the symmetrical aerofoil sections generate less lift than the cambered aerofoil section? **Angle of attack is the angle between the chord line and the relative airflow. At the same angle of attack, the cross sectional area of the symmetrical section upper surface "streamtube" is larger.**

(c) Why does the cambered aerofoil section of 12% thickness generate a small amount of lift at slightly negative angles of attack? **At small negative angles of attack, a cambered aerofoil is still providing a reduced cross sectional area "streamtube" over the top surface, generating a small pressure differential.** (Ref. Page 4 - 6 & 7).

(d) For a given angle of attack, the symmetrical aerofoil section of 6% thickness generates the smallest amount of lift. In what way can this be a favourable characteristic? **At the high speeds at which modern high speed jet transport aircraft operate, a thin wing can generate the required lift force with minimum drag caused by the formation of shock waves. (This will be fully explained in later chapters).**

(e) What are the disadvantages of the symmetrical aerofoil section of 6% thickness? **It will give a high minimum speed, requiring complex high lift devices to enable the aircraft to use existing runways.**

PRINCIPLES OF FLIGHT   **LIFT**

SELF ASSESSMENT QUESTIONS

1. To maintain altitude, what must be done as Indicated Air Speed (IAS) is reduced:

    a) Decrease angle of attack to reduce the drag.
    b) Increase angle of attack to maintain the correct lift force.
    c) Deploy the speed brakes to increase drag.
    d) Reduce thrust.

2. If more lift force is required because of greater operating weight, what must be done to fly at the angle of attack which corresponds to $C_{L\,MAX}$:

    a) Increase the angle of attack.
    b) Nothing, the angle of attack for $C_{L\,MAX}$ is constant.
    c) It is impossible to fly at the angle of attack that corresponds to $C_{L\,MAX}$.
    d) Increase the Indicated Air Speed (IAS).

3. Which of the following statements is correct:

    1 - To generate a constant lift force, any adjustment in IAS must be accompanied by a change in angle of attack.
    2 - For a constant lift force, each IAS requires a specific angle of attack.
    3 - Minimum IAS is determined by $C_{L\,MAX}$.
    4 - The greater the operating weight, the higher the minimum IAS.

    a) 1, 2 and 4
    b) 4 only
    c) 2, 3 and 4
    d) 1, 2, 3 and 4

4. What effect does landing at high altitude airports have on ground speed with comparable conditions relative to temperature, wind, and aeroplane weight:

    a) Higher than at low altitude.
    b) The same as at low altitude.
    c) Lower than at low altitude.
    d) Dynamic pressure will be the same at any altitude.

5. What flight condition should be expected when an aircraft leaves ground effect:

    a) A decrease in parasite drag permitting a lower angle of attack.
    b) An increase in induced drag and a requirement for a higher angle of attack.
    c) An increase in dynamic stability.
    d) A decrease in induced drag requiring a smaller angle of attack.

PRINCIPLES OF FLIGHT   LIFT

6. What will be the ratio between airspeed and lift if the angle of attack and other factors remain constant and airspeed is doubled. Lift will be:

   a) Two times greater.
   b) Four times greater.
   c) The same.
   d) One quarter.

7. What true airspeed and angle of attack should be used to generate the same amount of lift as altitude is increased:

   a) A higher true airspeed for any given angle of attack.
   b) The same true airspeed and angle of attack.
   c) A lower true airspeed and higher angle of attack.
   d) A constant angle of attack and true air speed.

8. How can an aeroplane produce the same lift in ground effect as when out of ground effect:

   a) A lower angle of attack.
   b) A higher angle of attack.
   c) The same angle of attack.
   d) The same angle of attack, but a lower IAS.

9. By changing the angle of attack of a wing, the pilot can control the aeroplane's:

   a) Lift and airspeed, but not drag.
   b) Lift, gross weight, and drag.
   c) Lift, airspeed, and drag.
   d) Lift and drag, but not airspeed.

10. Which flight conditions of a large jet aeroplane create the most severe flight hazard by generating wingtip vortices of the greatest strength:

    a) Heavy, slow, gear and flaps up.
    b) Heavy, fast, gear and flaps down.
    c) Heavy, slow, gear and flaps down.
    d) Weight, gear and flaps make no difference.

11. Hazardous vortex turbulence that might be encountered behind large aircraft is created only when that aircraft is:

    a) Using high power settings.
    b) Operating at high airspeeds.
    c) Developing lift.
    d) Operating at high altitude.

PRINCIPLES OF FLIGHT LIFT

12. Wingtip vortices created by large aircraft tend to:

   a) Rise from the surface to traffic pattern altitude.
   b) Sink below the aircraft generating the turbulence.
   c) Accumulate and remain for a period of time at the point where the takeoff roll began.
   d) Dissipate very slowly when the surface wind is strong.

13. How does the wake turbulence vortex circulate around each wingtip, when viewed from the rear:

   a) Inward, upward, and around the wingtip.
   b) Counterclockwise.
   c) Outward, upward, and around the wingtip.
   d) Outward, downward and around the wingtip.

14. Which statement is true concerning the wake turbulence produced by a large transport aircraft:

   a) Wake turbulence behind a propeller-driven aircraft is negligible because jet engine thrust is a necessary factor in the formation of vortices.
   b) Vortices can be avoided by flying 300 feet below and behind the flightpath of the generating aircraft.
   c) The vortex characteristics of any given aircraft may be altered by extending the flaps or changing the speed.
   d) Vortices can be avoided by flying downwind of, and below the flight path of the generating aircraft.

15. What effect would a light crosswind have on the wingtip vortices generated by a large aeroplane that has just taken off:

   a) The downwind vortex will tend to remain on the runway longer than the upwind vortex.
   b) A crosswind will rapidly dissipate the strength of both vortices.
   c) A crosswind will move both vortices clear of the runway.
   d) The upwind vortex will tend to remain on the runway longer than the downwind vortex.

16. To avoid the wingtip vortices of a departing jet aeroplane during takeoff, the pilot should:

   a) Remain below the flightpath of the jet aeroplane.
   b) Climb above and stay upwind of the jet aeroplane's flightpath.
   c) Lift off at a point well past the jet aeroplane's flightpath.
   d) Remain below and downwind of the jet aeroplane's flightpath.

PRINCIPLES OF FLIGHT   LIFT

17. What wind condition prolongs the hazards of wake turbulence on a landing runway for the longest period of time:

   a) Light quartering headwind.
   b) Light quartering tailwind.
   c) Direct tailwind.
   d) Strong, direct crosswind.

18. If you take off behind a heavy jet that has just landed, you should plan to lift off:

   a) Prior to the point where the jet touched down.
   b) At the point where the jet touched down and on the upwind edge of the runway.
   c) Before the point where the jet touched down and on the downwind edge of the runway.
   d) Beyond the point where the jet touched down.

19. The adverse effects of ice, snow, or frost on aircraft performance and flight characteristics include decreased lift and:

   a) Increased thrust.
   b) A decreased stall speed.
   c) An increased stall speed.
   d) An aircraft will always stall at the same indicated airspeed.

20. Lift on a wing is most properly defined as the:

   a) Differential pressure acting perpendicular to the chord of the wing.
   b) Force acting perpendicular to the relative wind.
   c) Reduced pressure resulting from a laminar flow over the upper camber of an aerofoil, which acts perpendicular to the mean camber.
   d) Force acting parallel with the relative wind and in the opposite direction.

21. Which statement is true relative to changing angle of attack:

   a) A decrease in angle of attack will increase pressure below the wing, and decrease drag.
   b) An increase in angle of attack will decrease pressure below the wing, and increase drag.
   c) An increase in angle of attack will increase drag.
   d) An increase in angle of attack will decrease the lift coefficient.

22. The angle of attack of a wing directly controls the:

   a) Angle of incidence of the wing.
   b) Distribution of pressures acting on the wing.
   c) Amount of airflow above and below the wing.
   d) Dynamic pressure acting in the airflow.

PRINCIPLES OF FLIGHT LIFT

23. In theory, if the angle of attack and other factors remain constant and the airspeed is doubled, the lift produced at the higher speed will be:

    a) The same as at the lower speed.
    b) Two times greater than at the lower speed.
    c) Four times greater than at the lower speed.
    d) One quarter as much.

24. An aircraft wing is designed to produce lift resulting from a difference in the:

    a) Negative air pressure below and a vacuum above the wing's surface.
    b) Vacuum below the wing's surface and greater air pressure above the wing's surface.
    c) Higher air pressure below the wing's surface and lower air pressure above the wing's surface.
    d) Higher pressure at the leading edge than at the trailing edge.

25. On a wing, the force of lift acts perpendicular to, and the force of drag acts parallel to the:

    a) Camber line.
    b) Longitudinal axis.
    c) Chord line.
    d) Flightpath.

26. Which statement is true, regarding the opposing forces acting on an aeroplane in steady-state level flight:

    a) Thrust is greater than drag and weight and lift are equal.
    b) These forces are equal.
    c) Thrust is greater than drag and lift is greater than weight.
    d) Thrust is slightly greater than Lift, but the drag and weight are equal.

27. At higher elevation airports the pilot should know that indicated airspeed:

    a) Will be unchanged, but ground speed will be faster.
    b) Will be higher, but ground speed will be unchanged.
    c) Should be increased to compensate for the thinner air.
    d) Should be higher to obtain a higher landing speed.

28. An aeroplane leaving ground effect will:

    a) Experience a reduction in ground friction and require a slight power reduction.
    b) Require a lower angle of attack to maintain the same lift coefficient.
    c) Experience a reduction in induced drag and require a smaller angle of attack
    d) Experience an increase in induced drag and require more thrust.

PRINCIPLES OF FLIGHT — LIFT

29. If the same angle of attack is maintained in ground effect as when out of ground effect, lift will:

    a) Increase, and induced drag will increase.
    b) Increase, and induced drag will decrease.
    c) Decrease, and induced drag will increase.
    d) Decrease and induced drag will decrease.

30. Which is true regarding the force of lift in steady, unaccelerated flight:

    a) There is a corresponding indicated airspeed required for every angle of attack to generate sufficient lift to maintain altitude.
    b) An aerofoil will always stall at the same indicated airspeed; therefore, an increase in weight will require an increase in speed to generate sufficient lift to maintain altitude.
    c) At lower airspeeds the angle of attack must be less to generate sufficient lift to maintain altitude.
    d) The lift force must be exactly equal to the drag force.

31. At a given Indicated Air Speed, what effect will an increase in air density have on lift and drag:

    a) Lift will increase but drag will decrease.
    b) Lift and drag will increase.
    c) Lift and drag will decrease.
    d) Lift and drag will remain the same.

32. If the angle of attack is increased beyond the critical angle of attack, the wing will no longer produce sufficient lift to support the weight of the aircraft:

    a) Unless the airspeed is greater than the normal stall speed.
    b) Regardless of airspeed or pitch attitude.
    c) Unless the pitch attitude is on or below the natural horizon.
    d) In which case, the control column should be pulled-back immediately.

PRINCIPLES OF FLIGHT LIFT

33. GIVEN THAT:

   Aircraft A.
   Wingspan: 51 m
   Average wing chord: 4 m

   Aircraft B.
   Wingspan: 48 m
   Average wing chord: 3.5 m

   Determine the correct aspect ratio and wing area.

   a) Aircraft A has an aspect ratio of 13.7, and has a larger wing area than aircraft B.
   b) Aircraft B has an aspect ratio of 13.7, and has a smaller wing area than aircraft A.
   c) Aircraft B has an aspect ratio of 12.75, and has a smaller wing area than aircraft A.
   d) Aircraft A has an aspect ratio of 12.75, and has a smaller wing area than aircraft B.

34. Aspect ratio of the wing is defined as the ratio of the:

   a) Wingspan to the wing root.
   b) Square of the chord to the wing span.
   c) Wing span to the average chord.
   d) Square of the wing area to the span.

35. What changes to aircraft control must be made to maintain altitude while the airspeed is being decreased:

   a) Increase the angle of attack to compensate for the decreasing dynamic pressure.
   b) Maintain a constant angle of attack until the desired airspeed is reached, then increase the angle of attack.
   c) Increase angle of attack to produce more lift than weight.
   d) Decrease the angle of attack to compensate for the decrease in drag.

36. Take-off from an airfield with a low density altitude will result in:

   a) a longer take-off run.
   b) a higher than standard IAS before lift off.
   c) a higher TAS for the same lift off IAS.
   d) a shorter take off run because of the lower TAS required for the same IAS.

INTENTIONALLY LEFT BLANK

PRINCIPLES OF FLIGHT — LIFT

No	A	B	C	D	REF	No	A	B	C	D	REF
1		B				19			C		
2				D		20		B			
3				D		21			C		
4	A					22		B			
5		B				23			C		
6		B				24			C		
7	A					25				D	
8	A					26		B			
9			C			27	A				
10	A					28				D	
11			C			29		B			
12		B				30	A				
13			C			31				D	
14			C			32		B			
15				D		33		B			
16		B				34			C		
17		B				35	A				
18				D		36				D	

INTENTIONALLY LEFT BLANK

CHAPTER 6 - DRAG

Contents

	Page
INTRODUCTION	6 - 1
PARASITE DRAG	6 - 2
SKIN FRICTION DRAG	
SURFACE CONDITION	
SPEED OF FLOW	
ADVERSE PRESSURE GRADIENT	6 - 3
FORM (PRESSURE) DRAG	
LAMINAR AND TURBULENT SEPARATION	6 - 4
STREAMLINING	
PROFILE DRAG	
INTERFERENCE DRAG	6 - 5
FACTORS AFFECTING PARASITE DRAG	
INDUCED DRAG	6 - 6
WING TIP VORTICES	
INDUCED DOWNWASH	
FACTORS THAT AFFECT INDUCED DRAG	6 - 8
SIZE OF THE LIFT FORCE	
SPEED OF THE AIRCRAFT	
ASPECT RATIO OF THE WING	
THE INDUCED DRAG COEFFICIENT	6 - 11
METHODS OF REDUCING INDUCED DRAG	6 - 12
WING END-PLATE	
TIP TANKS	
WINGLETS	
WINGTIP SHAPE	
EFFECT OF LIFT ON PARASITE DRAG	6 - 13
EFFECT OF CONFIGURATION	
EFFECT OF ALTITUDE	
EFFECT OF SPEED	
AEROPLANE TOTAL DRAG	6 - 14
THE EFFECT OF AIRCRAFT GROSS WEIGHT	6 - 16
THE EFFECT OF ALTITUDE	6 - 17
THE EFFECT OF CONFIGURATION	
SPEED STABILITY	6 - 18
POWER REQUIRED	6 - 20
VMP/VMD RELATIONSHIP	6 - 21
SUMMARY	6 - 22
SELF ASSESSMENT QUESTIONS	6 - 24
ANSWERS	6 - 33

```
                    TOTAL DRAG
            ┌───────────┴───────────┐
      PARASITE DRAG            INDUCED DRAG      WAVE
   ┌────────┼────────┐                           DRAG
SKIN FRICTION  FORM    INTERFERENCE
   DRAG       DRAG        DRAG
      └───┬───┘
       PROFILE
        DRAG
```

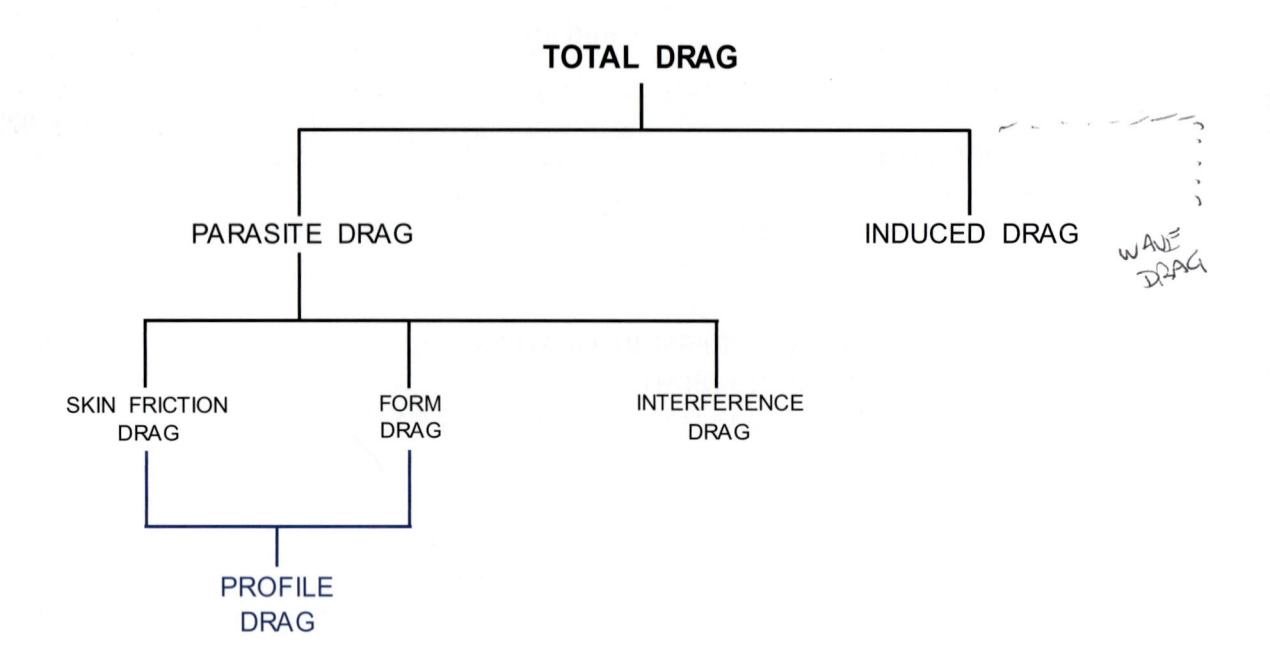

Figure 6.0 Total Drag

PRINCIPLES OF FLIGHT — DRAG

6.1 INTRODUCTION

Drag is the force which resists the forward motion of the aircraft. Drag acts parallel to and in the same direction as the relative airflow (in the opposite direction to the flight path). Please remember that when considering airflow velocity it does not make any difference to the airflow pattern whether the aircraft is moving through the air or the air is flowing past the aircraft: it is the relative velocity which is the important factor.

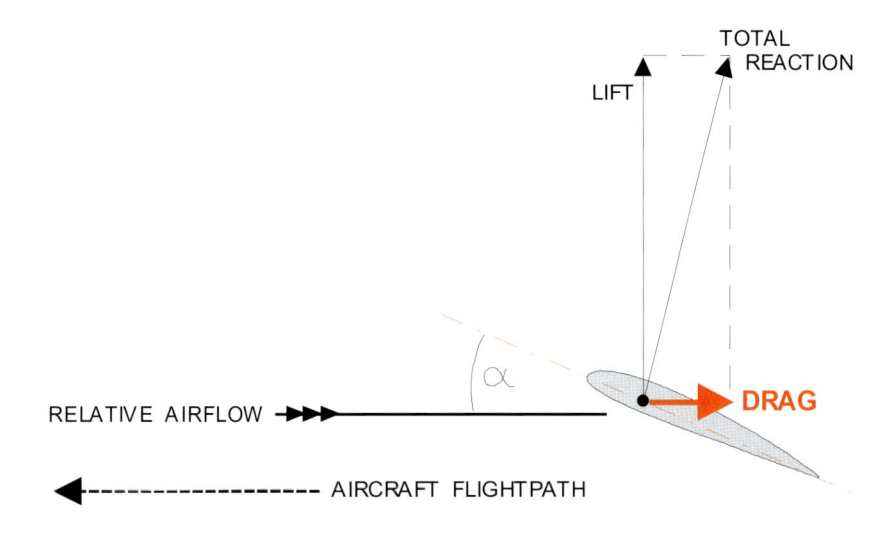

Figure 6.1

Every part of an aeroplane exposed to the airflow produces different types of resistance to forward motion which contribute to the Total Drag. Total Drag is sub-divided into two main types:

    (1)   PARASITE DRAG - independent of lift generation, and

    (2)   INDUCED DRAG - the result of lift generation.

Parasite drag is further sub-divided into:

    a)   Skin Friction Drag

    b)   Form (Pressure) Drag, and

    c)   Interference Drag

Note: Skin Friction and Form Drag are together known as PROFILE DRAG.

Induced drag will be considered later. We will first consider the elements of parasite drag.

PRINCIPLES OF FLIGHT — DRAG

6.2 PARASITE DRAG

If an aircraft were flying at zero lift angle of attack the only drag present would be parasite drag. Parasite drag is made-up of 'Skin Friction', 'Form' and 'Interference' Drag.

6.2.1 SKIN FRICTION DRAG:
Particles of air in direct contact with the surface are accelerated to the speed of the aircraft and are carried along with it. Adjacent particles will be accelerated by contact with the lower particles, but their velocity will be slightly less than the aircraft because the viscosity of air is low. As distance from the surface increases less and less acceleration of the layers of air takes place. Therefore, over the entire surface there will exist a layer of air whose relative velocity ranges from zero at the surface to a maximum at the boundary of the air affected by the presence of the aircraft. The layer of air extending from the surface to the point where no viscous effect is detectable is known as the **boundary layer.** In flight, the nature of the boundary layer will determine the maximum lift coefficient, the stalling characteristics, the value of form drag, and to some extent the high speed characteristics of an aircraft.

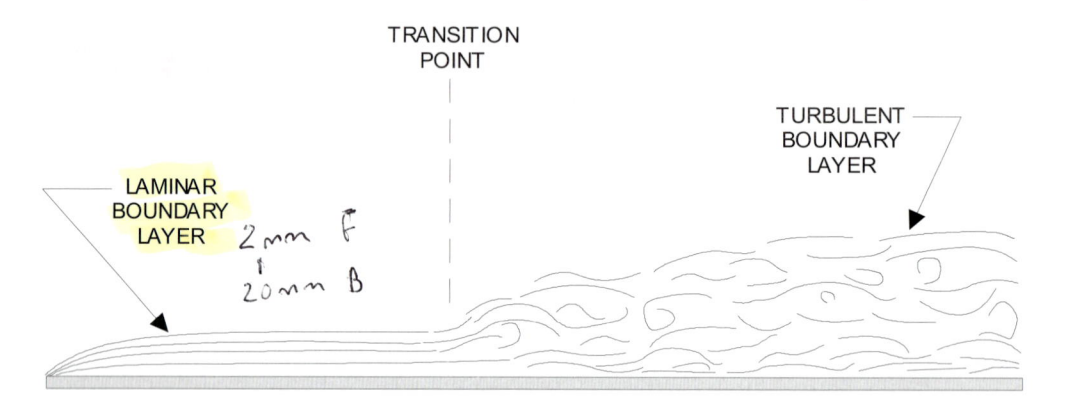

Figure 6.2

Consider the flow of air across a flat surface, as in Fig 6.2. The boundary layer will exist in two forms, either laminar or turbulent. In general, the flow at the front will be laminar and become turbulent some distance back, known as the transition point. **The increased rate of change in velocity at the surface in the turbulent flow will give more skin friction than the laminar flow.** A turbulent boundary layer also has a higher level of kinetic energy than a laminar layer.

Forward movement of the transition point will increase skin friction because there will be a greater area of turbulent flow. The position of the transition point is dependent upon:

a) **Surface condition** - The thin laminar layer is extremely sensitive to surface irregularities. Any roughness on the skin of a leading portion of an aircraft will cause transition to turbulence at that point and the thickening, turbulent boundary layer will spread out fanwise down-stream causing a marked increase in skin friction drag.

PRINCIPLES OF FLIGHT

DRAG

b) **Adverse pressure gradient** (Fig. 6.3) - A laminar layer cannot exist when pressure is rising in the direction of flow. On a curved surface, such as an aerofoil, the transition point is usually at, or near to the point of maximum thickness. Because of the adverse pressure gradient existing on a curved surface the transition point will be further forward than if the surface was flat.

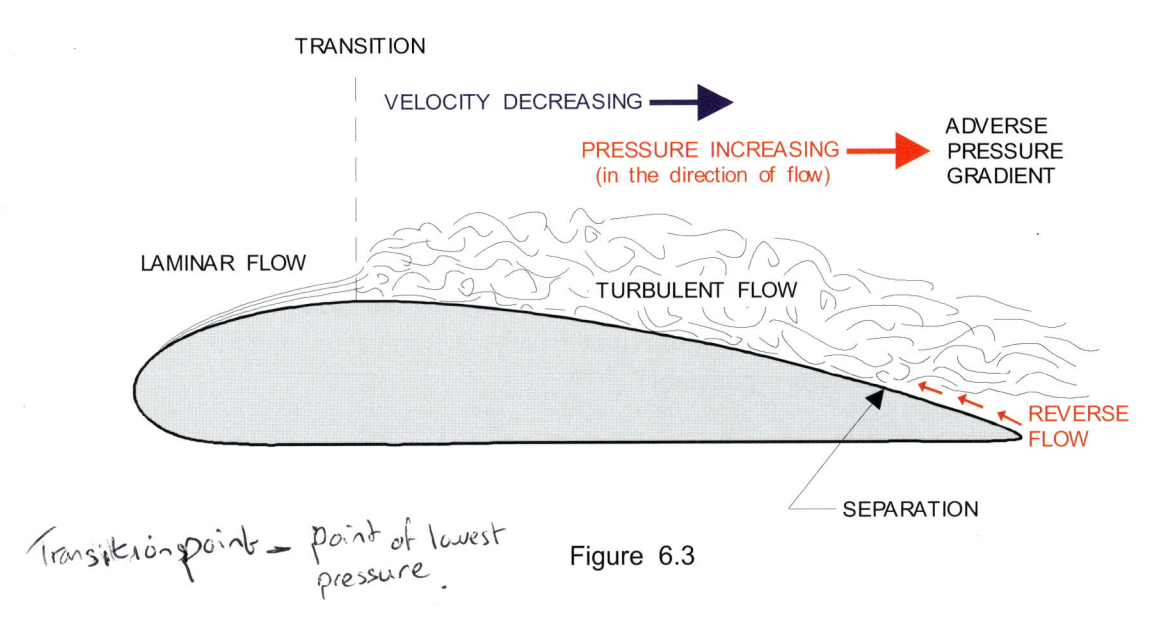

Figure 6.3

Transition point - point of lowest pressure.

NB: The vertical scale of the boundary layer in the above sketch is greatly exaggerated. Typically, boundary layer thickness is from 2 millimetres at the leading edge, increasing to about 20 millimetres at the trailing edge.

6.2.2 FORM (PRESSURE) DRAG: Results from the pressure at the leading edge of a body being greater than the pressure at the trailing edge. Overall, skin friction causes a continual reduction of boundary layer kinetic energy as flow continues back along the surface. The adverse pressure gradient behind the transition point will cause an additional reduction in kinetic energy of the boundary layer. If the boundary layer does not have sufficient kinetic energy in the presence of the adverse pressure gradient, the lower levels of the boundary layer stop moving (stagnate). The upper levels of the boundary layer will overrun at this point (separation point) and the boundary layer will separate from the surface at the separation point. See Fig. 6.3. Also, surface flow aft of the separation point will be forward, toward the separation point - a flow reversal. Because of separation there will be a lower pressure at the trailing edge than the leading edge. An aerodynamic force will act in the direction of the lower pressure - form drag.

Separation will occur when the boundary layer does not have sufficient kinetic energy in the presence of a given adverse pressure gradient.

PRINCIPLES OF FLIGHT — DRAG

Loss of kinetic energy in the boundary layer can be caused by various factors.

a) As angle of attack increases, the transition point moves closer to the leading edge and the adverse pressure gradient becomes stronger. This causes the separation point to move forward. Eventually, boundary layer separation will occur so close to the leading edge that there will be insufficient wing area to provide the required lift force, C_L will decrease and stall occurs.

b) When a shock wave forms on the upper surface, the increase of static pressure through the shock wave will create an extreme adverse pressure gradient. If the shock wave is sufficiently strong, separation will occur immediately behind the shock wave. This will be explained fully in Chapter 13 - High Speed Flight.

Laminar and Turbulent Separation: Separation has been shown to be caused by the airflow meeting an adverse pressure gradient, but it is found that a turbulent boundary layer is more resistant to separation than a laminar one when meeting the same pressure gradient. In this respect the turbulent boundary layer is preferable to the laminar one, but from the point of view of drag the laminar flow is preferable.

Streamlining: Each part of an aircraft will be subject to form (pressure) drag. To reduce form drag it is necessary to delay separation to a point as close to the trailing edge as possible. Streamlining increases the ratio between the length and depth of a body, reducing the curvature of the surfaces and thus the adverse pressure gradient. Fineness ratio is the measure of streamlining. It has been found that the ideal fineness ratio is 3:1, as illustrated in Fig. 6.4.

NB: The addition of fairings and fillets (see Glossary, Page 1-10) at the junction of components exposed to the airflow is also referred to as "Streamlining".

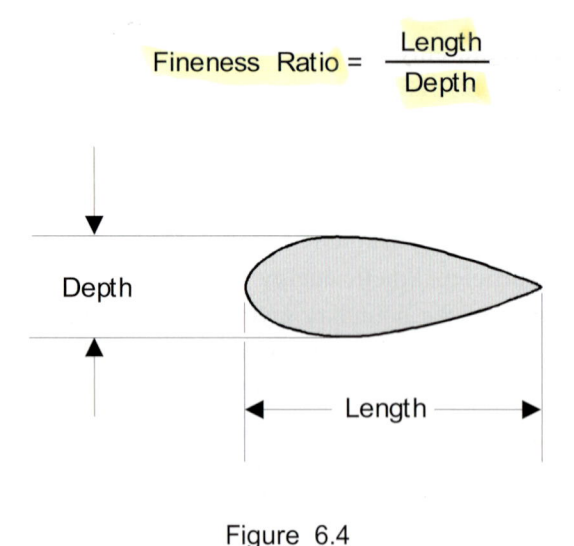

$$\text{Fineness Ratio} = \frac{\text{Length}}{\text{Depth}}$$

Figure 6.4

Profile Drag: The combination of skin friction and form drag is known as profile drag. It can be considered that these drags result from the "profile" (or cross-sectional area) of the aircraft presented to the relative airflow.

PRINCIPLES OF FLIGHT — DRAG

6.2.3 INTERFERENCE DRAG: When considering a complete aircraft, parasite drag will be greater than the sum of the parts. Additional drag results from boundary layer 'interference' at wing/fuselage, wing/engine nacelle and other such junctions. Filleting is necessary to minimise interference drag. *[streamlining]*

6.2.4 FACTORS AFFECTING PARASITE DRAG

1. Indicated Air Speed

    Parasite Drag varies directly with the square of the Indicated Air Speed (IAS).

    If IAS is doubled the Parasite Drag will be four times greater - if IAS is halved the Parasite Drag will be one quarter of its previous value.

2. Configuration

    Parasite Drag varies directly in proportion to the frontal area presented to the airflow; this is known as 'Parasite Area'. If flaps are deployed, the undercarriage lowered, speed brakes selected or roll control spoilers operated, 'Parasite Area' is increased and Parasite drag will increase.

3. Airframe Contamination

    Contamination by ice, frost, snow, mud or slush will increase the Parasite Drag Coefficient, and in the case of severe airframe icing, the area.

THE PARASITE DRAG FORMULA   *[At zero lift α]*

$$D_P = \tfrac{1}{2} \rho \, V^2 \, C_{Dp} \, S$$

where,

D_P	=	Parasite Drag
$\tfrac{1}{2}\rho V^2$	=	Dynamic Pressure (Q)
C_{Dp}	=	Parasite Drag Coefficient
S	=	Area (Parasite Area)

PRINCIPLES OF FLIGHT

DRAG

6.3 INDUCED DRAG

Induced drag is an undesirable by-product of lift. Wingtip vortices modify upwash and downwash in the vicinity of the wing which produces a rearward component to the lift vector known as induced drag.

The lower the IAS, the higher the angle of attack - the stronger the vortices.

The stronger the vortices - the greater the induced drag.

Wing Tip Vortices: Airflow over the top surface of a wing is at a lower pressure than that beneath. The trailing edge and the wing tips are where the airflows interact, Fig. 6.5. The pressure differential modifies the directions of flow, inducing a span-wise vector towards the root on the upper surface and towards the tip on the lower surface. "Conventionally", an aircraft is viewed from the rear. An anti-clockwise vortex will be induced at the right wing-tip and a clock-wise vortex at the left wing-tip, Fig. 6.6. At higher angles of attack (Lower IAS) the decreased chordwise vector will increase the resultant spanwise flow, making the vortices stronger.

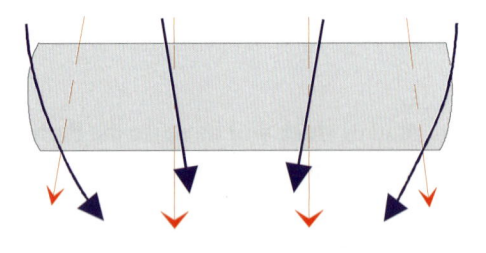

Figure 6.5

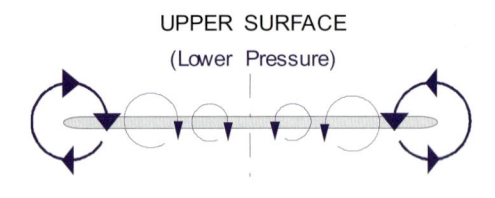

Figure 6.6

UPPER SURFACE
(Lower Pressure)

Induced Downwash: Wingtip vortices create certain vertical velocity components in the airflow in the vicinity of the wing, both in front of and behind it, Fig. 6.8. These vertical velocities strengthen upwash and downwash which reduces the effective angle of attack. The stronger the vortices, the greater the reduction in effective angle of attack.

Due to the localised reduction in effective angle of attack, the overall lift generated by a **wing** will be below the value that would be generated if there were no spanwise pressure differential. It is the production of lift itself which reduces the magnitude of the lift force being generated.

To replace the lift lost by the increased upwash and downwash the **wing** must be flown at a higher angle of attack, than would otherwise be necessary. This increases drag. This extra drag is called **Induced drag**, Fig. 6.9.

PRINCIPLES OF FLIGHT   **DRAG**

RELATIVE AIRFLOW

EFFECTIVE AIRFLOW

Tip vortices increase upwash over outer portions of span

Tip vortices increase downwash over outer portions of span

INCREASED DOWNWASH AND UPWASH REDUCES EFFECTIVE ANGLE OF ATTACK OVER OUTER PORTIONS OF SPAN

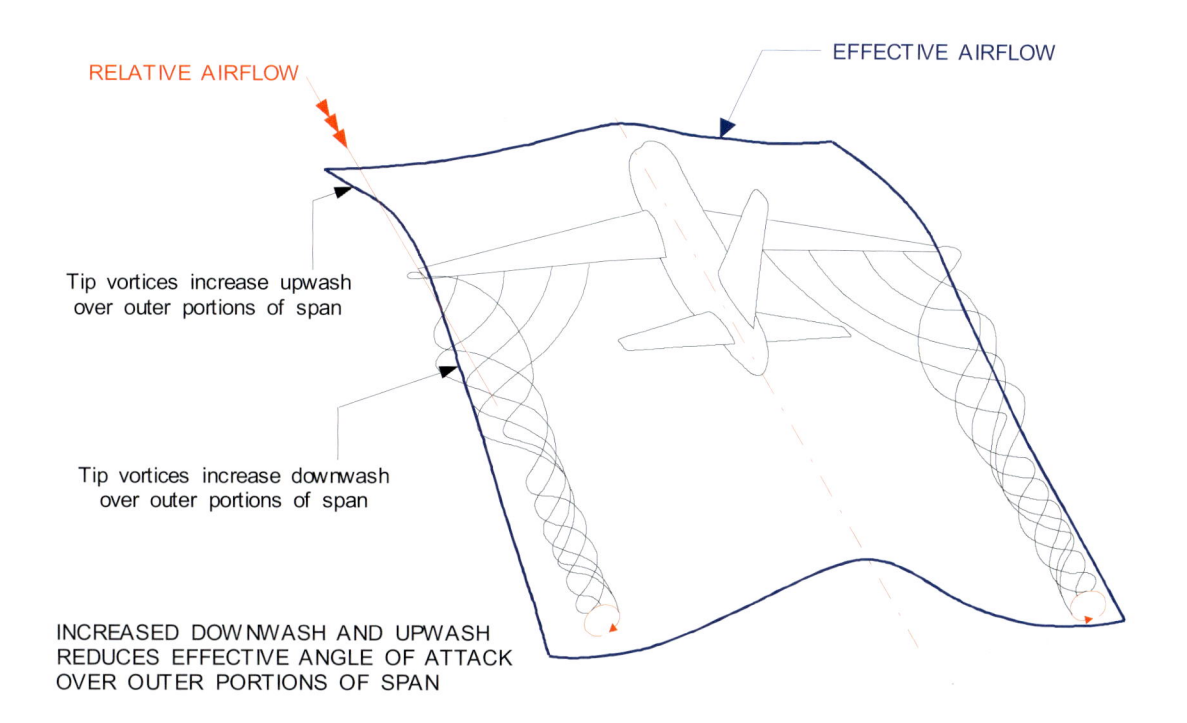

Figure 6.7

Upwash Increased

Vertical Velocities in the vicinity of the wing are a function of tip vortex strength

Downwash Increased

V
Relative Airflow

EFFECTIVE AIRFLOW

Angular deflection of effective airflow is a function of both vortex strength and True Air Speed (TAS).

Induced Downwash

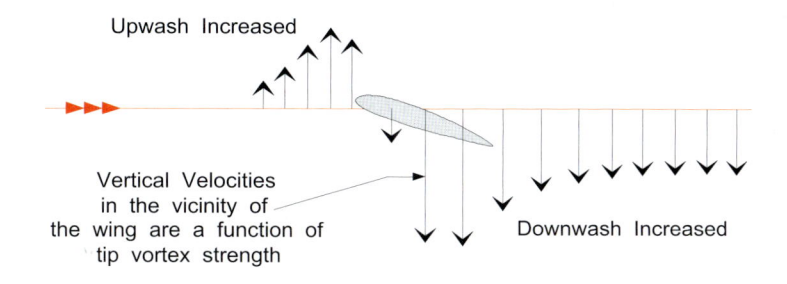

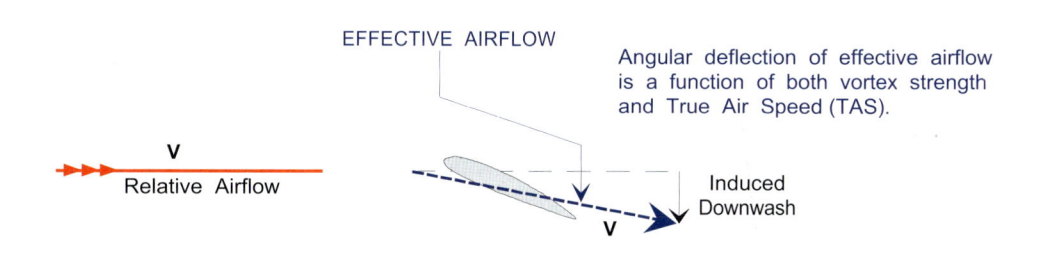

V

Figure 6.8

PRINCIPLES OF FLIGHT
DRAG

α_e = effective angle of attack
α_i = induced angle of attack

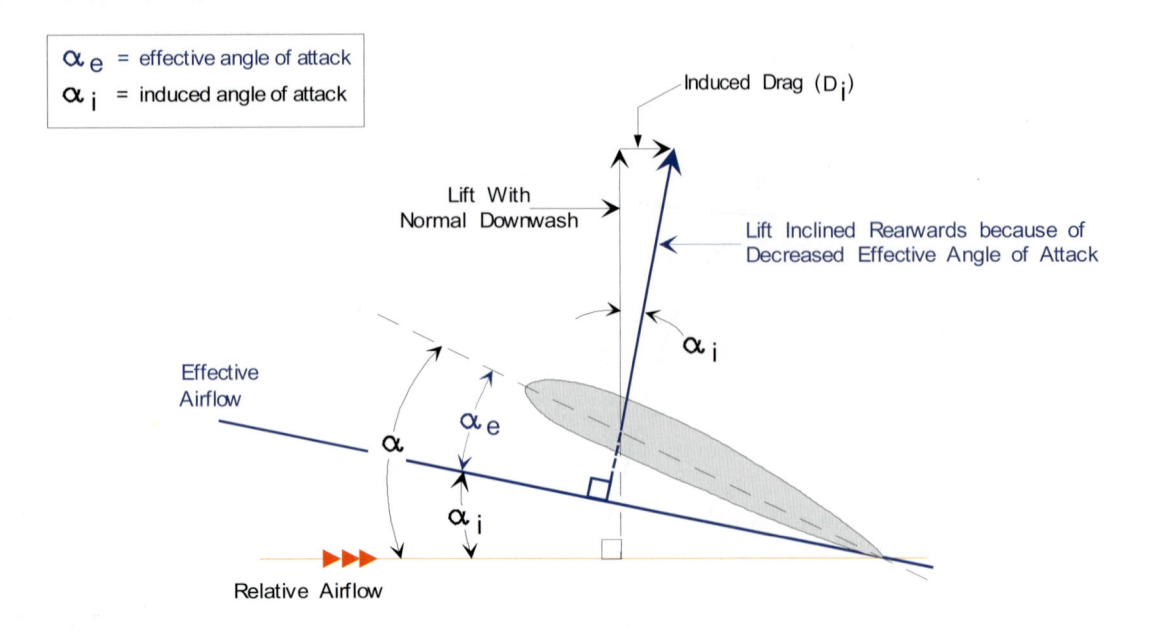

Figure 6.9

Factors that Affect Induced Drag:

(a) **The size of the lift force** - Because induced drag is a component of the lift force, the greater the lift, the greater will be the induced drag. Lift must be equal to weight in level flight so induced drag will depend on the weight of the aircraft. Induced drag will be greater at higher aircraft weights. Certain manoeuvres require the lift force to be greater than the aircraft weight. The relationship of lift to weight is known as the "Load Factor" (or 'g'). For example, lift is greater than weight during a steady turn so induced drag will be higher during a steady turn than in straight and level flight. Therefore, induced drag also increases as the Load Factor increases. **Induced drag will increase in proportion to the square of the lift force.**

$$\text{Load Factor} = \frac{\text{Lift}}{\text{Weight}}$$

(b) **The speed of the aircraft** - Induced drag decreases with increasing speed (for a constant lift force). This is because as speed increases the downwash caused by the tip vortices becomes less significant, the rearward inclination of the lift is less, and therefore induced drag is less. **Induced drag varies inversely as the square of the speed.** (Refer to page 6 - 11 for a detailed explanation)

(c) **The aspect ratio of the wing** - The tip vortices of a high aspect ratio wing affect a smaller proportion of the span so the overall change in downwash will be less, giving a smaller rearward tilt to the lift force. Induced drag therefore decreases as aspect ratio increases (for a given lift force). **The induced drag coefficient is inversely proportional to the aspect ratio.**

PRINCIPLES OF FLIGHT DRAG

From the previous three factors it is possible to develop the following equation:

$$C_{D_i} = \propto \frac{(C_L)^2}{AR}$$

It can be seen that the relationship for the induced drag coefficient, (C_{D_i}), emphasises the need of a high aspect ratio wing for aeroplane configurations designed to operate at the higher lift coefficients during the major portion of their flight, i.e. conventional high speed jet transport aircraft.

The effect of aspect ratio on lift and drag characteristics is shown in Figs. 6.10 and 6.11. The basic aerofoil section properties are shown on these plots and these properties would be typical only of a wing planform of extremely high (infinite) aspect ratio. When a wing of some finite aspect ratio is constructed of this basic section, the principal differences will be in the lift and drag characteristics - the moment characteristics remain essentially the same.

The effect of increasing aspect ratio on the lift curve, Fig. 6.10, is to decrease the wing angle of attack necessary to produce a given lift coefficient. Higher aspect ratio wings are more sensitive to changes in angle of attack, but require a smaller angles of attack for maximum lift.

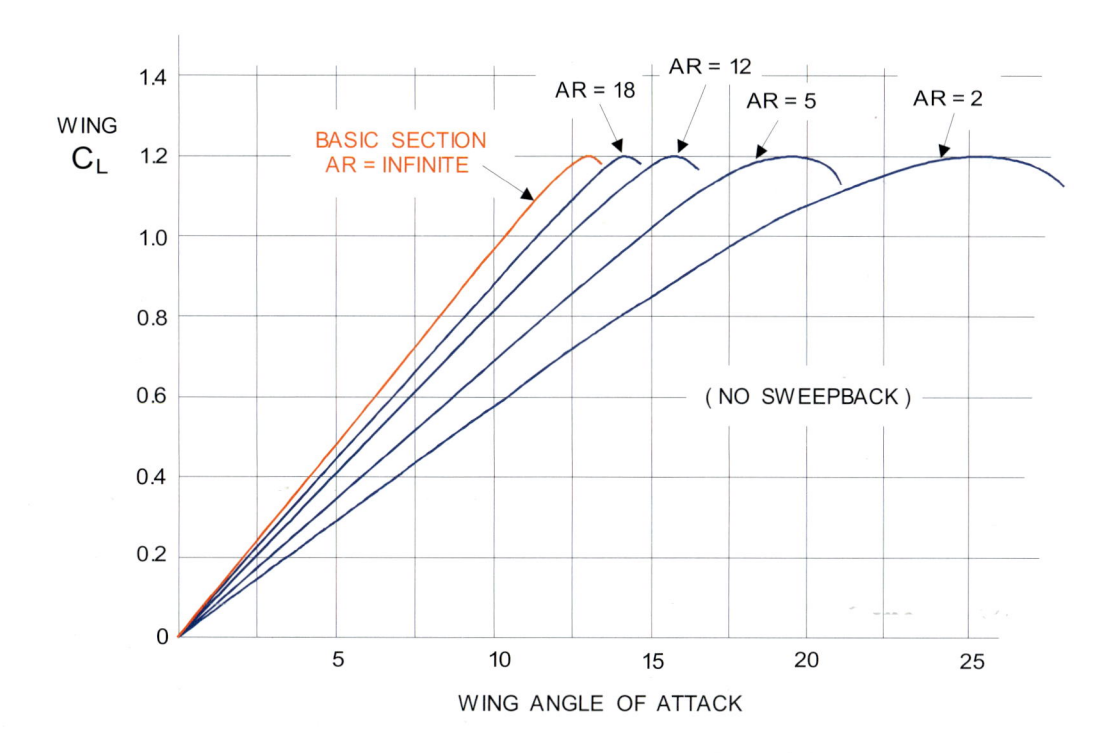

Figure 6.10

PRINCIPLES OF FLIGHT   **DRAG**

From Fig. 6.11 it can be seen that at any lift coefficient, a higher aspect ratio gives a lower wing drag coefficient since the induced drag coefficient varies inversely with aspect ratio. When the aspect ratio is high the induced drag varies only slightly with lift. At high lift coefficients (low IAS), the induced drag is very high and increases very rapidly with lift coefficient.

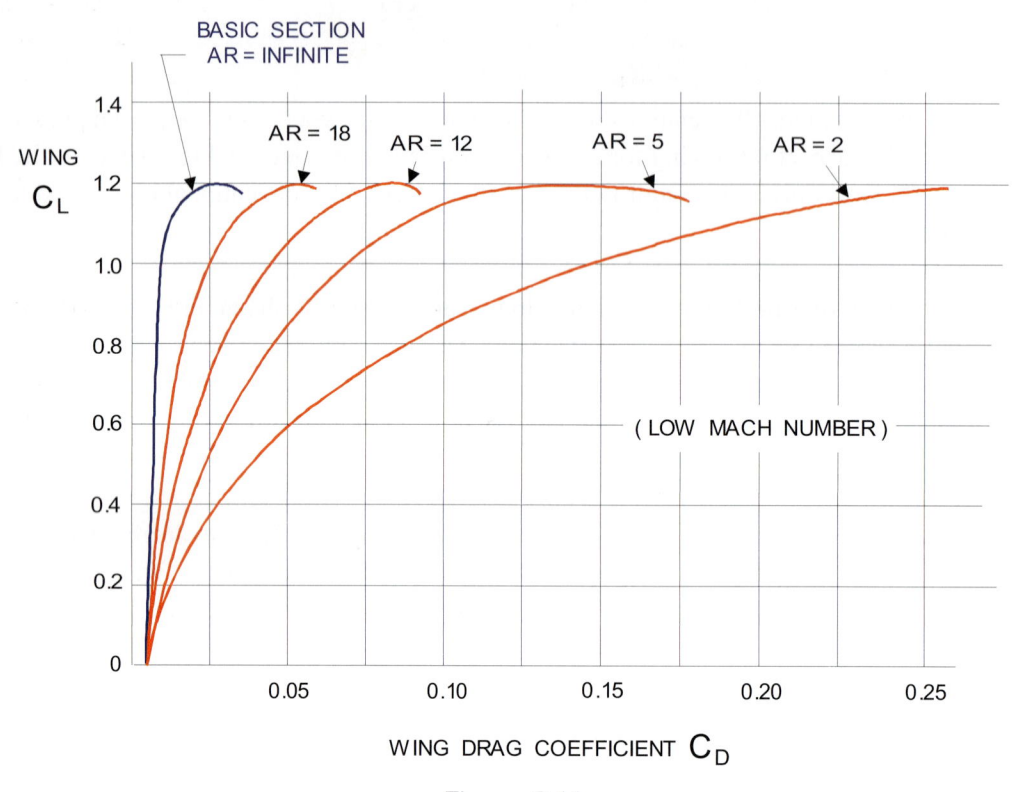

Figure 6.11

The lift and drag curves for a high aspect ratio wing, Figs. 6.10 and 6.11, show continued strong increase in C_L with α up to stall and large changes in C_D only at the point of stall.

Continuing to increase aspect ratio is restricted by the following considerations.

Very high aspect ratio wings will experience the following:-

a) **Excessive wing bending moments:** which can be reduced by carrying fuel in the wings and mounting the engines in pods beneath the wing.

b) **Reduced rate of roll** (particularly at low airspeed): This is caused by the down-going wing (only while it is actually moving down) experiencing an increased effective angle of attack. The increased effective angle of attack is due to the resultant of the forward TAS of the wing and the angular TAS of the tip. The higher the aspect ratio, the greater the vertical TAS of the tip for a given roll rate, leading to a greater increase in effective angle of attack. The higher the effective angle of attack at the tip, the greater the resistance to roll. This phenomena is called **aerodynamic damping** and will be covered in more detail in later chapters.

c) **Reduced ground clearance in roll during take-off and landing.**

PRINCIPLES OF FLIGHT — DRAG

The Induced Drag Coefficient (C_{Di})

$$D_i = \tfrac{1}{2}\rho V^2 \; C_{Di} \; S$$

This equation would seem to imply that induced drag (D_i) increases with speed, but the induced drag coefficient (C_{Di}) is proportional to C_L^2 and inversely proportional to wing aspect ratio. As speed increases, **to maintain a constant lift force** C_L must be reduced. Thus, with an increase in speed C_{Di} decreases:

$$C_{Di} = \frac{C_L^2}{AR}$$

The following example illustrates the change in C_{Di} with speed, which leads to the change in D_i.

If an aircraft's speed is increased from 80 kt (41 m/s) to 160 kt (82 m/s) the dynamic pressure will be four times greater. (Sea level ISA density is used in the example, but any constant density will give the same result).

$$Q = \tfrac{1}{2}\rho V^2$$

$$Q = 0.5 \times 1.225 \times 41 \times 41 = 1029.6$$

$$Q = 0.5 \times 1.225 \times 82 \times 82 = 4118.4$$

Referring to the lift formula: $L = Q \; C_L \; S$

If dynamic pressure is four times greater because speed is doubled, C_L must be reduced to ¼ of its previous value to maintain a constant lift force.

Applying 1/4 of the previous C_L to the C_{Di} formula: $C_{Di} = \dfrac{C_L^2}{AR}$

$$C_{Di} = \frac{(\tfrac{1}{4})^2}{AR} \quad \text{because AR is constant} \quad C_{Di} = (\tfrac{1}{4})^2 = \tfrac{1}{16}$$

If 1/16 of the previous C_{Di} is applied to the Induced drag formula:

$$D_i = (Q \times 4) \times \tfrac{1}{16} = \tfrac{1}{4}$$

Conclusion: If speed is doubled in level flight: dynamic pressure will be four times greater, C_L must be decreased to 1/4 of its previous value, C_{Di} will be 1/16 of its previous value and D_i will be reduced to 1/4 of its previous value.

If speed is halved in level flight: dynamic pressure will be 1/4 of its previous value, C_L will need to be four times greater, C_{Di} will be 16 times greater, giving four times more D_i

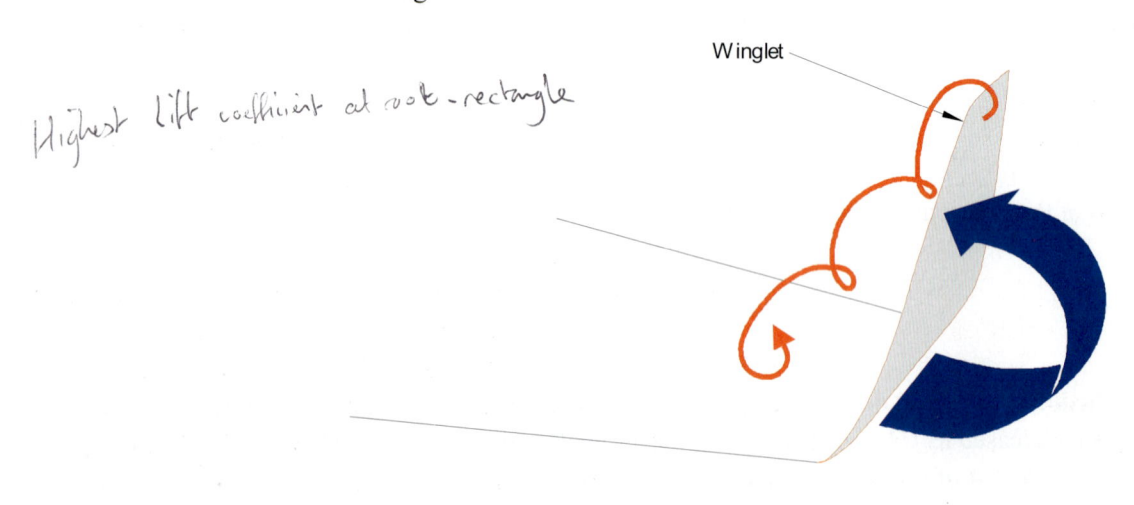

PRINCIPLES OF FLIGHT — DRAG

6.4 METHODS OF REDUCING INDUCED DRAG

Induced drag is low at high speeds, but at low speeds it comprises over half the total drag. Induced drag depends on the strength of the trailing vortices, and it has been shown that a high aspect ratio wing reduces the strength of the vortices for a given lift force. However, very high aspect ratios increase the wing root bending moment, reduce the rate of roll and give reduced ground clearance in roll during take-off and landing, therefore aspect ratio has to be kept within practical limits. The following list itemises other methods used to minimise induced drag by weakening the wing tip vortices.

a) **Wing End-plates:** A flat plate placed at the wing tip will restrict the tip vortices and have a similar effect to an increased aspect ratio, but without the extra bending loads. However, the plate itself will cause parasite drag, and at higher speeds there may be no overall saving in drag.

b) **Tip Tanks:** Fuel tanks placed at the wing tips will have a similar beneficial effect to an end plate, will reduce the induced drag, and will also reduce the wing root bending moment.

c) **Winglets:** Small vertical aerofoils which form part of the wing tip (Fig. 6.12). Shaped and angled to the induced airflow, they generate a small forward force (i.e. "negative drag", or thrust). Winglets partly block the air flowing from the bottom to the top surface of the wing, reducing the strength of the tip vortex. In addition, the small vortex generated by the winglet interacts with and further reduces the strength of the main wingtip vortex.

d) **Wing tip shape:** The shape of the wing tip can affect the strength of the tip vortices, and designs such as turned down or turned up wing tips have been used to reduce induced drag.

Figure 6.12

6.5 EFFECT OF LIFT ON PARASITE DRAG

The sum of drag due to form, friction and interference is termed "parasite" drag because it is not directly associated with the development of lift. While parasite drag is not directly associated with the production of lift, in reality it does vary with lift. The variation of parasite drag coefficient, C_{Dp}, with lift coefficient, C_L, is shown for a typical aeroplane in Fig. 6.13.

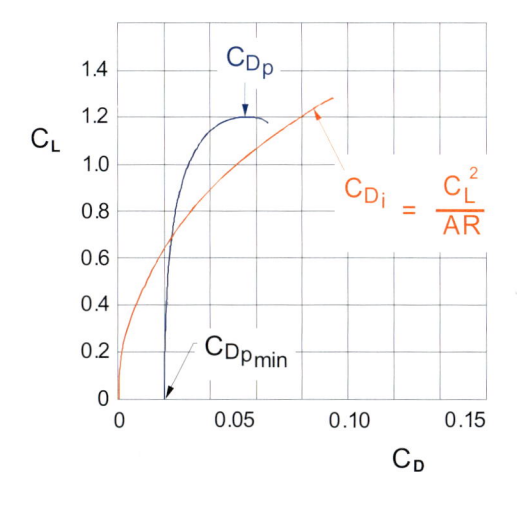

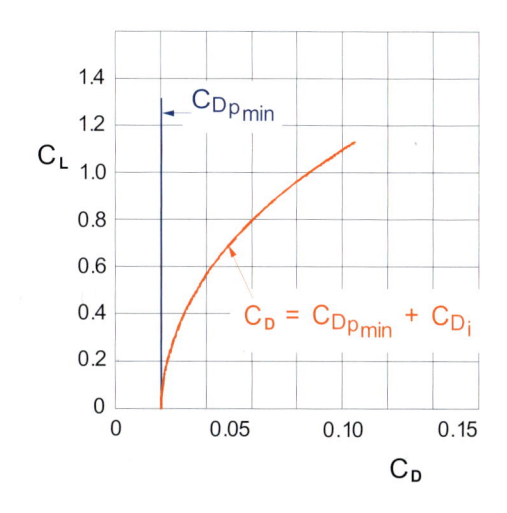

Figure 6.13

Figure 6.14

However, the part of parasite drag above the minimum at zero lift is included with the induced drag coefficient. Fig. 6.14.

Effect of Configuration: Parasite drag, D_p, is unaffected by lift, but is variable with dynamic pressure and area. If all other factors are held constant, parasite drag varies significantly with frontal area. As an example, lowering the landing gear and flaps might increase the parasite area by as much as 80%. At any given IAS this aeroplane would experience an 80% increase in parasite drag.

Effect of Altitude: In most phases of flight the aircraft will be flown at a constant IAS, the dynamic pressure and, thus parasite drag will not vary. The TAS would be higher at altitude to provide the same IAS.

Effect of Speed: The effect of speed alone on parasite drag is the most important. If all other factors are held constant, doubling the speed will give four times the dynamic pressure and hence, four times the parasite drag, (or one quarter as much parasite drag at half the original speed). This variation of parasite drag with speed points out that parasite drag will be of greatest importance at high IAS and of much lower significance at low dynamic pressures. To illustrate this fact, an aeroplane in flight just above the stall speed could have a parasite drag which is only 25% of the total drag. However, this same aeroplane at maximum level flight speed would have a parasite drag which is very nearly 100% of the total drag. The predominance of parasite drag at high flight speeds emphasises the necessity for great aerodynamic cleanliness (streamlining) to obtain high speed performance.

PRINCIPLES OF FLIGHT   DRAG

6.6   AEROPLANE TOTAL DRAG

The total drag of an aeroplane in flight is the sum of induced and parasite drag. Fig. 6.15 illustrates the variation of total drag with IAS for a given aeroplane in level flight at a particular weight and configuration.

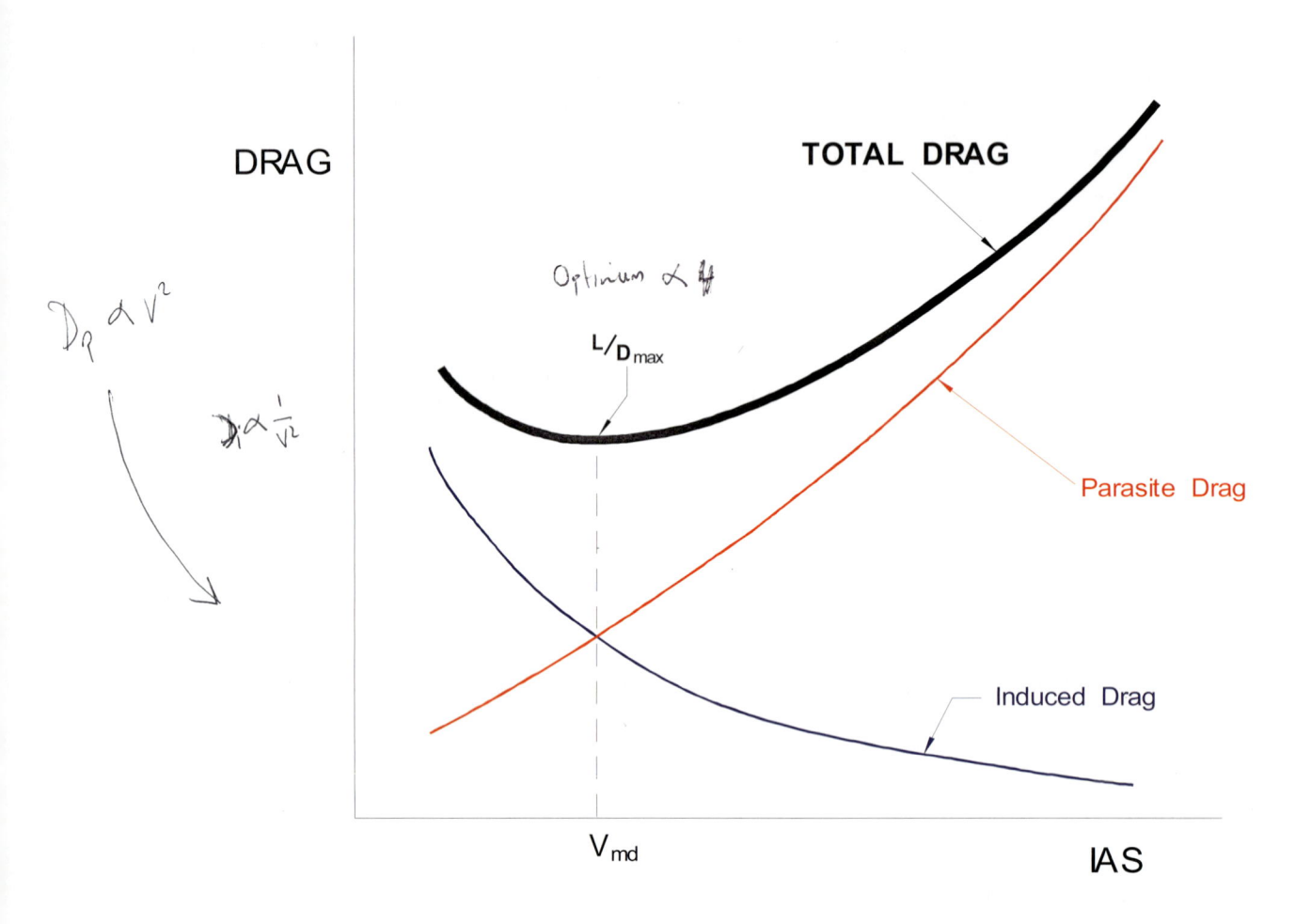

[Figure 6.15: Graph showing DRAG vs IAS with TOTAL DRAG curve (minimum at V_{md}, corresponding to L/D_{max} and Optimum α), Parasite Drag curve (increasing), and Induced Drag curve (decreasing). Handwritten annotations: $D_p \propto V^2$ and $D_i \propto \frac{1}{V^2}$]

Figure 6.15

Fig. 6.15 shows the predominance of induced drag at low speed and parasite drag at high speed. Because of the particular manner in which parasite and induced drags vary with speed **the speed at which total drag is a minimum (V_{md}) occurs when the induced and parasite drag are equal**. The speed for minimum drag is an important reference for many items of aeroplane performance. Range, endurance, climb, glide, manoeuvre, landing and take-off performance are all based on some relationship involving the aeroplane total drag curve. Since flying at V_{md} incurs the least total drag for lift-equal-weight flight, the aeroplane will also be at L/D_{max} angle of attack (approximately 4°).

PRINCIPLES OF FLIGHT — DRAG

It is important to remember that L/D_{max} is obtained at a specific angle of attack and also that the maximum Lift/Drag ratio is a measure of aerodynamic efficiency.

Corresponds to V_{MD} at level flight.

NB: If an aircraft is operated at the L/D_{max} angle of attack, drag will be a minimum while generating the required lift force. Any angle of attack lower or higher than that for L/D_{max} increases the drag for a given lift force; greater drag requires more thrust, which would be inefficient, and expensive. It must also be noted that if IAS is varied, L/D will vary.

Fig. 5.4 illustrated L/D ratio plotted against angle of attack. An alternative presentation of L/D is a polar diagram in which C_L is plotted against C_D, as illustrated in Fig. 6.16.

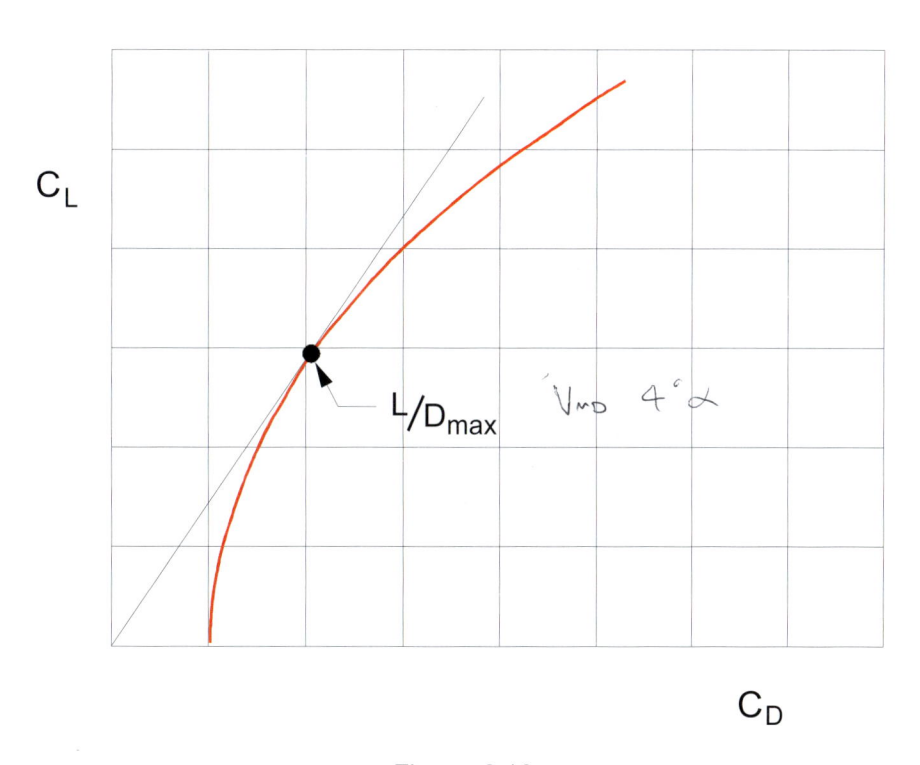

Figure 6.16

[Polar diagram with C_L on vertical axis and C_D on horizontal axis, showing L/D_{max} at tangent point; annotation: V_{MD} 4° α]

The C_L / C_D, whole aeroplane polar diagram in Fig. 6.16 shows C_L increasing initially much more rapidly than C_D, but that ultimately C_D increases more rapidly. The condition for maximum Lift/Drag ratio may be found from the drag polar by drawing the tangent to the curve from the origin.

NB: This is a very common method of displaying L/D ratio, so the display in Fig. 6.16 should become well known.

PRINCIPLES OF FLIGHT — DRAG

6.7 THE EFFECT OF AIRCRAFT GROSS WEIGHT ON TOTAL DRAG

The effect of variation in aircraft gross weight on total drag can be seen from Fig. 6.17. As fuel is consumed gross weight will decrease. As the aircraft weight decreases less lift is required (lower C_L) which will reduce induced drag. Total drag will be less and V_{md} will occur at a lower IAS.

If an aircraft is operated at a higher gross weight, more lift will be required. If more lift is generated, induced drag will be higher. Total drag will be greater and V_{md} will occur at a higher IAS. If an aircraft is manoeuvred so that the load factor is increased, the result will be similar to that caused by an increase in gross weight. i.e. induced drag will increase.

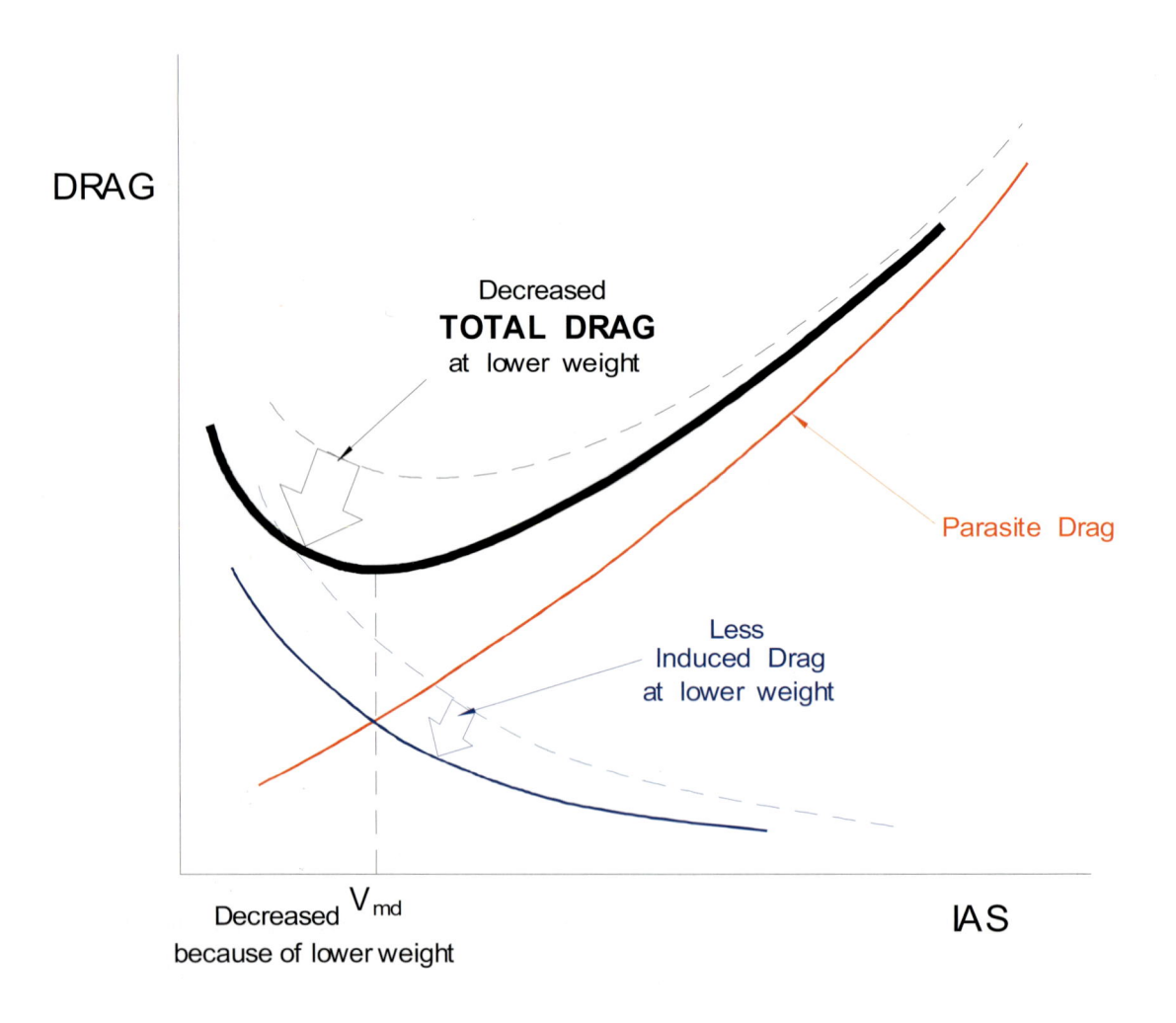

Figure 6.17

PRINCIPLES OF FLIGHT DRAG

6.8 THE EFFECT OF ALTITUDE ON TOTAL DRAG

Aircraft usually operate within limits of Indicated Air Speed (IAS), so it is relevant to consider the variation of drag with IAS. If an aircraft is flown at a constant IAS, dynamic pressure will be constant. As density decreases with increasing altitude, TAS must be increased to maintain the constant IAS ($Q = \frac{1}{2} \rho V^2$). If the aircraft is flown at a constant IAS, drag will not vary with altitude.

6.9 THE EFFECT OF CONFIGURATION ON TOTAL DRAG

Extension of the landing gear, airbrakes, or flaps will increase parasite drag, but will not substantially affect induced drag. The effect of increasing parasite drag is to increase total drag at any IAS but to decrease the speed V_{md} compared to the clean aircraft, (Fig. 6.18).

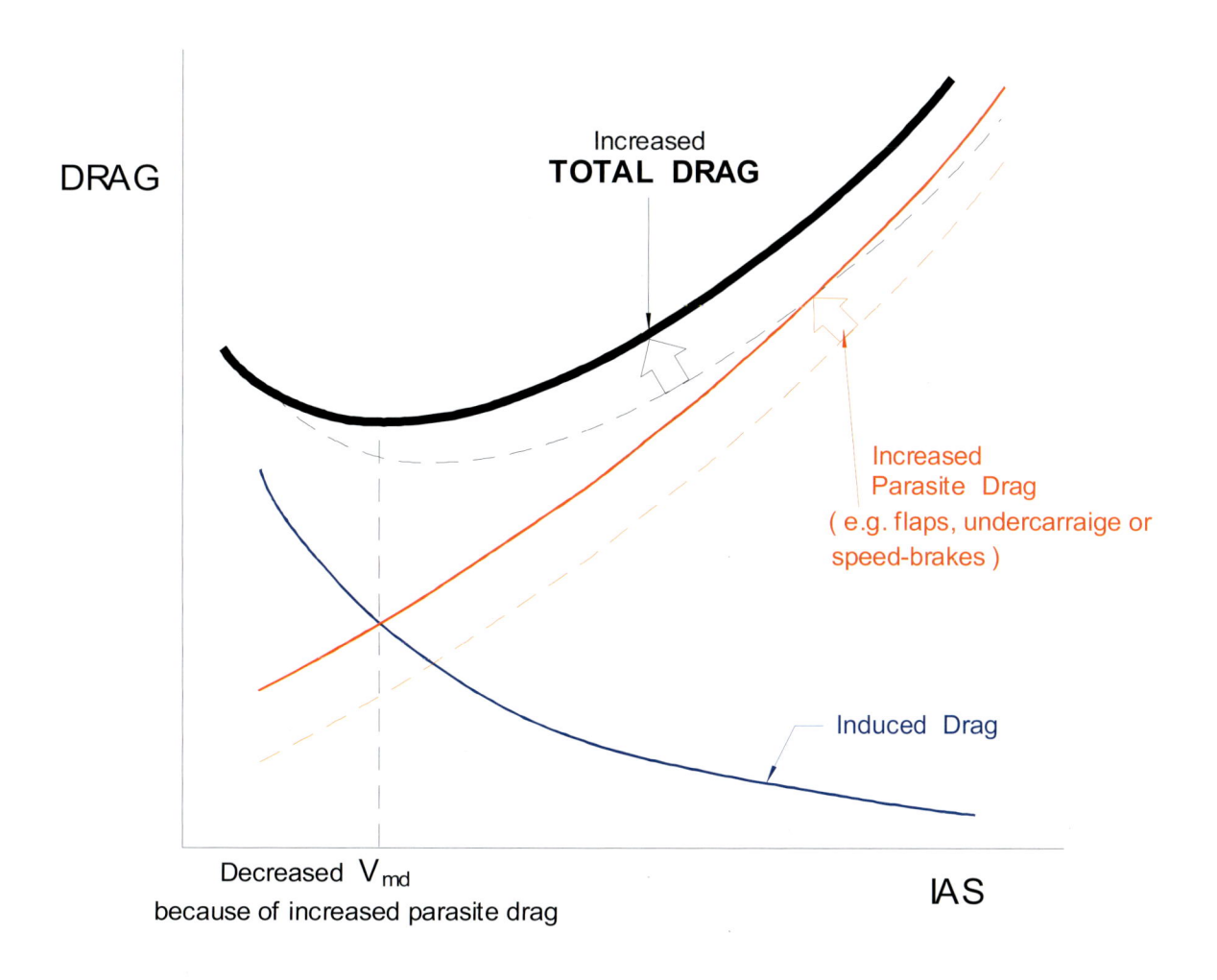

Figure 6.18

PRINCIPLES OF FLIGHT DRAG

6.10 SPEED STABILITY

For an aircraft to be in steady flight the aircraft must be in equilibrium - there can be no out of balance forces or moments. When an aircraft is trimmed to fly at a steady speed, thrust and drag are equal. Therefore, when an aircraft is in steady flight it can be said that the term DRAG and the term 'THRUST REQUIRED' have the same meaning.

Consequently, an alternative to considering DRAG against IAS as in the graph of Fig. 6.15, the term 'THRUST REQUIRED' can be substituted for drag.

For an aircraft in steady flight, if there is a variation in speed **with no change in throttle setting**, (which is called 'THRUST AVAILABLE'), depending on the trim speed, there will be either an excess or a deficiency of thrust available. This phenomena is illustrated in Fig. 6.19.

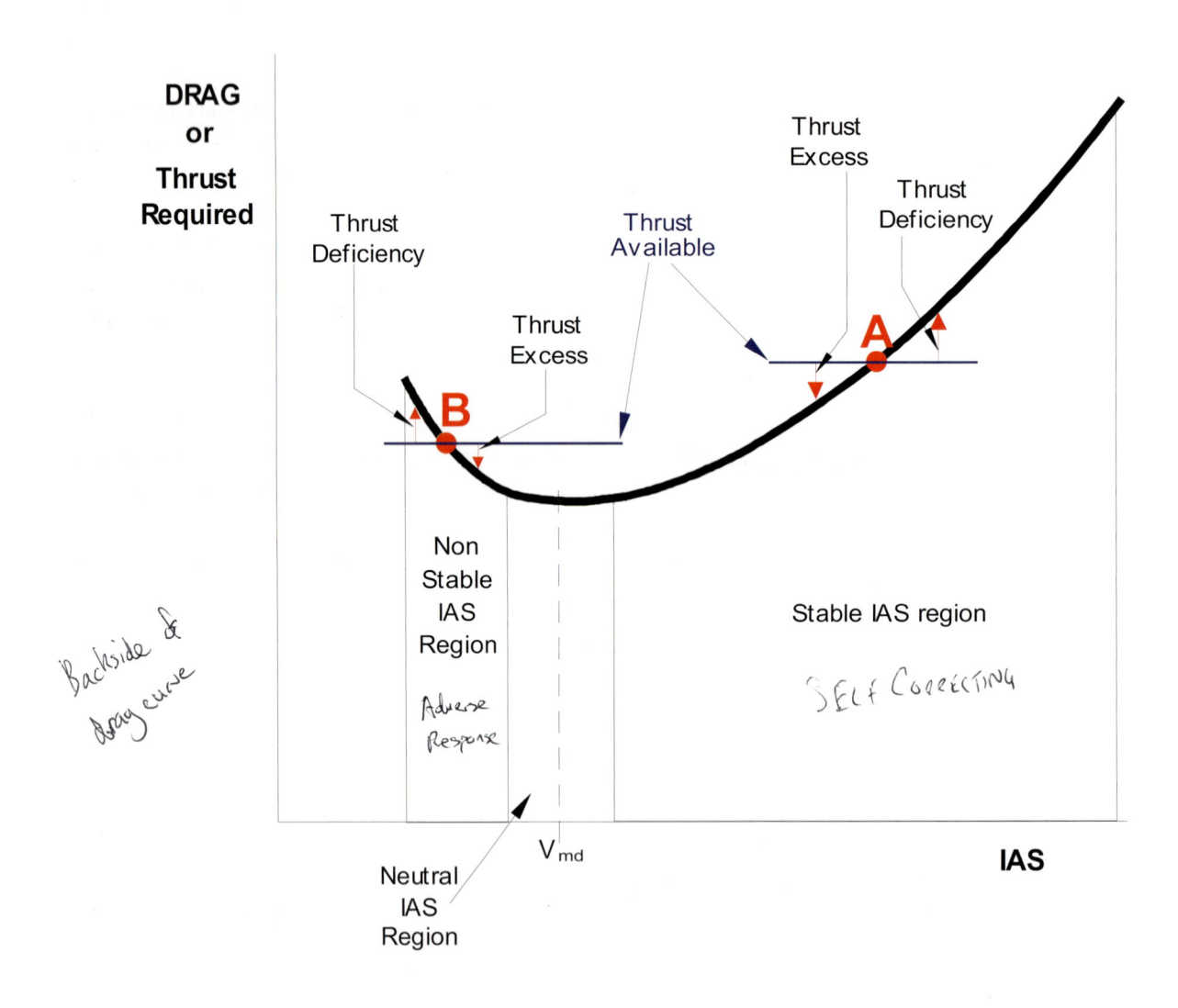

Figure 6.19

If an aircraft is established in steady flight at point 'A' in Fig. 6.19, lift is equal to weight and the thrust available is set to match the thrust required. If the aircraft is disturbed to some airspeed slightly greater than point 'A', a thrust deficiency will exist and, if the aircraft is disturbed to some airspeed slightly lower than point 'A', a thrust excess will exist. This relationship provides a tendency for the aircraft to return to the equilibrium of point 'A' and resume the original trim speed. Steady flight at speeds greater than V_{md} is characterised by a relatively strong tendency of the aircraft to maintain the trim speed quite naturally; **the aircraft is speed stable.**

Speed stability is an important consideration, particularly at speeds at and below V_{md}, most often encountered during the approach to landing phase of flight.

If an aircraft is established in steady flight at point 'B' in Fig. 6.19, lift is equal to weight and the thrust available is set to match the thrust required. If the aircraft is disturbed and goes faster than the trim speed there will be a decrease in drag giving an excess of thrust which will cause the aircraft to accelerate. If a disturbance slows the aircraft below the trim speed there will be an increase in drag which will give a thrust deficiency causing the aircraft to slow further. This relationship is basically unstable because the variation of excess thrust to either side of point 'B' tends to magnify any original disturbance. Steady flight at speeds less than V_{md} is characterised by a tendency for the aircraft to drift away from the trim speed **and the aircraft is speed unstable.** If a disturbance reduces speed it will naturally continue to reduce. If a disturbance increases speed it will continue to drift up to V_{md}. For this reason, the pilot must closely monitor IAS during the approach phase of flight. Any tendency for the aircraft to slow down must be countered **immediately** by a 'generous' application of thrust to quickly return to the desired trim speed.

Consider Fig. 6.19. If an aircraft **maintains a constant IAS** in the speed unstable region, the addition of parasite drag by selecting undercarriage down or by deploying flaps has the benefit of reducing V_{md} which can improve speed stability by moving the speed stable region to the left.

At speeds very close to V_{md} an aircraft usually exhibits no tendency towards either speed stability or speed instability - the neutral IAS region.

PRINCIPLES OF FLIGHT — DRAG

6.11 POWER REQUIRED (Introduction)

We will now consider the relationship between Thrust, Drag and Power. These sound like engine considerations which might be better studied in Book 4, but it has already been shown that Drag can also be referred to as 'Thrust Required' and you will now see that a similar relationship exists with 'Power Required' - they are both important airframe considerations.

1. Thrust is a FORCE (a push or a pull), used to oppose Drag,

   but Power is the RATE of doing WORK, or $\quad \text{POWER} = \dfrac{\text{WORK}}{\text{TIME}}$

   and $\quad$ WORK = FORCE x DISTANCE

   so POWER must be $\dfrac{\text{FORCE x DISTANCE}}{\text{TIME}}$

   For Power Required:

   a) Which Force?
      Drag.

   b) Distance divided by time is speed.

      Which speed?
      The only speed there is - the speed of the aircraft through the air, True Air Speed (TAS).

   Therefore, **POWER REQUIRED = DRAG x TAS**

2. If an aircraft climbs at a constant IAS, Drag will remain constant, **but TAS must be increased - so Power Required will increase.**

It is necessary to consider Power Required when studying Principles of Flight because Work must be done on the aircraft to "raise" it to a higher altitude when climbing. Logically, maximum work can be done on the aircraft in the minimum time when the power available from the engine(s) is greatest and the power required by the airframe is least.

For easy reference, associate the word POWER with the word RATE. e.g. minimum rate of descent is achieved in a steady glide when the aircraft is flown at the minimum power required speed (V_{MP}).

These and other considerations will be examined more fully during the study of Aircraft Performance in Book 6 and Flight Mechanics in Chapter 12 of this Book.

PRINCIPLES OF FLIGHT — DRAG

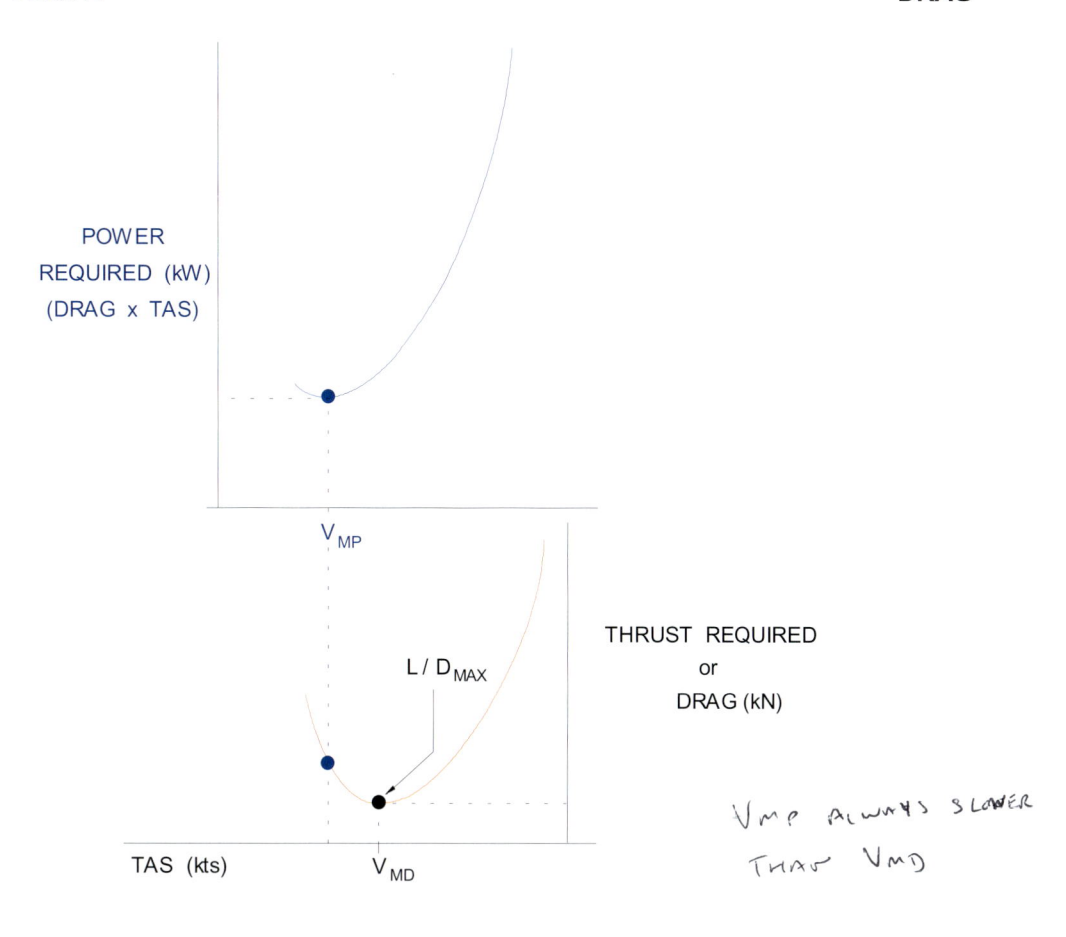

Figure 6.20

Figure 6.20 is drawn for sea level conditions where TAS = IAS and is valid for one particular aircraft, for one weight, only in level flight, and shows how a graph of TAS against 'Power Required' has been constructed from a TAS/Drag curve by multiplying each value of drag by the appropriate TAS and converting it to kilowatts.

The speed for minimum power required is known as V_{MP} and is an Indicated Air Speed (IAS).

Note that the speed corresponding to minimum Power Required (V_{MP}), is slower than the speed for minimum drag (V_{MD}).

Effect of Altitude: An aircraft flying at V_{MD} will experience constant drag at any altitude because V_{MD} is an IAS. At altitude the TAS for a given IAS is higher, but the power required also increases by the amount (Power Required = Drag x TAS). So the ratio of TAS to Power Required is unaffected and V_{MP} will remain slower than V_{MD}.

This information primarily concerns aircraft performance, but the relationship of speed for minimum power required (V_{MP}) and speed for minimum drag (V_{MD}) is important for the study of rate and angle of descent in a steady glide, outlined in Chapter 12.

PRINCIPLES OF FLIGHT — DRAG

6.11 SUMMARY

(1) Parasite drag is made up of:

    (a) Skin friction drag.

    (b) Form (Pressure) drag.

        Skin friction plus Form drag is known as Profile Drag.

    (c) Interference drag.

Parasite Drag varies directly as the square of the Indicated Air Speed (IAS) - Double the speed, four times the parasite drag. Halve the speed, one quarter the parasite drag.

The designer can minimise Parasite Drag by:-

    (i) Streamlining.
    (ii) Filleting and
    (iii) The use of laminar flow wing sections.

Flight crews must ensure the airframe, and the wing in particular, is not contaminated by ice, snow, mud or slush.

(2) Induced drag:-

    (a) Spanwise airflow generates wingtip vortices.

    (b) The higher the C_L (the lower the IAS) the stronger the wingtip vortices.

    (c) Wingtip vortices strengthen downwash.

    (d) Strengthened downwash inclines wing lift rearwards.

    (e) The greater the rearward inclination of wing lift the greater the Induced Drag.

Induced Drag varies inversely as the square of the Indicated Air Speed (IAS) - Halve the speed, 16 times the induced drag coefficient (C_{Di}) and four times the induced drag (D_i). Double the speed, one sixteenth the C_{Di} and one quarter the D_i.

The designer can minimise Induced Drag by:-

    (i) Using a high aspect ratio wing planform.
    (ii) A tapered wing planform with wing twist and/or spanwise camber variation, or
    (iii) Incorporation of wing end-plates, tip tanks, winglets or various wing tip shapes.

PRINCIPLES OF FLIGHT   DRAG

(3)   Total drag.

    (a)   Total drag is the sum of Parasite and Induced drag.

    (b)   Total drag is a minimum when Parasite and Induced drag are equal.

    (c)   At low IAS Induced drag is dominant.

    (d)   At high IAS Parasite drag dominates.

    (e)   The IAS at which Parasite and Induced drag are equal is called minimum drag speed (V_{md}).

    (f)   As gross weight decreases in flight Induced drag decreases, Total drag decreases and V_{md} decreases.

    (g)   At a constant IAS, altitude has no affect on Total drag, but TAS will increase as density decreases with increasing altitude.

    (h)   Configuration changes which increase the "Parasite Area", such as undercarriage, flaps or speed brakes, increases Parasite drag, increases Total drag and decreases V_{md}.

(4)   Speed stability.

    (a)   An aircraft flying at a steady IAS higher than V_{md} with a fixed throttle setting will have speed stability.

    (b)   An aircraft flying at a steady IAS at V_{md} or slower with a fixed throttle setting will usually NOT have speed stability.

    (c)   If an aircraft flying at a steady IAS and a fixed throttle setting within the non-stable IAS region encounters a disturbance which slow the aircraft, the aircraft will tend to slow further; IAS will tend to continue to decrease and Total drag increase.

(5)   Power Required

    (a) V_{MP}, the Indicated Air Speed for minimum 'Power Required' is slower than the minimum drag speed (V_{MD}).

    (b)   Maximum TAS/Power ratio (1·32 V_{MP}) occurs at V_{MD}.

PRINCIPLES OF FLIGHT   DRAG

SELF ASSESSMENT QUESTIONS

1. What is the effect on total drag of an aircraft if the airspeed decreases in level flight below that speed for maximum L/D?

    a) Drag increases because of increased induced drag.
    b) Drag decreases because of lower induced drag.
    c) Drag increases because of increased parasite drag.
    d) Drag decreases because of lower parasite drag.

2. By changing the angle of attack of a wing, the pilot can control the airplane's:

    a) lift and airspeed, but not drag.
    b) lift, gross weight, and drag.
    c) lift, airspeed, and drag.
    d) lift and drag, but not airspeed.

3. What is the relationship between induced and parasite drag when the gross weight is increased?

    a) Parasite drag increases more than induced drag.
    b) Induced drag increases more than parasite drag.
    c) Both parasite and induced drag are equally increased.
    d) Both parasite and induced drag are equally decreased.

4. In theory, if the airspeed of an airplane is doubled while in level flight, parasite drag will become:

    a) twice as great.
    b) half as great.
    c) four times greater.
    d) one quarter as much.

5. As airspeed decreases in level flight below that speed for maximum lift/drag ratio, total drag of an aeroplane:

    a) decreases because of lower parasite drag.
    b) increases because of increased parasite drag.
    c) increases because of increased induced drag.
    d) decreases because of lower induced drag.

6. (Refer to annex 'A') At the airspeed represented by point B, in steady flight, the airplane will

   a) have its maximum L/D ratio.
   b) have its minimum L/D ratio.
   c) be developing its maximum coefficient of lift.
   d) be developing its minimum coefficient of drag

7. Which statement is true relative to changing angle of attack?

   a) A decrease in angle of attack will increase pressure below the wing, and decrease drag.
   b) An increase in angle of attack will decrease pressure below the wing, and increase drag.
   c) An increase in angle of attack will increase drag.
   d) A decrease in angle of attack will decrease pressure below the wing and increase drag.

8. On a wing, the force of lift acts perpendicular to, and the force of drag acts parallel to the:

   a) flightpath.
   b) longitudinal axis.
   c) chord line.
   d) longitudinal datum

9. That portion of the aircraft's total drag created by the production of lift is called:

   a) induced drag, and is greatly affected by changes in airspeed.
   b) induced drag, and is not affected by changes in airspeed.
   c) parasite drag, and is greatly affected by changes in airspeed.
   d) parasite drag, which is inversely proportional to the square of the airspeed

10. The best L/D ratio of an aircraft occurs when parasite drag is:

    a) a minimum.
    b) less than induced drag.
    c) greater than induced drag.
    d) equal to induced drag.

11. An aircraft has a L/D ratio of 15:1 at 50 kts in calm air. What would the L/D ratio be with a direct headwind of 25 kts?

    a) 30 : 1
    b) 15 : 1
    c) 25 : 1
    d) 7.5 : 1

PRINCIPLES OF FLIGHT   DRAG

12. Which is true regarding aerodynamic drag?

    a)   Induced drag is a by-product of lift and is greatly affected by changes in airspeed.
    b)   All aerodynamic drag is created entirely by the production of lift.
    c)   Induced drag is created entirely by air resistance.
    d)   Parasite drag is a by-product of lift.

13. At a given True Air Speed, what effect will increased air density have on the lift and drag of an aircraft?

    a)   Lift will increase but drag will decrease.
    b)   Lift and drag will increase.
    c)   Lift and drag will decrease.
    d)   Lift and drag will remain the same.

14. If the Indicated Air Speed of an aircraft is increased from 50 kts to 100 kts, parasite drag will be:

    a)   four times greater.
    b)   six times greater.
    c)   two times greater.
    d)   one quarter as much.

15. If the Indicated Air Speed of an aircraft is decreased from 100 kts to 50 kts, induced drag will be:

    a)   two times greater.
    b)   four times greater.
    c)   half as much.
    d)   one quarter as much.

16. The best L/D ratio of an aircraft in a given configuration is a value that:

    a)   varies with Indicated Air Speed.
    b)   varies depending upon the weight being carried.
    c)   varies with air density.
    d)   remains constant regardless of Indicated Air Speed changes.

17. The tendency of an aircraft to develop forces which restore it to its original condition, when disturbed from a condition of steady flight, is known as:

    a)   manoeuverability.
    b)   controllability.
    c)   stability.
    d)   instability.

18. As Indicated Air Speed increases in level flight, the total drag of an aircraft becomes greater than the total drag produced at the maximum lift/drag speed because of the:

    a) decrease in induced drag only.
    b) increase in induced drag.
    c) increase in parasite drag.
    d) decrease in parasite drag only.

19. The resistance, or skin friction, due to the viscosity of the air as it passes along the surface of a wing is a type of:

    a) induced drag.
    b) form drag.
    c) parasite drag.
    d) interference drag.

20. Which relationship is correct when comparing drag and airspeed?

    a) Parasite drag varies inversely as the square of the airspeed.
    b) Induced drag increases as the square of the airspeed.
    c) Parasite drag increases as the square of the lift coefficient divided by the aspect ratio.
    d) Induced drag varies inversely as the square of the airspeed.

21. If the same angle of attack is maintained in ground effect as when out of ground effect, lift will:

    a) decrease, and parasite drag will decrease.
    b) increase, and induced drag will decrease.
    c) decrease, and parasite drag will increase.
    d) increase and induced drag will increase.

22. Which statement is true regarding aeroplane flight at L/Dmax?

    a) Any angle of attack other than that for L/Dmax increases parasite drag.
    b) Any angle of attack other than that for L/Dmax increases the lift/drag ratio.
    c) Any angle of attack other than that for L/Dmax increases total drag for a given aeroplane's lift.
    d) Any angle of attack other than that for L/Dmax increases the lift and reduces the drag.

23. Aspect ratio of a wing is defined as the ratio of the:

    a) square of the chord to the wingspan.
    b) wingspan to the wing root.
    c) area squared to the chord.
    d) wingspan to the mean chord.

PRINCIPLES OF FLIGHT   DRAG

24. A wing with a very high aspect ratio (in comparison with a low aspect ratio wing) will have:

   a) poor control qualities at low airspeeds.
   b) increased drag at high angles of attack.
   c) a low stall speed.
   d) reduced bending moment on its attachment points.

25. At a constant velocity in airflow, a high aspect ratio wing will have (in comparison with a low aspect ratio wing):

   a) increased drag, especially at a low angle of attack.
   b) decreased drag, especially at a high angle of attack.
   c) increased drag, especially at a high angle of attack.
   d) decreased drag, especially at low angles of attack.

26. (Refer to annex 'B') Which aircraft has the highest aspect ratio?

   a) 3.
   b) 4.
   c) 2.
   d) 1.

27. (Refer to annex 'B') Which aircraft has the lowest aspect ratio?

   a) 4.
   b) 2.
   c) 3.
   d) 1.

28. (Refer to annex 'B') Consider only aspect ratio (other factors remain constant). Which aircraft will generate greatest lift?

   a) 1.
   b) 2.
   c) 3.
   d) 4.

29. (Refer to annex 'B') Consider only aspect ratio (other factors remain constant). Which aircraft will generate greatest drag?

   a) 1.
   b) 4.
   c) 3.
   d) 2.

30. What happens to total drag when accelerating from C_{Lmax} to maximum speed?

    a) Increases.
    b) Increases then decreases.
    c) Decreases.
    d) Decreases then increases.

31. (Refer to annex 'C'), the whole aircraft CL against CD polar. Point 'B' represents:

    1 - Best Lift/Drag ratio.
    2 - The critical angle of attack.
    3 - Recommended approach speed.
    4 - Never exceed speed (V_{NE}).

    a) 1 and 2
    b) 1 only
    c) 2 only
    d) 4 only

32. If the Indicated Air Speed of an aircraft in level flight is increased from 100 kt to 200 kt, what change will occur in (i) TAS (ii) C_{Di} (iii) D_i ?

	(i)	(ii)	(iii)
a)	2	1/4	1/16
b)	0	4	16
c)	4	1/16	1/4
d)	2	1/16	1/4

INTENTIONALLY

LEFT

BLANK

PRINCIPLES OF FLIGHT   DRAG

ANNEX 'A'

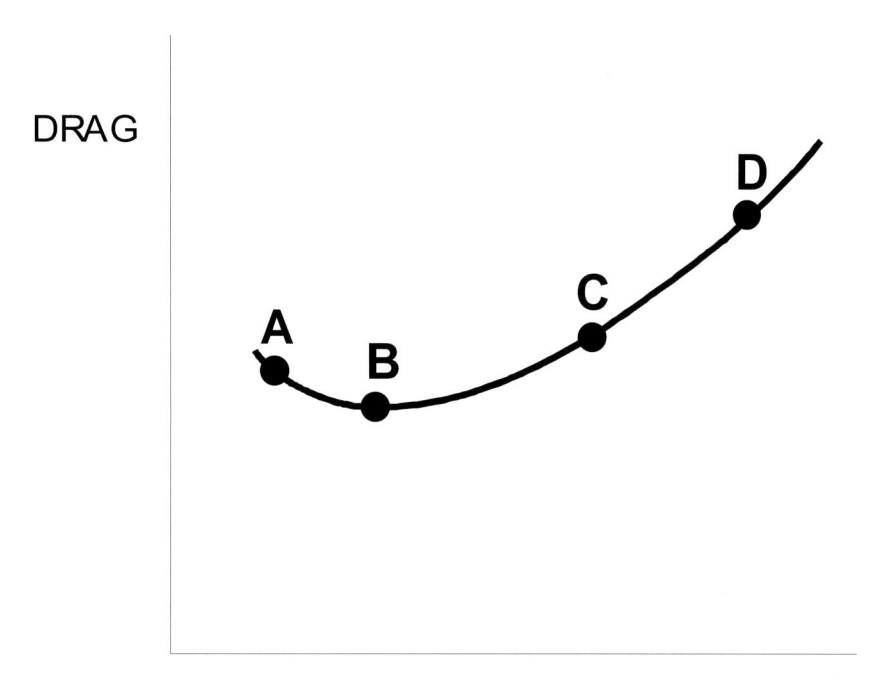

DRAG

```
              D
           C
     A
       B
```

IAS

ANNEX 'B'

Aircraft 1. Span 22.5 metres   5.625
             Chord 4 metres

Aircraft 2. Wing Area 90 square metres   22.5
             Span 45 metres

Aircraft 3. Span 30 metres   10
             Chord 3 metres

Aircraft 4. Wing Area 90 square metres   17.8
             Span 40 metres

PRINCIPLES OF FLIGHT DRAG

ANNEX 'C'

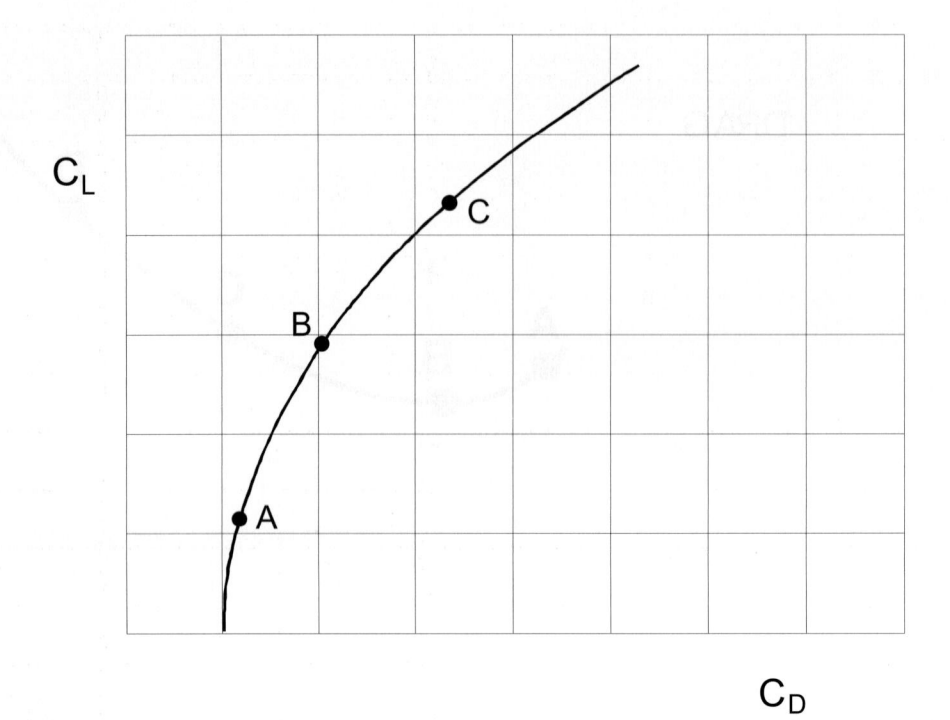

PRINCIPLES OF FLIGHT — DRAG

ANSWERS

No	A	B	C	D	REF	No	A	B	C	D	REF
1	A					17			C		
2			C			18			C		
3		B				19			C		
4			C			20				D	
5			C			21		B			
6	A					22			C		
7			C			23				D	
8	A					24	A				
9	A					25		B			
10				D		26			C		
11		B				27				D	
12	A					28		B			
13		B				29	A				
14	A					30				D	
15		B				31		B			
16				D		32				D	

CHAPTER 7 - STALLING

Contents

	Page
INTRODUCTION	7 - 1
CAUSE OF THE STALL	
THE LIFT CURVE	7 - 2
STALL RECOVERY	
AIRCRAFT BEHAVIOUR CLOSE TO THE STALL	7 - 3
USE OF FLIGHT CONTROLS CLOSE TO THE STALL	
STALL RECOGNITION	7 - 4
STALL SPEED	
STALL WARNING	7 - 6
ARTIFICIAL STALL WARNING DEVICES	
STICK SHAKER	7 - 7
STALL WARNING VANE	7 - 8
ANGLE OF ATTACK VANE	7 - 9
ANGLE OF ATTACK PROBE	
BASIC STALL REQUIREMENTS	7 - 10
WING DESIGN CHARACTERISTICS	
THE EFFECT OF AEROFOIL SECTION	
THE EFFECT OF WING PLAN FORM	7 - 12
RECTANGULAR WING	
TAPERED WING	7 - 13
WASHOUT	
THICKNESS AND CAMBER	
LEADING EDGE SLOTS	
STALL STRIPS	7 - 14
VORTEX GENERATORS	7 - 15
SWEPT BACK WING	7 - 16
TIP STALL AND PITCH-UP	
WING FENCES	7 - 17
VORTILONS	
SAW TOOTH LEADING EDGE	
KEY FACTS 1 - SELF STUDY	7 - 18
SUPER STALL (DEEP STALL)	7 - 22
SUPER STALL PREVENTION - STICK PUSHER	7 - 23
FACTORS THAT EFFECT STALL SPEED	7 - 24
1G STALL SPEED	
WEIGHT CHANGE	7 - 25
COMPOSITION AND RESOLUTION OF FORCES	7 - 26
PARALLELOGRAM OF FORCES	
BASIC TRIGONOMETRY	
LIFT INCREASE IN A LEVEL TURN	7 - 27

FACTORS THAT EFFECT STALL SPEED - CONTINUED.
    LOAD FACTOR .... 7 - 28
    HIGH LIFT DEVICES .... 7 - 29
    CG POSITION .... 7 - 30
    LANDING GEAR POSITION .... 7 - 31
    ENGINE POWER .... 7 - 32
        PROPELLER
        JET
    MACH NUMBER .... 7 - 34
    WING CONTAMINATION .... 7 - 36
        ICE
        FROST
        SNOW
    WARNING TO PILOT OF ICING-INDUCED STALLS .... 7 - 38
    STABILISER STALL DUE TO ICE .... 7 - 39
    EFFECTS OF HEAVY RAIN ON STALL SPEED
    STALL AND RECOVERY CHARACTERISTICS OF CANARDS
SPINNING .... 7 - 40
    PRIMARY CAUSES OF A SPIN
    PHASES OF A SPIN .... 7 - 41
    EFFECT OF MASS & BALANCE ON SPINS .... 7 - 42
    SPIN RECOVERY
SPECIAL PHENOMENA OF STALL .... 7 - 44
    CROSSED-CONTROL STALL
    ACCELERATED STALL
    SECONDARY STALL
    LARGE AIRCRAFT
    SMALL AIRCRAFT .... 7 - 45
        POWER ON AND POWER OFF
    CLIMBING AND DESCENDING TURNS .... 7 - 46
HIGH SPEED BUFFET
ANSWERS (V_S IN 25° AND 30° BANK) .... 7 - 48
KEY FACTS 2 - SELF STUDY .... 7 - 49
SELF ASSESSMENT QUESTIONS .... 7 - 53
KEY FACTS 1 AND 2 (COMPLETE) .... 7 - 63

NB: Throughout this chapter reference will be made to JAR stall requirements etc, but it must be emphasised that these references are for training purposes only and are not subject to amendment action.

PRINCIPLES OF FLIGHT   STALLING

7.1   INTRODUCTION

Stalling is a potentially hazardous manoeuvre involving loss of height and loss of control. A pilot must be able to clearly and unmistakably identify an impending stall, so that it can be prevented. Different types of aircraft exhibit various stall characteristics; some less desirable than others. Airworthiness authorities specify minimum stall qualities that an aircraft must possess.

7.2   CAUSE OF THE STALL

The C_L of an aerofoil increases with angle of attack up to a maximum ($C_{L\,MAX}$). Any further increase above this stalling, or **critical angle of attack,** will make it impossible for the airflow to smoothly follow the upper wing contour, the flow will separate from the surface, causing C_L to decrease and drag to increase rapidly. Since the $C_{L\,MAX}$ of an aerofoil corresponds to the minimum steady flight speed (the 1g stall speed), it is an important point of reference.

A stall is caused by airflow separation. Separation can occur when either the boundary layer has insufficient kinetic energy or the adverse pressure gradient becomes too great.

Fig. 7.1 shows that at low angles of attack virtually no flow separation occurs before the trailing edge, the flow being attached over the rear part of the surface in the form of a turbulent boundary layer.

As angle of attack increases, the adverse pressure gradient increases, reducing the kinetic energy, and the boundary layer will begin to separate from the surface at the trailing edge.

Further increase in angle of attack makes the separation point move forward and the wing area that generates a pressure differential becomes smaller. At angles of attack higher than approximately 16°, the extremely steep adverse pressure gradient will have caused so much separation that insufficient lift is generated to balance the aircraft weight.

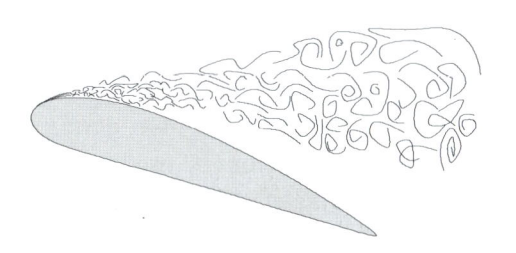

Figure 7.1

It is important to remember that the angle of attack is the angle between the chord line and the relative airflow. Therefore, if the angle of attack is increased up to or beyond the critical angle, an aeroplane can be stalled at any airspeed or flight attitude.

> An aeroplane can be stalled at any airspeed or attitude

7 - 1

PRINCIPLES OF FLIGHT   STALLING

7.3 THE LIFT CURVE

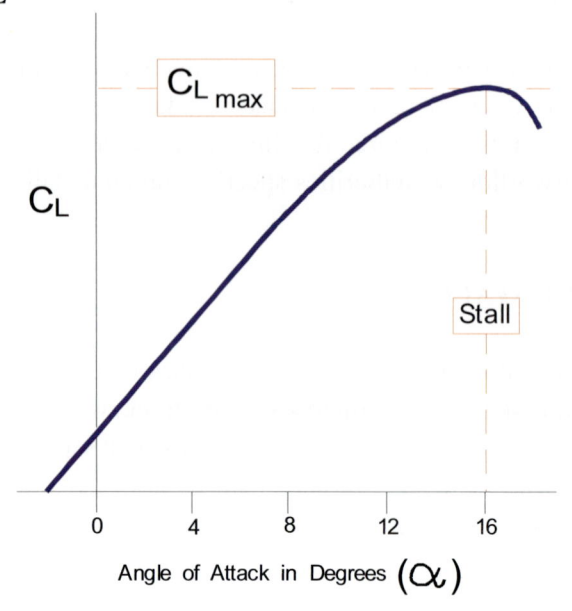

Figure 7.2

Fig. 7.2 shows that as the angle of attack increases from the zero lift value, the curve is linear over a considerable range. As the effects of separation begin to be felt, the slope of the curve begins to fall off. Eventually, lift reaches a maximum and begins to decrease. The angle at which it does so is called the stalling angle or critical angle of attack, and the corresponding value of lift coefficient is $C_{L\,MAX}$. A typical stalling angle is about 16°.

7.4 STALL RECOVERY

To recover from a stall or prevent a full stall, the angle of attack must be decreased to reduce the adverse pressure gradient. This may consist of merely releasing back pressure, or it may be necessary to smoothly move the pitch control forward, depending on the aircraft design and severity of the stall. (Excessive forward movement of the pitch control however, may impose a negative load on the wing and delay recovery). For most modern jet transport aircraft it is usually sufficient to lower the nose to the horizon or just below, while applying maximum authorised power to minimise height loss.

On straight wing aircraft the rudder should be used to prevent wing drop during stall and recovery. On swept wing aircraft it is recommended that the ailerons be used to prevent wing drop, with a small amount of smoothly applied co-ordinated rudder. (The rudder on modern high speed jet transport aircraft is very powerful and careless use can give too much roll, leading to pilot induced oscillation - PIO).

Allow airspeed to increase and recover lost altitude with moderate back pressure on the pitch control. Pulling too hard could trigger a secondary stall, or worse, could exceed the limit load factor and damage the aircraft structure. As angle of attack reduces below the critical angle, the adverse pressure gradient will decrease, airflow will re-attach, and lift and drag will return to their normal values.

PRINCIPLES OF FLIGHT **STALLING**

7.5 AIRCRAFT BEHAVIOUR CLOSE TO THE STALL

Stall characteristics vary with different types of aircraft. However, for modern aircraft during most normal manoeuvres, the onset of stall is gradual. The first indications of a stall may be provided by any or all of the following:-

a) unresponsive flight controls,

b) a stall warning or stall prevention device, or

c) aerodynamic buffet.

The detailed behaviour of various aircraft types will be discussed later.

7.6 USE OF FLIGHT CONTROLS CLOSE TO THE STALL

At low speeds normally associated with stalling, dynamic pressure is at a very low value and greater control deflection will be required to achieve the same response; also the flying controls will feel unresponsive or "mushy". If an accidental stall does occur it is vitally important that the stall and recovery should occur without too much wing drop. Moving a control surface modifies the chord line and hence the angle of attack. An aircraft being flown close to the stall angle may have one wing that produces slightly less lift than the other; that wing will tend to drop. Trying to lift a dropping wing with aileron will increase its angle of attack, Fig. 7.3, and may cause the wing to stall completely, resulting in that wing dropping at an increased rate. **At speeds close to the stall ailerons must be used with caution.** On straight wing aircraft the rudder should be used to yaw the aircraft just enough to increase the speed of a dropping wing to maintain a wings level attitude. Swept wing aircraft basic stall requirements are designed to enable the ailerons to be used successfully up to 'stall recognition' (Page 7-4 and Para. 7.11), but small amounts of rudder can be used if smoothly applied and co-ordinated with the ailerons.

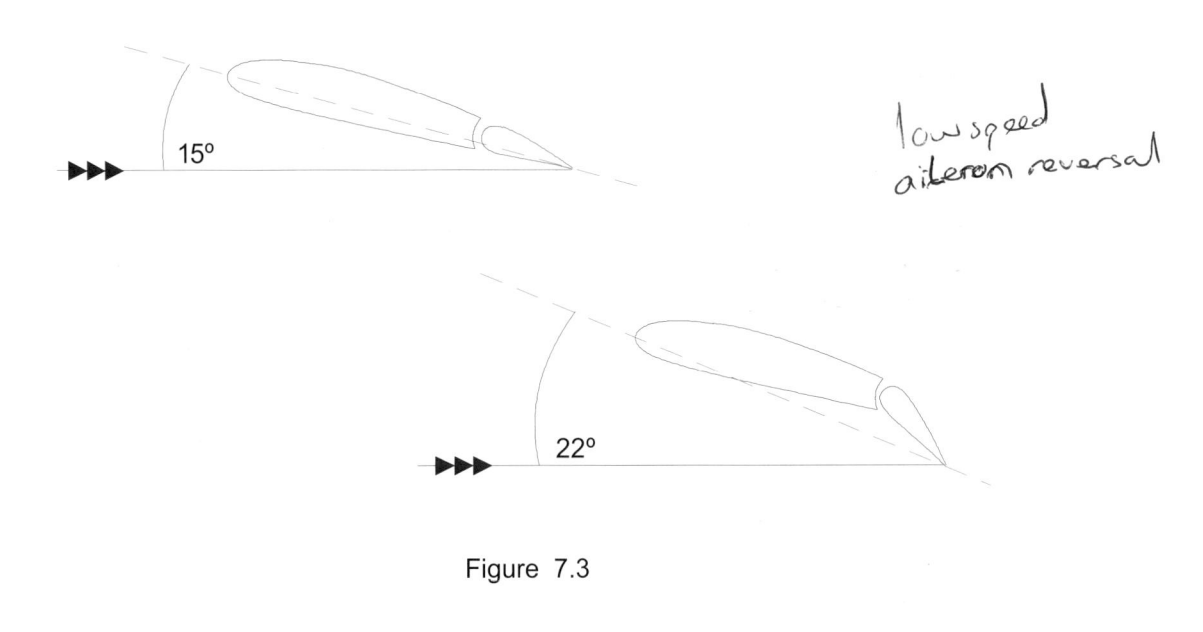

[handwritten annotation: low speed aileron reversal]

Figure 7.3

PRINCIPLES OF FLIGHT — STALLING

7.7 STALL RECOGNITION

The aeroplane is considered stalled when the behaviour of the aeroplane gives the pilot a clear and distinctive indication of an acceptable nature that the aeroplane is stalled.

Acceptable indications of a stall, occurring either individually or in combination, are:-

(1) A nose-down pitch that cannot be readily arrested;

(2) Buffeting, of a magnitude and severity that is a strong and effective deterrent to further speed reduction; or increasing α or

(3) The pitch control reaches the aft stop and no further increase in pitch attitude occurs when the control is held full aft for a short time before recovery is initiated.

7.8 STALL SPEED

It is necessary to fly at slow speeds (high angles of attack) during take-off and landing in order to keep the required runway lengths to a reasonable minimum. **There must be an adequate safety margin between the minimum speed allowed for normal operations and the stall speed.**

Prototype aircraft are stalled and stall speeds established for inclusion in the Flight Manual during the flight testing that takes place before type certification.

'Small' aircraft (JAR-23) use V_{S0} and V_{S1} on which to base the stall speed.

For 'Large' aircraft (JAR-25) a reference stall speed, V_{SR}, is used.

a) The reference stall speed (V_{SR}) is a calibrated airspeed defined by the aircraft manufacturer. V_{SR} may not be less than a 1-g stall speed. V_{SR} is expressed as:-

$$V_{SR} \geq \frac{V_{CLMAX}}{\sqrt{n_{ZW}}}$$

Where:-

V_{CLMAX} = Calibrated airspeed obtained when the load factor corrected lift coefficient is first a maximum during the manoeuvre prescribed in sub-paragraph (c) of this paragraph.

In addition, when the manoeuvre is limited by a device that abruptly pushes the nose down at a selected angle of attack (e.g. a stick pusher), V_{CLMAX} may not be less than the speed existing at the instant the device operates.

n_{ZW} = Load factor normal to the flight path at V_{CLMAX}

PRINCIPLES OF FLIGHT   **STALLING**

> **NB** On aircraft without a stick pusher, V_{SR} can be considered to be the same as the 1g stall speed (V_{S1g}). But it is impossible to fly at speeds less than that at which the stick pusher activates, so for aircraft fitted with a stick pusher, V_{SR} will be 2 knots or 2% greater than the speed at which the stick pusher activates. (See Figures 7.3a and 7.3b for an illustration of the designations of stall speed and stall warning).

From the 'sample' aeroplane on Page 5-6, the speed at C_{LMAX} was 150 kts. This can be considered as that aeroplane's V_{CLMAX}. **At 1g, V_{SR} would therefore be 150 kts.**

(b) V_{CLMAX} is determined with:-

        (1)   Zero thrust at the stall speed

        (2)   Propeller pitch controls (if applicable) in the take-off position

        (3)   The aeroplane in other respects (such as flaps and landing gear) in the condition existing in the test or performance standard in which V_{SR} is being used

        (4)   The weight used when V_{SR} is being used as a factor to determine compliance with a required performance standard

        (5)   The centre of gravity position that results in the highest value of reference stall speed; and

        (6)   The aeroplane trimmed for straight flight at a speed selected by the manufacturer, but not less than $1\cdot13\ V_{SR}$ and not greater than $1\cdot3\ V_{SR}$.

(c)   Starting from the stabilised trim condition [see (b)(6) above], apply the longitudinal control to decelerate the aeroplane so that the speed reduction does not exceed one knot per second.

(d)   In addition to the requirements of sub-paragraph (a) of this paragraph, when a device that abruptly pushes the nose down at a selected angle of attack (e.g. a stick pusher) is installed, the reference stall speed V_{SR}, may not be less than 2 knots or 2%, whichever is the greater, above the speed at which the device operates.

V_{SR} will vary with each of the above conditions. Additional factors which affect V_{SR} are load factor, thrust in excess of zero and wing contamination. All these effects will be detailed later.

> Density altitude does not effect indicated stall speed

PRINCIPLES OF FLIGHT   **STALLING**

7.9 STALL WARNING

Having established a stall speed for each configuration there must be clear and distinctive warning, **sufficiently in advance of the stall**, for the stall itself to be avoided.

(a) Stall warning with sufficient margin to prevent inadvertent stalling with the flaps and landing gear in any normal position must be clear and distinctive to the pilot in straight and turning flight.

(b) The warning may be furnished either through the inherent aerodynamic qualities of the aeroplane or by a device that will give clearly distinguishable indications under expected conditions of flight. **However, a visual stall warning device that requires the attention of the crew within the cockpit is not acceptable by itself.** If a warning device is used, it must provide a warning in each of the aeroplane configurations prescribed in sub-paragraph (a) of this paragraph at the speed prescribed in sub-paragraph (c) and (d) of this paragraph.

(c) When the speed is reduced at rates not exceeding 1 knot per second, stall warning must begin, in each normal configuration, at a speed, V_{SW}, exceeding the speed at which the stall is identified in accordance with Paragraph 7.7 **by not less than 5 knots or 5% CAS, whichever is the greater.** Once initiated, stall warning must continue until the angle of attack is reduced to approximately that at which stall warning began.

(d) In addition to the requirements of sub-paragraph (c) of this paragraph, when the speed is reduced at rates not exceeding one knot per second, in straight flight with engines idling and CG position specified in Paragraph 7.8 (b)(5), V_{SW}, in each normal configuration must exceed V_{SR} by not less than 3 knots or 3% CAS, whichever is greater.

(e) The stall warning margin must be sufficient to allow the pilot to prevent stalling (as defined in Paragraph 7.7) when recovery is initiated not less than one second after the onset of stall warning in slow-down turns with at least 1·5g load factor normal to the flight path and airspeed deceleration rates of at least 2 knots per second, with the flaps and landing gear in any normal position, with the aeroplane trimmed for straight flight at a speed of 1·3 V_{SR}, and with the power or thrust necessary to maintain level flight at 1·3 V_{SR}.

(f) Stall warning must also be provided in each abnormal configuration of the high lift devices that is likely to be used in flight following system failures (including all configurations covered by Flight Manual procedures).

PRINCIPLES OF FLIGHT   STALLING

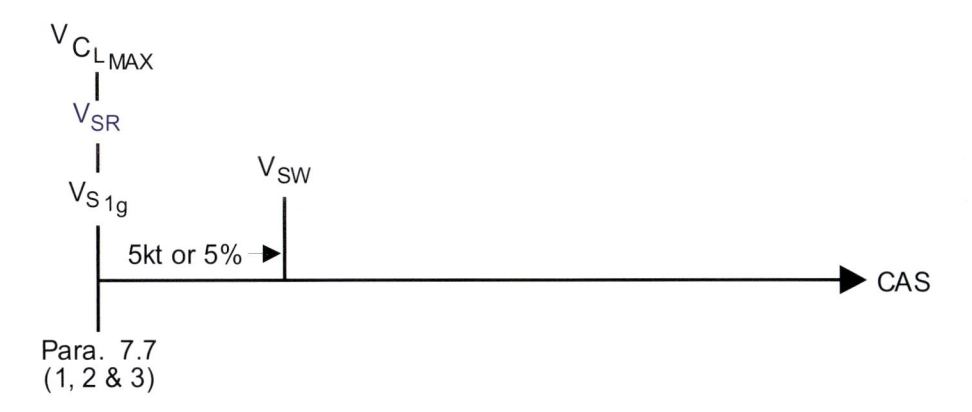

Figure 7.3a Aircraft without stick pusher

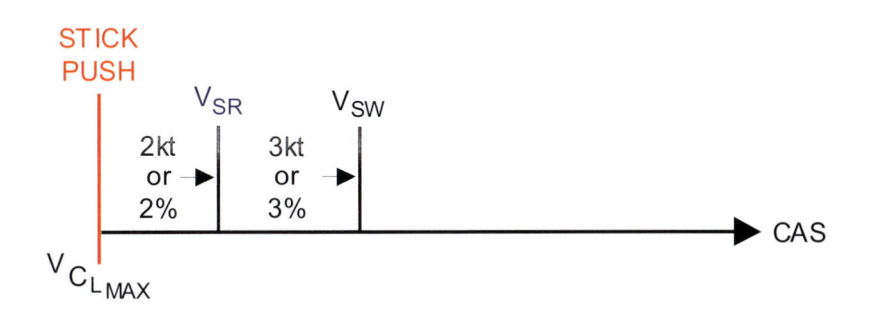

Figure 7.3b Aircraft fitted with Stick Pusher

7.10 ARTIFICIAL STALL WARNING DEVICES

Adequate stall warning **may** be provided by the airflow separating comparatively early and giving aerodynamic buffet by shaking the wing and by buffeting the tailplane, perhaps transmitted up the elevator control run and shaking the control column, but this is not usually sufficient, so a device which simulates natural buffet is usually fitted to all aircraft.

Artificial stall warning on small aircraft is usually given by a buzzer or horn. The artificial stall warning device used on modern large aircraft is a stick shaker, in conjunction with lights and a noise-maker.

Stick shaker: A stick shaker represents what it is replacing; it shakes the stick and is a tactile warning. If the stick shaker activates when the pilot's hands are not on the controls: when the aircraft is on autopilot, for example, a very quiet stick shaker could not function as a stall warning so a noise maker is added in parallel.

The stick shaker is a pair of simple electric motors, one clamped to each pilot's control column, rotating an out of balance weight. When the motor runs it shakes the stick.

PRINCIPLES OF FLIGHT **STALLING**

An artificial stall warning device can receive its signal from a number of different types of detector switch, all activated by changes in angle of attack,

FLAPPER SWITCH
(activated by movement of stagnation point)

STAGNATION POINT
(has moved downwards and backwards around leading edge)

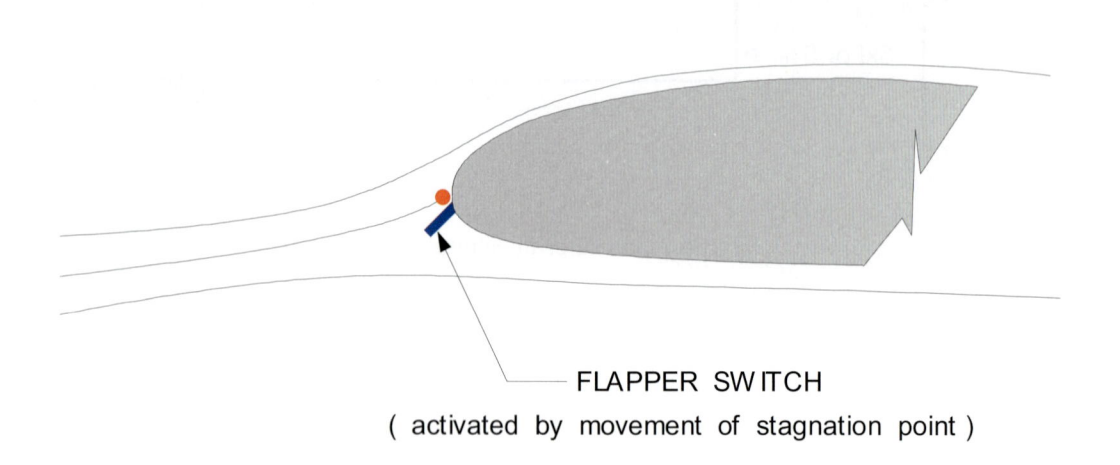

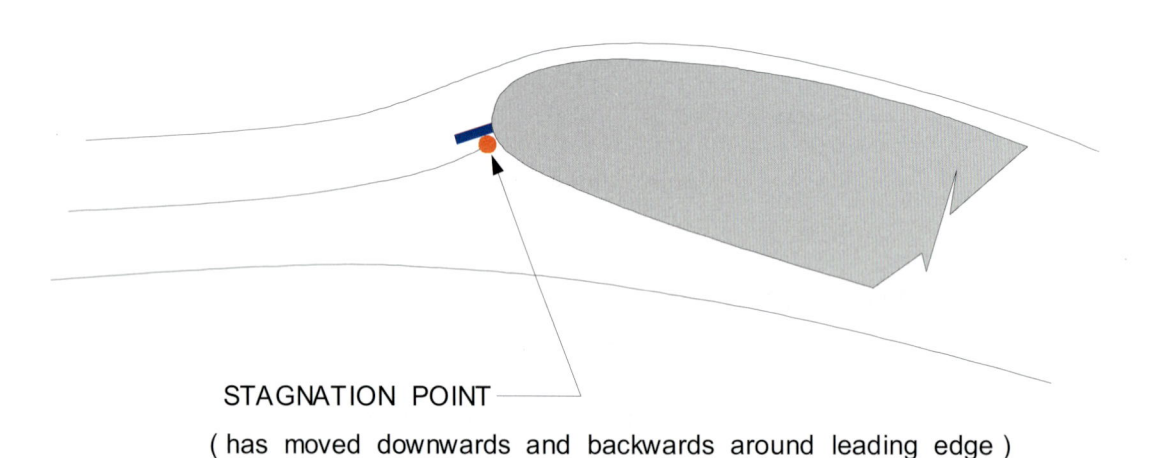

Figure 7.4   Flapper Switch

Flapper switch (leading edge stall warning vane): Fig. 7.4. As angle of attack increases, the stagnation point moves downwards and backwards around the leading edge. The flapper switch is so located, that at the appropriate angle of attack, the stagnation point moves to its underside, and the increased pressure lifts and closes the switch.

PRINCIPLES OF FLIGHT

STALLING

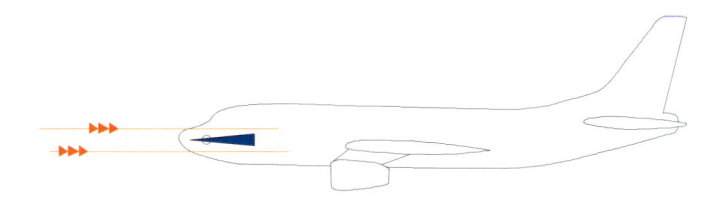

AS ANGLE OF ATTACK INCREASES, VANE ROTATES RELATIVE TO FUSELAGE

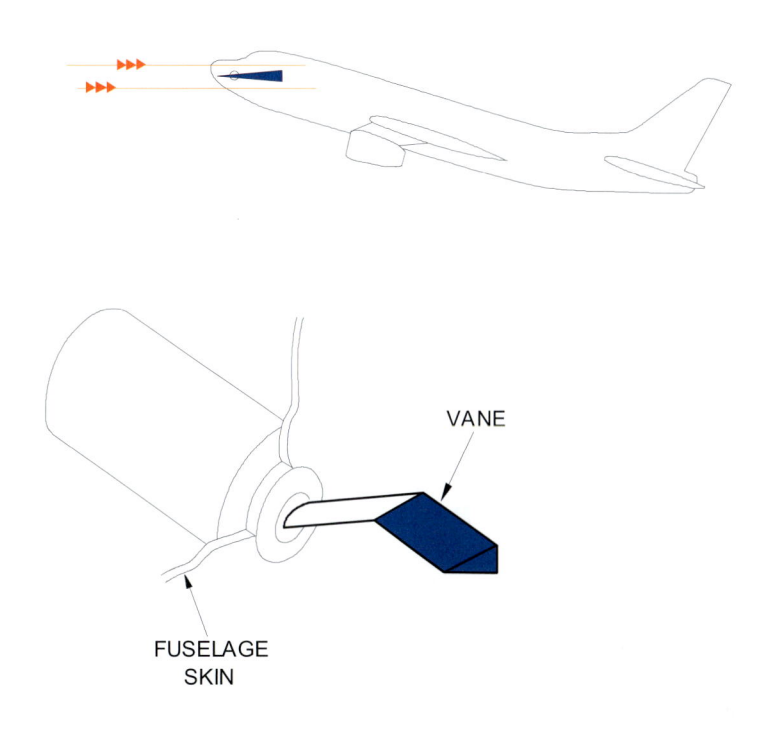

Figure 7.5 Angle of Attack Vane

Angle of attack vane: Fig. 7.5. Mounted on the side of the fuselage, the vane streamlines with the relative airflow and the fuselage rotates around it. The stick shaker is activated at the appropriate angle of attack.

Angle of attack probe: Also mounted on the side of the fuselage; consists of slots in a probe, which are sensitive to changes in angle of relative airflow.

All of these sense angle of attack and, therefore, automatically take care of changes in aircraft mass; the majority also compute the **rate of change of angle of attack** and give earlier warning in the case of faster rates of approach to the stall. The detectors are usually datum compensated for configuration changes and are always heated or anti-iced. There are usually sensors on both sides to counteract any sideslip effect.

PRINCIPLES OF FLIGHT STALLING

7.11 BASIC STALL REQUIREMENTS (JAR and FAR)

(a) It must be possible to **produce and to correct roll and yaw** by unreversed use of aileron and rudder controls, up to the time the aeroplane is stalled. **No abnormal nose-up pitching** may occur. The **longitudinal control force must be positive** up to and throughout the stall. In addition, it must be possible to promptly **prevent stalling** and **to recover from a stall by normal use of the controls**.

[margin note: needs to have a tougher control as it increases.]

(b) For level wing stalls, the roll occurring between the stall and the completion of the recovery may not exceed approximately 20°.

(c) For turning flight stalls, the action of the aeroplane after the stall may not be so violent or extreme as to make it difficult, with normal piloting skill, to effect a prompt recovery and to regain control of the aeroplane. The maximum bank angle that occurs during the recovery may not exceed:

  (1) Approximately 60 degrees in the original direction of the turn, or 30 degrees in the opposite direction, for deceleration rates up to 1 knot per second; and

  (2) Approximately 90 degrees in the original direction of the turn, or 60 degrees in the opposite direction, for deceleration rates in excess of 1 knot per second.

7.12 WING DESIGN CHARACTERISTICS

It has been shown that stalling is due to airflow separation, characterised by a loss of lift, and an increase in drag, that will cause the aircraft to lose height. This is generally true, but there are aspects of aircraft behaviour and handling at or near the stall which depend on the design of the wing aerofoil section and planform.

7.13 THE EFFECT OF AEROFOIL SECTION

Shape of the aerofoil section will influence the manner in which it stalls. With some sections, stall occurs very suddenly and the drop in lift is very marked. With others, the approach to stall is more gradual, and the decrease in lift is less disastrous.

In general, an aeroplane should not stall too suddenly, and the pilot should have adequate warning, in terms of handling qualities, of the approach of a stall. This warning generally takes the form of buffeting and general lack of response to the controls. If a particular wing design stalls too suddenly, it will be necessary to provide some sort of artificial pre-stall warning device or even a stall prevention device.

> A given aerofoil section will always stall at the same angle of attack

PRINCIPLES OF FLIGHT **STALLING**

Features of aerofoil section design which affect behaviour near the stall are:

a) leading edge radius,

b) thickness-chord ratio,

c) camber, and particularly the amount of camber near the leading edge, and

d) chordwise location of the points of maximum thickness and maximum camber.

Generally, the sharper the nose (small leading edge radius), the thinner the aerofoil section, or the further aft the position of maximum thickness and camber, the more sudden will be the stall. i.e. an aerofoil section designed for efficient operation at higher speeds, Fig. 7.6.

The stall characteristics of the above listed aerofoil sections can be used to either encourage a stall to occur, or delay stalling, at a particular location on the wing span.

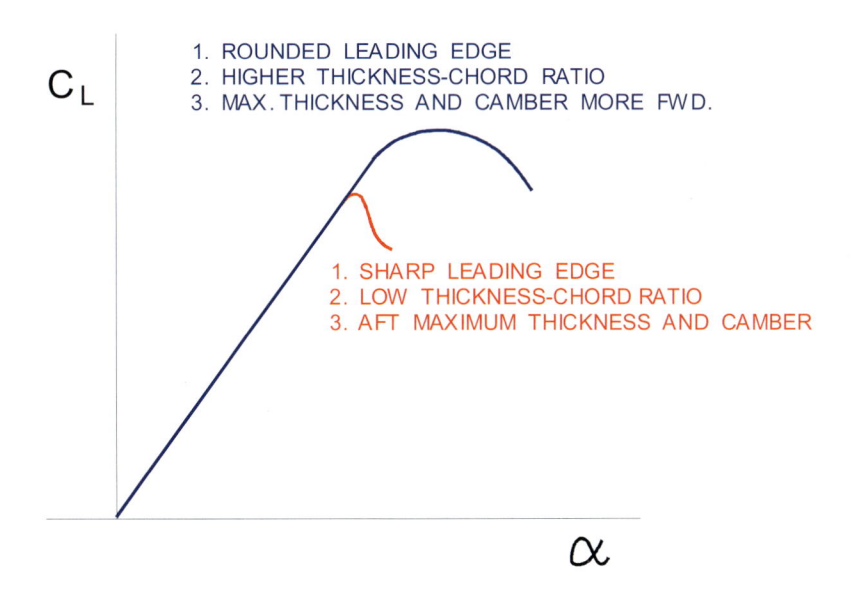

Figure 7.6

PRINCIPLES OF FLIGHT   STALLING

7.14   THE EFFECT OF WING PLAN FORM

On basic wing plan forms, airflow separation will not occur simultaneously at all spanwise locations.

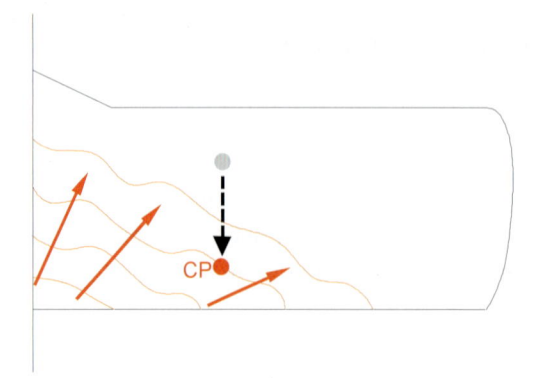

STRONG TIP VORTICES DECREASE EFFECTIVE ANGLE OF ATTACK AT WING TIP, THUS DELAYING TIP STALL.

CP MOVES REARWARDS, AIRCRAFT NOSE DROPS.

Figure 7.7   Rectangular Wing

The Rectangular Wing: Fig. 7.7. On a rectangular wing, separation tends to begin at the root, and spreads out towards the tip. Reduction in lift initially occurs inboard near the aircraft CG, and if it occurs on one wing before the other, there is **little tendency for the aircraft to roll**. The aircraft loses height, but in doing so remains more or less wings level. **Loss of lift is felt ahead of the centre of gravity of the aircraft and the CP moves rearwards, so the nose drops and angle of attack is reduced.** Thus, there is a natural tendency for the aircraft to move away from the high angle of attack which gave rise to the stall. The separated airflow from the root immerses the rear fuselage and tail area, and aerodynamic buffet can provide a warning of the approaching stall. Being located outside of the area of separated airflow, the ailerons tend to remain effective when the stalling process starts. All of these factors give the most desirable kind of response to a stall (Ref. para. 7.7, 7.9(b), and 7.11):-

a)   Aileron effectiveness,

b)   nose drop,

c)   aerodynamic buffet, and

d)   absence of violent wing drop.

Unfortunately, a rectangular wing has unacceptable wing bending characteristics and is not very aerodynamically efficient, so most modern aircraft have a tapered and/or swept planform.

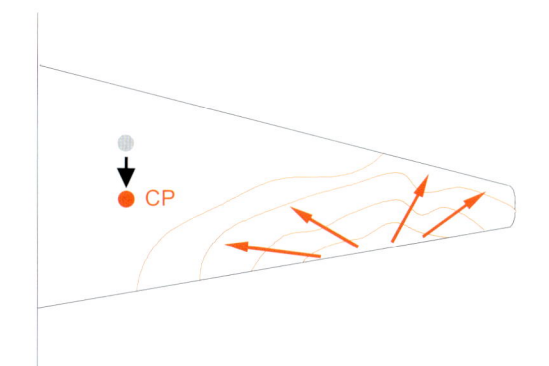

PRINCIPLES OF FLIGHT

STALLING

Figure 7.8 Tapered Wing

The Tapered Wing: Fig. 7.8. Separation tends to occur first in the region of the wing tips, reducing lift in those areas. If an actual wing were allowed to stall in this way, stalling would give aileron buffet, and perhaps violent wing drop. (Wing drop at the stall gives an increased tendency for an aircraft to enter a spin). There would be no buffet on the tail, no strong nose down pitching moment, and very little, if any, aileron effectiveness. To give favourable stall characteristics, a tapered wing must be modified using one or more of the following:-

a) Geometric twist (**washout**), a decrease in incidence from root to tip. This decreases the angle of attack at the tip, and the root will tend to stall first.

b) The aerofoil section may be varied throughout the span such that sections with **greater thickness and camber** are located near the tip. The higher $C_{L\ MAX}$ of such sections delays stall so that the root will tend to stall first.

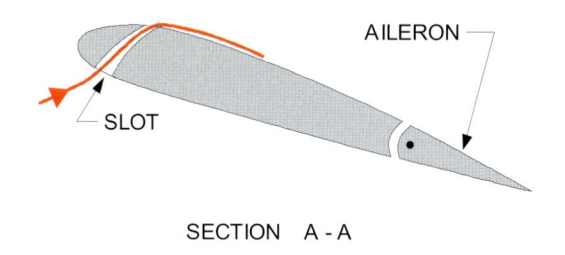

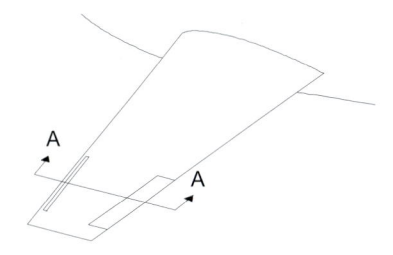

Figure 7.9 Leading Edge Slot

c) Leading edge **slots**, Fig. 7.9, towards the tip re-energise (increase the kinetic energy of) the boundary layer. They increase local $C_{L\ MAX}$ and are useful, both for delaying separation at the tip, and retaining aileron effectiveness. The function of slats and slots will be fully described in Chapter 8.

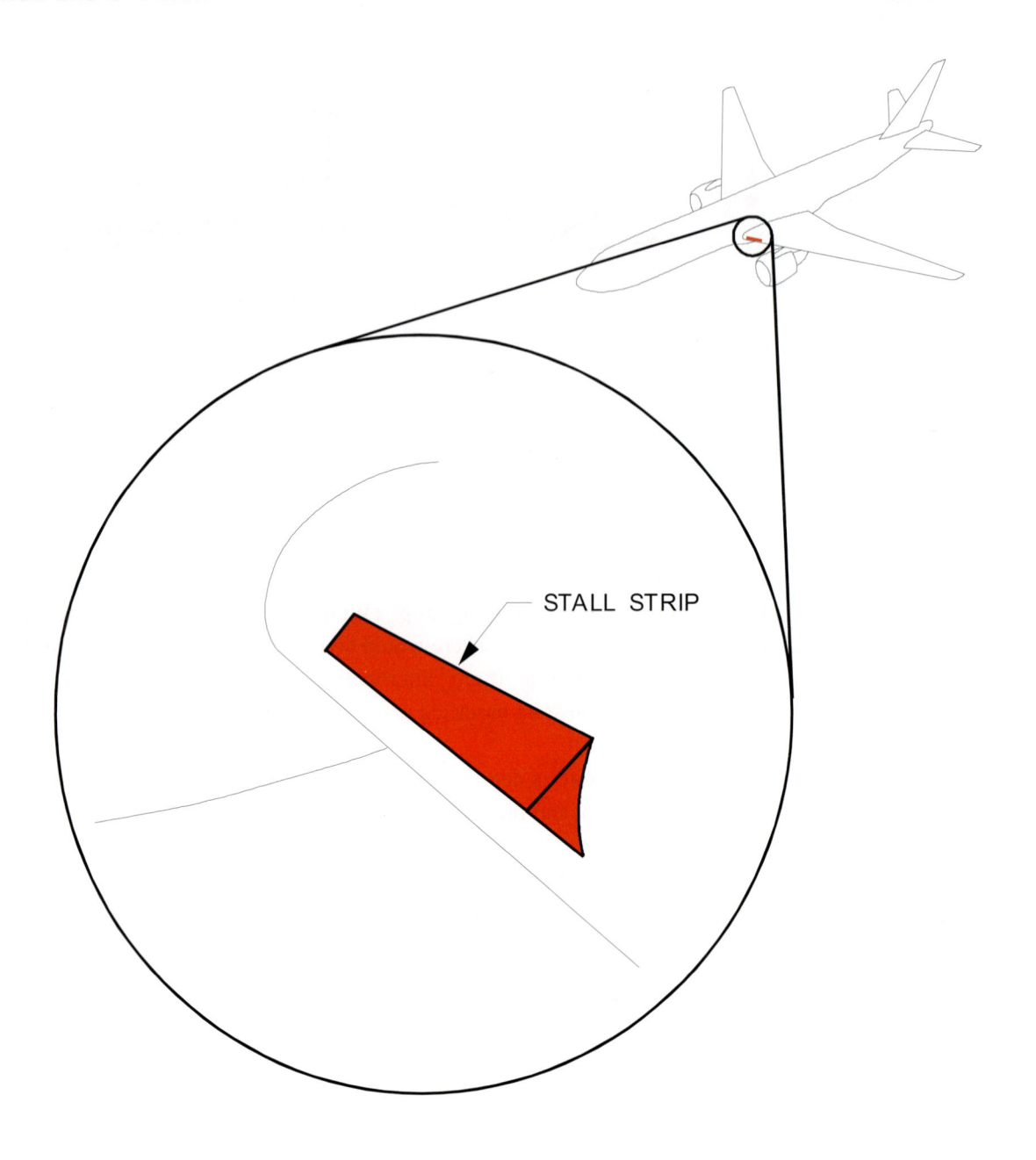

Figure 7.10   Stall Strip

d) Another method for improving the stall pattern is by forcing a stall to occur from the root. An aerofoil section with a smaller leading edge radius at the root would promote airflow separation at a lower angle of attack but decrease overall wing efficiency. The same result can be accomplished by attaching **stall strips** (small triangular strips), Fig. 7.10, to the wing leading edge.

At higher angles of attack stall strips promote separation, but will not effect the efficiency of the wing in the cruise.

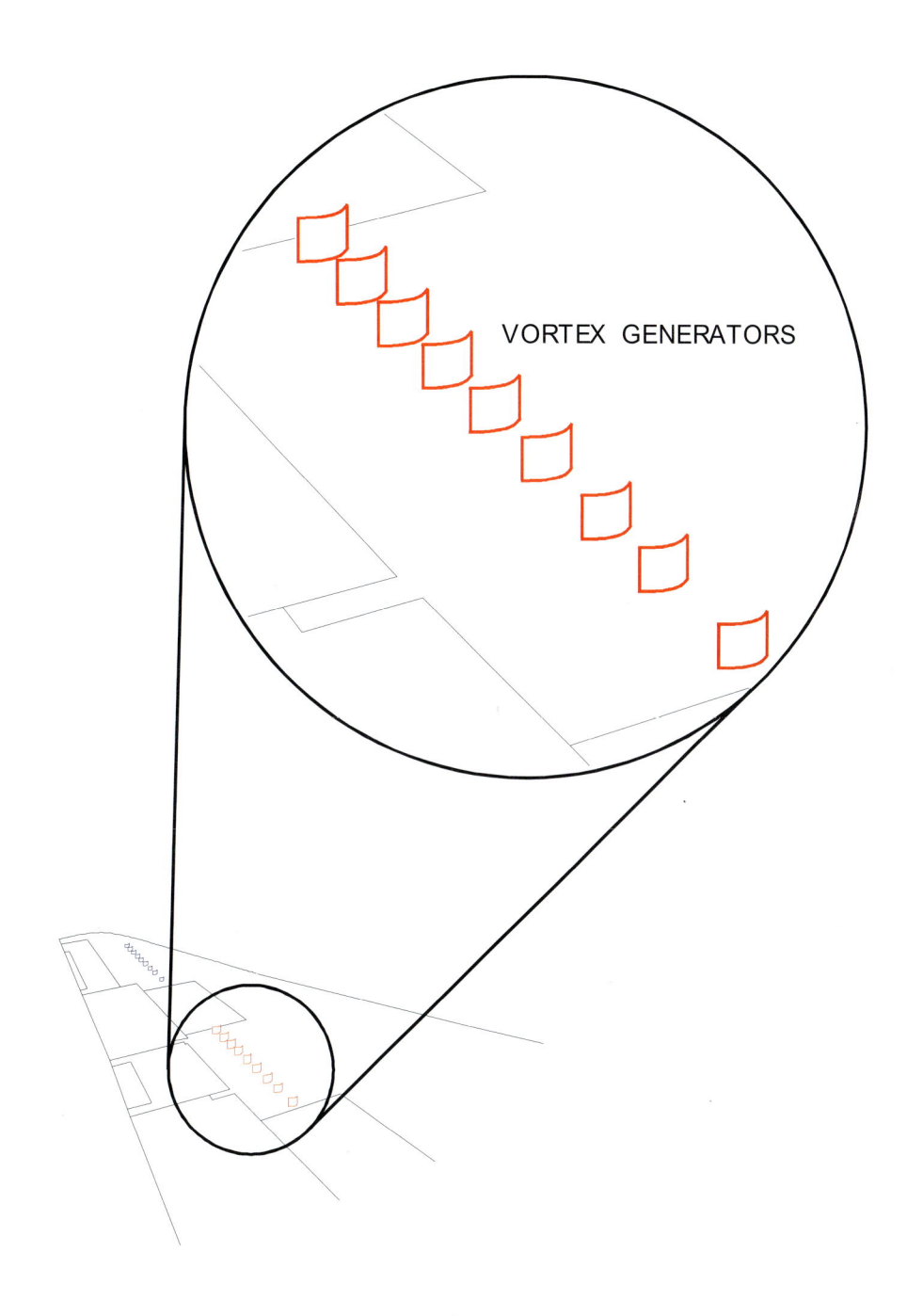

Figure 7.11 Vortex Generators

e) **Vortex generators**, Fig. 7.11, are rows of small, thin aerofoil shaped blades which project vertically (about 2·5cm) into the airstream. They each generate a small vortex which causes the free stream flow of high energy air to mix with and add kinetic energy to the boundary layer. This re-energises the boundary layer and tends to delay separation.

PRINCIPLES OF FLIGHT — STALLING

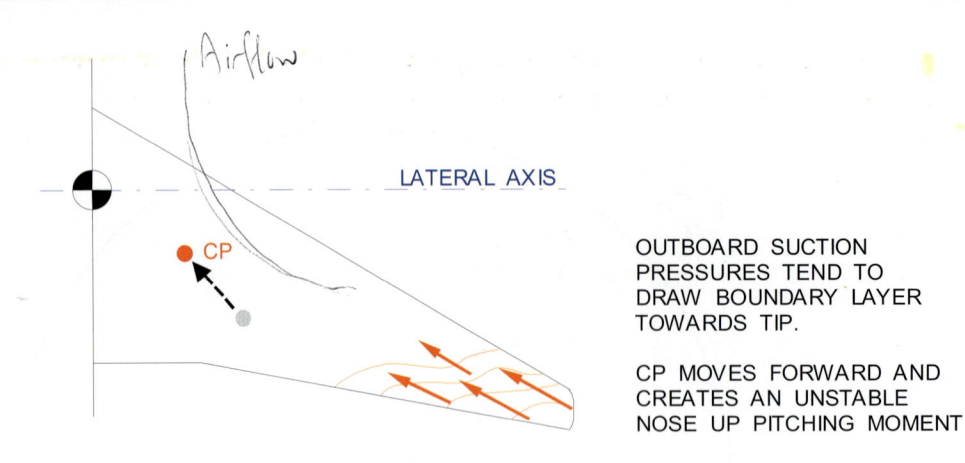

Figure 7.12 — Swept wing showing airflow, CP position, and lateral axis. Labels: OUTBOARD SUCTION PRESSURES TEND TO DRAW BOUNDARY LAYER TOWARDS TIP. CP MOVES FORWARD AND CREATES AN UNSTABLE NOSE UP PITCHING MOMENT.

Figure 7.12

Sweepback: Fig. 7.12. A swept wing is fitted to allow a higher maximum speed, but it has an increased tendency to stall first near the tips. **Loss of lift at the tips moves the CP forward, giving a nose up pitching moment**.

Effective lift production is concentrated inboard and the maximum downwash now impacts the tailplane, Fig. 7.13, adding to the nose up pitching moment.

Pitch-up: As soon as a swept wing begins to stall, both forward CP movement and increased downwash at the tailplane cause the aircraft nose to rise rapidly, further increasing the angle of attack. This is a very undesirable and unacceptable response at the stall and can result in complete loss of control in pitch from which it may be very difficult, or even impossible, to recover. **This phenomenon is known as pitch-up, and is a very dangerous characteristic of many high speed, swept wing aircraft.**

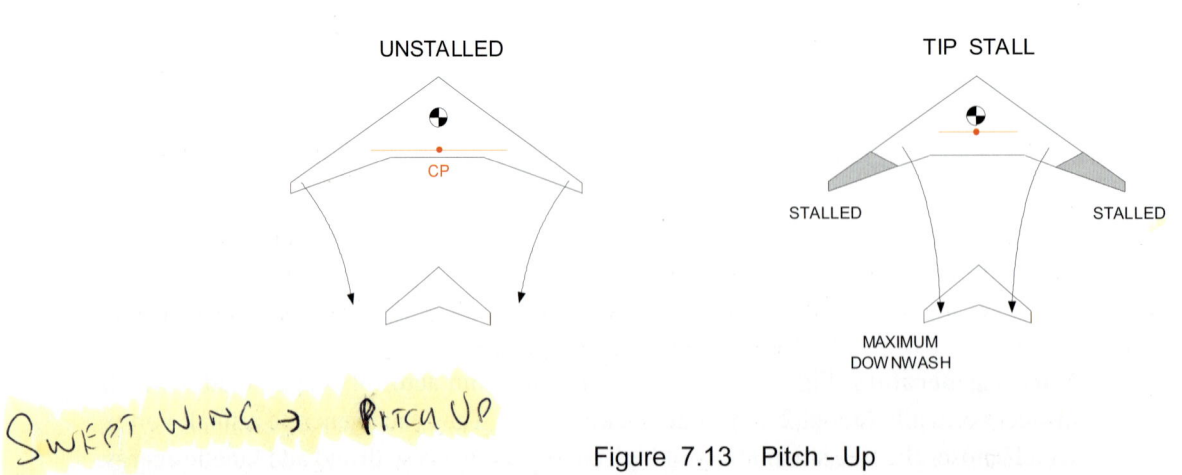

Figure 7.13 Pitch - Up

PRINCIPLES OF FLIGHT — STALLING

The tendency of a swept back wing to tip stall is due to the induced spanwise flow of the boundary layer from root to tip. The following design features can be incorporated to minimise this effect and give a swept wing aircraft more acceptable stall characteristics:-

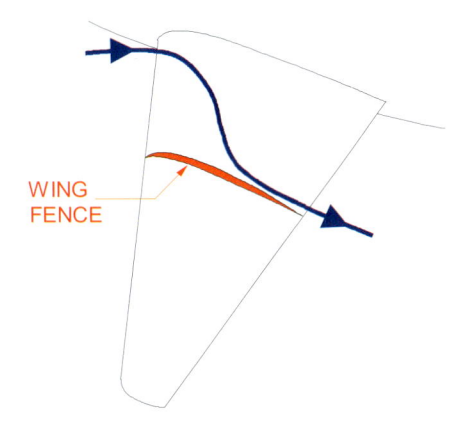

Figure 7.14 Wing Fence

Wing fences (boundary layer fences), Fig. 7.14, are thin metal fences which generally extend from the leading edge to the trailing edge on the top surface and are intended to prevent outward drift of the boundary layer.

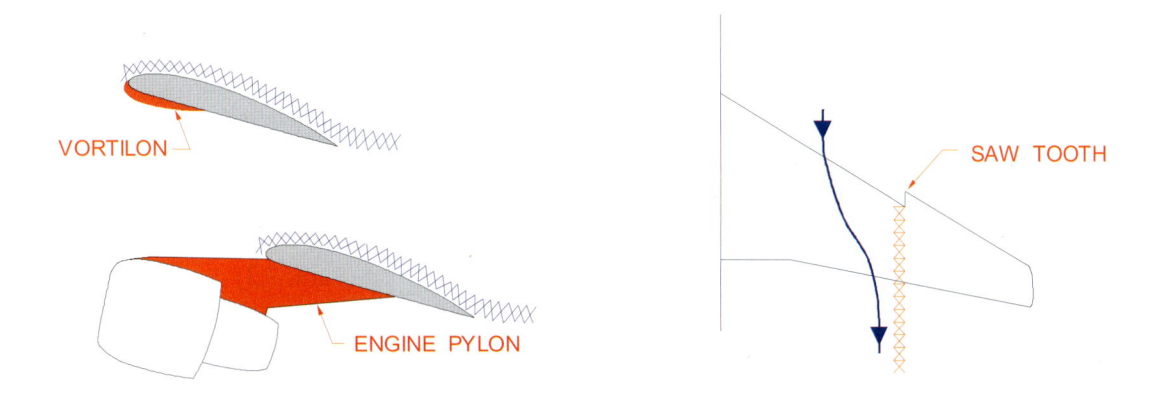

Figure 7.15 Vortilon

Figure 7.16 Saw Tooth

Vortilons, Fig. 7.15, are also thin metal fences, but are smaller than a full chordwise fence. They are situated on the underside of the wing leading edge. The support pylons of pod mounted engines on the wing also act in the same way. At high angles of attack a small but intense vortex is shed over the wing top surface which acts as an aerodynamic wing fence.

Saw tooth leading edge, Fig. 7.16, will also generate a strong vortex over the wing upper surface at high angles of attack, minimising spanwise flow of the boundary layer. (Rarely used on modern high speed jet transport aircraft).

PRINCIPLES OF FLIGHT   STALLING

The following four pages contain a revision aid to encourage students to become familiar with any new terminology, together with the key elements of 'stalling'.

KEY FACTS 1 - Self Study

Insert the missing words in these statements, using the foregoing paragraphs for reference.

Stalling involves loss of _____ and loss of _____. (Para. 7.1)

A pilot must be able to clearly and unmistakably _____ a stall. (Para. 7.1)

A stall is caused by airflow _____. (Para. 7.2)

Separation can occur when either the boundary layer has insufficient _____ energy or the _____ _____ gradient becomes too great. (Para. 7.2)

Adverse pressure gradient increases with increase in angle of _____. (Para. 7.2)

Alternative names for the angle of attack at which stall occurs are the _____ angle and the _____ angle of attack. (Para. 7.3)

The coefficient of lift at which a stall occurs is _____. (Para. 7.3)

A stall can occur at any _____ or flight _____. (Para. 7.2)

A typical stalling angle is approximately ____°. (Para. 7.3)

To recover from a stall the angle of _____ must be _____. (Para. 7.4)

Maximum power is applied during stall recovery to minimise _____ loss. (Para. 7.4)

7 - 18

PRINCIPLES OF FLIGHT   STALLING

On small aircraft, the _____ should be used to prevent wing _____ at the stall. (Para. 7.4)

On swept wing aircraft the _____ should be used to prevent wing _____ at the stall.(Para. 7.4)

Recover height lost during stall recovery with moderate _____ pressure on the _____ control. (Para. 7.4)

The first indications of a stall may be _____ flight controls, stall _____ device or aerodynamic _____. (Para. 7.5)

At speeds close to the stall, _____ must be used with caution to _____ a dropping wing. (Para. 7.6)

Acceptable indications of a stall are: (Para. 7.7)
    (1)   a nose _____ pitch that can not be readily arrested.
    (2)   severe _____.
    (3)   pitch control reaching _____ stop and no further increase in _____ attitude occurs.

Reference stall speed (V_{SR}) is a CAS defined by the _____ _____ .(Para. 7.8(a))

V_{SR} may not be _____ than a ____ stall speed. (Para. 7.8(a))

When a device that abruptly pushes the _____ _____ at a selected angle of _____ is installed, V_{SR} may not be _____ than ___ knots or ___ %, whichever is _____, above the speed at which the _____ operates. (Para. 7.8(d))

Stall warning with sufficient _____ to prevent inadvertent stalling must be _____ and _____ to the pilot in straight and turning flight. (Para. 7.9(a))

Acceptable stall warning may consist of the inherent _____ qualities of the aeroplane or by a _____ that will give clearly distinguishable indications under expected conditions of flight. (Para. 7.9(b))

PRINCIPLES OF FLIGHT **STALLING**

Stall warning must begin at a speed exceeding the stall speed by not less than __ knots or __ % CAS, whichever is the greater. (Para. 7.9(c))

Artificial stall warning on a small aircraft is usually given by a _____ or _____. (Para. 7.10)

Artificial stall warning on a large aircraft is usually given by a _____ shaker, in conjunction with _____ and a noisemaker. (Para. 7.10)

An artificial stall warning device can be activated by a _____ switch, an angle of _____ vane or an angle of attack _____. (Para. 7.10)

Most angle of attack sensors compute the _____ of change of angle of attack to give _____ warning in the case of accelerated rates of stall approach. (Para. 7.10)

JAR required stall characteristics, up to the time the aeroplane is stalled, are:- (Para. 7.11)

a) It must be possible to produce and correct ____ by unreversed use of the _____ and _____
b) No abnormal nose up _____ may occur
c) Longitudinal control force must be _____
d) It must be possible to promptly prevent _____ and recover from a stall by normal use of the _____
e) There should be no excessive ____ between the stall and completion of recovery
f) For turning flight stalls, the action of the aeroplane after the stall may not be so _____ or _____ as to make it difficult, with normal piloting _____, to effect prompt _____ and to regain _____ of the aeroplane

An aerofoil section with a small leading edge _____ will stall at a _____ angle of attack and the stall will be more _____. (Para. 7.13)

An aerofoil section with a large thickness-chord ratio will stall at a _____ angle of attack and will stall more _____. (Para. 7.13)

An aerofoil section with camber near the _____ _____ will stall at a higher angle of attack. (Para. 7.13)

7 - 20 © Oxford Aviation Services Limited

PRINCIPLES OF FLIGHT					STALLING

A rectangular wing plan form will tend to stall at the _____ first. (Para. 7.14)

A rectangular wing planform usually has ideal stall characteristics, these are:- (Para. 7.14)

    a)   Aileron _____ at the stall
    b)   Nose _____ at the stall
    c)   Aerodynamic _____ at the stall
    d)   Absence of violent wing _____ at the stall

To give a wing with a tapered planform the desired stall characteristics, the following devices can be included in the design:- (Para. 7.14)

    a)   _____ (decreasing incidence from root to tip)
    b)   An aerofoil section with _____ thickness and camber at the tip
    c)   Leading edge _____ at the tip
    d)   Stall _____ fitted to the wing inboard leading edge
    e)   _____ generators which re-energise the _____ layer at the tip

A swept back wing has an increased tendency to tip stall due to the spanwise flow of boundary layer from root to tip on the wing top surface. Methods of delaying tip stall on a swept wing planform are:- (Para. 7.14)

    a)   Wing _____, thin metal fences which generally extend from the leading edge to the trailing edge on the wing top surface
    b)   _____, also thin metal fences, but smaller and are situated on the underside of the wing leading edge
    c)   Saw _____ leading edge, generates vortices over wing top surface at high angles of attack
    d)   Engine _____ of pod mounted wing engines also act as vortilons
    e)   _____ generators are also used to delay tip stall on a swept wing

Tip stall on a swept wing planform gives a tendency for the aircraft to _____-___ at the stall. This is due to the ___ moving forwards when the wing tips stall _____. (Para. 7.14)

KEY FACTS 1, WITH WORD INSERTS CAN BE FOUND ON PAGE 7 - 63

PRINCIPLES OF FLIGHT STALLING

7.15 SUPER STALL (DEEP STALL)

A swept-back wing tends to stall first near the tips. Since the tips are situated well aft of the CG, the loss of lift at the tips causes the pitch attitude to increase rapidly and further increase the angle of attack. Fig. 7.17.

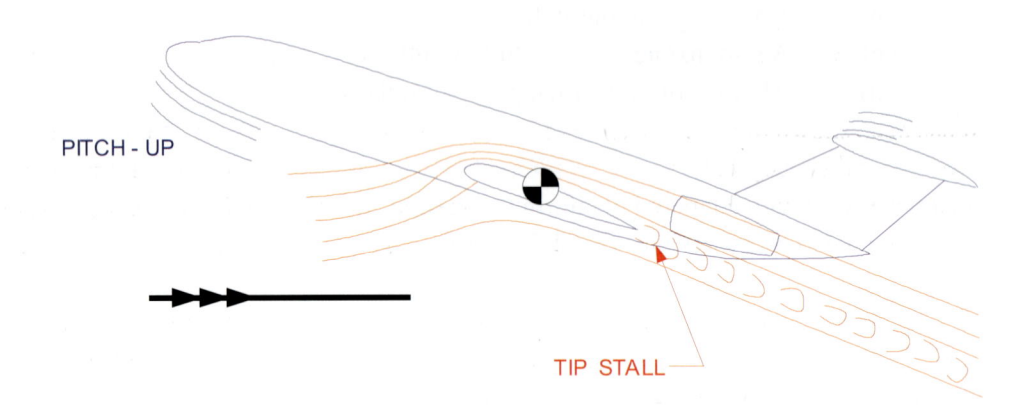

Figure 7.17   Pitch - up

This "automatic" increase in angle of attack, caused by pitch-up, stalls more of the wing. Drag will increase rapidly, lift will reduce, and the aeroplane will start to sink **at a constant, nose high, pitch attitude**. This results in a rapid additional increase in angle of attack, Fig. 7.18.

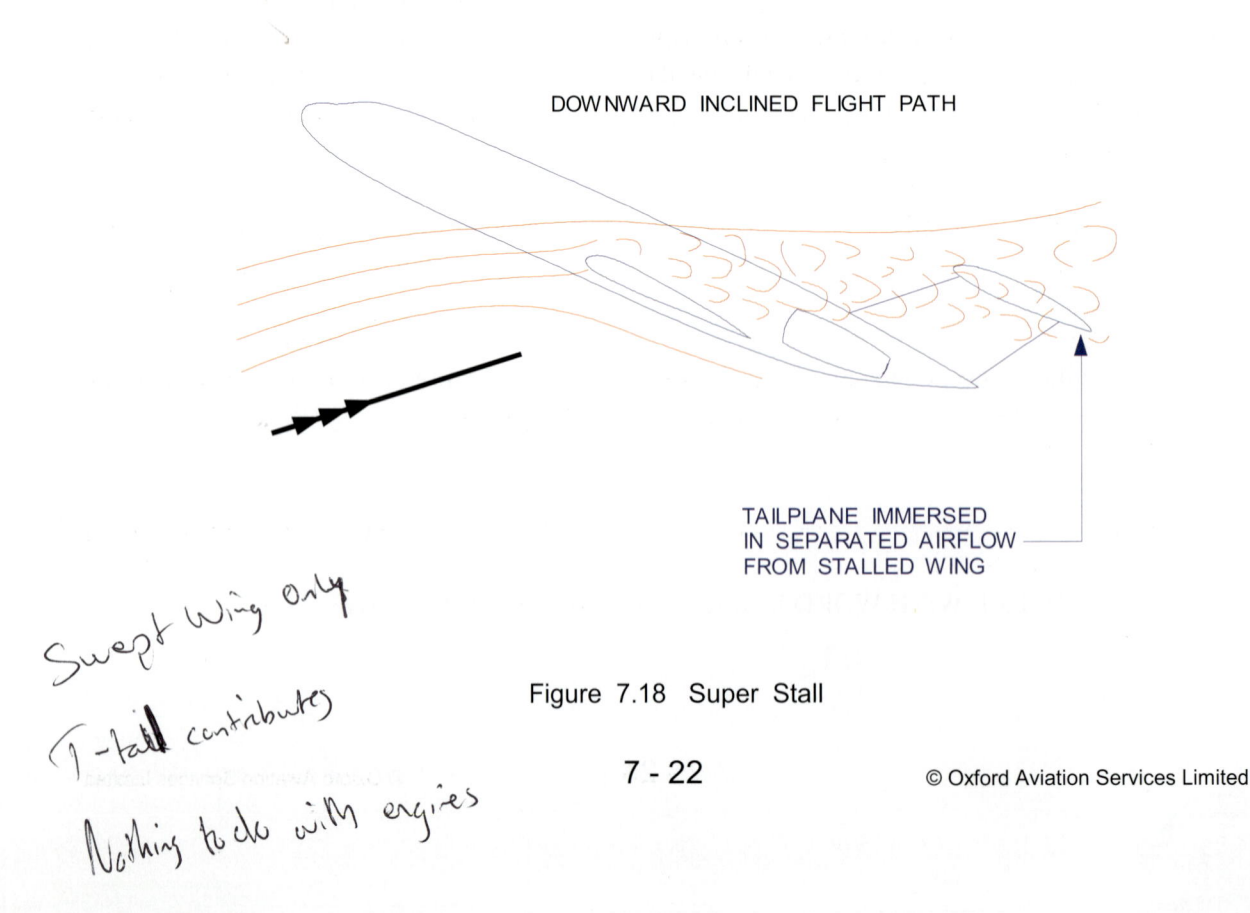

Figure 7.18 Super Stall

Separated airflow from the stalled wing will immerse a high-set tailplane in low energy turbulent air, Fig. 7.18. Elevator effectiveness is greatly reduced making it impossible for the pilot to decrease the angle of attack. The aeroplane will become stabilized in what is known as the "super-stall" or "deep-stall" condition.

Clearly, the combination of a swept-back wing and a high mounted tailplane ('T'-Tail) are the factors involved in the "super or deep-stall". Of the two:-

THE SWEPT-BACK WING IS THE MAJOR CONTRIBUTORY FACTOR.

It has been shown that the tendency for a swept-back wing to pitch-up can be reduced by design modifications (wing fences, vortilons and saw tooth leading edge) which minimise the root-to-tip spanwise flow of the boundary layer. These devices **delay** tip stall. Vortex generators are also frequently used on a swept wing to delay tip stall and improve the stall characteristics.

The wing root can also be encouraged to stall first. This can be done by modifying the aerofoil section at the root, fitting stall strips and by fitting less efficient leading edge flaps (Kruger flaps) to the inboard section of the wing.

Aircraft such as the DC-9, MD-80, Boeing 727, Fokker 28 and others, have swept-back wings and high mounted tailplanes ('T'-Tail). They also have rear, fuselage mounted engines. The only contribution rear mounted engines make is that they are the reason the designer placed the tailplane on top of the fin in the first place. In-and-of-itself, mounting the engines on the rear fuselage does not contribute to super stall.

7.16 SUPER STALL PREVENTION - STICK PUSHER

An aircraft design which exhibits super-stall characteristics must be fitted with **a device to prevent it from ever stalling.** This device is a stick pusher. Once such an aircraft begins to stall it is too late; the progression to super stall is too fast for a human to respond, and the aircraft cannot then be un-stalled.

A stick pusher is a device attached to the elevator control system, which physically pushes the control column forward, reducing the angle of attack before super-stall can occur.

The force of the push is typically about 80 lbs. This is regarded as being high enough to be effective, but not too high to hold in a runaway situation. Provision is made to "dump" the stick pusher system in the event of a malfunction. Once dumped, the pusher cannot normally be reset in flight.

Once actuated, the stick pusher will automatically disengage once the angle of attack reduces below a suitable value.

PRINCIPLES OF FLIGHT — STALLING

7.17 FACTORS THAT AFFECT STALL SPEED

Paragraph 7.8 details the CAS at which an aircraft stalls (V_{SR}). We know that stalling is caused by exceeding the critical angle of attack. Stalling has nothing to do with the speed of the aircraft; **the critical angle of attack can be exceeded at any aircraft speed.** However, it has been shown that if an aircraft is flown in straight and level flight and speed reduced at a rate not exceeding 1 knot per second, the CAS at which it stalls can be identified. It is upon this reference stall speed (V_{SR}) that the recommended take-off, manoeuvre, approach and landing speeds are based, to give an adequate margin from the stall during normal operations (1·05 V_{SR}, 1·1 V_{SR}, 1·2 V_{SR}, 1·3 V_{SR} etc).

Factors which can affect V_{SR} are:

$$V_{S1g} = \sqrt{\frac{L}{\frac{1}{2}\rho \, C_{L\,MAX} \, S}}$$

a) Changes in weight. *Increase V_{S1g}*
b) Manoeuvring the aircraft (increasing the load factor). *Increase*
c) Configuration changes (changes in CL_{MAX} and pitching moment).
d) Engine thrust and propeller slipstream *Decrease*
e) Mach number
f) Wing contamination *Increase*
g) Heavy rain

7.18 1g STALL SPEED

In straight and level flight the weight of the aircraft is balanced by the lift.

$$\text{Load Factor (n) or 'g'} = \frac{\text{Lift}}{\text{Weight}}$$

While (n) is the correct symbol for load factor, the relationship between lift and weight has for years been popularly known as 'g'. (1g corresponds to the force acting on us in every day life). If more lift is generated than weight the load factor or 'g' will be greater than one; the force acting on the aircraft and everything in it, including the pilot will be greater.

If Lift = Weight, the load factor will be **one** and from the lift formula:

$$L = \tfrac{1}{2} \rho \, V^2 \, C_L \, S$$

it can be seen that lift will change whenever any of the other factors in the formula change. **We consider density (ρ) and wing area (S) constant for this example.** If the engine is throttled back, drag will reduce speed (V) and, from the formula, it can be seen that lift would decrease. To keep lift constant and maintain 1g flight at a reduced speed, C_L must be increased by increasing the angle of attack.

PRINCIPLES OF FLIGHT — STALLING

Any further reduction in speed would need a further increase in angle of attack; each succeeding lower CAS corresponding to a greater angle of attack. Eventually, at a certain CAS, the wing reaches its stalling angle ($C_{L\,MAX}$), beyond which any further increase in angle of attack, in an attempt to maintain lift, will precipitate a stall. We can transpose the lift formula to show this relationship:-

$$V_{S1g} = \sqrt{\frac{L}{\frac{1}{2}\rho\, C_{L_{max}}\, S}}$$

Density altitude does not effect indicated stall speed

7.19 EFFECT OF WEIGHT CHANGE ON STALL SPEED

At $C_{L\,MAX}$ for 1g flight, a change in weight requires a change in lift and it can be seen from the V_{S1g} formula that, for instance, an increase in weight (lift) will increase V_{S1g}

The relationship between basic stalling speeds at two different weights can be obtained from the following formula:-

$$V_{S1g\,new} = V_{S1g\,old} \sqrt{\frac{new\ weight}{old\ weight}}$$

The angle of attack at which stall occurs will NOT be affected by the weight. (Provided that the appropriate value of $C_{L\,MAX}$ is not affected by speed - as it will be at speeds greater than 0·4M, ref. para. 7.29). **To maintain a given angle of attack in level flight, it is necessary to change the dynamic pressure (CAS) if the weight is changed.**

As an example: at a weight of 588,600 N an aircraft stalls at 150 Kt CAS, what is the V_{S1g} stall speed at a weight of 470,880 N?

$$V_{S1g\,new} = 150 \sqrt{\frac{470880}{588600}}$$

$$= 134\ knots\ CAS$$

Weight does not effect stall angle

It should be noted that a 20% reduction in weight has resulted in an approximate 10% reduction in stall speed. (As a "rule of thumb", this relationship can be used to save calculator batteries, and time in the exam!). The change in stall speed due to an increase in weight can be calculated in the same way.

PRINCIPLES OF FLIGHT STALLING

7.20 COMPOSITION AND RESOLUTION OF FORCES

A force is a vector quantity. It has magnitude and direction, and can be represented by a straight line, passing through the point at which it is applied, its length representing the magnitude of the force, and its direction corresponding to that in which the force is acting.

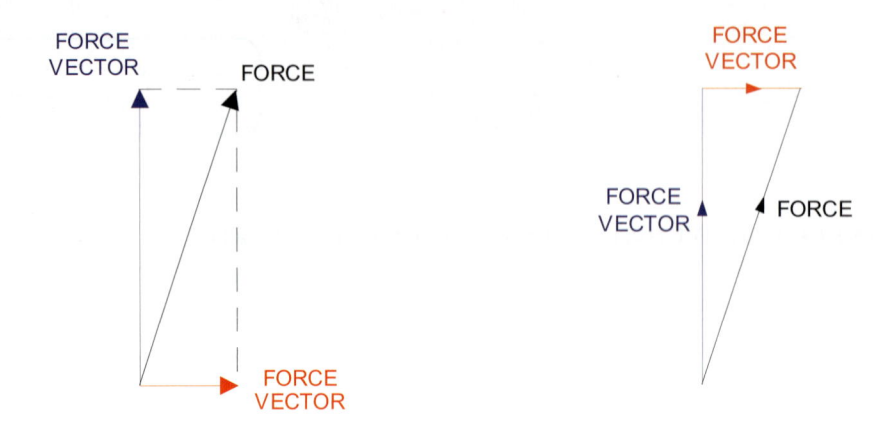

Figure 7.19 The Resolution of A Force Into Two Vectors

As vector quantities, forces can be added or subtracted to form a resultant force, or they can be **resolved - split into two or more component parts by the simple process of drawing the vectors to represent them.** Fig. 7.19.

7.21 THE PARALLELOGRAM OF FORCES

If three forces which act at a point are in equilibrium, they can be represented by the sides of a triangle taken in order. This is called the principle of the triangle of forces, and the so called parallelogram of forces is really the same thing, two sides and the diagonal of the parallelogram corresponding to the triangle.

7.22 USING TRIGONOMETRY TO SOLVE A PARALLELOGRAM OF FORCES

If one of the angles and the length of one of the sides of a right angled triangle is known, it is possible to calculate the length of the other sides. In a parallelogram of forces the sides of the triangle represent the magnitude of the force vectors, so it is possible to calculate the magnitude of the forces.

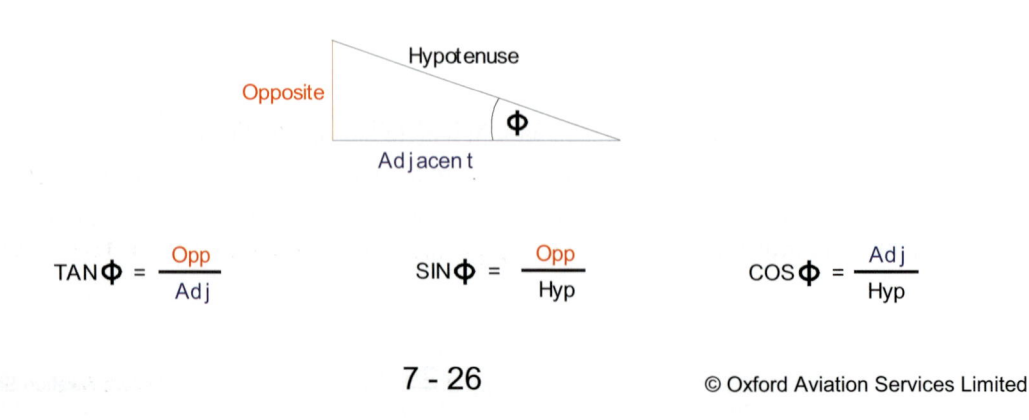

$$\text{TAN}\,\phi = \frac{\text{Opp}}{\text{Adj}} \qquad \text{SIN}\,\phi = \frac{\text{Opp}}{\text{Hyp}} \qquad \text{COS}\,\phi = \frac{\text{Adj}}{\text{Hyp}}$$

PRINCIPLES OF FLIGHT   STALLING

7.23   LIFT INCREASE IN A LEVEL TURN

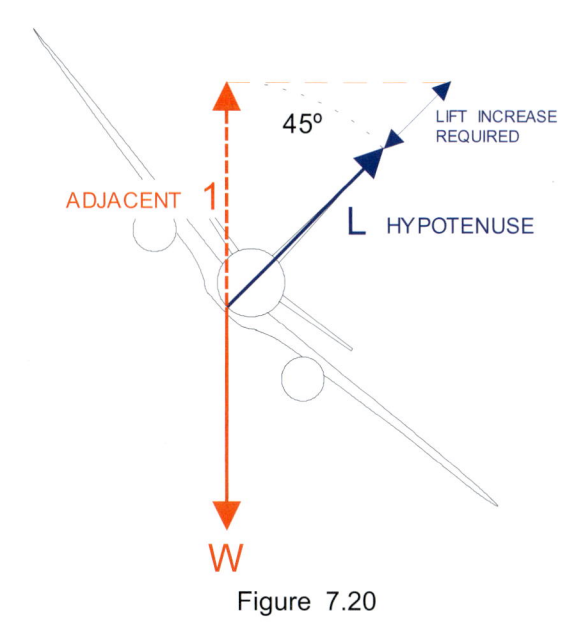

Figure 7.20

Fig. 7.20 shows an aircraft in a level, 45° bank turn. Weight always acts vertically downwards. For the aircraft to maintain altitude, the UP force must be the same as the DOWN force. Lift is inclined from the horizontal by the bank angle of 45° and can be resolved into two components, or vectors; one vertical and one horizontal. It can be SEEN from the illustration that in a level turn, lift must be increased in order to produce an upwards force vector equal to weight. We know the vertical force must be equal to the weight, so the vertical force can represented by (1). The relationship between the vertical force and lift can be found using trigonometry, where φ (phi) is the bank angle:-

$$\cos \phi = \frac{ADJ\,(1)}{HYP\,(L)} \quad \text{transposing this formula gives,} \quad L = \frac{1}{\cos \phi}$$

$$L = \frac{1}{0.707} = 1.41$$

This shows that :-

In a 45° bank, LIFT must be greater than weight by a factor of 1.41

Another way of saying the same thing: in a level 45° bank turn, lift must be increased by 41%

Be aware of % changes in lift and % changes in Vs.

PRINCIPLES OF FLIGHT   **STALLING**

7.24 EFFECT OF LOAD FACTOR ON STALL SPEED

It has been demonstrated that to bank an aircraft and maintain altitude, lift has to be greater than weight. And that, additional lift in a turn is obtained by increasing the angle of attack. To consider the relationship between lift and weight we use Load Factor.

$$\text{LOAD FACTOR (n) or 'g'} = \frac{\text{LIFT}}{\text{WEIGHT}}$$

(a) Increasing lift in a turn, increases the load factor.

(b) **As bank angle increases, load factor increases.**

In straight and level flight at $C_{L\ MAX}$ it would be impossible to turn AND maintain altitude. Trying to increase lift would stall the aircraft. If a turn was started at an IAS above the stall speed, at some bank angle C_L would reach its maximum and the aircraft would stall at a speed higher than the 1g stall speed.

The increase of lift in a level turn is a function of the bank angle only. Using the following formula, it is possible to calculate stall speed as a function of bank angle or load factor.

$$V_{S_t} = V_S \sqrt{\frac{1}{\cos \phi}}$$

> Load factor does not effect stall angle

where: V_{S_t} is the stall speed in a turn

Using our example aeroplane: the 1g stall speed is 150 knots CAS, what will be the stall speed in a 45° bank?

$$V_{S_t} = 150 \sqrt{\frac{1}{0.707}} = 178 \text{ knots CAS}$$

In a 60° bank the stall speed will be:

$$V_{S_t} = 150 \sqrt{\frac{1}{0.5}} = 212 \text{ knots CAS}$$

Stall speed in a 45° bank is 19% greater than V_{S1g} and in a 60° bank the stall speed is 41% greater than V_{S1g}, and since these are ratio's, this will be true for any aircraft.

PRINCIPLES OF FLIGHT — STALLING

As bank angle is increased, stall speed will increase at an increasing rate. While operating at high C_L, during take-off and landing in particular, only moderate bank angles should be used to manoeuvre the aircraft. For a modern high speed jet transport aircraft, the absolute maximum bank angle which should be used in service is 30° (excluding emergency manoeuvres). The normal maximum would be 25°, at higher altitude the normal maximum is 10° to 15°.

If the 1g stall speed is 150 kt, calculate the stall speed in a 25° and a 30° bank turn. (Answers on page 7 - 48).

If the stall speed in a 15° bank turn is 153 kt CAS and it is necessary to calculate the stall speed in a 45° bank turn, you would need to calculate the 1g stall speed first, as follows:-

$$V_{St} = V_{S1g} \sqrt{\frac{1}{\cos 15°}} \quad \text{transposition gives} \quad V_{S1g} = \frac{V_{St}}{\sqrt{\frac{1}{\cos 15°}}}$$

$$V_{S1g} = \frac{153}{1.02} = 150 \text{ kt CAS}$$

PTO for exam Q.

7.25 EFFECT OF HIGH LIFT DEVICES ON STALL SPEED

Modern high speed jet transport aircraft have swept wings with relatively low thickness/chord ratio's (e.g. 12% for an A310). The overall value of C_{LMAX} for these wings is fairly low and the clean stalling speed correspondingly high. In order to reduce the landing and take off speeds, various devices are used to increase the usable value of C_{LMAX}. In addition to decreasing the stall speed, these high-lift devices will usually alter the stalling characteristics. The devices include:-

a) leading-edge flaps and slats

b) trailing edge flaps

From the 1g stall formula:

$$V_{S1g} = \sqrt{\frac{L}{\frac{1}{2} \rho\, C_{L_{max}}\, S}}$$

it can be seen that an increase in C_{LMAX} will reduce the stall speed. It is possible, with the most modern high lift devices, to increase C_{LMAX} by as much as 100%. High lift devices will be fully described in chapter 8. High lift devices decrease stall speed, hence minimum flight speed, so provide a shorter take-off and landing run - this is their sole purpose.

PRINCIPLES OF FLIGHT — STALLING

7.26 EFFECT OF CG POSITION ON STALL SPEED

JAR 25.103(b) states that V_{CLMAX} is determined with the CG position that results in the highest value of reference stall speed.

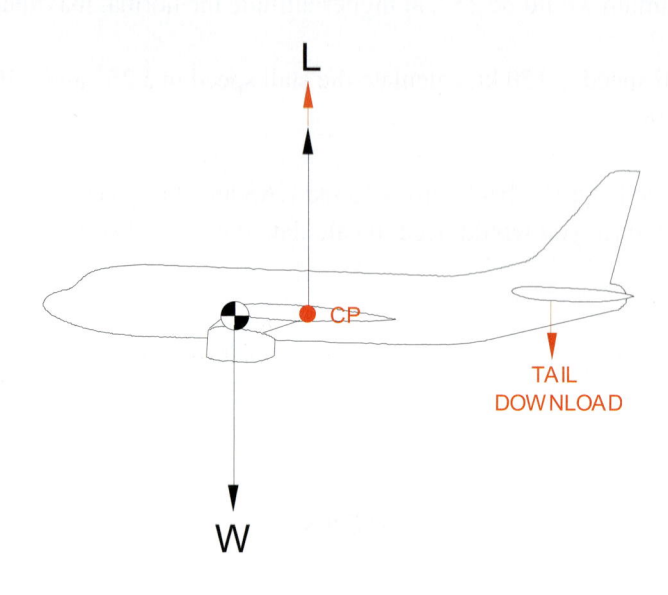

Figure 7.21

If the CG is in front of the CP, Fig. 7.21, giving a nose down pitching moment and there is no thrust/drag moment to oppose it, the tailplane must provide a down load to maintain equilibrium. Lift must be increased to maintain an upwards force equal to the increased downwards force. From the 1g stall formula it can be seen that C_{LMAX} will be divisible into the increased lift force more times.

$$V_{S_{1g}} = \sqrt{\frac{L}{\frac{1}{2} \rho \; C_{L_{max}} \; S}}$$

Forward movement of the CG increases stall speed.

From page 7.29 JAA Q
In level flight at 1.3 Vs, what is the approximate bank angle which the A/C will stall?

$$\frac{1}{1.3^2} = \cos\phi$$

$$\frac{1}{1.69} = 0.59 = \cos\phi \quad \therefore \quad \phi = 54°$$

PRINCIPLES OF FLIGHT **STALLING**

7.27 EFFECT OF LANDING GEAR ON THE STALL SPEED

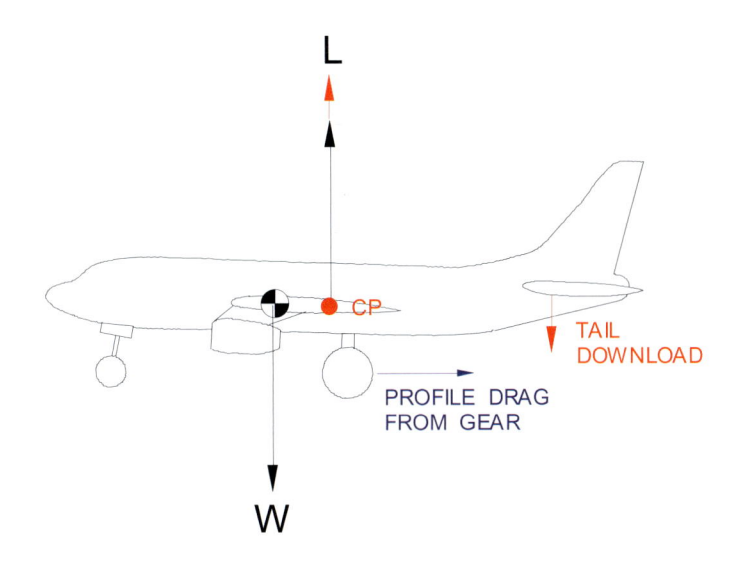

Figure 7.22

From Fig. 7.22 it can be seen that with the undercarriage down, profile drag below the CG is increased. This will give a nose down pitching moment which must be balanced by increasing the tail down load. Lift must be increased to balance the increased downwards force.

(CG movement due to the direction in which the undercarriage extends will have an insignificant influence on stall speed). By far the greater influence is the increased profile drag of the gear when it is extended.

Extending the undercarriage increases stall speed.

PRINCIPLES OF FLIGHT

STALLING

7.28 EFFECT OF ENGINE POWER ON STALL SPEED

JAR 25.103(b) states that V_{CLMAX} is determined with zero thrust at the stall speed.

When establishing V_{CLMAX} the engines must be at zero thrust and it is assumed that the weight of the aircraft is entirely supported by lift. If thrust is applied close to the stall the nose high attitude of the aircraft produces a vertical component of thrust, Fig. 7.24, which assists in supporting the weight and less lift is required. Aircraft with propellers will have an additional effect caused by the propeller slipstream.

The most important factors affecting this relationship are engine type (propeller or jet), thrust to weight ratio and inclination of the thrust vector at C_{LMAX}.

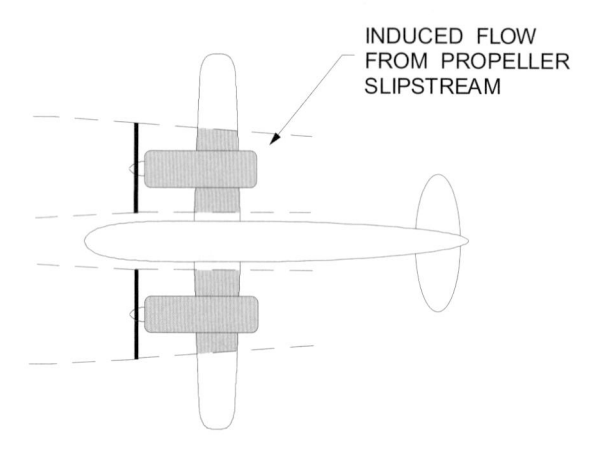

Figure 7.23

Propeller: Fig. 7.23. The slipstream velocity behind the propeller is greater than the free stream flow, depending on the thrust developed. Thus, when the propeller aeroplane is at low airspeeds and high power, the dynamic pressure within the propeller slipstream is much greater than that outside and this generates much more lift than at zero thrust. The lift of the aeroplane at a given angle of attack and airspeed will be greatly affected. If the aircraft is in the landing flare, reducing power suddenly will cause a significant reduction in lift and a heavy landing could result. On the other hand, a potentially heavy landing can be avoided by a judicious 'blast' from the engines.

Jet: The typical jet aircraft does not experience the induced flow velocities encountered in propeller driven aeroplanes, thus the only significant factor is the vertical component of thrust, Fig. 7.24. Since this vertical component contributes to supporting the weight of the aircraft, less aerodynamic lift is required to hold the aeroplane in flight. If the thrust is large and is given a large inclination at maximum lift angle, the effect on stall speed can be very large. Since there is very little induced flow from the jet, the angle of attack at stall is essentially the same power-on as power-off.

PRINCIPLES OF FLIGHT — STALLING

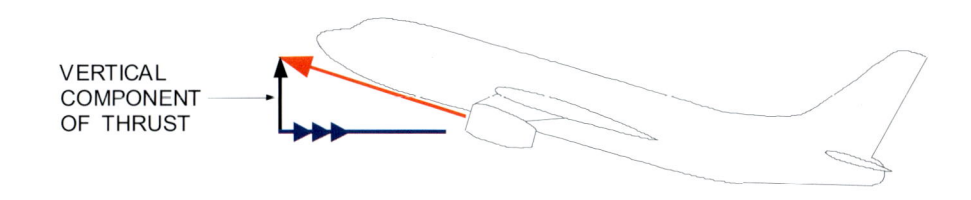

Figure 7.24

Power-on stall speed is less than power-off. This will be shown to be significant during the study of windshear in chapter 15.

PRINCIPLES OF FLIGHT STALLING

7.29 EFFECT OF MACH NUMBER (COMPRESSIBILITY) ON STALL SPEED

As an aircraft flies faster, the streamline pattern around the wing changes. Faster than about four tenths the speed of sound (0·4M) these changes start to become significant. This phenomena is known as compressibility. This will be discussed fully in Chapter 13.

Pressure waves, generated by the passage of a wing through the air, propagate ahead of the wing at the speed of sound. These pressure waves upwash air ahead of the wing towards the lower pressure on the top surface.

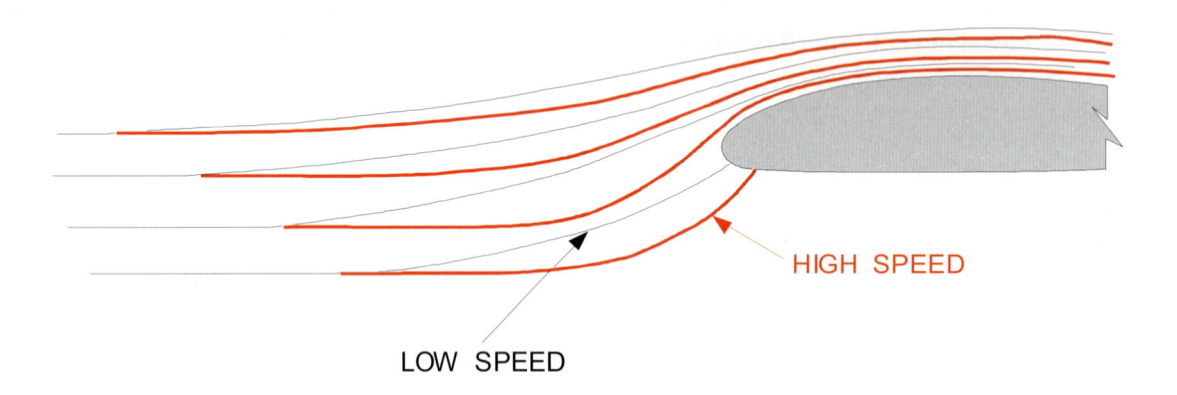

Figure 7.25

Fig. 7.25 shows that at low speed, the streamline pattern is affected far ahead of the wing and the air has a certain distance in which to upwash. As speed increases the wing gets closer to its leading pressure wave and the streamline pattern is affected a shorter distance ahead, so must approach the wing at a steeper angle.

This change in the streamline pattern accentuates the adverse pressure gradient near the leading edge and flow separation occurs at a reduced angle of attack. Above 0·4M $C_{L\,MAX}$ decreases as shown in Fig. 7.26.

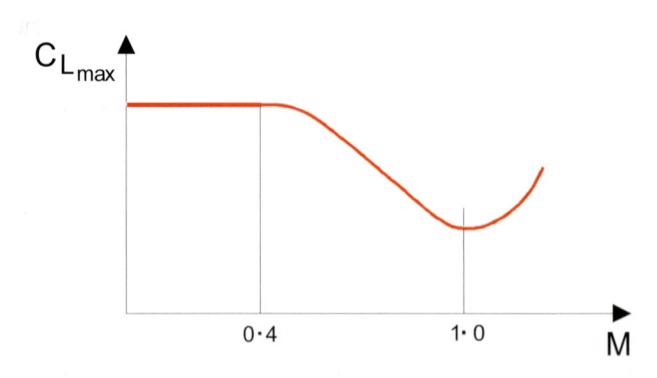

Figure 7.26

PRINCIPLES OF FLIGHT — STALLING

Referring to the 1g stall speed formula:

$$V_{S_{1g}} = \sqrt{\frac{L}{\frac{1}{2} \rho\, C_{L_{max}}\, S}}$$

If $C_{L_{MAX}}$ decreases, $V_{S_{1g}}$ will increase.

To maintain a constant EAS as altitude increases, TAS is increased. Also, outside air temperature decreases with increasing altitude, causing the local speed of sound to decrease. Mach number is proportional to TAS and inversely proportional to the local speed of sound (a):

$$M = \frac{TAS}{a}$$

Therefore, at a constant EAS, Mach number will increase as altitude increases.

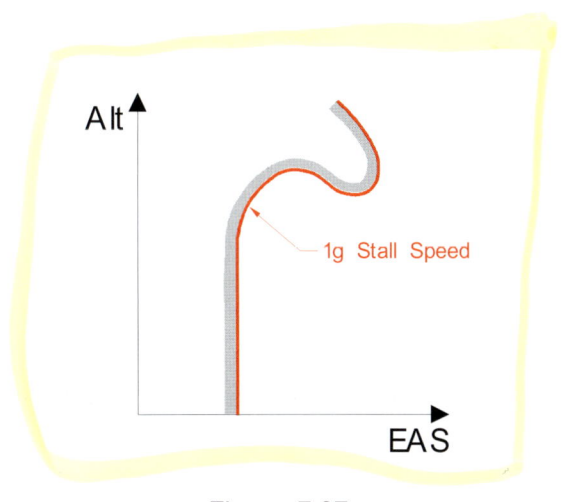

Figure 7.27

Fig. 7.27 shows the variation of stalling speed with altitude at constant load factor (n). Such a curve is called the stalling boundary for the given load factor, in which altitude is plotted against equivalent airspeed. At this load factor (1g), the aircraft cannot fly at speeds to the left of this boundary. It is clear that over the lower range of altitude, stall speed does not vary with altitude. This is because at these low altitudes, the Mach number at V_S is less than 0·4 M, too low for compressibility effects to be present. Eventually (approximately 30,000 ft), Mach number at V_S has increased with altitude to such an extent that these effects are important, and the rise in stalling speed with altitude is apparent.

Using the example aeroplane from earlier, the $V_{S_{1g}}$ of 150 kt is equal to M0·4 at approximately 29,000 ft using ISA values.

As altitude increases, stall speed is initially constant then increases, due to compressibility.

PRINCIPLES OF FLIGHT   STALLING

7.30 EFFECT OF WING CONTAMINATION ON STALL SPEED

Refer to:-
AIC 104/1998 "Frost Ice and Snow on Aircraft", and
AIC 98/1999 "Turbo-Prop and other Propeller Driven Aeroplanes: Icing Induced Stalls".

Any contamination on the wing, but particularly ice, frost or snow, will drastically alter the aerodynamic contour and affect the nature of the boundary layer.

ICE The formation of ice on the leading edge of the wing will produce:-

a) Large changes in the local contour, leading to severe local adverse pressure gradients.

b) High surface friction and a considerable reduction of boundary layer kinetic energy.

These cause a large decrease in $C_{L\ MAX}$ and can increase stall speed by approximately 30% **with no change in angle of attack.**

The added weight of the ice will also increase the stall speed, but the major factor is the reduction in $C_{L\ MAX}$.

FROST The effect of frost is more subtle. The accumulation of a hard coat of frost on the wing upper surface will produce a surface texture of considerable roughness.

Tests have shown that ice, snow or frost, with the thickness and surface roughness similar to medium or coarse sandpaper on the leading edge and upper surface of a wing can reduce lift by as much as 30% (10% to 15% increase in stall speed) and increases drag by 40%.

While the basic shape and aerodynamic contour is unchanged, the increase in surface roughness increases skin friction and reduces the kinetic energy of the boundary layer. Separation will occur at an angle of attack and lift coefficients lower than for the clean smooth wing.

SNOW The effect of snow can be similar to frost in that it will increase surface roughness. If there is a coating of snow on the aircraft it must be removed before flight. Not only will the snow itself increase skin friction drag, but may obscure airframe icing. Snow will NOT blow-off during taxi or take-off.

The pilot in command is legally required to ensure the aeroplane is aerodynamically clean at the time of take-off. It is very important that the holdover time of any de-icing or anti-icing fluid applied to the airframe is known. If this time will be exceeded before take-off, the aircraft must be treated again.

PRINCIPLES OF FLIGHT

STALLING

While the reduction in $C_{L\,MAX}$ due to frost formation is not usually as great as that due to ice formation, it is usually unexpected because it may be thought that large changes in the aerodynamic shape (such as due to ice) are necessary to reduce $C_{L\,MAX}$. However, kinetic energy of the boundary layer is an important factor influencing separation of the airflow and this energy is reduced by an increase in surface roughness. The general effects of ice and frost formation on $C_{L\,MAX}$ is typified by the illustrations in Fig. 7.28.

> Ice, frost and snow change the aerofoil section, decrease the stall angle and increase the stall speed

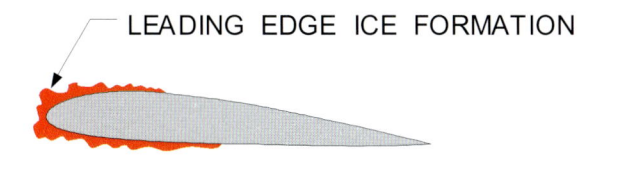

LEADING EDGE ICE FORMATION

UPPER SURFACE FROST

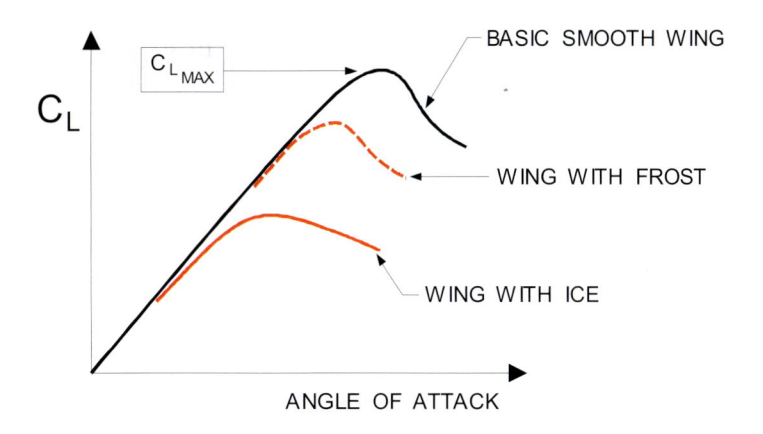

Figure 7.28

The increase in stall speed due to ice formation is not easy to quantify, as the accumulation and shape of the ice formation is impossible to predict. **Even a little ice is too much.** Ice or frost must never be allowed to remain on any aerodynamic surfaces in flight, nor must ice, frost, snow or other contamination be allowed to remain on the aircraft immediately before flight.

PRINCIPLES OF FLIGHT   **STALLING**

7.31 WARNING TO THE PILOT OF ICING-INDUCED STALLS

There have been recent cases involving loss of control in icing conditions due to undetected stalling at speeds significantly above the normal stalling speed, accompanied by violent roll oscillations.

Control of an aeroplane can be lost as a result of an icing-induced stall, the onset of which can be so insidious* as to be difficult to detect.

The following advice is offered on the recognition of, and the recovery from, insidious icing-induced wing-stalls:-

a) Loss of performance in icing conditions may indicate a serious build-up of airframe icing (even if this cannot be seen) which causes a gradual loss of lift and a significant increase in drag;

b) this build-up of ice can cause the aeroplane to stall at approximately 30% above the normal stall speed;

c) The longitudinal characteristics of an icing-induced wing-stall can be so gentle that the pilot may not be aware that it has occurred;

d) the stall warning system installed on the aeroplane may not alert the pilot to the insidious icing-induced wing-stall (angle of attack will be below that required to trigger the switch), so should not be relied upon to give a warning of this condition. Airframe buffet, however, may assist in identifying the onset of wing-stall;

e) the first clue may be a roll control problem. This can appear as a gradually increasing roll oscillation or a violent wing drop;

f) a combination of rolling oscillation and onset of high drag can cause the aeroplane to enter a high rate of descent unless prompt recovery action is taken;

g) if a roll control problem develops in icing conditions, the pilot should suspect that the aeroplane has entered an icing-induced wing-stall and should take immediate stall recovery action (decrease the angle of attack). The de-icing system should also be activated. If the aeroplane is fitted with an anti-icing system this should have been activated prior to entry into icing conditions in accordance with the Flight Manual/Operations Manual procedures and recommendations. If the anti-icing system has not been in use then it should be immediately activated. Consideration should also be given to leaving icing conditions by adjusting track and/or altitude if possible.

*Insidious - advancing imperceptibly: without warning

PRINCIPLES OF FLIGHT　　　　　　　　　　　　　　　　　　　　　STALLING

7.32　STABILISER STALL DUE TO ICE

The tailplane is an aerofoil, and because it is thinner than the wing, it is likely to experience icing before the wing does. The effect will be the same as for the wing, the stall will occur at a lower angle of attack. The tailplane is normally operating at a negative angle of attack, producing a download, so if the tailplane stalls and the download is lost, the nose of the aircraft will drop and longitudinal control will be lost.

Stalling of an ice contaminated tailplane could be precipitated by extension of the wing flaps. Lowering the flaps increases the downwash, and this increases the negative angle of attack of the tailplane. If the tailplane has ice contamination this could be sufficient to cause it to stall. Recovery procedure in this situation would be to retract the flaps again, thus reducing the downwash.

7.33　EFFECT OF HEAVY RAIN ON STALL SPEED

WEIGHT: Heavy rain will form a film of water on an aircraft and increase its weight slightly, maybe as much as 1 - 2%, this in itself will increase stall speed.

AERODYNAMIC EFFECT: The film of water will distort the aerofoil, roughen the surface, and alter the airflow pattern on the whole aircraft. $C_{L\,MAX}$ will decrease causing stall speed to increase.

DRAG: The film of water will increase interference drag, profile drag [skin friction] and form drag. In light rain, drag may increase by 5%, moderate 20% and heavy rain up to 30%. This obviously increases thrust required.

IMPACT: An additional consideration, while not affecting stall speed, is the effect of the impact of heavy rain on the aircraft. Momentum will be lost and airspeed will decrease, requiring increased thrust. At the same time, heavy rain will also be driving the aircraft downwards. The volume of rain in any given situation will vary, but an aircraft on final approach which suddenly enters a torrential downpour of heavy rain will be subject to a loss of momentum and a decrease in altitude, similar to the effect of microburst windshear. (Chapt. 16).

7.34　STALL AND RECOVERY CHARACTERISTICS OF CANARDS

With the conventional rear tailplane configuration the wing stalls before the tailplane, and longitudinal control and stability are maintained at the stall. On a canard layout if the wing stalls first, stability is lost, but if the foreplane stalls first then control is lost and the maximum value of C_L is reduced.

PRINCIPLES OF FLIGHT   STALLING

7.35   SPINNING   *autorotation*

When an aircraft is accidentally or deliberately stalled, the motion of the aircraft may in some cases develop into a spin. The important characteristics of a spin are:-

a)   the aircraft is descending along a steep helical path about a vertical spin axis,

b)   the angle of attack of both wings is well above the stall angle,

c)   the aircraft has a high rate of rotation about the vertical spin axis,

d)   viewed from above, the aircraft executes a circular path about the spin axis, and the radius of the helix is usually less than the semi-span of the wing,

e)   the aircraft may be in the "erect" or "inverted" position in the spin.

The spin is one of the most complex of all flight manoeuvres. A spin may be defined as an aggravated stall resulting in autorotation, which means the rotation is stable and will continue due to aerodynamic forces if nothing intervenes. During the spin the wings remain unequally stalled.

7.36   PRIMARY CAUSES OF A SPIN

A stall must occur before a spin can take place. A spin occurs when one wing stalls more than the other, Fig. 7.29. The wing that is more stalled will drop and the nose of the aircraft will yaw in the direction of the lower wing.

The cause of an accidental spin is exceeding the critical angle of attack while performing a manoeuvre with either too much or not enough rudder input for the amount of aileron being used (crossed-controls). If the correct stall recovery is not initiated promptly, the stall could develop into a spin.

Co-ordinated use of the flight controls is important, especially during flight at low airspeed and high angle of attack. Although most pilots are able to maintain co-ordinated flight during routine manoeuvres, this ability often deteriorates when distractions occur and their attention is divided between important tasks. Distractions that have caused problems include preoccupation with situations inside or outside the flight deck, manoeuvring to avoid other aircraft, and manoeuvring to clear obstacles during take-off, climb, approach or landing.

A spin may also develop if forces on the aircraft are unbalanced in other ways, for example, from yaw forces due to an engine failure on a multi-engine aircraft, or if the CG is laterally displaced by an unbalanced fuel load.

PRINCIPLES OF FLIGHT
STALLING

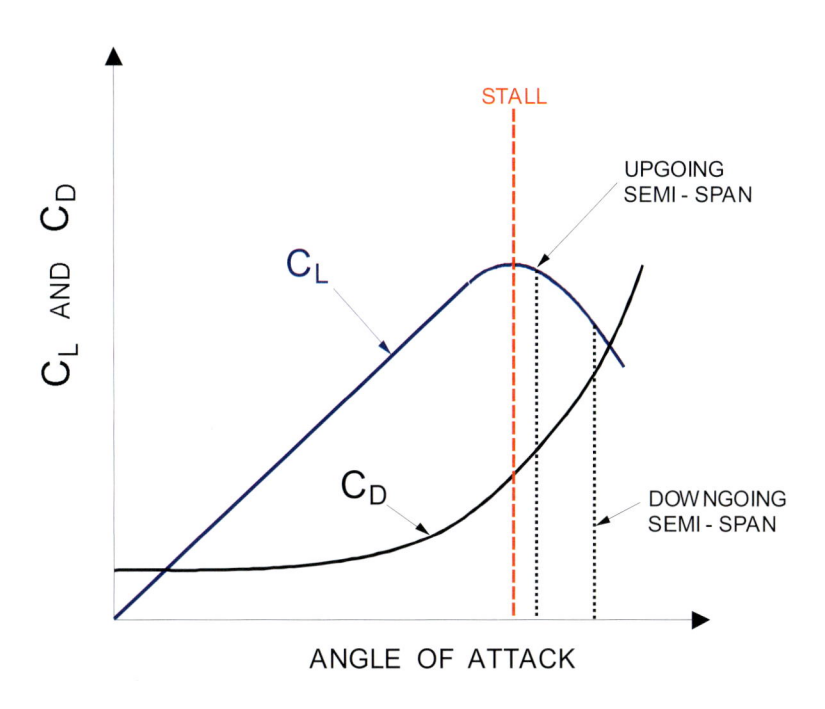

Figure 7.29

7.37 PHASES OF A SPIN

There are three phases of a spin.

1. The **incipient spin** is the first phase, and exists from the time the aeroplane stalls and rotation starts until the spin is fully developed.

2. A **fully developed spin** exists from the time the angular rotation rates, airspeed, and vertical descent rate are stabilized from one turn to the next.

3. The third phase, **spin recovery**, begins when the anti-spin forces overcome the pro-spin forces.

If an aircraft is near the critical angle of attack, and more lift is lost from one wing than the other, that wing will drop. Its relative airflow will be inclined upwards, increasing its effective angle of attack. As the aeroplane rolls around its CG, the rising wing has a reduced effective angle of attack and remains less stalled than the other. This situation of unbalanced lift tends to increase as the aeroplane yaws towards the low wing, accelerating the high, outside wing and slowing the inner, lower wing. As with any stall, the nose drops, and as inertia forces begin to take effect, the spin usually stabilizes at a steady rate of rotation and descent.

PRINCIPLES OF FLIGHT

It is vitally important that recovery from an unintentional spin is begun as soon as possible, since many aeroplanes will not easily recover from a fully developed spin, and others continue for several turns before recovery inputs become effective. Recovery from an incipient spin normally requires less altitude and time than the recovery from a fully developed spin. Every aeroplane spins differently, and an individual aeroplane's spin characteristics vary depending on configuration, loading, and other factors.

7.38 THE EFFECT OF MASS AND BALANCE ON SPINS

Both the total mass of the aircraft and its distribution influence the spin characteristics of the aeroplane. Higher masses generally mean slower initial spin rates, but as the spin progresses, spin rates may tend to increase. The higher angular momentum extends the time and altitude necessary for recovery from a spin in a heavily loaded aeroplane.

CG location is even more significant, affecting the aeroplane's resistance to spin as well as all phases of the spin itself.

a) CG towards the forward limit makes an aircraft more stable, and control forces will be higher which makes it less likely that large, abrupt control movements will be made. When trimmed, the aeroplane will tend to return to level flight if the controls are released, but the stall speed will be higher.

b) CG towards the aft limit decreases longitudinal static stability and reduces pitch control forces, which tends to make the aeroplane easier to stall. Once a spin is entered, the further aft the CG, the flatter the spin attitude.

c) If the CG is outside the aft limit, or if power is not reduced promptly, the spin is more likely to go flat. A flat spin is characterised by a near level pitch and roll attitude with the spin axis near the CG. Although the altitude lost in each turn of a flat spin may be less than in a normal spin, the extreme yaw rate (often exceeding 400° per second) results in a high descent rate. The relative airflow in a flat spin is nearly straight up, keeping the wings at high angles of attack. More importantly, the upward flow over the tail may render the elevator and rudder ineffective, making recovery impossible.

7.39 SPIN RECOVERY

Recovery from a simple stall is achieved by reducing the angle of attack which restores the airflow over the wing; spin recovery additionally involves stopping the rotation. **The extremely complex aerodynamics of a spin may dictate vastly different recovery procedures for different aeroplanes, so no universal spin recovery procedure can exist for all aeroplanes.**

The recommended recovery procedure for some aeroplanes is simply to reduce power to idle and release pressure on the controls. At the other extreme, the design of some aircraft is such that recovery from a developed spin requires definite control movements, precisely timed to coincide with certain points in the rotation, for several turns.

PRINCIPLES OF FLIGHT — STALLING

The following is a general recovery procedure for erect spins. Always refer to the Flight Manual for the particular aircraft being flown and follow the manufacturers recommendations.

1. Move the throttle or throttles to idle. This minimises altitude loss and reduces the possibility of a flat spin developing. It also eliminates possible asymmetric thrust in multi-engine aeroplanes. Engine torque and gyroscopic propeller effect can increase the angle of attack or the rate of rotation in single-engine aeroplanes, aggravating the spin.

2. Neutralise the ailerons. Aileron position is often a contributory factor to flat spins, or to higher rotation rates in normal spins.

3. Apply full rudder against the spin. Spin direction is most reliably determined from the turn co-ordinator. Do not use the ball in the slip indicator, its indications are not reliable and may be affected by its location within the flight deck.

4. Move the elevator control briskly to approximately the neutral position. Some aircraft merely require a relaxation of back pressure, while others require full forward pitch control travel.

The above four items can be accomplished simultaneously.

5. Hold the recommended control positions until rotation stops.

6. As rotation stops, neutralise the rudder. If rudder deflection is maintained after rotation stops, the aircraft may enter a spin in the other direction!

7. Recover from the resulting dive with gradual back pressure on the pitch control.

    a) Pulling too hard could trigger a secondary stall, or exceed the limit load factor and damage the aircraft structure.

    b) Recovering too slowly from the dive could allow the aeroplane to exceed its airspeed limits, particularly in aerodynamically clean aeroplanes.

    Avoiding excessive speed build-up during recovery is another reason for closing the throttles during spin recovery

    c) Add power as you resume normal flight, being careful to observe power and rpm limitations.

Equilibrium: The sum of the moments is zero, and the sum of the forces is zero.

PRINCIPLES OF FLIGHT — STALLING

7.40 SPECIAL PHENOMENA OF STALL

CROSSED-CONTROL STALL

A crossed-control stall can occur when flying at high angles of attack while applying rudder in the opposite direction to aileron, or too much rudder in the same direction as aileron. This will be displayed by the ball in the slip indicator being displaced from neutral.

Crossed-control stalls can occur with little or no warning; one wing will stall a long time before the other and a quite violent wing drop can occur. The "instinctive" reaction to stop the wing drop with aileron must be resisted (ref. para 7.6). The rudder should be used to keep the aircraft in balanced, co-ordinated flight at all times (ball in the middle), especially at low airspeeds/high angles of attack.

ACCELERATED STALL

An accelerated stall is caused by abrupt or excessive control movement. An accelerated stall can occur during a sudden change in the flight path, during manoeuvres such as steep turns or a rapid recovery from a dive. It is called an 'accelerated stall' because it occurs at a load factor greater than 1g. An accelerated stall is usually more violent than a 1g stall, and is often unexpected because of the relatively high airspeed.

SECONDARY STALL

A secondary stall may be triggered while attempting to recover from a stall. This usually happens as a result of trying to hasten the stall recovery; either by not decreasing the angle of attack enough at stall warning or by not allowing sufficient time for the aircraft to begin flying again before attempting to regain lost altitude. With full power still applied, relax the back pressure and allow the aeroplane to fly before reapplying moderate back pressure to regain lost height.

LARGE AIRCRAFT

During airline 'type' conversion training on large aircraft, full stalls are not practised. To familiarise pilots with the characteristics of their aircraft, only the approach to stall (stick shaker activation) is carried out.

(a) Jet Aircraft (swept wing): there are no special considerations during the approach to the stall.

    (i) Power-Off stall: at stick shaker, smoothly lower the nose to the horizon, or just below, to un-stall the wing; simultaneously increase power to the maximum recommended to minimise height loss, prevent wing drop with roll control, raise the gear and select take-off flaps.

    (ii) Power-On stall: as with power-off.

(b) Multi-engine propeller.

  (i) Power-Off stall: at stick shaker, smoothly lower the nose to the horizon, or just below, to un-stall the wing; simultaneously increase power to the maximum recommended to minimise height loss, prevent wing drop with rudder and aileron control, raise the gear and select take-off flaps.

  (ii) Power-On stall: as with power-off.

The primary difference between jet and propeller aircraft is the rapidly changing propeller torque and slipstream that will be evident during power application. It is essential for the pilot to maintain co-ordination between rudder and aileron while applying the control inputs required to counter the changing rolling and yawing moments generated by the propeller when the engine is at high power settings or during rapid applications of power. Yaw must be prevented during a stall and recovery.

SMALL AIRCRAFT

(c) Single engine propeller

  (i) Power-Off stall: at stall warning, smoothly lower the nose to the horizon, or just below, to un-stall the wing; simultaneously increase power to the maximum recommended to minimise height loss, prevent wing drop with rudder and raise the gear if applicable.

  (ii) Power-on stall and recovery in a **single engine propeller** aircraft has additional complications. At the high nose attitude and low airspeed associated with a power-on stall, there will be considerable "turning effects" from the propeller. (These are fully detailed in Chapt. 16).

To maintain co-ordinated flight during the approach to, and recovery from, a power-on stall, the pilot of a **single engine propeller** aircraft must compensate for the turning effects of the propeller with the correct combination of rudder and aileron. It is essential to maintain co-ordinated flight (ball in the middle) when close to the stall AND during recovery. Any yawing tendency could easily develop into a spin. When the aircraft nose drops at the stall, gyroscopic effect will also be apparent, increasing the nose left yawing moment - with a clockwise rotating propeller.

An accidental power-on stall, during take-off or go-around, when a pilot's attention is diverted, could easily turn into a spin. It is essential that correct stall recovery action is taken at the first indication of a stall. (Forward movement of the pitch control; neutralise the roll control; and prevent wing drop with the rudder).

PRINCIPLES OF FLIGHT   STALLING

STALL AND RECOVERY IN A CLIMBING AND DESCENDING TURN

When an aircraft is in a level co-ordinated turn at a constant bank angle, the inside wing is moving through the air more slowly than the outside wing and consequently generates less lift. If the ailerons are held neutral, the aircraft has a tendency to continue to roll in the direction of bank (over-banking tendency). Rather than return the ailerons to neutral when the required degree of bank angle is reached, the pilot must hold aileron opposite to the direction of bank; the lower the airspeed, the greater the aileron input required.

The inner (lower) wing may have a greater effective angle of attack due to the lowered aileron and may reach the critical angle of attack first. The rudder must be used at all times to maintain co-ordinated flight (ball in the middle).

In a climbing turn, airspeed will be lower and in a **single engine propeller** aircraft, the rolling and yawing forces generated by the propeller and its slipstream will add their own requirements for unusual rudder and aileron inputs. e.g. for an aircraft with a clockwise rotating propeller in a climbing turn to the left at low speed it may be necessary for the pilot to be holding a lot of right roll aileron and right rudder. If an aircraft in this situation were to stall, the gross control deflections can make the aircraft yaw or roll violently. Correct co-ordination of the controls is essential, in all phases of flight, to prevent the possibility of an accidental spin.

CONCLUSIONS

In whatever configuration, attitude, or power setting a stall warning occurs, the correct pilot action is to decrease the angle of attack below the stall angle to un-stall the wing, apply maximum allowable power to minimise altitude loss and prevent any yaw from developing to minimise the possibility of spinning (pretty much, in that order). "Keep the ball in the middle".

7.41 HIGH SPEED BUFFET (SHOCK STALL)

When explaining the basic Principles of Flight, we consider air to be incompressible at speeds less than four tenths the speed of sound (0·4M). That is, pressure is considered to have no effect on air density. At speeds higher than 0·4M it is no longer practical to make that assumption because density changes in the airflow around the aircraft begin to make differences to the behaviour of the aircraft.

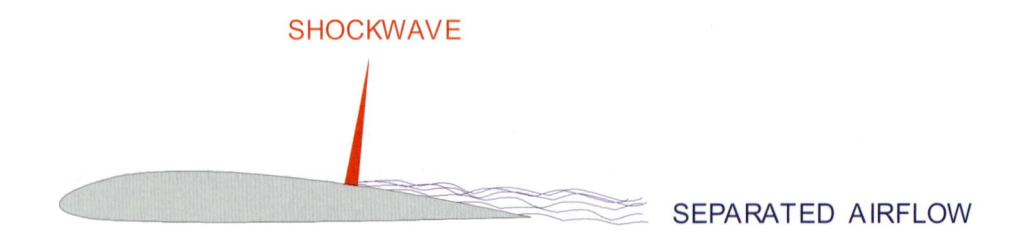

Figure 7.30 Shock Induced Stall

PRINCIPLES OF FLIGHT   STALLING

At high altitude, a large high speed jet transport aircraft will be cruising at a speed marginally above its critical Mach number, and will have a small shock wave on the wing. If such an aircraft over speeds the shock wave will rapidly grow larger, causing the static pressure to increase sharply in the immediate vicinity of the shock wave. The locally **increased adverse pressure gradient** will cause the boundary layer to separate immediately behind the shock wave, Fig 7.30. This is called a 'shock stall'. The separated airflow will engulf the tail area in a very active turbulent wake and cause severe airframe buffeting - a very undesirable phenomenon.

High speed buffet (shock stall) can seriously damage the aircraft structure, so an artificial warning device is installed that will alert the pilot if the aircraft exceeds its maximum operational speed limit (V_{MO}/M_{MO})* by even a small margin. The high speed warning is aural ("clacker", horn or siren) and is easily distinguishable from the "low speed" high angle of attack "stick shaker" warning.

We have seen that approaching the critical angle of attack can cause airframe buffeting ("low speed" buffet) and we have now shown that flying too fast will also cause airframe buffeting ("high speed" buffet). ANY airframe buffeting is undesirable and can quickly lead to structural damage, besides upsetting the passengers.

It will be shown that at high cruising altitudes (36,000 to 42,000 ft) the margin between the high angle of attack stall warning and the high speed warning, may be as little as 15 kt.

*VMO is the maximum operating Indicated Air Speed,
  MMO is the maximum operating Mach number. (These will be fully discussed in Chapter 14).

NB: It is operationally necessary to fly as fast as economically possible and designers are constantly trying to increase the maximum speed at which aircraft can fly, without experiencing any undesirable characteristics. During certification flight testing the projected maximum speeds are investigated and **maximum operating speeds** are established. The maximum operating speed limit (V_{MO}/M_{MO}) gives a speed margin into which the aircraft can momentarily overspeed and be recovered by the pilot before any undesirable characteristics occur. (Tuck, loss of control effectiveness, and several stability problems - these will all be detailed in later chapters).

PRINCIPLES OF FLIGHT   **STALLING**

ANSWERS:

Stall speed in a 25° and 30° bank if V_{S1g} = 150 kt CAS. (with % comparisons)

    25° = 158 kt CAS (5% increase in stall speed above V_{S1g}) [lift 10% greater]

    30° = 161 kt CAS (7% increase in stall speed above V_{S1g}) [lift 15% greater]

    45° = 178 kt CAS (19% increase in stall speed above V_{S1g}) [lift 41% greater]

    60° = 212 kt CAS (41% increase in stall speed above V_{S1g}) [lift 100% greater]

PRINCIPLES OF FLIGHT   **STALLING**

KEY FACTS 2 - Self Study

Insert the missing words in these statements, using the foregoing paragraphs for reference.

The swept-back wing is the major contributory factor to _____ stall. (Para. 7.15).

An aircraft design with super stall tendencies must be fitted with a stick _____. (Para. 7.16).

Factors which can affect V_{SR} are: (Para. 7.17).

    a)   Changes in _____
    b)   Manoeuvring the aircraft (increasing the _____ _____)
    c)   Configuration changes (changes in _____ and _____ moment)
    d)   Engine _____ and propeller _____
    e)   _____ number
    f)   Wing _____
    g)   Heavy _____

In straight and level flight the load factor is _____. (Para. 7.18).

At a higher weight, the stall speed of an aircraft will be _____ (Para. 7.19)

If the weight is decreased by 50% the stall speed will _____ by approximately ____%. (Para. 7.19).

Load factor varies with _____ _____. (Para. 7.24)

The increase in stall speed in a turn is proportional to the square root of the _____ _____. (Para. 7.24).

High lift devices will _____ the stall speed because $C_{L\ MAX}$ is _____. (Para. 7.25)

Forward CG movement will _____ stall speed due to the increased tail _____ load. (Para. 7.26).

Lowering the landing gear will increase stall speed due to the increased tail _____ load. (Para. 7.27).

Increased engine power will decrease stall speed due to propeller _____ and/or the _____ inclination of thrust. (Para. 7.28).

The effect of increasing Mach number on stall speed begin at _____ M. (Para. 7.29).

The effects of compressibility increases stall speed by decreasing _____. (Para. 7.29)

PRINCIPLES OF FLIGHT   **STALLING**

The formation of ice on the leading edge of the wing can _____ stall speed by ____ %. (Para. 7.30).

Frost formation on the wing can _____ stall speed by ____ %. (Para. 7.30).

An aircraft must be free of all _____, _____ and ____ immediately before _____. (Para. 7.30)

Airframe contamination _____ stall speed by reducing _____, increasing the adverse _____ _____ and/or reducing the _____ energy of the boundary layer. (Para. 7.30).

Indications of an icing-induced stall can be loss of aircraft _____, _____ oscillations or _____ drop and high rate of _____. Artificial stall warning will be _____, but aerodynamic _____ may assist in identifying the onset of wing stall. (Para. 7.31).

Very heavy ____ can _____ the stall speed due to the film of water altering the _____ contour of the wing. (Para. 7.33).

A _____ must occur before a spin can take place. (Para. 7.36).

In a steady spin, _____ wings are stalled, one more than the other. (Para. 7.36).

A spin may also develop if forces on the aircraft are unbalanced in other ways, for example, from yaw forces due to an _____ failure on a multi-engine aircraft, or if the ____ is laterally displaced by an unbalanced _____ load. (Para. 7.36).

The following is a general recovery procedure for erect spins:- (Para. 7.39).

1. Move the throttle or throttles to _____.
2. _____ the ailerons.
3. Apply full _____ against the spin.
4. Move the _____ control briskly to approximately the neutral position.
5. _____ the recommended control positions until rotation stops.
6. As rotation stops, neutralise the _____.
7. Recover from the resulting dive with _____ back pressure on the _____ control.

A crossed-control stall can be avoided by maintaining the ___ of the slip indicator in the _____. (Para. 7.40).

A stall can occur at any _____ or flight _____ if the _____ angle of attack is exceeded. (Para. 7.2 and 7.40).

A secondary stall can be triggered either by not _____ the angle of _____ enough at stall warning or by not allowing sufficient ___ for the aircraft to begin _____ again before attempting to _____ lost altitude. (Para. 7.40).

PRINCIPLES OF FLIGHT **STALLING**

An added complication during an accidental stall and recovery of a single engine propeller aircraft is due to the _____ and _____ forces generated by the _____. It is essential to maintain balanced, co-ordinated flight, particularly at ____ airspeed, high angles of _____. (Para. 7.40).

In whatever configuration, attitude, or power setting a stall warning occurs, the correct pilot action is to _____ the angle of attack below the _____ angle to un-stall the ____, apply maximum allowable _____ to minimise altitude loss and prevent any ____ from developing to minimise the possibility of _____. "Keep the _____ in the middle". (Para. 7.40).

If a large shockwave forms on the wing, due to an inadvertent overspeed. The locally increased _____ pressure gradient will cause the _____ _____ to separate immediately _____ the shock wave. This is called '_____ stall'. (Para. 7.41).

KEY FACTS 2, WITH WORD INSERTS CAN BE FOUND ON PAGE 7 - 66

INTENTIONALLY LEFT BLANK

SELF ASSESSMENT QUESTIONS

1. An aeroplane will stall at the same:

    a) angle of attack and attitude with relation to the horizon
    b) airspeed regardless of the attitude with relation to the horizon
    c) angle of attack regardless of the attitude with relation to the horizon
    d) indicated airspeed regardless of altitude, bank angle and load factor

2. A typical stalling angle of attack for a wing without sweepback is:

    a) 4°
    b) 16°
    c) 30°
    d) 45°

3. If the aircraft weight is increased without change of C of G position, the stalling angle of attack will:

    a) remain the same.
    b) decrease.
    c) increase.
    d) the position of the CG does not affect the stall speed.

4. If the angle of attack is increased above the stalling angle:

    a) lift and drag will both decrease.
    b) lift will decrease and drag will increase.
    c) lift will increase and drag will decrease.
    d) lift and drag will both increase.

5. The angle of attack at which an aeroplane stalls:

    a) will occur at smaller angles of attack flying downwind than when flying upwind
    b) is dependent upon the speed of the airflow over the wing
    c) is a function of speed and density altitude
    d) will remain constant regardless of gross weight

6. An aircraft whose weight is 237402 N stalls at 132 kt. At a weight of 356103 N it would stall at:

    a) 88 kt
    b) 162 kt
    c) 108 kt
    d) 172 kt

PRINCIPLES OF FLIGHT — STALLING

7. For an aircraft with a 1g stalling speed of 60 kt IAS, the stalling speed in a steady 60° turn would be:

    a) 43 kt
    b) 60 kt
    c) 84 kt
    d) 120 kt

8. For an aircraft in a steady turn the stalling speed would be:

    a) the same as in level flight
    b) at a lower speed than in level flight
    c) at a higher speed than in level flight, and a lower angle of attack.
    d) at a higher speed than in level flight and at the same angle of attack.

9. Formation of ice on the wing leading edge will:

    a) not affect the stalling speed.
    b) cause the aircraft to stall at a higher speed and a higher angle of attack.
    c) cause the aircraft to stall at a higher speed and a lower angle of attack.
    d) cause the aircraft to stall at a lower speed.

10. Dividing lift by weight gives:

    a) wing loading
    b) lift/drag ratio
    c) aspect ratio
    d) load factor

11. The stalling speed of an aeroplane is most affected by:

    a) changes in air density
    b) variations in aeroplane loading
    c) variations in flight altitude
    d) changes in pitch attitude

12. Stalling may be delayed to a higher angle of attack by:

    a) increasing the adverse pressure gradient
    b) increasing the surface roughness of the wing top surface
    c) distortion of the leading edge by ice build-up
    d) increasing the kinetic energy of the boundary layer

PRINCIPLES OF FLIGHT **STALLING**

13. A stall inducer strip will:

    a) cause the wing to stall first at the root
    b) cause the wing to stall at the tip first
    c) delay wing root stall
    d) re-energise the boundary layer at the wing root

14. On a highly tapered wing without wing twist the stall will commence:

    a) simultaneously across the whole span.
    b) at the centre of the span.
    c) at the root.
    d) at the tip.

15. Sweepback on a wing will:

    a) reduce induced drag at low speed.
    b) increase the tendency to tip stall.
    c) reduce the tendency to tip stall.
    d) cause the stall to occur at a lower angle of attack.

16. The purpose of a boundary layer fence on a swept wing is:

    a) to re-energise the boundary layer and prevent separation.
    b) to control spanwise flow and delay tip stall.
    c) to generate a vortex over the upper surface of the wing.
    d) to maintain a laminar boundary layer.

17. A wing with washout would have:

    a) the tip chord less than the root chord.
    b) the tip incidence less than the root incidence.
    c) the tip incidence greater than the root incidence.
    d) the tip camber less than the root camber.

18. On an untapered wing without twist the downwash:

    a) increases from root to tip.
    b) increases from tip to root.
    c) is constant across the span.
    d) is greatest at centre span, less at root and tip.

19. A wing of constant thickness which is not swept back:

    a) will stall at the tip first due to the increase in spanwise flow.
    b) could drop a wing at the stall due to the lack of any particular stall inducing characteristics.
    c) will pitch nose down approaching the stall due to the forward movement of the centre of pressure.
    d) will stall evenly across the span.

20. Slots increase the stalling angle of attack by:

    a) Increasing leading edge camber.
    b) delaying separation.
    c) Reducing the effective angle of attack.
    d) Reducing span-wise flow.

21. A rectangular wing, when compared to other wing planforms, has a tendency to stall first at the:

    a) wing root providing adequate stall warning
    b) wingtip providing inadequate stall warning
    c) wingtip providing adequate stall warning
    d) leading edge, where the wing root joins the fuselage

22. Vortex generators are used:

    a) to reduce induced drag
    b) to reduce boundary layer separation
    c) to induce a root stall
    d) to counteract the effect of the wing-tip vortices.

23. A stick shaker is:

    a) an overspeed warning device that operates at high Mach numbers.
    b) an artificial stability device.
    c) a device to vibrate the control column to give a stall warning.
    d) a device to prevent a stall by giving a pitch down.

24. A stall warning device must be set to operate:

    a) at the stalling speed.
    b) at a speed just below the stalling speed.
    c) at a speed about 5% to 10% above the stalling speed.
    d) at a speed about 20% above the stalling speed.

25. Just before the stall the wing leading edge stagnation point is positioned:

   a) above the stall warning vane
   b) below the stall warning vane
   c) on top of the stall warning vane
   d) on top of the leading edge because of the extremely high angle of attack

26. A wing mounted stall warning detector vane would be situated:

   a) on the upper surface at about mid chord.
   b) on the lower surface at about mid chord.
   c) at the leading edge on the lower surface.
   d) at the leading edge on the upper surface.

27. The input data to a stall warning device (e.g. stick shaker) system is:

   a) angle of attack only.
   b) angle of attack, and in some systems rate of change of angle of attack.
   c) airspeed only.
   d) airspeed and sometimes rate of change of airspeed.

28. A stick pusher is:

   a) a device to prevent an aircraft from stalling.
   b) a type of trim system.
   c) a device to assist the pilot to move the controls at high speed.
   d) a device which automatically compensates for pitch changes at high speed.

29. In a developed spin:

   a) the angle of attack of both wings will be positive
   b) the angle of attack of both wings will be negative
   c) the angle of attack of one wing will be positive and the other will be negative
   d) the down going wing will be stalled and the up going wing will not be stalled

30. To recover from a spin, the elevators should be:

   a) moved up to increase the angle of attack
   b) moved down to reduce the angle of attack
   c) set to neutral
   d) allowed to float

31. High speed buffet (shock stall) is caused by:

    a) the boundary layer separating in front of a shockwave at high angles of attack
    b) the boundary layer separating immediately behind the shock wave
    c) the shock wave striking the tail of the aircraft
    d) the shock wave striking the fuselage

32. In a 30° bank level turn, the stall speed will be increased by:

    a) 7%
    b) 30%
    c) 1.07%
    d) 15%

33. Heavy rain can increase the stall speed of an aircraft for which of the following reasons?

    a) Water increases the viscosity of air
    b) Heavy rain can block the pitot tube, giving false airspeed indications
    c) The extra weight and distortion of the aerodynamic surfaces by the film of water
    d) The impact of heavy rain will slow the aircraft

34. If the tailplane is supplying a download and stalls due to contamination by ice:

    a) the wing will stall and the aircraft will pitch-up due to the weight of the ice behind the aircraft CG
    b) the increased weight on the tailplane due to the ice formation will pitch the aircraft nose up, which will stall the wing
    c) because it was supplying a download the aircraft will pitch nose up
    d) the aircraft will pitch nose down

35. Indications of an icing-induced stall can be:

    1. An artificial stall warning device
    2. Airspeed close to the normal stall speed
    3. Violent roll oscillations
    4. Airframe buffet
    5. Violent wing drop
    6. Extremely high rate of descent while in a 'normal' flight attitude

    a) 1, 2, 4 and 5
    b) 1, 3 and 5
    c) 1, 4 and 6
    d) 3, 4, 5 and 6

PRINCIPLES OF FLIGHT   STALLING

36. If a light single engine propeller aircraft is stalled, power-on, in a climbing turn to the left, which of the following is the preferred recovery action?

   a) elevator stick forward, ailerons stick neutral, rudder to prevent wing drop.
   b) elevator stick neutral, rudder neutral, ailerons to prevent wing drop, power to idle.
   c) elevator stick forward, ailerons and rudder to prevent wing drop.
   d) elevator stick neutral, rudder neutral, ailerons stick neutral, power to idle.

37. If the stick shaker activates on a swept wing jet transport aircraft immediately after take-off while turning, which of the following statements contains the preferred course of action?

   a) Decrease the angle of attack
   b) Increase thrust
   c) Monitor the instruments to ensure it is not a spurious warning
   d) Decrease the bank angle

INTENTIONALLY

LEFT

BLANK

PRINCIPLES OF FLIGHT — STALLING

No	A	B	C	D	REF	No	A	B	C	D	REF
1			C		Para. 7.2	20		B			Page 7 - 12(c)
2		B			Para. 7.3	21	A				Para. 7.14
3	A				Para 7.19	22		B			Page 7 - 14(e)
4		B			Para. 7.2	23			C		Para. 7.10
5				D	Para. 7.19	24			C		Para. 7.9(c)
6		B			Para. 7.19	25		B			Fig. 7.4
7			C		Para. 7.24	26			C		Fig. 7.4
8				D	Para. 7.24	27		B			Para. 7.10
9			C		Para. 7.30	28	A				Para. 7.16
10				D	Para. 7.24	29	A				Para. 7.35
11		B			Para. 7.24	30		B			Para. 7.39
12				D	Page 7 - 12(c)	31		B			Para. 7.41
13	A				Page 7 - 13(d)	32	A				Para. 7.24
14				D	Fig. 7.8	33			C		Para. 7.33
15		B			Page 7 - 15	34				D	Para. 7.32
16		B			Page 7 - 16	35				D	Para. 7.31
17		B			Page 7 - 12(a)	36	A				Para. 7.40
18	A				Fig. 7.7	37	A				Para.7.40
19		B			Para. 7.14						

INTENTIONALLY

LEFT

BLANK

PRINCIPLES OF FLIGHT   STALLING

KEY FACTS 1 - Correct Statements

Stalling involves loss of **height** and loss of **control**

A pilot must be able to clearly and unmistakably **identify** a stall

A stall is caused by airflow **separation**

Separation can occur when either the boundary layer has insufficient **kinetic** energy or the **adverse pressure** gradient becomes too great.

Adverse pressure gradient increases with increase in angle of **attack**

Alternative names for the angle of attack at which stall occurs are the **stall** angle and the **critical** angle of attack

The coefficient of lift at which a stall occurs is $C_{L\,MAX}$

A stall can occur at any **airspeed** or flight **attitude**

A typical stalling angle is approximately **16°**

To recover from a stall the angle of **attack** must be **decreased**

Maximum power is applied during stall recovery to minimise **height** loss

On small aircraft, the **rudder** should be used to prevent wing **drop** at the stall

On swept wing aircraft the **ailerons** should be used to prevent wing **drop** at the stall

Recover height lost during stall recovery with moderate **back** pressure on the **elevator** control

The first indications of a stall may be **unresponsive** flight controls, stall **warning** device or aerodynamic **buffet**

At speeds close to the stall, **ailerons** must be used with caution to **lift** a dropping wing

Acceptable indications of a stall are:

  (1)   a nose **down** pitch that can not be readily arrested

  (2)   severe **buffeting**

  (3)   pitch control reaching **aft** stop and no further increase in **pitch** attitude occurs

PRINCIPLES OF FLIGHT — STALLING

Reference stall speed (V_{SR}) is a CAS defined by the **aircraft manufacturer**.

V_{SR} may not be **less** than a **1g** stall speed.

When a device that abruptly pushes the **nose down** at a selected angle of **attack** is installed, V_{SR} may not be **less** than **2** knots or **2 %**, whichever is **greater**, above the speed at which the **device** operates.

Stall warning with sufficient **margin** to prevent inadvertent stalling must be **clear** and **distinctive** to the pilot in straight and turning flight

Acceptable stall warning may consist of the inherent **aerodynamic** qualities of the aeroplane or by a **device** that will give clearly distinguishable indications under expected conditions of flight

Stall warning must begin at a speed exceeding the stall speed by not less than **5** knots or **5 %** CAS, whichever is the greater.

Artificial stall warning on a small aircraft is usually given by a **horn** or **buzzer**

Artificial stall warning on a large aircraft is usually given by a **stick** shaker, in conjunction with **lights** and a noisemaker

An artificial stall warning device can be activated by a **flapper** switch, an angle of **attack** vane or an angle of attack **probe**

Most angle of attack sensors compute the **rate** of change of angle of attack to give **earlier** warning in the case of accelerated rates of stall approach

JAR required stall characteristics, up to the time the aeroplane is stalled, are:-

a) It must be possible to produce and correct **yaw** by unreversed use of the **ailerons** and **rudder**
b) No abnormal nose up **pitching** may occur
c) Longitudinal control force must be **positive**
d) It must be possible to promptly prevent **stalling** and recover from a stall by normal use of the **controls**
e) There should be no excessive **roll** between the stall and completion of recovery
f) For turning flight stalls, the action of the aeroplane after the stall may not be so **violent** or **extreme** as to make it difficult, with normal piloting **skill**, to effect prompt **recovery** and to regain **control** of the aeroplane

An aerofoil section with a small leading edge **radius** will stall at a **smaller** angle of attack and the stall will be more **sudden**

An aerofoil section with a large thickness-chord ratio will stall at a **higher** angle of attack and will stall more **gently**

An aerofoil section with camber near the **leading edge** will stall at a higher angle of attack

A rectangular wing plan form will tend to stall at the **root** first

A rectangular wing planform usually has ideal stall characteristics, these are:-

  a) Aileron **effectiveness** at the stall
  b) Nose **drop** at the stall
  c) Aerodynamic **buffet** at the stall
  d) Absence of violent wing **drop** at the stall

To give a wing with a tapered planform the desired stall characteristics, the following devices can be included in the design:-

  a) **Washout** (decreasing incidence from root to tip)
  b) An aerofoil section with **greater** thickness and camber at the tip
  c) Leading edge **slots** at the tip
  d) Stall **strips** fitted to the wing inboard leading edge
  e) **Vortex** generators which re-energise the **boundary** layer at the tip

A swept back wing has an increased tendency to tip stall due to the spanwise flow of boundary layer from root to tip on the wing top surface. Methods of delaying tip stall on a swept wing planform are:-

  a) Wing **fences**, thin metal fences which generally extend from the leading edge to the trailing edge on the wing top surface
  b) **Vortilons**, also thin metal fences, but smaller and are situated on the underside of the wing leading edge
  c) Saw **tooth** leading edge, generates vortices over wing top surface at high angles of attack
  d) Engine **pylons** of pod mounted wing engines also act as vortilons
  e) **Vortex** generators are also used to delay tip stall on a swept wing

Tip stall on a swept wing planform gives a tendency for the aircraft to **pitch-up** at the stall. This is due to the **CP** moving forwards when the wing tips stall **first**.

PRINCIPLES OF FLIGHT

STALLING

KEY FACTS 2 - Correct Statements

The swept-back wing is the major contributory factor to **super** stall.

An aircraft design with super stall tendencies must be fitted with a stick **pusher**.

Factors which can affect V_{SR} are:

a) Changes in **weight**.
b) Manoeuvring the aircraft (increasing the **load factor**).
c) Configuration changes (changes in $C_{L\,MAX}$ and **pitching** moment).
d) Engine **thrust** and propeller **slipstream**
e) **Mach** number
f) Wing **contamination**
g) Heavy **rain**

In straight and level flight the load factor is **one**.

At a higher weight, the stall speed of an aircraft will be **higher**.

If the weight is decreased by 50% the stall speed will **decrease** by approximately **25%**.

Load factor varies with **bank angle**.

The increase in stall speed in a turn is proportional to the square root of the **load factor**.

High lift devices will **decrease** the stall speed because $C_{L\,MAX}$ is **increased**.

Forward CG movement will **increase** stall speed due to the increased tail **down** load.

Lowering the landing gear will increase stall speed due to the increased tail **down** load.

Increased engine power will decrease stall speed due to propeller **slipstream** and/or the **upwards** inclination of thrust.

The effect of increasing Mach number on stall speed begin at **0·4M**.

The effects of compressibility increases stall speed by decreasing $C_{L\,MAX}$.

PRINCIPLES OF FLIGHT — STALLING

The formation of ice on the leading edge of the wing can **increase** stall speed by **30%**.

Frost formation on the wing can **increase** stall speed by **15%**.

An aircraft must be free of all **snow**, **frost** and **ice** immediately before **flight**.

Airframe contamination **increases** stall speed by reducing $C_{L\ MAX}$, increasing the adverse **pressure gradient** and/or reducing the **kinetic** energy of the boundary layer.

Indications of an icing-induced stall can be loss of aircraft **performance**, **roll** oscillations or **wing** drop and high rate of **descent**. Artificial stall warning will be **absent**, but aerodynamic **buffet** may assist in identifying the onset of wing stall.

Very heavy **rain** can **increase** the stall speed due to the film of water altering the **aerodynamic** contour of the wing.

A **stall** must occur before a spin can take place.

In a steady spin, **both** wings are stalled, one more than the other.

A spin may also develop if forces on the aircraft are unbalanced in other ways, for example, from yaw forces due to an **engine** failure on a multi-engine aircraft, or if the **CG** is laterally displaced by an unbalanced **fuel** load.

The following is a general recovery procedure for erect spins:-

1. Move the throttle or throttles to **idle**.
2. **Neutralise** the ailerons.
3. Apply full **rudder** against the spin.
4. Move the **elevator** control briskly to approximately the neutral position.
5. **Hold** the recommended control positions until rotation stops.
6. As rotation stops, neutralise the **rudder**.
7. Recover from the resulting dive with **gradual** back pressure on the **pitch** control.

A crossed-control stall can be avoided by maintaining the **ball** of the slip indicator in the **middle**.

A stall can occur at any **speed** or flight **attitude** if the **critical** angle of attack is exceeded.

A secondary stall can be triggered either by not **decreasing** the angle of **attack** enough at stall warning or by not allowing sufficient **time** for the aircraft to begin **flying** again before attempting to **regain** lost altitude.

PRINCIPLES OF FLIGHT — STALLING

An added complication during an accidental stall and recovery of a single engine propeller aircraft is due to the **rolling** and **yawing** forces generated by the **propeller**. It is essential to maintain balanced, co-ordinated flight, particularly at **low** airspeed, high angles of **attack.**

In whatever configuration, attitude, or power setting a stall warning occurs, the correct pilot action is to **decrease** the angle of attack below the **stall** angle to un-stall the **wing**, apply maximum allowable **power** to minimise altitude loss and prevent any **yaw** from developing to minimise the possibility of **spinning**. "Keep the **ball** in the middle".

If a large shockwave forms on the wing, due to an inadvertent overspeed. The locally increased **adverse** pressure gradient will cause the **boundary layer** to separate immediately **behind** the shock wave. This is called '**shock** stall'.

CHAPTER 8 - HIGH LIFT DEVICES

Contents

	Page
PURPOSE OF HIGH LIFT DEVICES	8 - 1
TAKE-OFF AND LANDING SPEEDS	
$C_{L\,MAX}$ AUGMENTATION	
FLAPS	
TRAILING EDGE FLAPS	
PLAIN FLAP	
SPLIT FLAP	8 - 2
SLOTTED AND MULTIPLE SLOTTED FLAPS	
FOWLER FLAP	8 - 3
COMPARISON OF TRAILING EDGE FLAPS	
$C_{L\,MAX}$ AND STALLING ANGLE	8 - 4
DRAG	8 - 5
LIFT / DRAG RATIO	8 - 6
PITCHING MOMENT	
CENTRE OF PRESSURE MOVEMENT	
CHANGE OF DOWNWASH	
OVERALL PITCH CHANGE	8 - 7
AIRCRAFT ATTITUDE WITH FLAPS LOWERED	
LEADING EDGE HIGH LIFT DEVICES	8 - 8
LEADING EDGE FLAPS	
KRUEGER FLAP	
VARIABLE CAMBER LEADING EDGE FLAP	8 - 9
EFFECT OF LEADING EDGE FLAPS ON LIFT	
LEADING EDGE SLOTS	8 - 10
LEADING EDGE SLAT	
AUTOMATIC SLOTS	8 - 12
DISADVANTAGES OF THE SLOT	
DRAG AND PITCHING MOMENT OF LEADING EDGE DEVICES	
TRAILING EDGE PLUS LEADING EDGE DEVICES	
SEQUENCE OF OPERATION	8 - 13
ASYMMETRY OF HIGH LIFT DEVICES	8 - 14
FLAP LOAD RELIEF SYSTEM	
CHOICE OF FLAP SETTING FOR TAKE-OFF CLIMB AND LANDING	
MANAGEMENT OF HIGH LIFT DEVICES	8 - 16
FLAP RETRACTION AFTER TAKE OFF	
FLAP EXTENSION PRIOR TO LANDING	8 - 18
SELF ASSESSMENT QUESTIONS	8 - 19
ANSWERS	8 - 25

PRINCIPLES OF FLIGHT — HIGH LIFT DEVICES

8.1 PURPOSE OF HIGH LIFT DEVICES

Aircraft are fitted with high lift devices to reduce the take-off and landing distances. This permits operation at greater weights from given runway lengths and enables greater payloads to be carried.

8.2 TAKE-OFF AND LANDING SPEEDS

The take-off and landing distances depend on the speeds required at the screen, and these are laid down in the performance regulations. For both take-off and landing, one of the requirements is for a safe margin above the stalling speed ($1.2\ V_{S1}$ for take-off and $1.3\ V_{SO}$ for landing). The stalling speed is determined by the C_{LMAX} of the wing, and so to obtain the lowest possible distances, the C_{LMAX}, must be as high as possible.

8.3 C_{LMAX} AUGMENTATION

One of the main factors which determine the C_{LMAX} of an aerofoil section is the camber. It has been shown (Pages 5-8 and 5-9) that increasing the camber of an aerofoil section increases the C_L at a given angle of attack and increases C_{LMAX}. For take-off and landing a cambered section is desirable, but this would give high drag at cruising speeds and require a very nose down attitude. It is usual to select a less cambered aerofoil section to optimise cruise and modify the section for take-off and landing by the use of flaps.

8.4 FLAPS

A flap is a hinged portion of the trailing or leading edge which can be deflected downwards and so produce an increase of camber. For low speed aerofoils the flaps will be on the trailing edge only, but on high speed aerofoils where the leading edge may be symmetrical or have a negative camber, there will usually be flaps on both the leading edge and the trailing edge.

8.5 TRAILING EDGE FLAPS

The basic principle of the flap has been adapted in many ways. The more commonly used types of trailing edge flap are considered below.

8.6 PLAIN FLAP

The plain flap, illustrated in Fig. 8.1, has a simple construction and gives a good increase in C_{LMAX}, although with fairly high drag. It is used mainly on low speed aircraft and where very short take-off and landing is not required.

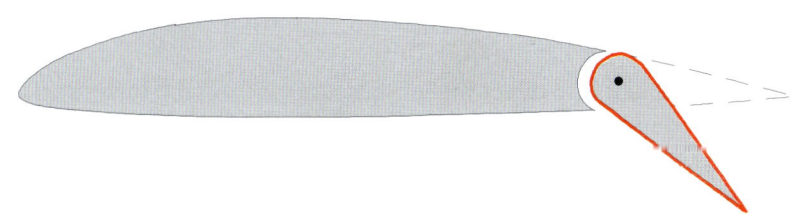

Figure 8.1 Plain Flap

PRINCIPLES OF FLIGHT   **HIGH LIFT DEVICES**

8.7 SPLIT FLAP

The flap forms part of the lower surface of the wing trailing edge, the upper surface contour being unaffected when the flap is lowered.

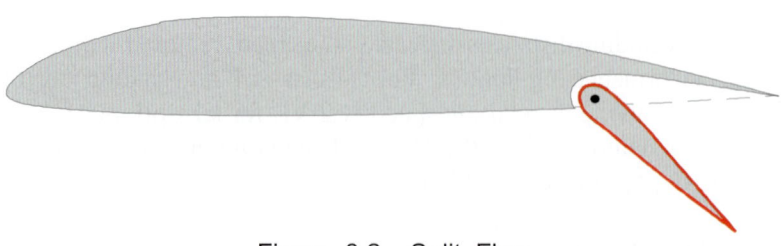

Figure 8.2   Split Flap

The split flap gives about the same increase in lift as the plain flap at low angles of attack, but gives slightly more at higher angles as the upper surface camber is not increased and so separation is delayed. The drag however is higher than for the plain flap due to the increased depth of the wake.

8.8 SLOTTED AND MULTIPLE SLOTTED FLAPS

When the slotted flap is lowered a slot or gap is opened between the flap and the wing.

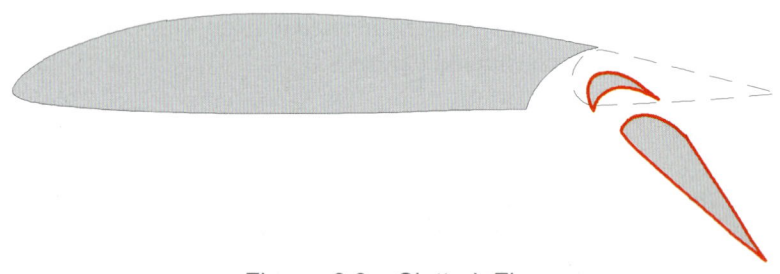

Figure 8.3   Slotted Flap

The purpose of the slot is to direct higher pressure air from the lower surface over the flap and re-energise the boundary layer. This delays the separation of the airflow on the upper surface of the flap. The slotted flap gives a bigger increase in C_{LMAX} than the plain or split flap and much less drag, but has a more complex construction.

PRINCIPLES OF FLIGHT   **HIGH LIFT DEVICES**

8.9 THE FOWLER FLAP

The Fowler flap, Fig. 8.4, **moves rearwards and then down**, initially giving an increase in wing area and then an increase in camber. The Fowler flap may be slotted.

First selection moves flap rearwards only.

Fowler Flap

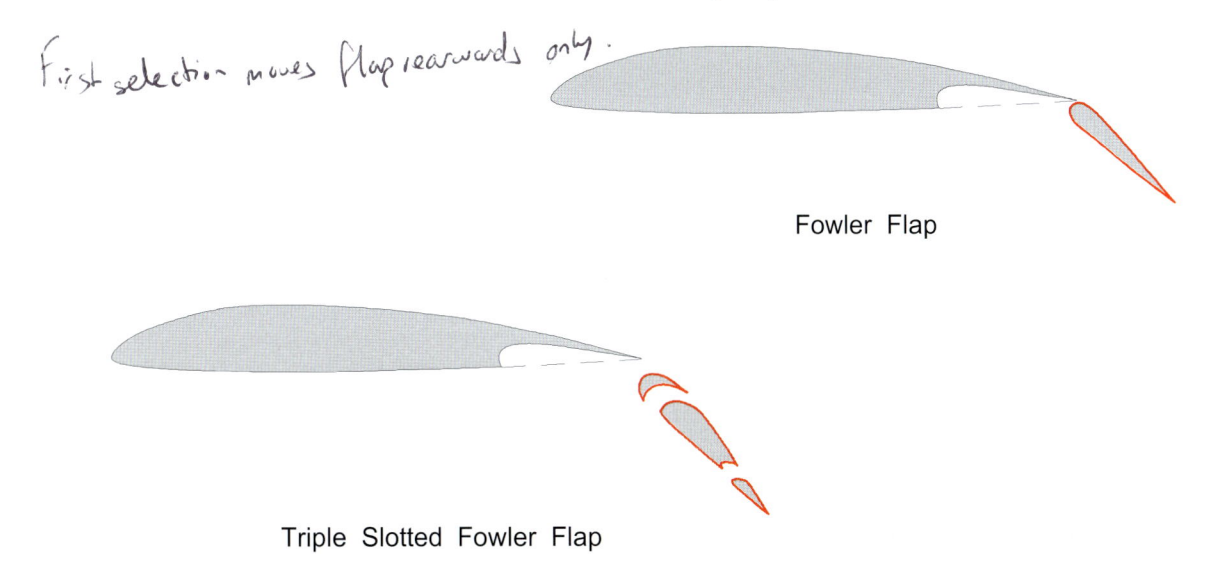

Triple Slotted Fowler Flap

Figure 8.4

Because of the combined effects of increased area and camber, the Fowler flap gives the greatest increase in lift of the flaps considered, and also gives the least drag because of the slot and the reduction of thickness : chord ratio. However the change of pitching moment is greater because of the rearward extension of the chord.

8.10 COMPARISON OF TRAILING EDGE FLAPS

Figure 8.5 shows a comparison of the lift curves for the flaps considered above, for the same angle of flap deflection. It should be noted however that the different types of flap do not all give their greatest increase in lift at the same flap angle.

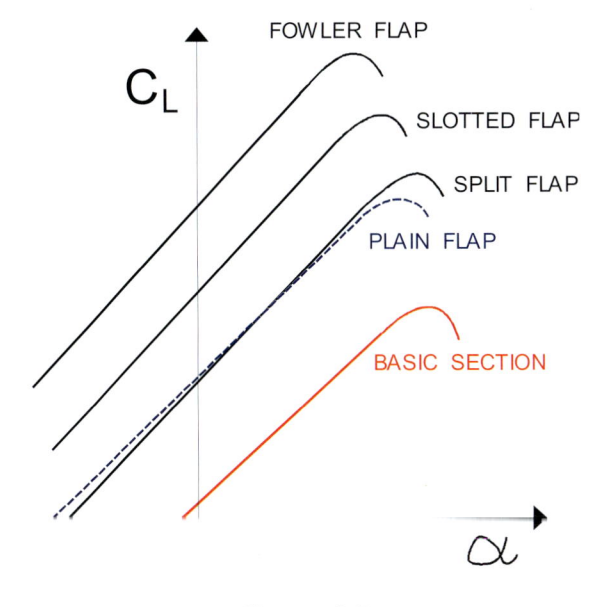

Figure 8.5

PRINCIPLES OF FLIGHT   HIGH LIFT DEVICES

Figure 8.6 shows the variation of the lift increment with increasing flap angle. It can be seen that the increments are reducing as the flap angle increases, and that beyond some optimum flap angle the increments decrease.

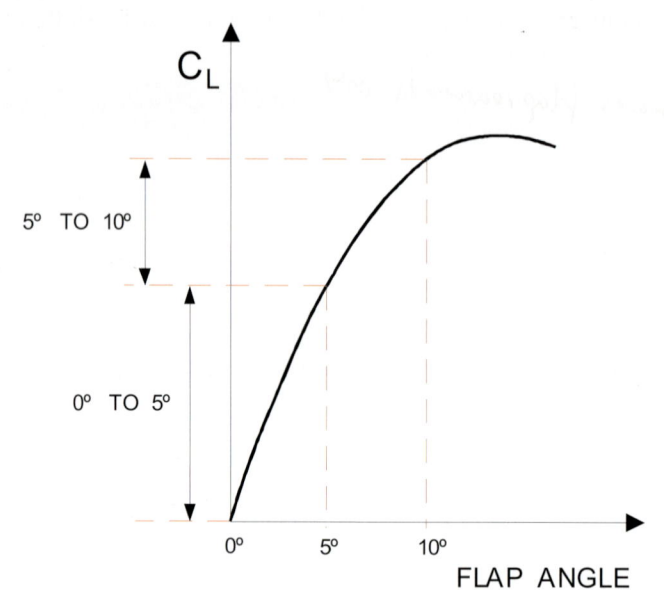

Figure 8.6

8.11 $C_{L\,MAX}$ AND STALLING ANGLE

It can be seen from Figure 8.5 that with the flap lowered $C_{L\,MAX}$ is increased, but the stalling angle is reduced. This is because lowering the flap increases the effective angle of attack.

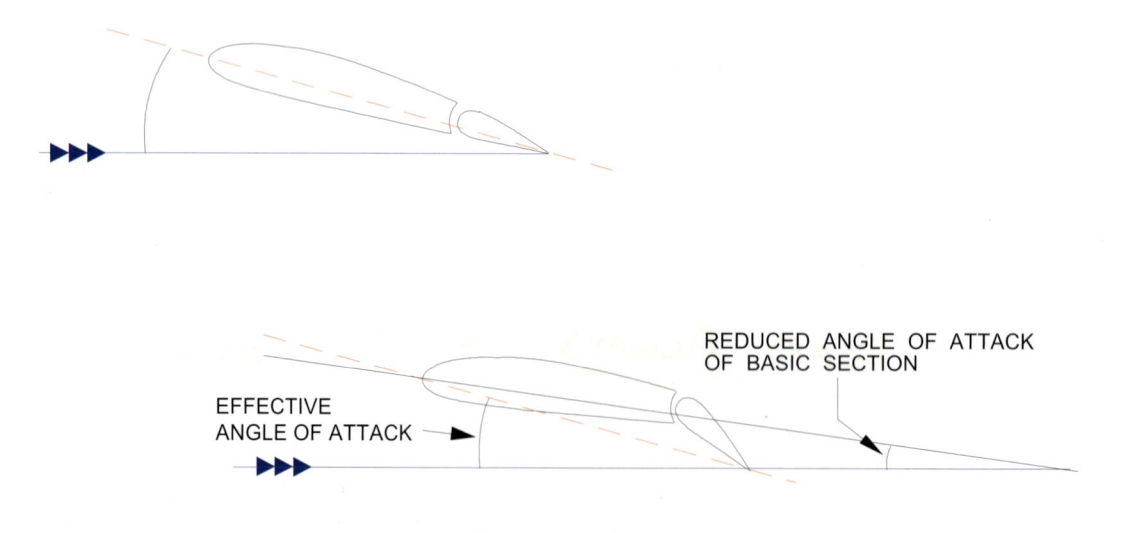

Figure 8.7

It is conventional to plot the $C_L \sim \alpha$ curve using the angle of attack for the basic section. Consequently, as shown in Fig. 8.7, at the stalling angle of attack for the section with flap lowered, the basic wing section is at a reduced angle.

FLAPS REDUCE ABILITY TO CLIMB.

PRINCIPLES OF FLIGHT   **HIGH LIFT DEVICES**

8.12 DRAG

Fig. 8.8 shows a comparison of the drag polar curves for the various types of flap. It can be seen that for a given flap deflection the drag produced by the different types of flap varies considerably, the split flap giving the highest drag and the Fowler flap the least.

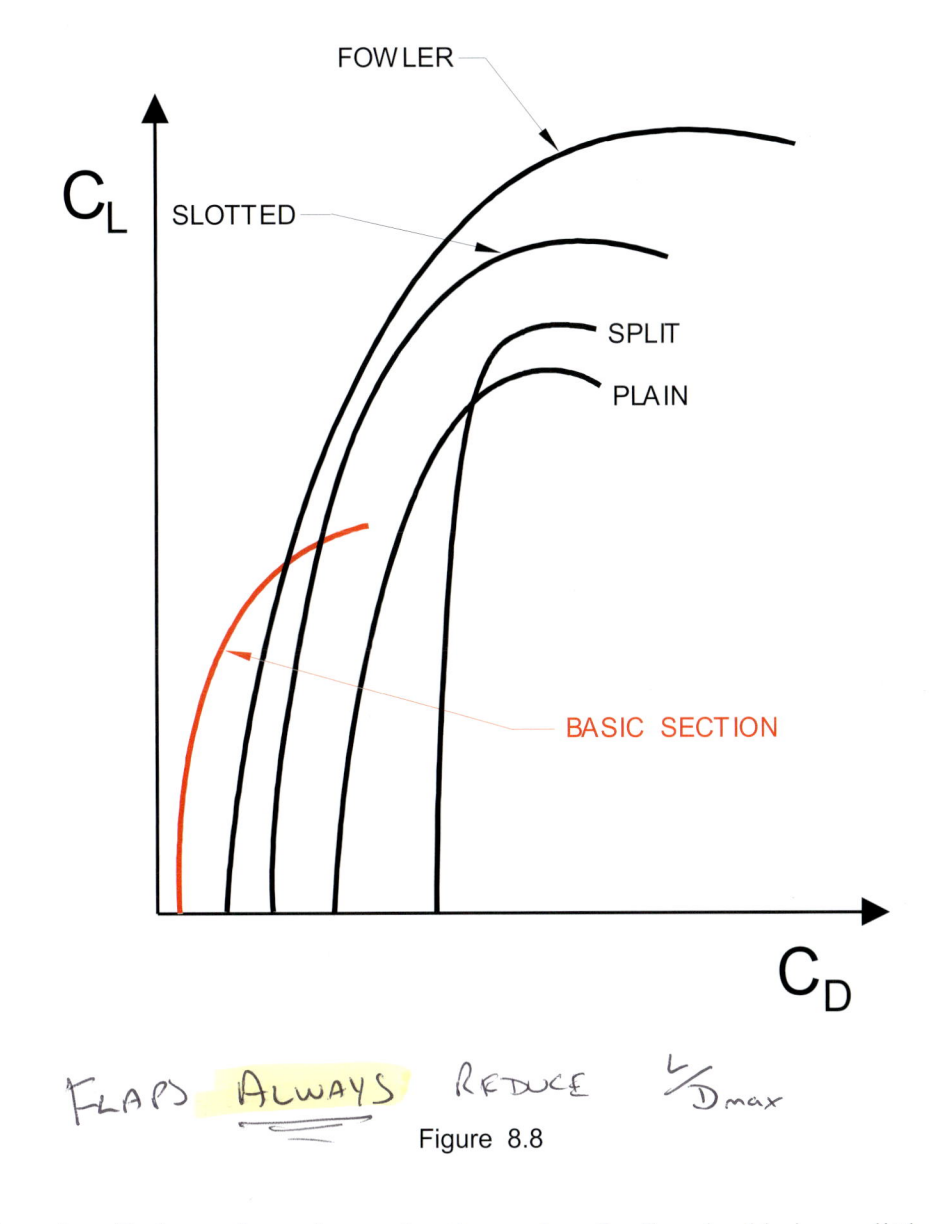

FLAPS ALWAYS REDUCE L/D_{max}

Figure 8.8

During take-off, drag reduces the acceleration, and so the flap should give as little drag as possible. For landing however, drag adds to the braking force and so the flap drag is beneficial. The addition of drag during approach also improves speed stability, see Para. 6.11.

As in the case of the lift increments, the drag increments with increasing flap angle are not constant, the increments in drag get larger as the flap angle increases.

PRINCIPLES OF FLIGHT　　　　　　　　　　　　　　　HIGH LIFT DEVICES

8.13　LIFT / DRAG RATIO

Lowering flap increases both the lift and the drag, but not in the same proportion. Although the lift is the larger force, the proportional increase in the drag is greater, and so the maximum obtainable **lift / drag ratio** decreases. The maximum lift / drag ratio occurs where the tangent from the origin of the drag polar touches the curve, and the gradient of the tangent line is a measure of the maximum lift / drag ratio (Figure 8.9).

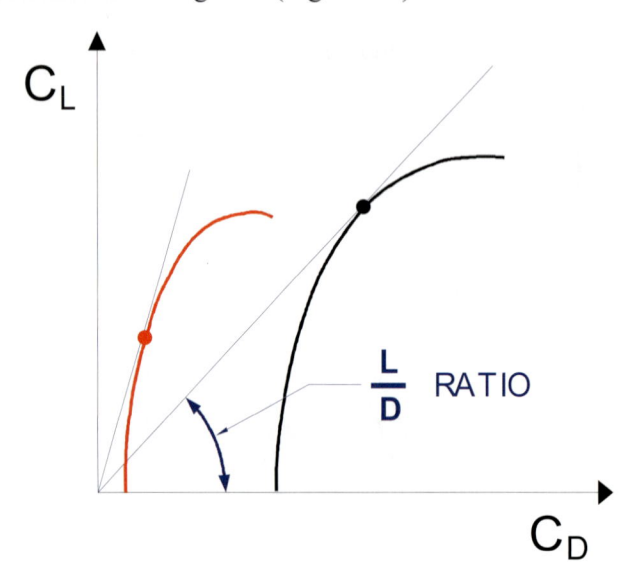

Figure 8.9　L / D Ratio

The lift / drag ratio is a measure of aerodynamic efficiency and affects the aircraft's performance in areas such as range, climb angle and glide angle. With flaps lowered, range will be decreased, climb angle reduced and glide angle increased.

8.14　PITCHING MOMENT

Flap movement, up or down, will usually cause a change of pitching moment. This is due to Centre of Pressure (CP) movement and downwash at the tailplane.

8.15　CENTRE OF PRESSURE MOVEMENT

Moving a trailing edge flap will modify the pressure distribution over the whole chord of the aerofoil, but the greatest changes will occur in the region of the flap. When flap is lowered, the Centre of Pressure will move rearwards giving a nose down pitching moment, Fig. 8.10a. In the case of a Fowler flap, rearward movement of the flap will also cause the CP to move aft, resulting in an even greater increase in the nose-down pitching moment.

8.16　CHANGE OF DOWNWASH

Tailplane effective angle of attack is determined by the downwash from the wing. If the flaps are lowered the downwash will increase and the tailplane angle of attack will decrease, causing a nose-up pitching moment, Fig. 8.10b.

PRINCIPLES OF FLIGHT   HIGH LIFT DEVICES

WING | TAILPLANE

CP (wing, flaps up) — DOWNWASH

CP (wing, flaps down, moved aft) — INCREASED DOWNWASH

NOSE DOWN PITCHING MOMENT | NOSE UP PITCHING MOMENT

Figure 8.10a   Figure 8.10b

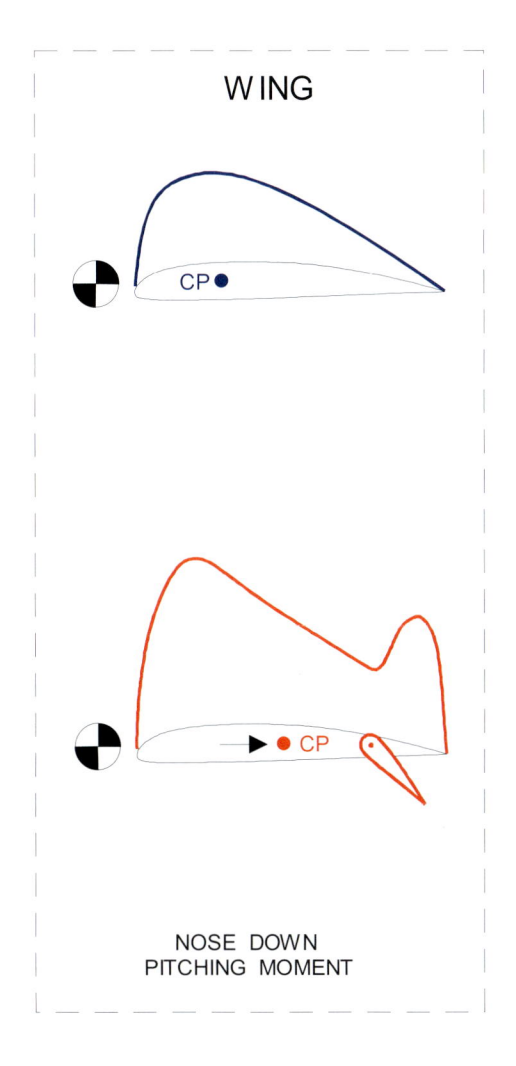

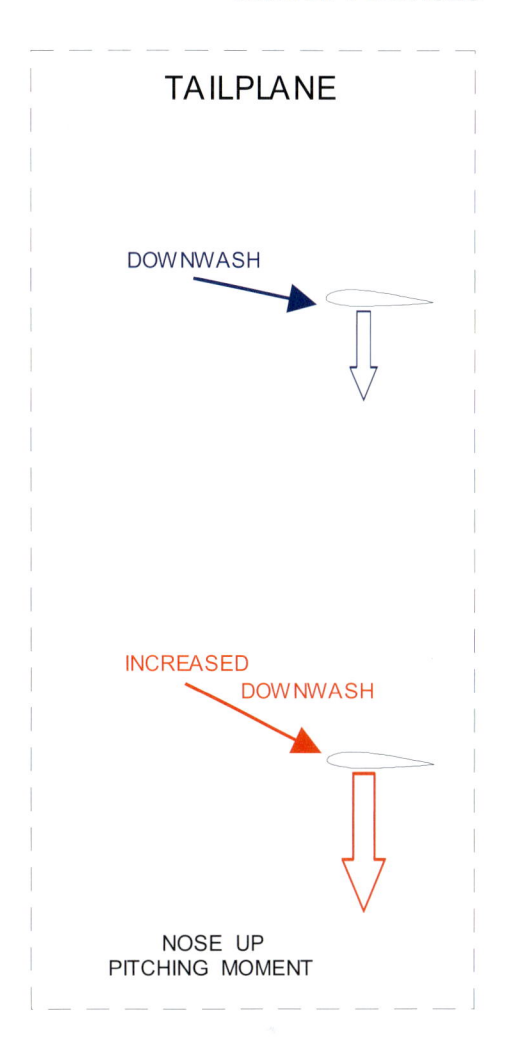

Fowler Flap with T-tail, nose down.

8.17 OVERALL PITCH CHANGE

The resultant aircraft pitching moment will depend upon which of the two effects is dominant. The pitching moment will be influenced by the type of flap, the position of the wing and relative position of the tailplane, and may be nose-up, nose-down, or almost zero. For example, on flap extension, a tailplane mounted on top of the fin will be less influenced by the change of downwash, resulting in an increased aircraft nose down pitching moment.

8.18 AIRCRAFT ATTITUDE WITH FLAPS LOWERED

When the aircraft is in steady flight the lift must be equal to the weight. If the flaps are lowered but the speed kept constant, lift will increase, and to maintain it at its original value the angle of attack must be decreased. The aircraft will therefore fly in a more nose-down attitude if the flaps are down. On the approach to landing this is an advantage as it gives better visibility of the landing area.

PRINCIPLES OF FLIGHT   HIGH LIFT DEVICES

8.19 LEADING EDGE HIGH LIFT DEVICES

There are two forms of leading edge high lift device commonly in use, the leading edge flap and the leading edge slot or slat.

8.20 LEADING EDGE FLAPS

On high speed aerofoil sections the leading edge may have very little camber and have a small radius. This can give flow separation just aft of the leading edge at quite low angles of attack. This can be remedied by utilising a leading edge flap which increases the leading edge camber.

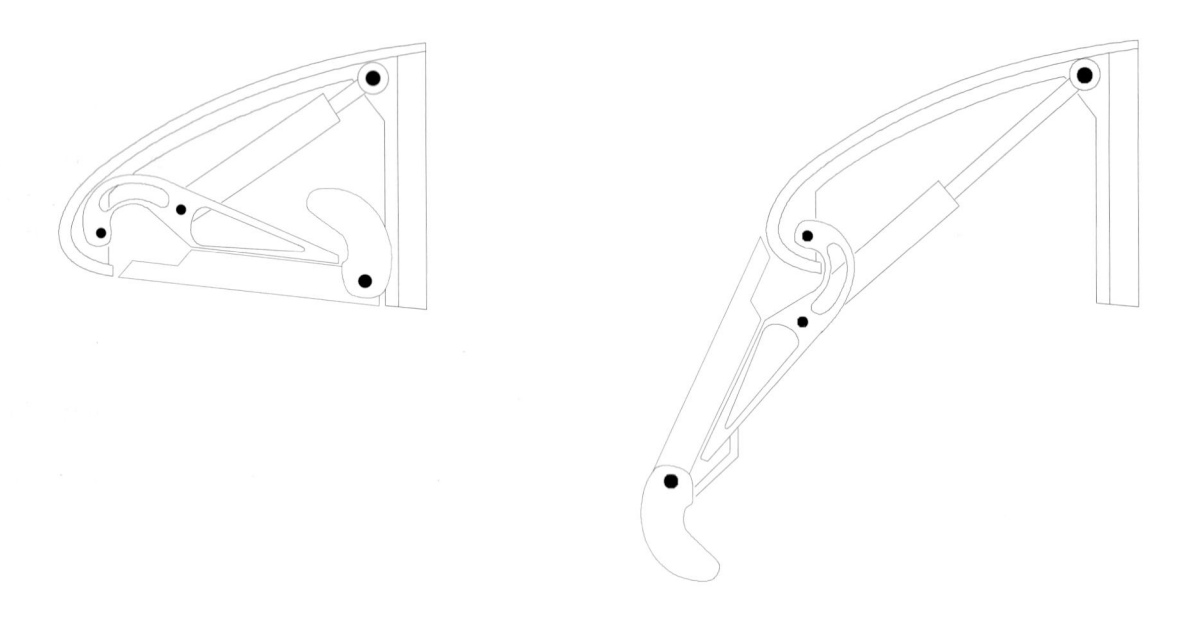

Figure 8.11   Krueger flap

8.20.1 KRUEGER FLAP

The Krueger flap is part of the lower surface of the leading edge, which can be rotated about its forward edge as shown in Fig. 8.11. To promote root stall on a swept wing, Krueger flaps are used on the inboard section because they are less efficient than the variable camber shown opposite.

PRINCIPLES OF FLIGHT
HIGH LIFT DEVICES

EXTENDED

RETRACTED

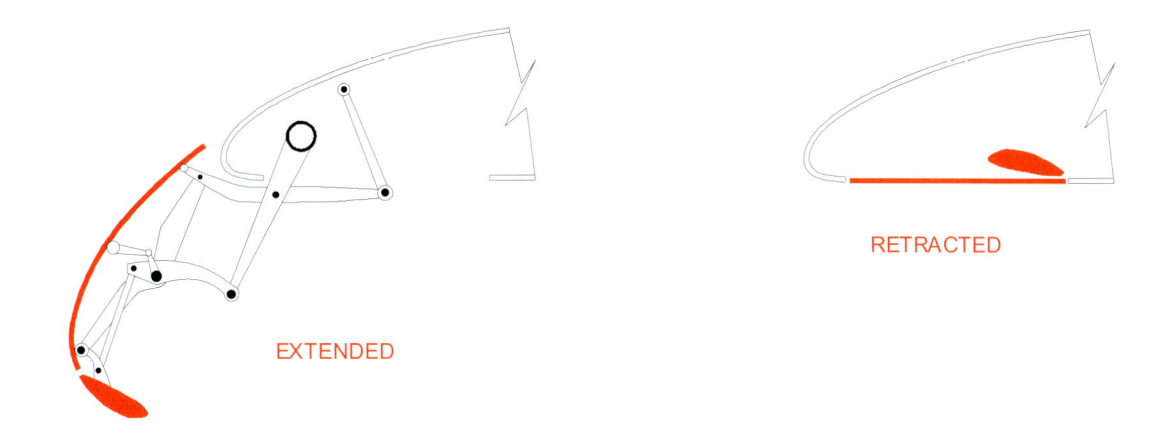

Figure 8.12 Variable camber leading edge flap

8.20.2 VARIABLE CAMBER LEADING EDGE FLAP

To improve efficiency by giving a better leading edge profile, the camber of a leading edge flap may be increased as it is deployed. Unlike trailing edge flaps which can be selected to intermediate positions, leading edge devices are either fully extended (deployed) or retracted (stowed).

8.21 EFFECT OF LEADING EDGE FLAPS ON LIFT

The main effect of the leading edge flap is to delay separation, so **increase the stalling angle** and the corresponding $C_{L\ MAX}$. However there will be some increase of lift at lower angles of attack due to the increased camber of the aerofoil section. Figure 8.13 shows the effect of these flaps on the lift curve.

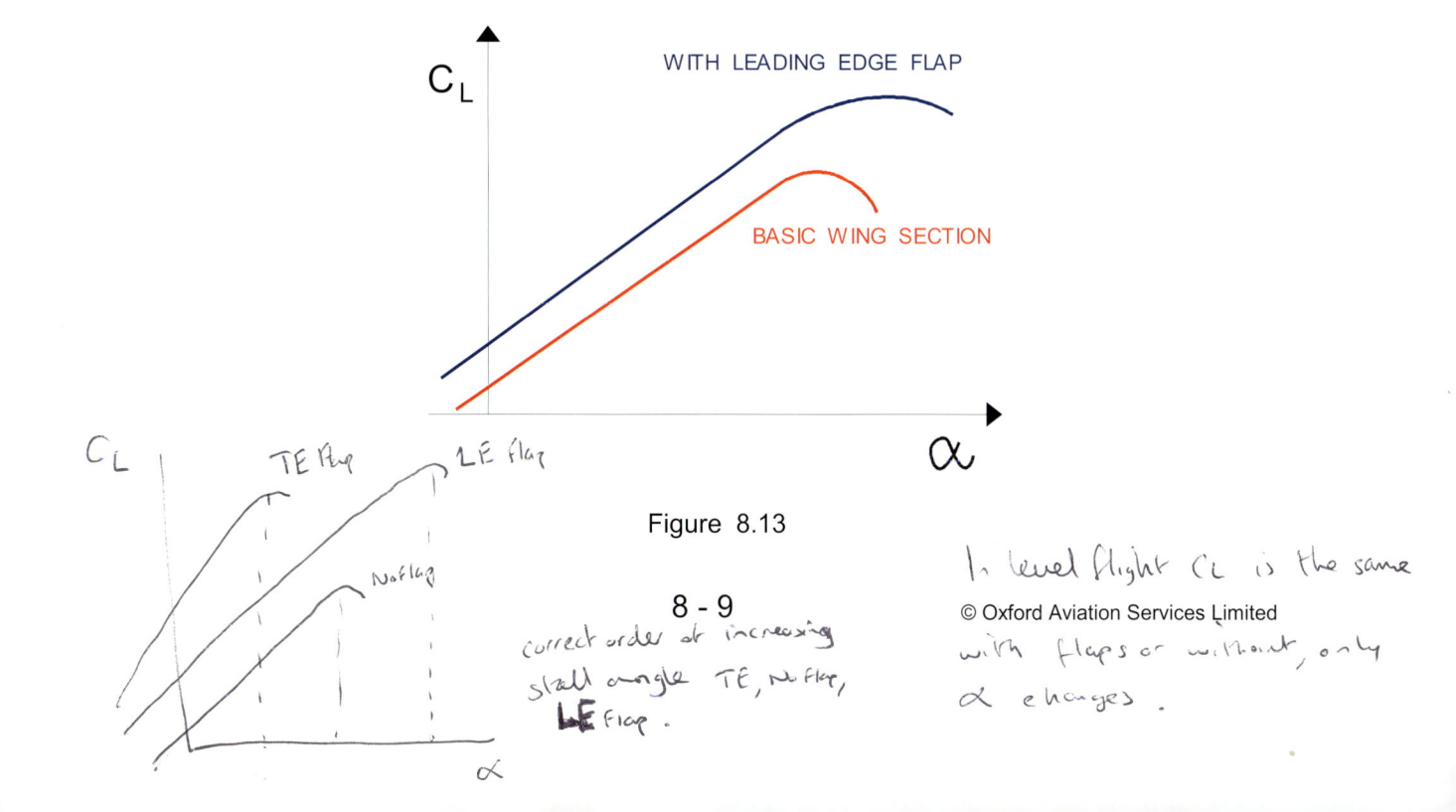

Figure 8.13

PRINCIPLES OF FLIGHT HIGH LIFT DEVICES

8.22 LEADING EDGE SLOTS

A leading edge slot is a gap from the lower surface to the upper surface of the leading edge, and may be fixed, or created by moving part of the leading edge (the slat) forwards.

$C_{L_{max}}$ WING   (Given Adverse Pressure Gradient)

SLAT

SLAT OPEN - Boundary Layer Re - Energised

(Same Adverse Pressure Gradient)

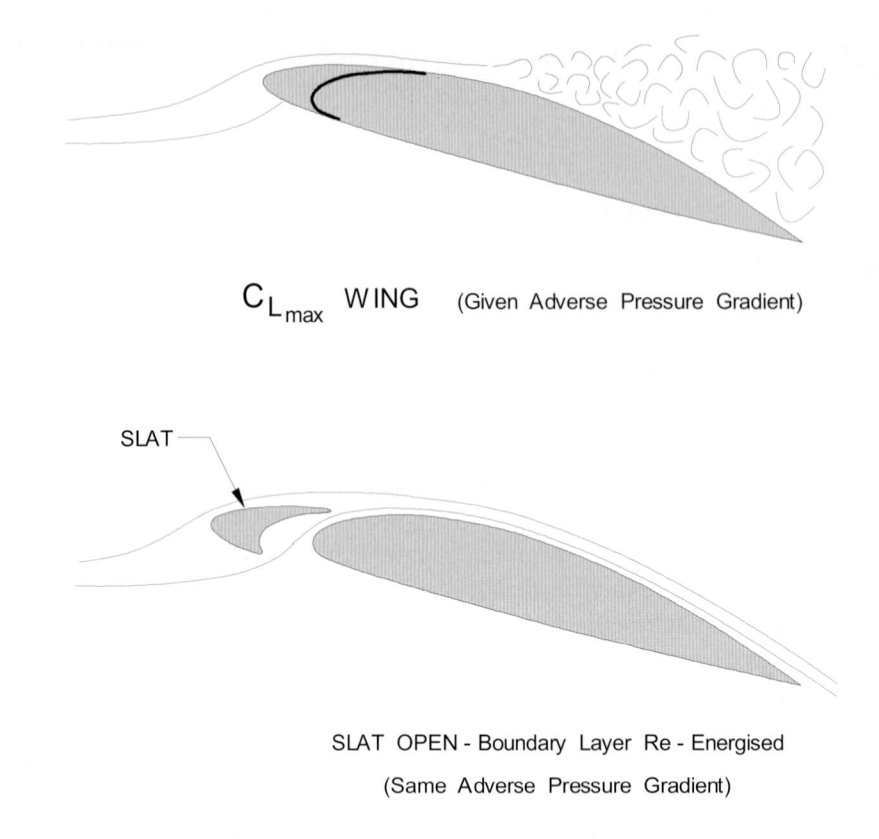

Figure 8.14   Leading edge slat

8.23 LEADING EDGE SLAT

A slat is a small auxiliary aerofoil attached to the leading edge of the wing, Fig. 8.14. When deployed, the slat forms a slot which allows passage of air from the high pressure region below the wing to the low pressure region above it. Additional Kinetic Energy is added to the airflow through the slot by the slat forming a convergent duct.

When slats are deployed the boundary layer is re-energised

If Kinetic Energy is added to the boundary layer, boundary layer separation will be delayed to a much higher angle of attack. At approximately 25°, the increased adverse pressure gradient will once again overwhelm the Kinetic Energy of the boundary layer and separation will occur.

If the slot is permanently open, i.e. a fixed slot, the extra drag at high speed is an unnecessary disadvantage, so most slats in commercial use are opened and closed by a control mechanism.

The slot can be closed for high speed flight and opened for low speeds, usually in conjunction with the trailing edge flaps and actuated by the same selector on the flight deck.

PRINCIPLES OF FLIGHT **HIGH LIFT DEVICES**

The graph at Fig.8.15 shows the comparative figures for a slatted and un-slatted wing of the same basic dimensions.

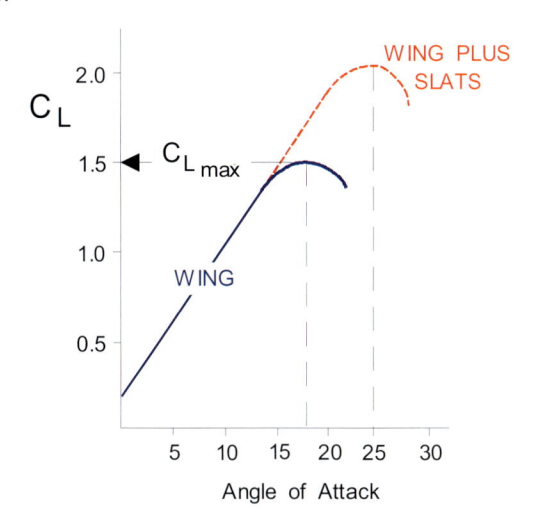

Figure 8.15

The effect of the slat is to prolong the lift curve by delaying boundary layer separation until a higher angle of attack. When operating at high angles of attack the slat itself is generating a high lift coefficient because of its marked camber. The action of the slat is to flatten the marked peak of the low-pressure envelope at high angles of attack and to change it to one with a more gradual pressure gradient. The flattening of the lift distribution envelope means that the boundary layer does not undergo the sudden thickening that occurred through having to negotiate the very steep adverse pressure gradient that existed immediately behind the former suction peak, and so it retains much of its Kinetic Energy, thus enabling it to penetrate almost the full chord of the wing before separating. Fig. 8.16 shows the alleviating effect of the slat on the low pressure peak and that, although flatter, the area of the low pressure region, which is proportional to its strength, is unchanged or even increased. **The 'suction' peak does not move forward, so the effect of the slot on pitching moment is insignificant.**

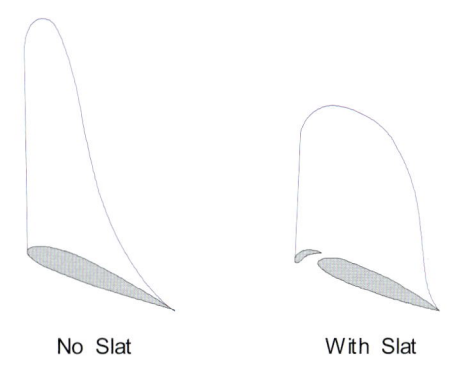

Figure 8.16

8.24 AUTOMATIC SLOTS

On some aircraft the slots are not controlled by the pilot, but operate automatically. Their movement is caused by the changes of pressure which occur around the leading edge as the angle of attack increases. At low angles of attack the high pressures around the stagnation point keep the slat in the closed position. At high angles of attack the stagnation point has moved underneath the leading edge and 'suction' pressures occur on the upper surface of the slat. These pressures cause the slat to move forward and create the slot.

This system is used mainly on small aircraft as a stall protection system. On larger aircraft the position of the slats is selected when required by the pilot, their movement being controlled electrically or hydraulically.

8.25 DISADVANTAGES OF THE SLOT

The slot can give increases in C_{LMAX} of the same magnitude as the trailing edge flap, but whereas the trailing edge flap gives its C_{LMAX} at slightly less than the normal stalling angle, the slot requires a much increased angle of attack to give its C_{LMAX}. In flight this means that the aircraft will have a very nose-up attitude at low speeds and on the approach to land, visibility of the landing area could be restricted.

8.26 DRAG AND PITCHING MOMENT OF LEADING EDGE DEVICES

Compared to trailing edge flaps the changes of drag and pitching moment resulting from the operation of leading edge devices are small.

8.27 TRAILING EDGE PLUS LEADING EDGE DEVICES

Most large transport aircraft employ both trailing edge and leading edge devices. Fig. 8.17 shows the effect on the lift curve of both types of device.

PRINCIPLES OF FLIGHT **HIGH LIFT DEVICES**

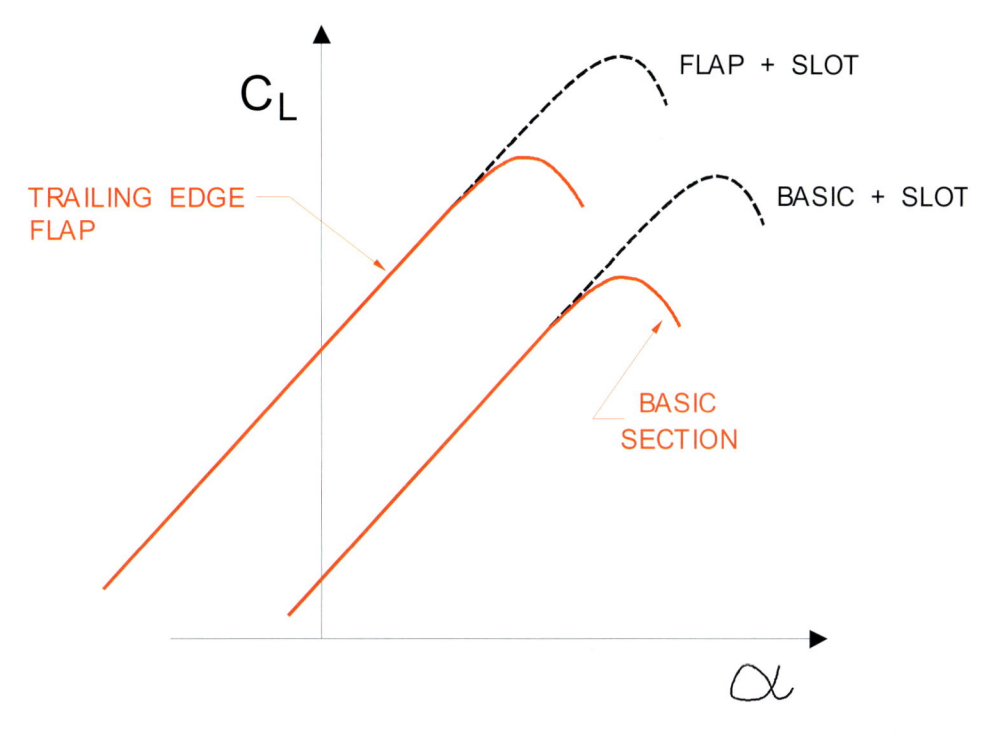

Figure 8.17

8.28 SEQUENCE OF OPERATION

For some aerofoils the sequence of flap operation is critical. Lowering a trailing edge flap increases both the downwash and the upwash. For a high speed aerofoil, an increase of upwash at the leading edge when the angle of attack is already fairly high, could cause the wing to stall. The leading edge device must therefore be deployed before the trailing edge flap is lowered. When the flaps are retracted the trailing edge flap must be retracted before the leading edge device is raised.

PRINCIPLES OF FLIGHT　　　　　　　　　　　HIGH LIFT DEVICES

8.29　ASYMMETRY OF HIGH LIFT DEVICES

Deployment of high lift devices can produce large changes of lift, drag and pitching moment. If the movement of the devices is not symmetrical on the two wings, the unbalanced forces could cause severe roll control problems. On many flap control systems the deflection on the two sides is compared while the flaps are moving, and if one side should fail, movement on the other side is automatically stopped. However on less sophisticated systems, a failure of the operating mechanism could lead to an asymmetric situation. The difference in lift will cause a rolling moment which must be opposed by the ailerons, and the difference in drag will cause a yawing moment which must be opposed by the rudder. Whether the controls will be adequate to maintain straight and level flight will depend on the degree of asymmetry and the control power available.

8.30　FLAP LOAD RELIEF SYSTEM

On large high speed jet transport aircraft, a device is fitted in the flap operating system to prevent the flaps deploying if the aircraft speed is too high. The pilot can select the flaps, but they will not extend until the airspeed is below the flap extend speed (V_{FE}). If a selection is made, and the flaps do not run because the speed is too high, they will extend as soon as the airspeed decreases to an appropriate value.

8.31　CHOICE OF FLAP SETTING FOR TAKE-OFF, CLIMB AND LANDING

1. TAKEOFF
Takeoff distance depends upon unstick speed and rate of acceleration to that speed.

a)　　Lowest unstick speed will be possible at the highest C_{LMAX} and this will be achieved at a large flap angle, Fig. 8.18.

b)　　But large flap angles also give high drag, Fig. 8.19, which will reduce acceleration and increase the distance required to accelerate to unstick speed.

c)　　A lower flap angle will give a higher unstick speed, but better acceleration, and so give a shorter distance to unstick.

Thus there will be some optimum setting which will give the shortest possible take-off distance. If leading edge devices are fitted they will be used for take-off as they increase the C_{LMAX} for any trailing edge flap setting.

2. CLIMB
After take-off, a minimum climb gradient is required in the take-off configuration. Climb gradient is reduced by flap, so if climb gradient is limiting, a lesser flap angle may be selected even though it gives a longer take-off distance.

3. LANDING
Landing distance will depend on touchdown speed and deceleration. The lowest touchdown speed will be given by the highest C_{LMAX}, obtained at a large flap angle, Fig. 8.18. Large flap angle will also give high drag, Fig. 8.19, and so good deceleration. For landing, a large flap angle will be used. Leading edge devices will also be used to obtain the highest possible C_{LMAX}.

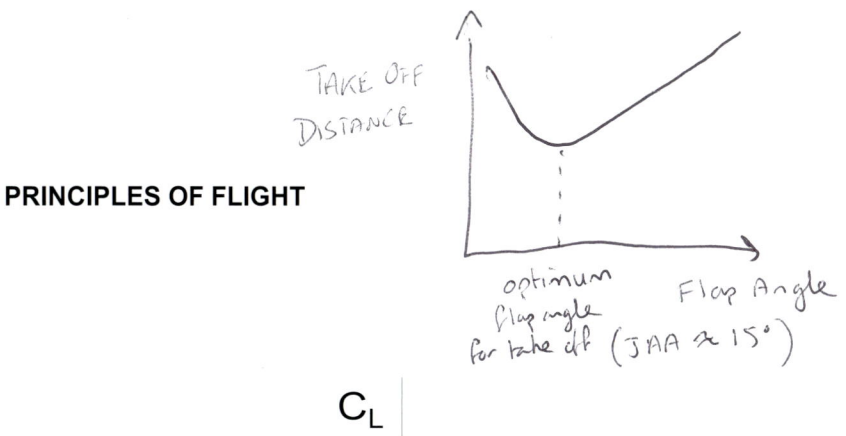

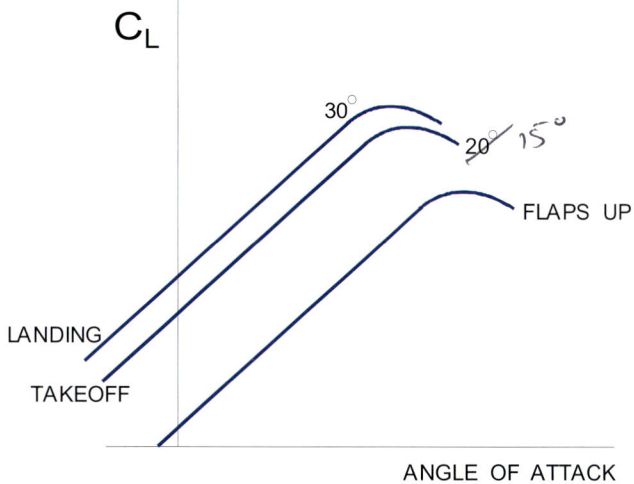

PRINCIPLES OF FLIGHT   **HIGH LIFT DEVICES**

[Handwritten graph: Take off distance vs Flap Angle, showing a curve with minimum at "optimum flap angle for take off (JAA ≈ 15°)"]

Figure 8.18

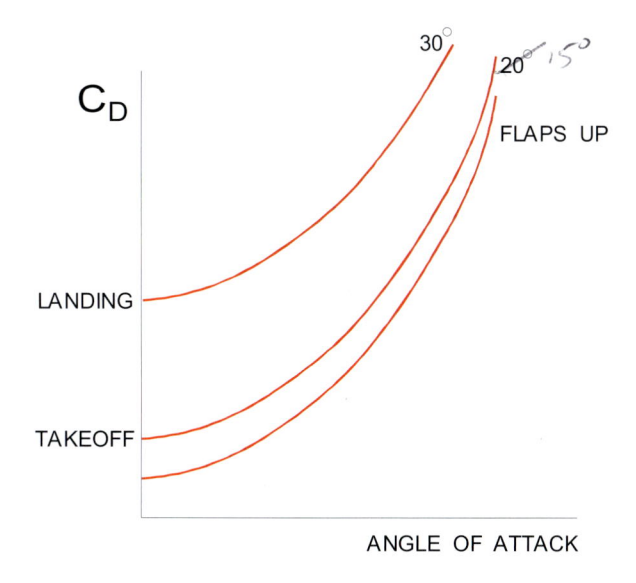

Figure 8.19

PRINCIPLES OF FLIGHT   HIGH LIFT DEVICES

8.32 MANAGEMENT OF HIGH LIFT DEVICES

To take full advantage of the capabilities of flaps the flight crew must properly manage their retraction and extension.

FLAP RETRACTION AFTER TAKE OFF

With reference to Fig. 8.20, assume the aircraft has just taken off with flaps extended and is at point 'A' on the lift curve. If the flaps are retracted, with no change made to either angle of attack or IAS, the coefficient of lift will reduce to point 'C' and the aircraft will sink.

1. From point 'A' on the lift curve the aircraft should be accelerated to point 'B.

2. From point 'B', as the flaps are retracted the angle of attack should be increased to point 'C' to maintain the coefficient of lift constant.

The pilot should not retract the flaps until the aircraft has sufficient IAS. Of course, this same factor must be considered for any intermediate flap position between extended and retracted. (Refer to Page 5-6 for a review of the Interpretation of the Lift Curve if necessary.)

As the configuration is altered from the flaps down to the flaps up or "clean" configuration, three important changes take place:

a) Changes of pressure distribution on the wing generates a nose up pitching moment. But reduced wing downwash increasing the tailplane effective angle of attack generates a nose down pitching moment. The resultant, actual, pitching moment experienced by the aircraft will depend upon which of these two pitching moments is dominant.
    (Ref. Para. 8.15)

b) With reference to Fig. 8.21, the retraction of flaps ('B' to 'C') causes a reduction of drag coefficient. This drag reduction improves the acceleration of the aircraft.

c) Flap retraction usually takes place in stages and movement of the flaps between stages will take a finite period of time. It has been stated that as flaps are retracted, an increase in angle of attack is required to maintain the same lift coefficient.

    If aircraft acceleration is low throughout the flap retraction speed range, the angle of attack must be increased an appreciable amount to prevent the aircraft from sinking. This situation is typical after take off when gross weight and density altitude are high.

    However, most modern jet transport aircraft have enough acceleration throughout the flap retraction speed range that the resultant rapid gain in airspeed requires a much less noticeable increase in angle of attack.

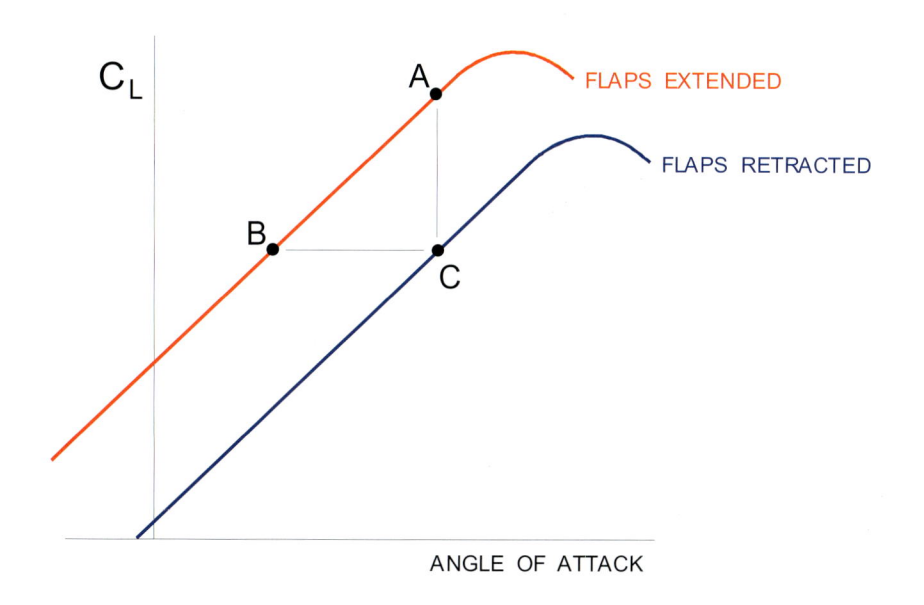

At level flight the CL does nothing as flaps raised or lowered.

PRINCIPLES OF FLIGHT **HIGH LIFT DEVICES**

Figure 8.20

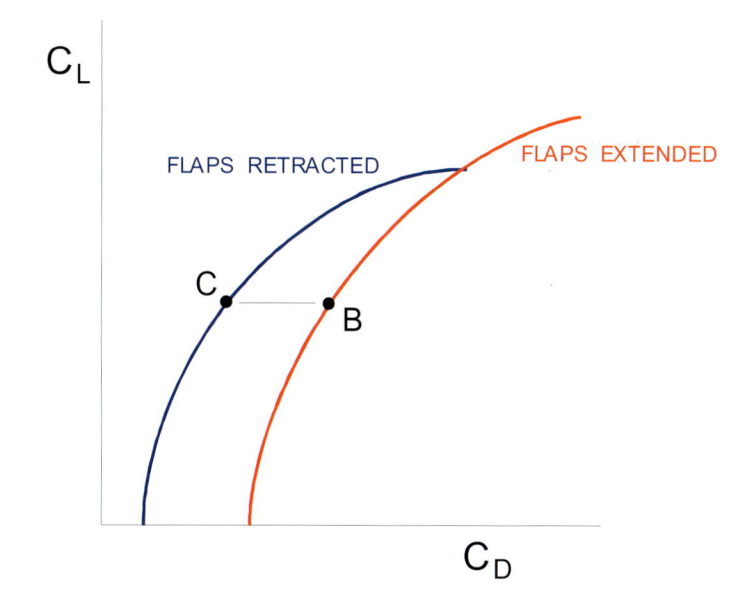

Figure 8.21

8 - 17 © Oxford Aviation Services Limited

PRINCIPLES OF FLIGHT   **HIGH LIFT DEVICES**

FLAP EXTENSION PRIOR TO LANDING

With reference to Fig. 8.22, assume the aircraft is in level flight in the terminal area prior to landing and is at point 'A' on the lift curve. If the flaps are extended, with no change made to angle of attack, the coefficient of lift will increase to point 'C' and the aircraft will gain altitude (balloon).

1. From point 'A', as the flaps are extended the angle of attack should be decreased to point 'B' to maintain the coefficient of lift constant.

2. From point 'B' on the lift curve the aircraft should be decelerated to point 'C'.

(Refer to Page 5-6 for a review of the Interpretation of the Lift Curve if necessary.)

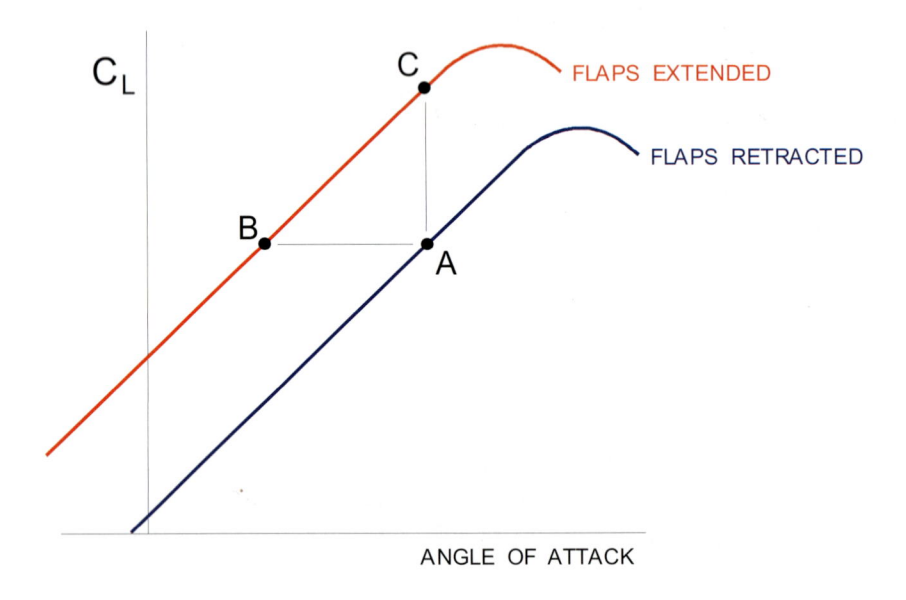

Figure 8.22 Deployment of flaps for landing

SELF ASSESSMENT QUESTIONS

1. With the flaps lowered, the stalling speed will:

   a) increase.
   b) decrease.
   c) increase, but occur at a higher angle of attack.
   d) remain the same.

2. When flaps are lowered the stalling angle of attack of the wing:

   a) remains the same, but $C_{L\,max}$ increases.
   b) increases and $C_{L\,max}$ increases.
   c) decreases, but $C_{L\,max}$ increases.
   d) decreases, but $C_{L\,max}$ remains the same.

3. With full flap, the maximum Lift/drag ratio:

   a) increases and the stalling angle increases
   b) decreases and the stalling speed decreases
   c) remains the same and the stalling angle remains the same
   d) remains the same and the stalling angle decreases

4. When a leading edge slot is opened, the stalling speed will:

   a) increase
   b) decrease
   c) remain the same but will occur at a higher angle of attack.
   d) remain the same but will occur at a lower angle of attack.

5. The purpose of a leading edge droop is:

   a) to give a more cambered section for high speed flight.
   b) to increase the wing area for take-off and landing.
   c) to increase wing camber, and delay separation of the airflow when trailing edge flaps are lowered.
   d) to decrease the lift during the landing run.

6. Lowering flaps sometimes produces a pitch moment change due to:

   a) decrease of the angle of incidence.
   b) movement of the centre of pressure.
   c) movement of the centre of gravity.
   d) increased angle of attack of the tailplane.

7. Which type of flap would give the greatest change in pitching moment?

    a) Split
    b) Plain
    c) Fowler
    d) Plain slotted

8. A split flap is:

    a) a flap divided into sections which open to form slots through the flap.
    b) a flap manufactured in several sections to allow for wing flexing.
    c) a flap which can move up or down from the neutral position.
    d) a flap where the upper surface contour of the wing trailing edge is fixed and only the lower surface contour is altered when the flaps are lowered

9. If the flaps are lowered in flight, with the airspeed kept constant, to maintain level flight the angle of attack:

    a) must be reduced.
    b) must be increased.
    c) must be kept constant but power must be increased.
    d) must be kept constant and power required will be constant.

10. If flaps are lowered during the take-off run:

    a) the lift would not change until the aircraft is airborne.
    b) the lift would increase when the flaps are lowered.
    c) the lift would decrease.
    d) the acceleration would increase.

11. When flaps are lowered the spanwise flow on the upper surface of the wing:

    a) does not change.
    b) increase towards the tip.
    c) increases towards the root.
    d) increases in speed but has no change of direction.

12. If a landing is to be made without flaps the landing speed must be:

    a) reduced.
    b) increased.
    c) the same as for a landing with flaps.
    d) the same as for a landing with flaps but with a steeper approach.

PRINCIPLES OF FLIGHT   **HIGH LIFT DEVICES**

13. Lowering the flaps during a landing approach:

    a) increases the angle of descent without increasing the airspeed
    b) decreases the angle of descent without increasing power
    c) eliminates floating
    d) permits approaches at a higher indicated airspeed

14. With reference to Annex A , the type of flap illustrated is a:

    a) Slotted Krueger flap
    b) Slotted Variable camber flap
    c) Slotted Slat
    d) Slotted Fowler flap

15. With reference to Annex F , the type of flap illustrated is a:

    a) Slat
    b) Fowler flap
    c) Krueger flap
    d) Variable camber flap

INTENTIONALLY LEFT BLANK

PRINCIPLES OF FLIGHT HIGH LIFT DEVICES

Annex A

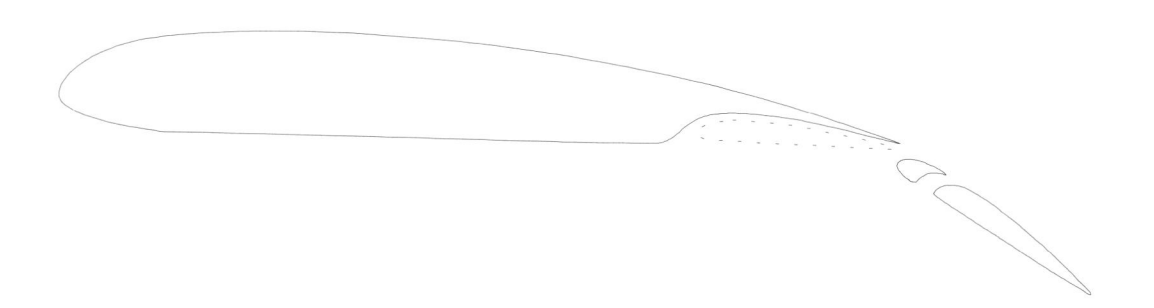

Annex F

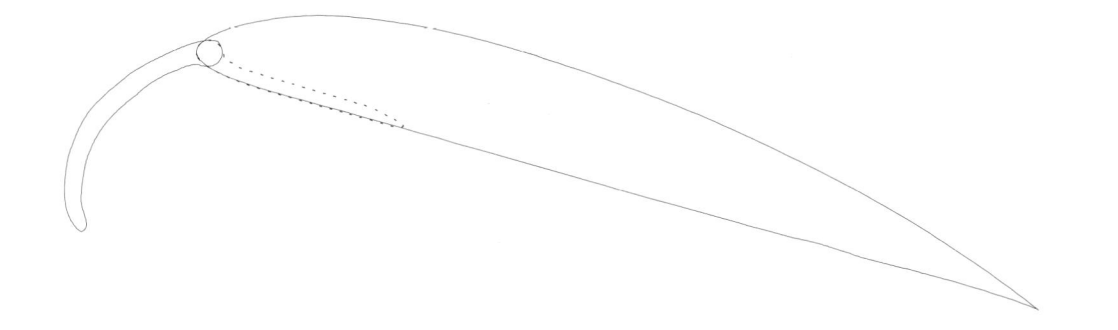

INTENTIONALLY

LEFT

BLANK

ANSWERS

No	A	B	C	D	REF
1		B			
2			C		
3		B			
4		B			
5			C		
6		B			
7			C		
8				D	
9	A				
10		B			
11			C		
12		B			
13	A				
14				D	
15				D	

CHAPTER 9 - AIRFRAME CONTAMINATION

Contents

	Page
INTRODUCTION	9 - 1
TYPES OF CONTAMINATION	
EFFECT OF FROST AND ICE ON THE AIRCRAFT	
EFFECT ON INSTRUMENTS	9 - 2
EFFECT ON CONTROLS	
WATER CONTAMINATION	
AIRFRAME AGING	
SELF ASSESSMENT QUESTIONS	9 - 3
ANSWERS	9 - 5

PRINCIPLES OF FLIGHT   **AIRFRAME CONTAMINATION**

9.1 INTRODUCTION

The airframe may become contaminated by ice, frost or water either whilst it is flight, or when standing on the ground.

The meteorological conditions that cause ice and frost to form are dealt with elsewhere, but the effect is an accumulation of ice or frost on the surface of the aircraft which will affect its performance and handling.

9.2 TYPES OF CONTAMINATION

a)   **Frost**. Frost can form on the surface of the aircraft either when it is standing on the ground when the temperature falls below 0°C, or in flight, if the aircraft, after flying in a region where the temperature is below 0°C, moves into a warmer layer of air. It consists of a fairly thin coating of crystalline ice.

b)   **Ice**. The main forms of icing are clear ice, rime ice and rain ice. Clear ice (glaze ice) is a translucent layer of ice with a smooth surface, caused by large super cooled water droplets, striking the leading edges of the airframe. As there is some delay in freezing, there is some flow back along the surface behind the leading edge.

Rime ice forms when small supercooled water droplets strike the leading edges and freeze almost immediately so that there is no flow back. It is a white opaque formation.

Rain ice is caused by rain which becomes supercooled by falling from an inversion into air which is below 0°C. It does not freeze immediately and forms considerable flow back, and builds up very quickly.

9.3 EFFECT OF FROST AND ICE ON THE AIRCRAFT

The formation of ice and frost on the airframe will:

a)   modify the profile of the aerofoil

b)   increase the roughness of the aircraft surface

c)   increase the weight of the aircraft

The main effect of frost will be to increase the surface roughness and this will increase the energy loss in the boundary layer. The skin friction drag will increase and the boundary layer will have an earlier separation, giving a reduced $C_{L\,MAX}$. Take-off with frost on the wings could result in a stall after lift off if the normal take-off speed is used.

Tests have shown that frost, ice or snow with the thickness and surface roughness of medium or coarse sandpaper, reduces lift by as much as 30% and increases drag by 40%

Ice will normally form on and behind the leading edges of wings and tailplane and can result in severe distortion of the leading edge profile. This will give a large increase in drag and a substantial decrease in $C_{L\,MAX}$.

The reduced $C_{L\,MAX}$ of the wing will give a higher stalling speed and the decreased $C_{L\,MAX}$ of the tailplane could cause it to stall when the aircraft is flying at low speed, particularly if the wing downwash is increased as a result of flap extension.

Tailplane stall will result in loss of longitudinal control. Clear ice and rain ice especially can add considerable weight to the airframe, and this will in turn give a higher stalling speed, as well as increased induced drag. The margin of thrust to drag will be decreased, reducing the ability to climb. Increased power will be required to maintain height, resulting in increased fuel consumption.

Ice formation on propeller blades can upset the balance of the propeller and cause severe vibration, particularly if pieces of ice break off from one blade. Pieces of ice shed from propellers can also cause damage to the fuselage.

9.4 EFFECT ON INSTRUMENTS

Formation of ice on static vents and pitot heads could cause errors in the readings of pressure instruments, and eventually, failure to show any reading.

9.5 EFFECT ON CONTROLS

Any moveable surface could become jammed by ice forming in the gaps around the control, or by pieces of ice breaking off and becoming jammed in the control gaps. The controls could become difficult to operate or immovable.

9.6 WATER CONTAMINATION

If the wings are contaminated with water due to heavy rain, the boundary layer may become turbulent further forward on the wing, particularly if the section is of the laminar flow type. This will cause increased drag and may disrupt the boundary layer resulting in a significantly higher stall speed.

Adjustments to operational speed should be made in accordance with the recommendations of the aircraft manufacturer or aircraft operator, when taking-off and landing in heavy rain.

9.7 AIRFRAME AGING

Over a period of years the condition of the airframe will deteriorate due to small scratches, minor damage, repairs, and general accumulation of dirt and grease.

The overall effect of this will be to increase the drag of the aircraft (mainly skin friction drag) with a consequent increase in fuel consumption. The cost of operating the aircraft will therefore increase with the age of the airframe. The normal deterioration of the airframe is allowed for in the performance charts of the aeroplane.

SELF ASSESSMENT QUESTIONS

1. After an aircraft has been exposed to severe weather:

    a) snow should be removed but smooth ice may be left.
    b) all snow and ice should be removed.
    c) loose snow may be left but ice must be removed.
    d) providing the contamination is not too thick, it may be left in place.

2. Icing conditions may be encountered in the atmosphere when:

    a) relative humidity is low and temperature rises.
    b) pressure is high and humidity falls.
    c) relative humidity is high and temperature is low.
    d) relative pressure is high and temperature is high.

3. Which is an effect of ice, snow, or frost formation on an aeroplane?

    a) Increased angle of attack for stalls.
    b) Increased stall speed.
    c) Increased pitch down tendencies.
    d) Decreased speed for stalling

4. Frost covering the upper surface of an aircraft wing will usually cause:

    a) the aircraft to stall at an angle of attack that is lower than normal
    b) no problems to pilots
    c) drag factors so large that sufficient speed cannot be obtained for take-off
    d) the aircraft to stall at an angle of attack that is higher than normal

5. If it is suspected that ice may have formed on the tailplane and longitudinal control difficulties are experienced following flap selection, the prudent action to take would be:

    a) immediately decrease the flap setting
    b) allow the speed to increase
    c) select a greater flap deflection because this will increase $C_{L\,max}$
    d) reduce the angle of attack

PRINCIPLES OF FLIGHT   **AIRFRAME CONTAMINATION**

6. When considering in-flight airframe contamination with frost or ice, which of the following statements is correct?

    a) Build-up can be identified by the ice detection equipment fitted to the aircraft.
    b) The pilot can visually identify build-up on the wings, tailplane or flight controls by looking through the flight deck windows; at night by using the ice detection lights.
    c) Visual evidence of the accumulation of airframe icing may not exist.
    d) Due to the high speed of modern aircraft, significant airframe contamination with frost, ice or snow will not occur.

7. In the event of an icing-induced wing stall, which of the following indications will reliably be available to the flight crew?

    1 - Activation of the stall warning device (horn or stick shaker).
    2 - The aircraft pitching nose down.
    3 - Loss of elevator effectiveness.
    4 - Airframe buffet.
    5 - A roll control problem (increasing roll oscillation or violent wing drop).
    6 - A high rate of descent.

    a) 1, 2, 3, 4, 5 and 6
    b) 1, 3 and 4
    c) 1, 4 and 6
    d) 4, 5 and 6

PRINCIPLES OF FLIGHT **AIRFRAME CONTAMINATION**

ANSWERS

No	A	B	C	D	REF
1		B			
2			C		
3		B			
4	A				
5	A				
6			C		
7				D	

INTENTIONALLY

LEFT

BLANK

CHAPTER 10 - STABILITY AND CONTROL

Contents

	Page
INTRODUCTION	10 - 1
STATIC STABILITY	
AEROPLANE REFERENCE AXES	10 - 4
STATIC LONGITUDINAL STABILITY	10 - 5
NEUTRAL POINT	10 - 9
STATIC MARGIN	10 - 10
TRIM AND CONTROLLABILITY	10 - 11
KEY FACTS 1 (SELF STUDY)	10 - 14
GRAPHIC PRESENTATION	10 - 17
CONTRIBUTION OF THE COMPONENT SURFACES	10 - 20
WING	
FUSELAGE AND NACELLES	10 - 22
HORIZONTAL TAIL	
LONGITUDINAL DIHEDRAL	10 - 23
DOWNWASH	10 - 24
POWER-OFF STABILITY	10 - 25
EFFECT OF CG POSITION	10 - 26
POWER EFFECTS	10 - 27
HIGH LIFT DEVICES	10 - 29
CONTROL FORCE STABILITY	10 - 30
MANOEUVRE STABILITY	10 - 35
STICK FORCE PER 'G'	10 - 36
TAILORING CONTROL FORCES	10 - 38
STICK CENTRING SPRING	
DOWN SPRING	
BOBWEIGHT	10 - 39
LONGITUDINAL CONTROL	10 - 40
MANOEUVRING CONTROL REQUIREMENTS	
TAKE OFF CONTROL REQUIREMENTS	10 - 41
LANDING CONTROL REQUIREMENTS	10 - 42
DYNAMIC STABILITY	10 - 43
LONGITUDINAL DYNAMIC STABILITY	10 - 47
LONG PERIOD OSCILLATION (PHUGOID)	10 - 48
SHORT PERIOD OSCILLATION	10 - 49

DIRECTIONAL STABILITY AND CONTROL .... 10 - 51
    SIDESLIP ANGLE .... 10 - 52
    STATIC DIRECTIONAL STABILITY .... 10 - 53
    CONTRIBUTION OF THE AEROPLANE COMPONENTS .... 10 - 54
        FUSELAGE
        DORSAL AND VENTRAL FINS .... 10 - 55
        FIN .... 10 - 57
        WING AND NACELLES .... 10 - 58
        POWER EFFECTS .... 10 - 60
        CRITICAL CONDITION
        CG POSITION
        HIGH ANGLE OF ATTACK .... 10 - 61
        VENTRAL FIN
LATERAL STABILITY AND CONTROL .... 10 - 62
    STATIC LATERAL STABILITY .... 10 - 63
    CONTRIBUTION OF THE AEROPLANE COMPONENTS .... 10 - 65
        WING
        WING POSITION .... 10 - 66
        SWEEPBACK .... 10 - 67
        FIN .... 10 - 68
        PARTIAL SPAN FLAPS .... 10 - 69
LATERAL DYNAMIC EFFECTS .... 10 - 70
    SPIRAL DIVERGENCE
    DUTCH ROLL
PILOT INDUCED OSCILLATIONS (PIO) .... 10 - 71
HIGH MACH NUMBERS .... 10 - 72
MACH TRIM
KEY FACTS 2 (SELF STUDY) .... 10 - 73
SUMMARY .... 10 - 77
SELF ASSESSMENT QUESTIONS .... 10 - 81
    ANSWERS .... 10 - 87
KEY FACTS 1 (ANSWERS) .... 10 - 89
KEY FACTS 2 (ANSWERS) .... 10 - 92

PRINCIPLES OF FLIGHT   STABILITY AND CONTROL

10.1 INTRODUCTION

Stability is the tendency of an aircraft to return to a steady state of flight without any help from the pilot, after being disturbed by an external force.

An aircraft must have the following qualities:

    a)   Adequate stability to maintain a uniform flight condition.

    b)   The ability to recover from various disturbing influences.

    c)   Sufficient stability to minimise the workload of the pilot and

    d)   Proper response to the controls so that it may achieve its design performance with adequate manoeuvrability.

There are two broad categories of stability, **static** and **dynamic**. Dynamic stability will be considered later.

10.2 STATIC STABILITY   *[handwritten: INITIAL REACTION]*

An aircraft is in a state of equilibrium (trim) when the sum of all forces is zero **and** the sum of all moments is zero; there are no accelerations and the aircraft will continue in steady flight. If equilibrium is disturbed by a gust, or deflection of the controls, the aircraft will experience accelerations due to an unbalance of moments or forces.

The type of **static stability** an aircraft possesses is defined by its **initial tendency**, following the removal of some disturbing force.

    1 -   **Positive static stability** (or static stability) exists if an aircraft is disturbed from equilibrium and has the tendency to return to equilibrium.

    2 -   **Neutral static stability** exists if an aircraft is subject to a disturbance and has neither the tendency to return nor the tendency to continue in the displacement direction.

    3 -   **Negative static stability** (or static instability) exists if an aircraft has a tendency to continue in the direction of disturbance.

Examples of the three types of static stability are shown in Fig's. 10.1, 10.2 and 10.3

PRINCIPLES OF FLIGHT **STABILITY AND CONTROL**

Fig. 10.1, illustrates the condition of **positive static stability** (or static stability). The ball is displaced from equilibrium at the bottom of the trough. When the disturbing force is removed, the initial tendency of the ball is to return towards the equilibrium condition. The ball may roll back and forth through the point of equilibrium but displacement to either side creates the initial tendency to return.

POSITIVE STATIC STABILITY

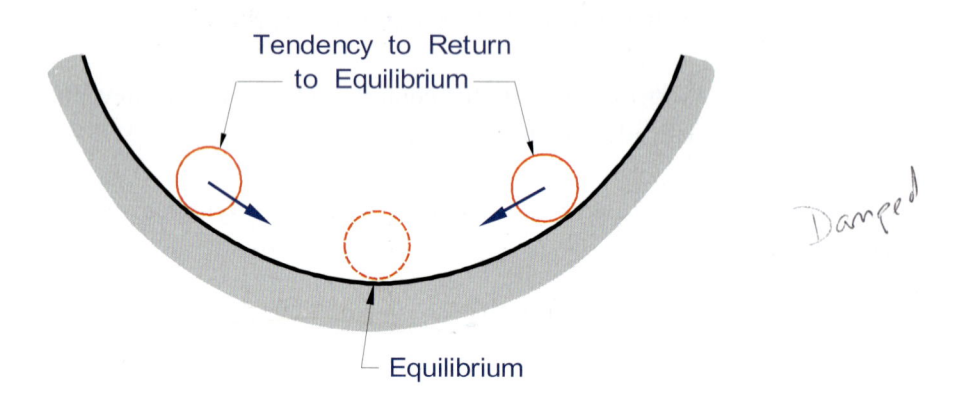

Damped

Figure 10.1

Fig. 10.2, illustrates the condition of **neutral static stability**. The ball encounters a new equilibrium at any point of displacement and has no tendency to return to its original equilibrium.

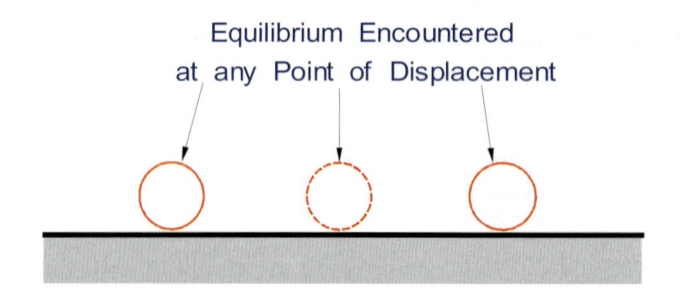

NEUTRAL STATIC STABILITY

Figure 10.2

Fig. 10.3, illustrates the condition of **negative static stability** (or static instability). Displacement from equilibrium at the hilltop gives a tendency for greater displacement.

NEGATIVE STATIC STABILITY

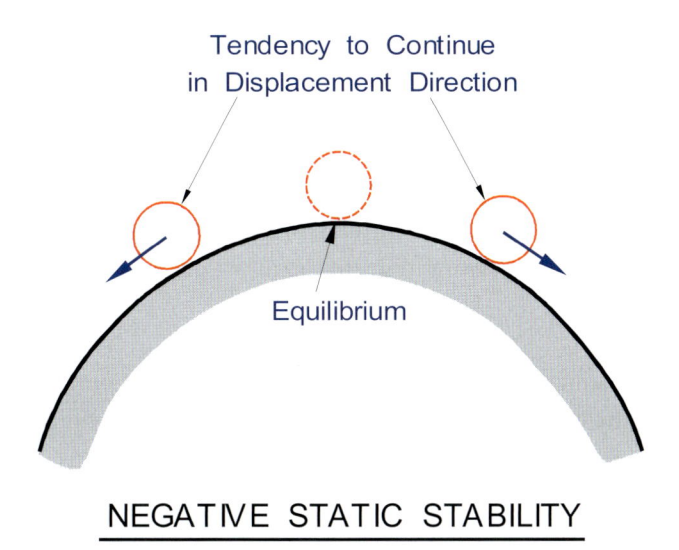

Figure 10.3

The term "static" is applied to this form of stability since any resulting motion is not considered. Only the **initial tendency** to return to equilibrium is considered in static stability.

The static longitudinal stability of an aircraft is assessed by it being displaced from some trimmed angle of attack.

If the aerodynamic pitching moments created by this displacement tend to return the aircraft to the equilibrium angle of attack the aircraft has **positive static longitudinal stability**.

PRINCIPLES OF FLIGHT   **STABILITY AND CONTROL**

10.3 AEROPLANE REFERENCE AXES

In order to visualise the forces and moments on the aircraft, it is necessary to establish a set of reference axes **passing through the centre of gravity**. Figure 10.4 illustrates a conventional right hand axis system.

The **longitudinal axis** passes through the CG from nose to tail. A moment about this axis is a rolling moment, L, a roll to the right is a positive rolling moment.

The **normal axis** passes "vertically" through the CG at 90° to the longitudinal axis. A moment about the normal axis is a yawing moment, N, and a positive yawing moment would yaw the aircraft to the right.

The **lateral axis** is a line passing through the CG, parallel to a line passing through the wing tips. A moment about the lateral axis is a pitching moment, M, and a positive pitching moment is nose up.

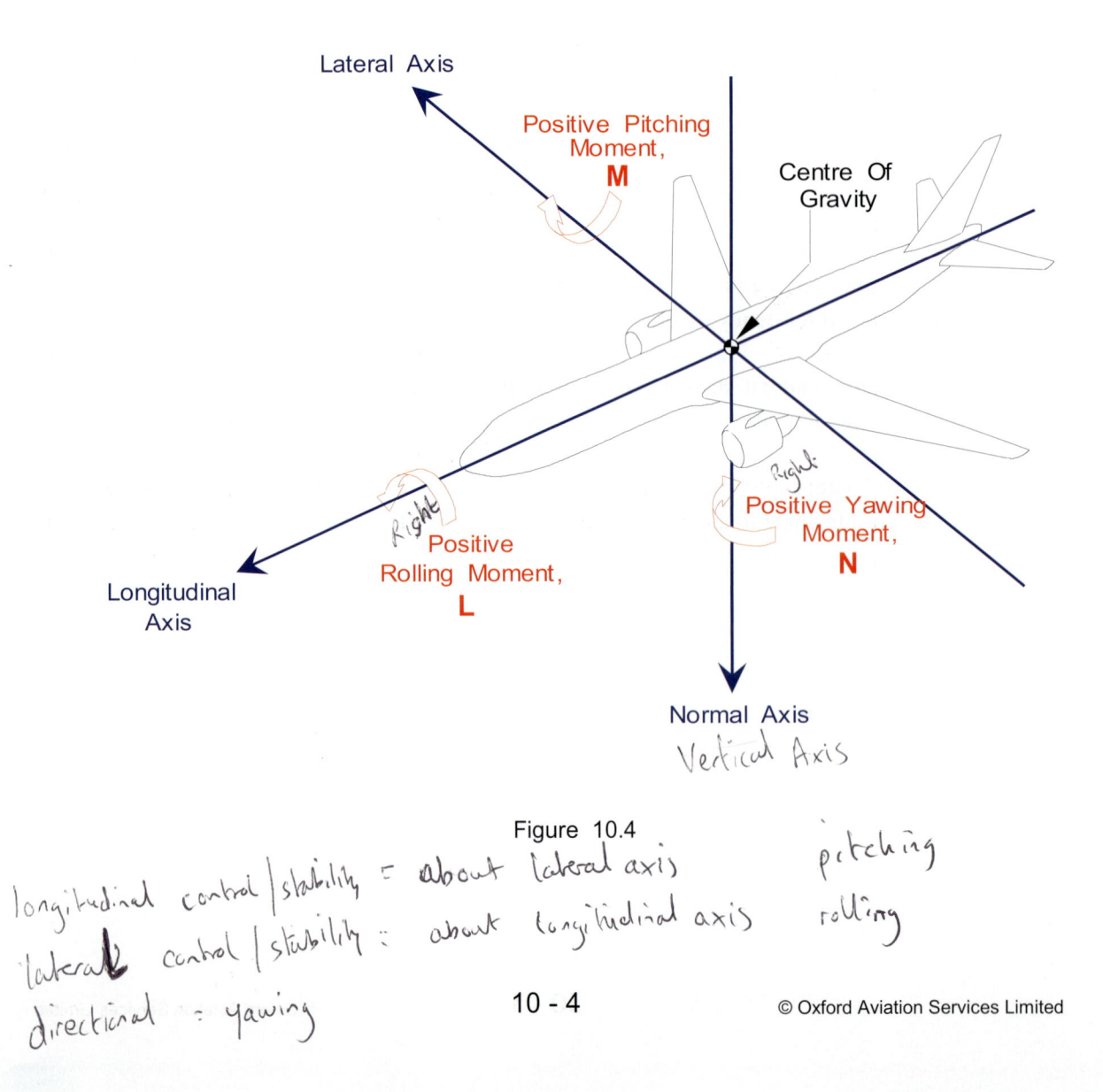

Figure 10.4

[handwritten notes:]
Vertical Axis
longitudinal control/stability = about lateral axis — pitching
lateral control/stability = about longitudinal axis — rolling
directional = yawing

PRINCIPLES OF FLIGHT   **STABILITY AND CONTROL**

10.4 STATIC LONGITUDINAL STABILITY

Longitudinal stability is motion about the lateral axis. To avoid confusion, consider the axis about which the particular type of stability takes place. Thus, lateral stability is about the longitudinal axis (rolling), directional stability is about the normal axis (yawing) and longitudinal stability is about the lateral axis (pitching). Static longitudinal stability is considered first because it can be studied in isolation; in general it does not interact with motions about the other two axes. Lateral and directional stability tend to interact (coupled motion), and these will be studied later.

a)   An aircraft will exhibit **static longitudinal stability** if it tends to return towards the trim angle of attack when displaced by a gust **OR** a control input.

        (i)   It is essential that an aircraft has positive static longitudinal stability. If it is stable, an aeroplane is safe and easy to fly since it seeks and tends to maintain a trimmed condition of flight. It also follows that control deflections and control "feel" (stick force) must be logical, both in direction and magnitude.

b)   If the aircraft is **neutrally stable**, it tends to remain at any displacement to which it is disturbed.

        (i)   Neutral static longitudinal stability usually defines the lower limit of aeroplane stability since it is the boundary between stability and instability. The aeroplane with neutral static stability may be excessively responsive to controls and the aircraft has no tendency to return to trim following a disturbance - generally this would not be acceptable.

c)   The aircraft which is **unstable** will continue to pitch in the disturbed direction until the displacement is resisted by opposing control forces.

        (i)   The aeroplane with negative static longitudinal stability is inherently divergent from any intended trim condition. If it is at all possible to fly the aircraft, it cannot be trimmed and illogical control forces and deflections are required to provide equilibrium with a change of attitude and airspeed - clearly, this would be totally unacceptable.

PRINCIPLES OF FLIGHT — STABILITY AND CONTROL

For the study of stability it is convenient to consider the changes in magnitude of lift force due to changes in angle of attack, acting through a stationary point; the aerodynamic centre (AC). It will be remembered that the location of the AC is at the quarter chord (or 25% aft of the leading edge). It should be noted that the pitching moment about the AC is negative (nose down) and that this negative (nose down) pitching moment about the AC does not change with changes in angle of attack. Fig. 10.5.

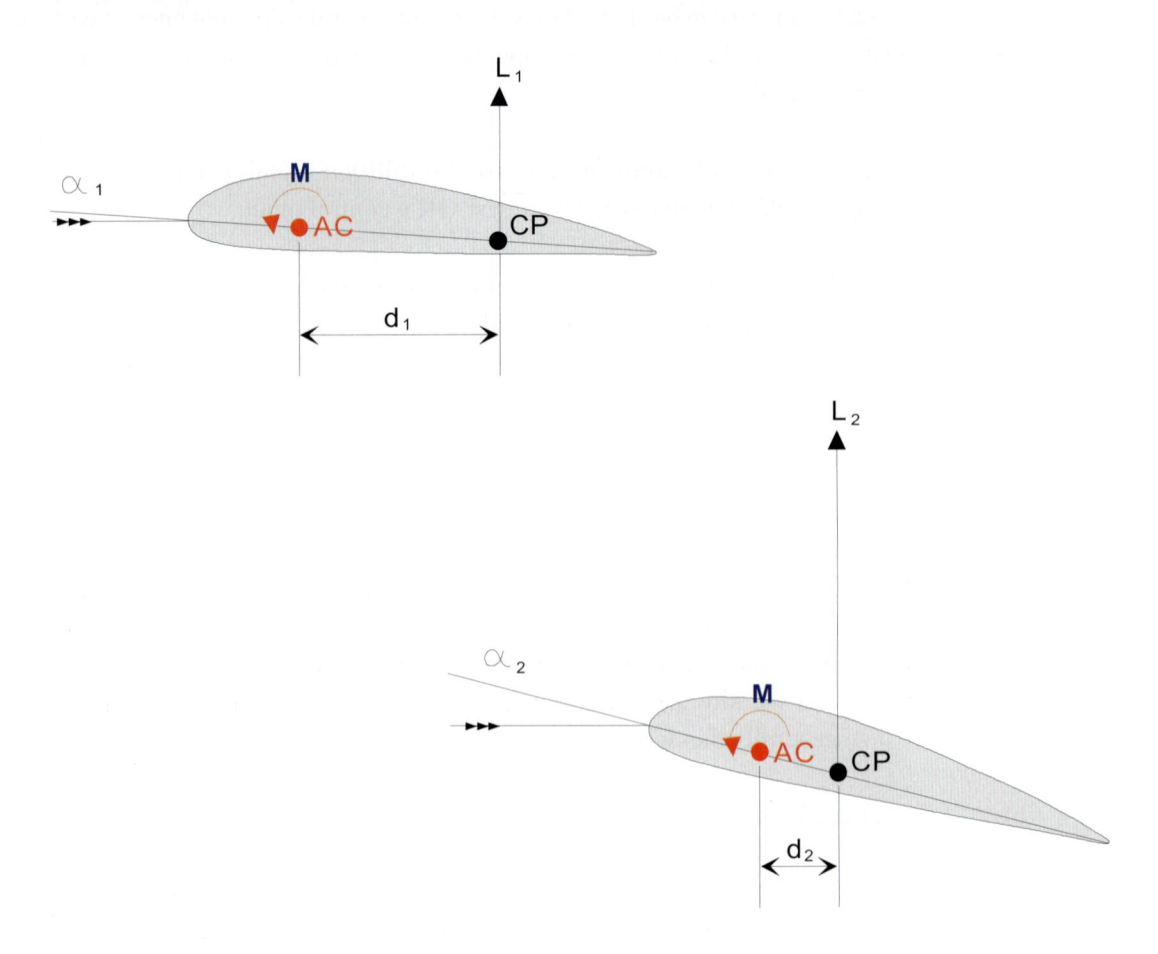

MOMENT (M) REMAINS THE SAME AT "NORMAL" ANGLES OF ATTACK BECAUSE

$L_1 \times d_1$ at α_1 = $L_2 \times d_2$ at α_2

Figure 10.5   Aerodynamic Centre (AC)

The pitching moment about the AC remains constant as the angle of attack is increased because the magnitude of the lift force increases but acts through a smaller arm due to the CP moving forward. It is only at the AC (25% chord) that this will occur. If a point in front of, or to the rear of the AC were considered, the pitching moment would change with angle of attack.

For the study of stability we will consider the lift to act at the AC. **The AC is a stationary point located at the 25% chord, only when the airflow is subsonic.**

PRINCIPLES OF FLIGHT   **STABILITY AND CONTROL**

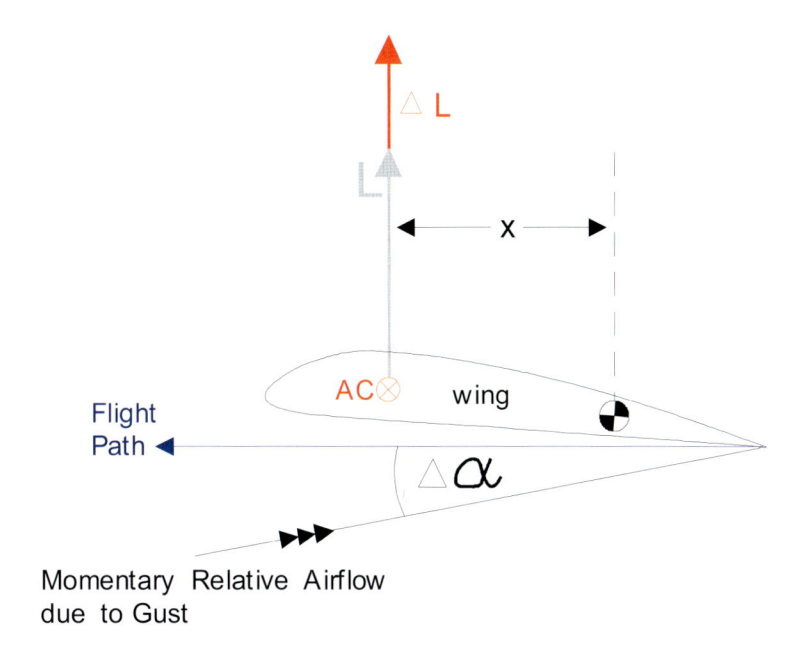

Figure 10.6   A wing alone is unstable

A wing considered alone is statically unstable, because the AC is in front of the CG, Fig. 10.6. A vertical gust will momentarily increases the angle of attack and increase lift (ΔL), which, when multiplied by arm 'x', will generate a positive (nose up) pitching moment about the CG. This will tend to increase the angle of attack further, an unstable pitching moment. The wing on its own would rotate nose up about the CG, Fig.10.7.

AN AIRCRAFT ROTATES AROUND ITS CG

UNSTABLE (NOSE UP) PITCHING MOMENT ABOUT THE CG

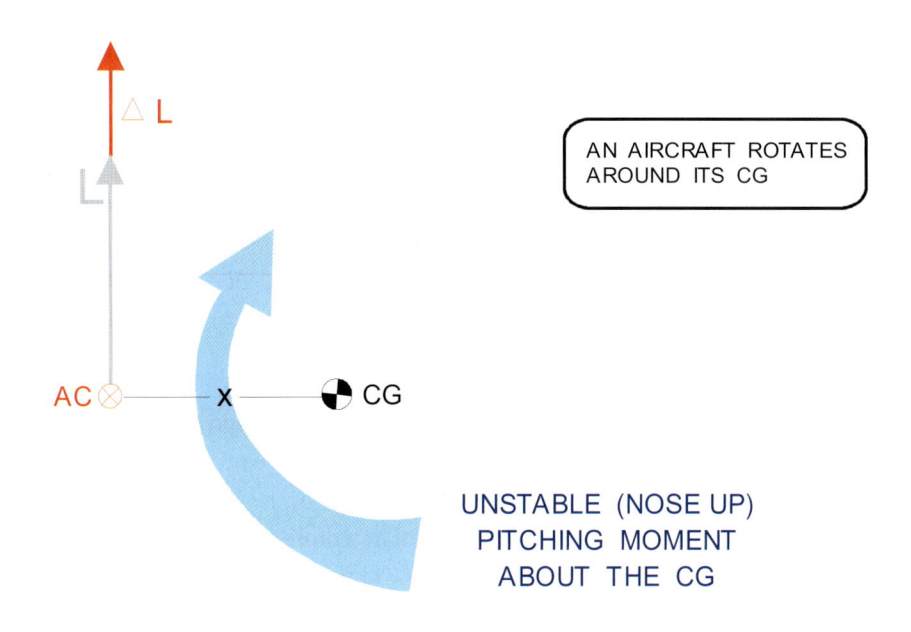

Figure 10.7

PRINCIPLES OF FLIGHT   **STABILITY AND CONTROL**

Now consider a wing together with a tailplane. The tailplane is positioned to generate a stabilising pitching moment about the aircraft CG. The same vertical gust will increases the angle of attack of the tailplane and increase tailplane lift (ΔLt), which, when multiplied by arm 'y', will generate a negative (nose down) pitching moment about the aircraft CG.

If the tail moment is greater than the wing moment the sum of the moments will not be zero and the resultant nose down moment will give an angular acceleration about the CG. The nose down angular acceleration about the CG will return the aircraft towards its original position of equilibrium. The greater the tail moment relative to the wing moment, the greater the rate of acceleration towards the original equilibrium position. (Too much angular acceleration is not good).

wing destabilising
tailplane stabilising

$\Delta \alpha$	= Change in angle of attack due to gust		L_t	= Tailplane lift
AC	= Aerodynamic Centre		ΔL_t	= Change in tailplane lift
L	= Wing lift		x	= Arm from wing AC to aircraft CG
ΔL	= Change in wing lift		y	= Arm from tailplane AC to aircraft CG

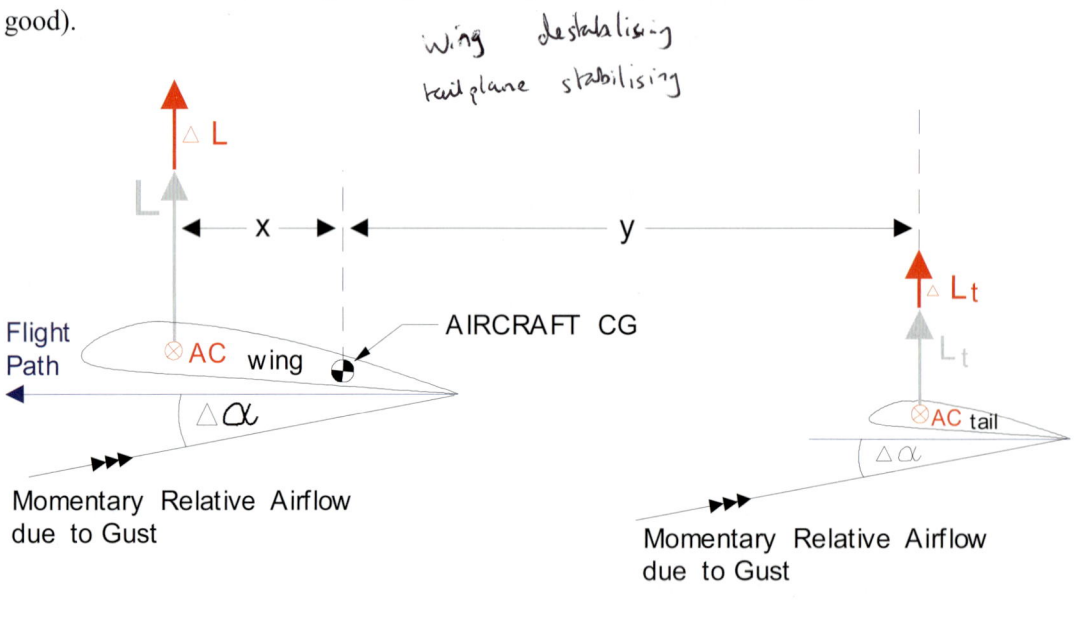

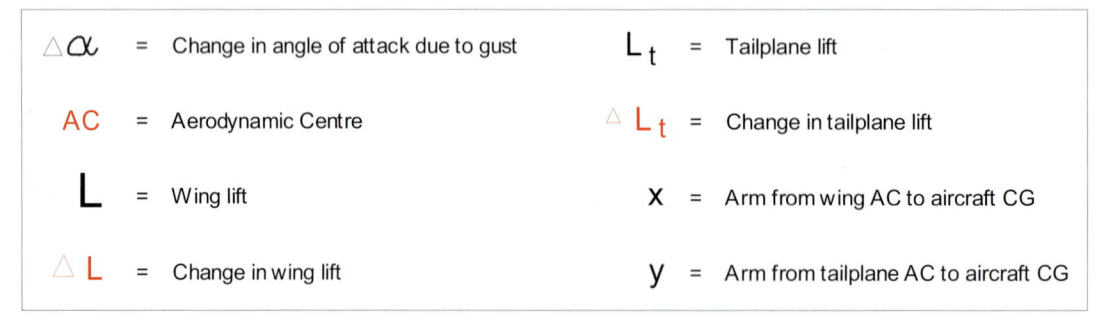

Figure 10.8

There are two moments to consider; the wing moment and the tail moment. The wing moment is a function of the change in wing lift multiplied by arm 'x'. The tail moment is a function of the change in tailplane lift multiplied by arm 'y', Fig. 10.8. The length of both arms is dependent upon CG position. If the CG is considered in a more forward position, the tail arm is larger and the wing arm is smaller. A more forward CG position increases static longitudinal stability.

If the nose down (negative) tail moment is greater than the nose up (positive) wing moment, the aircraft will have **static longitudinal stability.**

PRINCIPLES OF FLIGHT   **STABILITY AND CONTROL**

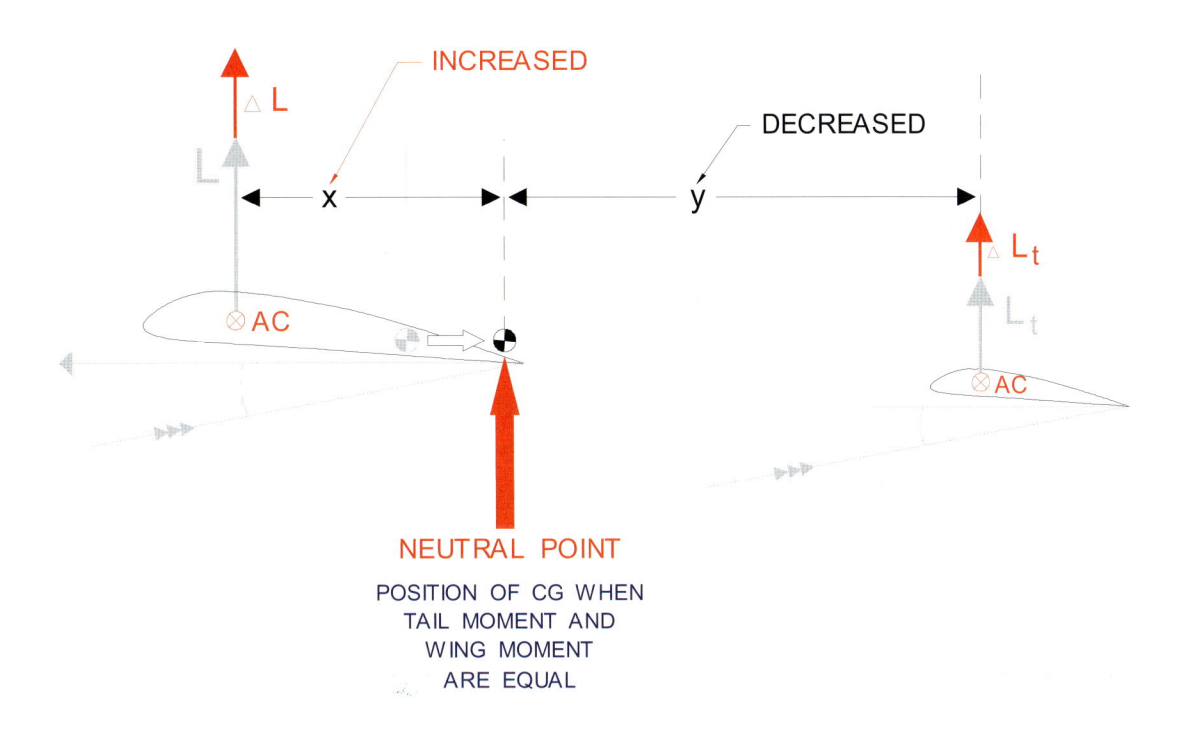

Figure 10.9 Neutral Point

10.5 NEUTRAL POINT

If you consider the CG moving rearwards from a position of static longitudinal stability:-

a) the tail arm 'y' will decrease and the wing arm 'x' will increase; consequently,

b) the (negative) tail moment will decrease and the (positive) wing moment will increase, Fig. 10.9.

Eventually the CG will reach a position at which the tail moment is the same as the wing moment. If a vertical gust were to displace the aircraft nose up, the sum of the moments will be zero and there will be no angular acceleration about the CG to return the aircraft towards its original position of equilibrium.

Because there is no resultant moment, **either nose up or nose down**, the aircraft will remain in its new position of equilibrium; the aircraft will have **neutral** static longitudinal stability. Para. 10.4 (b).

The position of the CG when the sum of the changes in the tail moment and wing moment caused by the gust is zero, is known as the **neutral point**, Fig. 10.9.

PRINCIPLES OF FLIGHT — STABILITY AND CONTROL

10.6 STATIC MARGIN

We have established that: with the CG on the neutral point the aircraft will have neutral static longitudinal stability. i.e. the sum changes in the wing moment and the tail moment caused by a disturbance is zero.

If the CG is positioned just forward of the neutral point, the tail moment will be slightly greater than the wing moment (arm 'y' increased and arm 'x' decreased). A vertical gust which increases the angle of attack will generate a small nose down angular acceleration about the CG, which will gently return the aircraft towards its original position of trim (equilibrium).

The further forward the CG, the greater the nose down angular acceleration about the CG - the greater the degree of static longitudinal stability.

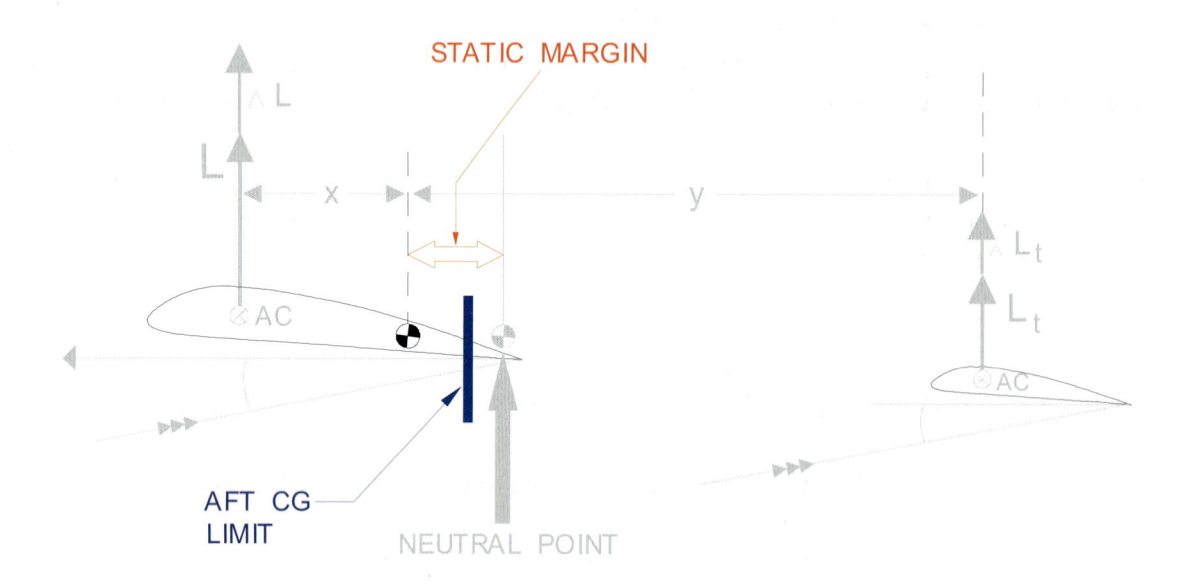

Figure 10.10   Static Margin & Aft CG Limit

The neutral point is an important point of reference in the study of static longitudinal stability. In practice, the CG will never be allowed to move so far aft that it reached the neutral point. The aircraft would be much too sensitive to the controls. Para.10.4 (b).

It has been stated that the further forward the CG is from the neutral point, the greater the static longitudinal stability. The distance the CG is forward of the neutral point will give a measure of the static longitudinal stability; this distance is called the static margin, Fig. 10.10. The greater the static margin, the greater the static longitudinal stability.

A certain amount of static longitudinal stability is always required, so the **aft CG limit** will be positioned some distance forward of the neutral point. The distance between the neutral point and the aft CG limit gives the required **minimum static stability margin**.

PRINCIPLES OF FLIGHT   **STABILITY AND CONTROL**

10.7 TRIM AND CONTROLLABILITY

An aircraft is said to be trimmed (in trim) if all moments in pitch, roll, and yaw are equal to zero. The establishment of **trim** (equilibrium) at various conditions of flight may be accomplished by:-

a)   pilot effort,

b)   trim tabs,

c)   variable incidence trimming tailplane,

d)   moving fuel between the wing tanks and an aft located trim tank, or

e)   bias of a surface actuator (powered flying controls).

> STATIC STABILITY RESISTS PILOT EFFORT AND GUSTS

The term **controllability** refers to the ability of the aircraft to respond to control surface displacement and achieve the desired condition of flight. Adequate controllability must be available to perform takeoff and landing and accomplish the various manoeuvres in flight.

A contradiction exists between stability and controllability. **A high degree of stability gives reduced controllability**. The relationship between static stability and controllability is demonstrated by the following four illustrations.

POSITIVE STATIC STABILITY

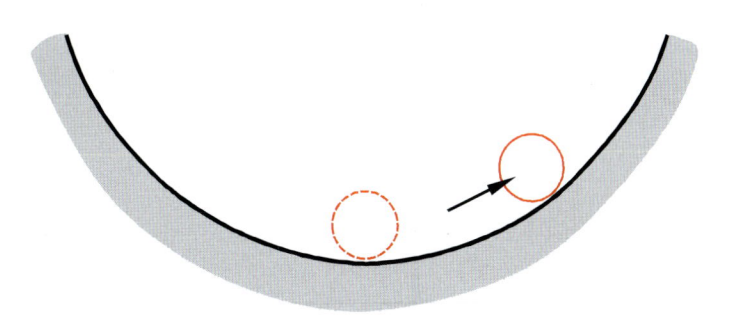

Figure 10.11

Degrees of static stability are illustrated by a ball placed on various surfaces. Positive static stability is shown by the ball in a trough, Fig. 10.11; if the ball is displaced from equilibrium at the bottom of the trough, there is an initial tendency to return to equilibrium. If it is desired to "control" the ball and maintain it in the displaced position, a force must be supplied in the direction of displacement to balance the inherent tendency to return to equilibrium.

This same stable tendency in an aircraft resists displacement from trim equally, **whether by pilot effort on the controls (stick force) or atmospheric disturbance.**

PRINCIPLES OF FLIGHT **STABILITY AND CONTROL**

INCREASED POSITIVE STATIC STABILITY

INCREASED STATIC STABILITY INCREASES STICK FORCE

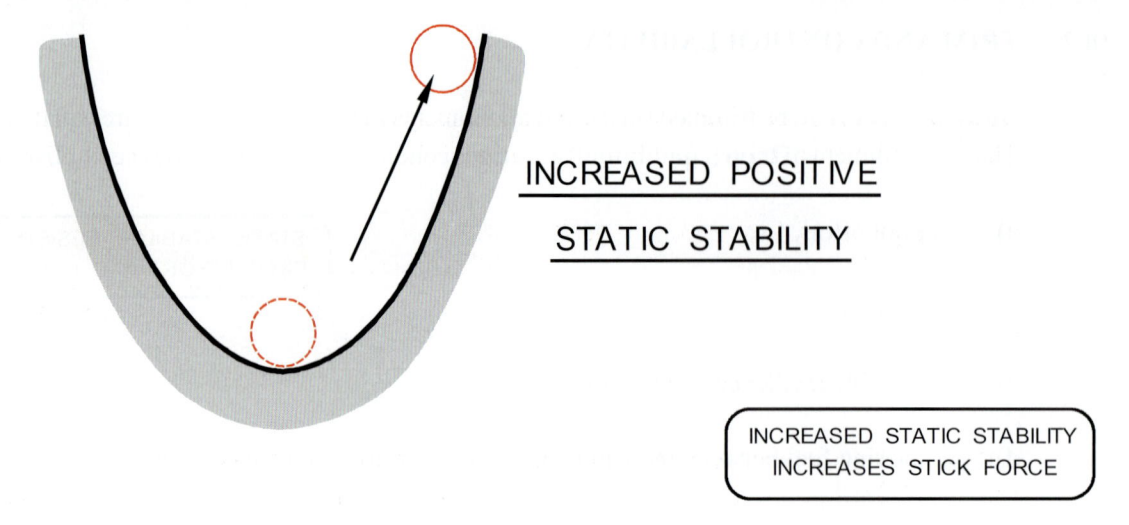

Figure 10.12

The effect of increased static stability (forward CG movement) on controllability is illustrated by the ball in a steeper trough, Fig. 10.12. A greater force is required to "control" the ball to the same position of displacement when the static stability is increased. In this manner, a large degree of static stability tends to make the aircraft less controllable. It is necessary to achieve the proper proportion between static stability and controllability during the design of an aircraft because **too much static stability** (Forward CG position) **reduces controllability**. The forward CG limit is set to ensure minimum controllability, Fig. 10.13.

FWD CG LIMIT
HIGH STICK FORCE

AFT CG LIMIT
LOW STICK FORCE

STATIC MARGIN

NEUTRAL POINT

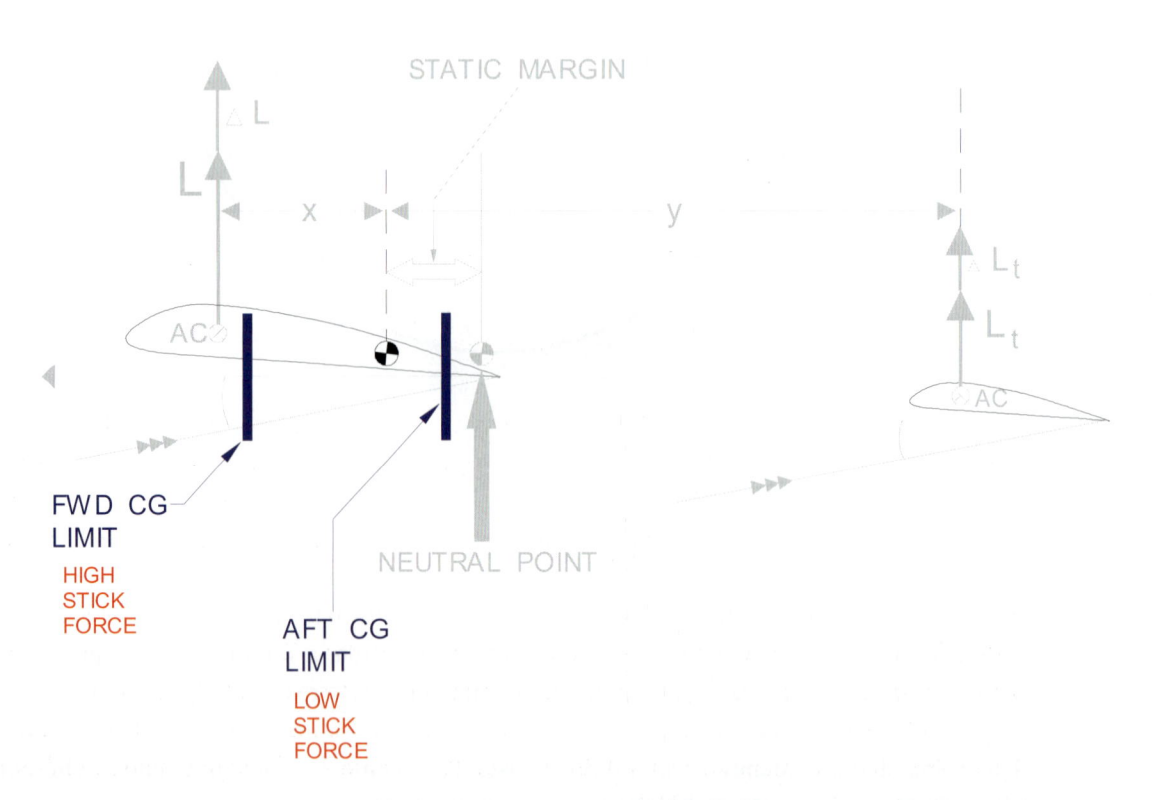

Figure 10.13   Fwd & Aft CG Limits

PRINCIPLES OF FLIGHT   STABILITY AND CONTROL

NEUTRAL STATIC STABILITY

Figure 10.14

> DECREASED STATIC STABILITY REDUCES STICK FORCE

The effect of reduced static stability on controllability is shown by the ball on a flat surface, Fig. 10.14. If neutral static stability existed (CG on the neutral point), the ball may be displaced from equilibrium and there is no tendency to return. A new point of equilibrium is obtained and no force is required to maintain the displacement. As static stability approaches zero, controllability increases to infinity and the only resistance to displacement is a resistance to the motion of displacement, aerodynamic damping. For this reason, **decreased static stability** (Aft CG movement) **increases controllability**. If the stability of the aircraft is too low, control deflections may create exaggerated displacements of the aircraft.

NEGATIVE STATIC STABILITY

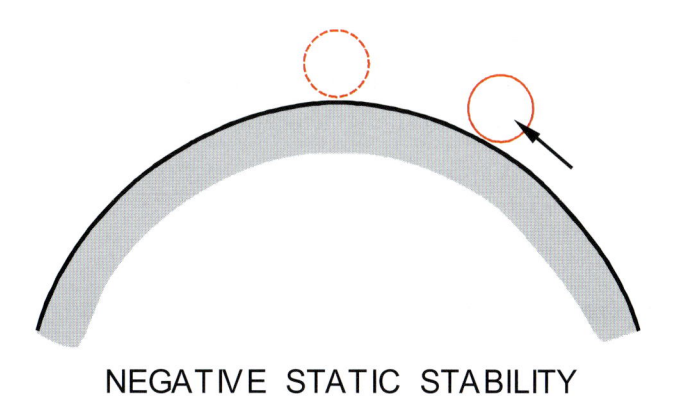

Figure 10.15

The effect of static instability on controllability (CG aft of the neutral point) is shown in Fig. 10.15 by the ball on a hill. If the ball is displaced from equilibrium at the top of the hill, the initial tendency is for the ball to continue in the displaced direction. In order to "control" the ball at this position of displacement, a force must be applied **opposite** to the direction of displacement.

This effect would be apparent during flight by an unstable "feel" to the aircraft. If the controls were deflected to increase the angle of attack, the aircraft would need to be 'held' at the higher angle of attack by a push force to keep the aircraft from continuing in the nose up direction. The pilot would be supplying the stability by his attempt to maintain the equilibrium, this is totally unacceptable!

PRINCIPLES OF FLIGHT   STABILITY AND CONTROL

KEY FACTS 1 - Self Study (Insert the missing words, with reference to the preceding paragraphs).

Stability is the _____ of an aircraft to return to a _____ state of flight, after being disturbed by an external _____, without any help from the _____. (Para. 10.1).

There are two broad categories of stability; _____ and _____ . (Para. 10.1).

An aircraft is in a state of _____ (trim) when the sum of all forces is ____ and the sum of all _____ is zero. (Para. 10.2).

The type of static stability an aircraft possesses is defined by its _____ tendency, following the removal of some disturbing force. (Para. 10.2).

The three different types of static stability are: (Para. 10.2).
a) _____ static stability exists if an aircraft is disturbed from equilibrium and has the tendency to return to equilibrium.
b) _____ static stability exists if an aircraft is subject to a disturbance and has neither the tendency to return nor the tendency to continue in the displacement direction.
c) _____ static stability exists if an aircraft has a tendency to continue in the direction of disturbance.

The longitudinal axis passes through the ____ from _____ to _____. (Para. 10.3)

The normal axis passes "vertically" through the ___ at __° to the _____ axis. (Para. 10.3)

The lateral axis is a line passing through the ___, parallel to a line passing through the ____ tips. (Para. 10.3).

The three reference axes all pass through the _____ ___ _____. (Para. 10.3)

Lateral stability involves motion about the _____ axis (_____). (Para. 10.4).

Longitudinal stability involves motion about the _____ axis (_____). (Para. 10.4).

Directional stability involves motion about the _____ axis (_____). (Para. 10.4).

PRINCIPLES OF FLIGHT   STABILITY AND CONTROL

We consider the changes in _____ of lift force due to changes in angle of _____, acting through a _____ point; the _____ _____. (Page 10 - 6)

The aerodynamic centre (AC) is located at the ___% chord position. (Page 10 - 6)

The _____ pitching moment about the AC remains _____ at normal angles of attack. (Page 10 - 6).

A wing on its own is statically _____ because the ___ is in front of the ___. (Page 10 - 7).

An upward vertical gust will momentarily _____ the angle of attack of the wing. The _____ lift force magnitude acting through the ___ will increase the _____ pitching moment about the ___. This is an _____ pitching moment. (Page 10 - 7).

The _____ is positioned to generate a _____ pitching moment about the aircraft ___. (Page 10 - 8).

If the tail moment is greater than the wing moment the sum of the moments will not be ____ and the resultant nose _____ moment will give an angular _____ about the ____. (Page 10 - 8).

The _____ the tail moment relative to the wing moment, the _____ the rate of return _____ the original _____ position. (Page 10 - 8).

The tail moment is increased by moving the aircraft ___ forwards, which _____ the tail arm and decreases the _____ arm. (Page 10 - 8).

If the nose down (_____) tail moment is greater than the nose up (_____) wing moment, the aircraft will have _____ _____ stability. (Page 10 - 8).

The position of the CG when changes in the sum of the tail moment and wing moment due to a disturbance is zero, is known as the _____ _____. (Para. 10.5).

The further forward the ___, the _____ the nose down angular _____ about the ___ - the _____ the degree of _____ _____ stability. (Para. 10.6).

The _____ the ___ is forward of the _____ point will give a measure of the _____ longitudinal stability; this distance is called the static _____. (Para. 10.6).

The greater the static margin, the _____ the _____ _____ stability. (Para. 10.6).

The ____ CG limit will be positioned some distance _____ of the _____ _____. (Para. 10.6).

The distance between the _____ limit and the neutral point gives the required _____ static stability _____. (Para. 10.6).

PRINCIPLES OF FLIGHT — STABILITY AND CONTROL

An aircraft is said to be _____ if all _____ in pitch, roll, and yaw are equal to _____. (Para. 10.7).

Trim (_____) is the function of the _____ and may be accomplished by:- (Para. 10.7).
a) _____ effort
b) trim _____,
c) moving _____ between the wing _____ and an aft located _____ tank, or
d) bias of a surface _____ (_____ flying controls).

The term _____ refers to the ability of the aircraft to respond to control surface displacement and achieve the desired _____ of flight. (Para. 10.7).

A high degree of stability tends to reduce the _____ of the aircraft. (Para. 10.7).

The stable tendency of an aircraft resists displacement from ___ equally, whether by ____ effort on the controls (_____ force) or _____. (Para. 10.7).

If the CG moves forward, static longitudinal stability _____ and controllability _____ (stick force _____). (Para. 10.7).

If the CG moves aft, static longitudinal stability _____ and controllability _____ (stick force _____). (Para. 10.7).

With the CG on the forward limit, static longitudinal stability is _____, controllability is ____ and stick force is _____. (Para. 10.7).

With the CG on the aft limit, static longitudinal stability is _____, controllability is _____ and stick force is ____. (Para. 10.7).

The aft CG limit is set to ensure a _____ degree of static longitudinal stability. (Para. 10.7).

The fwd CG limit is set to ensure a _____ degree of controllability under the worst circumstance. (Para. 10.7).

KEY FACTS 1, WITH THE MISSING WORDS INSERTED CAN BE FOUND ON PAGE 10 - 89.

10.8 GRAPHIC PRESENTATION OF STATIC LONGITUDINAL STABILITY

Static longitudinal stability depends upon the relationship of angle of attack and pitching moment. It is necessary to study the pitching moment contribution of each component of the aircraft. In a manner similar to all other aerodynamic forces, the pitching moment about the lateral axis is studied in the coefficient form.

$$M = C_M \, Q \, S \, (MAC)$$

or

$$C_M = \frac{M}{Q \, S \, (MAC)}$$

where,

M = pitching moment about the CG
(positive if in a nose-up direction)

Q = dynamic pressure

S = wing area

MAC = mean aerodynamic chord

C_M = pitching moment coefficient

The pitching moment coefficients contributed by all the various components of the aircraft are summed up and plotted versus lift coefficient (angle of attack).

Study of the plots of C_M versus C_L is a convenient way to relate the static longitudinal stability of an aeroplane.

PRINCIPLES OF FLIGHT

STABILITY AND CONTROL

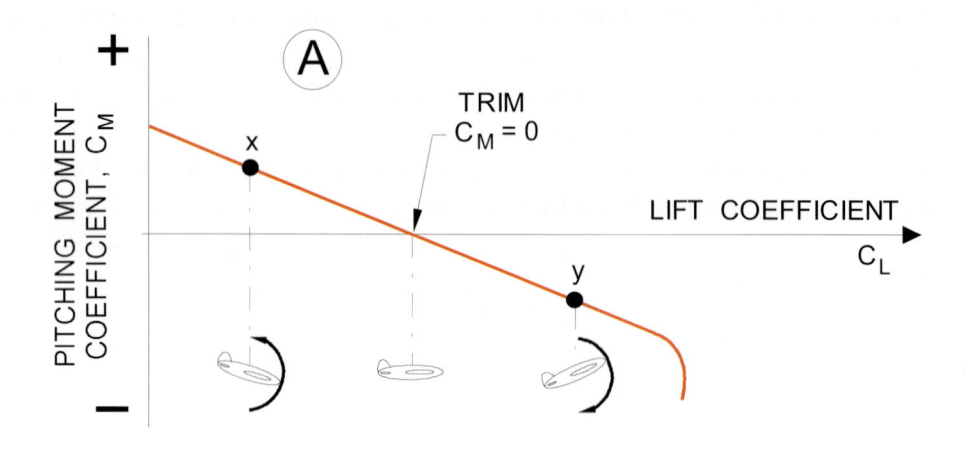

Graph A illustrates the variation of pitching moment coefficient (C_M) with lift coefficient (C_L) for an aeroplane with positive static longitudinal stability. Evidence of static stability is shown by a tendency to return to equilibrium, or **"trim"**, upon displacement. The aeroplane described by graph A is in trim or equilibrium when $C_M = 0$ and, if the aeroplane is disturbed to some different C_L the pitching moment change tends to return the aircraft to the point of trim. If the aeroplane were disturbed to some higher C_L (point y), a negative or nose-down pitching moment is developed which tends to decrease angle of attack back to the trim point. If the aeroplane were disturbed to some lower C_L (point x), a positive or nose up pitching moment is developed which tends to increase the angle of attack back to the trim point. Thus, positive static longitudinal stability is indicated by a negative slope of C_M versus C_L. The degree of static longitudinal stability is indicated by the slope of the curve (red line).

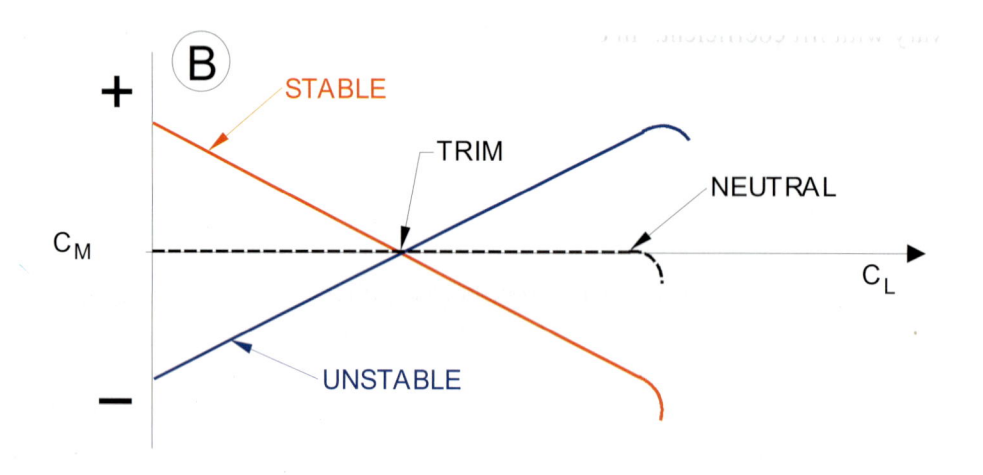

Graph B provides comparison of a stable and an unstable condition. Positive static stability is indicated by the red curve with negative slope. Neutral static stability would be the result if the curve had zero slope. If neutral stability exists, the aeroplane could be disturbed to some higher or lower lift coefficient without change in pitching moment coefficient.

PRINCIPLES OF FLIGHT **STABILITY AND CONTROL**

Such a condition would indicate that the aeroplane would have no tendency to return to some original equilibrium and would not hold trim. An aeroplane which demonstrates a positive slope of the C_M versus C_L curve (blue line) would be unstable. If the unstable aeroplane were subject to any disturbance from equilibrium at the trim point, the changes in pitching moment would only magnify the disturbance. When the unstable aeroplane is disturbed to some higher C_L a positive change in C_M occurs which would illustrate a tendency for continued, greater displacement. When the unstable aeroplane is disturbed to some lower C_L a negative change in C_M takes place which tends to create continued displacement.

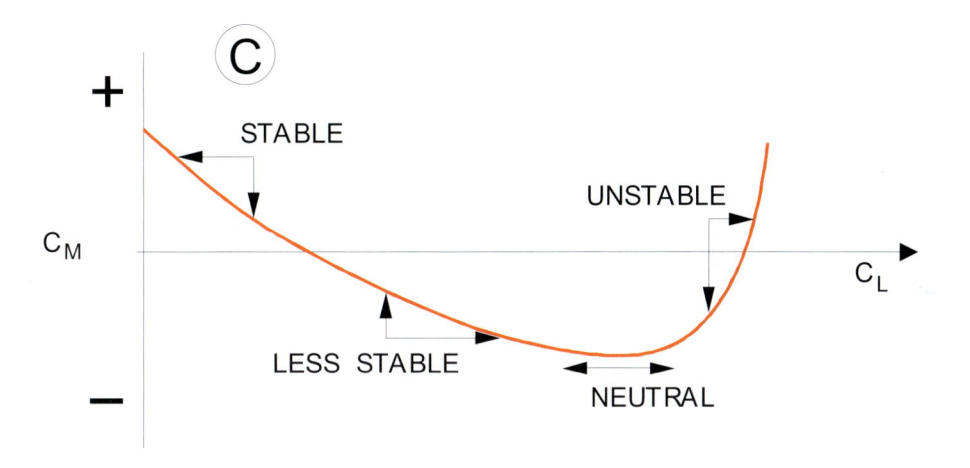

Ordinarily, the static longitudinal stability of a conventional aeroplane configuration does not vary with lift coefficient. In other words, the slope of C_M versus C_L does not change with C_L. However, if:

    a)   the aeroplane has sweepback,

    b)   there is a large contribution of 'power effect' on stability, or

    c)   there are significant changes in downwash at the horizontal tail,

noticeable changes in static stability can occur at high lift coefficients (low speed). This condition is illustrated by graph C. The curve of C_M versus C_L of this illustration shows a good stable slope at low values of C_L (high speed). Increasing C_L gives a slight decrease in the negative slope hence a decrease in stability occurs. With continued increase in C_L the slope becomes zero and neutral stability exists. Eventually, the slope becomes positive and the aeroplane becomes unstable or "pitch-up" results.

Remember, at any lift coefficient, the static stability of the aeroplane is depicted by the slope of the curve of C_M versus C_L.

PRINCIPLES OF FLIGHT **STABILITY AND CONTROL**

10.9 CONTRIBUTION OF THE COMPONENT SURFACES

The net pitching moment about the lateral axis is due to the contribution of each of the component surfaces acting in their appropriate flow fields.

By studying the contribution of each component, their effect on static stability may be appreciated. It is necessary to recall that the pitching moment coefficient is defined as:

$$C_M = \frac{M}{Q \; S \; (MAC)}$$

Thus, any pitching moment coefficient (C_M) - regardless of source - has the common denominator of dynamic pressure (Q), wing area (S), and wing mean aerodynamic chord (MAC). This common denominator is applied to the pitching moments contributed by the:

a) fuselage and nacelles,

b) horizontal tail, and

c) power effects as well as pitching moments contributed by the wing.

WING: The contribution of the wing to stability depends primarily on the location of the aerodynamic centre (AC) with respect to the aeroplane centre of gravity. Generally, **the aerodynamic centre is defined as the point on the wing Mean Aerodynamic Chord (MAC) where the wing pitching moment coefficient does not vary with lift coefficient.** All changes in lift coefficient effectively take place at the wing aerodynamic centre. Thus, if the wing experiences some change in lift coefficient, the pitching moment created will be a direct function of the relative location of the AC and CG.

*The degree of positive camber of the wing has no effect on longitudinal stability. The pitching moment about the AC is always negative regardless of angle of attack.

Stability is given by the development of restoring moments. As the wing AC is forward of the CG, the wing contributes an unstable pitching moment to the aircraft, as shown in Fig. 10.16.

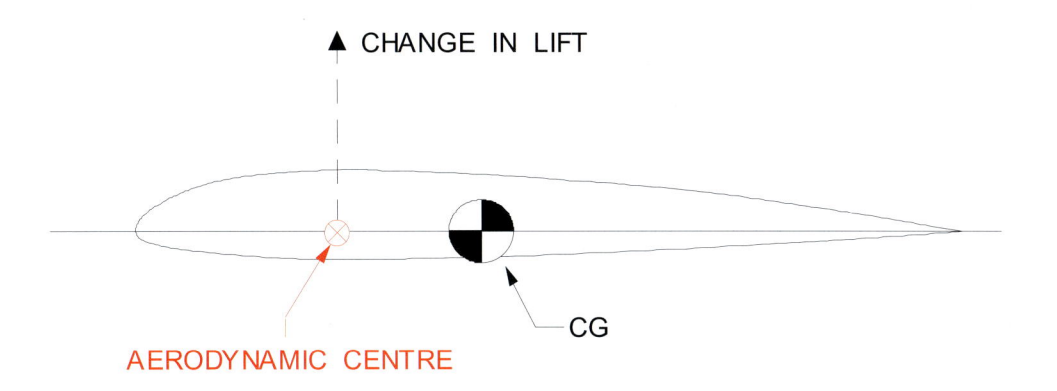

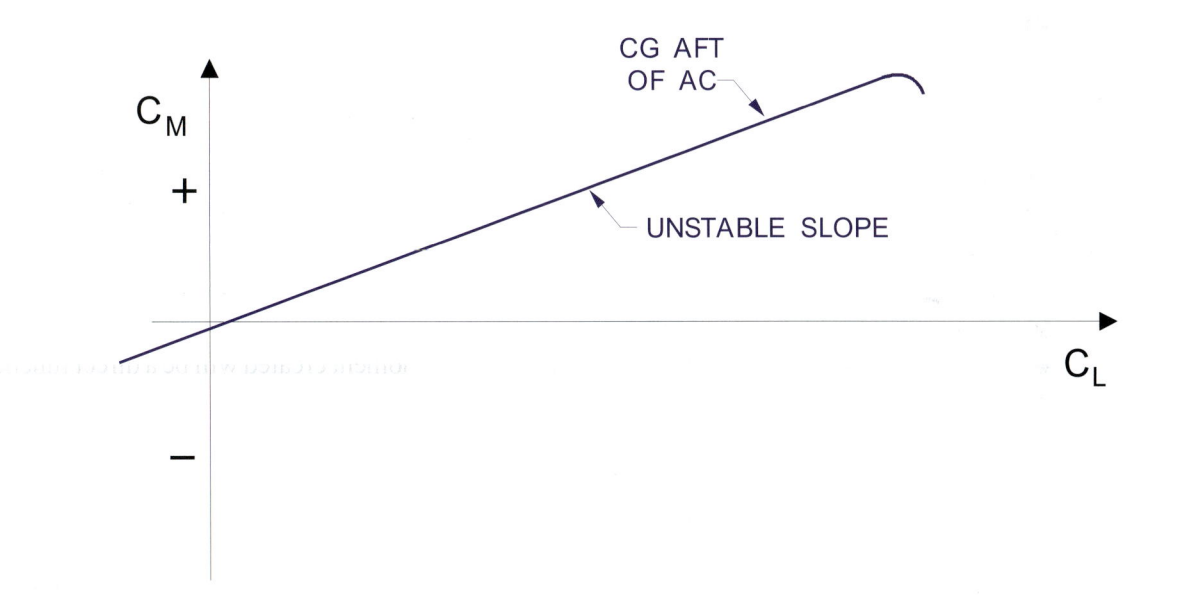

Figure 10.16   Unstable Wing Contribution

Since the wing is the predominating aerodynamic surface of an aeroplane, any change in the wing contribution may produce a significant change in the aeroplane stability.

PRINCIPLES OF FLIGHT   **STABILITY AND CONTROL**

SYMMETRICAL BODY (fuselage or nacelle)

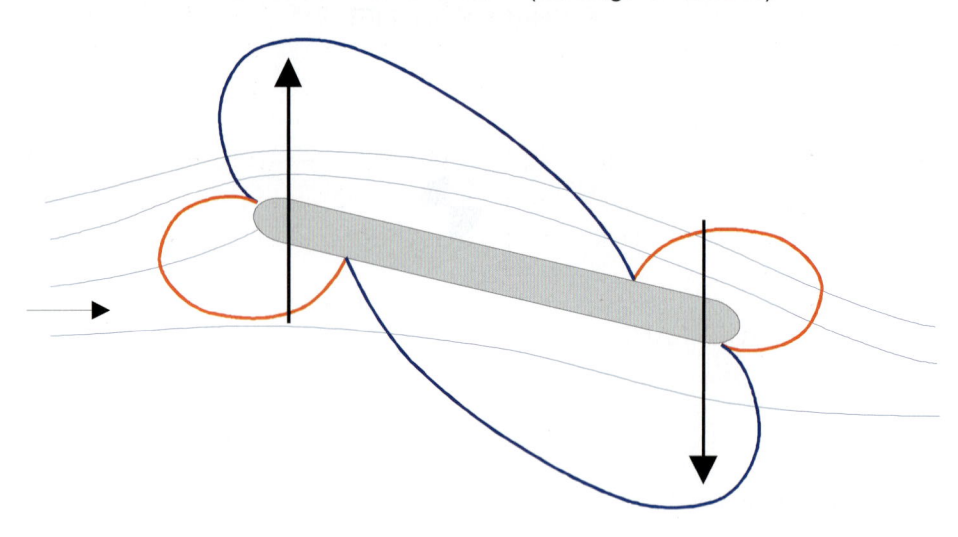

Figure 10.17

FUSELAGE AND NACELLES: In most cases, the contribution of the fuselage and nacelles is destabilising. A symmetrical body in an airflow develops an unstable pitching moment when given an angle of attack. In fact, an increase in angle of attack produces an increase in the unstable pitching moment without the development of lift. Fig. 10.17 illustrates the pressure distribution which creates this unstable moment on the body. An increase in angle of attack causes an increase in the unstable pitching moment but a negligible increase in lift.

HORIZONTAL TAIL: The horizontal tail usually provides the greatest stabilising influence of all the components of the aeroplane.

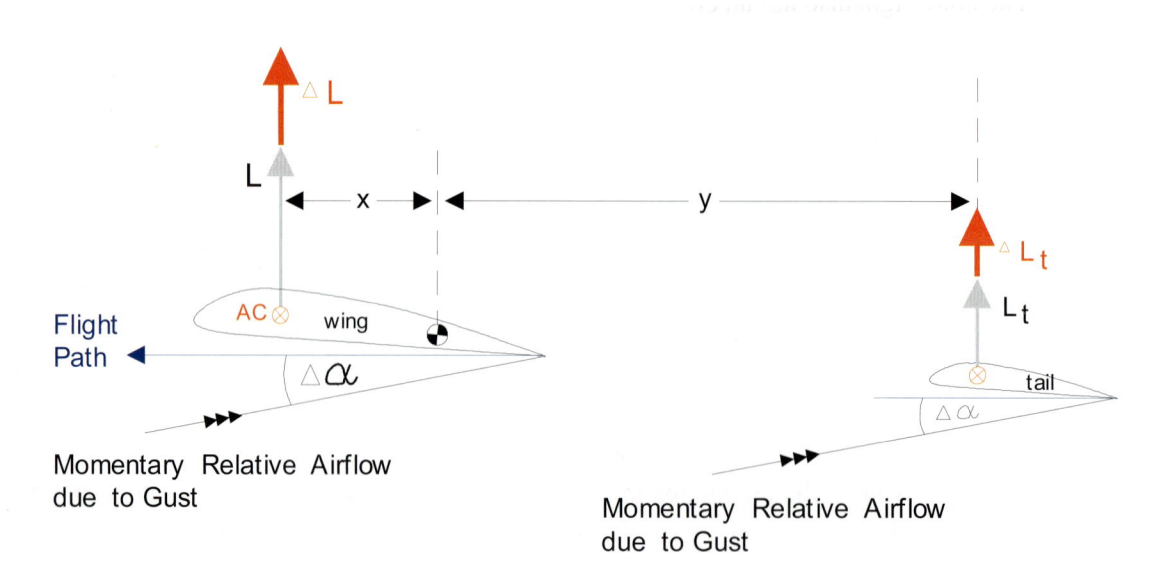

Figure 10.18

PRINCIPLES OF FLIGHT   STABILITY AND CONTROL

To appreciate the contribution of the horizontal tail to stability, inspect Fig. 10.18. If the aeroplane is given an increase in angle of attack (by a gust OR control displacement), an increase in tail lift will occur at the aerodynamic centre of the tail. An increase in lift at the horizontal tail produces a negative (stabilising) moment about the aircraft CG.

For a given vertical gust velocity and aircraft TAS, the wing moment is essentially determined by the CG position. BUT, the tail moment is determined by the CG position AND the effectiveness of the tailplane. For a given moment arm (CG position), the effectiveness of the tailplane is dependent upon:

a) Downwash from the wing

b) Dynamic pressure at the tailplane

c) Longitudinal dihedral

Downwash from the wing and dynamic pressure at the tailplane will be discussed in due course, but the effect of longitudinal dihedral is shown below.

LONGITUDINAL DIHEDRAL: The difference between tailplane and wing incidence. For longitudinal static stability the tailplane incidence is smaller. As illustrated in Fig. 10.19, this will generate a greater percentage increase in tailplane lift than wing lift for a given vertical gust.

This guarantees that the positive contribution of the tailplane to static longitudinal stability will be sufficient to overcome the sum of the de-stabilising moments from the other components of the aeroplane.

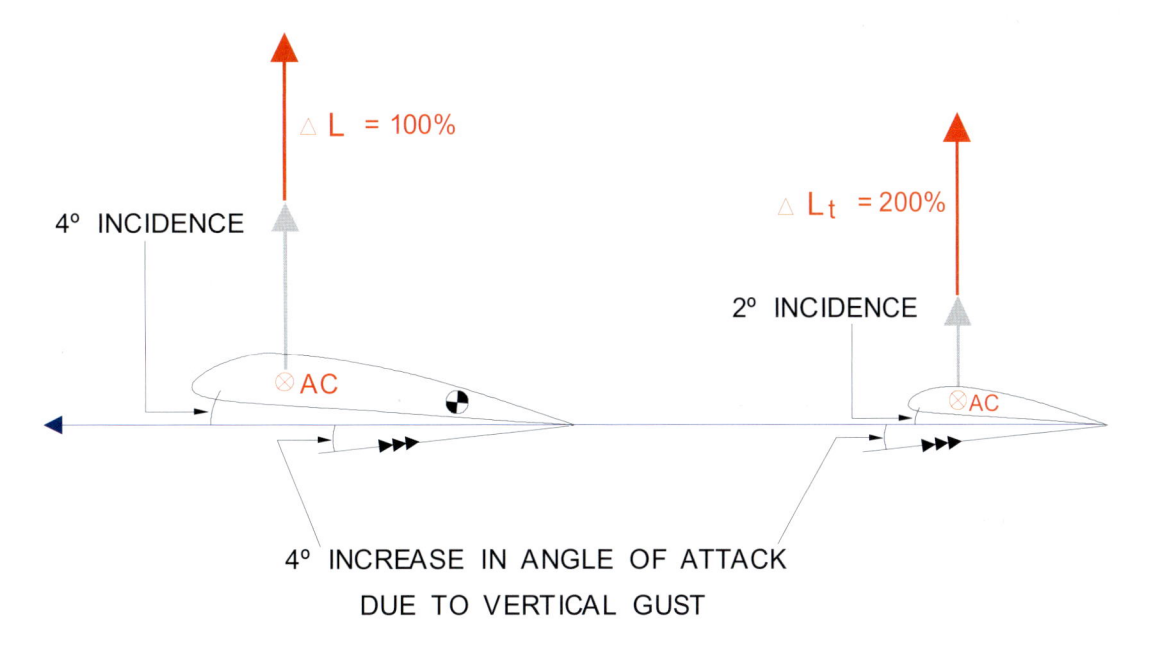

Figure 10.19 Longitudinal Dihedral

PRINCIPLES OF FLIGHT   STABILITY AND CONTROL

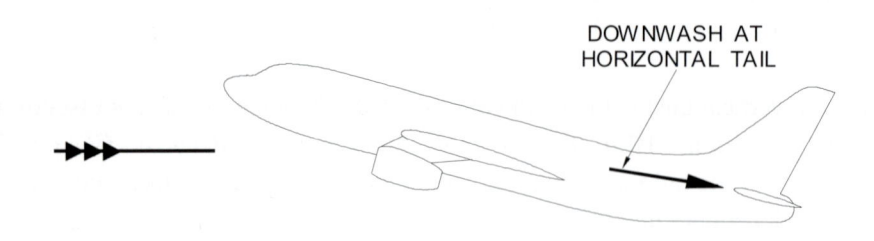

Figure 10.20

Downwash Destabilising

DOWNWASH DECREASES LONGITUDINAL STATIC STABILITY

DOWNWASH: It should be appreciated that the flow at the horizontal tail does not have the same flow direction or dynamic pressure as the free stream. Due to the wing wake, fuselage boundary layer, and power effects, the dynamic pressure at the horizontal tail may be greatly different from the dynamic pressure of the free stream. In most instances, the dynamic pressure at the tail is usually less and this reduces the efficiency of the tail.

When the aeroplane is given a change in angle of attack, the horizontal tail does not experience the same change in angle of attack as the wing, Fig. 10.20.

Because of the increase in downwash behind the wing, the horizontal tail will experience a smaller change in angle of attack, e.g., if a 10° change in wing angle of attack causes a 4° increase in downwash at the horizontal tail, the horizontal tail experiences only a 6° change in angle of attack. In this manner, the downwash at the horizontal tail reduces the contribution to stability.

Any factor which alters the rate of change of downwash at the horizontal tail (e.g. flaps or propeller slipstream) will directly affect the tail contribution and aeroplane stability. **Downwash decreases static longitudinal stability.**

PRINCIPLES OF FLIGHT   **STABILITY AND CONTROL**

10.10 POWER-OFF STABILITY

When the aerodynamic stability of a configuration is of interest, power effects are neglected and the stability is considered by a buildup of the contributing components.

Fig. 10.21 illustrates a typical buildup of the components of a conventional aeroplane configuration. If the CG is arbitrarily set at 30 percent MAC, the contribution of the wing alone is destabilising, as indicated by the positive slope of C_M versus C_L. The combination of the wing and fuselage increases the instability. The contribution of the tail alone is highly stabilizing from the large negative slope of the curve. The contribution of the tail must be sufficiently stabilising so that the complete configuration will exhibit positive static stability at the anticipated CG locations.

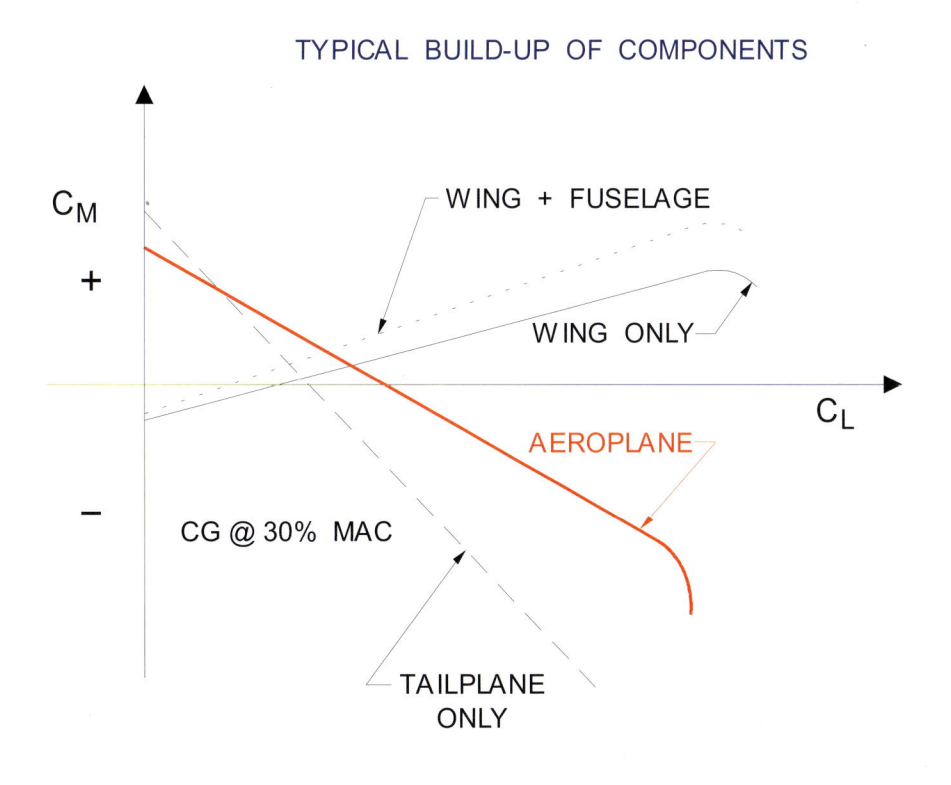

Figure 10.21

EFFECT OF CG POSITION

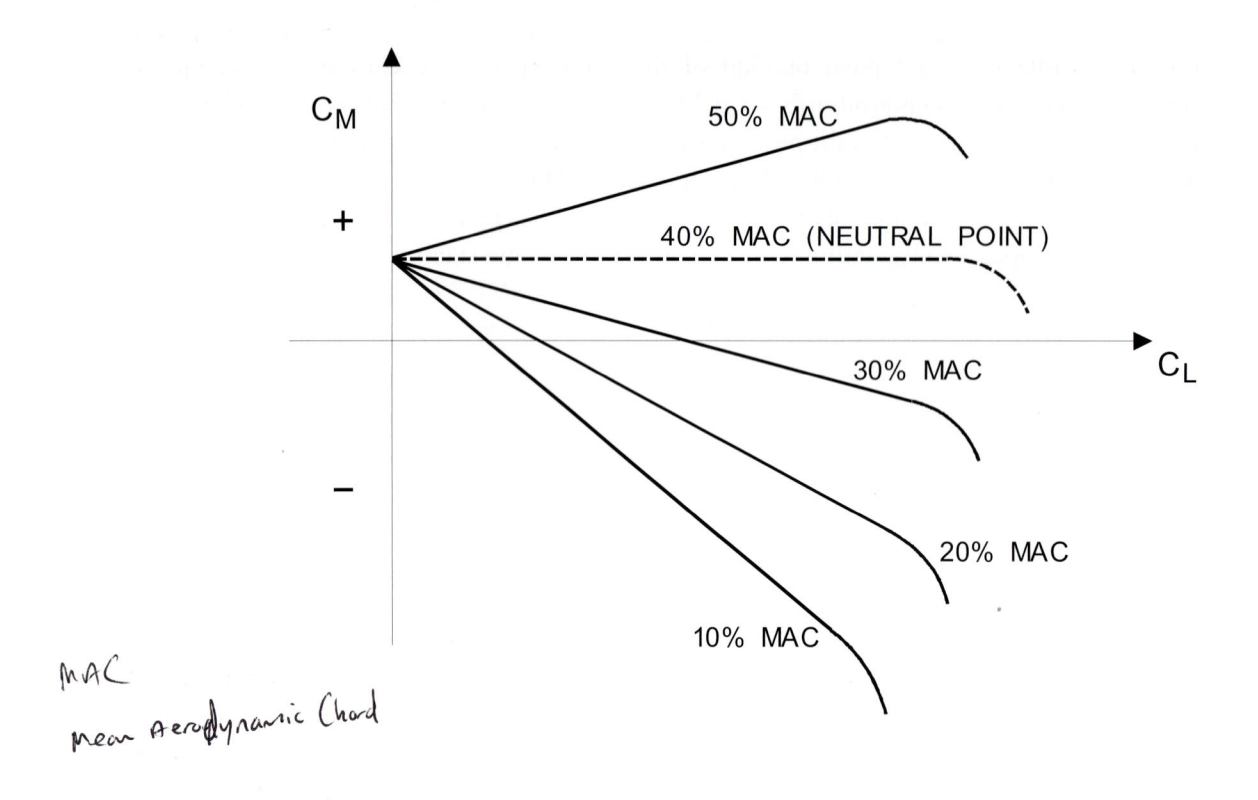

Figure 10.22

10.11 EFFECT OF CG POSITION

A variation of CG position can cause large changes in the static longitudinal stability. In the conventional aeroplane configuration, the large changes in stability with CG variation are primarily due to the large changes in the wing contribution. If the incidence of all surfaces remains fixed, the effect of CG position on static longitudinal stability is typified by the chart in Fig. 10.22. As the CG is gradually moved aft, the aeroplane static stability decreases, then becomes neutral then unstable. The CG position which produces zero slope and neutral static stability is referred to as the "neutral point." The neutral point may be imagined as the effective aerodynamic centre of the entire aeroplane configuration, i.e., **with the CG at the neutral point, all changes in net lift effectively occur at that point and no change in pitching moment results. The neutral point defines the most aft CG position without static instability.**

PRINCIPLES OF FLIGHT   STABILITY AND CONTROL

10.12 POWER EFFECTS

The effects of power may cause significant changes in trim lift coefficient and static longitudinal stability. Since the contribution to stability is evaluated by the change in moment coefficients, **power effects will be most significant when the aeroplane operates at high power and low airspeeds such as during approach and while taking-off.**

DESTABILISING

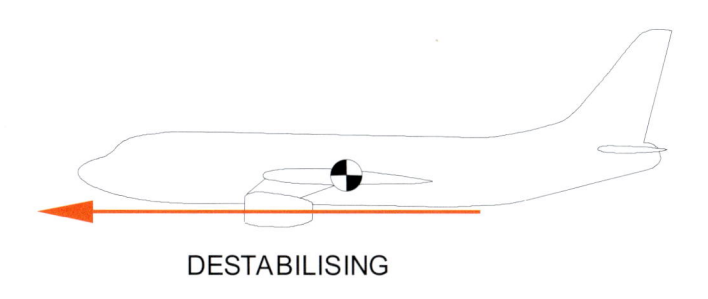

Figure 10.23

The effects of power are considered in two main categories. First, there are the direct effects resulting from the forces created by the propulsion unit. Next, there are the indirect effects of the slipstream and other associated flow which alter the forces and moments of the aerodynamic surfaces. The direct effects of power are illustrated in Fig. 10.23. The vertical location of the thrust line defines one of the direct contributions to stability. If the thrust line is below the CG, as illustrated, a thrust increase will produce a positive or nose up moment and the effect is destabilising.

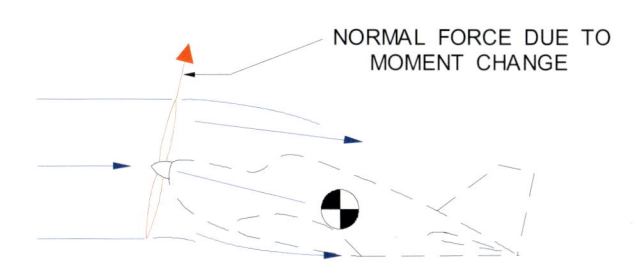

Figure 10.24

A propeller located ahead of the CG contributes a destabilising effect. As shown in Fig. 10.24, a rotating propeller inclined to the relative airflow causes a deflection of the airflow. The momentum change of the slipstream creates a normal force at the plane of the propeller. As this normal force will increase with an increase in aeroplane angle of attack, the effect will be destabilising when the propeller is ahead of the CG. **The magnitude of the unstable contribution depends on the distance from the CG to the propeller and is largest at high power and low dynamic pressure.**

PRINCIPLES OF FLIGHT **STABILITY AND CONTROL**

WING, NACELLE AND FUSELAGE MOMENTS AFFECTED BY SLIPSTREAM

DYNAMIC PRESSURE AT TAIL AFFECTED BY SLIPSTREAM

WING LIFT AFFECTED BY SLIPSTREAM

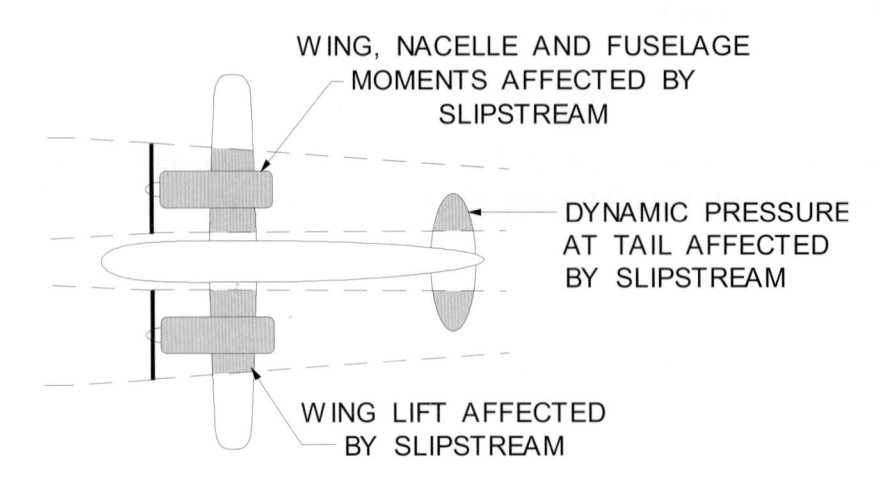

Figure 10.25

The indirect effects of power are of greatest concern in the propeller powered aeroplane rather than the jet powered aeroplane. As shown in Fig. 10.25, the propeller powered aeroplane creates slipstream velocities on the various surfaces which are different from the flow field typical of power-off flight. Since the various wing, nacelle, and fuselage surfaces are partly or wholly immersed in this slipstream, the contribution of these components to stability can be quite different from the power-off flight condition. Ordinarily, the change of fuselage and nacelle contribution with power is relatively small. The added lift on the portion of the wing immersed in the slipstream requires that the aeroplane operate at a lower angle of attack to produce the same effective lift coefficient. Generally, this reduction in angle of attack to effect the same C_L reduces the tail contribution to stability. However, the increase in dynamic pressure at the tail tends to increase the effectiveness of the tail and may be a stabilising effect. The magnitude of this contribution due to the slipstream velocity on the tail will depend on the CG position and trim lift coefficient.

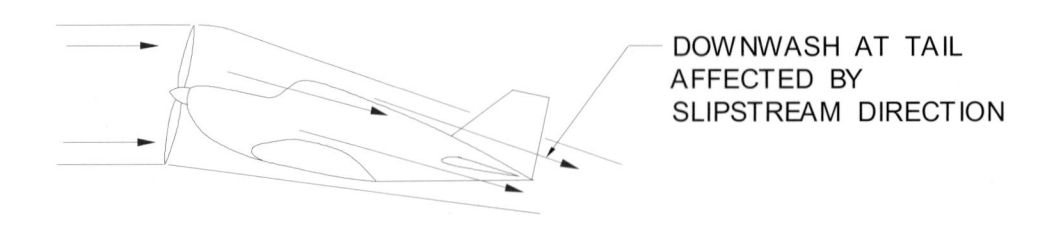

DOWNWASH AT TAIL AFFECTED BY SLIPSTREAM DIRECTION

Figure 10.26

The deflection of the slipstream shown in Fig. 10.26 by the normal force at the propeller tends to increase the downwash at the horizontal tail and reduce the contribution to stability.

PRINCIPLES OF FLIGHT **STABILITY AND CONTROL**

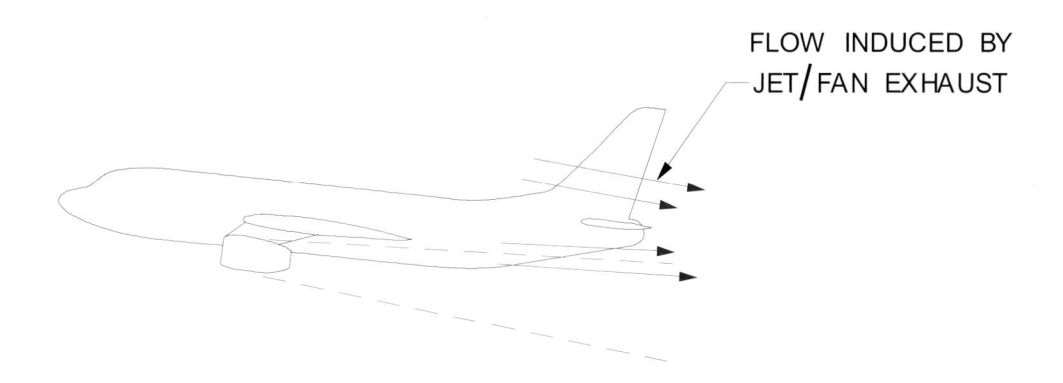

Figure 10.27

Essentially the same destabilising effect is produced by the flow induced at the exhaust of turbo-jet/fan engines, Fig. 10.27. Ordinarily, the induced flow at the horizontal tail of a jet aeroplane is slight and is destabilising when the jet passes underneath the horizontal tail. The magnitude of the indirect power effects on stability tends to be greatest at high C_L, high power, and low flight speeds.

CONCLUSIONS TO THE EFFECTS OF POWER

The combined direct and indirect power effects contribute to a general reduction of static stability at high power, high C_L and low dynamic pressure. It is generally true that any aeroplane will experience the lowest level of static longitudinal stability under these conditions. Because of the greater magnitude of both direct and indirect power effects, the propeller powered aeroplane usually experiences a greater effect than the jet powered aeroplane.

10.13 HIGH LIFT DEVICES

An additional effect on stability can be from the extension of high lift devices. High lift devices tend to increase downwash at the tail and reduce the dynamic pressure at the tail, both of which are destabilising. However, high lift devices may prevent an unstable contribution of the wing at high C_L. While the effect of high lift devices depends on the aeroplane configuration, the usual effect is destabilising. **Hence, the aeroplane may experience the most critical forward neutral point during the power approach or overshoot/missed approach. During this condition of flight the static stability is usually the weakest and particular attention must be given to precise control of the aeroplane.**

The power - on neutral point may set the most aft limit of CG position.

PRINCIPLES OF FLIGHT   **STABILITY AND CONTROL**

10.14 CONTROL FORCE STABILITY

The static longitudinal stability of an aeroplane is defined by the **tendency** to return to equilibrium upon displacement. In other words, a stable aeroplane will resist displacement from trim or equilibrium. The control forces of the aeroplane should reflect the stability of the aeroplane and provide suitable reference to the pilot for precise control of the aeroplane.

EFFECT OF ELEVATOR DEFLECTION

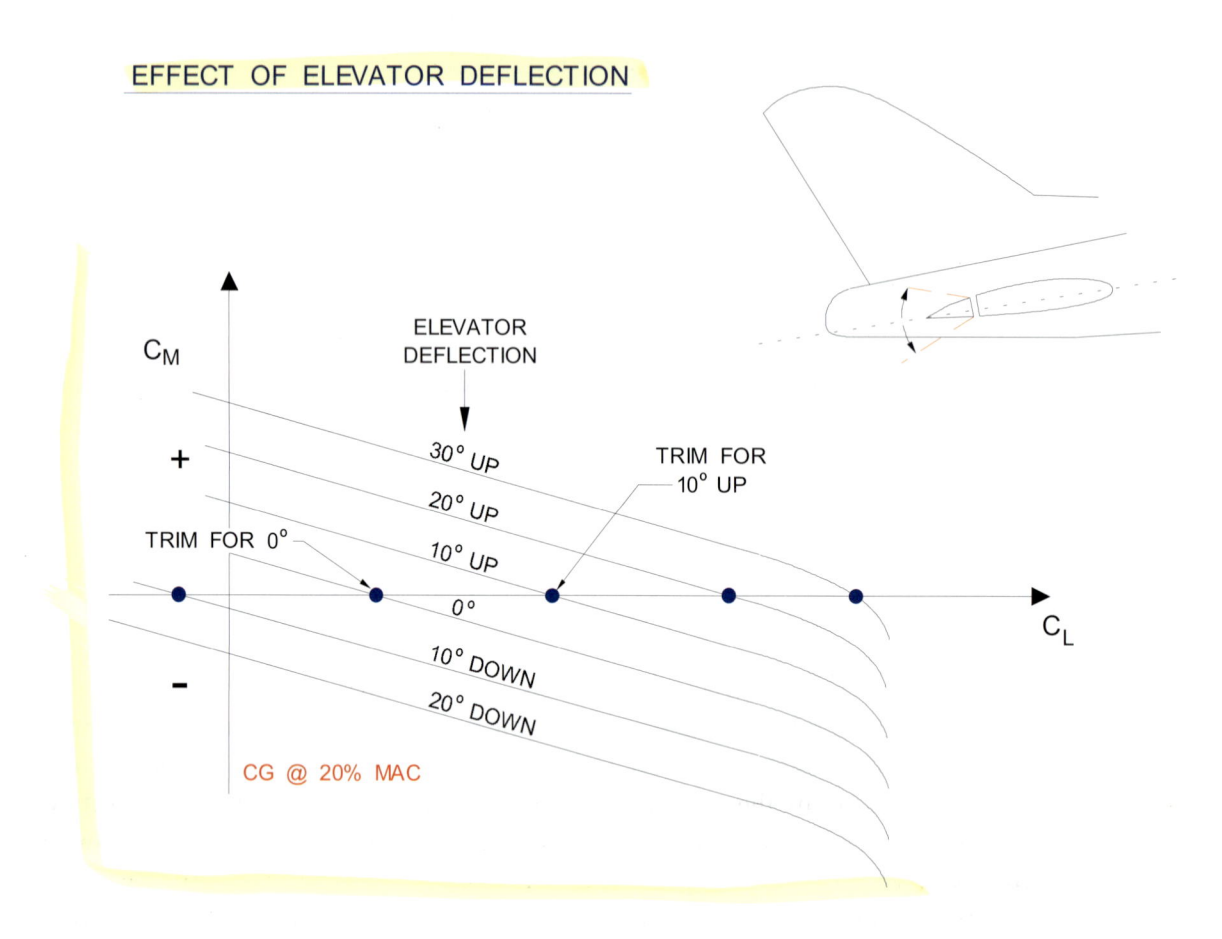

Figure 10.28

The effect of elevator deflection on pitching moments is illustrated by the graph of Fig. 10.28. If the elevators of the aeroplane are held at zero deflection, the resulting line of C_M versus C_L for $0°$ depicts the static stability and trim lift coefficient. If the elevators are held at a deflection of $10°$ up (aircraft trimmed at a lower speed), the aeroplane static stability is unchanged but the trim lift coefficient is increased.

> A CHANGE IN ELEVATOR POSITION DOES NOT ALTER THE TAIL CONTRIBUTION TO STABILITY

PRINCIPLES OF FLIGHT   **STABILITY AND CONTROL**

As the elevator is held in various positions, equilibrium (trim) will occur at various lift coefficients, and the trim C_L can be correlated with elevator deflection as shown in Fig. 10.29.

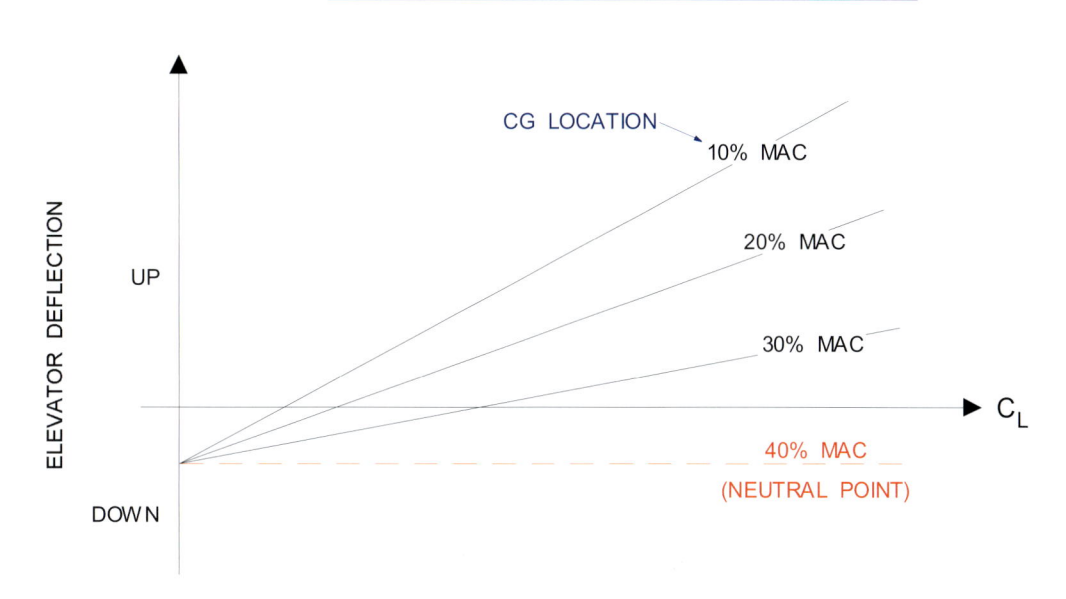

Figure 10.29

When the CG position of the aeroplane is fixed, each elevator position corresponds to a particular trim lift coefficient. As the CG is moved aft the slope of this line decreases and the decrease in stability is evident by a given control displacement causing a greater change in trim lift coefficient. **This is evidence that decreasing stability causes increased controllability and, of course, increasing stability decreases controllability.**

If the CG is moved aft until the line of trim C_L versus elevator deflection has zero slope, neutral static stability is obtained.

PRINCIPLES OF FLIGHT   STABILITY AND CONTROL

Figure 10.30

Since each value of lift coefficient corresponds to a particular value of dynamic pressure required to support an aeroplane in level flight, trim airspeed can be correlated with elevator deflection as in the graph of Fig. 10.30.

If the CG location is ahead of the neutral point and control position is directly related to surface deflection, the aeroplane will give evidence of **stick position stability**. In other words, the aeroplane will require the stick to be moved aft to increase the angle of attack and trim at a lower airspeed and to be moved forward to decrease the angle of attack and trim at a higher airspeed.

It is highly desirable to have an aeroplane demonstrate this feature. If the aeroplane were to have stick position instability, the aeroplane would require the stick to be moved aft to trim at a higher airspeed or to be moved forward to trim at a lower airspeed.

There is an increment of force dependent on the trim tab setting which varies with the dynamic pressure or the square of equivalent airspeed. Fig.10.31 indicates the variation of stick force with airspeed and illustrates the effect of tab setting on stick force.

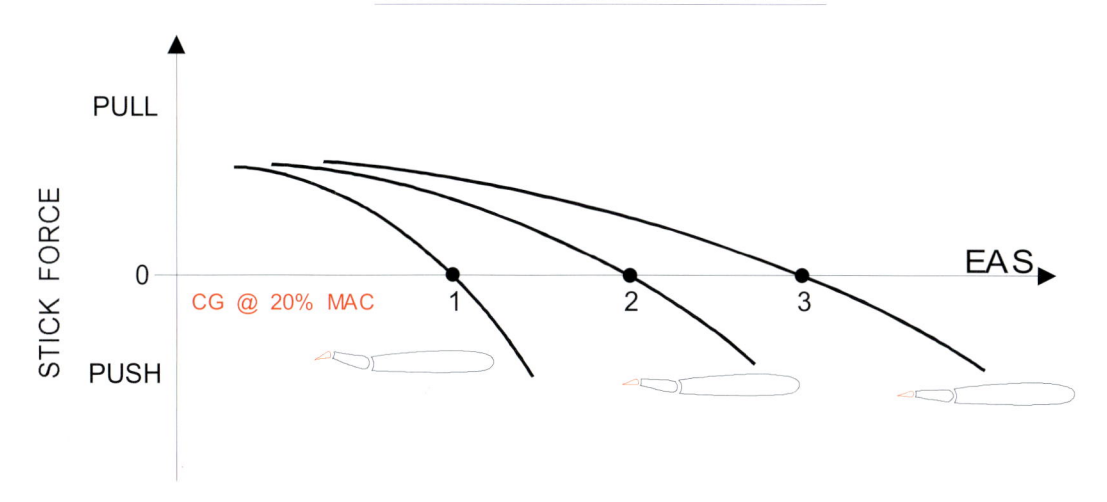

Figure 10.31

In order to trim the aeroplane at point (1) a certain amount of up elevator is required and zero stick force is obtained with the use of the trim tab. To trim the aeroplane for higher speeds corresponding to points (2) and (3), less and less aircraft nose-up tab is required.

Note that when the aeroplane is properly trimmed, a push force is required to increase airspeed and a pull force is required to decrease airspeed. In this manner, the aeroplane would have positive stick force stability with a stable "feel" for airspeed.

PRINCIPLES OF FLIGHT   **STABILITY AND CONTROL**

EFFECT OF CG POSITION

Figure 10.32

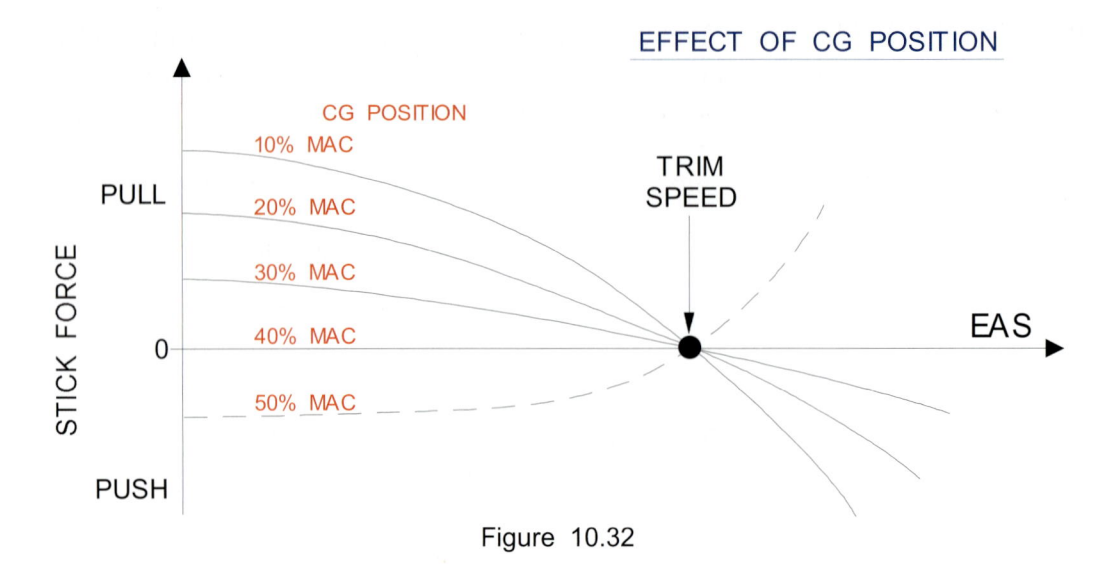

If the CG of the aeroplane were varied while maintaining trim at a constant airspeed, the effect of CG position on stick force stability could be appreciated. As illustrated in Fig. 10.32, moving the CG aft decreases the slope of the line of stick force through the trim speed. Thus, on decreasing stick-force stability it is evident that smaller stick forces are necessary to displace the aeroplane from the trim speed. When the stick force gradient (or slope) becomes zero, the CG is at the neutral point and neutral stability exists. If the CG is aft of the neutral point, stick force instability will exist, e.g. the aeroplane will require a push force at a lower speed or a pull force at a higher speed. It should be noted that the stick force gradient is low at low airspeeds and when the aeroplane is at low speeds, high power, and a CG position near the aft limit, the "feel" for airspeed will be weak.

EFFECT OF CONTROL SYSTEM FRICTION

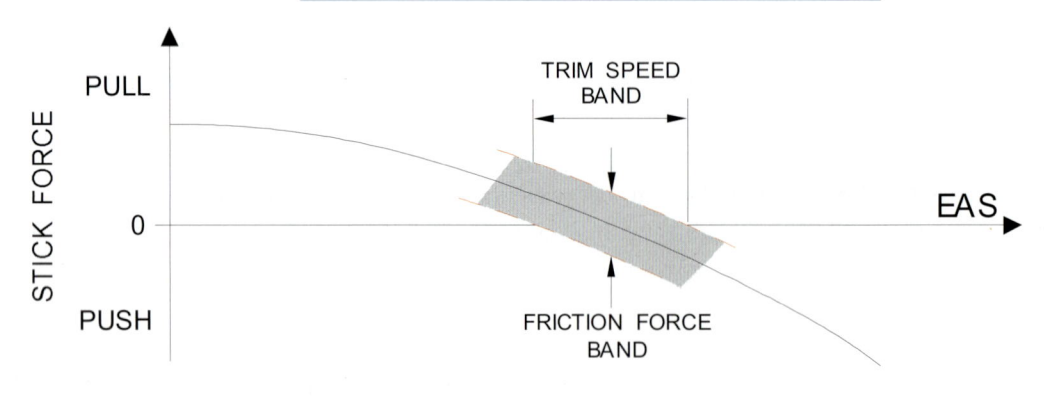

Figure 10.33

Control system friction can create very undesirable effects on control forces. Fig. 10.33 illustrates that the control force versus airspeed is a band rather than a line. A wide friction force band can completely mask the stick force stability when the stick force stability is low. Modern flight control systems require precise maintenance to minimize the friction force band and preserve proper feel to the aeroplane.

PRINCIPLES OF FLIGHT **STABILITY AND CONTROL**

10.15 MANOEUVRE STABILITY

When the pilot pitches the aircraft, it rotates about the CG and the tailplane is subject to a pitching velocity, in this example, downwards. Due to the pitching velocity in manoeuvring flight, the longitudinal stability of the aeroplane is slightly greater than in steady flight conditions.

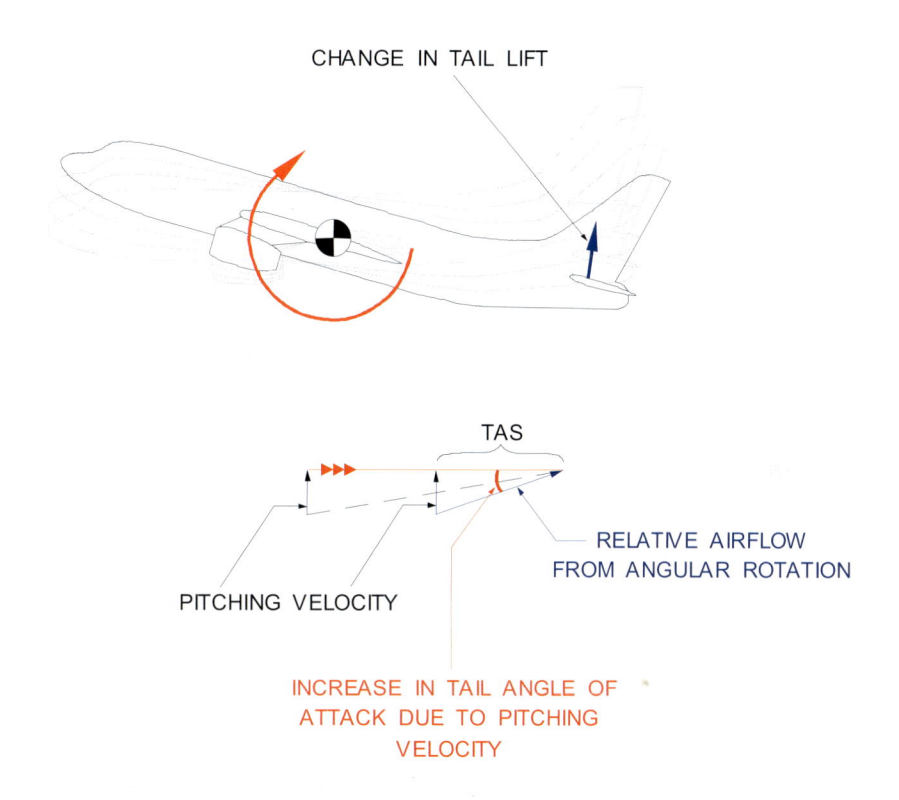

Figure 10.34   Aerodynamic Damping

Fig. 10.34 shows that the tailplane experiences an upwards component of airflow due to its downwards pitching velocity. The vector addition of this vertical component to the TAS provides an increase in effective angle of attack of the tail, which creates an increase in tail lift, opposing the nose up pitch displacement.

Since the negative pitching moment opposes the nose up pitch displacement but is **due** to the nose up pitching motion, the effect is a damping in pitch (aerodynamic damping).

It can be seen that an increase in TAS, for a given pitching velocity, decreases the angle of attack due to pitching velocity

> INCREASING ALTITUDE AT A CONSTANT IAS DECREASES AERODYNAMIC DAMPING

PRINCIPLES OF FLIGHT
STABILITY AND CONTROL

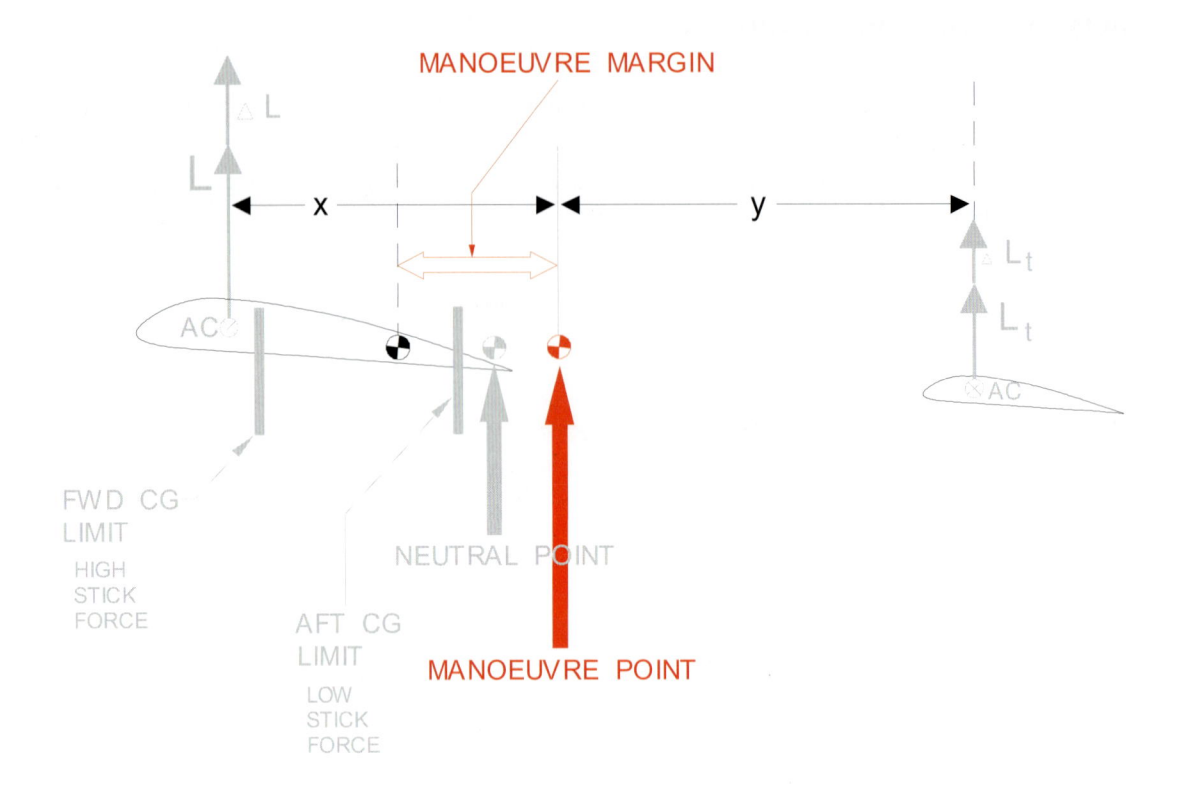

Figure 10.35   Manoeuvre Point

The pitching moment from aerodynamic damping will give greater stability in manoeuvres than is apparent in steady flight. The CG position when the tail moment would be the same as the wing moment during manoeuvring is known as the **manoeuvre point** and this "neutral point" will be further aft than for 1g flight, as shown in Fig.10.35.

In most cases the manoeuvre point will not be a critical item; if the aeroplane demonstrates static stability in 1g flight, it will definitely have stability in manoeuvring flight.

10.16   STICK FORCE PER 'g'

The most direct appreciation of the manoeuvring stability of an aeroplane is obtained from a plot of stick force versus load factor such as shown in Fig. 10.36. The aeroplane with positive manoeuvring stability should demonstrate a steady increase in stick force with increase in load factor or "g". The manoeuvring stick force gradient - or stick force per "g" - must be positive but should be of the proper magnitude. The stick force gradient must not be excessively high or the aeroplane will be difficult and tiring to manoeuver. Also, the stick force gradient must not be too low or the aeroplane may be overstressed inadvertently when light control forces exist.

PRINCIPLES OF FLIGHT   STABILITY AND CONTROL

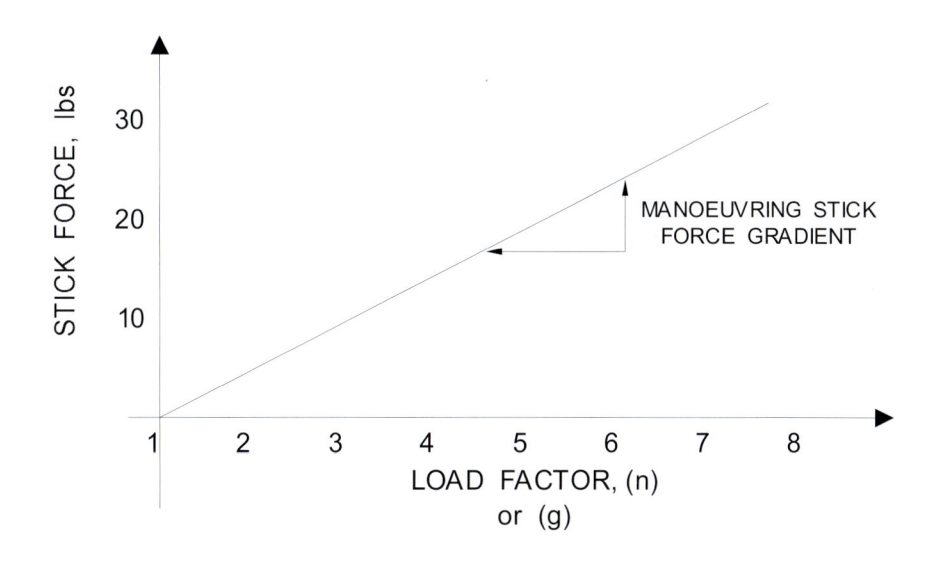

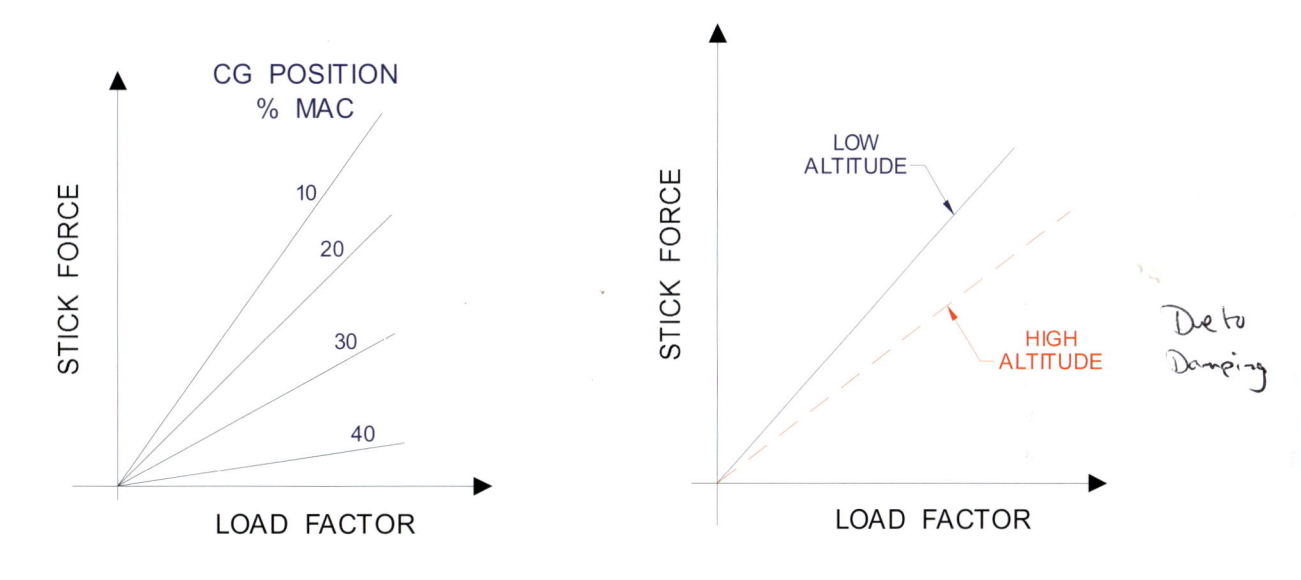

Figure 10.36

When the aeroplane has high static stability, the manoeuvring stability will be high and a high stick force gradient will result, Fig. 10.36. A possibility exists that the forward CG limit could be set to prevent an excessively high manoeuvring stick force gradient. As the CG moves aft, the stick force gradient decreases with decreasing manoeuvring stability and the lower limit of stick force gradient may be reached.

When asked to calculate 'stick force per g', remember that the aircraft is at 1g to start with. So 1g must be subtracted from the 'g' limit before dividing by the pull force.

The pitch damping of the aeroplane is related to air density. At high altitudes, the high TAS reduces the change in tail angle of attack for a given pitching velocity and reduces the pitch damping. Thus, a decrease in manoeuvring stick force stability can be expected with increased altitude.

PRINCIPLES OF FLIGHT — STABILITY AND CONTROL

10.17 TAILORING CONTROL FORCES

Control forces should reflect the stability of the aeroplane but, at the same time, should be of a tolerable magnitude. A manual flying control system may employ an infinite variety of techniques to provide satisfactory control forces throughout the speed, CG and altitude range of the aircraft.

EFFECT OF STICK CENTRING SPRING

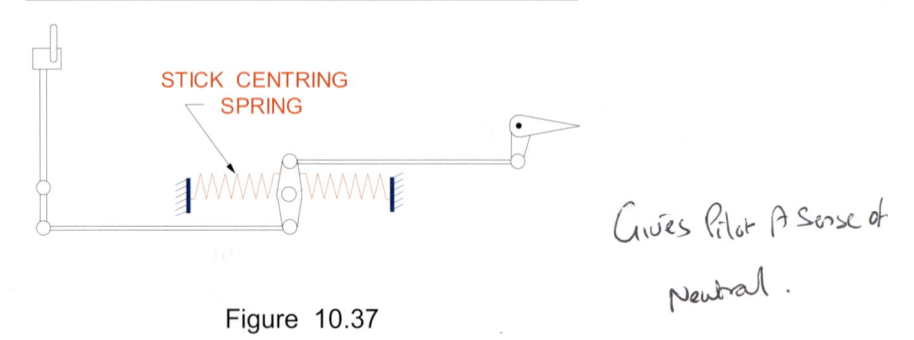

Figure 10.37

10.17.1 STICK CENTRING SPRING

If a spring is added to the control system as shown in Fig 10.37, it will tend to centre the stick and provide a force increment depending on stick displacement.

When the control system has a fixed gearing between stick position and surface deflection, the centring spring will provide a contribution to stick force stability according to stick position.

The contribution to stick force stability will be largest at low flight speeds where relatively large control deflections are required. The contribution will be smallest at high airspeed because of the smaller control deflections required. Thus, the stick centring spring will increase the airspeed and manoeuvring stick force stability but the contribution decreases at high airspeeds.

A variation of this device would be a spring stiffness which would be controlled to vary with dynamic pressure (Q - Feel). In that case, the contribution of the spring to stick force stability would not diminish with speed.

10.17.2 DOWN SPRING

A down spring added to a control system is a means of increasing airspeed stick force stability without a change in aeroplane static stability.

As shown in Fig. 10.38, a down spring consists of a long pre-loaded spring attached to the control system which tends to rotate the elevators down (aircraft nose down). The effect of the down spring is to contribute an increment of pull force independent of control deflection or airspeed.

EFFECT OF DOWNSPRING

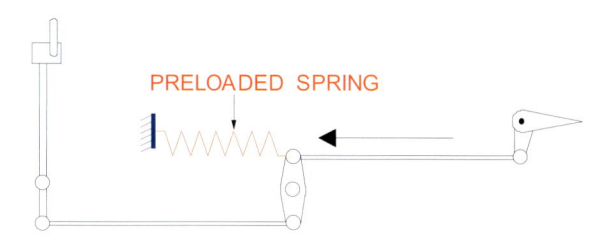

Figure 10.38

When the down spring is added to the control system of an aeroplane and the aeroplane is re-trimmed for the original speed, the airspeed stick force gradient is increased and there is a stronger feel for airspeed. The down spring would provide a "synthetic" improvement to an aeroplane deficient in airspeed stick force stability. Since the force increment from the down spring is unaffected by stick position or normal acceleration, the manoeuvring stick force stability would be unchanged.

10.17.3 BOBWEIGHT

The bobweight is an effective device for improving stick force stability. As shown in Fig. 10.39, the bobweight consists of an eccentric mass attached to the control system which, in unaccelerated flight, contributes an increment of pull force identical to the down spring. In fact, a bobweight added to the control system of an aeroplane produces an effect identical to the down spring. The bobweight will increase the airspeed stick force gradient and increase the feel for airspeed.

The bobweight also has an effect on the manoeuvring stick force gradient since the bobweight mass is subjected to the same acceleration as the aeroplane. Thus, the bobweight will provide an increment of stick force in direct proportion to the manoeuvring acceleration of the aeroplane (load factor applied). This will prevent the pilot applying too much 'g' during manoeuvres; the more you pull back, the more resistance the bobweight adds to the control system.

EFFECT OF BOBWEIGHT

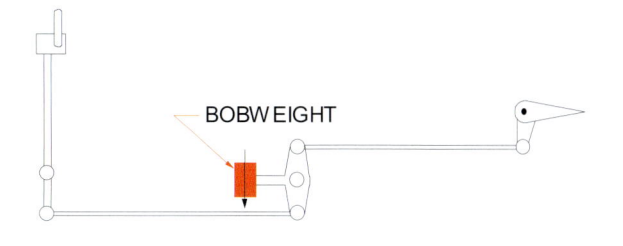

Figure 10.39

PRINCIPLES OF FLIGHT — STABILITY AND CONTROL

10.18 LONGITUDINAL CONTROL

To be satisfactory, an aeroplane must have adequate controllability as well as adequate stability. An aeroplane with high static longitudinal stability will exhibit great resistance to displacement from equilibrium. Hence, the most critical conditions of controllability will occur when the aeroplane has high static stability, i.e., **the lower limits of controllability will set the upper limits of static stability.** (Fwd. CG limit).

There are three principal conditions of flight which provide the critical requirements of longitudinal control power (manoeuvring, take-off and landing). Any one or combination of these conditions can determine the overall longitudinal control power and set a limit to the forward CG position.

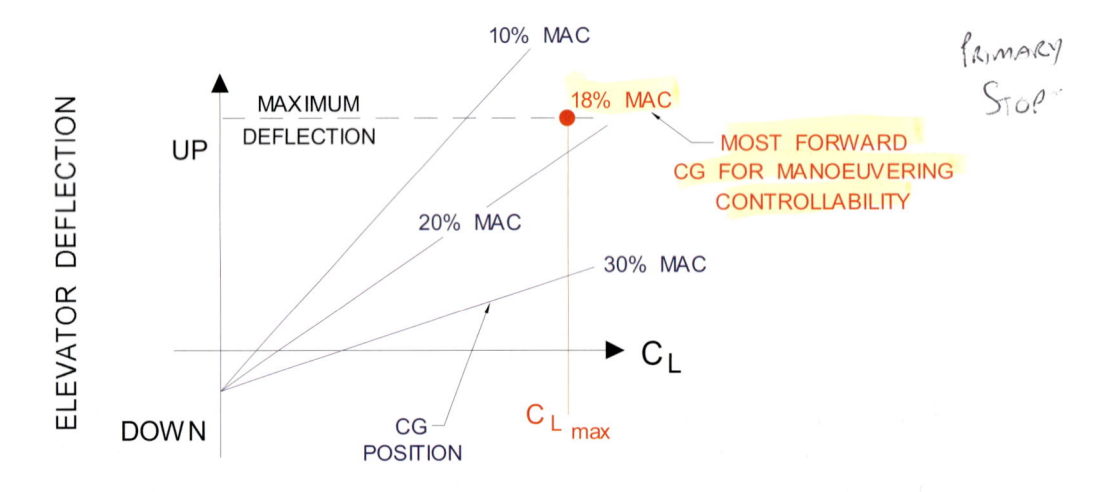

Figure 10.40

10.19 MANOEUVRING CONTROL REQUIREMENT

The aeroplane should have sufficient longitudinal control power to attain the maximum usable lift coefficient or the limit load factor during manoeuvres. As shown in Fig. 10.40, forward movement of the CG increases the longitudinal stability of an aeroplane and requires larger control deflections to produce changes in trim lift coefficient. For the example shown, the maximum effective deflection of the elevator is not capable of trimming the aeroplane at $C_{L\,max}$ for CG positions ahead of 18 percent MAC.

This particular control requirement can be most critical for an aeroplane in supersonic flight. Supersonic flight is usually accompanied by large increases in static longitudinal stability (due to aft CP movement) and a reduction in the effectiveness of control surfaces. In order to cope with these trends, powerful all-moving surfaces must be used to attain limit load factor or maximum usable C_L in supersonic flight. This requirement is so important that once satisfied, the supersonic configuration usually has sufficient longitudinal control power for all other conditions of flight.

PRINCIPLES OF FLIGHT STABILITY AND CONTROL

10.20 TAKEOFF CONTROL REQUIREMENT

At take-off, the aeroplane must have sufficient elevator control power to assume the takeoff attitude prior to reaching takeoff speed.

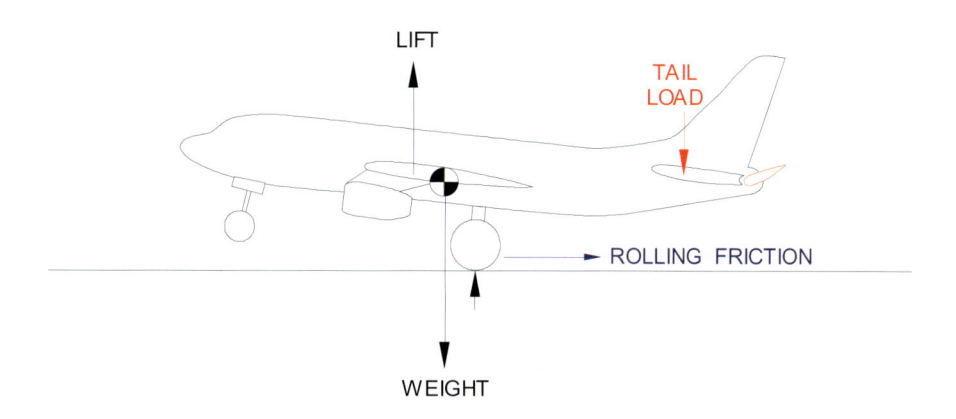

Figure 10.41

Fig. 10.41 illustrates the principal forces acting on an aeroplane during takeoff roll. When the aeroplane is in the three point attitude at some speed less than the stall speed, the wing lift will be less than the weight of the aeroplane. As the elevators must be capable of rotating to the takeoff attitude, the critical condition will be with zero load on the nose wheel and the net of lift and weight supported on the main gear.

Rolling friction resulting from the normal force on the main gear creates an adverse nose down moment.

Also, the CG ahead of the main gear contributes a nose down moment and this consideration could decide the most aft location of the main landing gear during design.

To balance these two nose down moments, the horizontal tail must be capable of producing a nose up moment big enough to attain the takeoff attitude at the specified speed.

The propeller aeroplane at take-off power may induce considerable slipstream velocity at the horizontal tail which can provide an increase in the efficiency of the surface. The jet aeroplane does not experience a similar magnitude of this effect since the induced velocities from the jet are relatively small compared to the slipstream velocities from a propeller.

PRINCIPLES OF FLIGHT — STABILITY AND CONTROL

10.21 LANDING CONTROL REQUIREMENT

At landing, the aeroplane must have sufficient control power to ensure adequate control at specified landing speeds. The most critical requirement will exist when the CG is in the most forward position, flaps are fully extended, and power is set at idle. This configuration will provide the most stable condition which is most demanding of controllability.

The landing control requirement has one particular difference from the manoeuvring control requirement of free flight. As the aeroplane approaches the surface, there will be a change in the three-dimensional flow over the aeroplane due to ground effect. A wing in proximity to the ground plane will experience a decrease in tip vortices and downwash at a given lift coefficient. The decrease in downwash at the tail tends to increase the static stability and produce a nose down moment from the reduction in download on the tail. Thus, the aeroplane just off the runway surface, Fig. 10.42, will require additional control deflection to trim at a given lift coefficient and the landing control requirement may be critical in the design of longitudinal control power.

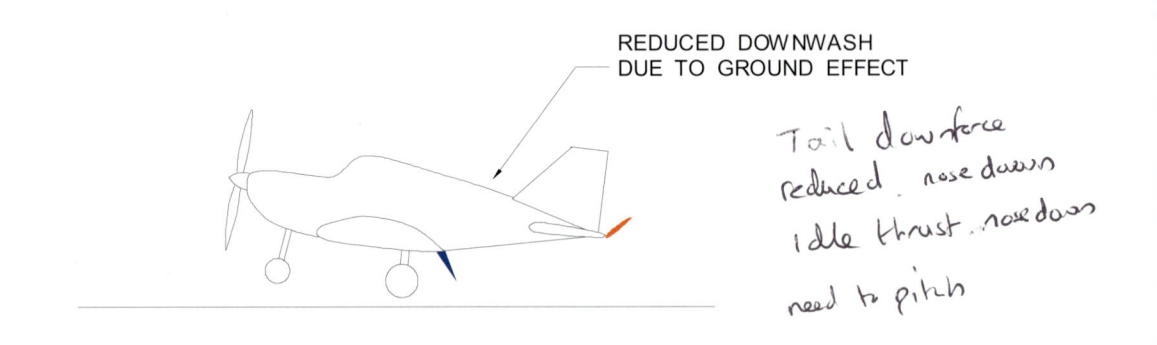

Figure 10.42

As an example of ground effect, a typical propeller powered aeroplane may require as much as 15° more up elevator to trim at $C_{L\ MAX}$ in ground effect than in free flight.

In some cases the effectiveness of the elevator is adversely affected by the use of trim tabs. **If trim is used to excess in trimming stick forces, the effectiveness of the elevator may be reduced to hinder landing or takeoff control.**

Each of the three principal conditions requiring adequate longitudinal control are critical for high static stability. If the forward CG limit is exceeded, the aeroplane may encounter a deficiency of controllability in any of these conditions.

The forward CG limit is set by the minimum permissible controllability

The aft CG limit is set by the minimum permissible stability.

PRINCIPLES OF FLIGHT   STABILITY AND CONTROL

10.22   DYNAMIC STABILITY

While **static** stability is concerned with the **initial tendency** of an aircraft to return to equilibrium, dynamic stability is defined by the resulting **motion with time**. If an aircraft is disturbed from equilibrium, the time history of the resulting motion indicates its dynamic stability. In general, an aircraft will demonstrate positive dynamic stability if the amplitude of motion decreases with time. The various conditions of possible dynamic behaviour are illustrated in the following six history diagrams. The nonoscillatory modes shown in diagrams A, B and C depict the time histories possible without cyclic motion.

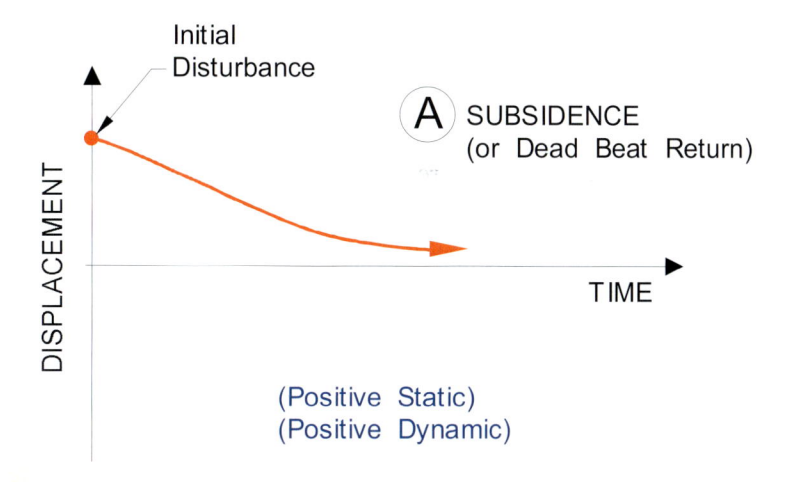

Chart A illustrates a system which is given an initial disturbance and the motion simply subsides without oscillation, the mode is termed "subsidence" or "deadbeat return." Such a motion indicates **positive static stability** by the initial tendency to return to equilibrium and **positive dynamic stability** since the amplitude decreases with time.

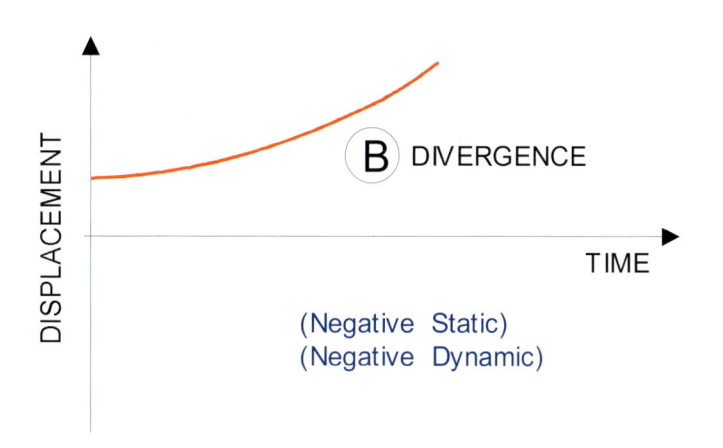

Chart B illustrates the mode of "divergence" by a non-cyclic increase of amplitude with time. The initial tendency to continue in the displacement direction is evidence of **static instability** and the increasing amplitude is proof of **dynamic instability**.

10 - 43

PRINCIPLES OF FLIGHT   STABILITY AND CONTROL

C
NEUTRAL STATIC STABILITY

(Neutral Static)
(Neutral Dynamic)

DISPLACEMENT / TIME

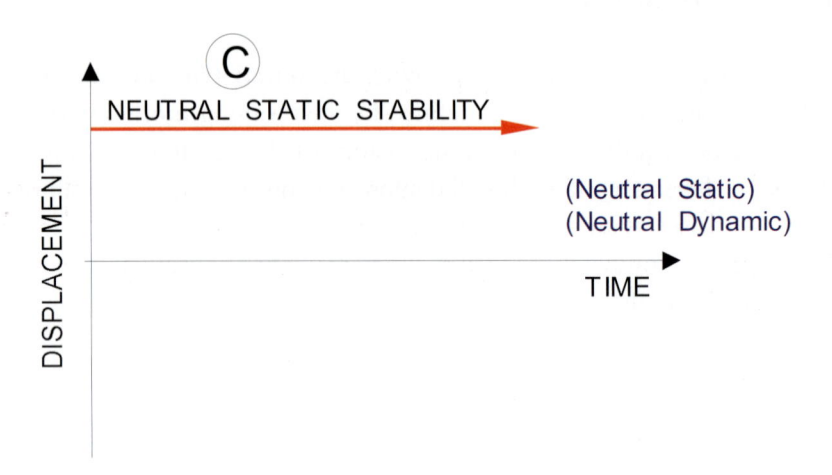

Chart C illustrates the mode of pure neutral stability. If the original disturbance creates a displacement which then remains constant, the lack of tendency for motion and the constant amplitude indicate **neutral static** and **neutral dynamic stability**.

The oscillatory modes shown in diagrams D, E and F depict the time histories possible with cyclic motion. One feature common to each of these modes is that positive static stability is demonstrated by the initial tendency to return to equilibrium conditions. However, the resulting dynamic behaviour may be stable, neutral, or unstable.

D
DAMPED OSCILLATION

(Positive Static)
(Positive Dynamic)

DISPLACEMENT / TIME

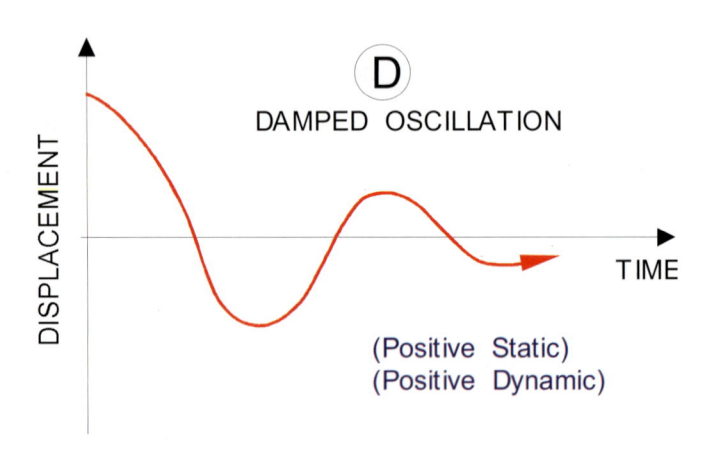

Chart D illustrates the mode of a damped oscillation where the amplitude decreases with time. The reduction of amplitude with time indicates there is **resistance to motion** and that **energy is being dissipated**. Dissipation of energy or **damping** is necessary to provide positive dynamic stability.

PRINCIPLES OF FLIGHT   **STABILITY AND CONTROL**

E   UNDAMPED OSCILLATION

(Positive Static)
(Neutral Dynamic)

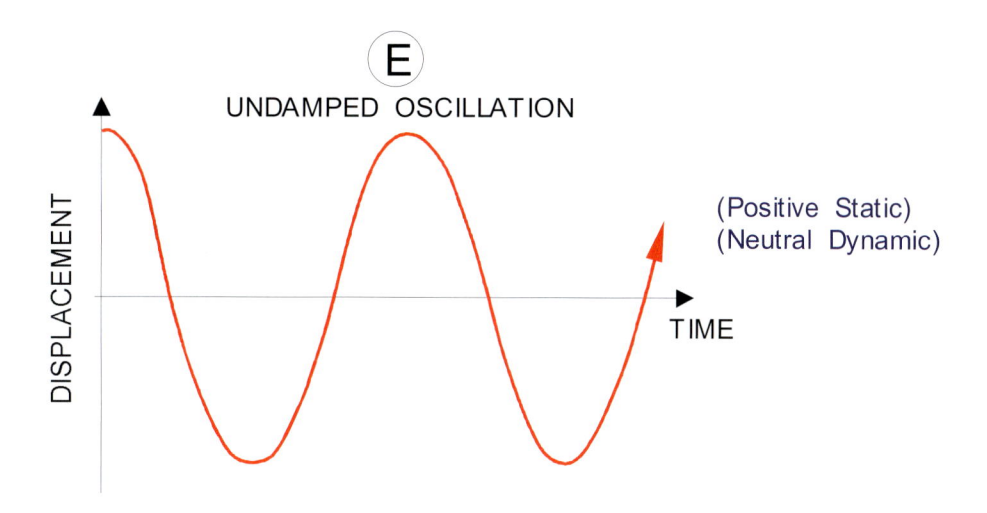

If there is no damping in the system, the mode of chart E is the result, an undamped oscillation. Without damping, the oscillation continues with no reduction of amplitude with time. While such an oscillation indicates **positive static stability**, **neutral dynamic stability** exists. Positive damping is necessary to eliminate the continued oscillation. As an example, a car with worn shock absorbers (or "dampers") lacks sufficient dynamic stability and the continued oscillatory motion is both unpleasant and potentially dangerous. In the same sense, an aircraft must have sufficient damping to rapidly dissipate any oscillatory motion which would affect the safe operation of the aircraft. When natural **aerodynamic damping** cannot be obtained, artificial damping must be provided to give the necessary positive dynamic stability.

F   DIVERGENT OSCILLATION

(Positive Static)
(Negative Dynamic)

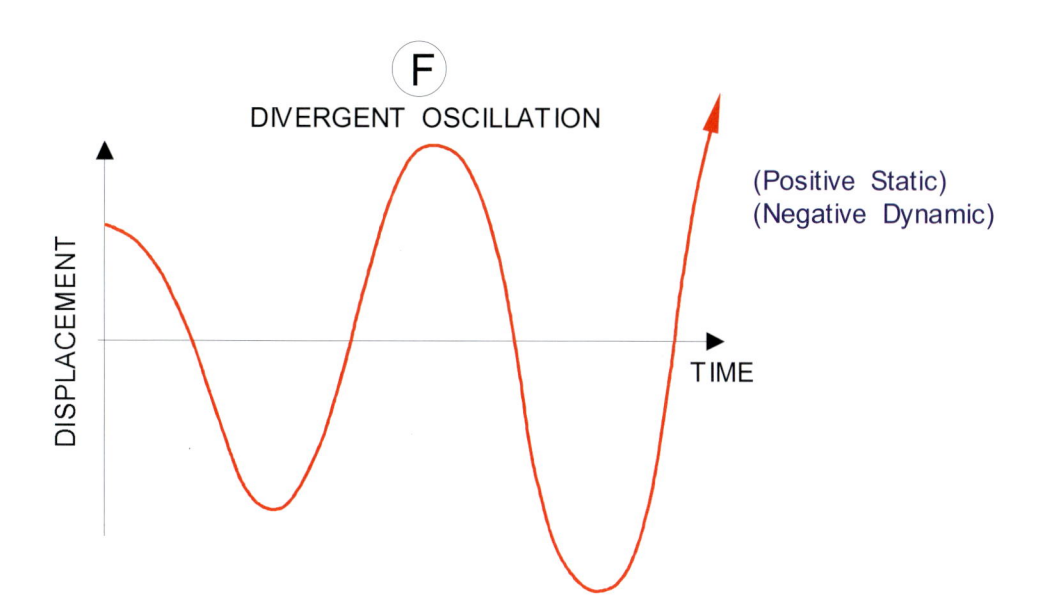

Chart F illustrates the mode of a divergent oscillation. This motion is **statically stable** since it tends to return to the equilibrium position. However, each subsequent return to equilibrium is with increasing velocity such that amplitude continues to increase with time. Thus, **dynamic instability** exists.

Divergent oscillation results when energy is supplied to the motion rather than dissipated by positive damping. An example of divergent oscillation occurs if a pilot unknowingly makes control inputs which are near the natural frequency of the aeroplane in pitch; energy is added to the system, negative damping exists, and **Pilot Induced Oscillation** (P.I.O.) results.

The existence of static stability does not guarantee the existence of dynamic stability. However, the existence of dynamic stability implies the existence of static stability.

> IF AN AIRCRAFT IS STATICALLY UNSTABLE, IT CANNOT BE DYNAMICALLY STABLE

Any aircraft must demonstrate the required degrees of static and dynamic stability. If the aircraft were allowed to have static instability with a rapid rate of divergence, it would be very difficult, if not impossible to fly. In addition, positive dynamic stability is mandatory in certain areas to prevent objectionable continued oscillations of the aircraft.

PRINCIPLES OF FLIGHT   STABILITY AND CONTROL

10.23 LONGITUDINAL DYNAMIC STABILITY.

The considerations of longitudinal **dynamic** stability are concerned with the time history response of the aeroplane to disturbances, i.e., the variation of displacement amplitude with time following a disturbance.

From previous definition:

a) dynamic stability will exist when the amplitude of motion decreases with time and

b) dynamic instability will exist if the amplitude increases with time.

An aeroplane must demonstrate positive dynamic stability for the major longitudinal motions. In addition, the aeroplane must demonstrate a certain degree of longitudinal stability by reducing the amplitude of motion at a certain rate. The required degree of dynamic stability is usually specified by the time necessary for the amplitude to reduce to one-half the original value: the time to damp to half-amplitude.

The aeroplane in free flight has six degrees of freedom: rotation in roll, pitch, and yaw and translation in the horizontal, vertical, and lateral directions. In the case of longitudinal dynamic stability, the degrees of freedom can be limited to pitch rotation, plus vertical and horizontal translation.

Since the aeroplane is usually symmetrical from left to right, there will be no need to consider coupling between longitudinal and lateral / directional motions.

Thus, the principal variables in the longitudinal motion of an aeroplane will be:

1. The pitch attitude of the aeroplane.

2. The angle of attack (which will differ from the pitch attitude by the inclination of the flight path).

3. True airspeed (TAS)

The longitudinal dynamic stability of an aeroplane generally consists of two basic modes of oscillation:-

     a) long period oscillation (phugoid)

     b) short period motion

While the longitudinal motion of the aeroplane may consist of a combination of these modes, the characteristics of each mode are sufficiently distinct that each oscillatory tendency may be studied separately.

PRINCIPLES OF FLIGHT   **STABILITY AND CONTROL**

10.24 LONG PERIOD OSCILLATION (PHUGOID)

The first mode of dynamic longitudinal stability consists of a **long period oscillation** referred to as the **phugoid**.

The phugoid or long period oscillation involves noticeable variations in:-

i)   pitch attitude,

ii)   altitude and

iii)   airspeed, but

iv)   **nearly constant angle of attack**. (not much change in load factor)

The phugoid is a gradual interchange of potential and kinetic energy about some equilibrium airspeed and altitude. Fig. 10.43 illustrates the characteristic motion of the phugoid.

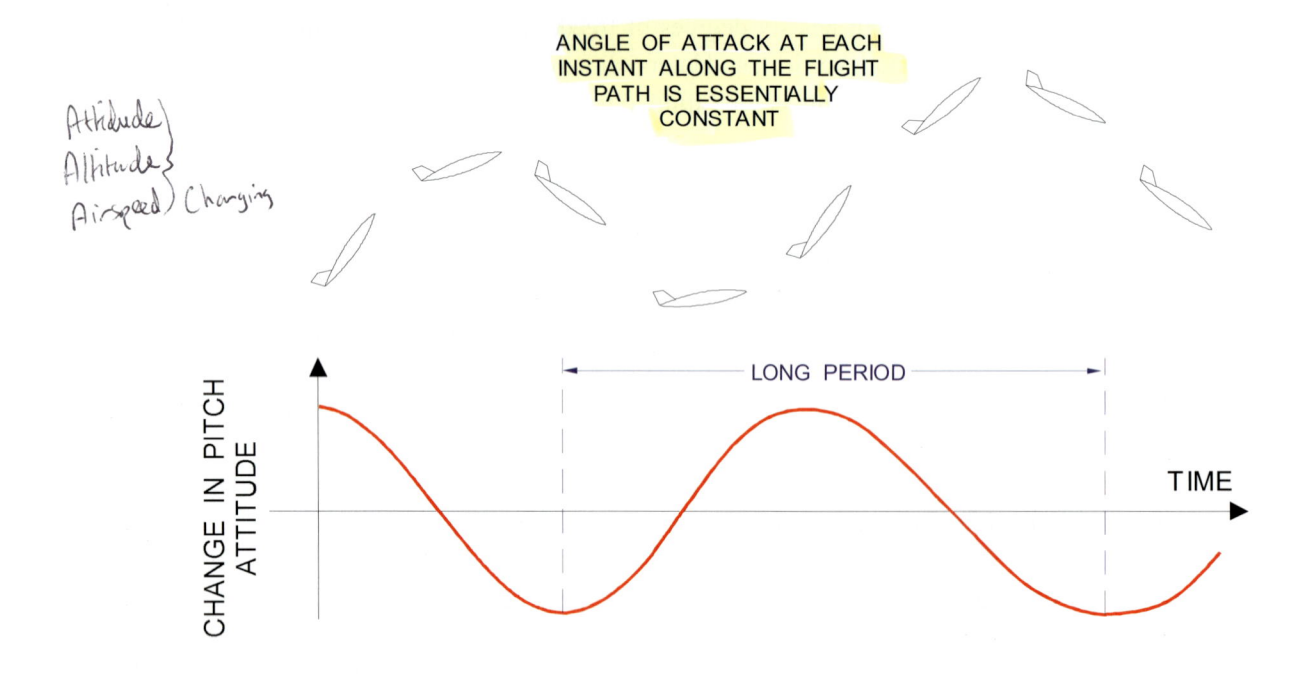

Figure 10.43   Long Period Oscillation (Phugoid)

The period of oscillation in the phugoid is between 1 and 2 minutes. Since the pitch rate is quite low and only negligible changes in angle of attack take place, damping of the phugoid is weak. However, such weak damping does not necessarily have any great consequence. Since the period of oscillation is so great, **long period oscillation is easily controlled by the pilot**. Due to the nature of the phugoid, it is not necessary to make any specific aerodynamic provisions to counteract it.

PRINCIPLES OF FLIGHT STABILITY AND CONTROL

10.25 SHORT PERIOD OSCILLATION

The second mode of dynamic longitudinal stability is the **short period** oscillation.

Short period oscillation involves significant changes in angle of attack (load factor), with approximately constant speed, height and pitch attitude; it consists of rapid pitch oscillations during which the aeroplane is constantly being restored towards equilibrium by its static stability and **the amplitude of the short period oscillations being decreased by pitch damping**.

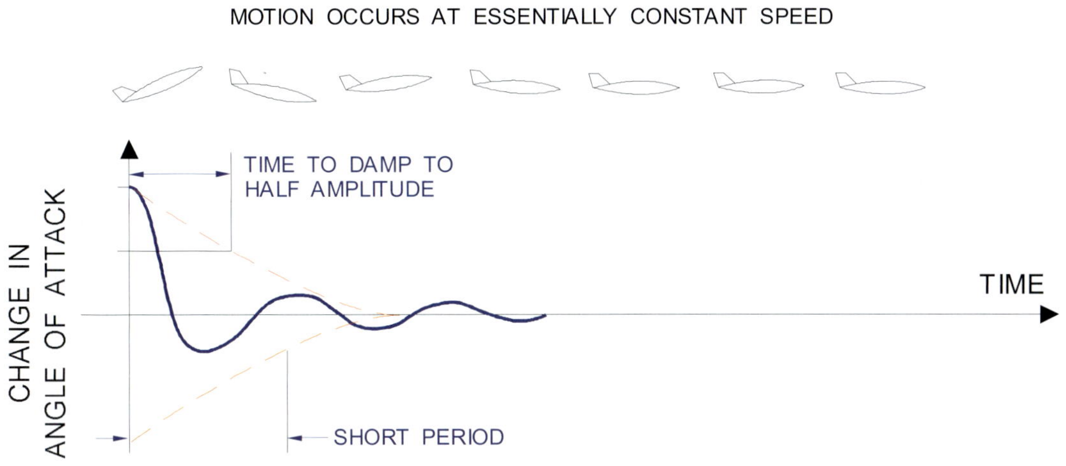

Figure 10.44   Short Period Oscillation

Short period oscillation at high dynamic pressures with large changes in angle of attack could produce severe 'g' loads. (Large changes in load factor).

Shown in Fig. 10.44, the second mode has relatively short periods that correspond closely with the normal pilot response lag time, e.g., 1 or 2 seconds or less. There is the possibility that an attempt by the pilot to forcibly damp an oscillation may actually reinforce the oscillation (PIO) and produce instability.

Short period oscillation is not easily controlled by the pilot.

If short period oscillation occurs, release the controls; the aeroplane is designed to demonstrate the necessary damping. Even an attempt by the pilot to hold the controls stationary when the aeroplane is oscillating may result in a small unstable input into the control system which can reinforce the oscillation to produce failing flight loads.

Modern large high speed jet transport aircraft are fitted with pitch dampers, which automatically compensate for any dynamic longitudinal instability.

PRINCIPLES OF FLIGHT STABILITY AND CONTROL

Of the two modes of dynamic longitudinal stability, the **short period oscillation is of greatest importance**. The short period oscillation can generate damaging flight loads due to the rapid changes in 'g' loading, and it is adversely affected by pilot response lag (PIO).

It has been stated that the amplitude of the oscillations are decreased by pitch damping, so the problems of dynamic stability can become acute under the conditions of flight where reduced aerodynamic damping occurs.

High altitude, and consequently low density (high TAS), reduces aerodynamic damping, as detailed in paragraph 10.15.

> DYNAMIC STABILITY IS REDUCED AT HIGH ALTITUDE DUE TO REDUCED AERODYNAMIC DAMPING

PRINCIPLES OF FLIGHT — STABILITY AND CONTROL

10.26 DIRECTIONAL STABILITY AND CONTROL

The directional stability of an aeroplane is essentially the "weathercock" stability and involves moments about the Normal axis and their relationship with yaw or **sideslip angle**. An aeroplane which has static directional stability will tend to return to equilibrium when subjected to some disturbance. Evidence of static directional stability would be the development of yawing moments which tend to restore the aeroplane to equilibrium.

SIDESLIP — AIRFLOW IS EITHER SIDE (HORIZONTALLY) OF THE LONGITUDINAL AXIS.

DEFINITIONS

The axis system of an aeroplane defines a positive yawing moment, N, as a moment about the normal axis which tends to rotate the nose to the right. As in other aerodynamic considerations, it is convenient to consider yawing moments in the coefficient form so that static stability can be evaluated independent of weight, altitude, speed, etc. The yawing moment, N, is defined in the coefficient form by the following equation:

$$N = C_n \, Q \, S \, b$$

or

$$C_n = \frac{N}{Q \, S \, b}$$

where,

- N = yawing moment (positive to the right)
- Q = dynamic pressure
- S = wing area
- b = wing span
- C_n = yawing moment coefficient (positive to the right)

The yawing moment coefficient, C_n is based on the wing dimensions S and b as the wing is the characteristic surface of the aeroplane.

PRINCIPLES OF FLIGHT   **STABILITY AND CONTROL**

10.27 SIDESLIP ANGLE

The sideslip angle relates the displacement of the aeroplane centerline from the relative airflow. Sideslip angle is provided the symbol β (beta) and is positive when the relative wind is displaced to the right of the aeroplane centerline. Fig. 10.45 illustrates the definitions of sideslip angle.

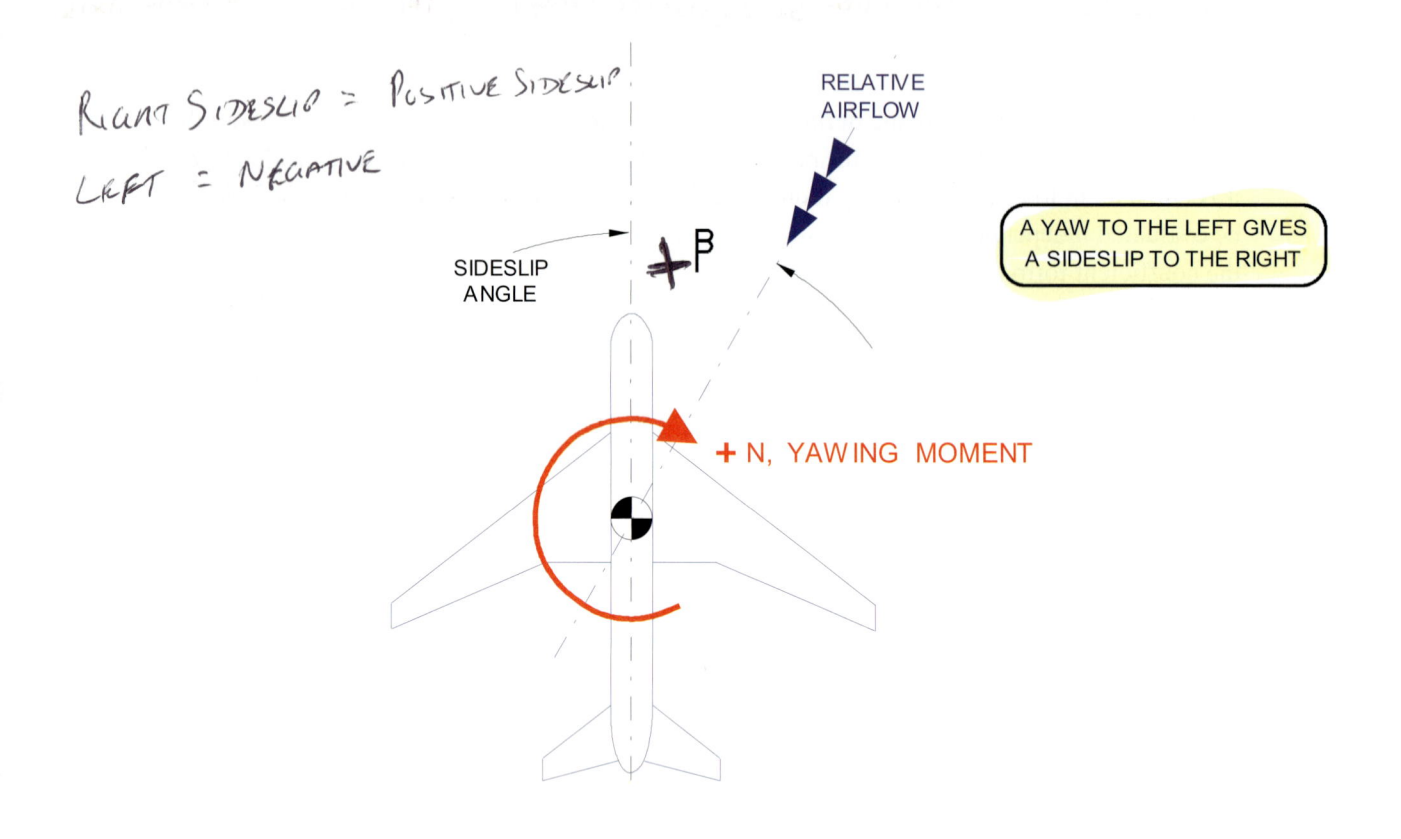

[Handwritten annotation: RIGHT SIDESLIP = POSITIVE SIDESLIP; LEFT = NEGATIVE]

Figure 10.45 Sideslip Angle (β)

The sideslip angle, β, is essentially the "directional angle of attack" of the aeroplane and is the primary reference in directional stability as well as lateral stability considerations. Static directional stability of the aeroplane is appreciated by response to sideslip.

PRINCIPLES OF FLIGHT   STABILITY AND CONTROL

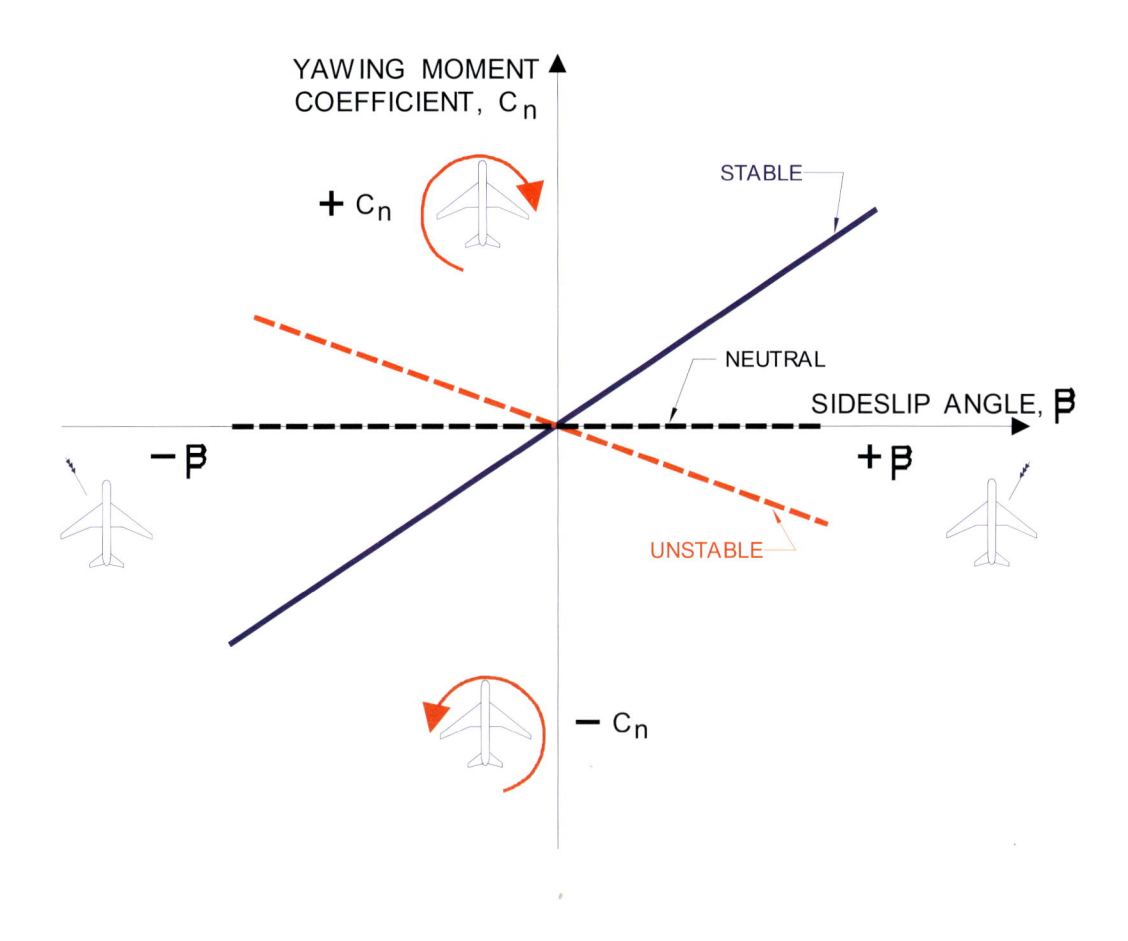

Figure 10.46

10.28 STATIC DIRECTIONAL STABILITY

Static directional stability can be illustrated by a graph of yawing moment coefficient, C_n versus sideslip angle, β, such as shown in Fig 10.46. When the aeroplane is subject to a positive sideslip angle, static directional stability will be evident if a positive yawing moment coefficient results. Thus, when the relative airflow comes from the right ($+\beta$) a yawing moment to the right ($+C_n$) should be created which tends to "weathercock" the aeroplane and return the nose into the wind. Static directional stability will exist when the curve of C_n versus β has a positive slope and the degree of stability will be a function of the slope of this curve. If the curve has zero slope, there is no tendency to return to equilibrium and neutral static directional stability exists. When the curve of C_n versus β has a negative slope, the yawing moments developed by sideslip tend to diverge rather than restore and static directional instability exists.

PRINCIPLES OF FLIGHT   **STABILITY AND CONTROL**

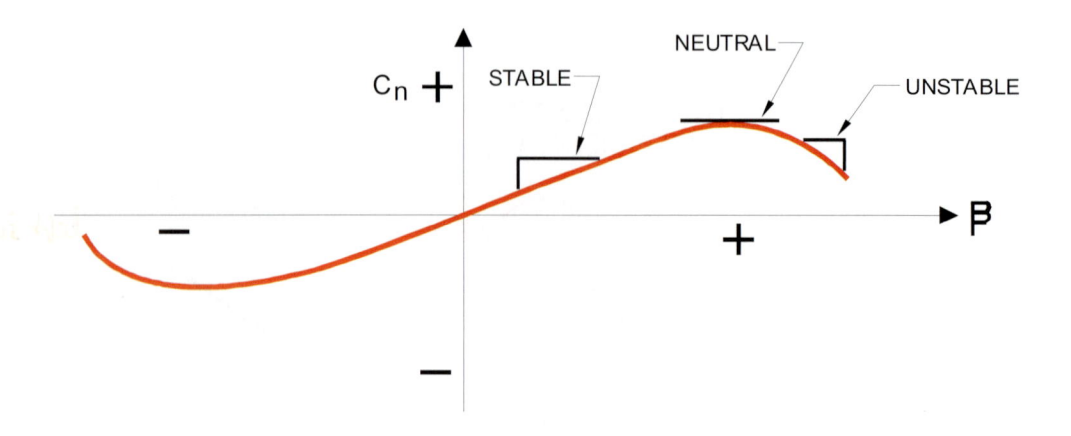

Figure 10.47

Fig. 10.47 illustrates the fact that the instantaneous slope of the curve of C_n versus β will describe the static directional stability of the aeroplane.

a)   At small angles of sideslip a strong positive slope depicts strong directional stability.

b)   Large angles of sideslip produce zero slope and neutral stability.

c)   At very high sideslip the negative slope of the curve indicates directional instability.

This decay of directional stability with increased sideslip is not an unusual condition. However, directional instability should not occur at the angles of sideslip of ordinary flight conditions.

Static directional stability must be in evidence for all the critical conditions of flight. Generally, good directional stability is a fundamental quality directly affecting the pilots' impression of an aeroplane.

10.29 CONTRIBUTION OF THE AEROPLANE COMPONENTS.

Because the contribution of each component depends upon and is related to the others, it is necessary to study each separately.

FUSELAGE: The fuselage is destabilizing, Fig. 10.48. It is an aerodynamic body and a condition of sideslip can be likened to an "angle of attack", so that an aerodynamic side force is created. This side force acts through the fuselage aerodynamic centre (AC), which is close to the quarter-length point. If this aerodynamic centre is ahead of aircraft centre of gravity, as is usually the case, the effect is de-stabilizing.

PRINCIPLES OF FLIGHT — STABILITY AND CONTROL

FUSELAGE (Plan View)

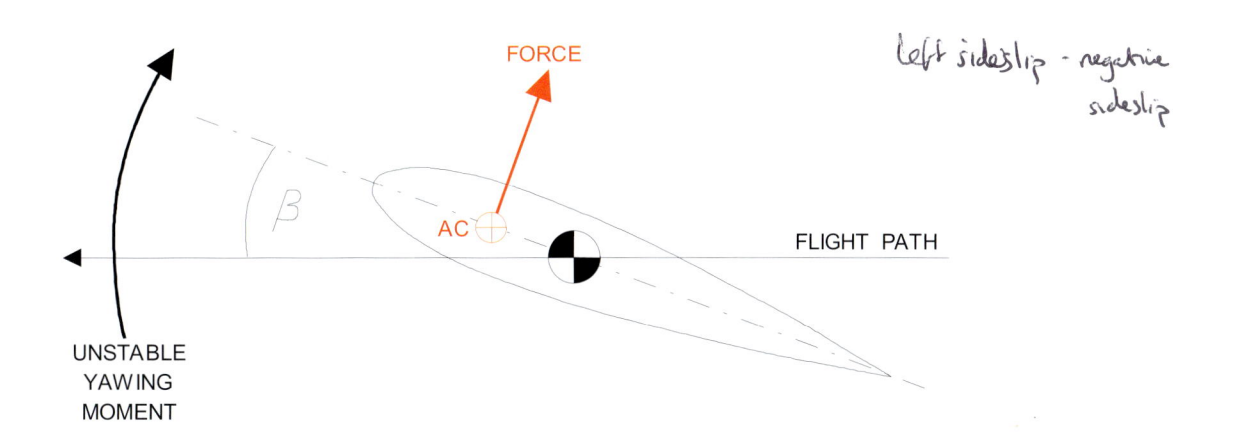

left sideslip - negative sideslip

Figure 10.48

DORSAL AND VENTRAL FINS: To overcome the instability in the fuselage it is possible to incorporate into the overall design, dorsal or ventral fins. A dorsal fin is a small aerofoil, of very low aspect ratio, mounted on top of the fuselage near the rear. A ventral fin is mounted below. Such fins are shown in Fig. 10.49.

fins - low aspect ratio

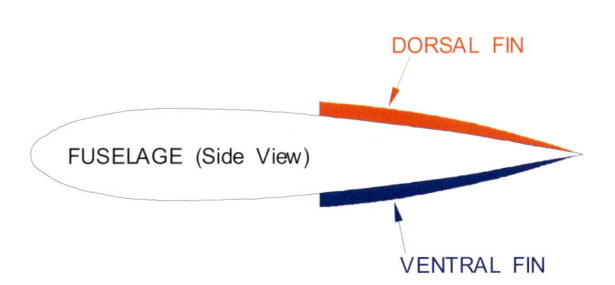

Figure 10.49

If the aircraft is yawed to the right the dorsal and ventral fins will create a side force to the right. The line of action of this force is well aft of the aircraft CG, giving a yawing moment to the left (a stabilising effect). However, at small angles of yaw they are ineffective.

PRINCIPLES OF FLIGHT   STABILITY AND CONTROL

The side force created by dorsal and ventral fins at small sideslip angles will be very small because:-

a)   the dorsal and ventral fins are at a low angle of attack,

b)   they have a small surface area, and

c)   their aspect ratio is very low, resulting in small lift-curve slope. Fig. 10.50.

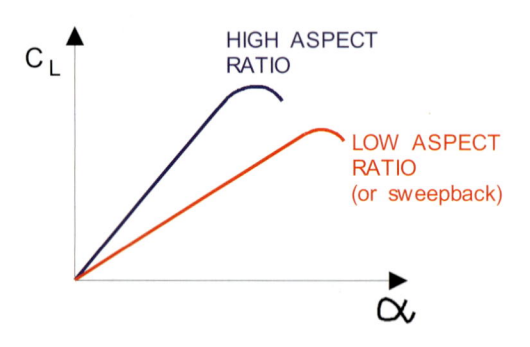

Figure 10.50

When fitted with dorsal and ventral fins a fuselage which is unstable in yaw, will remain unstable at low sideslip angles. Dorsal and ventral fins become more effective at relatively high sideslip angles. Due to their low aspect ratio they do not tend to stall at any sideslip angle which an aircraft is likely to experience in service.

The effectiveness of dorsal and ventral fins increases with increasing sideslip angle, so that the combination of a fuselage with dorsal or ventral fin is stable at large sideslip angles.

While dorsal and ventral fins contribute in exactly the same way to directional static stability, a dorsal fin contributes positively to lateral static stability, while a ventral fin is destabilising in this mode, as will be demonstrated later. For this reason, the dorsal fin is much more common.

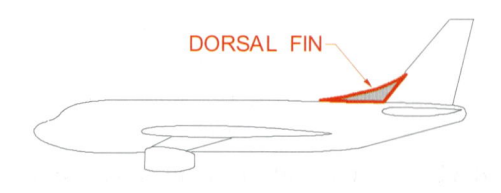

Figure 10.51

PRINCIPLES OF FLIGHT   **STABILITY AND CONTROL**

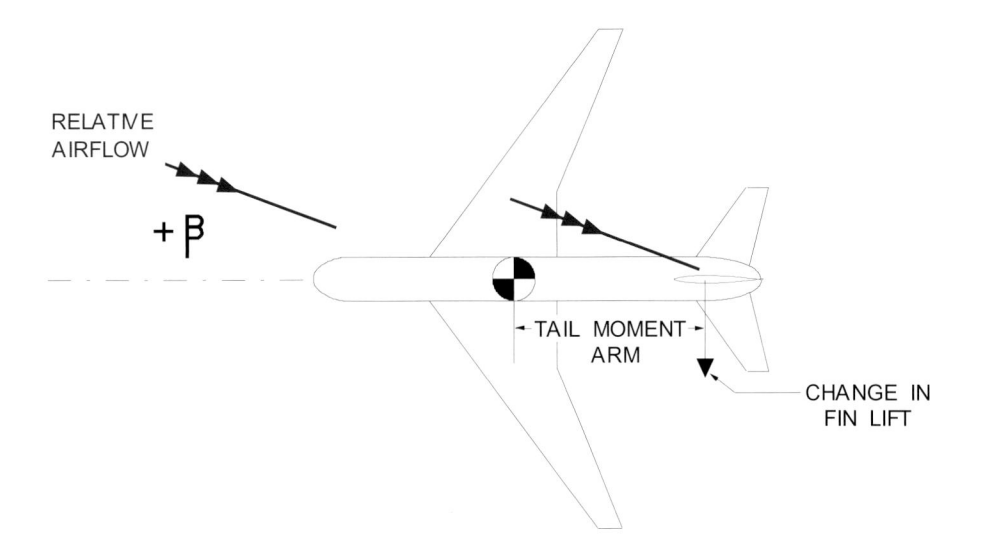

Figure 10.52

FIN: The fin (vertical stabiliser) is the major source of directional stability for the aeroplane. As shown in Fig. 10.52, in a sideslip the fin will experience a change in angle of attack. The change in lift (side force) on the fin creates a yawing moment about the centre of gravity which tends to yaw the aeroplane into the relative airflow. The magnitude of the fin contribution to static directional stability depends on both the change in fin lift and the fin moment arm. Clearly, the fin moment arm is a powerful factor.

The contribution of the fin to directional stability depends on its ability to produce changes in lift, or side force, for a given change in sideslip angle. The contribution of the fin is a direct function of its area. The required directional stability may be obtained by increasing the fin area. However, increased surface area has the obvious disadvantage of increased parasite drag.

The lift curve slope of the fin determines how sensitive the surface is to change in angle of attack. While it is desirable to have a high lift curve slope for the fin, a high aspect ratio surface is not necessarily practical or desirable - bending, lower stalling angle (Fig.10.51), hangar roof clearance, etc. The stall angle of the surface must be sufficiently great to prevent stall and subsequent loss of effectiveness at expected sideslip angles. (sweepback or low aspect ratio increases the stalling angle of attack of the fin).

The flow field in which the fin operates is affected by other components of the aeroplane as well as power effects. The dynamic pressure at the fin could depend on the slipstream of a propeller or the boundary layer of the fuselage. Also, the local flow direction at the fin is influenced by the wing wake, fuselage crossflow, induced flow of the horizontal tail, or the direction of slipstream from a propeller. Each of these factors must be considered as possibly affecting the contribution of the fin to directional stability.

A high mounted tailplane ('T' - tail) makes the fin more effective by acting as an "end plate".

The side force on the fin may still be relatively small compared to that on the fuselage, which is destabilising, but because its line of action is far aft of the CG, the yawing moment it creates is relatively large, and gives overall stability to the fuselage-fin combination. The principle behind the effect of the fin as a stabiliser is just the same as in the case of the dorsal or ventral fin. However, because it is much larger, and in particular, has a much higher aspect ratio, it is effective at low angles of sideslip. It remains effective until the angle of sideslip is such that the fin angle of attack approaches its stalling angle, but above this value the side force on the fin decreases with increasing sideslip angle, and the fin ceases to be effective as a stabiliser. It is at this point that the dorsal or ventral fin becomes important. Because it stalls at a very much higher angle of attack, it takes over the stabilising role of the fin at large angles of sideslip.

WING and NACELLES: The contribution of the wing to static directional stability is usually small.

a) The contribution of a straight wing alone is usually negligible.

b) **Sweepback produces a stabilizing effect**, which increases with increase in C_L (i.e. at lower IAS).

c) Engine nacelles on the wings produce a contribution that will depend on such factors as their size and position and the shape of the wing planform. On a straight wing, they usually produce a destabilising effect.

A swept wing provides a stable contribution depending on the amount of sweepback but the contribution is relatively weak when compared with other components. Consider a sideslipping swept wing, as illustrated in Fig. 10.53.

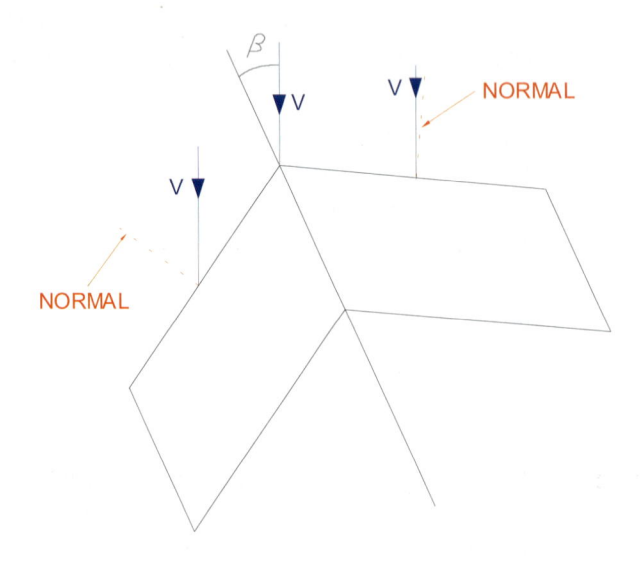

Figure 10.53

PRINCIPLES OF FLIGHT STABILITY AND CONTROL

The inclination of the forward, right, wing to the relative airflow is greater than that of the rearward wing, so there is more lift, and hence more induced drag on the right side, (the influence of increased lift on the forward wing will be explained when lateral static stability is considered). The result of this discrepancy in drag on the two sides of the wing is a yawing moment to the right, which tends to eliminate the sideslip. This is a stabilising effect, and may be important if the sweepback angle is quite large.

Fig. 10.54 illustrates a typical buildup of the directional stability of an aeroplane by separating the contribution of the fuselage and fin. As shown by the graph of Cn versus β, the contribution of the fuselage is destabilising but the instability decreases at large sideslip angles. The contribution of the fin alone is highly stabilising up to the point where the surface begins to stall. The contribution of the fin must be large enough so that the complete aeroplane (wing-fuselage-fin combination) exhibits the required degree of stability.

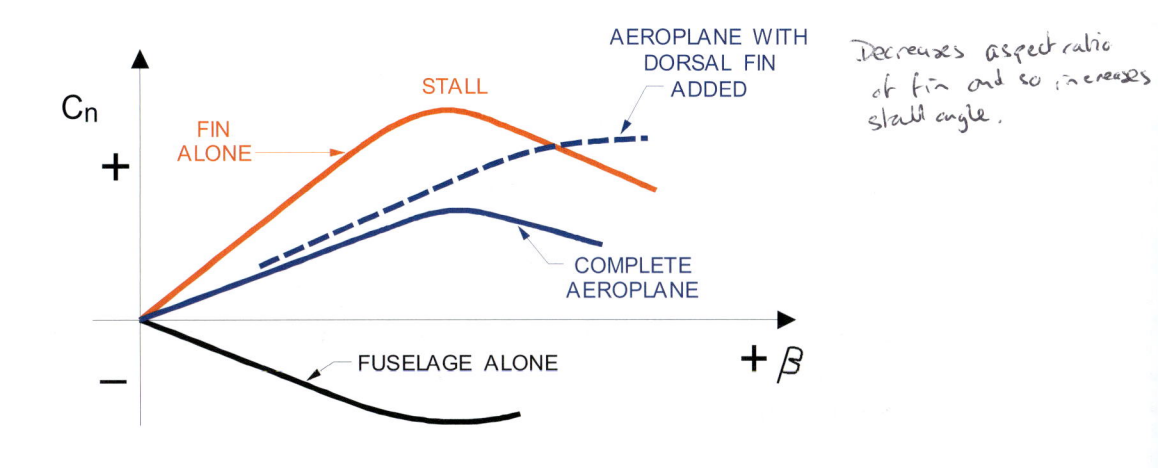

Figure 10.54

The dorsal fin has a powerful effect on preserving the directional stability at large angles of sideslip which would produce stall of the fin.

The addition of a dorsal fin to the aeroplane will reduce the decay of directional stability at high sideslip in two ways.

a) The least obvious but most important effect is a large increase in the fuselage stability at large sideslip angles.

b) In addition, the effective aspect ratio of the fin is reduced which increases the stall angle for the surface.

By this twofold effect, the addition of the dorsal fin is a very useful device. The decreased lift curve slope of a sweptback fin will also decrease the tendency for the fin to stall at high sideslip angles.

PRINCIPLES OF FLIGHT   STABILITY AND CONTROL

POWER EFFECT: The effects of power on static directional stability are similar to the power effects on static longitudinal stability. The direct effect is confined to the normal force at the propeller plane and, of course, is destabilising when the propeller is located ahead of the CG. In addition, the air in the slipstream behind a propeller spirals around the fuselage, and this results in a sidewash at the fin (from the left with a clockwise rotating propeller). The indirect effects of power induced velocities and flow direction changes at the fin (spiral slipstream effect) are quite significant for the propeller driven aeroplane and can produce large directional trim changes. As in the longitudinal case, the indirect effects are negligible for the jet powered aeroplane.

The contribution of the direct and indirect power effects to static directional stability is greatest for the propeller powered aeroplane and usually slight for the jet powered aeroplane. In either case, the general effect of power is destabilising and the **greatest contribution will occur at high power and low dynamic pressure.**

CRITICAL CONDITIONS: The most critical conditions of static directional stability are usually the combination of several separate effects. The combination which produces the most critical condition is much dependent upon the type of aeroplane. **In addition, there exists a coupling of lateral and directional effects such that the required degree of static directional stability may be determined by some of these coupled conditions.**

CENTRE OF GRAVITY POSITION: Centre of gravity position has a relatively negligible effect on static directional stability. The usual range of CG position on any aeroplane is set by the limits of **longitudinal** stability and control. Within this limiting range of CG position, no significant changes take place in the contribution of the vertical tail, fuselage, nacelles, etc. Hence, static directional stability is essentially unaffected by the variation of CG position within the longitudinal limits.

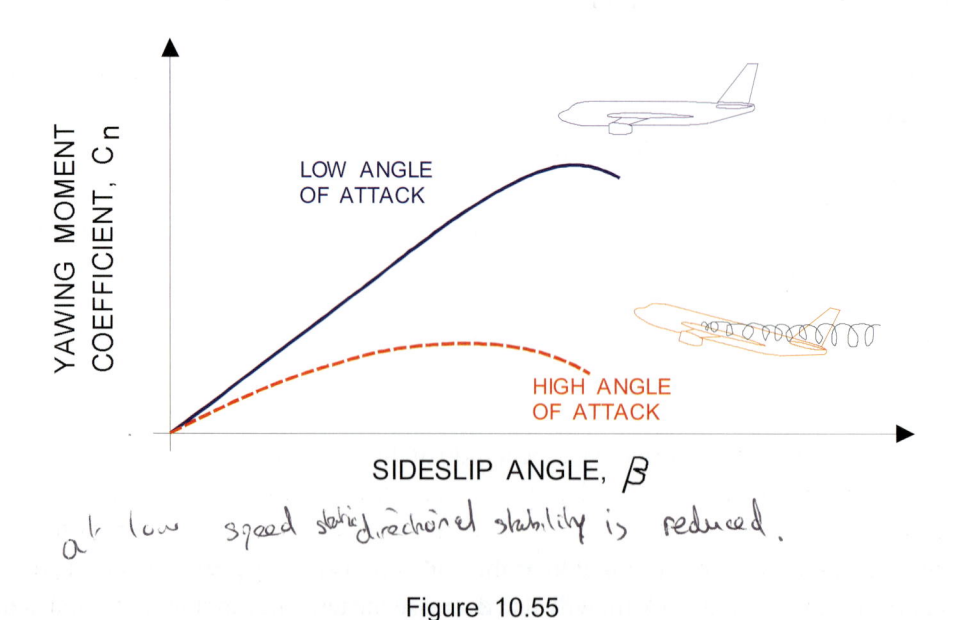

at low speed static directional stability is reduced.

Figure 10.55

PRINCIPLES OF FLIGHT   STABILITY AND CONTROL

HIGH ANGLE OF ATTACK: When the aeroplane is at a **high angle of attack** a decrease in static directional stability can be anticipated. As shown by Fig. 10.55, a high angle of attack reduces the stable slope of the curve of Cn versus β. The decrease in static directional stability is due in great part to the reduction in the contribution of the fin. At high angles of attack, the effectiveness of the fin is reduced because of increase in the fuselage boundary layer at the fin location. The decay of directional stability with angle of attack is most significant for an aeroplane with sweepback since this configuration requires a high angle of attack to achieve high lift coefficients.

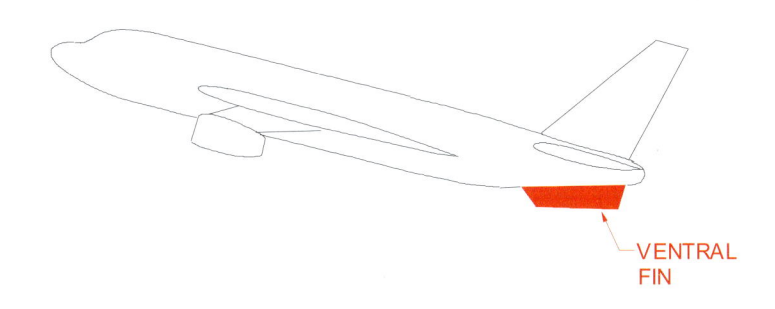

Figure 10.56 Ventral Fin

VENTRAL FIN: Ventral fins may be added as an additional contribution to directional stability, Fig. 10.56. Landing clearance requirements may limit their size, require them to be retractable, or require two smaller ventral fins to be fitted instead of one large one.

The most critical demands of static directional stability will occur from some combination of the following effects:

1) high angle of sideslip

2) high power at low airspeed

3) high angle of attack

4) high Mach number

The propeller powered aeroplane may have such considerable power effects that the critical conditions may occur at low speed while the effect of high Mach numbers may produce the critical conditions for the typical transonic, jet powered aeroplane. In addition, the coupling of lateral and directional effects may require prescribed degrees of directional stability.

PRINCIPLES OF FLIGHT   **STABILITY AND CONTROL**

10.30 LATERAL STABILITY AND CONTROL

The static lateral stability of an aeroplane involves consideration of rolling moments due to sideslip. If an aeroplane has favourable rolling moment due to sideslip, a lateral displacement from wing level flight produces sideslip and the sideslip creates rolling moments tending to return the aeroplane to wing level flight. By this action, static lateral stability will be evident. Of course, a sideslip will produce yawing moments depending on the nature of the static directional stability but the consideration of static lateral stability will involve only the relationship of rolling moments and sideslip.

DEFINITIONS

The axis system of an aeroplane defines a positive rolling, L, as a moment about the longitudinal axis which tends to rotate the right wing down. As in other aerodynamic considerations, it is convenient to consider rolling moments in the coefficient form so that lateral stability can be evaluated independent of weight, altitude, speeds, etc. The rolling moment, L, is defined in the coefficient form by the following equation:

$$L = C_l \, Q \, S \, b$$

or

$$C_l = \frac{L}{Q \, S \, b}$$

where,

L = rolling moment (positive to the right)
Q = dynamic pressure
S = wing area
b = wing span
C_l = rolling moment coefficient (positive to the right)

The angle of sideslip, β has been defined previously as the angle between the aeroplane centerline and the relative wind and is positive when the relative wind is to the right of the centerline.

PRINCIPLES OF FLIGHT   **STABILITY AND CONTROL**

10.31 STATIC LATERAL STABILITY

Static lateral stability can be illustrated by a graph of rolling moment coefficient, C_l, versus sideslip angle, β, such as shown in Fig. 10.57. When the aeroplane is subject to a positive sideslip angle, lateral stability will be evident if a negative rolling moment coefficient results. Thus, when the relative airflow comes from the right ($+\beta$), a rolling moment to the left ($-C_l$) should be created which tends to roll the aeroplane to the left. Lateral stability will exist when the curve of C_l versus β has a negative slope and the degree of stability will be a function of the slope of this curve. If the slope of the curve is zero, neutral lateral stability exists; if the slope is positive lateral instability is present.

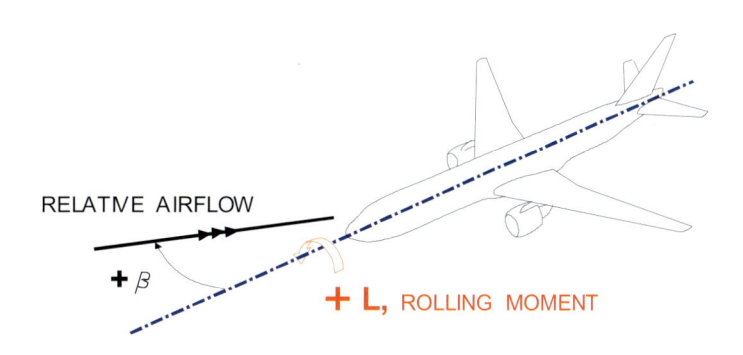

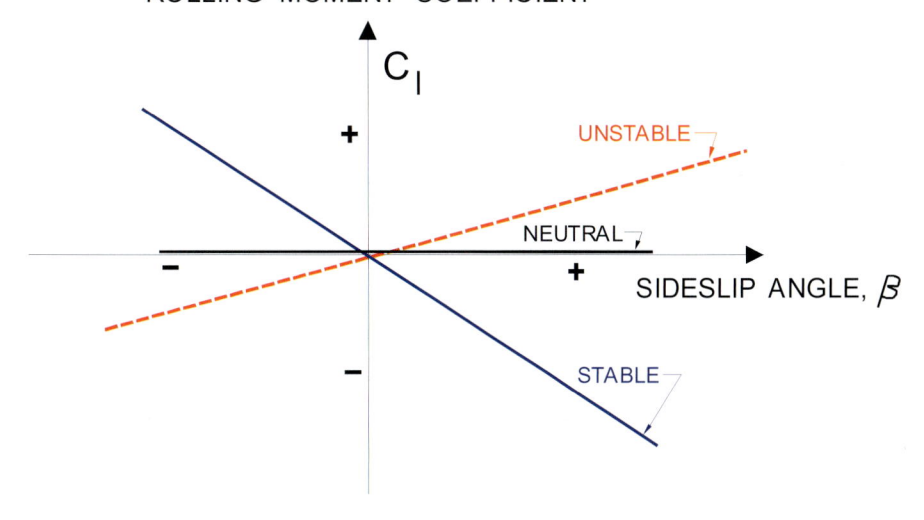

Figure 10.57

PRINCIPLES OF FLIGHT   STABILITY AND CONTROL

It is desirable to have static lateral stability (favourable roll due to sideslip), Fig. 10.58. However, the required magnitude of lateral stability is determined by many factors. Excessive roll due to sideslip complicates crosswind take-off and landing and may lead to undesirable **oscillatory coupling** with the directional motion of the aeroplane. In addition, high lateral stability may combine with adverse yaw to hinder rolling performance. Generally, good handling qualities are obtained with a relatively light, or weak positive, lateral stability.

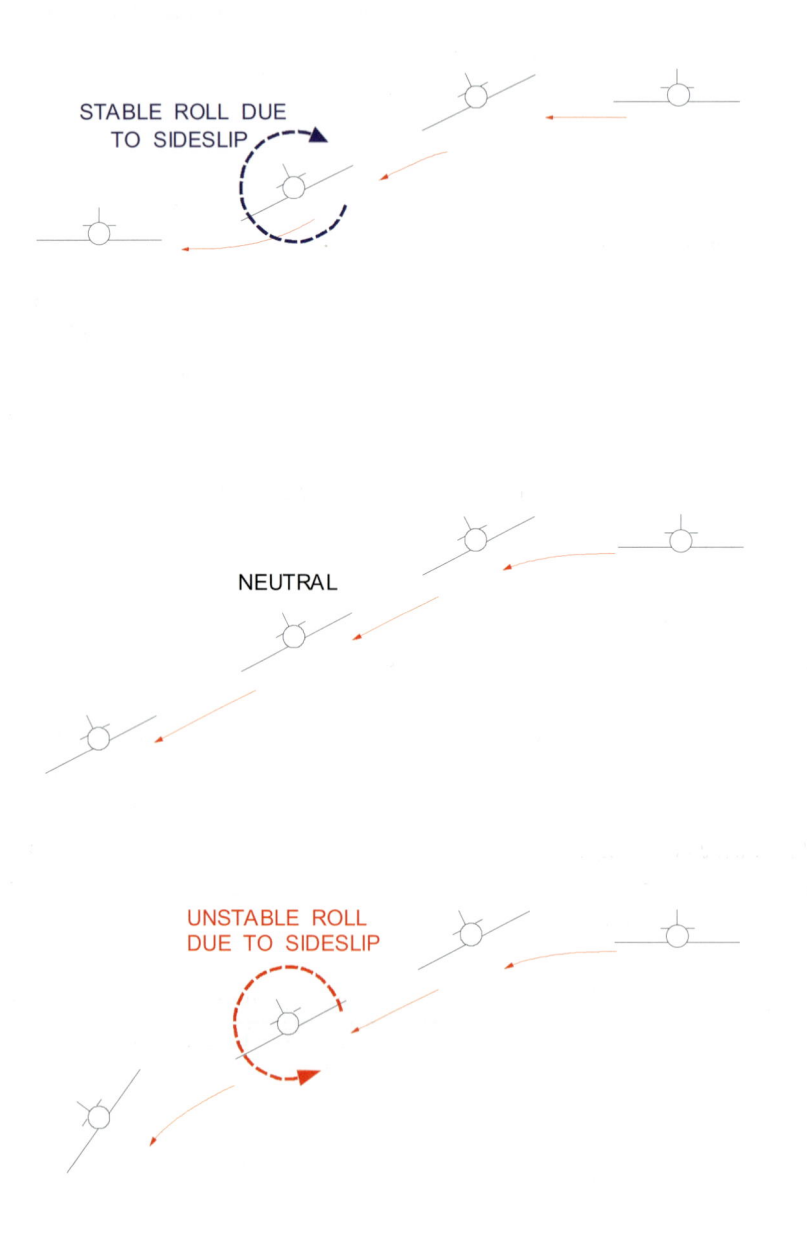

Figure 10.58   Static Lateral Stability

PRINCIPLES OF FLIGHT **STABILITY AND CONTROL**

10.32 CONTRIBUTION OF THE AEROPLANE COMPONENTS.

In order to appreciate the development of lateral stability in an aeroplane, each of the components which contribute must be inspected. **There will be interference between the components, which will alter the contribution to stability of each component on the aeroplane.**

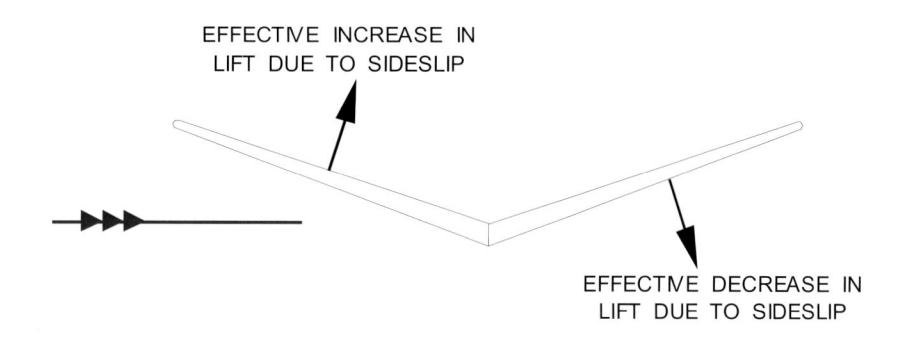

Figure 10.59   Geometric Dihedral

WING: The principal surface contributing to the lateral stability of an aeroplane is the wing. The effect of *geometric dihedral is a powerful contribution to lateral stability.

As shown in Fig. 10.59, a wing with geometric dihedral will develop stable rolling moments with sideslip. If the relative wind comes from the side, the wing into the wind is subject to an increase in angle of attack and develops an increase in lift. The wing away from the wind is subject to a decrease in angle of attack and develops a decrease in lift. The changes in lift gives a rolling moment tending to raise the into-wind wing, hence **geometric dihedral contributes a stable roll due to sideslip**.

Since geometric dihedral is so powerful in producing lateral stability it is taken as a common denominator of the lateral stability contribution of all other components. Generally, the contribution of wing position, flaps, power, etc., is expressed as **"DIHEDRAL EFFECT"**.

*Geometric Dihedral: The angle between the plane of each wing and the horizontal, when the aircraft is unbanked and level; positive when the wing lies above the horizontal, as in Fig. 10.59. Negative geometric dihedral is used on some aircraft, and is known as anhedral.

PRINCIPLES OF FLIGHT
STABILITY AND CONTROL

WING POSITION: The contribution of the **fuselage** alone is usually quite small; depending on the location of the resultant aerodynamic side force on the fuselage.

However, the effect of the **wing - fuselage - tail** combination is significant since the vertical placement of the wing on the fuselage can greatly affect the combination. A wing located at the mid wing position will generally exhibit a "dihedral effect" no different from that of the wing alone.

Fig. 10.60 illustrates the effect of wing position on static lateral stability.

a) A low wing position gives an unstable contribution. The direction of relative airflow decreases the effective angle of attack of the wing into wind and increases the effective angle of attack of the wing out of wind - tending to increase the rolling moment.

b) A high wing location gives a stable contribution. The direction of relative airflow increases the effective angle of attack of the wing into wind and decreases the effective angle of attack of the wing out of wind, tending to decrease the rolling moment.

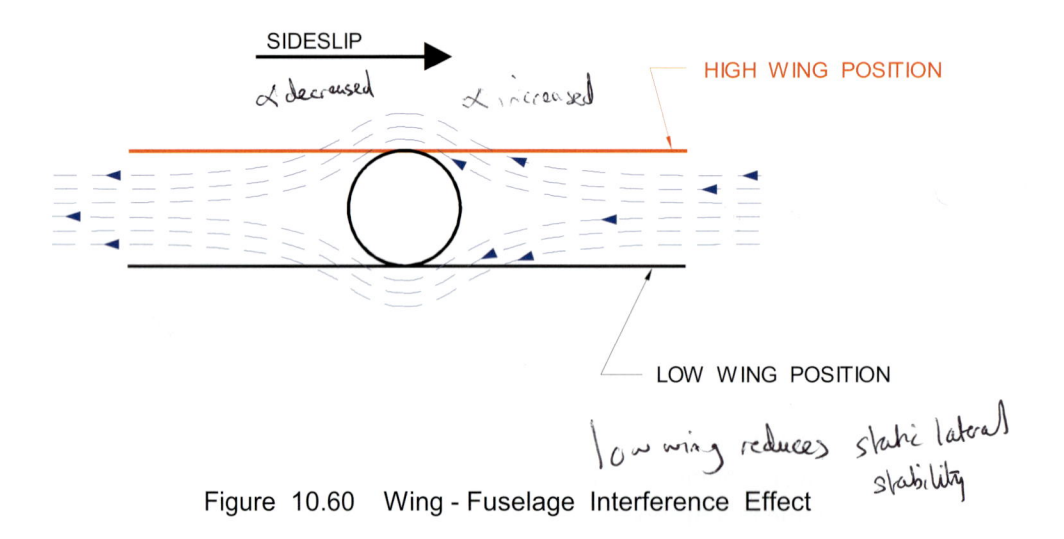

[Handwritten annotations on figure: α decreased, α increased; low wing reduces static lateral stability]

Figure 10.60   Wing - Fuselage Interference Effect

The magnitude of "dihedral effect" contributed by the vertical position of the wing is large and may require a noticeable dihedral angle for the low wing configuration. **A high wing position, on the other hand, usually requires no geometric dihedral at all.**

PRINCIPLES OF FLIGHT — STABILITY AND CONTROL

SWEEPBACK: The contribution of sweepback to "dihedral effect" is important because of the nature of the contribution. As shown in Figs. 10.61 and 10.62, if the wing is at a positive lift coefficient, the wing into the wind has less sweep and an increase in lift and the wing out of the wind has more sweep and a decrease in lift; a negative rolling moment will be generated, tending to roll the wings towards level. In this manner **the swept back wing contributes a positive "dihedral effect".** (A swept forward wing would give a negative dihedral effect).

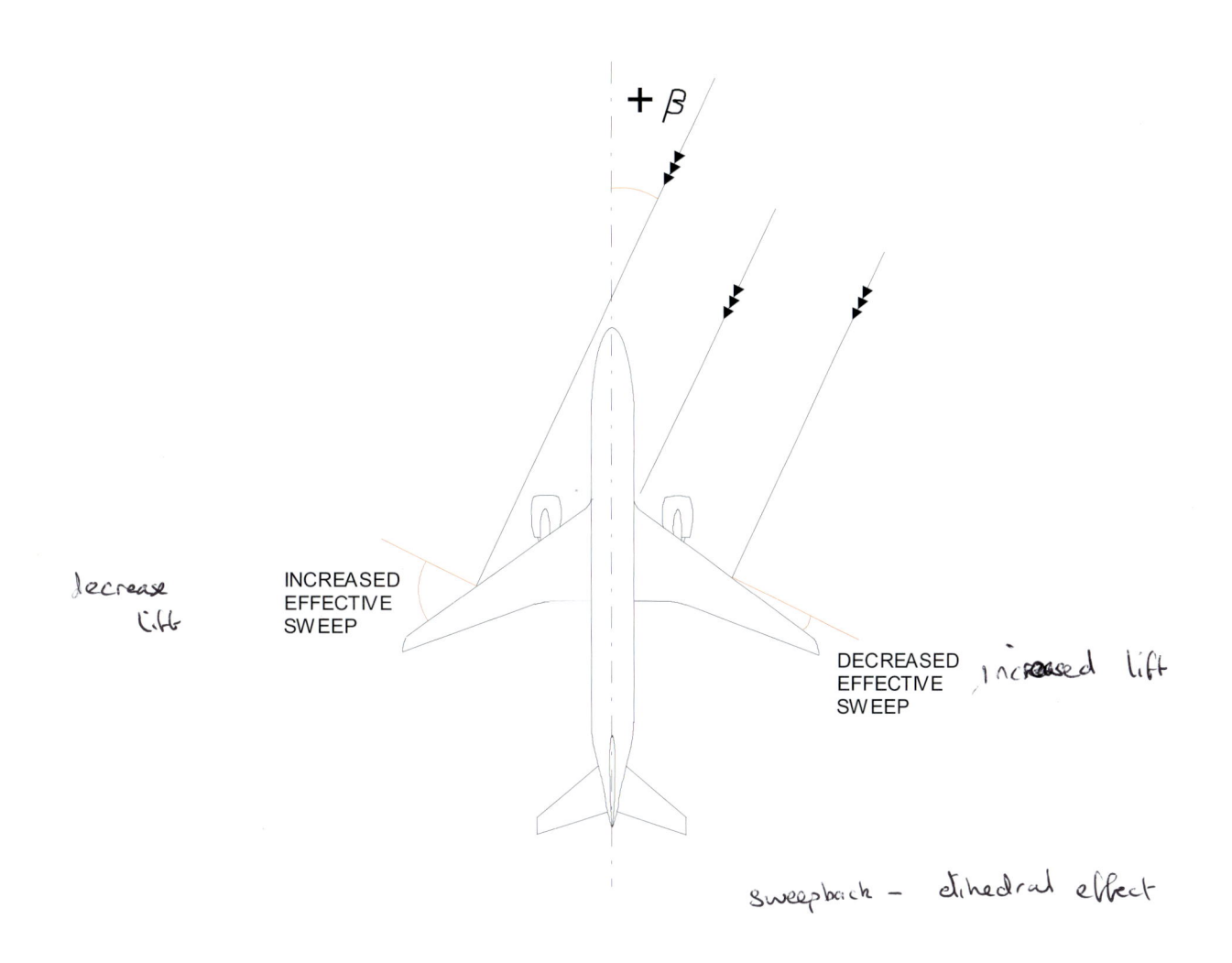

Figure 10.61 The Effect of Sweepback

The contribution of sweepback to "dihedral effect" is proportional to the wing lift coefficient as well as the angle of sweepback. Because high speed flight requires a large amount of sweepback, an excessively high "dihedral effect" will be present at low speeds (high C_L). **An aircraft with a swept back wing requires less geometric dihedral than a straight wing.**

PRINCIPLES OF FLIGHT — STABILITY AND CONTROL

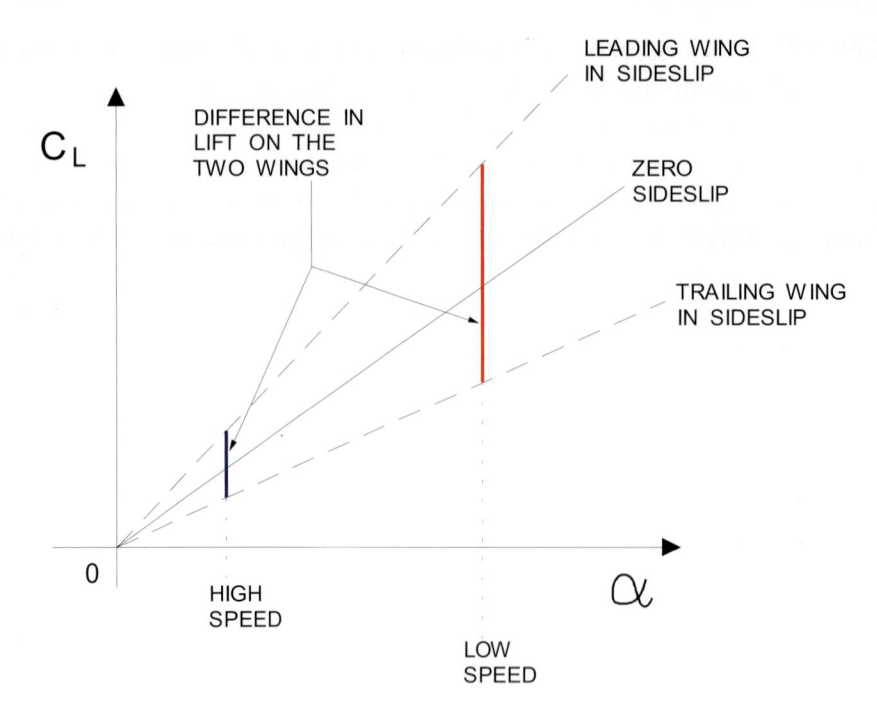

Figure 10.62 Effect of speed on 'dihedral effect' of swept wing

The fin can provide a small "dihedral effect" contribution, Fig. 10.63. If the fin is large, the side force produced by sideslip may produce a rolling moment as well as the important yawing moment contribution. **The fin contribution to purely lateral static stability, is usually very small.**

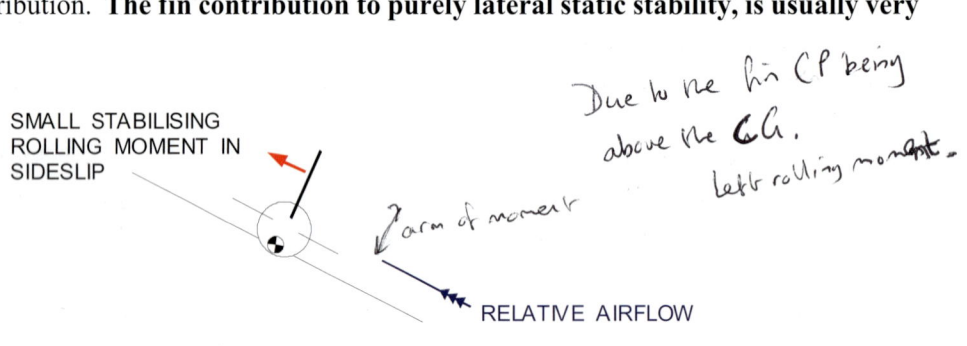

Figure 10.63 Fin Contribution

The ventral fin, being below the aircraft CG, has a negative influence on lateral static stability, as illustrated in Fig. 10.63a.

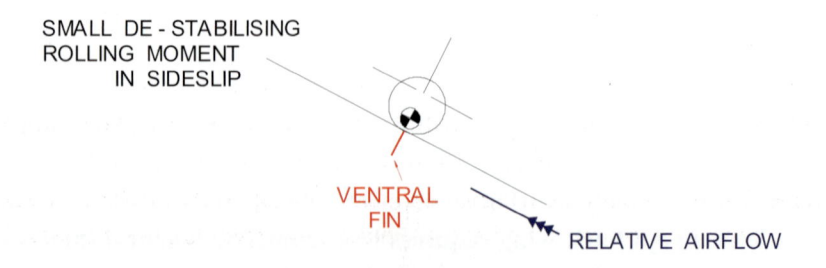

Figure 10.63a Ventral Fin Contribution

Generally, the "dihedral effect" should not be too great since high roll due to sideslip can create certain problems.

Excessive "dihedral effect" can lead to "Dutch roll," difficult rudder coordination in rolling manoeuvres, or place extreme demands for lateral control power during crosswind takeoff and landing. If the airplane demonstrates satisfactory "dihedral effect" during cruise, certain exceptions can be tolerated when the airplane is in the takeoff and landing configuration. Since the effects of flaps and power are destabilizing and reduce the "dihedral effect", a certain amount of negative "dihedral effect" may be possible due to these sources.

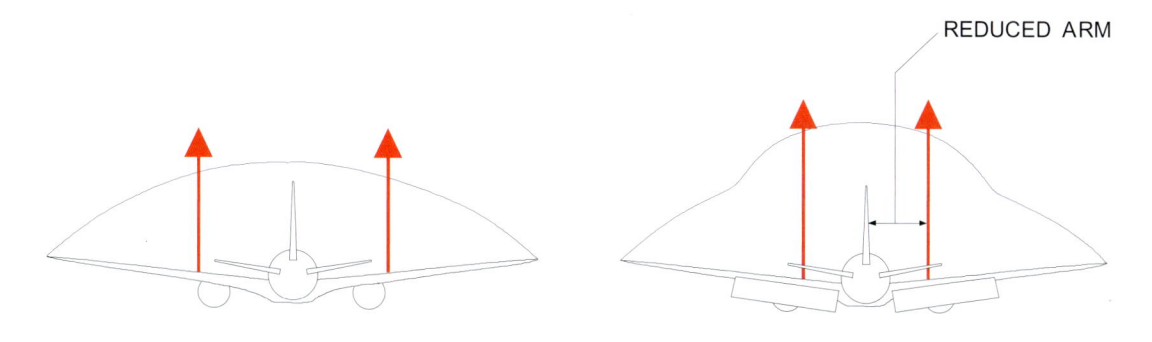

Figure 10.64 Partial Span Flaps Reduce Lateral Stability

The deflection of flaps causes the inboard sections of the wing to become relatively more effective and these sections have a small spanwise moment arm, Fig. 10.64. Therefore, the changes in wing lift due to sideslip occur closer inboard and the dihedral effect is reduced.

The effect of power on "dihedral effect" is negligible for the jet aeroplane but considerable for the propeller driven aeroplane. The propeller slipstream at high power and low airspeed makes the inboard wing sections much more effective and reduces the dihedral effect.

The reduction in "dihedral effect" is most critical when the flap and power effects are combined, e.g., the propeller driven aeroplane in a power-on approach.

With certain exceptions during the conditions of landing and takeoff, the "dihedral effect" or lateral stability should be positive but light. The problems created by excessive "dihedral effect" are considerable and difficult to contend with. Lateral stability will be evident to a pilot by stick forces and displacements required to maintain sideslip. Positive stick force stability will be evident by stick forces required in the direction of the controlled sideslip.

CONCLUSION: the designer is faced with a dilemma. An aircraft is given sweepback to increase the speed at which it can operate, but a by-product of sweepback is static lateral stability. A sweptback wing requires much less geometric dihedral than a straight wing. If a requirement also exists for the wing to be mounted on top of the fuselage, an additional "dihedral effect" is present. A high mounted and sweptback wing would give excessive "dihedral effect", so anhedral is used to reduce "dihedral effect" to the required level.

PRINCIPLES OF FLIGHT   STABILITY AND CONTROL

10.33 LATERAL DYNAMIC EFFECTS

Previous discussion has separated the lateral and directional response of the aeroplane to sideslip, in order to give each the required detailed study.

However, when an aeroplane is placed in a sideslip, the lateral and directional response will be coupled, i.e. sideslip will simultaneously produce a rolling and a yawing moment.

The principal effects which determine the lateral dynamic characteristics of an aeroplane are:

1) Rolling moment due to sideslip or "dihedral effect" (static lateral stability).

2) Yawing moment due to sideslip or static directional stability.

10.34 SPIRAL DIVERGENCE

Spiral divergence will exist when static directional stability is very large when compared to the "dihedral effect".

The character of spiral divergence is not violent. The aeroplane, when disturbed from the equilibrium of level flight, begins a slow spiral which gradually increases to a spiral dive. When a small sideslip is introduced, the strong directional stability tends to restore the nose into the wind while the relatively weak "dihedral effect" lags in restoring the aeroplane laterally. The rate of divergence in the spiral motion is usually so gradual that the pilot can control the tendency without difficulty.

10.35 DUTCH ROLL

Dutch roll will occur when the "dihedral effect" is large when compared to static directional stability.

Dutch roll is a coupled lateral and directional oscillation which is objectionable because of the oscillatory nature.

When a yaw is introduced, the strong "dihedral effect" will roll the aircraft due to the lift increase on the wing into wind. The increased induced drag on the rising wing will yaw the aircraft in the opposite direction, reversing the coupled oscillations.

Aircraft with a tendency to Dutch Roll are fitted with a Yaw Damper. This automatically displaces the rudder proportional to the rate of yaw to damp-out the oscillations.

If the Yaw Damper fails in flight, it is recommended that the ailerons be used by the pilot to damp-out Dutch Roll. Because of the response lag, if the pilot uses the rudder, pilot induced oscillation (PIO) will result and the Dutch Roll may very quickly become divergent, leading to loss of control.

PRINCIPLES OF FLIGHT   STABILITY AND CONTROL

Dutch roll is objectionable, and spiral divergence is tolerable if the rate of divergence is low. For this reason the "dihedral effect" should be no more than that required for satisfactory lateral stability.

If the static directional stability is made adequate to prevent objectionable Dutch roll, this will automatically be sufficient to prevent directional divergence. Since the more important handling qualities are a result of high static directional stability and minimum necessary "dihedral effect", most aeroplanes demonstrate a mild spiral tendency. As previously mentioned, a weak spiral tendency is of little concern to the pilot and certainly preferable to Dutch roll.

The contribution of sweepback to the lateral dynamics of an aeroplane is significant. Since the "dihedral effect" from sweepback is a function of lift coefficient, the dynamic characteristics may vary throughout the flight speed range.

When the swept wing aeroplane is at low C_L the "dihedral effect" is small and the spiral tendency may be apparent. When the swept wing aeroplane is at high C_L the "dihedral effect" is increased and the Dutch Roll oscillatory tendency is increased.

10.36 PILOT INDUCED OSCILLATIONS (PIO)

Certain undesirable motions may occur due to inadvertent action on the controls. This can occur about any of the axes, but the most important condition exists with the short period longitudinal motion of the aeroplane where pilot control system response lag can produce an unstable oscillation. The coupling possible in the pilot/control system/aeroplane combination is capable of producing damaging flight loads and loss of control of the aeroplane.

When the normal human response lag and control system lag are coupled with the aeroplane motion, inadvertent control reactions by the pilot may furnish negative damping to the oscillatory motion and dynamic instability will exist.

Since short period motion is of relatively high frequency, the amplitude of the pitching oscillation can reach dangerous proportions in an unbelievably short time.

When pilot induced oscillation is encountered, the most effective solution is an immediate release of the controls. Any attempt to forcibly damp the oscillation simply continues the excitation and amplifies the oscillation. Freeing the controls removes the unstable (but inadvertent) excitation and allows the aeroplane to recover by virtue of its inherent dynamic stability.

10.37 HIGH MACH NUMBERS

Generally, flight at high Mach numbers will take place at high altitude, hence the effect of high altitude must be separated for study. Aerodynamic damping is due to moments created by pitching, rolling, or yawing of the aircraft. These moments are derived from the changes in angles of attack of the tail, wing and fin surfaces with angular rotation (see Fig. 10.35).

Higher TAS common to high altitude flight reduces the angle of attack changes and reduces aerodynamic damping. In fact, aerodynamic damping is proportional to the square root of the relative density, similar to the proportion of True Air Speed to Equivalent Air Speed. Thus, at an ISA altitude of 40,000 ft., aerodynamic damping would be reduced to one-half the ISA sea level value.

10.38 MACH TRIM

As speed increases beyond the Critical Mach number (M_{CRIT}), shock wave formation at the root of a swept back wing will:

a) reduce lift forward of the CG, and

b) reduce downwash at the tailplane.

Together, these factors will generate a nose down pitching moment. At high Mach numbers, an aircraft will become unstable with respect to speed; instead of an increasing push force being required as speed increases, a pull force becomes necessary to prevent the aircraft accelerating further. This is potentially dangerous. A small increase in Mach number will give a nose down pitch which will further increase the Mach number. This in turn leads to a further increase in the nose down pitching moment. This unfavourable high speed characteristic, known as **"Mach Tuck"**, **"High Speed Tuck"** or **"Tuck Under"** would restrict the maximum operating speed of a modern high speed jet transport aircraft.

To maintain the required stick force gradient at high Mach numbers, a Mach trim system must be fitted. This device, sensitive to Mach number, may:

a) deflect the elevator up

b) decrease the incidence of the variable incidence trimming tailplane or

c) move the CG rearwards by transferring fuel from the wings to a rear trim tank

by an amount greater than that required merely to compensate for the trim change. This ensures the required stick force gradient is maintained in the cruise at high Mach numbers.

Whichever method of trim is used by a particular manufacturer, **a Mach trim system will adjust longitudinal trim and operates only at high Mach numbers.**

PRINCIPLES OF FLIGHT   STABILITY AND CONTROL

KEY FACTS 2 - Self Study (Insert the missing words, with reference to the preceding paragraphs).

Positive static longitudinal stability is indicated by a _____ slope of C_M versus C_L. The degree of _____ longitudinal stability is indicated by the _____ of the curve. (Para. 10.8).

The net pitching moment about the _____ axis is due to the contribution of each of the component _____ acting in their appropriate _____ fields. (Para. 10.9).

In most cases, the contribution of the fuselage and nacelles is _____. (Para. 10.9).

(Para. 10.9) Noticeable changes in static stability can occur at high C_L (low speed) if:
a)   the aeroplane has _____,
b)   there is a large contribution of '_____ effect', or
c)   there are significant changes in _____ at the horizontal tail,

The horizontal tail usually provides the _____ stabilising influence of all the components of the aeroplane. (Para. 10.9).

_____ decreases static longitudinal stability. (Para. 10.9).

If the thrust line is below the CG, a thrust increase will produce a _____ or nose ___ moment and the effect is _____. (Para. 10.12).

High lift devices tend to _____ downwash at the tail and _____ the dynamic pressure at the tail, both of which are _____. (Para. 10.13).

An increase in TAS, for a given pitching velocity, _____ aerodynamic damping. (Para. 10.15).

The aeroplane with positive manoeuvring stability should demonstrate a steady _____ in stick force with _____ in load factor or "___". (Para. 10.16).

The stick force gradient must not be excessively _____ or the aeroplane will be difficult and tiring to manoeuver. Also, the stick force gradient must not be too _____ or the aeroplane may be overstressed inadvertently when light control forces exist. (Para. 10.16).

When the aeroplane has high static stability, the manoeuvring stability will be _____ and a ___ stick force gradient will result. The _____ CG limit could be set to prevent an excessively high manoeuvring stick force gradient. As the CG moves aft, the stick force gradient _____ with _____ manoeuvring stability and the _____ limit of stick force gradient may be reached. (Para. 10.16).

At high altitudes, the high TAS _____ the change in tail angle of attack for a given pitching velocity and _____ the pitch damping. Thus, a decrease in manoeuvring stick force stability can be expected with _____ altitude. (Para. 10.16).

10 - 73

PRINCIPLES OF FLIGHT   **STABILITY AND CONTROL**

A flying control system may employ _____ springs, _____ springs or ____ weights to provide satisfactory control forces throughout the speed, CG and altitude range of an aircraft. (Para. 10.17).

While static stability is concerned with the initial tendency of an aircraft to return to equilibrium, dynamic stability is defined by the resulting _____ with _____. (Para. 10.22).

An aircraft will demonstrate positive dynamic stability if the _____ of motion _____ with time. (Para. 10.22).

When natural aerodynamic damping cannot be obtained, _____ damping must be provided to give the necessary positive dynamic stability. (Para. 10.22).

(Para. 10.23) The longitudinal dynamic stability of an aeroplane generally consists of two basic modes of oscillation:-
a) _____ period (phugoid)
b) _____ period

The phugoid oscillation occurs with nearly constant _____ of _____. (Para. 10.24).

The period of oscillation is so great, the pilot is easily able to counteract ____ _____ oscillation. (Para. 10.24).

Short period oscillation involves significant changes in _____ of _____. (Para. 10.25).

Short period oscillation is ____ _____ controlled by the pilot. (Para. 10.25).

The problems of dynamic stability can become acute at _____ altitude because of _____ aerodynamic _____. (Para. 10.25).

To overcome the directional instability in the fuselage it is possible to incorporate into the overall design, _____ or _____ fins. (Para. 10.29).

The _____ is the major source of directional stability for the aeroplane. (Para. 10.29).

A ___ - tail makes the fin more effective by acting as an "____ plate". (Para. 10.29).

Because the _____ fin stalls at a very much higher angle of attack, it takes over the stabilising role of the fin at large angles of sideslip. (Para. 10.29).

_____ produces a directional stabilising effect, which increases with increase in C_L. (Para. 10.29).

PRINCIPLES OF FLIGHT   STABILITY AND CONTROL

_____ fins increase directional stability at _____ angles of attack. Landing clearance requirements may limit their size, require them to be retractable, or require two smaller ventral fins to be fitted instead of one large one. (Para. 10.29).

Generally, good handling qualities are obtained with a relatively _____, or ____ positive, lateral stability. (Para. 10.31).

The principal surface contributing to the lateral stability of an aeroplane is the _____. The effect of geometric _____ is a powerful contribution to lateral stability. (Para. 10.31).

A low wing position gives an _____ contribution to static lateral stability. (Para. 10.32).

A _____ wing location gives a stable contribution to static lateral stability. (Para. 10.32).

The magnitude of "dihedral effect" contributed by the vertical position of the wing is _____ and may require a noticeable dihedral angle for the _____ wing configuration. A high wing position, on the other hand, usually requires ___ geometric _____ at all. (Para. 10.32).

The _____ back wing contributes a positive "dihedral effect". (Para. 10.32).

An aircraft with a swept back wing requires _____ geometric dihedral than a straight wing. (Para. 10.32).

The fin contribution to purely lateral static stability, is usually very _____. (Para. 10.32).

Excessive "dihedral effect" can lead to "_____ roll," difficult rudder coordination in _____ manoeuvres, or place extreme demands for _____ control power during crosswind takeoff and landing. (Para. 10.32).

Deploying partial span flaps gives a _____ dihedral effect. (Para. 10.32).

A sweptback wing requires much less geometric dihedral than a straight wing. If a requirement also exists for the wing to be mounted on top of the fuselage, an additional "dihedral effect" is present. A high mounted and sweptback wing would give excessive "dihedral effect", so _____ is used to reduce "dihedral effect" to the required level. (Para. 10.32).

When an aeroplane is placed in a sideslip, the lateral and directional response will be _____, i.e. sideslip will simultaneously produce a _____ and a _____ moment. (Para. 10.33).

Spiral divergence will exist when static directional stability is very _____ when compared to the "dihedral effect". (Para. 10.34).

The rate of divergence in the spiral motion is usually so _____ that the pilot can control the tendency without _____. (Para. 10.34).

10 - 75
© Oxford Aviation Services Limited

PRINCIPLES OF FLIGHT STABILITY AND CONTROL

Dutch roll will occur when the "dihedral effect" is _____ when compared to static directional stability. (Para. 10.35).

Aircraft which Dutch Roll are fitted with a _____ Damper. This automatically displaces the rudder proportional to the _____ of yaw to damp-out the oscillations. (Para. 10.35).

If the Yaw Damper fails in flight, it is recommended that the _____ be used by the pilot to damp-out Dutch Roll. (Para. 10.35).

If the pilot uses the _____, pilot induced oscillation (PIO) will result and the Dutch Roll may very quickly become _____, leading to loss of _____. (Para. 10.35).

When the swept wing aeroplane is at low C_L the "dihedral effect" is small and the _____ tendency may be apparent. When the swept wing aeroplane is at high C_L the "dihedral effect" is increased and the _____ _____ oscillatory tendency is increased. (Para. 10.35).

When pilot induced oscillation is encountered, the most effective solution is an immediate _____ of the controls. Any attempt to forcibly damp the oscillation simply _____ the excitation and _____ the oscillation. (Para. 10.36).

Higher TAS common to high altitude flight _____ the _____ of _____ changes and reduces aerodynamic _____. (Para. 10.37).

Mach Tuck is caused by ___ of lift in front of the ___ and _____ downwash at the tail due to the formation of a _____ on a swept back wing at _____ Mach numbers. (Para. 10.38).

The Mach trim system will adjust _____ _____ to maintain the required _____ _____ gradient and operates only at _____ Mach numbers. (Para. 10.38).

KEY FACTS 2, WITH THE MISSING WORDS INSERTED CAN BE FOUND ON PAGE 10 - 92.

PRINCIPLES OF FLIGHT — STABILITY AND CONTROL

10.39 SUMMARY - Self Study

Stability is the inherent quality of an aircraft to correct for conditions that may disturb its equilibrium and to return to, or continue on its origin flight path. An aircraft can have two basic types of stability: **static** and **dynamic,** and three condition of each type: **positive, neutral,** and **negative.**

Static stability describes the initial reaction of an aircraft after it has been disturbed from equilibrium about one or more of its three axes.

> **Positive static stability** is the condition of stability in which restorative forces are set-up that will tend to return an aircraft to its original condition anytime it's disturbed from a condition of equilibrium. If an aircraft has an initial tendency to return to its original attitude of equilibrium, it has **positive static stability.** (statically stable).
>
> An aircraft with **neutral static stability** produces neither forces that tend to return it to its original condition, nor cause it to depart further from this condition. If an aircraft tends to remain in its new, disturbed state, it has **neutral static stability.** (statically neutral).
>
> If an aircraft has **negative static stability,** anytime it is disturbed from a condition of equilibrium, forces are set up that will tend to cause it to depart further from its original condition. Negative static stability is a highly undesirable characteristic as it can cause loss of control. When an aircraft continues to diverge, it exhibits **negative static stability.** (statically unstable).
>
> Most aeroplanes have positive static stability in pitch and yaw, and are close to neutrally statically stable in roll.

PRINCIPLES OF FLIGHT   STABILITY AND CONTROL

When an aircraft exhibits positive static stability about any of its three axes, the term **"dynamic stability"** describes the long term tendency of the aircraft.

When an aircraft is disturbed from equilibrium and then tries to return, it will invariably overshoot the original ATTITUDE (due to its momentum) and then start to return again. This results in a series of oscillations.

> **Positive dynamic stability** is a condition in which the forces of static stability decrease with time. Positive dynamic stability is desirable. If oscillations become smaller with time, an aircraft has **positive dynamic stability**. (dynamically stable).
>
> **Neutral dynamic stability** causes an aircraft to hunt back and forth around a condition of equilibrium, with the corrections getting neither larger or smaller. (dynamically neutral). Neutral dynamic stability is undesirable.
>
> If an aircraft diverges further away from its original attitude with each oscillation, it has **negative dynamic stability.** Negative dynamic stability causes the forces of static stability to increase with time. (dynamically unstable). Negative dynamic stability is extremely undesirable.

The overall design of an aircraft contributes to its **stability** (or lack of it) about each of its three axes of motion.

The vertical stabiliser (**fin**) is the primary source of **directional stability** (yaw).

The horizontal stabiliser (**tailplane**) is the primary source of **longitudinal stability** (pitch).

The **wing** is the primary source of **lateral stability** (roll).

CG location also affects stability.

> If the CG is close to its aft limit, an aircraft will be less stable in both pitch and yaw.
>
> As the CG is moves forward, stability increases.

Even though an aeroplane will be less stable with an aft CG, it will have some desirable aerodynamic characteristics due to reduced aerodynamic loading of the horizontal tail surface. This type of an aeroplane will have a slightly lower stall speed and will cruise faster for a given power setting.

PRINCIPLES OF FLIGHT   **STABILITY AND CONTROL**

Manoeuverability is the quality of an aircraft that permits it to be manoeuvred easily and to withstand the stresses imposed by those manoeuvres.

Controllability is the capability of an aircraft to respond to the pilot's control, especially with regard to flight path and attitude.

An aircraft is longitudinally stable if it returns to a condition of level flight after a disturbance in pitch, caused by either a gust or displacement of the elevator by the pilot. The location of the CG and the effectiveness of the tailplane determines the longitudinal stability, and thus the controllability of an aircraft.

Increasing stability about any axis:-

a)   Decreases manoeuverability and controllability, and

b)   Increases stick (or pedal) forces.

Phugoid oscillation is a long-period oscillation in which the pitch attitude, airspeed, and altitude vary, but the angle of attack remains relatively constant. It is a gradual interchange of potential and kinetic energy about some equilibrium airspeed and altitude. An aircraft experiencing longitudinal phugoid oscillation is demonstrating positive static stability, and it is **easily controlled by the pilot.**

An aircraft will return towards wing level after a wing drop if it has **static lateral stability.**

The wing of most aircraft has a positive geometric dihedral angle (dihedral). This is the angle produced by the wing tips being higher than the wing root. If the left wing drops in flight, an aircraft will momentarily begin to slip to the left, and the effective angle of attack of the left wing will increase and the effective angle of attack of the right wing will decrease. The change in angle of attack of both wings will cause the wing to return back towards a level attitude.

Sweepback also has a "dihedral effect". This is a by-product. A wing is swept back to give an aircraft a higher M_{CRIT}. An aircraft with a swept-back wing will not require as much geometrical dihedral as a straight wing.

Some aircraft have the wing mounted on top of the fuselage for various reasons. Also as a by-product, a high mounted wing will give a "dihedral effect" due to the direction of airflow around the fuselage and wing during a sideslip. An aircraft with a high mounted wing does not require as much geometric dihedral.

An aircraft which has a high mounted, swept-back wing will have so much lateral stability that the wing is usually given anhedral (negative dihedral).

Too much static lateral stability could result in dynamic instability - Dutch Roll.

PRINCIPLES OF FLIGHT
STABILITY AND CONTROL

Static Directional stability is the tendency of the nose of an aircraft to yaw towards the relative airflow. It is achieved by the keel surface behind the CG being larger than that in front of the CG.

A sweptback wing also provides a measure of static directional stability.

Too much static directional stability could result in dynamic instability - Spiral Instability.

Interaction between static lateral stability and static directional stability. If a wing drops and the aircraft begins to slip to the side, directional stability will cause the nose to yaw into the relative airflow.

"Dihedral effect" tends to roll an aircraft when a wing drops, and directional stability causes the nose to yaw into the direction of the low wing.

These two forces interact (coupled motion):-

1. An aircraft with strong static directional stability and weak "dihedral effect" will have a tendency towards **spiral instability**.

    When a wing drops, the nose will yaw toward the low wing and the airplane will begin to turn. The increased speed of the wing on the outside of the turn will increase the angle of bank, and the reduction in the vertical component of lift will force the nose to a low pitch angle. This will cause the aircraft to enter a descending spiral.

2. An aircraft with strong "dihedral effect" and weak directional stability will have a tendency towards **dutch roll instability**.

A Mach Trim system maintains the required stick force gradient at high Mach numbers by adjusting the longitudinal trim. The Mach Trim system only operates at high Mach numbers.

SELF ASSESSMENT QUESTIONS

1. An aeroplane which is inherently stable will:

   a) require less effort to control.
   b) be difficult to stall.
   c) not spin.
   d) have a built-in tendency to return to its original state following the removal of any disturbing force.

2. After a disturbance in pitch an aircraft oscillates in pitch with increasing amplitude. It is:

   a) statically and dynamically unstable.
   b) statically stable but dynamically unstable.
   c) statically unstable but dynamically stable.
   d) statically and dynamically stable.

3. Longitudinal stability is given by:

   a) the fin.
   b) the wing dihedral.
   c) the horizontal tailplane.
   d) the ailerons.

4. An aircraft is constructed with dihedral to provide:

   a) lateral stability about the longitudinal axis.
   b) longitudinal stability about the lateral axis.
   c) lateral stability about the normal axis.
   d) directional stability about the normal axis.

5. Lateral stability is reduced by increasing:

   a) Anhedral.
   b) Dihedral.
   c) Sweepback.
   d) Fuselage and fin area.

6. If the wing AC is forward of the CG:

   a) changes in lift produce a wing pitching moment which acts to reduce the change of lift.
   b) changes in lift produce a wing pitching moment which acts to increase the change of lift.
   c) changes in lift give no change in wing pitching moment.
   d) when the aircraft sideslips the CG causes the nose to turn into the sideslip thus applying a restoring moment.

PRINCIPLES OF FLIGHT																																STABILITY AND CONTROL

7. The longitudinal static stability of an aircraft:

   a) is reduced by the effects of wing downwash.
   b) is increased by the effects of wing downwash.
   c) is not affected by wing downwash.
   d) is reduced for nose up displacements, but increased for nose down displacements by the effects of wing downwash.

8. To ensure some degree of longitudinal stability in flight, the position of the CG:

   a) must always coincide with the AC.
   b) must be forward of the Neutral Point.
   c) must be aft of the Neutral Point.
   d) must not be forward of the aft CG limit.

9. When the CG is close to the forward limit:

   a) very small forces are required on the control column to produce pitch.
   b) longitudinal stability is reduced.
   c) very high stick forces are required to pitch because the aircraft is very stable.
   d) stick forces are the same as for an aft CG.

10. The static margin is equal to the distance between:

    a) the CG and the AC.
    b) the AC and the neutral point.
    c) the CG and the neutral point.
    d) the CG and the CG datum point.

11. If a disturbing force causes the aircraft to roll:

    a) wing dihedral will cause a rolling moment which reduces the sideslip.
    b) the fin will cause a rolling moment which reduces the sideslip.
    c) dihedral will cause a yawing moment which reduces the sideslip.
    d) dihedral will cause a nose up pitching moment.

12. With flaps lowered, lateral stability:

    a) will be increased because of the effective increase of dihedral.
    b) will be increased because of increased lift.
    c) will be reduced because the centre of lift of each semi-span is closer to the wing root.
    d) will not be affected.

13. Dihedral gives a stabilising rolling moment by causing an increase in lift:

    a) on the up going wing when the aircraft rolls.
    b) on the down going wing when the aircraft rolls.
    c) on the lower wing if the aircraft is sideslipping.
    d) on the lower wing whenever the aircraft is in a banked attitude.

14. A high wing configuration with no dihedral, compared to a low wing configuration with no dihedral, will provide:

    a) greater longitudinal stability.
    b) the same degree of longitudinal stability as any other configuration because dihedral gives longitudinal stability.
    c) less lateral stability than a low wing configuration.
    d) greater lateral stability due to the airflow pattern around the fuselage when the aircraft is sideslipping increasing the effective angle of attack of the lower wing.

15. At a constant IAS, what affect will increasing altitude have on damping in roll:

    a) remains the same.
    b) increases because the TAS increases.
    c) decreases because the ailerons are less effective.
    d) decreases because the density decreases.

16. Sweepback of the wings will:

    a) not affect lateral stability.
    b) decrease lateral stability.
    c) increases lateral stability at high speeds only.
    d) increases lateral stability at all speeds.

17. At low forward speed:

    a) increased downwash from the wing will cause the elevators to be more responsive.
    b) due to the increased angle of attack of the wing the air will flow faster over the wing giving improved aileron control.
    c) a large sideslip angle could cause the fin to stall.
    d) a swept back wing will give an increased degree of longitudinal stability.

18. Following a lateral disturbance, an aircraft with Dutch roll instability will:

    a) go into a spiral dive.
    b) develop simultaneous oscillations in roll and yaw.
    c) develop oscillations in pitch.
    d) develop an unchecked roll.

19. To correct dutch roll on an aircraft with no automatic protection system:

    a) use roll inputs
    b) use yaw inputs
    c) move the CG
    d) reduce speed below M_{MO}

20. A yaw damper:

    a) increases rudder effectiveness.
    b) must be disengaged before making a turn.
    c) augments stability.
    d) increases the rate of yaw.

21. A wing which is inclined downwards from root to tip is said to have:

    a) wash out.
    b) taper.
    c) sweep.
    d) anhedral.

22. The lateral axis of an aircraft is a line which:

    a) passes through the wing tips.
    b) passes through the centre of pressure, at right angles to the direction of the airflow.
    c) passes through the quarter chord point of the wing root, at right angles to the longitudinal axis.
    d) passes through the centre of gravity, parallel to a line through the wing tips.

23. Loading an aircraft so that the CG exceeds the aft limits could result in:

    a) loss of longitudinal stability, and the nose to pitch up at slow speeds
    b) excessive upward force on the tail, and the nose to pitch down
    c) excessive load factor in turns
    d) high stick forces

24. The tendency of an aircraft to suffer from dutch roll instability can be reduced:

    a) by sweeping the wings
    b) by giving the wings anhedral
    c) by reducing the size of the fin
    d) by longitudinal dihedral

25. What determines the longitudinal static stability of an aeroplane?

    a) The relationship of thrust and lift to weight and drag
    b) The effectiveness of the horizontal stabilizer, rudder, and rudder trim tab
    c) The location of the CG with respect to the AC
    d) the size of the pitching moment which can be generated by the elevator

26. Dihedral angle is:

    a) the angle between the main plane and the longitudinal axis
    b) the angle measured between the main plane and the normal axis
    c) the angle between the quarter chord line and the horizontal datum
    d) the upward and outward inclination of the main planes to the horizontal datum

27. Stability around the normal axis:

    a) is increased if the keel surface behind the CG is increased
    b) is given by the lateral dihedral
    c) depends on the longitudinal dihedral
    d) is greater if the wing has no sweepback

28. The Centre of Gravity of an aircraft is found to be within limits for take-off::

    a) the C of G will be within limits for landing
    b) the C of G for landing must be checked, allowing for fuel consumed
    c) the C of G will not change during the flight
    d) the flight crew can adjust the CG during flight to keep it within acceptable limits for landing

PRINCIPLES OF FLIGHT **STABILITY AND CONTROL**

29. The ailerons are deployed and returned to neutral when the aircraft has attained a small angle of bank. If the aircraft then returns to a wings-level attitude without further control movement it is:

    a) neutrally stable
    b) statically and dynamically stable
    c) statically stable, dynamically neutral
    d) statically stable

30. The property which tends to decreases rate of displacement about any axis, but only while displacement is taking place, is known as:

    a) stability
    b) controllability
    c) aerodynamic damping
    d) manoeuverability

31. If an aircraft is loaded such that the stick force required to change the speed is zero

    a) the CG is on the neutral point
    b) the CG is behind the neutral point
    c) the CG is on the manouevre point
    d) the CG is on the forward CG limit

PRINCIPLES OF FLIGHT **STABILITY AND CONTROL**

ANSWERS

No	A	B	C	D	REF	No	A	B	C	D	REF
1				D		17			C		
2		B				18		B			
3			C			19	A				
4	A					20			C		
5	A					21				D	
6		B				22				D	
7	A					23	A				
8		B				24		B			
9			C			25			C		
10			C			26				D	
11	A					27	A				
12			C			28		B			
13			C			29		B			
14				D		30			C		
15				D		31	A				
16				D							

INTENTIONALLY

LEFT

BLANK

PRINCIPLES OF FLIGHT   STABILITY AND CONTROL

KEY FACTS 1 - Self Study

Stability is the **tendency** of an aircraft to return to a **steady** state of flight, after being disturbed by an external **force**, without any help from the **pilot**. (Para. 10.1).

There are two broad categories of stability; **static** and **dynamic**. (Para. 10.1).

An aircraft is in a state of **equilibrium** (trim) when the sum of all forces is **zero** and the sum of all **moments** is zero. (Para. 10.2).

The type of static stability an aircraft possesses is defined by its **initial** tendency, following the removal of some disturbing force. (Para. 10.2).

The three different types of static stability are: (Para. 10.2).
a) **Positive** static stability exists if an aircraft is disturbed from equilibrium and has the tendency to return to equilibrium.
b) **Neutral** static stability exists if an aircraft is subject to a disturbance and has neither the tendency to return nor the tendency to continue in the displacement direction.
c) **Negative** static stability exists if an aircraft has a tendency to continue in the direction of disturbance.

The longitudinal axis passes through the **CG** from **nose** to **tail**. (Para. 10.3)

The normal axis passes "vertically" through the **CG** at **90°** to the **longitudinal** axis. (Para. 10.3)

The lateral axis is a line passing through the **CG**, parallel to a line passing through the **wing** tips. (Para. 10.3).

The three reference axes all pass through the **centre of gravity**. (Para. 10.3)

Lateral stability involves motion about the **longitudinal** axis (**rolling**). (Para. 10.4).

Longitudinal stability involves motion about the **lateral** axis (**pitching**). (Para. 10.4).

Directional stability involves motion about the **normal** axis (**yawing**). (Para. 10.4).

PRINCIPLES OF FLIGHT   **STABILITY AND CONTROL**

We consider the changes in **magnitude** of lift force due to changes in angle of **attack**, acting through a **stationary** point; the **aerodynamic centre**. (Page 10 - 6)

The aerodynamic centre (AC) is located at the **25%** chord position. (Page 10 - 6)

The **negative** pitching moment about the AC remains **constant** at normal angles of attack. (Page 10 - 6).

A wing on its own is statically **unstable** because the **AC** is in front of the **CG**. (Page 10 - 7).

An upward vertical gust will momentarily **increase** the angle of attack of the wing. The **increased** lift force magnitude acting through the **AC** will increase the **positive** pitching moment about the **CG**. This is an **unstable** pitching moment. (Page 10 - 7).

The **tailplane** is positioned to generate a **stabilising** pitching moment about the aircraft **CG**. (Page 10 - 8).

If the tail moment is greater than the wing moment the sum of the moments will not be **zero** and the resultant nose **down** moment will give an angular **acceleration** about the **CG**. (Page 10 - 8).

The **greater** the tail moment relative to the wing moment, the **greater** the rate of return **towards** the original **equilibrium** position. (Page 10 - 8).

The tail moment is increased by moving the aircraft **CG** forwards, which **increases** the tail arm and decreases the **wing** arm. (Page 10 - 8).

If the nose down (**negative**) tail moment is greater than the nose up (**positive**) wing moment, the aircraft will have **static longitudinal** stability. (Page 10 - 8).

The position of the CG when changes in the sum of the tail moment and wing moment due to a disturbance is zero, is known as the **neutral point**. (Para. 10.5).

The further forward the **CG**, the **greater** the nose down angular **acceleration** about the **CG** - the **greater** the degree of **static longitudinal** stability. (Para. 10.6).

The **distance** the **CG** is forward of the **neutral** point will give a measure of the **static** longitudinal stability; this distance is called the static **margin**. (Para. 10.6).

The greater the static margin, the **greater** the **static longitudinal** stability. (Para. 10.6).

The **aft** CG limit will be positioned some distance **forward** of the **neutral point**. (Para. 10.6).

The distance between the **aft CG** limit and the neutral point gives the required **minimum** static stability **margin**. (Para. 10.6).

PRINCIPLES OF FLIGHT   **STABILITY AND CONTROL**

An aircraft is said to be **trimmed** if all **moments** in pitch, roll, and yaw are equal to **zero**. (Para. 10.7).

Trim (**equilibrium**) is the function of the **controls** and may be accomplished by:- (Para. 10.7).
a)   **pilot** effort
b)   trim **tabs**,
c)   moving **fuel** between the wing **tanks** and an aft located **trim** tank, or
d)   bias of a surface **actuator** (**powered** flying controls).

The term **controllability** refers to the ability of the aircraft to respond to control surface displacement and achieve the desired **condition** of flight. (Para. 10.7).

A high degree of stability tends to reduce the **controllability** of the aircraft. (Para. 10.7).

The stable tendency of an aircraft resists displacement from **trim** equally, whether by **pilot** effort on the controls (**stick** force) or **gusts**. (Para. 10.7).

If the CG moves forward, static longitudinal stability **increases** and controllability **decreases** (stick force **increases**). (Para. 10.7).

If the CG moves aft, static longitudinal stability **decreases** and controllability **increases** (stick force **decreases**). (Para. 10.7).

With the CG on the forward limit, static longitudinal stability is **greatest**, controllability is **least** and stick force is **high**. (Para. 10.7).

With the CG on the aft limit, static longitudinal stability is **least**, controllability is **greatest** and stick force is **low**. (Para. 10.7).

The aft CG limit is set to ensure a **minimum** degree of static longitudinal stability. (Para. 10.7).

The fwd CG limit is set to ensure a **minimum** degree of controllability under the worst circumstance. (Para. 10.7).

PRINCIPLES OF FLIGHT — STABILITY AND CONTROL

KEY FACTS 2 - Self Study

Positive static longitudinal stability is indicated by a **negative** slope of C_M versus C_L. The degree of **static** longitudinal stability is indicated by the **slope** of the curve. (Para. 10.8).

The net pitching moment about the **lateral** axis is due to the contribution of each of the component **surfaces** acting in their appropriate **flow** fields. (Para. 10.9).

In most cases, the contribution of the fuselage and nacelles is **destabilising.** (Para. 10.9).

(Para. 10.9) Noticeable changes in static stability can occur at high C_L (low speed) if:
a) the aeroplane has **sweepback**,
b) there is a large contribution of '**power** effect', or
c) there are significant changes in **downwash** at the horizontal tail,

The horizontal tail usually provides the **greatest** stabilising influence of all the components of the aeroplane. (Para. 10.9).

Downwash decreases static longitudinal stability. (Para. 10.9).

If the thrust line is below the CG, a thrust increase will produce a **positive** or nose **up** moment and the effect is **destabilizing**. (Para. 10.12).

High lift devices tend to **increase** downwash at the tail and **reduce** the dynamic pressure at the tail, both of which are **destabilizing**. (Para. 10.13).

An increase in TAS, for a given pitching velocity, **decreases** aerodynamic damping. (Para. 10.15).

The aeroplane with positive manoeuvring stability should demonstrate a steady **increase** in stick force with **increase** in load factor or "**g**". (Para. 10.16).

The stick force gradient must not be excessively **high** or the aeroplane will be difficult and tiring to manoeuver. Also, the stick force gradient must not be too **low** or the aeroplane may be overstressed inadvertently when light control forces exist. (Para. 10.16).

When the aeroplane has high static stability, the manoeuvring stability will be **high** and a **high** stick force gradient will result. The **forward** CG limit could be set to prevent an excessively high manoeuvring stick force gradient. As the CG moves aft, the stick force gradient **decreases** with **decreasing** manoeuvring stability and the **lower** limit of stick force gradient may be reached. (Para. 10.16).

At high altitudes, the high TAS **reduces** the change in tail angle of attack for a given pitching velocity and **reduces** the pitch damping. Thus, a decrease in manoeuvring stick force stability can be expected with **increased** altitude. (Para. 10.16).

A flying control system may employ **centring** springs, **down** springs or **bob** weights to provide satisfactory control forces throughout the speed, CG and altitude range of an aircraft. (Para. 10.17).

While static stability is concerned with the initial tendency of an aircraft to return to equilibrium, dynamic stability is defined by the resulting **motion** with **time**. (Para. 10.22).

An aircraft will demonstrate positive dynamic stability if the **amplitude** of motion **decreases** with time. (Para. 10.22).

When natural aerodynamic damping cannot be obtained, **artificial** damping must be provided to give the necessary positive dynamic stability. (Para. 10.22).

(Para. 10.23) The longitudinal dynamic stability of an aeroplane generally consists of two basic modes of oscillation:-
a) **long** period (phugoid)
b) **short** period

The phugoid oscillation occurs with nearly constant **angle** of **attack**. (Para. 10.24).

The period of oscillation is so great, the pilot is easily able to counteract **long period** oscillation. (Para. 10.24).

Short period oscillation involves significant changes in **angle** of **attack**. (Para. 10.25).

Short period oscillation is **not easily** controlled by the pilot. (Para. 10.25).

The problems of dynamic stability can become acute at **high** altitude because of **reduced** aerodynamic **damping**. (Para. 10.25).

To overcome the directional instability in the fuselage it is possible to incorporate into the overall design, **dorsal** or **ventral** fins. (Para. 10.29).

The **fin** is the major source of directional stability for the aeroplane. (Para. 10.29).

T - tail makes the fin more effective by acting as an "**end** plate". (Para. 10.29).

Because the **dorsal** fin stalls at a very much higher angle of attack, it takes over the stabilizing role of the fin at large angles of sideslip. (Para. 10.29).

Sweepback produces a directional stabilising effect, which increases with increase in C_L. (Para. 10.29).

PRINCIPLES OF FLIGHT   STABILITY AND CONTROL

Ventral fins increase directional stability at **high** angles of attack. Landing clearance requirements may limit their size, require them to be retractable, or require two smaller ventral fins to be fitted instead of one large one. (Para. 10.29).

Generally, good handling qualities are obtained with a relatively **light**, or **weak** positive, lateral stability. (Para. 10.31).

The principal surface contributing to the lateral stability of an aeroplane is the **wing**. The effect of geometric **dihedral** is a powerful contribution to lateral stability. (Para. 10.31).

A low wing position gives an **unstable** contribution to static lateral stability. (Para. 10.32).

A **high** wing location gives a stable contribution to static lateral stability. (Para. 10.32).

The magnitude of "dihedral effect" contributed by the vertical position of the wing is **large** and may require a noticeable dihedral angle for the **low** wing configuration. A high wing position, on the other hand, usually requires **no** geometric **dihedral** at all. (Para. 10.32).

The **swept** back wing contributes a positive "dihedral effect". (Para. 10.32).

An aircraft with a swept back wing requires **less** geometric dihedral than a straight wing. (Para. 10.32).

The fin contribution to purely lateral static stability, is usually very **small**. (Para. 10.32).

Excessive "dihedral effect" can lead to "**Dutch** roll," difficult rudder coordination in **rolling** manoeuvres, or place extreme demands for **lateral** control power during crosswind takeoff and landing. (Para. 10.32).

Deploying partial span flaps gives a **reduced** dihedral effect. (Para. 10.32).

A sweptback wing requires much less geometric dihedral than a straight wing. If a requirement also exists for the wing to be mounted on top of the fuselage, an additional "dihedral effect" is present. A high mounted and sweptback wing would give excessive "dihedral effect", so **anhedral** is used to reduce "dihedral effect" to the required level. (Para. 10.32).

When an aeroplane is placed in a sideslip, the lateral and directional response will be **coupled**, i.e. sideslip will simultaneously produce a **rolling** and a **yawing** moment. (Para. 10.33).

Spiral divergence will exist when static directional stability is very **large** when compared to the "dihedral effect". (Para. 10.34).

The rate of divergence in the spiral motion is usually so **gradual** that the pilot can control the tendency without **difficulty**. (Para. 10.34).

PRINCIPLES OF FLIGHT   **STABILITY AND CONTROL**

Dutch roll will occur when the "dihedral effect" is **large** when compared to static directional stability. (Para. 10.35).

Aircraft which Dutch Roll are fitted with a **Yaw** Damper. This automatically displaces the rudder proportional to the **rate** of yaw to damp-out the oscillations. (Para. 10.35).

If the Yaw Damper fails in flight, it is recommended that the **ailerons** be used by the pilot to damp-out Dutch Roll. (Para. 10.35).

If the pilot uses the **rudder**, pilot induced oscillation (PIO) will result and the Dutch Roll may very quickly become **divergent**, leading to loss of **control**. (Para. 10.35).

When the swept wing aeroplane is at low C_L the "dihedral effect" is small and the **spiral** tendency may be apparent. When the swept wing aeroplane is at high C_L the "dihedral effect" is increased and the **Dutch Roll** oscillatory tendency is increased. (Para. 10.35).

When pilot induced oscillation is encountered, the most effective solution is an immediate **release** of the controls. Any attempt to forcibly damp the oscillation simply **continues** the excitation and **amplifies** the oscillation. (Para. 10.36).

Higher TAS common to high altitude flight **reduces** the **angle** of **attack** changes and reduces aerodynamic **damping**. (Para. 10.37).

Mach Tuck is caused by **loss** of lift in front of the **CG** and **reduced** downwash at the tail due to the formation of a **shockwave** on a swept back wing at **high** Mach numbers. (Para. 10.38).

The Mach trim system will adjust **longitudinal trim** to maintain the required **stick force** gradient and operates only at **high** Mach numbers. (Para. 10.38).

INTENTIONALLY LEFT BLANK

CHAPTER 11 - CONTROLS

Contents

	Page
INTRODUCTION	11 - 1
HINGE MOMENTS	11 - 2
CONTROL BALANCING	11 - 3
AERODYNAMIC BALANCE	
INSET HINGE	
HORN BALANCE	
INTERNAL BALANCE	11 - 4
BALANCE TAB	
ANTI-BALANCE TAB	11 - 5
SERVO TAB	
SPRING TAB	
POWERED FLYING CONTROLS	11 - 6
POWER ASSISTED	
FULLY POWERED	11 - 7
ARTIFICIAL FEEL ('Q' FEEL)	
MASS BALANCE	11 - 8
LONGITUDINAL CONTROL	
EFFECT OF ELEVATOR DEFLECTION	
DIRECTION OF THE TAILPLANE LOAD	11 - 9
ELEVATOR ANGLE WITH 'G'	
EFFECT OF ICE ON THE TAILPLANE	
LATERAL CONTROL	
EFFECT OF AILERON DEFLECTION	11 - 10
EFFECT OF WINGSPAN ON RATE OF ROLL	
ADVERSE AILERON YAW	
DIFFERENTIAL AILERONS	11 - 11
FRISE AILERONS	
AILERON - RUDDER COUPLING	
ROLL CONTROL SPOILERS	
INBOARD AILERONS	11 - 12
FLAPERONS	
SPOILERS	11 - 13
COMBINED AILERON AND SPOILER CONTROLS	11 - 14
SPEED BRAKES	
TYPES OF SPEED BRAKE	
EFFECT OF SPEED BRAKES ON THE DRAG CURVE	11 - 15
GROUND SPOILERS (LIFT DUMPERS)	
DIRECTIONAL CONTROL	11 - 16
EFFECT OF RUDDER DEFLECTION	
FIN STALL	

ASYMMETRIC THRUST . . . . 11 - 17
RUDDER RATIO CHANGER
SECONDARY EFFECTS OF CONTROLS . . . . 11 - 18
YAWING MOMENT DUE TO ROLL
ROLLING MOMENT DUE TO YAW
TRIMMING . . . . 11 - 19
METHODS OF TRIMMING
      TRIM TAB . . . . 11 - 20
      FIXED TABS
      VARIABLE INCIDENCE TAILPLANE
      SPRING BIAS . . . . 11 - 22
      CG ADJUSTMENT
      ARTIFICIAL FEEL TRIM
SELF ASSESSMENT QUESTIONS . . . . 11 - 23
        ANSWERS . . . . 11 - 31

Important Defintions

Pitch Angle: The angle between the aircraft longitudinal axis and the horizon.

Roll Angle: The angle between the aircraft lateral axis and the horizon.

Yaw Angle: The angle between the aircraft longitudinal axis and the Relative airflow.

PRINCIPLES OF FLIGHT   **CONTROLS**

11.1 INTRODUCTION

All aircraft are fitted with a control system to enable the pilot to manoeuvre and trim the aircraft in flight about each of its three axes. The aerodynamic moments required to rotate the aircraft about the axes are usually supplied by means of 'flap' type control surfaces positioned at the extremities of the aircraft so that they have the longest possible moment arm about the CG. There are usually three separate control systems and three sets of control surfaces:

a)   **Rudder** for control in **yaw** about the **normal axis** (directional control).

b)   **Elevator** for control in **pitch** about the **lateral axis** (longitudinal control).

c)   **Ailerons** for control in **roll** about the **longitudinal axis** (lateral control). Spoilers may also be used to assist or replace the ailerons for roll control.

The effect of two of these controls may be combined in a single set of control surfaces:

d)   **Elevons:** combine the effects of elevator and aileron.

e)   **Ruddervator:** ('V' or butterfly tail), combine the effects of rudder and elevator.

f)   **Tailerons:** slab horizontal tail surfaces that move either together, as pitch control, or independently for control in roll.

The moment around an axis is produced by changing the aerodynamic force on the appropriate aerofoil. The magnitude of the force is a product of the dynamic pressure (IAS^2) and the angular displacement of the control surface. Aerodynamic force can be changed by:-

g)   adjusting the camber of the aerofoil.
h)   changing the incidence of the aerofoil.
i)   decreasing lift and increasing drag by "spoiling" the airflow.

Changing the camber of any aerofoil (wing, tailplane or fin) will change its lift. Deflecting a control surface effectively changes its camber. Fig. 11.1 shows the effect on C_L of movement of a control surface.

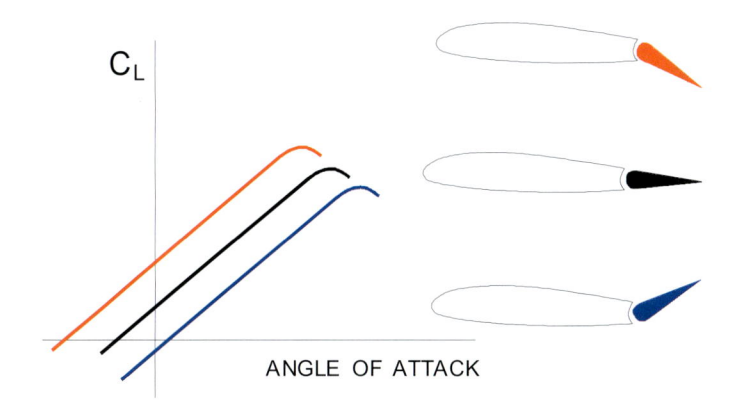

Figure 11.1   Control surface changes camber and lift

PRINCIPLES OF FLIGHT CONTROLS

Changing the incidence of an aerofoil will change its lift. The usual application of this system is for pitch control - the all moving (slab) tailplane. There is no elevator, when the pilot makes a pitch input the incidence of the whole tailplane changes.

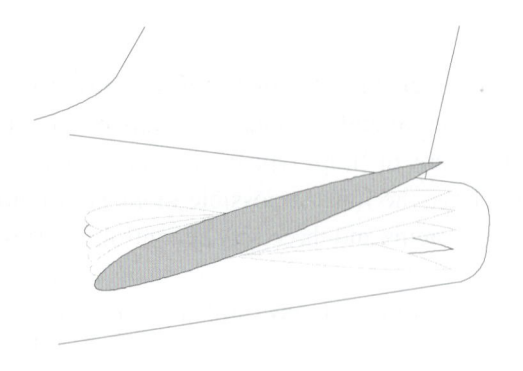

Figure 11.2 All moving (slab) tailplane

Spoilers are a device for reducing the lift of an aerofoil, by disturbing the airflow over the upper surface. They assist lateral control by moving up on the side with the up-going aileron, as illustrated in Fig. 11.3.

Figure 11.3 Spoilers

11.2 HINGE MOMENTS

If an aerodynamic force acts on a control surface, it will try to rotate the control around its hinge in the direction of the force. The moment is a product of the force (F) times the distance (d) from the hinge line to the control surface CP. This is called the hinge moment. The force is due to the surface area, the angular displacement of the control surface and the dynamic pressure.

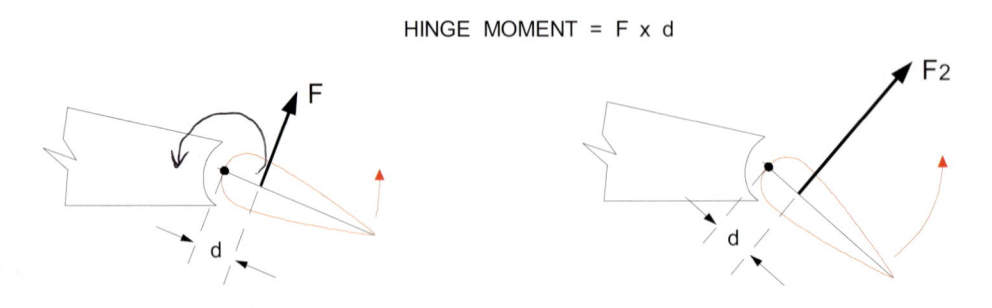

$$\text{HINGE MOMENT} = F \times d$$

Figure 11.4 Hinge moment (Feel)

To move the control surface to the required angular displacement and maintain it in that position the pilot has to overcome, then balance, the hinge moment by applying a force (stick force) to the cockpit control. The stick force will therefore depend on the size of the hinge moment.

PRINCIPLES OF FLIGHT   **CONTROLS**

11.3 CONTROL BALANCING

The aerodynamic force on the controls will depend on the area of the control surface, its angular displacement and the IAS. For large and fast aircraft the resulting aerodynamic force can give hinge moments / stick forces which are too high for easy operation of the controls.

The pilot will require assistance to move the controls in these conditions, and this can be done either by using (hydraulic) powered flying controls, or by using some form of aerodynamic balance.

11.3.1 AERODYNAMIC BALANCE

Aerodynamic balance involves using the aerodynamic forces on the control surface to reduce the hinge moment / stick force and may be done in several ways:

a) **Inset hinge:** If distance (d) is reduced the hinge moment will be reduced. The smaller the hinge moment, the smaller the stick force and the easier it will be for the pilot to move the controls. Setting the hinge back does not reduce the effectiveness of the control, only the hinge moment.

If the aerodynamic force (F2) were to move forward of the hinge, a condition known as "overbalance" would exist. As the force moved forward, a reduction then a reversal of the stick force would occur. This would be very dangerous and the designer must ensure the aerodynamic force can never move forward of the hinge.

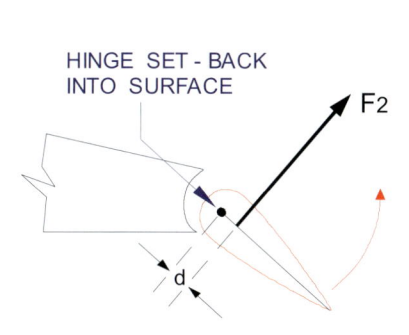

Figure 11.5   Inset hinge

b) **Horn Balance:** The principle of the horn balance is similar to that of the inset hinge, in that part of the surface is forward of the hinge line, and forces on this part of the surface give hinge moments which are in the opposite direction to the moments on the main part of the surface. The overall moment is therefore reduced, but not the control effectiveness.

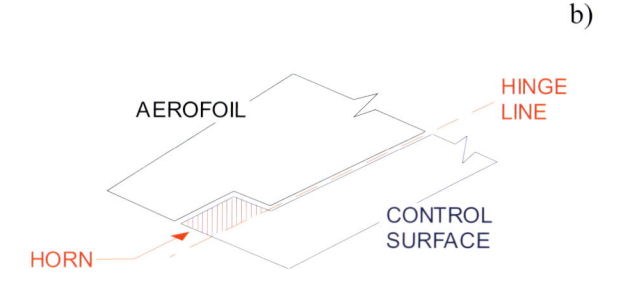

Figure 11.6   Horn balance

PRINCIPLES OF FLIGHT — CONTROLS

Balance panels

c) **Internal Balance:** This balance works on the same principle as the inset hinge, but the aerodynamic balance area is inside the wing.

Seal between leading edge of control surface and trailing edge of the wing.

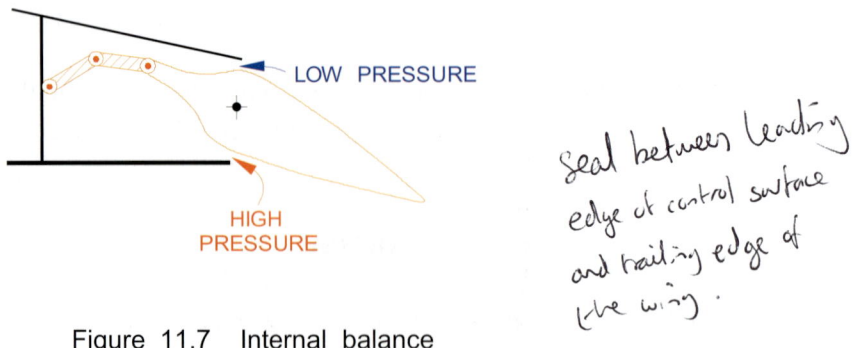

Figure 11.7   Internal balance

Movement of the control causes pressure changes on the aerofoil, and these pressure changes are felt on the balance area. For example, if the control surface is moved down, pressure above the aerofoil is reduced and pressure below it is increased. The reduced pressure is felt on the upper surface of the balance 'panel', and the increased pressure on the lower surface. The pressure difference on the balance therefore gives a hinge moment which is the opposite to the hinge moment on the main control surface, and the overall hinge moment is reduced.

See Page 11-22 for a Tab Quick Reference Guide.

d) **Balance Tab:** The preceding types of aerodynamic balance work by causing some of the dynamic pressure on the control surface to act forward of the hinge line. The balance tab provides a force acting on the control surface trailing edge opposite to the force on the main control surface. **The balance tab moves in the opposite direction to the control surface.** The pilot moves the surface, the surface moves the tab.

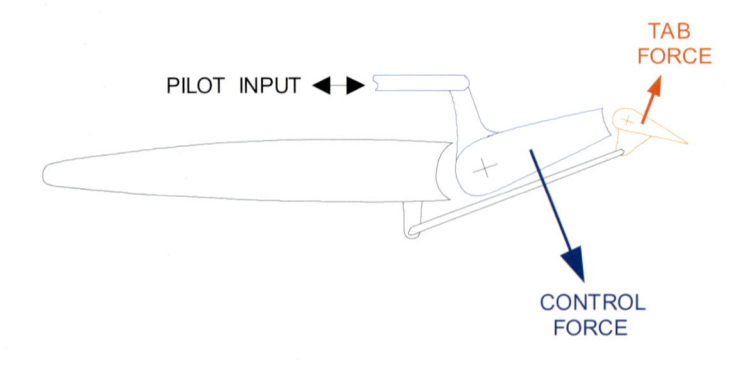

Figure 11.8   Balance Tab

Unlike the previous types of balance, the balance tab will give some reduction in control effectiveness, as the tab force is opposite to the control force.

PRINCIPLES OF FLIGHT   **CONTROLS**

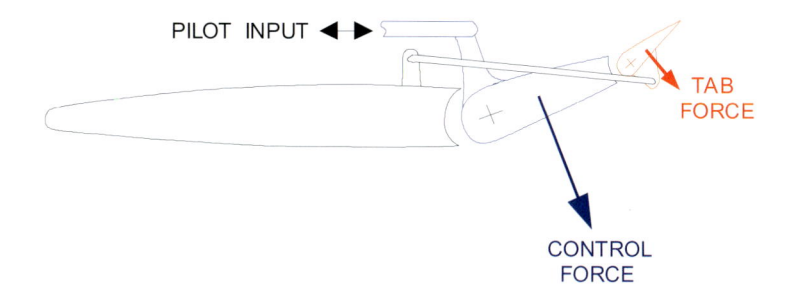

Figure 11.9   Anti - Balance tab

e)   **Anti-balance Tab: The anti-balance tab moves in the same direction as the control surface** and increases control effectiveness, but will increase the hinge moment and give heavier stick forces. The pilot moves the surface, the surface moves the tab.

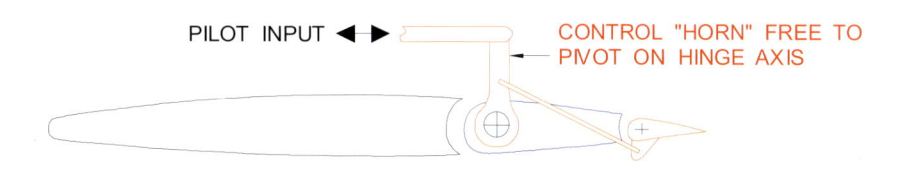

Figure 11.10   Servo Tab

f)   **Servo Tab: Pilot control input deflects the servo tab only**, the aerodynamic force on the tab then moves the control surface until an equilibrium position is reached. **If external control locks are fitted to the control surface on the ground, the cockpit control will still be free to move.** Older types of high speed jet transport aircraft (B707) successfully used servo tab controls, the disadvantage of the servo tab is reduced control effectiveness at low IAS.

[handwritten: Must remove]

Figure 11.11   Spring Tab

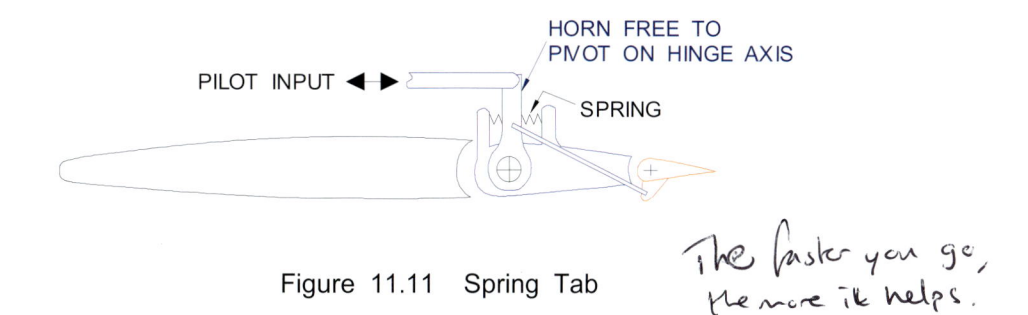

[handwritten: The faster you go, the more it helps.]

g)   **Spring Tab:** The spring tab is a modification of the servo tab, such that tab movement is proportional to the applied stick force. Maximum tab assistance is obtained at high speed when the stick forces are greatest. High dynamic pressure will prevent the surface from moving, so the spring is compressed by the pilot input and the tab moves the surface. The spring is not compressed at low IAS, so the pilot input deflects the control surface and the tab, increasing the surface area and control effectiveness at low speed.

PRINCIPLES OF FLIGHT CONTROLS

11.3.2 (HYDRAULIC) POWERED FLYING CONTROLS

If the required assistance for the pilot to move the controls cannot be provided by the preceding types of aerodynamic balance, then power assisted or fully powered controls have to be used.

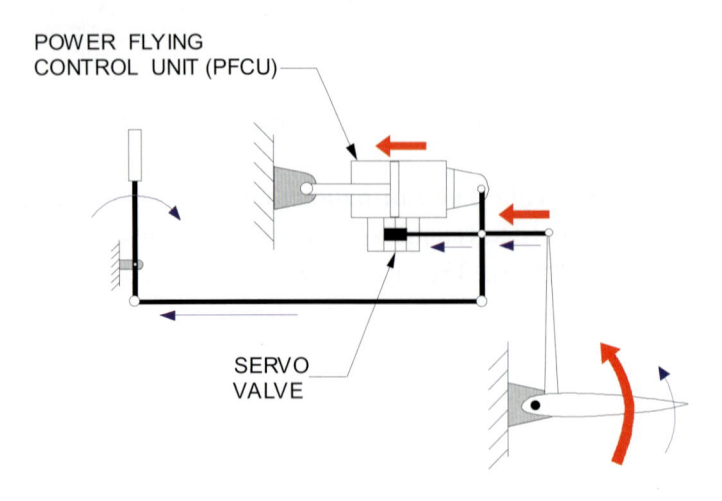

Figure 11.12   Power assisted flying control

a) **Power Assisted Controls**

With a power assisted flying control, Fig. 11.12, only a certain proportion of the force required to oppose the hinge moment is provided by the pilot, the hydraulic system provides most of the force. Although the pilot does not have to provide all the force required, the natural 'feel' of the controls is retained and the stick force increases as the square of the IAS, just as in a completely manual control.

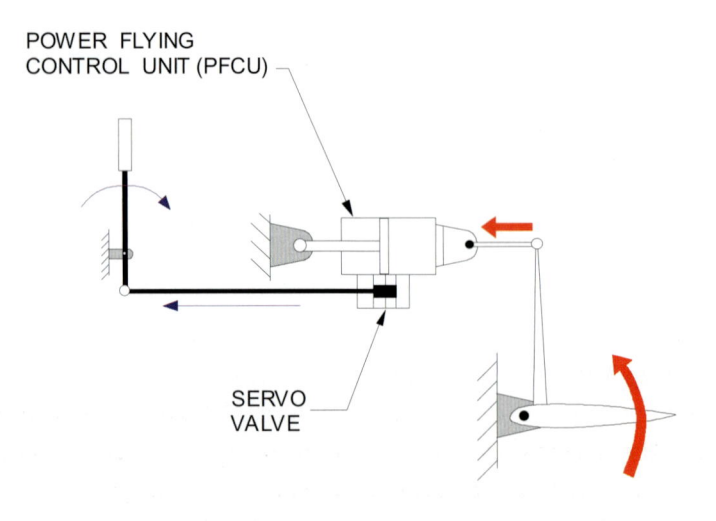

Figure 11.13   Fully powered flying control

PRINCIPLES OF FLIGHT CONTROLS

b) **Fully Powered Controls**

For bigger and/or faster aircraft, hinge moments are so large that fully powered controls must be used. In a fully powered control system, none of the force to move the control surface is supplied by the pilot. The only force the pilot supplies is that required to overcome system friction and to move the servo valve, all the necessary power to move the control surface is supplied by the aircraft's hydraulic system.

Fig. 11.13 shows that movement of the servo valve to the left allows hydraulic fluid to enter the left chamber of the PFCU. The body of the unit will move to the left, its movement being transferred to the control surface. As soon as the PFCU body reaches the position into which the pilot placed the servo valve, the PFCU body, and hence the control surface, stops moving. The unit is now locked in its new position by "incompressible" liquid trapped on both sides of the piston and will remain in that position until the servo valve is again moved by the pilot. Aerodynamic loads on the control surface are unable to move the cockpit controls, so powered flying controls are known as "irreversible" controls.

c) **Artificial Feel ('Q' Feel)**

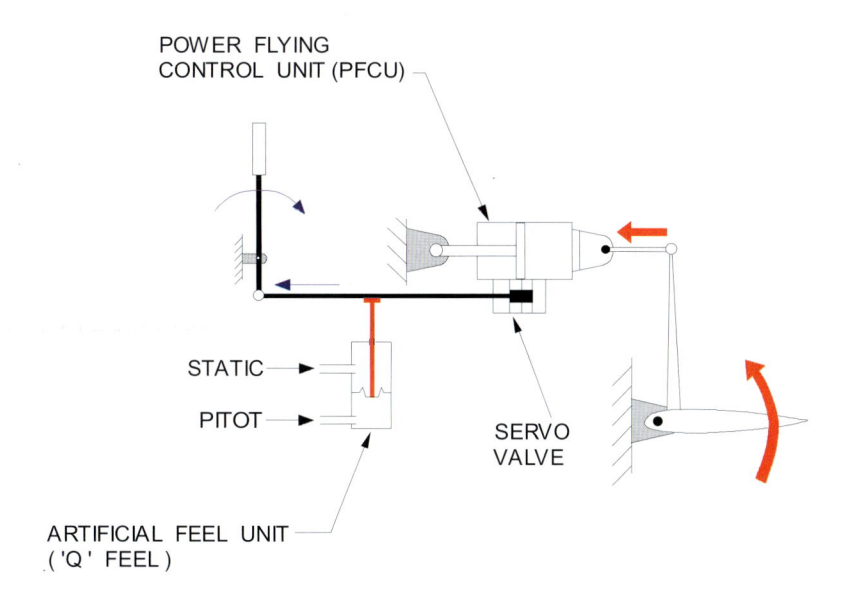

Figure 11.14 Artificial feel ('Q' feel)

With a fully powered flying control the pilot is unaware of the aerodynamic force on the controls, so it is necessary to incorporate "artificial" feel to prevent the aircraft from being overstressed. As shown schematically in Fig. 11.14, a device sensitive to dynamic pressure ($\frac{1}{2} \rho V^2$) or 'Q' is used. Pitot pressure is fed to one side of a chamber and static pressure to the other, which moves a diaphragm under the influence of changing dynamic pressure with airspeed and causes "regulated" hydraulic pressure to provide a resistance or "feel" on the pilot's input controls proportional to IAS^2, just as in a manual control. In addition, stick force should increase as stick displacement increases.

11.4 MASS BALANCE

Mass balance is a WEIGHT attached to the control surface forward of the hinge. Most control surfaces are mass balanced. The purpose of this is to prevent control surface flutter. Flutter is an oscillation of the control surface which can occur due to the bending and twisting of the structure under load. If the control surface CG is behind the hinge line, inertia will cause the surface to oscillate about its hinge line. The oscillations can be divergent, and cause structural failure. A detailed explanation of flutter is given in Chapter 14.

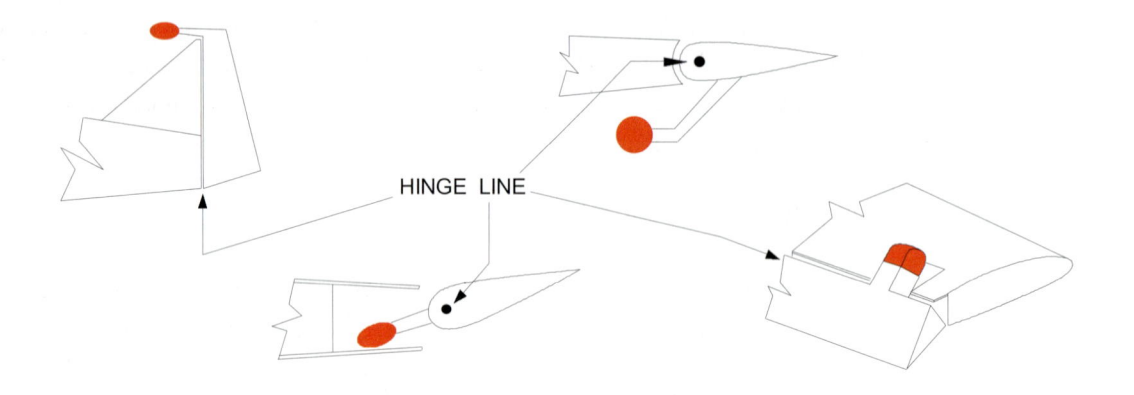

Figure 11.15   Mass balance weights

Flutter may be prevented by **adding weight to the control surface in front of the hinge line.** This brings the centre of gravity of the control forward to a position on, or slightly in front of the hinge, but always to the point required by the designers . This reduces the inertia moments about the hinge and prevents flutter developing. Fig. 11.15 illustrates some common methods of mass balancing.

11.5 LONGITUDINAL CONTROL

Control in pitch is usually obtained by elevators or by an all moving (slab) tailplane, and the controls must be adequate to balance the aircraft throughout its speed range at all permitted CG positions and configurations and to give an adequate rate of pitch for manoeuvres.

11.5.1 EFFECT OF ELEVATOR DEFLECTION

Suppose that the aircraft is flying in balance at a steady speed with the elevator neutral. If the elevator is deflected upwards, the tail will develop a download which will begin to pitch the aircraft nose upwards. As the angle of attack increases, the tailplane download decreases and the aircraft will reach an equilibrium pitch position. It will then remain in that pitch position with the elevator kept at the selected angle. If the elevator is returned to neutral the tail will develop an upload which will begin to pitch the aeroplane down again. At a given C G position there will be a given pitch attitude for each elevator position.

PRINCIPLES OF FLIGHT   **CONTROLS**

11.5.2 DIRECTION OF THE TAILPLANE LOAD

The elevator angle required to give balance depends on IAS and the CG position. At normal cruising speeds and CG positions, the elevator should ideally be approximately neutral. The tailplane will be giving a download, and consequently a nose-up pitching moment. This will balance the nose-down moment created by the wing with its centre of pressure fairly well aft. At higher than normal speeds the CP will move further rearwards giving a stronger nose-down pitch, and needing a larger down-load from the tailplane. However at higher speed the aircraft's angle of attack will be decreased, requiring some down elevator to provide the correct tail-load.

At lower than normal speeds the CP will move forward and the wing and fuselage may cause a nose-up pitching moment. The tailplane will be required to give an up-load for balance. At low speed the aircraft will be at a high angle of attack, and to reach this attitude the elevator will have been moved up.

11.5.3 ELEVATOR ANGLE WITH 'g'

When the aircraft is performing a pitching manoeuvre the tailplane angle of attack is increased by the effect of the rotational velocity and the aerodynamic damping is increased. This means that a larger elevator angle will be required than for the same conditions in 1g flight. The additional elevator angle required will be proportional to the 'g' being experienced. The elevator movement available should be sufficient to allow the design limit 'g' to be reached. **The most demanding requirement for elevator up authority will be when the aircraft is being flared for landing, in ground effect with most forward CG** (see Paragraph 10.21).

11.5.4 EFFECT OF ICE ON THE TAILPLANE

The tailplane is an aerofoil, usually symmetrical as it is required to produce both up and down loads. It is set at an angle of incidence which is less than that of the wing. This ensures that it will not stall before the wing, and so control can be maintained up to the stall. It is usually affected by the **downwash from the wing and this reduces its effective angle of attack**. Typically the tail will be at a negative angle of attack, producing a download for balance. If ice forms on the tailplane leading edge, its aerofoil shape will be distorted, and its stalling angle reduced. This could cause the tailplane to stall, particularly if the downwash is increased as result of lowering flaps. With the tailplane stalled its download would be reduced and the aircraft would pitch down and could not be recovered.

11.6 LATERAL CONTROL

Control in roll is usually obtained by ailerons or by spoilers, or by a combination of the two. The main requirement for lateral control is to achieve an adequate rate of roll.

On the ground with the control wheel in the neutral position both ailerons should be slightly below alignment with the wing trailing edge, "drooped". When airborne, the lower pressure on the top surface will "suck" both ailerons up into a position where they are perfectly aligned with the wing trailing edge, thus reducing drag.

11.6.1 EFFECT OF AILERON DEFLECTION (Aerodynamic Damping)

In steady level flight with the ailerons neutral, the lift on the two wings will be equal. If the control wheel is turned to the left, the left aileron will move up and the right aileron down. The up aileron will decrease the lift of the left wing which will begin to 'drop'. The downward movement of the wing creates a relative airflow upwards, which increases its effective angle of attack. The opposite effects will occur on the right (up going) wing.

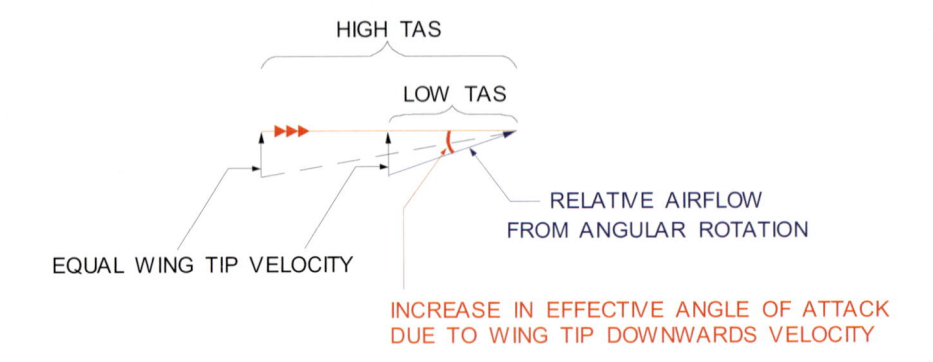

Figure 11.16 Aerodynamic damping in roll

The increased effective angle of attack of the down going wing increases its lift, which opposes the roll. This is called aerodynamic damping. The greater the rate of roll, the greater the damping. It can also be seen from Fig. 11.16 that the greater the TAS, the smaller the increase in effective angle of attack for a given roll rate.

The change in wing lift for a given aileron deflection depends on the IAS, but the change of effective angle of attack due to roll velocity depends on TAS. At high TAS (constant IAS, higher altitude) the change in effective angle of attack will be reduced and a higher rate of roll will be possible. Rate of roll therefore increases (aerodynamic damping decreases) with higher TAS for a given aileron deflection. **The aileron is known as a rate control** since a given aileron angle of deflection determines a **rate** of roll, not a roll displacement.

11.6.2 EFFECT OF WINGSPAN ON RATE OF ROLL

For a given rate of roll, the wing tip rolling velocity will increase with the wing span. Aerodynamic damping will therefore be greater if the span is greater. Under the same conditions, a short span wing will have a greater rate of roll than a large span wing.

11.6.3 ADVERSE AILERON YAW

The ailerons produce a rolling moment by increasing the lift on one wing and decreasing it on the other. The increased lift on the up-going wing gives an increase in the induced drag, whereas the reduced lift on the downgoing wing gives a decease in induced drag. The difference in drag on the two wings produces a yawing moment which is opposite to the rolling moment, that is, a roll to the left produces a yawing moment to the right. This is known as adverse aileron yaw.

PRINCIPLES OF FLIGHT CONTROLS

11.6.4 REDUCING ADVERSE AILERON YAW

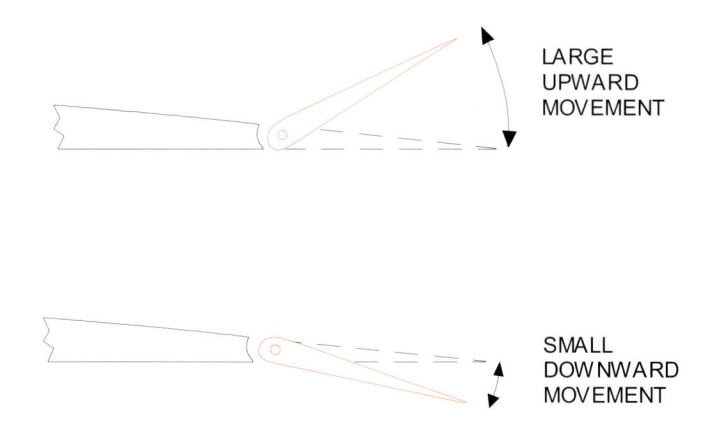

Figure 11.17   Differential ailerons

a) **Differential ailerons:** The aileron linkage causes the up-going aileron the move through a larger angle than the down-going aileron, Fig. 11.17. This increases the drag on the up aileron, and reduces it on the down aileron, and so reduces the difference in drag between the two wings.

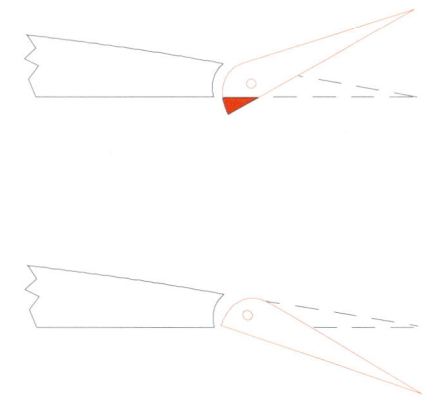

Figure 11.18   Frise ailerons

b) **Frise ailerons:** have an asymmetric leading edge, as illustrated in Fig. 11.18. The leading edge of the up-going aileron protrudes below the lower surface of the wing, causing high drag. The leading edge of the down-going aileron remains shrouded and causes less drag.

c) **Aileron-rudder coupling:** In this system the aileron and rudder controls are interconnected, so that when the ailerons are deflected the rudder automatically moves to counter the adverse yaw.

d) **Roll control spoilers:** If roll spoilers are used to augment the roll rate obtained from the ailerons, they will reduce the adverse yaw, as the down-going wing will have an increase in drag due to the raised spoiler.

PRINCIPLES OF FLIGHT   CONTROLS

11.6.5 INBOARD AILERONS

Ailerons are normally situated at the wing tips to give the greatest rolling moment for the force produced. However, this means they are also able to generate the maximum twisting loads on the wing. For instance, a down going aileron will twist the wing tip and decrease wing tip incidence. The wing is not a rigid structure and any twist will cause a decrease of aileron effectiveness. As IAS increases, a down going aileron will give more wing twist (decreased wing tip incidence). Eventually an IAS will be reached at which the decrease in tip incidence will give a larger down force than the up force produced by the aileron. This is called high speed "aileron reversal"; the wing will go down, rather than up as the pilot intended. To reduce this effect the ailerons could be mounted further inboard. Unfortunately, this would reduce aileron effectiveness at low speed.

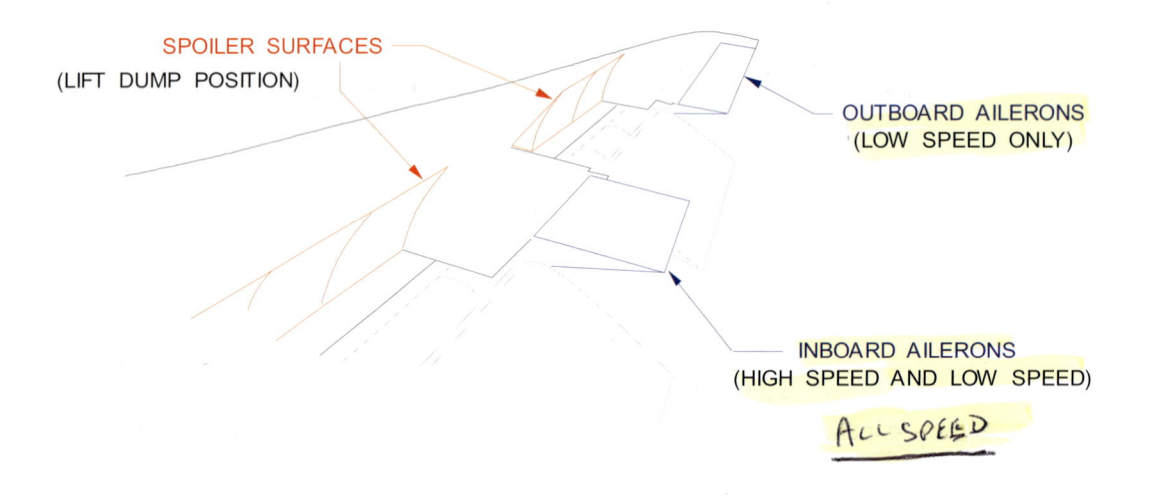

Figure 11.19   Inboard and outboard ailerons & Spoiler surfaces

Alternatively, two sets of ailerons may be fitted, as illustrated in Fig. 11.19. One set at the wing tips for use only at low speeds when the forces involved are low, and one set inboard for use at high speeds when the forces are greater and could cause greater structural distortion. Outboard (low speed) ailerons are "locked-out" as the flaps retract. At low speed both sets of ailerons work, but at high speed only the inboard ailerons respond to control input.

11.6.6 FLAPERONS

The flaps and the ailerons both occupy part of the wing trailing edge. For good take-off and landing performance the flaps need to be as large as possible, and for a good rate of roll the ailerons need to be as large as possible. However, the space available is limited, and one solution is to droop the ailerons symmetrically to augment the flap area. They then move differentially from the drooped position to give lateral control. Another system is to use the trailing edge moveable surfaces to perform the operation of both flaps and ailerons.

PRINCIPLES OF FLIGHT   CONTROLS

11.6.7 ROLL CONTROL SPOILERS

Spoilers may be used to give lateral control, in addition to, or instead of ailerons. Spoilers consist of movable panels on the upper wing surface, hinged at their forward edge, which can be raised hydraulically, as illustrated in Fig. 11.20. A raised spoiler will disturb the airflow over the wing and reduce lift.

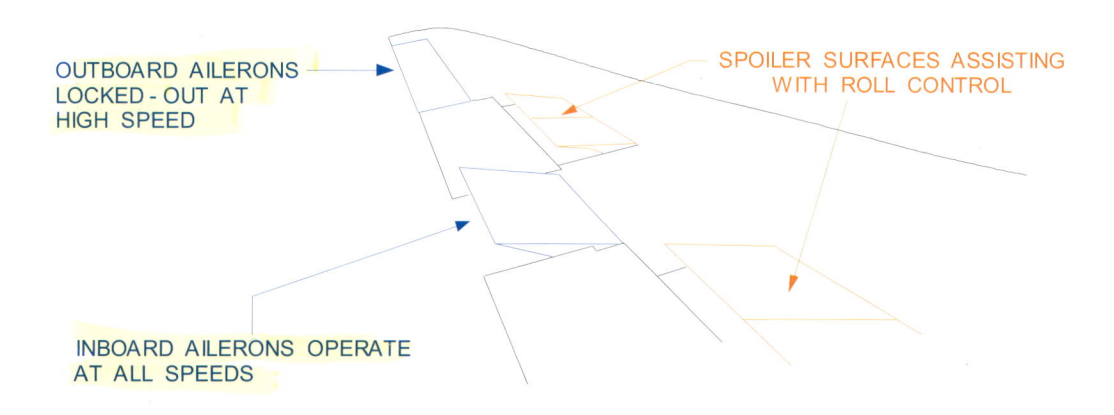

Figure 11.20   Roll control spoilers

To function as a lateral control, the spoilers rise on the wing with the up going aileron (down going wing), proportional to aileron input. On the wing with the down going aileron, they remain flush. Unlike ailerons, spoilers cannot give an increase of lift, so a roll manoeuvre controlled by spoilers will always give a net loss of lift. However the spoiler has several advantages compared to the aileron:

a)   **There is no adverse yaw:** The raised spoiler increases drag on that wing, so the yaw is in the same direction as the roll.

b)   **Wing twisting is reduced:** The aerodynamic force on the spoilers acts further forward than is the case with ailerons, reducing the moment which tends to twist the wing.

c)   At transonic speed its effectiveness is not reduced by shock induced separation.

d)   It cannot develop flutter.

e)   Spoilers do not occupy the trailing edge, which can then be utilised for flaps.

11.6.8 COMBINED AILERON AND SPOILER CONTROLS

On a few aircraft, lateral control is entirely by spoilers, but in the majority of applications the spoilers work in conjunction with the ailerons. Ailerons alone may be inadequate to achieve the required rate of roll at low speeds when the dynamic pressure is low, and at high speeds they may cause excessive wing twist and begin to lose effectiveness if there is shock induced separation. Spoilers can be used to augment the rate of roll, but may not be required to operate over the whole speed range. On some aircraft the spoilers are only required at low speed, and this can be achieved by making them inoperative when the flaps are retracted.

Movement of the cockpit control for lateral control is transmitted to a mixer unit which causes the spoiler to move up when the aileron moves up, but to remain retracted when the aileron moves down.

11.7 SPEED BRAKES

Speed brakes are devices to increase the drag of an aircraft when it is required to decelerate quickly or to descend rapidly. Rapid deceleration is required if turbulence is encountered at high speed, to slow down to the Rough Air Speed as quickly as possible. A high rate of descent may be required to conform to Air Traffic Control requirements, and particularly if an emergency descent is required.

11.7.1 TYPES OF SPEED BRAKE

Ideally the speed brake should produce an increase in drag with no loss of lift or change in pitching moment. The fuselage mounted speed brake is best suited to meet these requirements, Fig. 11.21.

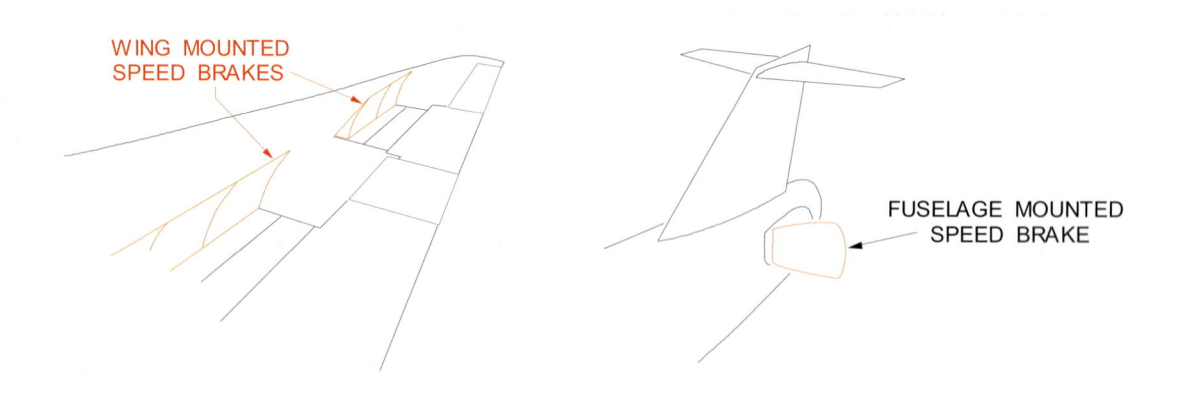

Figure 11.21 Wing mounted and fuselage mounted speed brakes

PRINCIPLES OF FLIGHT — CONTROLS

However, as the wing mounted spoiler gives an increase in drag, it is convenient to use the spoiler surfaces as speed brakes in addition to their lateral control function. To operate as speed brakes they are **controlled by a separate lever in the cockpit and activate symmetrically**. Speed brakes are normally cleared for operation up to V_{MO} / M_{MO} but may "blow back" from the fully extended position at high speeds. Spoilers will still function as a roll control whilst being used as speed brakes, by moving asymmetrically from the selected speed brake position.

An example is illustrated in Fig. 11.22. Speed brakes have been selected and then a turn to the left is initiated. The spoiler surfaces on the wing with the up going aileron will stay deployed, or modulate upwards, depending on the speed brake selection and the roll input. The spoiler surfaces on the wing with the down going aileron will modulate towards the stowed position. The spoiler surfaces on the wing with the down going aileron may partially or fully stow, again depending on the speed brake selection and the roll input.

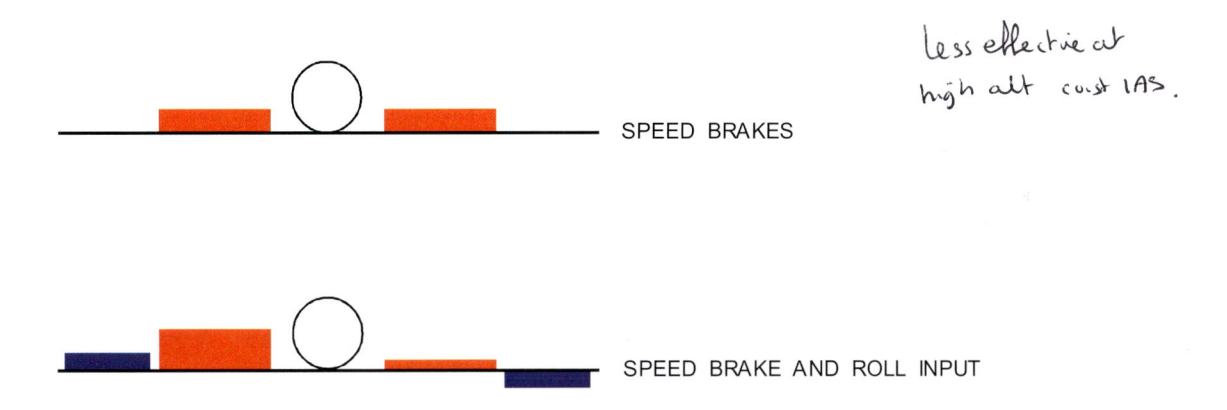

less effective at high alt const IAS.

Figure 11.22 Mixed speed brake and roll input

11.7.2 EFFECT OF SPEED BRAKES ON THE DRAG CURVE

The drag resulting from the operation of speed brakes is profile drag, so will not only increase the total drag but will also decrease V_{md}. This is an advantage at low speeds as the speed stability will be better than with the aircraft in the clean configuration.

11.7.3 GROUND SPOILERS (LIFT DUMPERS)

During the landing run the decelerating force is given by aerodynamic drag, reverse thrust and the wheel brakes. Wheel brake efficiency depends on the weight on the wheels, but this will be reduced by any lift that the wing is producing. Lift can be reduced by operating the speed brake lever to the lift dump position, Fig. 11.19. Both the wheel brake drag and the aerodynamic drag are increased, and the landing run reduced. On many aircraft types, additional spoiler surfaces are activated in the lift dumping selection than when airborne. These ground spoilers are made inoperative in flight by a switch on the undercarriage leg which is operated by the extension of the leg after take-off.

PRINCIPLES OF FLIGHT

11.8 DIRECTIONAL CONTROL

Control in yaw is obtained by the rudder. The rudder is required to:-

a) maintain directional control with asymmetric power

b) correct for crosswinds on take off and landing

c) correct for adverse yaw

d) recover from a spin

e) correct for changes in propeller turning moment on single engined aircraft

11.8.1 EFFECT OF RUDDER DEFLECTION

If the rudder is deflected to the left the aircraft will begin to yaw to the left. This will create a sideslip to the right. The sideslip airflow from the right acting on the fixed part of the fin will cause a side load to the left, opposing the effect of the rudder. As the yaw increases this damping force will increase until it balances the rudder force. The aircraft will then stop yawing, and will maintain that angle of yaw, with the rudder deflected to its original position. If the rudder is returned to the neutral position, both the fin and the rudder will give a force to the left which will return the aircraft to its original position with zero yaw. A given rudder angle will therefore correspond to a given yaw displacement.

11.8.2 FIN STALL

The sideslip angle is effectively the angle of attack of the fin, and as for any aerofoil, there will be a critical angle at which it will stall. If the rudder is deflected in the direction to correct the sideslip, the stalling angle will be reduced.

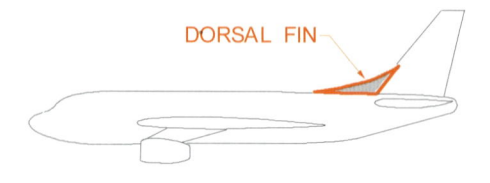

The stalling angle of an aerofoil is affected by its aspect ratio, and so the stalling angle of the fin could be increased by decreasing its aspect ratio. This can be done by fitting a dorsal fin, Fig. 11.23.

Figure 11.23

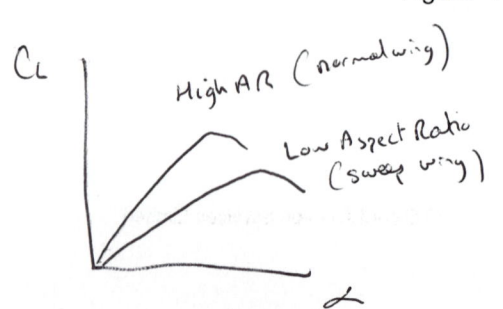

PRINCIPLES OF FLIGHT — CONTROLS

11.8.3 ASYMMETRIC THRUST *(STOP OR PREVENT YAW)*

For a twin engined aircraft, if engine failure occurs, the thrust from the operating engine will cause a yawing moment. This must be counteracted by the rudder. The rudder force will vary with speed squared, and so there will be a minimum speed at which the force will be sufficient to balance the engine yawing moment. This is the minimum control speed (V_{MC}).

11.8.4 RUDDER RATIO CHANGER

With a simple control system, full rudder pedal movement will provide full rudder deflection. With high speed aircraft, while it is necessary to have large rudder deflections available at low speed, when flying at high speed, full rudder deflection would cause excessive loads on the structure. To prevent this occurring a gear change system can be incorporated into the rudder control system. This may be a single gear change which gives a smaller rudder deflection for full pedal movement above a certain speed, or a progressive gear change which gives a decreasing rudder deflection with full pedal movement as speed increases, Fig. 11.24.

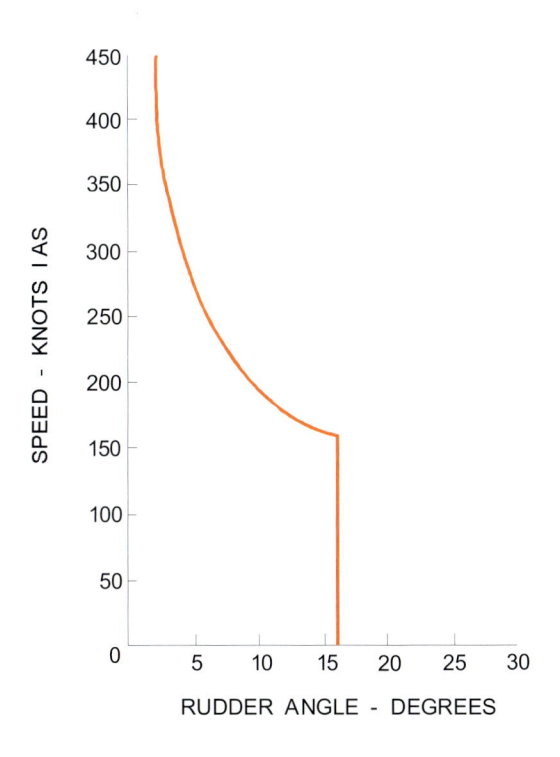

Figure 11.24   Rudder ratio

PRINCIPLES OF FLIGHT   CONTROLS

11.9 SECONDARY EFFECTS OF CONTROLS

The controls are designed to give a moment around a particular axis, but may additionally give a moment around a second axis. This coupling occurs particularly with the rolling and yawing moments.

11.9.1 YAWING MOMENT DUE TO ROLL

a) A rolling moment is normally produced by deflecting the ailerons, and it has been seen that they can also produce an adverse yawing moment due to the difference in drag on the two ailerons. Induced drag is increased on the wing with the down going aileron, making the aircraft, for instance, roll left and at the same time, yaw right.

b) If the aircraft is rolling, the down-going wing experiences an increased angle of attack and the up-going wing a decreased angle of attack, increasing the adverse yawing moment..

11.9.2 ROLLING MOMENT DUE TO YAW

a) If the aircraft is yawing to the left, the right wing has a higher velocity than the left wing and so will give more lift. The difference in lift will give a rolling moment to the left.

b) If the rudder is deflected to the left (to give yaw to the left) the force on the fin is to the right. This will give a small rolling moment to the right because the fin CP is above the aircraft CG. This effect is usually very small, but a high fin may give an adverse roll.

One way to counteract this effect is to interconnect the ailerons and rudder so that when the rudder is moved the ailerons move automatically to correct the adverse roll.

PRINCIPLES OF FLIGHT   **CONTROLS**

11.10 TRIMMING

An aeroplane is trimmed when it will maintain its attitude and speed without the pilot having to apply any load to the cockpit controls. If it is necessary for a control surface to be deflected to maintain balance of the aircraft, the pilot will need to apply a force to the cockpit control to hold the surface in its deflected position. **This force may be reduced to zero by operation of the trim controls.**

The aircraft may need to be trimmed in pitch as a result of :

a) changes of speed

b) changes of power

c) varying CG positions

Trimming in yaw will be needed :

d) on a multi-engined aircraft if there is asymmetric power

e) as a result of changes in propeller torque

Trimming in roll is less likely to be needed, but could be required if the configuration is asymmetric, or if there is a lateral displacement of the CG.

11.10.1 METHODS OF TRIMMING

Various methods of trimming are in use, the main ones are:

a) the trimming tab

b) variable incidence (trimming) tailplane

c) spring bias

d) CG adjustment

e) adjustment of the artificial feel unit

11.10.2 TRIM TAB

A trim tab is a small adjustable surface set into the trailing edge of a main control surface. It's deflection is controlled by a trim wheel or electrical switch in the cockpit, usually arranged to operate in an instinctive sense. To maintain the primary control surface in its required position, **the tab is moved in the opposite direction to the control surface**, until the tab moment balances the control surface hinge moment.

Fig. 11.25 shows (f x D) from tab opposes (F x d) from control surface. If the two moments are equal the control will be trimmed, i.e. the stick force will be zero. Operation of the trim tab will slightly reduce the force being produced by the main control surface.

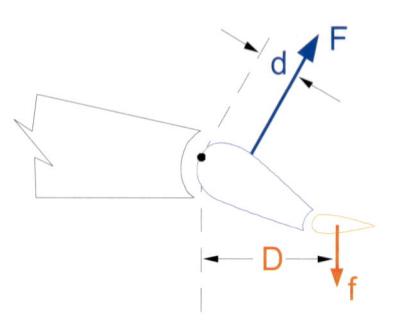

Figure 11.25

11.10.3 FIXED TABS

Some trim tabs are not adjustable in flight, but can be adjusted on the ground, to correct a permanent out of trim condition. They are usually found on ailerons and rudder. They operate in the same manner as the adjustable trim tab.

11.10.4 VARIABLE INCIDENCE (Trimming) TAILPLANE

This system of trimming may be used on manually operated and power operated controls. To trim, the tailplane incidence is adjusted by the trim wheel until the tailplane load is equal to the previous elevator balancing load required, Fig. 1.26. Stick force is now zero.

The main advantages of a variable incidence (trimming) tailplane are:

a) the drag is less in the trimmed state, as the aerofoil is more streamlined

b) trimming does not reduce the **effective range** of pitch control, as the elevator remains approximately neutral when the aircraft is trimmed.

c) it is very powerful and gives an increased ability to trim for larger CG and speed range.

The disadvantage of a variable incidence (trimming) tailplane is that it is more complex and heavy than a conventional trim tab system.

PRINCIPLES OF FLIGHT   **CONTROLS**

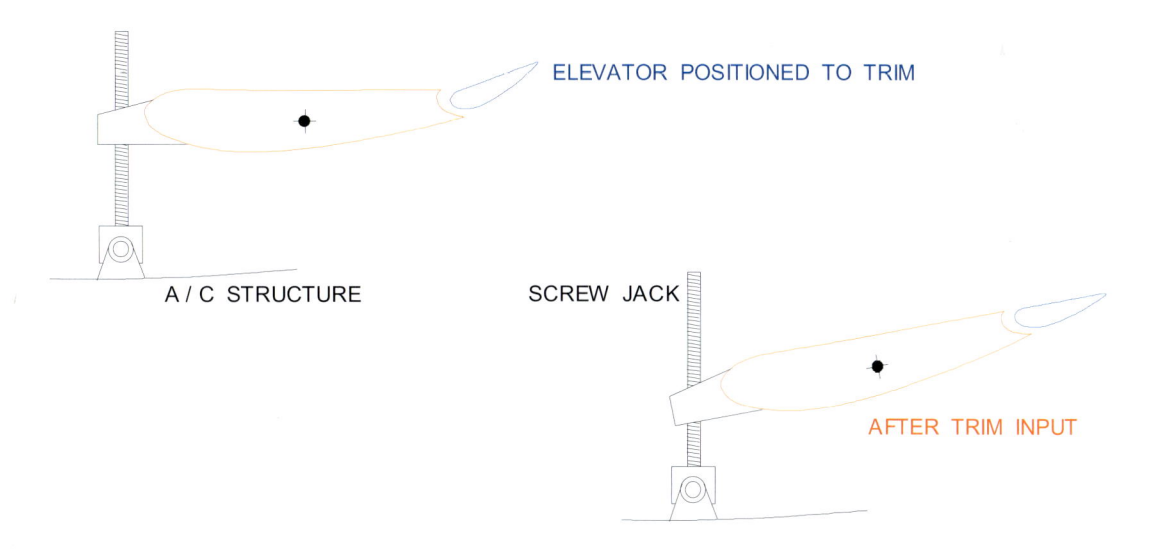

Figure 11.26   Variable incidence (trimming) tailplane

The amount of trim required will depend on the CG position, and recommended stabiliser take-off settings will be given in the aircraft Flight Manual. It is important that these are correctly set before take-off as incorrect settings could give either an excessive rate of pitch when the aircraft is rotated, leading to possible tail strikes, or very heavy stick forces on rotation, leading to increased take-off distances required.

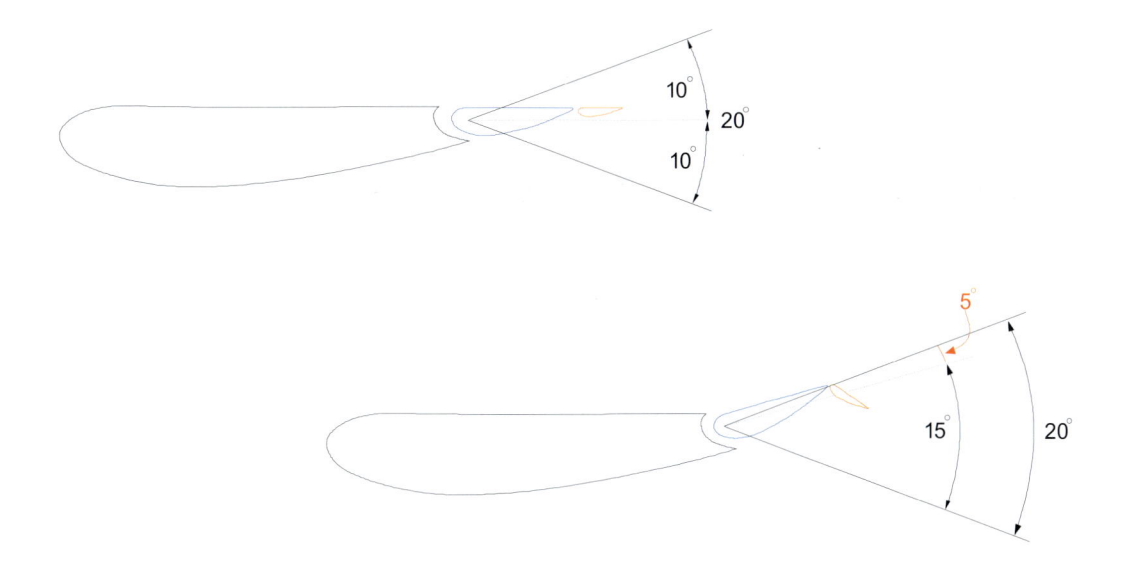

Figure 1.27   Reduced aircraft nose up pitch authority

The disadvantage of a "conventional" elevator and trim tab, Fig. 11.27, is that the aircraft nose up pitch authority reduces with forward CG movement. Forward CG positions will require the elevator to be trimmed more aircraft nose up. The illustration shows up elevator authority reduced from 10° to 5°.

PRINCIPLES OF FLIGHT   CONTROLS

11.10.5 SPRING BIAS

In the spring bias trim system, an adjustable spring force is used to decrease the stick force. No tab is required for this system.

11.10.6 CG ADJUSTMENT

If the flying controls are used for trimming, this results in an increase of drag due to the deflected surfaces. The out of balance pitching moment can be reduced by moving the CG, thus reducing the balancing load required and therefore the drag associated with it. This will give an increase of cruise range. CG movement is usually achieved by transferring fuel between tanks at the nose and tail of the aircraft.

11.10.7 ARTIFICIAL FEEL TRIM

If the flying controls are power operated, there is no feedback of the load on the control surface to the cockpit control. The feel on the controls has to be created artificially. When a control surface is moved the artificial feel unit provides a force to resist the movement of the cockpit control. To remove this force (i.e. to trim) the datum of the feel unit can be adjusted so that it no longer gives any load on the flight deck controls.

TABS - Quick Reference Guide

Type of Tab	Operated by	Movement Relative to Control Surface	Stick Force	Control Effectivenes
Balance	Control Surface	Opposite	Less	Reduced
Anti - Balance	Control Surface	Same	More	Increased
Servo	Pilot	Opposite	Less	Reduced
Spring	Pilot @ High Speed	Opposite @ High Speed	Less @ High Speed	Reduced @ High Speed
Trim	Trim Control ONLY	Opposite	Zero'd	Reduced

PRINCIPLES OF FLIGHT　　　　　　　　　　　　　　　　　　　　　　　　　**CONTROLS**

SELF ASSESSMENT QUESTIONS

1. An elevon is:

    a) an all moving tailplane that has no elevator
    b) the correct name for a V - tail
    c) a surface that extends into the airflow from the upper surface of the wing to reduce the lift
    d) a combined aileron and elevator fitted to an aircraft that does not have conventional horizontal stabiliser (tailplane)

2. When rolling at a steady rate the:

    a) up going wing experiences an increase in effective angle of attack
    b) rate of roll depends only on aileron deflection
    c) down going wing experiences an increase in effective angle of attack
    d) effective angle of attack of the up going and down going wings are equal

3. The control surface which gives longitudinal control is:

    a) the rudder.
    b) the ailerons.
    c) the elevators.
    d) the flaps.

4. Ailerons give:

    a) lateral control about the lateral axis.
    b) longitudinal control about the lateral axis.
    c) lateral control about the longitudinal axis.
    d) directional control about the normal axis.

5. Aileron reversal would be most likely to occur:

    a) with a rigid wing at high speed.
    b) with a flexible wing at high speed.
    c) with a rigid wing at low
    d) with a flexible wing at low speed.

6. If the ailerons are deflected to 10°, compared to 5°, this will cause:

    a) an increased angle of bank.
    b) an increased rate of roll.
    c) no change to either bank angle or roll rate.
    d) a reduction in the adverse yawing moment.

PRINCIPLES OF FLIGHT — CONTROLS

7. Yawing is a rotation around:

    a) the normal axis obtained by elevator.
    b) the lateral axis obtained by rudder.
    c) the longitudinal axis obtained by ailerons.
    d) the normal axis obtained by rudder.

8. If the control column is moved forward and to the left:

    a) the left aileron moves up, right aileron moves down, elevator moves up.
    b) the left aileron moves down, right aileron moves up, elevator moves down.
    c) the left aileron moves up, right aileron moves down, elevator down.
    d) the left aileron moves down, right aileron moves up, elevator moves up.

9. The secondary effect of yawing to port is to:

    a) roll to starboard
    b) pitch nose up
    c) roll first to starboard and then to port
    d) roll to port

10. Due to the AC of the fin being above the longitudinal axis, if the rudder is moved to the right, the force acting on the fin will give:

    a) a yawing moment to the left but no rolling moment.
    b) a rolling moment to the left.
    c) a rolling moment to the right.
    d) a yawing moment to the right but no rolling moment.

11. What should be the feel on a 'full and free' check of the controls:

    a) a gradual stiffening of the controls.
    b) rebound on reaching the stops.
    c) a solid stop.
    d) controls should not be moved to the stops.

12. The purpose of control locks on a flying control system is:

    a) to enable any free movement in the control system to be detected.
    b) to prevent structural damage to the controls in gusty conditions when the aircraft is on the ground.
    c) to keep the control surface rigid to permit ground handling.
    d) as a security measure.

PRINCIPLES OF FLIGHT   **CONTROLS**

13. An irreversible control:

    a) may be moved by operating the cockpit control but not by the aerodynamic loads acting on the control surface.
    b) has less movement in one direction than the other.
    c) may be moved either by the cockpit control or by a load on the control surface.
    d) is when the control locks are engaged.

14. Ailerons may be rigged slightly down (drooped):

    a) to increase the feel in the control circuit
    b) to correct for adverse aileron yaw
    c) to allow for up-float in flight to bring the aileron into the streamlined position
    d) to give a higher $C_{L\,max}$ for take-off

15. The tailplane shown has inverted camber. To cause the aircraft to pitch nose up the control column must be:

    a) the control column must be pushed forward
    b) the control column must be pulled backwards
    c) the control wheel must be rotated
    d) the incidence of the tailplane must be decreased because the negative camber will make it effective in the reverse sense

16. If an aileron is moved downward:

    a) the stalling angle of that wing is increased
    b) the stalling angle of that wing is decreased
    c) the stalling angle is not affected but the stalling speed is decreased

17. When rudder is used to give a coordinated turn to the left:

    a) the left pedal is moved forward, and the rudder moves right
    b) the right pedal is moved forward and the rudder moves left
    c) the left pedal is moved forward and the rudder moves left

18. The higher speed of the upper wing in a steady banked turn causes it to have more lift than the lower wing. This may be compensated for by:

    a) use of the rudder control
    b) operating the ailerons slightly in the opposite sense once the correct angle of bank has been reached
    c) increasing the nose up pitch by using the elevators

19. The purpose of a differential aileron control is to:

    a) give a yawing moment which opposes the turn
    b) reduce the yawing moment which opposes the turn
    c) give a pitching moment to prevent the nose from dropping in the turn
    d) improve the rate of roll

20. When displacing the ailerons from the neutral position:

    a) the up going aileron causes an increase in induced drag.
    b) the down going aileron causes an increase in induced drag.
    c) both cause an increase in induced drag.
    d) induced drag remains the same, the up going aileron causes a smaller increase in profile drag than the down going aileron.

21. The purpose of aerodynamic balance on a flying control is:

    a) to get the aircraft into balance.
    b) to prevent flutter of the flying control.
    c) to reduce the control load to zero.
    d) to make the control easier to move.

22. A horn balance on a control surface is:

    a) an arm projecting upward from the control surface to which the control cables are attached.
    b) a projection of the outer edge of the control surface forward of the hinge line.
    c) a rod projecting forward from the control surface with a weight on the end.
    d) a projection of the leading edge of the control surface below the wing undersurface.

23. An aileron could be balanced aerodynamically by:

    a) making the up aileron move through a larger angle than the down aileron.
    b) attaching a weight to the control surface forward of the hinge.
    c) having the control hinge set back behind the control surface leading edge.
    d) having springs in the control circuit to assist movement.

24. Control overbalance results in:

    a) a sudden increase in stick force
    b) a sudden reduction then reversal of stick force
    c) a sudden loss of effectiveness of the controls
    d) a gradual increase in stick force with increasing IAS

PRINCIPLES OF FLIGHT　　　　　　　　　　　　　　　　　　　　　　　　　**CONTROLS**

25. A control surface is mass balanced by:

    a) fitting a balance tab.
    b) attaching a weight acting forward of the hinge line.
    c) attaching a weight acting on the hinge line.
    d) attaching a weight acting behind the hinge line.

26. If the control wheel is turned to the right, a balance tab on the port aileron should:

    a) move up relative to the aileron
    b) move down relative to the aileron
    c) not move unless the aileron trim wheel is turned.
    d) move to the neutral position

27. The purpose of an anti-balance tab is to:

    a) trim the aircraft
    b) reduce the load required to move the controls at all speeds
    c) reduce the load required to move the controls at high speeds only
    d) give more feel to the controls

28. When the control column is pushed forward a balance tab on the elevator:

    a) will move up relative to the control surface.
    b) will move down relative to the control surface.
    c) will only move if the trim wheel is operated.
    d) moves to the neutral position.

29. The purpose of a spring tab is:

    a) to maintain a constant tension in the trim tab system.
    b) to increase the feel in the control system.
    c) to reduce the pilot's effort required to move the controls against high air loads.
    d) to compensate for temperature changes in cable tension.

30. The purpose of a trim tab is:

    a) to assist the pilot in initiating movement of the controls.
    b) to zero the load on the pilots controls in the flight attitude required.
    c) to provide feel to the controls at high speed.
    d) to increase the effectiveness of the controls.

PRINCIPLES OF FLIGHT   **CONTROLS**

31. To re-trim after failure of the right engine on a twin-engine aircraft:

    a) the rudder trim tab will move right and the rudder left.
    b) the trim tab will move left and the rudder right.
    c) the trim tab will move left and the rudder remain neutral.
    d) the trim tab will move right and the rudder remain neutral.

32. To trim an aircraft which tends to fly nose heavy with hands off, the top of the elevator trim wheel should be:

    a) moved forward to raise the nose and this would cause the elevator trim tab to move down, and the elevator to move up.
    b) moved backwards to raise the nose, and this would cause the elevator trim tab to move down, and the elevator to move up.
    c) moved backwards to raise the nose, and this would cause the elevator trim tab to move up, and the elevator to move up.
    d) be moved backwards to raise the nose, and this would cause the elevator trim tab to move up and cause the nose to rise.

33. To achieve the same degree of longitudinal trim, the trim drag from a variable incidence trimming tailplane would be:

    a) greater than that from an elevator.
    b) the same as that from an elevator.
    c) less than that from an elevator.

34. Following re-trimming for straight and level flight because of forward CG movement:

    a) nose up pitch authority will be reduced
    b) nose down pitch authority will be reduced
    c) longitudinal stability will be reduced
    d) tailplane down load will be reduced

35. An aircraft has a tendency to fly right wing low with hands off. It is trimmed with a tab on the left aileron. The trim tab will:

    a) move up, causing the left aileron to move up and right aileron to move down.
    b) move down, causing the left aileron to move up, right aileron remains neutral.
    c) move down causing the left aileron to move up, and right aileron to move down.
    d) move up causing the left wing to move down, ailerons remain neutral.

36. An aircraft takes off with the elevator control locks still in position. It is found to be nose heavy:

    a) backward movement of the trim wheel would increase nose heaviness.
    b) it would not be possible to move the trim wheel.
    c) backward movement of the trim wheel would reduce nose heaviness.
    d) operating the trim wheel would have no effect.

37. On a servo tab operated elevator, if the pilot's control column is pushed forward in flight:

    a) the servo tab will move down causing the elevator to move up.
    b) the elevator will move down causing the servo tab to move up.
    c) the elevator will move up causing the servo tab to move down.
    d) the servo tab will move up causing the elevator to move down.

38. If a cockpit control check is made on an aircraft with servo operated controls, and it is found that the cockpit controls move fully and freely in all directions:

    a) the control surfaces and servo tabs are free.
    b) the control surfaces are free but there could be locks on the servo tabs.
    c) there could be locks on the control surfaces and on the servo tabs.
    d) the servo tabs are free but there could be locks on the control surfaces.

39. In a servo operated aileron control system, turning the cockpit control wheel to the right in flight will cause the servo tab on the left aileron:

    a) to move up and the left aileron to move down
    b) to move down and the left aileron to move down
    c) to move down and the left aileron to move up
    d) to move up and the right aileron to move down

40. Spoilers on the upper surface of the wing may be used on landing:

    a) to give a nose down pitching moment
    b) to reduce the lift and so put more weight on the wheels, making the brakes more effective
    c) to cause drag and increase the lift from the flaps
    d) to reduce the touchdown speed

PRINCIPLES OF FLIGHT   **CONTROLS**

41. Wing mounted spoiler surfaces may be used as:

    a) air brakes
    b) lift dumpers
    c) lateral control
    d) all of the above

42. Spoilers, when used for roll control will:

    a) reinforce the boundary layer
    b) create turbulence at the wing root
    c) increase the camber at the wing root
    d) decrease lift on the upper wing surface when deployed asymmetrically

43. On an aircraft fitted with roll control spoilers, a roll to port is achieved by:

    a) deflecting the port spoiler up and starboard down
    b) deflecting the starboard spoiler down
    c) deflecting the port spoiler up
    d) deflecting the port spoiler down

44. In a fully power operated flying control system control feel is provided by:

    a) the friction in the control cable system.
    b) an artificial feel unit (Q - Feel)
    c) the aerodynamic loads on the control surface.
    d) the mass balance weights.

PRINCIPLES OF FLIGHT — CONTROLS

ANSWERS

No	A	B	C	D	REF	No	A	B	C	D	REF
1				D		23			C		
2			C			24		B			
3			C			25		B			
4			C			26	A				
5		B				27				D	
6		B				28	A				
7				D		29			C		
8			C			30		B			
9				D		31	A				
10		B				32		B			
11			C			33			C		
12		B				34	A				
13	A					35			C		
14			C			36	A				
15		B				37				D	
16		B				38				D	
17			C			39	A				
18		B				40		B			
19		B				41				D	
20		B				42				D	
21				D		43			C		
22		B				44		B			

INTENTIONALLY LEFT BLANK

CHAPTER 12 - FLIGHT MECHANICS

Contents

	Page
INTRODUCTION	12 - 1
STRAIGHT HORIZONTAL STEADY FLIGHT	
TAILPLANE AND ELEVATOR	12 - 2
BALANCE OF FORCES	12 - 3
STRAIGHT STEADY CLIMB	12 - 4
CLIMB ANGLE	12 - 5
EFFECT OF WEIGHT, ALTITUDE AND TEMPERATURE	
POWER ON DESCENT	12 - 6
EMERGENCY DESCENT	12 - 7
GLIDE	12 - 8
ANGLE OF DESCENT IN THE GLIDE	
EFFECT OF WEIGHT	12 - 9
EFFECT OF WIND	12 - 10
EFFECT OF CONFIGURATION	
RATE OF DESCENT IN THE GLIDE	
TURNING	
EFFECT OF WEIGHT ON TURNING	12 - 11
RADIUS AND RATE OF TURN	12 - 14
LOAD FACTOR IN THE TURN	12 - 16
'G' LIMIT ON TURNING	12 - 17
STALL LIMIT ON TURNING	
THRUST LIMIT ON TURNING	
MINIMUM TURN RADIUS	
TURN CO-ORDINATION	12 - 18
FLIGHT WITH ASYMMETRIC THRUST	12 - 20
YAWING MOMENT	
CRITICAL ENGINE	12 - 22
BALANCING THE YAWING MOMENT	12 - 23
ROLL AND YAW MOMENTS	12 - 24
MINIMUM CONTROL AIRSPEED	12 - 27
V_{MCA}	
FACTORS AFFECTING V_{MCA}	12 - 28
V_{MCG}	12 - 29
FACTORS AFFECTING V_{MCG}	
V_{MCL}	12 - 30
FACTORS AFFECTING V_{MCL}	12 - 31
SUMMARY OF MINIMUM CONTROL SPEEDS	
PERFORMANCE WITH ONE ENGINE INOPERATIVE	12 - 32
SINGLE ENGINE ANGLE OF CLIMB	
SINGLE ENGINE RATE OF CLIMB	
CONCLUSIONS	
SELF ASSESSMENT QUESTIONS	12 - 35
ANSWERS	12 - 43

PRINCIPLES OF FLIGHT   **FLIGHT MECHANICS**

12.1 INTRODUCTION

Flight Mechanics is the study of the forces acting on an aircraft in flight, and the response of the aircraft to those forces. For an aircraft to be in steady (unaccelerated) flight, the following conditions must exist:-

a)   The forces acting upward must exactly balance the forces acting downward,

b)   the forces acting forward must exactly balance the forces acting backward, and

c)   the sum of all moments must be zero.

This condition is known as equilibrium.

12.2 STRAIGHT HORIZONTAL STEADY FLIGHT

In straight and level flight there are four forces acting on the aircraft; LIFT, WEIGHT, THRUST and DRAG, as shown in Fig. 12.1.

Weight acts through the aircraft centre of gravity (CG), vertically downwards towards the centre of the earth. Alternatively, weight can be defined as acting parallel to the force of gravity.

Lift acts through the centre of pressure (CP), normal (at 90°) to the flight path.

For the purposes of this chapter (although not strictly true), thrust acts forwards, parallel to the flight path and drag acts backwards, parallel to the flight path.

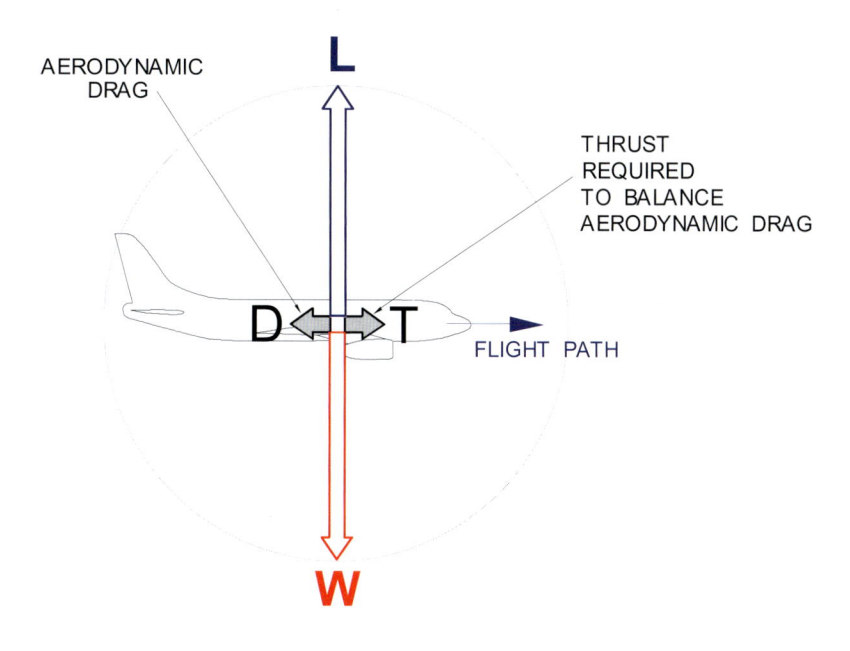

Figure 12.1   Forces in Level Flight

PRINCIPLES OF FLIGHT — FLIGHT MECHANICS

For an aircraft to be in steady level flight a condition of equilibrium must exist. This unaccelerated condition of flight is achieved with the aircraft trimmed with lift equal to weight and the throttles set for thrust to equal drag. It can be said that **for level flight the opposing forces must be equal**.

The L/D ratio of most modern aircraft is between 10 and 20 to 1. That is, lift is 10 to 20 times greater than drag.

The lines of action of thrust and drag lie very close together, so the moment of this couple is very small, and can be neglected for this study. The position of the CP and CG are variable and under most conditions of level flight are not coincident. The CP moves forward with increasing angle of attack and the CG moves with reduction in fuel. Generally, the CP is forward of the CG at low speed, giving a nose up pitching moment and behind the CG at high speed, giving a nose down pitching moment.

12.3 TAILPLANE AND ELEVATOR

The function of the tailplane is to maintain equilibrium by supply the force necessary to counter any pitching moments arising from CP and CG movement. With the CP behind the CG during normal cruise, as illustrated in Fig. 12.2, the tailplane must supply a down force.

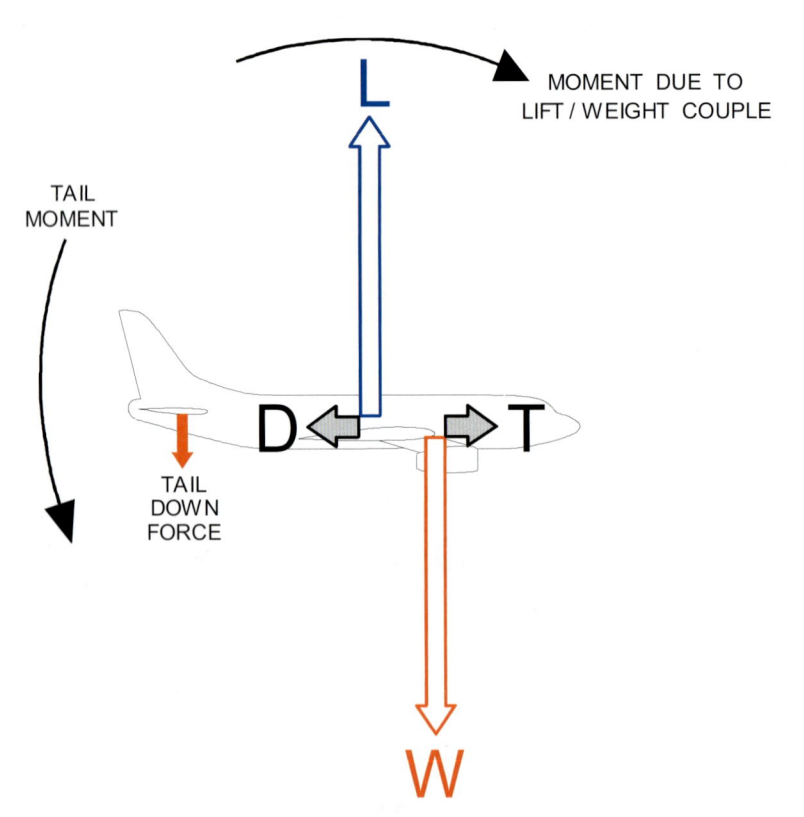

Figure 12.2 Tailplane Maintains Equilibrium

PRINCIPLES OF FLIGHT

FLIGHT MECHANICS

12.4 BALANCE OF FORCES

If the tailplane is producing a balancing force, this will add to or subtract from the lift force.

For a down load: Lift − tailplane force = Weight
For an up load: Lift + tailplane force = Weight

For steady level flight at a constant weight, the lift force required will be constant. At a steady speed the wing will give this lift at a given angle of attack. However if the speed is changed the angle of attack must change to maintain the same lift. As the lift changes with the square of the speed, but in direct proportion to the angle of attack, the angle of attack will vary as shown in Fig. 12.3 to give a constant lift.

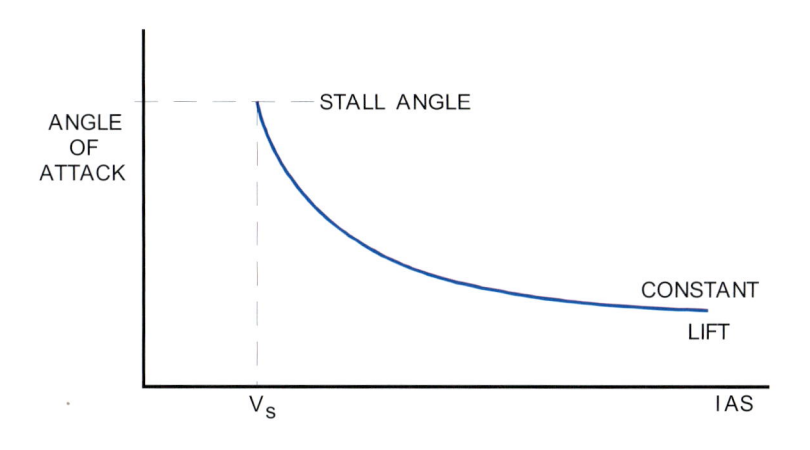

Figure 12.3   Variation of angle of attack with IAS

For steady level flight at a constant speed, the thrust must equal the drag. Drag increases with speed (above V_{md}) and so to maintain a higher speed, the thrust must be increased by opening the throttle.

To fly at the speed at point A, Fig. 12.4, requires a thrust of T_1 and to fly at point B requires a thrust of T_2. If the thrust is increased from T_1 to T_2 when the aircraft is at point A, the thrust will be greater then the drag, and the aircraft will accelerate in proportion to the 'excess' thrust AC until it reaches point B, where the thrust and the drag are again equal. If T_2 is the thrust available with the throttle fully open, then the speed at B is the maximum speed achievable in level flight.

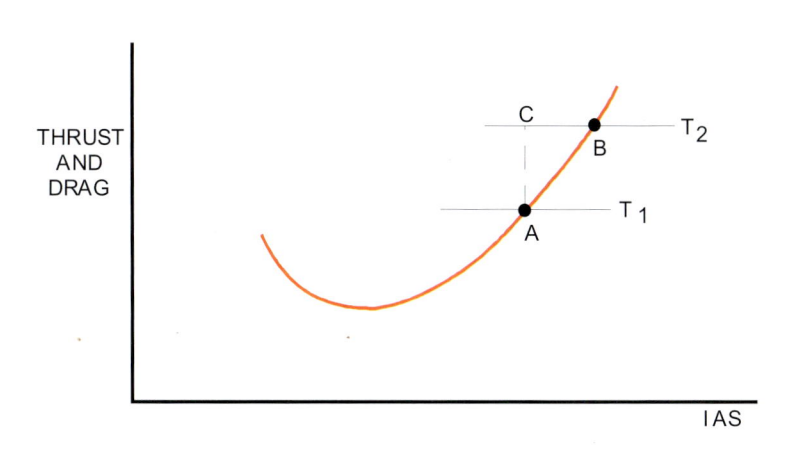

Figure 12.4   Balance of Thrust and Drag

PRINCIPLES OF FLIGHT **FLIGHT MECHANICS**

12.5 STRAIGHT STEADY CLIMB

Consider an aircraft in a straight steady climb along a straight flight path inclined at an angle (γ) to the horizontal. γ (gamma) is the symbol used for climb angle. The forces on the aircraft consist of Lift, normal to the flight path; Thrust and Drag, parallel to it; and Weight, parallel to the force of gravity. This system of forces is illustrated in Fig. 12.5.

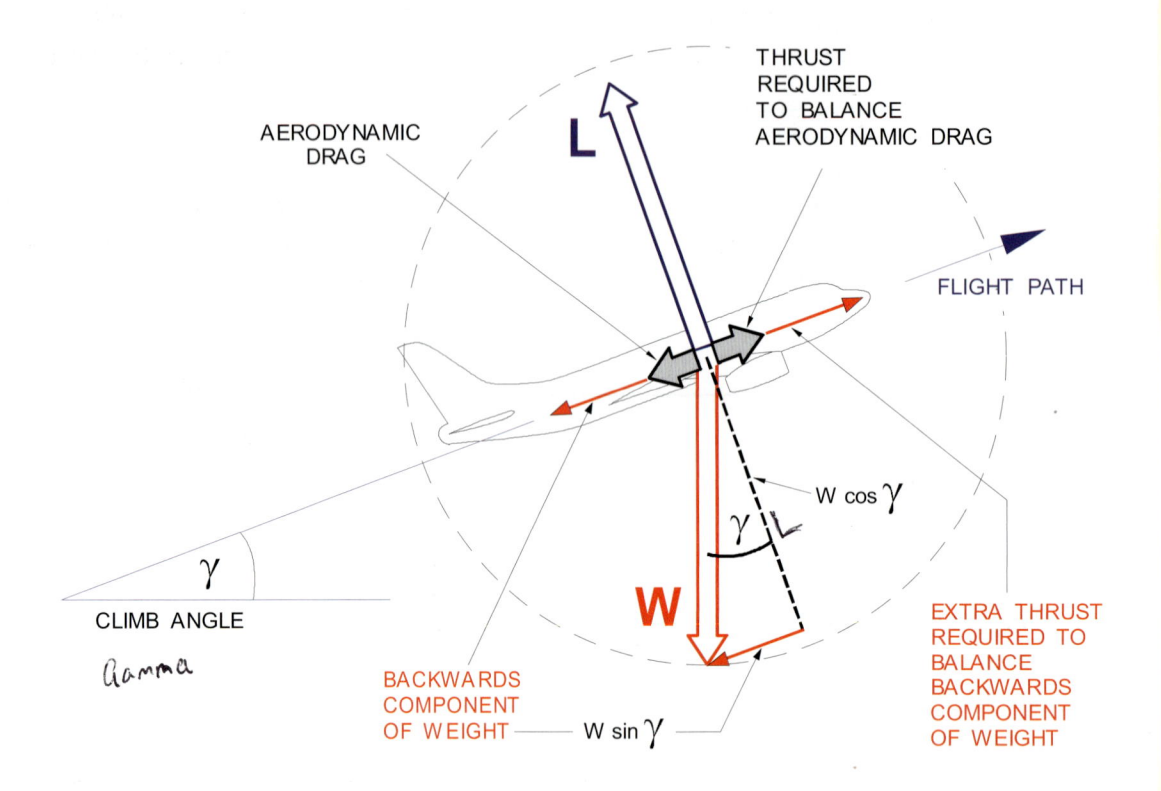

Figure 12.5 Forces in a Steady Climb

Weight is resolved into two components: one opposite Lift (W cos γ), and the other acting in the same direction as Drag (W sin γ), backwards along the flight path. The requirements for equilibrium are: Thrust must equal the sum of Drag plus the backwards component of Weight; and Lift must equal its opposing component of Weight. For equilibrium at a greater angle of climb, the Lift required will be less, and the backwards component of Weight will be greater.

$$L = W \cos \gamma$$
$$T = D + W \sin \gamma$$

In a straight steady climb, Lift is less than Weight because Lift only has to support a proportion of the weight, this proportion decreasing as the climb angle increases. (In a vertical climb no lift is required). The remaining proportion of Weight is supported by engine Thrust.

PRINCIPLES OF FLIGHT FLIGHT MECHANICS

It can be seen that for a straight steady climb the Thrust required is greater than Drag. This is to balance the backward component of Weight acting along the flight path.

$$\sin \gamma = \frac{T - D}{W}$$

The ability of an aircraft to climb depends upon EXCESS THRUST, available after opposing aerodynamic drag. The smaller the Drag for a given Thrust, the greater the ability to climb. **Drag will be less with flaps up, giving a larger climb angle** (improved climb gradient).

12.5.1 CLIMB ANGLE

Climb angle depends on "excess Thrust" (T - D) and the Weight. As both Thrust and Drag vary with IAS, excess Thrust will be greatest at one particular speed. This is the speed for maximum angle of climb, V_X. (see Fig. 12.27 for the propeller case).

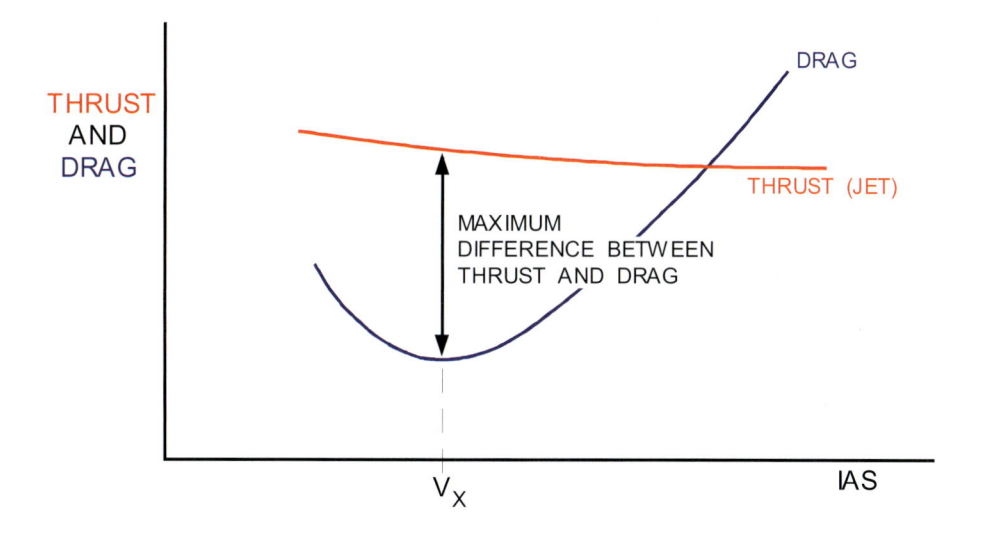

Figure 12.6   Variation of excess thrust with speed (JET)

The variation of Thrust with speed will depend on the type of engine. For a jet engine, where Thrust is fairly constant with speed, V_X will be near to V_{MD}, but for a propeller engined aircraft V_X will usually be below V_{MD}.

12.5.2 EFFECT OF WEIGHT, ALTITUDE AND TEMPERATURE.

The Drag of an aircraft at a given IAS is not affected by altitude or temperature, but higher Weight will increase Drag and reduce excess Thrust and consequently the climb angle.

Thrust available from the engine decreases with increasing altitude and increasing temperature, which also reduces excess Thrust. Climb angle therefore decreases with increasing Weight, altitude and temperature.

PRINCIPLES OF FLIGHT **FLIGHT MECHANICS**

12.6 POWER ON DESCENT

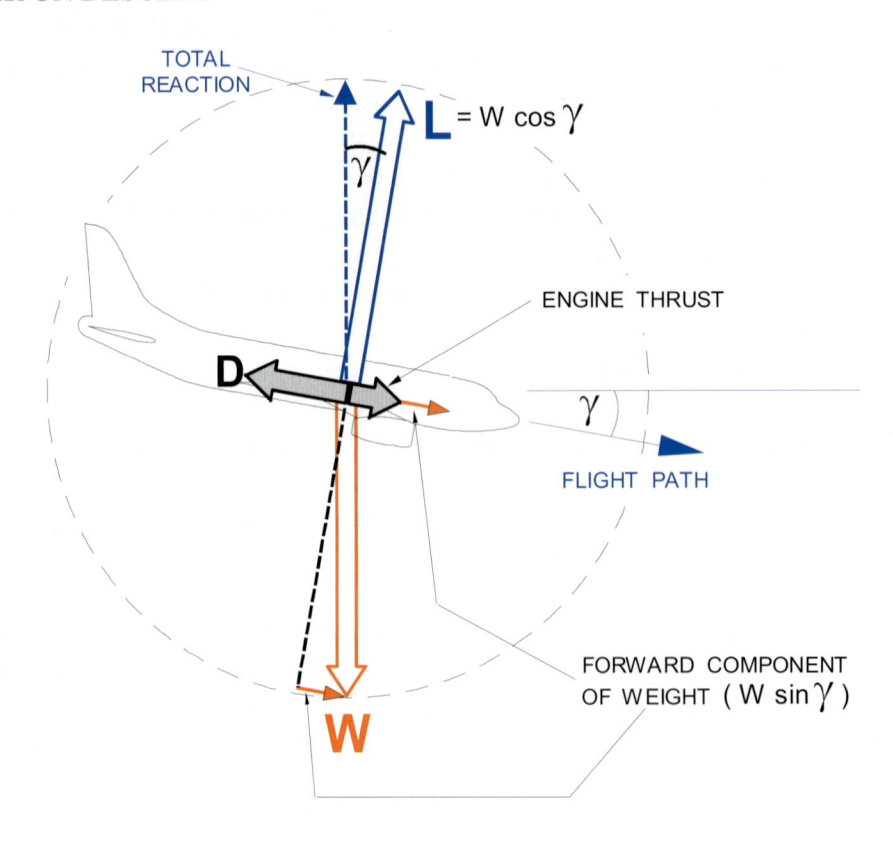

Figure 12.7 Forces in a Power - On Descent

Figure 12.7 illustrates the disposition of forces in a steady Power-On descent. The force of Weight is split into two components. One component (W cos γ) acts perpendicular to the flight path and is balanced by Lift, while the other component (W sin γ) acts forward along the flight path and 'adds' to the Thrust to balance Drag. If the nose of the aircraft is lowered with a constant Thrust setting the increased component of Weight acting forward along the flight path will cause an increase in IAS. The increased IAS will result in an increase in Drag which will eventually balance the increased forward force of Weight and equilibrium will be re-established.

If the throttle is closed the force of Thrust is removed and a larger forward component of Weight must be provided to balance Drag and maintain a constant IAS. This is accomplished by lowering the nose of the aeroplane to increase the descent angle (γ).

a) In a descent Lift is less than Weight. This is because Lift only has to balance the component of Weight perpendicular to the flight path (W cos γ).

b) In a descent Thrust is less than Drag. This is because Weight is giving a forward component in the same direction as Thrust (W sin γ).

PRINCIPLES OF FLIGHT   FLIGHT MECHANICS

12.7 EMERGENCY DESCENT

In the event of cabin pressurisation failure at high altitude it is necessary to descend as quickly as possible. The rate of descent can be increased by:

1. Reducing Thrust by closing the throttles.

2. Increasing Drag by:

    a) extending the speedbrakes,
    b) lowering the landing gear (at or below V_{LO}).

3. Increasing speed by lowering the nose.

    Speed can be increased in the clean configuration up to M_{MO} or V_{MO} depending on the altitude, or to the gear extended limit speed (V_{LE}) if the gear is down.

The overall rate of descent will be higher with the landing gear extended (lots of Drag), but if the gear operating limit speed (V_{LO}) is much less than the cruising speed the aircraft will have to be slowed down before the gear can be lowered (perhaps taking several minutes in level flight). So the initial rate of descent will be relatively low and the time spent at high altitude will be extended.

If the gear is not extended, throttles can be closed, speedbrakes extended and the nose lowered to accelerate the aircraft to M_{MO}/V_{MO} immediately, giving a higher initial rate of descent and getting the passengers down to a lower altitude without delay.

At high altitude the limiting speed will be M_{MO} and if an emergency descent is made at this Mach number the IAS will be increasing. At some altitude the IAS will reach V_{MO} and the nose must then be raised so as not to exceed V_{MO} for the remainder of the descent.

The rate of descent possible during an emergency descent can be quite high, so as the required level-off altitude is approached the rate of descent should be reduced progressively so as to give a smooth transition back to level flight.

12.8 GLIDE

In a glide without Thrust, the Weight component along the flight path must supply the propulsive force and balance Drag. In a glide there are only three forces acting on the aircraft, Lift, Weight and Drag.

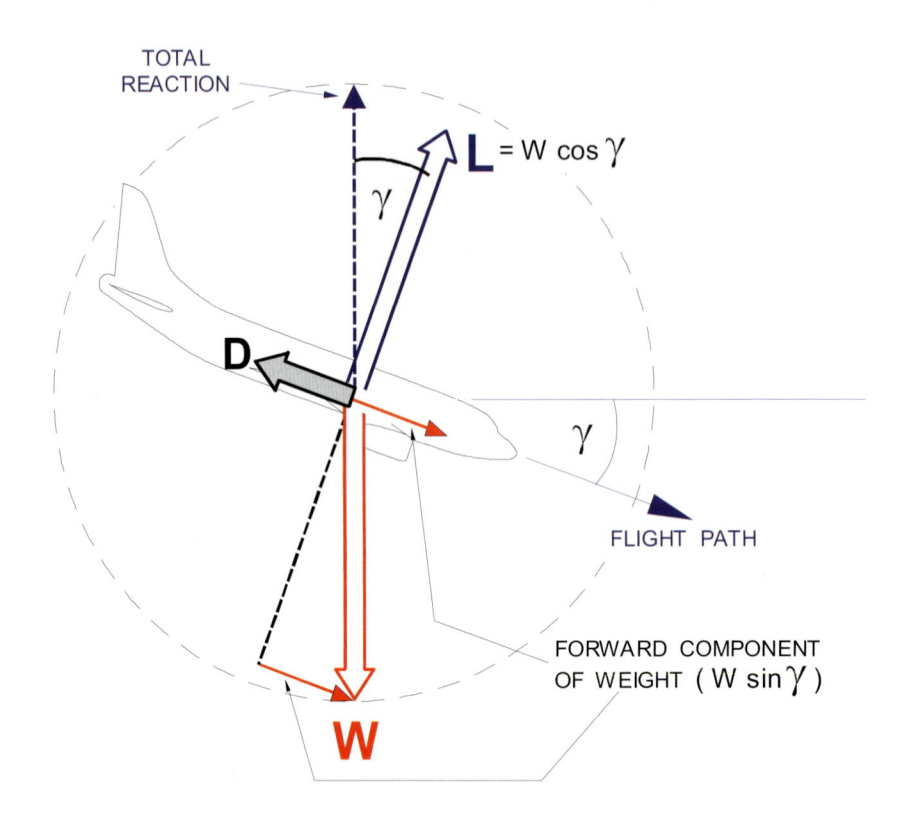

Figure 12.8 Forces in the Glide

Fig. 12.8 shows the disposition of forces in a steady glide. The forward component of Weight ($W \sin \gamma$) is a product of descent angle (γ); the greater the descent angle, the greater the forward component of weight (compare with Fig. 12.7). The forward component of weight must balance Drag for the aircraft to be in a steady glide. It follows that if Drag is reduced and Lift remains constant, the required balance of forces can be achieved at a smaller descent angle.

12.8.1 ANGLE OF DESCENT IN THE GLIDE

Glide angle is a function ONLY of the L/D ratio. The descent (glide) angle will be least when the L/D ratio is the greatest. L/D ratio is a maximum at the optimum angle of attack, and this also corresponds to the minimum drag speed (V_{MD}), Fig. 12.9. At speeds above or below V_{MD} the glide angle will be steeper.

Maximum distance in a glide can be achieved when the aircraft is flown at L/D_{MAX} (V_{MD}).

12.8.2 EFFECT OF WEIGHT

L/D $_{MAX}$ is independent of weight. Provided the aircraft is flown at its optimum angle of attack, the glide angle and glide distance will be the same whatever the weight. The speed corresponding to the optimum angle of attack, (V$_{MD}$) will however change with weight. V$_{MD}$ increases as weight increases.

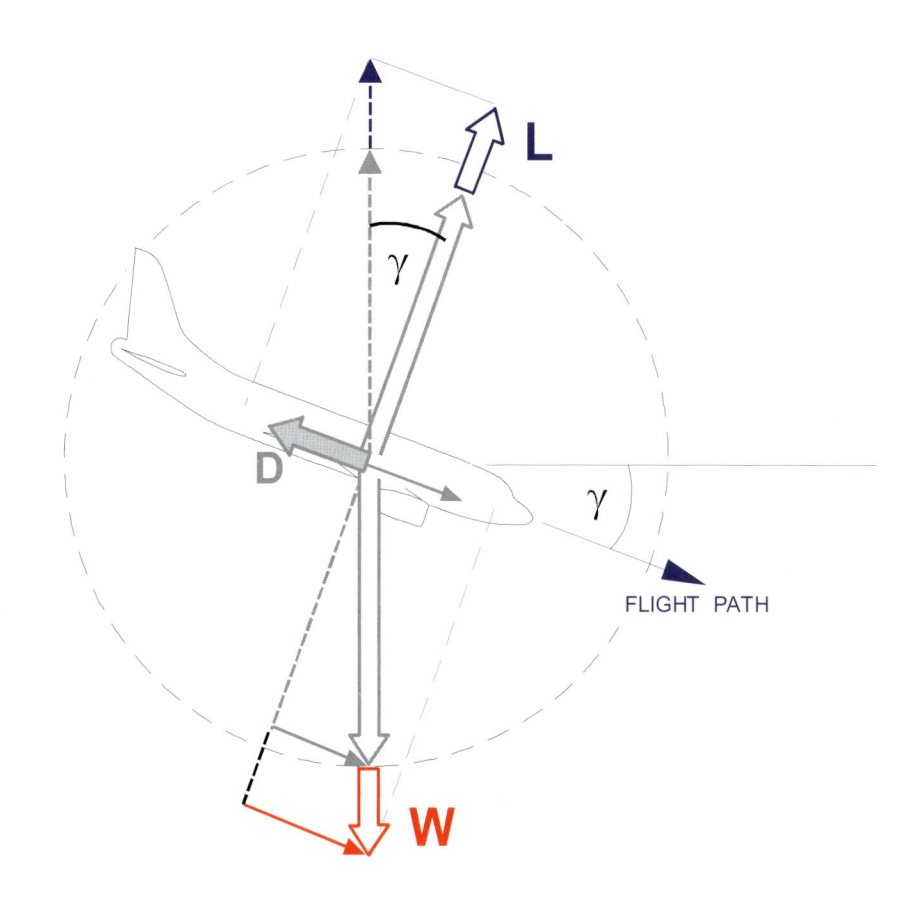

Figure 12.8a Increased Weight: no effect on glide range

As illustrated in Fig. 12.8a, a higher weight will give an increased forward component of weight and the aircraft will accelerate towards the resultant higher V$_{MD}$. As the aircraft accelerates, Lift increases and Drag will increase until it balances the increased forward component of Weight. Equilibrium is now re-established at the same L/D $_{MAX}$, but a higher IAS.

At a higher weight the aircraft will glide the same distance, but at a higher speed and consequently have an increased RATE of descent.

PRINCIPLES OF FLIGHT   FLIGHT MECHANICS

12.8.3 EFFECT OF WIND

The glide angle will determine the distance that the aircraft can glide for a given change of height.

$$\text{GLIDE DISTANCE} = \text{HEIGHT LOST} \times \frac{\text{LIFT (L)}}{\text{DRAG (D)}}$$

This distance would only be achieved in still air. If there is a wind the ground speed will change, and so the distance over the ground will change. **In a headwind the ground distance will be decreased and in a tailwind it will be increased.**

12.8.4 EFFECT OF CONFIGURATION

The maximum L/D ratio of an aircraft will be obtained in the clean configuration. Extension of flaps, spoilers, speedbrakes or landing gear etc. will reduce L/D_{MAX} and give a steeper glide angle, thus reducing glide range.

12.9 RATE OF DESCENT IN THE GLIDE

Minimum rate of descent in the glide is obtained at the IAS which produces minimum Power Required (V_{MP}). Flying at V_{MP} in a glide will enable the aircraft to stay airborne for as long as possible. As shown in Fig. 12.9, V_{MP} is a slower IAS than V_{MD}. Wind speed and direction has no effect on rate of descent. A frequently used method of showing the relationship of V_{MD} and V_{MP} is by use of the 'whole aeroplane C_L/C_D polar' curve, illustrated in Fig. 12.10.

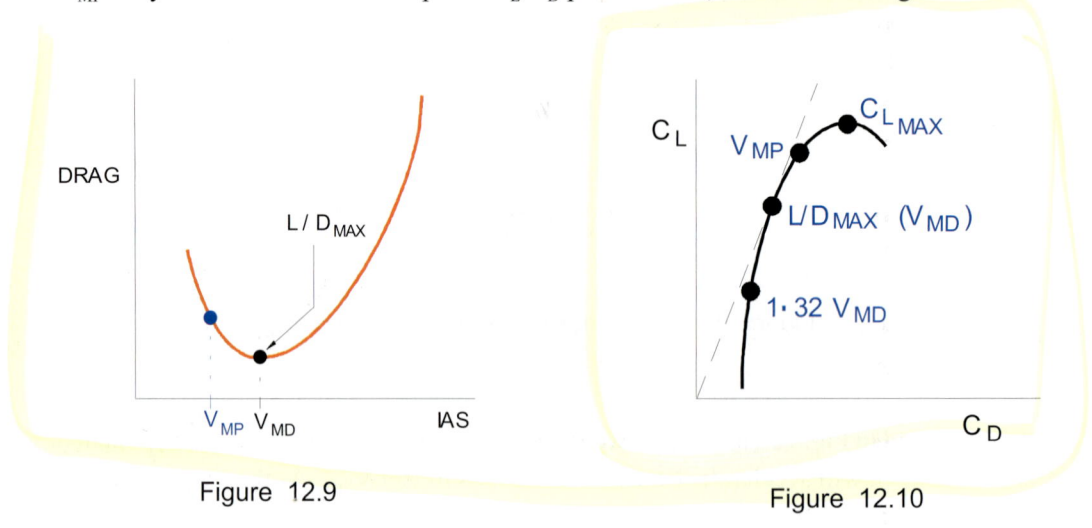

Figure 12.9   Figure 12.10

12.10 TURNING

For an aircraft to change direction, a force is required to deflect it towards the centre of the turn. This is called the centripetal force, Fig. 12.11. Banking the aircraft inclines the Lift. **It's the horizontal component of Lift which causes the aircraft to turn.** If the aircraft is banked and the angle of attack kept constant, the vertical component of lift will be too small to balance the weight and the aircraft will start to descend.

PRINCIPLES OF FLIGHT   **FLIGHT MECHANICS**

As the angle of bank increases, the angle of attack must be increased to bring about a greater total lift. The vertical component must be large enough to maintain level flight, while the horizontal component is large enough to produce the required centripetal force.

12.10.1 EFFECT OF WEIGHT ON TURNING

In a steady level turn, if thrust is ignored, lift provides a force to balance weight and centripetal force to turn the aircraft. **If the same TAS and angle of bank can be obtained, the radius of turn is basically independent of weight or the aircraft type.**

Not all aircraft can reach the same angle of bank at the same TAS. If weight increases, the vertical component of lift required increases, but the centripetal force to maintain the same radius of turn also increases in the same proportion. The lift required, although it is greater, has the same inclination to the vertical as before and the bank angle is the same, Fig. 12.12.

Figure 12.11   Forces in a turn

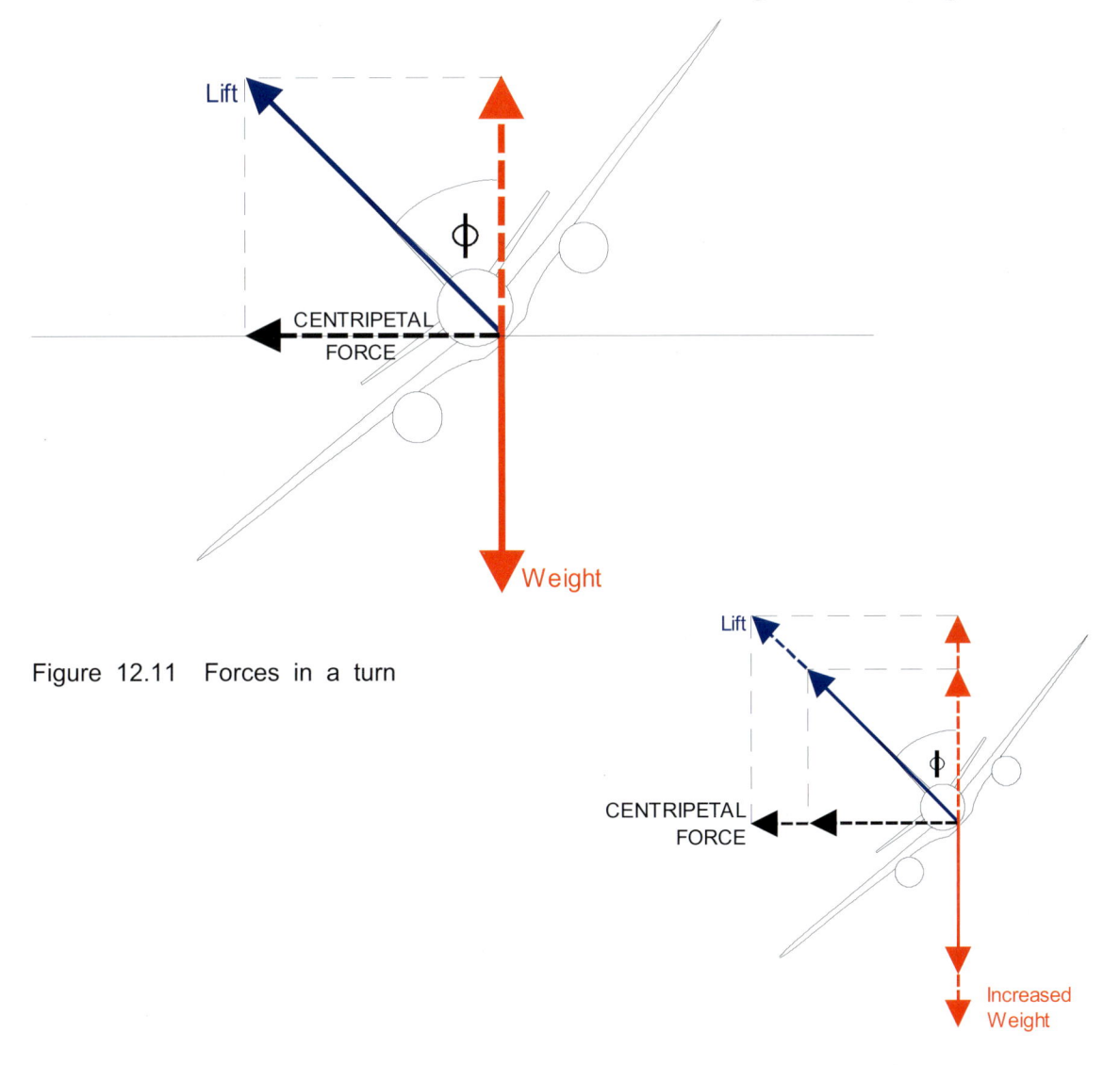

Figure 12.12   Bank angle and weight

PRINCIPLES OF FLIGHT   **FLIGHT MECHANICS**

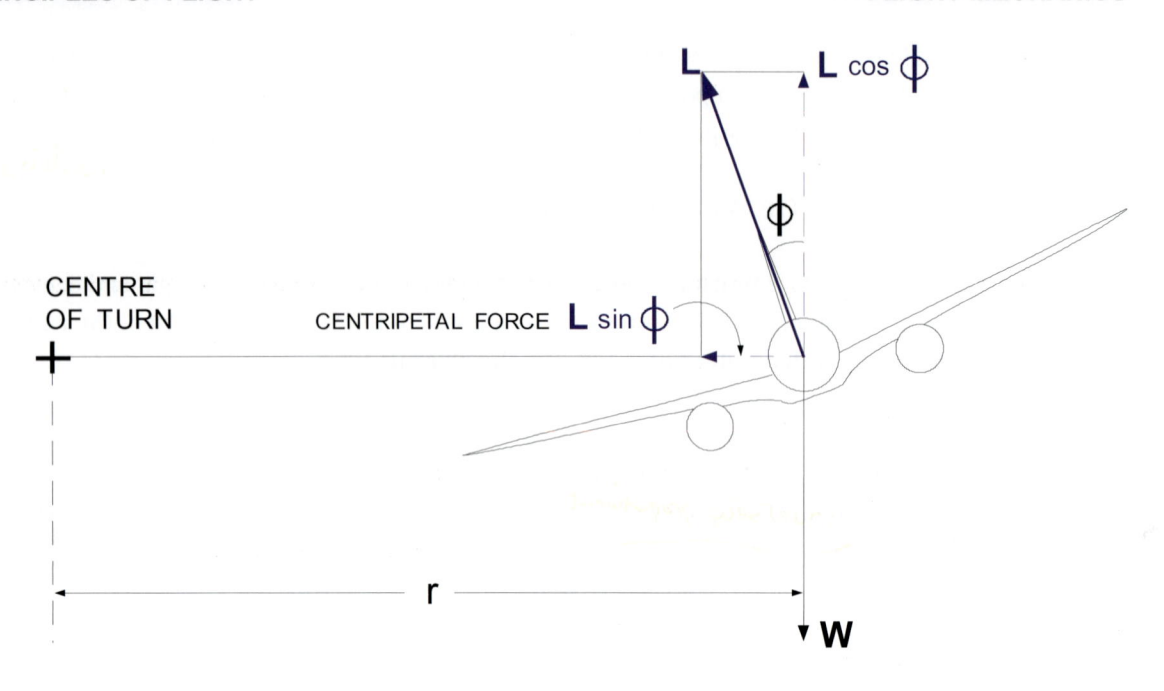

Figure 12.13 Forces acting in a steady turn

In a steady horizontal turn, Fig. 12.13, the conditions of equilibrium can be expressed in the form:

$$L \cos \phi = W \qquad (Eq\ 12.14)$$

$$L \sin \phi = \frac{W V^2}{r g} \qquad (Eq\ 12.15)$$

Where (L) is the wing lift in Newtons, (W) is the weight of the aircraft in Newtons, (V) the true air speed in m/s, (r) the radius of turn in metres, φ the angle of bank and (g) the acceleration of gravity constant of 9·81 m/s.

Dividing equation 12.15 by equation 12.14 we get:

$$\tan \phi = \frac{V^2}{r g} \qquad (Eq\ 12.16)$$

which is the basic turning equation relating (V), (r) and φ. Once two of these variables are known, the other two can be determined. From equation 12.16, the radius of turn is given by:

$$\text{turn radius} = \frac{V^2}{g \tan \phi} \qquad (Eq\ 12.17)$$

PRINCIPLES OF FLIGHT   **FLIGHT MECHANICS**

and the corresponding rate of turn (= V / r) by:

$$\text{rate of turn} = \frac{g \tan \phi}{V} \text{ radians / second} \qquad (Eq\ 12.18)$$

[handwritten annotation: $= \frac{V}{radius}$]

Rate of turn is the rate of change of heading or angular velocity of the turn. It may be expressed as degrees per minute, or by a Rate Number.

    Rate 1 turn is 180° per minute (3° per second)

    Rate 2 turn is 360° per minute (6° per second)

Rate of turn is ~~directly proportional~~ [handwritten: inversely proportional] to TAS and inversely proportional to the turn radius.

$$\text{Rate of turn} = \frac{\text{TAS}}{\text{Radius}}$$

For example: at a speed of 150 kt TAS (77 m/s), an aircraft performing a turn with a radius of 1480 metres would have a rate of turn of:

$$\frac{77}{1480} = 0.052 \text{ radians / sec}$$

there being 2π radians in a circle, $\quad \frac{360}{6.286} = 57.3°$ per radian

$$0.052 \times 57.3 = 3° \text{ per second (Rate one)}$$

a)   at a constant TAS, increasing the angle of bank decreases the turn radius and increases the rate of turn.

b)   to maintain a constant rate of turn, increasing speed requires an increased bank angle.

c)   at a constant bank angle, increasing speed increases the turn radius and decreases the rate of turn.

> In a constant rate turn, the angle of bank is dependent upon TAS

PRINCIPLES OF FLIGHT — FLIGHT MECHANICS

12.10.2 RADIUS AND RATE OF TURN

Two variables determine the rate of turn and radius of turn:-

a) Bank angle (φ). A steeper bank reduces turn radius and increases the rate of turn, but produces a higher load factor.

b) True air speed (TAS): Reducing speed reduces turn radius and increases the rate of turn, without increasing the load factor.

The radius of turn at **any given bank angle** (φ), varies directly with the square of the TAS:

$$\text{radius} = \frac{V^2}{g \tan \phi}$$

If speed is doubled, the turn radius will be four times greater, at a constant bank angle.

To appreciate the relationship between radius of turn and rate of turn at double the speed, consider:

$$\text{rate of turn} = \frac{V}{\text{radius}}$$

$$\text{rate of turn} = \frac{V\ (\times 2)}{\text{radius}\ (\times 4)} = \frac{1}{2}$$

If speed is doubled, the rate of turn will be half of its previous value, at a constant bank angle.

Because the rate of turn varies with TAS at any given bank angle, slower aeroplanes require less time and area to complete a turn than faster aeroplanes with the same bank angle, Fig.12.14.

A specific angle of bank and TAS will produce the same rate and radius of turn regardless of weight, CG position, or aeroplane type. It can also be seen from Fig.12.14 that increasing speed increases the turn radius and decreases the rate of turn. **The load factor remains the same because the bank angle has not changed.**

To increase the rate and decrease the radius of turn, steepen the bank and / or decrease the speed.

A given TAS and bank angle will produce a specific rate and radius of turn in any aeroplane. In a co-ordinated level turn, an increase in airspeed will increase the radius and decrease the rate of turn. **Load factor is directly related to bank angle, so the load factor for a given bank angle is the same at any speed.**

PRINCIPLES OF FLIGHT   **FLIGHT MECHANICS**

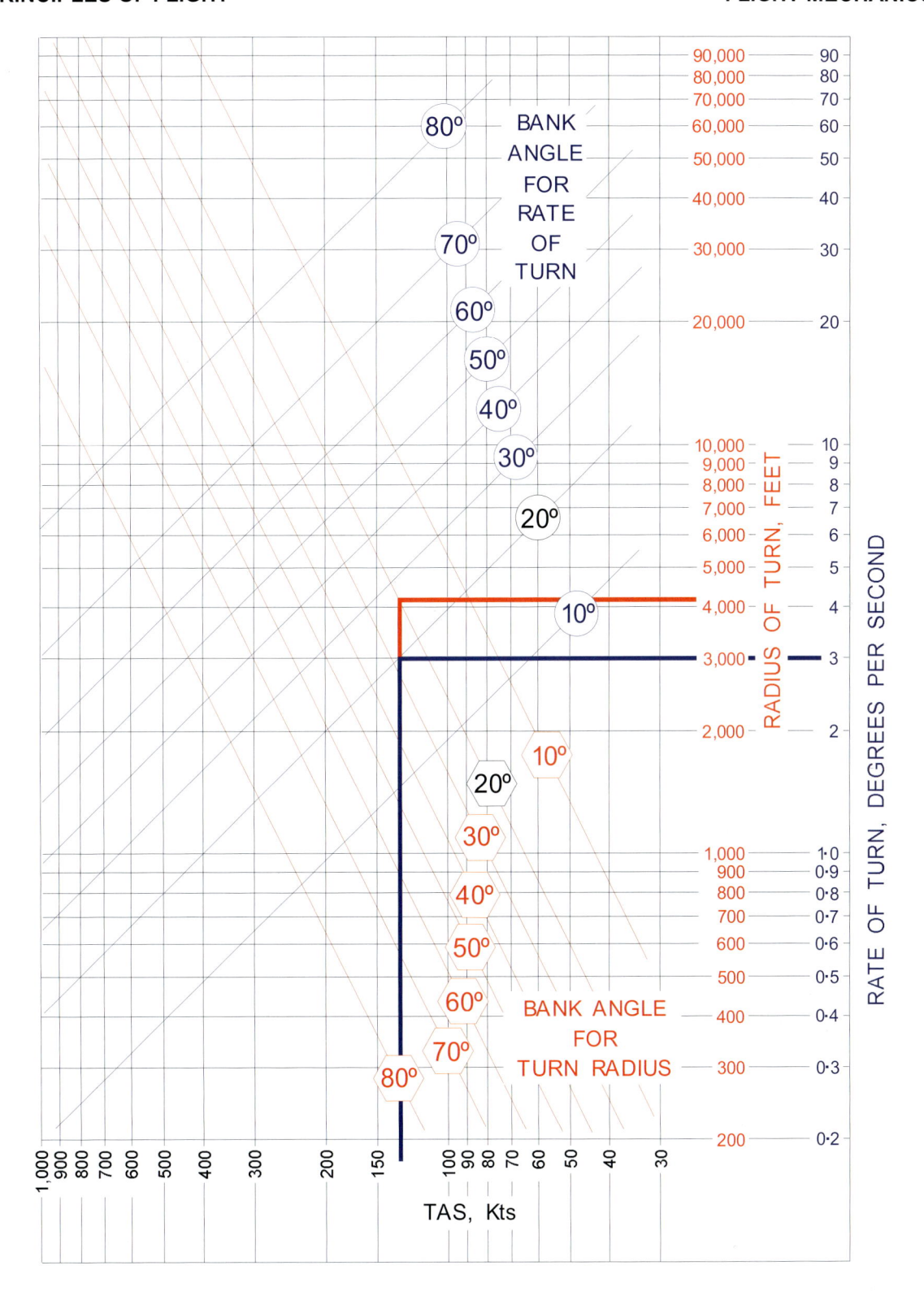

Figure 12.14 (For illustration purposes only). This chart will work for any aeroplane. The example shows that for a turn at 130 kts TAS and a bank angle of 20°, the radius will be 4,200 ft and the rate of turn will be 3° per second. At 260 kts TAS the radius will be 16,800 ft and the rate of turn will be 1·5° per second.

PRINCIPLES OF FLIGHT   FLIGHT MECHANICS

12.10.3 LOAD FACTOR IN THE TURN

When an aircraft is in a banked turn lift must be increased so as to maintain the vertical component of lift equal to weight, Fig. 12.15.

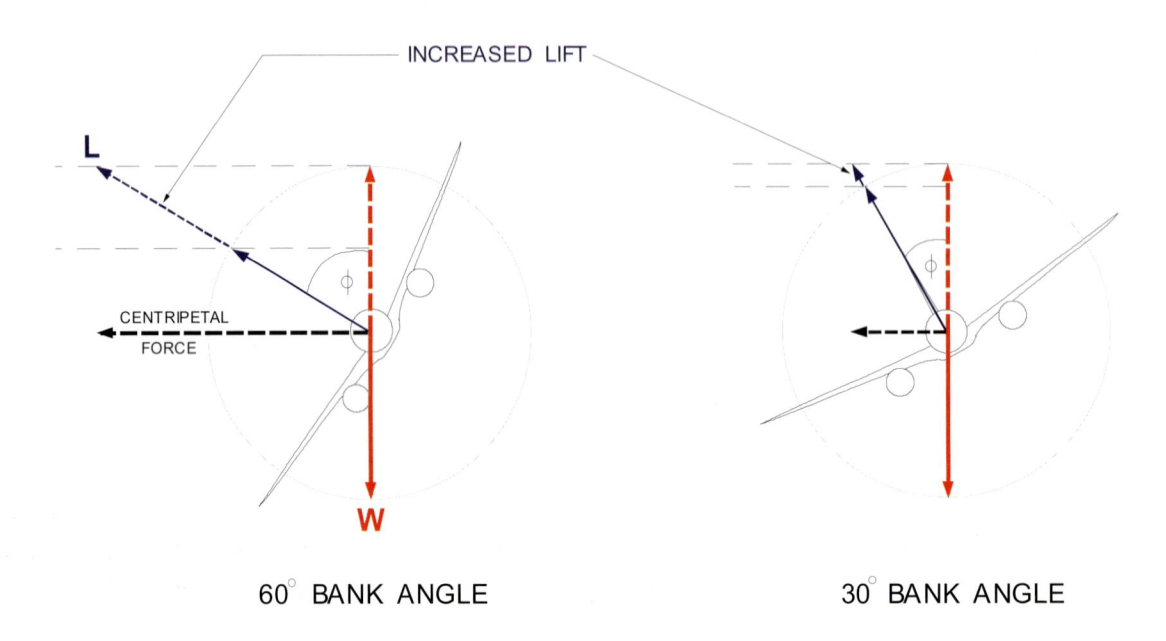

Figure 12.15   Increased lift required in a turn

This relationship may be expressed as:

$$\text{Load factor (n)} = \frac{L}{W} = \frac{1}{\cos \phi} = \sec \phi \qquad \text{(Eq 12.19)}$$

Refer to Page 7 - 24 and 7 - 25 for the full trigonometrical explanation.

Fig. 12.16 shows the relationship between load factor and bank angle. This chart will be effective for any aircraft. It can be seen that load factor (n) increases with bank angle at an increasing rate.

Load factor in the turn is a function ONLY of bank angle.

> Constant bank angle, constant load factor

PRINCIPLES OF FLIGHT **FLIGHT MECHANICS**

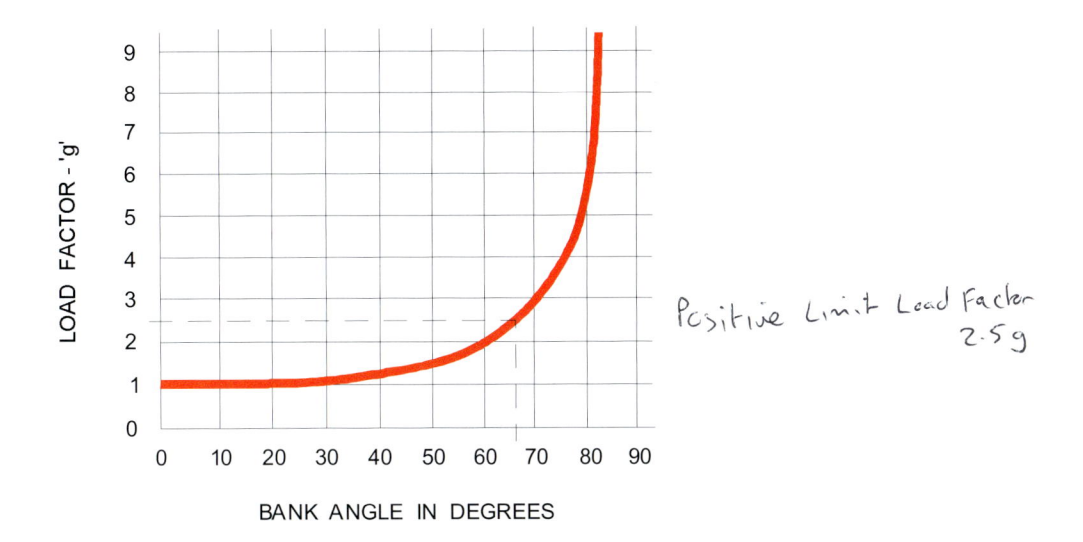

Figure 12.16   Relationship between 'g' and bank angle

Positive Limit Load Factor 2.5 g

12.10.4   'g' LIMIT ON TURNING

For each aircraft there is a design limit load factor. For modern high speed jet transport aircraft the positive limit load factor is 2·5 g. From Fig. 12.16 it can be seen that this would occur at a bank angle of 67° and this will determine a turn radius, depending on the TAS. This will be the minimum radius permissible at that 'g' if the strength limit is not to be exceeded.

12.10.5   STALL LIMIT ON TURNING

If speed is kept constant, but the bank angle increased, the angle of attack must also be increased to provide the increased lift required. Eventually the stalling angle will be reached and no further increase in bank angle (and decrease in turn radius) is possible. Because the stalling speed varies with weight, this boundary will be a function of weight.

weight increases min turning radius

12.10.6   THRUST LIMIT ON TURNING

During a turn lift must be greater than during level flight, and this will result in increased induced drag. To balance this additional drag, more thrust is required in a turn than for level flight at the same speed. The greater the bank angle the greater will be the thrust required, and eventually the throttle will be fully open. No further increase in bank angle (and decrease in turn radius) is then possible. The relative positions of the thrust boundary and the strength boundary will depend on the limit load factor and thrust available.

12.10.7   MINIMUM TURN RADIUS

If the thrust available is adequate, the minimum radius of turn occurs at the intersection of the stall limit and the strength limit. The speed at this point is V_A the maximum manoeuvring speed. The heavier the aircraft, the greater the minimum radius of turn.

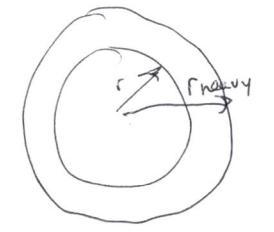

PRINCIPLES OF FLIGHT FLIGHT MECHANICS

12.10.8 TURN CO-ORDINATION

Adverse aileron yaw, engine torque, propeller gyroscopic precession, asymmetric thrust and spiral slipstream all give the possibility of unco-ordinated flight. Unco-ordinated flight exists when the aircraft is sideslipping. Indication of sideslip is given to the pilot by the inclinometer portion (ball) of the turn co-ordinator, Fig. 12.17. The miniature aeroplane indicates **rate of turn**.

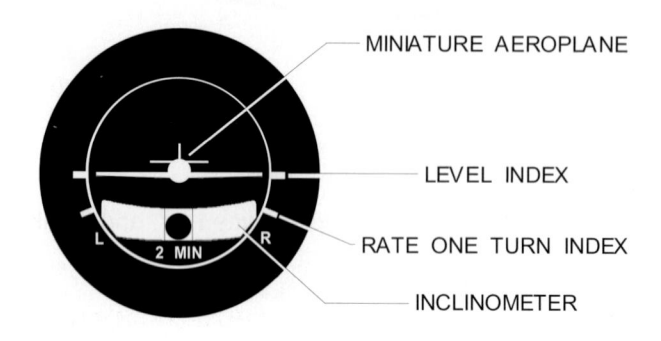

Figure 12.17 Turn co-ordinator

Co-ordinated flight is maintained by keeping the ball centred between the reference lines with rudder. To do this, apply rudder pressure on the side where the ball is deflected. The simple rule, "step on the ball," is a useful way to remember which rudder to apply.

If aileron and rudder are co-ordinated during a turn, the ball will remain centred and there will be no sideslip. If the aircraft is sideslipping, the ball moves away from the centre of the tube. Sideslipping towards the centre of the turn, moves the ball to the inside of the turn. Sideslipping towards the outside of the turn, moves the ball to the outside of the turn. To correct for these conditions and maintain co-ordinated flight, "step on the ball." Bank angle may also be varied to help restore co-ordinated flight from a sideslip. The following illustrations give examples.

PRINCIPLES OF FLIGHT   **FLIGHT MECHANICS**

Fig. 12.18 shows the aircraft in a rate 1 co-ordinated turn to the right.

Figure 12.18

Fig. 12.19 shows the aircraft in an unco-ordinated turn to the right; it will be sideslipping towards the centre of the turn (slipping turn). Using "step on the ball," the turn can be co-ordinated by applying right rudder pressure to centre the ball. The ball can also be centred by decreasing the bank angle.

Figure 12.19

Fig. 12.20 also shows the aircraft in an unco-ordinated turn to the right; it will be sideslipping towards the outside of the turn (skidding turn). Using "step on the ball," the turn can be co-ordinated by applying left rudder pressure. The ball can also be centred by increasing the bank angle.

Figure 12.20

PRINCIPLES OF FLIGHT

12.11 FLIGHT WITH ASYMMETRIC THRUST

INTRODUCTION

When an engine fails on a multi engine aircraft there will be a decrease in thrust and an increase in drag on the side with the failed engine:

a)   airspeed will decay

b)   the nose will drop and

c)   most significantly, **there will be an immediate yawing moment towards the failed (dead) engine.**

Fig. 12.21 shows the forces and moments acting on an aircraft following failure of the left (port) engine. The aircraft has a yawing moment towards the dead engine. The pilot has applied rudder to stop the yaw. **The vital action when an engine fails is to STOP THE YAW !**

12.11.1 YAWING MOMENT

The yawing moment is the product of thrust from the operating engine, multiplied by the distance between the thrust line and the CG (thrust arm) plus the drag from the failed engine, multiplied by the distance between the engine centre line and the CG. The strength of the yawing moment will depend on:

a)   how much thrust the operating engine is developing (throttle setting and density altitude)

b)   the distance between the thrust line and the CG (thrust arm)

c)   how much drag is being produced by the failed engine.

The rudder moment, which balances the yawing moment, is the product of the rudder force multiplied by the distance between the fin CP and the CG (rudder arm). This statement will be modified by factors yet to be introduced. Thus, at this preliminary stage, the ability of the pilot to counteract the yawing moment due to asymmetric thrust will depend on:

d)   rudder displacement (affecting rudder force)

e)   CG position (affecting rudder arm)

f)   the IAS (affecting rudder force)

PRINCIPLES OF FLIGHT   **FLIGHT MECHANICS**

Assume the rudder is at full deflection, CG is at the rear limit (shortest rudder arm) and the IAS (dynamic pressure) is just sufficient for the rudder force to give a rudder moment equal to the yawing moment - there will be no yaw. But, any decrease in IAS will cause the aircraft to yaw **uncontrollably** towards the failed engine. The **uncontrollable** yaw to the left, in this example, will cause the aircraft to roll **uncontrollably** to the left due to greater lift on the right wing. The aircraft will enter a spiral dive to the left (impossible to stop with the flight controls alone); if near the ground, disaster will result. In these extreme circumstances near the ground the ONLY way to regain control of the aeroplane is to close the throttle(s) on the operating engine(s). This removes the yawing moment and the aircraft can be force-landed under control.

Thus there is a **minimum IAS at which directional control can be maintained** following engine failure on a multi engine aircraft. This minimum IAS is called V_{MC} (minimum control speed).

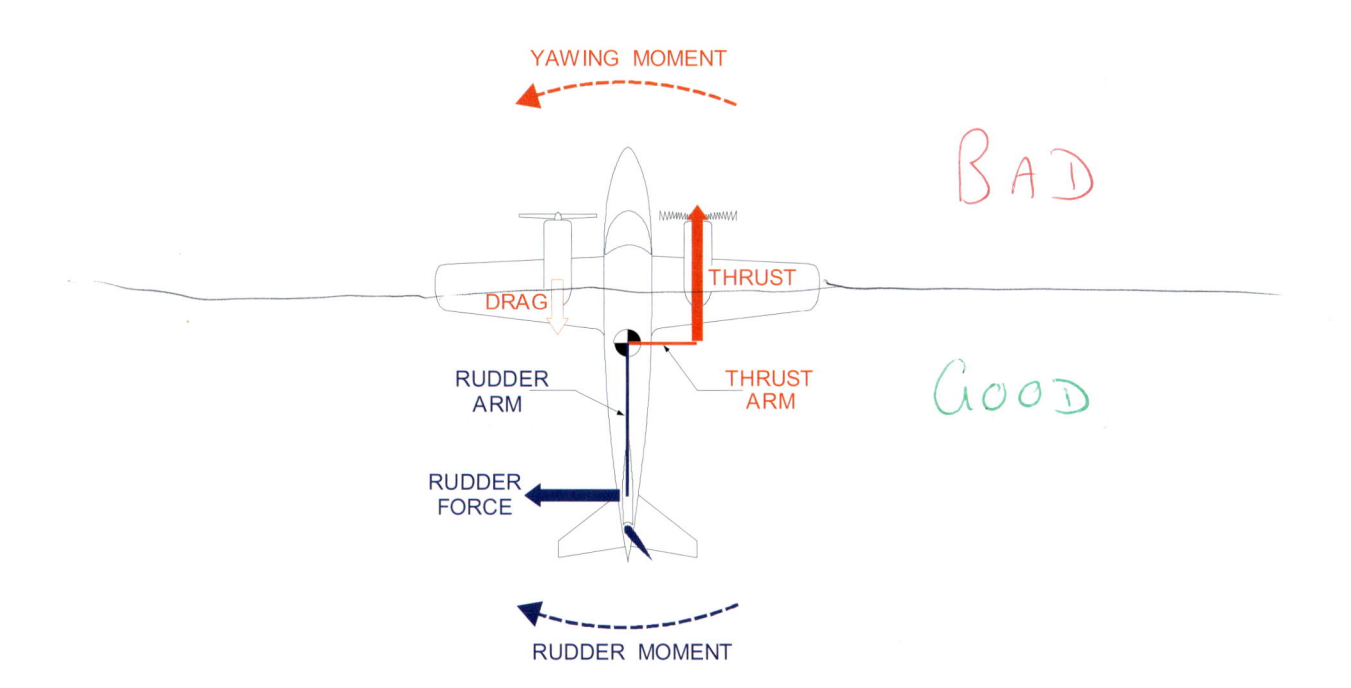

Figure 12.21 Asymmetric thrust

V_{MCA} AIRBORNE
V_{MCG} GROUND
V_{MCL} LANDING (LANDING CONFIG)

PRINCIPLES OF FLIGHT — FLIGHT MECHANICS

12.11.2 CRITICAL ENGINE

One of the factors influencing the yawing moment following engine failure on a multi engine aircraft is the length of the thrust arm (distance from the CG to the thrust line of the operating engine).

In the case of a propeller engine aircraft the length of the thrust arm is determined by the asymmetric effect of the propeller. At a positive angle of attack the thrust line of a clockwise rotating propeller, when viewed from the rear, is displaced to the right of the engine centre line. This is because the down going blade generates more thrust than the up going blade (Chapter 16). If both engines rotate clockwise, the starboard (right) engine will have a longer thrust arm than the port (left) engine.

If the left engine fails the thrust of the right engine acts through a longer thrust arm and will give a bigger yawing moment; a higher IAS (V_{MC}) would be necessary to maintain directional control. So at a given IAS the situation would be more critical if the left engine failed, Fig. 12.22.

The critical engine is the engine, the failure of which would give the biggest yawing moment.

To overcome the disadvantage of having a critical engine on smaller twins, their engines may be designed to counter-rotate. This means that the left engine rotates clockwise and the right engine rotates anti-clockwise, giving both engines the smallest possible thrust arm. Larger turbo - props (e.g. King Air etc. and larger) rotate in the same direction. In the case of a four engined jet aircraft the critical engine is either of the outboard engines.

NB: If all the propellers on a multi engine aircraft rotate in the same direction, they are sometimes called 'co-rotating' propellers.

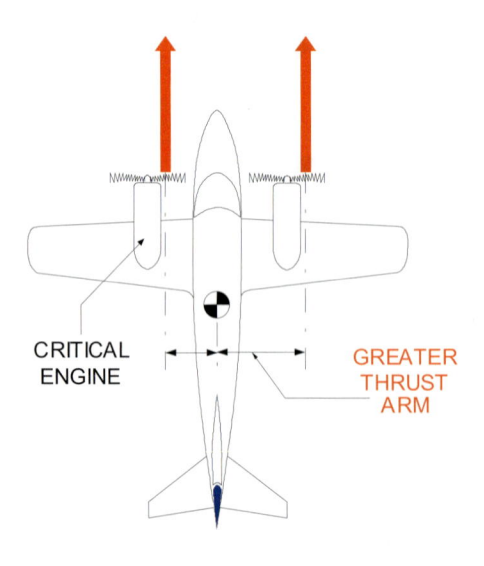

Figure 12.22 Critical engine

PRINCIPLES OF FLIGHT   **FLIGHT MECHANICS**

12.11.3 BALANCING THE YAWING MOMENTS AND FORCES

Although the moments are balanced in Fig. 12.21 the forces are not balanced. The unbalanced side force from the rudder can be balanced in two ways:

a)   with the wings level and

b)   by banking slightly towards the live engine (preferred method).

Rudder to Stop Yaw - Wings Level: Rudder is used to prevent yaw and the wings are maintained level with aileron. Yawing towards the live engine gives a sideslip force on the keel surfaces behind the CG opposite to the rudder force, Fig. 12.23. **If the sideslip angle is too large the fin could stall.** The turn indicator will be central and so will the slip indicator.

NB: Asymmetric thrust is the exception to the rule of co-ordinated flight being indicated to the pilot by the ball centred in the inclinometer.

This method of balancing the side force from the rudder gives reduced climb performance because of the excessive parasite drag generated, so is not the recommended method for critical situations, such as engine failure just after take-off or go-around. This technique can be used for initial control following an engine failure in the cruise.

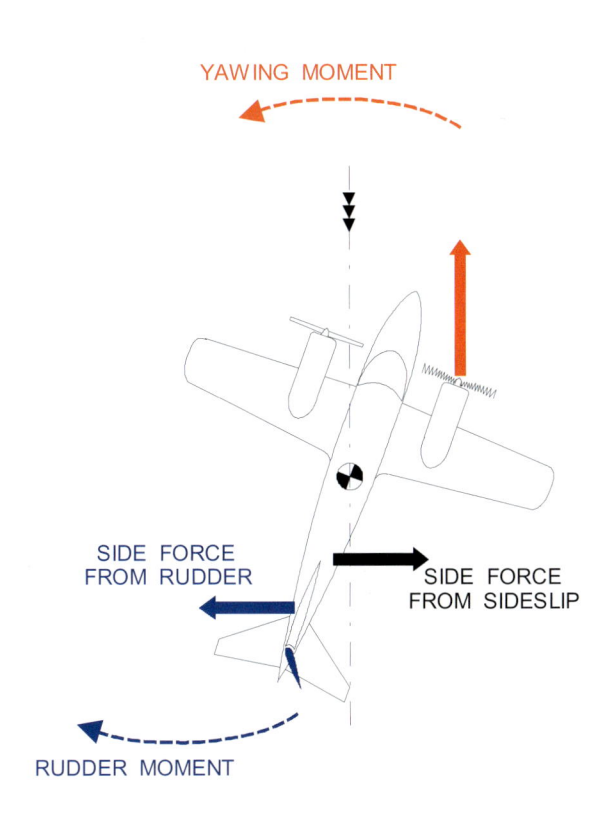

Figure 12.23 Wings level method

The advantage of the 'wings level' method of balancing the forces is the strong visual horizontal references available to the pilot, both inside and outside the aircraft.

The disadvantages are that if the sideslip angle is too large the fin could stall and the ability to climb is reduced due to excessive parasite drag.

PRINCIPLES OF FLIGHT FLIGHT MECHANICS

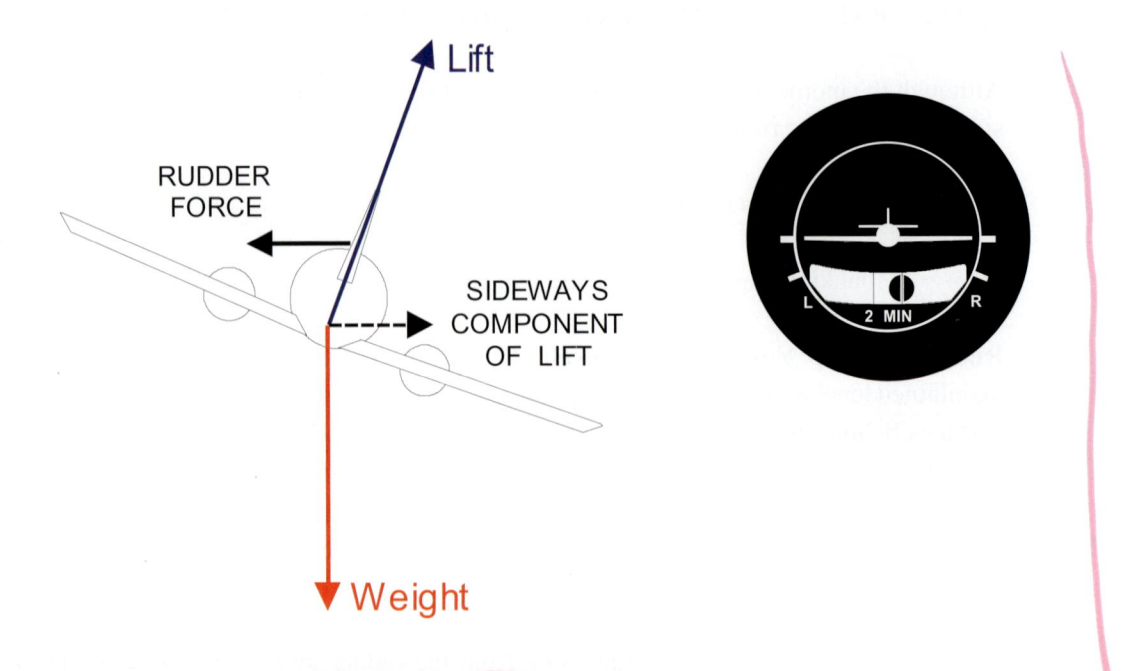

Figure 12.24 Max. 5° bank towards live engine

Rudder to Stop Yaw - Bank Towards Live Engine: It is more aerodynamically efficient to balance the rudder sideforce by banking towards the live engine, Fig. 12.24, so that lift gives a sideways component opposite to the rudder force. **The angle of bank must not exceed 5°**, to prevent excessive loss of vertical lift component.

Banking towards the live engine also reduces the side force on the fin from sideslip, which effectively reduces the yawing moment and gives more rudder authority to stop the yaw.

The cockpit indication will be the turn needle central with the slip indicator (ball) one half diameter displaced towards the live engine. The 'ball' is not centred, but the aircraft is not sideslipping. This method produces minimum drag and gives the best ability to climb.

12.11.4 ROLL AND YAW MOMENTS WITH ASYMMETRIC THRUST

The rolling and yawing moments and the power of the flight controls to balance them will determine the controllability of an aircraft with asymmetric thrust. Rolling and yawing moments with asymmetric thrust are affected by:

a) **Thrust on the live engine:** The greater the thrust, the greater the yawing moment from the live engine. The further the engine is mounted out on the wing (increased thrust arm), the larger the yawing moment. Thrust is greatest at low speed and full throttle.

b) **Altitude:** Thrust reduces with increasing altitude and / or increasing temperature (high density altitude). The worst case for engine failure is low density altitude, i.e. immediately after take-off on a cold day at a sea level airport.

PRINCIPLES OF FLIGHT   **FLIGHT MECHANICS**

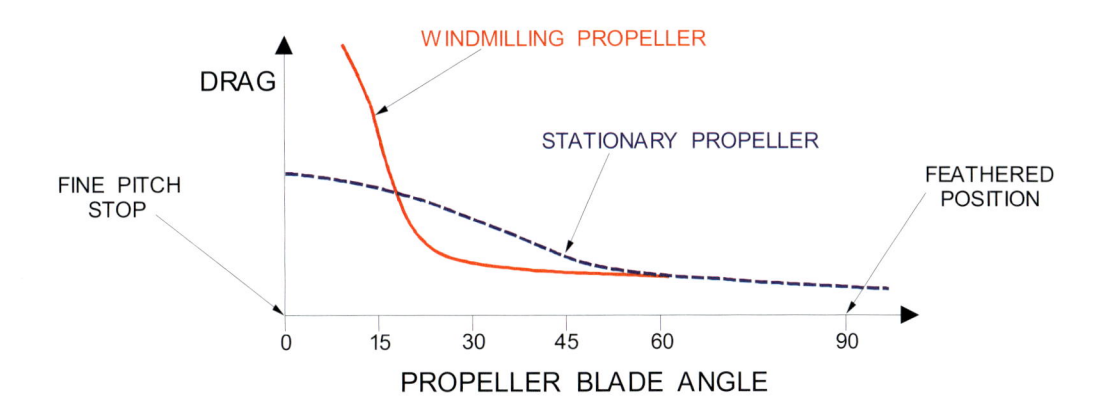

Figure 12.25 Propeller drag

    c)   **Drag from the dead engine and propeller:** Drag from the dead engine always adds to the yawing moment. The size of the contribution depends upon whether the propeller is windmilling, stopped or feathered, Fig.12.25. This effect will be absent on an aircraft powered by jet engines.

        i)   Drag from a windmilling propeller is high. It is being driven by the relative airflow, and is generating both drag and torque.

        ii)   If a propeller is stationary it is generating drag, but no torque. Drag from a stationary propeller is less than from one which is windmilling.

        iii)   A feathered propeller generates the least drag. There is no torque because it is not rotating and the parasite drag is a minimum because the blades are edge on to the relative airflow.

    The drag on the dead engine can also be reduced by closing the cowl flap.

    d)   **Asymmetric blade effect (also known as 'P Factor):** Described in Para. 12.26. If both engines rotate clockwise, the right engine has a longer thrust arm. Failure of the left engine will give a larger yawing moment. This effect will be absent on an aircraft with counter rotating propellers, contra-rotating propellers or jet engines.

    e)   **CG position:** The aircraft rotates about the CG. The fore and aft CG location has no effect on the yawing moment from a failed engine, but will influence the rudder arm, hence the rudder moment. CG on the aft limit will give the smallest rudder arm and the least ability to oppose the yawing moment from a failed engine.

NB: Contra-rotating propellers are mounted on the same shaft and are driven in opposite directions, usually by the same engine

PRINCIPLES OF FLIGHT FLIGHT MECHANICS

f) **Torque reaction:** When the engine turns the propeller, the equal and opposite reaction tries to turn the engine in the other direction. Following failure of one engine on an aircraft with propellers which rotate in the same direction (usually clockwise when viewed from the rear), the torque tries to roll the aircraft to the left. Failure of the left engine therefore gives the biggest rolling moment to the left. With counter rotating engines, both the asymmetric blade effect (P Factor) and the torque reaction are minimised and there is no longer a critical engine. This effect will be absent on an aircraft powered by jet engines.

g) **Difference in lift due to slipstream:** Engine failure on one side will give a loss of induced lift from the propeller slipstream on that side. Total lift will reduce giving a tendency to descend, but more importantly, there will be a rolling moment towards the dead engine; a greater rolling moment towards the dead engine will occur if the trailing edge flaps are deployed because of the higher initial C_L. This effect will be absent on an aircraft powered by jet engines.

h) **Rolling moment due to sideslip:** If the aircraft is flying with yaw to balance the rudder force, there will be a sideslip. In Fig. 12.23 the aircraft is sideslipping to the left. The dihedral of the left wing (with the dead engine) will cause the lift of the left wing to increase, which will compensate some of the lift loss due to the loss of the propeller slipstream.

i) **Weight:** Any weight increase will require a higher angle of attack at a given speed.

   (i) This will increase the asymmetric blade effect (P Factor) and give a bigger yawing moment.

   (ii) The fin and rudder will be masked to a greater extent by disturbed airflow from the wing and fuselage, making the rudder and fin less effective; consequently the available rudder moment will be reduced.

j) **Airspeed:** The effectiveness of the flying controls depends upon dynamic pressure, assuming full control displacement. An accurate measure of dynamic pressure at low airspeeds is given by the Calibrated Air Speed (CAS). CAS is IAS corrected for position error. At low airspeed / high C_L the pressures sensed by the pitot / static system are affected by the high angle of attack, so must be compensated to make the IAS reflect a more accurate measure of dynamic pressure. A higher IAS means more control effectiveness and consequently a larger available rudder moment to balance the yawing moment from the failed engine. A lower IAS will reduce the available rudder moment, if the other parameters remain the same. **IAS is the vital element in control of the aircraft with asymmetric thrust.**

PRINCIPLES OF FLIGHT
FLIGHT MECHANICS

12.11.5 MINIMUM CONTROL AIRSPEED

It has been shown that when a multi engine aircraft suffers an engine failure several variables affect both the yawing moment and the rudder moment which is used to oppose it. It has also been shown that there is a minimum IAS (V_{MC}), below which it is impossible for the pilot to maintain directional control with asymmetric thrust.

Airworthiness Authorities, in this case the JAA, have laid down conditions which must be satisfied when establishing the minimum airspeeds for inclusion in the flight Manual of a new aircraft type. As in most other cases, the conditions under which the minimum control airspeeds are established are 'worst case'. A factor of safety is built into these speeds to allow for aircraft age and average pilot response time.

Because there are distinct variations in the handling qualities of the aircraft when in certain configurations, minimum control airspeed (V_{MC}) has three separate specifications:

a) V_{MCA} Minimum control speed - airborne

b) V_{MCG} Minimum control speed - on the ground

c) V_{MCL} Minimum control speed - in the landing configuration

12.11.6 V_{MCA} (JAR 25.149 paraphrased)

V_{MCA} is the calibrated airspeed, at which, **when the critical engine is suddenly made inoperative**, it is possible to maintain control of the aeroplane with that engine still inoperative, and maintain straight flight with an angle of bank of not more than 5°.

V_{MCA} may not exceed 1·13 V_{SR} with:-

a)   maximum available take-off power or thrust on the engines;
b)   the aeroplane trimmed for take-off;
c)   the most unfavourable CG position;
d)   maximum sea level take-off weight;
e)   the aeroplane in its most critical take-off configuration (but with gear up); and
f)   the aeroplane airborne and the ground effect negligible; and
g)   If applicable, the propeller of the inoperative engine;
         (i)   windmilling; or
         (ii)   feathered, if the aeroplane has an automatic feathering device.

The rudder forces required to maintain control at V_{MCA} may not exceed 150 lb nor may it be necessary to reduce power or thrust on the operative engines.

NB: There is no performance requirement, just directional control.

PRINCIPLES OF FLIGHT FLIGHT MECHANICS

12.11.7 FACTORS AFFECTING V_{MCA}

ANGLE OF BANK: Banking towards the live engine reduces the rudder deflection required and so allows a lower V_{MCA}. 5° maximum is stipulated because larger bank angles would significantly reduce the vertical component of lift; the angle of attack would have to be increased with the added penalty of higher induced drag.

CG POSITION: Because the aircraft rotates around the CG, the position of the CG directly affects the length of the rudder arm and thus the power of the rudder and fin to maintain directional stability and control. The 'worst case' is with the CG at the aft limit. If the requirements can be met in this configuration, the ability to maintain directional control will be enhanced at any other CG location.

AILERON EFFECTIVENESS: At low airspeed, dynamic pressure is low which reduces the effectiveness of all the flying controls for a given angle of displacement. This affect on the rudder has already been discussed, but the ailerons will be affected in a similar way. In Fig. 12.23 and 12.24 (right roll input) the wings are maintained either level or at the required bank angle with the ailerons. At reduced airspeed, greater right roll aileron displacement must be used to keep the wings in the required position. The 'down' aileron on the left side will add to the yawing moment because of its increased induced drag. At low IAS (increased C_L) the large angle of down aileron could stall that wing and give an uncontrollable roll towards the dead engine. V_{MCA} must be high enough to prevent this unwelcome possibility.

FLAP POSITION: Flap position affects lift / drag ratio, nose down pitching moment and the stalling speed. With asymmetric thrust, flaps reduces climb performance, increases the margin above stall, but does not directly affect V_{MCA}. However, if take-off flap is used, the difference in lift between the two wings due to propeller slipstream is further increased. This increases the rolling moment, requires increased aileron deflection and indirectly increases V_{MCA}.

UNDERCARRIAGE: The undercarriage increases drag and reduces performance. The increased keel surface in front of the CG decreases directional stability slightly, thus the fin and rudder are opposed in sideslip conditions and this will slightly increase V_{MCA}.

ALTITUDE AND TEMPERATURE: V_{MCA} is affected by the amount of thrust being developed by the operating engine. As altitude and/ or temperature increases, the thrust from an unsupercharged engine will decrease. Therefore, V_{MCA} decreases with an increase in altitude and/or temperature.

RELATIONSHIP BETWEEN V_S AND V_{MCA}: V_S is constant with increasing altitude, so can be represented by a straight line in Fig. 12.26. (It was shown in Chapter 7 that stall speed does increase at higher altitudes, but for this study, we are only dealing with lower altitudes).
Fig. 12.26 shows that at about 3000 ft, V_S and V_{MCA} typically correspond. So above this altitude, the stall speed is higher than V_{MCA}. If the aircraft is slowed following an engine failure with full power on the operating engine the aircraft can stall before reaching V_{MCA}. The margin above loss of control is reduced; in this case by stalling.

PRINCIPLES OF FLIGHT — FLIGHT MECHANICS

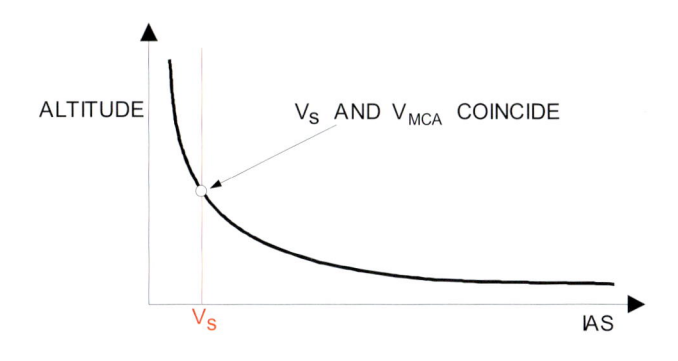

Figure 12.26 V_S and V_{MCA}

(handwritten: $V_1 \geq V_{MCG}$)

12.11.8 V_{MCG} (JAR 25.149 paraphrased)

V_{MCG}, the minimum control speed on the ground, is the calibrated airspeed during the take-off run, at which, when the critical engine is suddenly made inoperative, it is possible to maintain control of the aeroplane with the use of primary aerodynamic controls alone (**without the use of nose-wheel steering**) to enable the take-off to be safely continued using normal piloting skill. The rudder control forces may not exceed 150 pounds (68.1 kg) and, until the aeroplane becomes airborne, the lateral control may only be used to the extent of keeping the wings level. In the determination of V_{MCG}, assuming that the path of the aeroplane accelerating with all engines operating is along the centre of the runway, its path from the point at which the critical engine is made inoperative to the point at which recovery to a direction parallel to the centreline is completed may not deviate more than 30ft (9.144 m) laterally from the centre-line at any point. As for V_{MCA}, this must be established with:

   a)   maximum available take-off power or thrust on the engines;

   b)   the aeroplane trimmed for take-off;

   c)   the most unfavourable CG position;

   d)   maximum sea level take-off weight.

12.11.9 FACTORS AFFECTING V_{MCG}

ALTITUDE AND TEMPERATURE: V_{MCG} is affected by the amount of thrust being developed by the operating engine. As altitude and/or temperature increases, the thrust from an unsupercharged engine will decrease. Therefore, V_{MCG} decreases with an increase in altitude and/or temperature.

(handwritten: Vmca is a higher IAS than Vmca)

NOSE-WHEEL STEERING: Nosewheel steering is designed for taxiing - making large and sharp turns at low speed, turning off the runway and parking. When taking-off on wet, icy or slippery runways, the nosewheel begins to hydroplane between 70 and 90 knots (depending on tyre pressure and depth of water or slush) and has very little steering effect. Once the aircraft is moving, the nosewheel doesn't do much except turn sideways and skid.

V_{MCG} is established during flight testing, usually on a dry runway. If nosewheel steering were used by the test pilot it would give a false, low speed at which it was possible to maintain directional control on the ground after the critical engine is suddenly made inoperative. At this speed on a slippery runway - even if nosewheel steering were used by a line pilot, it would not give the required assistance in maintaining directional control following an engine failure and the aircraft would depart the side of the runway. The regulations ensure that limits are established in a "worst case" set of circumstances, in order to give the maximum safety factor during normal operations.

RUDDER ARM: When the aircraft is on the ground it rotates about the main undercarriage, which is aft of the CG. Therefore the rudder arm is shorter when the aircraft is on the ground. It will be found that on most aircraft V_{MCG} is higher than V_{MCA}.

12.11.10 V_{MCL} (JAR 25.149 paraphrased)

V_{MCL}, the minimum control speed during approach and landing with all engines operating, is the calibrated airspeed at which, when the critical engine is suddenly made inoperative, it is possible to maintain control of the aeroplane with that engine still inoperative, and maintain straight flight with an angle of bank of not more than 5°.

V_{MCL} must be established with:-

a)   the aeroplane in the most critical configuration for approach and landing with all engines operating;

b)   the most unfavourable CG;

c)   the aeroplane trimmed for approach with all engines operating;

d)   the most unfavourable weight;

e)   for propeller aeroplanes, the propeller of the inoperative engine in the position it achieves without pilot action; and

f)   go-around power or thrust setting on the operating engines(s).

PRINCIPLES OF FLIGHT   **FLIGHT MECHANICS**

In demonstrating V_{MCL}:-

a) the rudder force may not exceed 150 lb;

b) the aeroplane may not exhibit hazardous flight characteristics or require exceptional piloting skill, alertness or strength;

c) **lateral control must be sufficient to roll the aeroplane, from an initial condition of steady flight, through an angle of 20° in the direction necessary to initiate a turn away from the inoperative engine(s), in not more than 5 seconds.**

12.11.11 FACTORS AFFECTING V_{MCL}

AILERON EFFECTIVENESS: At low airspeed, dynamic pressure is low which reduces the effectiveness of all the flying controls for a given angle of displacement. This affect on the rudder has already been discussed, but the ailerons will be affected in a similar way. At reduced airspeed, greater aileron displacement must be used to obtain the required roll response. The 'down' aileron on the left side will also add to the yawing moment because of its increased induced drag and may stall the wing at low IAS (high C_L). Adequate aileron effectiveness is clearly very important when considering V_{MCL}, because this minimum control speed contains a roll requirement, not just directional control.

SUMMARY OF MINIMUM CONTROL SPEEDS

JAR 25.149 sets out the criteria to be used when establishing the minimum control speeds for certification of a new aircraft. The speeds so established will be included in the aircraft's Flight Manual.

From careful study of the above extracts, several things can be noted:-

a) nose wheel steering may not be used when establishing V_{MCG}. Its use would artificially decrease V_{MCG}. In service, when operating from a slippery runway, nose wheel steering would be ineffective so it might be impossible to directionally control the aircraft when at or above the stated V_{MCG}.

b) **V_{MCL} includes a roll requirement**, not merely directional control, as with the other speeds.

c) The thrust developed by an engine depends on the air density, and so thrust will decrease with increasing altitude and temperature. The yawing moment due to asymmetric thrust will therefore decrease with altitude and temperature, and so control can be maintained at a lower IAS. V_{MC} therefore decreases with increasing altitude and temperature (higher density altitude).

12.11.12 PERFORMANCE WITH ONE ENGINE INOPERATIVE

It was shown in paragraph 12.5 that an aircraft's ability to climb depends upon the excess thrust available, after aerodynamic drag is balanced. If a twin engined aircraft loses an engine, total thrust is reduced by 50%, but the excess thrust (the thrust, minus aerodynamic drag) is reduced by more than 50%, Fig. 12.27. The ability to climb may be reduced as much as 80%.

12.11.13 SINGLE ENGINE ANGLE OF CLIMB

Angle of climb is determined by excess thrust available. Climb angle will be a maximum when the aircraft is flown at the IAS where excess thrust is a maximum (maximum thrust to drag ratio). Since thrust decreases with forward speed and total drag increases below and above the minimum drag speed (V_{IMD}), the best angle of climb is achieved at a speed below V_{IMD} but a safe margin above the stall speed. The airspeed for maximum angle of climb is V_X for all engines operating and V_{XSE} for best single engine angle of climb.

12.11.14 SINGLE ENGINE RATE OF CLIMB

Rate of climb is determined by excess power available. Power is the rate of doing work and work is force times distance moved, so power is force times distance moved in a given time, i.e. thrust or drag times TAS (thrust or drag because they are both forces and TAS because it is the only speed there is!). Although thrust reduces with forward speed, total power available increases to a point because of the speed factor. Similarly, power required is a measure of drag times TAS, so excess power available determines the available rate of climb. The airspeed for best rate of climb is V_Y for all engines operating and V_{YSE} for best single engine rate of climb.

V_Y and V_{YSE} are higher than V_X and V_{XSE} and provide a safer margin above both stall and V_{MCA}. Under most circumstances V_Y and V_{YSE} are the best speeds to use. On small twin engine aircraft V_{YSE} is marked on the Air Speed Indicator by a blue radial line and is called 'blue line speed'.

12.11.15 CONCLUSIONS

At a given altitude, airspeed and throttle position, excess thrust depends on the amount of drag being generated, and this will depend on configuration, weight and whether turns are required to be made. The control surface deflections required to balance asymmetric thrust will also cause an increase in drag. It is essential therefore that after losing an engine, particularly during take-off or during a go-around, **drag is reduced and no turns are made until well away from the ground.**

Drag can be reduced by feathering the propeller of the inoperative engine, raising the undercarriage, carefully raising the flaps, closing the cowl flap on the inoperative engine and banking the aircraft no more than 5° towards the operating engine. Flying at V_{YSE} (blue line speed) with maximum continuous thrust on the operating engine will provide maximum climb performance and optimum control over the aeroplane.

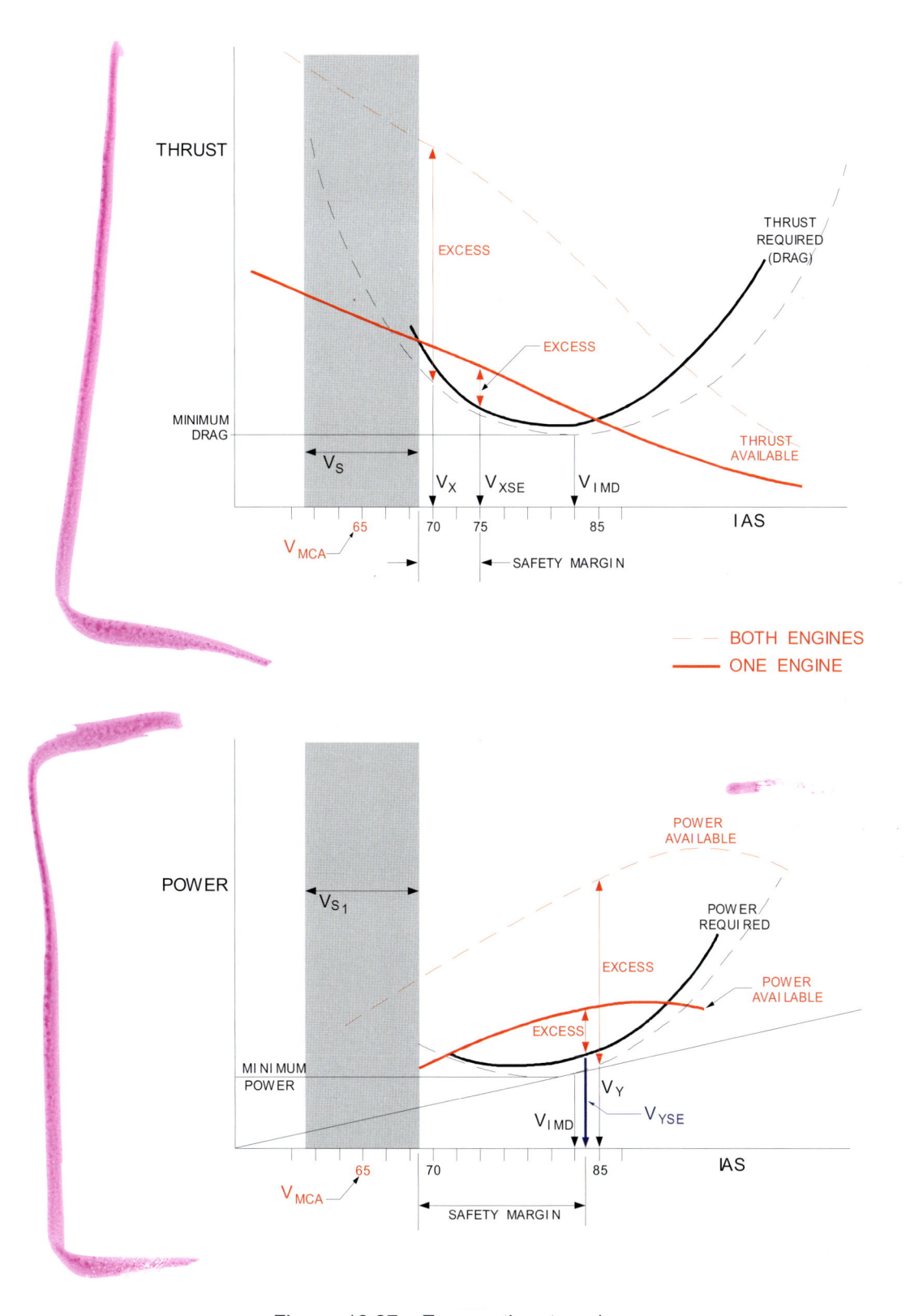

Figure 12.27 Excess thrust and excess power

INTENTIONALLY

LEFT

BLANK

PRINCIPLES OF FLIGHT **FLIGHT MECHANICS**

SELF ASSESSMENT QUESTIONS

1. In straight and level powered flight the following principal forces act on an aircraft:

    a) thrust, lift, weight.
    b) thrust, lift, drag, weight.
    c) thrust, lift, drag.
    d) lift, drag, weight.

2. For an aircraft in level flight, if the wing CP is aft of the CG and there is no thrust/drag couple, the tailplane load must be:

    a) upward
    b) downward
    c) zero
    d) forward

3. When considering the forces acting upon an aeroplane in straight-and-level flight at constant airspeed, which statement is correct?

    a) weight acts vertically toward the centre of the Earth
    b) lift acts perpendicular to the chord line and must be greater than weight
    c) thrust acts forward parallel to the relative wind and is greater than drag
    d) lift acts in the opposite direction to the aircraft weight

4. The horizontal stabilizer usually provides a download in level flight because:

    a) the main plane lift is always positive
    b) the lift/weight and thrust/drag couples combine to give a nose down pitch
    c) the lift produced is greater than required at high speed
    d) this configuration gives less interference

5. The reason a light general aviation aircraft tends to nose down during power reduction is that the:

    a) thrust line acts horizontally and above the force of drag
    b) centre of gravity is located forward of the centre of pressure
    c) centre of pressure is located forward of the centre of gravity
    d) force of drag acts horizontally and above the thrust line

6. To give the best obstacle clearance on take off, take off should be made with:

    a) flaps partially extended and at best rate of climb speed (Vy).
    b) flaps partially extended and at best angle of climb speed (Vx).
    c) flaps retracted and at best rate of climb speed (Vy).
    d) flaps retracted and at best angle of climb speed (Vx).

7. The angle of climb is proportional to:

    a) the amount by which the lift exceeds the weight.
    b) the amount by which the thrust exceeds the drag.
    c) the amount by which the thrust exceeds the weight.
    d) the angle of attack of the wing.

8. In a climb at a steady speed, the thrust is:

    a) equal to the aerodynamic drag.
    b) greater than the aerodynamic drag.
    c) less than the aerodynamic drag.
    d) equal to the weight component along the flight path.

9. A constant rate of climb in an aeroplane is determined by:

    a) wind speed
    b) the aircraft weight
    c) excess engine power
    d) excess airspeed

10. Assume that after take-off a turn is made to a downwind heading. In regard to the ground, the aeroplane will climb at:

    a) a greater rate into the wind than downwind
    b) a steeper angle downwind than into the wind
    c) the same angle upwind or downwind
    d) a steeper angle into the wind than downwind

11. What effect does high density altitude have on aircraft performance?

    a) It increases takeoff performance
    b) It increases engine performance
    c) It reduces climb performance

PRINCIPLES OF FLIGHT   **FLIGHT MECHANICS**

12. During a steady climb the lift force is:

    a) less than the weight.
    b) exactly equal to the weight.
    c) equal to the weight plus the drag.
    d) greater than the weight.

13. In a steady climb the wing lift is:

    a) equal to the weight
    b) greater than the weight
    c) equal to the weight component perpendicular to the flight path
    d) equal to the vertical component of weight

14. During a glide the following forces act on an aircraft:

    a) lift, weight, thrust.
    b) lift, drag, weight.
    c) drag, thrust, weight.
    d) lift and weight only.

15. For a glider having a maximum L/D ratio of 20 : 1, the flattest glide angle that could be achieved in still air would be:

    a) 1 ft in 10 ft
    b) 1 ft in 20 ft
    c) 1 ft in 40 ft
    d) 1 ft in 200 ft

16. To cover the greatest distance when gliding the gliding speed must be:

    a) near to the stalling speed.
    b) as high as possible within VNE limits.
    c) about 30% faster than Vmd.
    d) the one that gives the highest L/D ratio.

17. If the weight of an aircraft is increased the maximum gliding range:

    a) decreases.
    b) increases.
    c) remains the same, and rate of descent is unchanged.
    d) remains the same, but rate of descent increases.

18. When gliding into a headwind, the ground distance covered will be:

    a) less than in still air.
    b) the same as in still air but the glide angle will be steeper.
    c) the same as in still air but the glide angle will be flatter.
    d) greater than in still air.

19. During a 'power-on' glide the forces acting on an aircraft are:

    a) lift, drag and weight.
    b) lift, thrust and weight.
    c) lift, drag, thrust and weight.
    d) lift and weight only.

20. If airbrakes are extended during a glide, and speed maintained, the rate of descent will:

    a) increase and glide angle will be steeper.
    b) increase, but glide angle will remain the same.
    c) decrease.
    d) remain the same.

21. An aircraft has a L/D ratio of 16:1 at 50 kt in calm air. What would the approximate GLIDE RATIO be with a direct headwind of 25 kt?

    a) 32:1
    b) 16:1
    c) 8:1
    d) 4:1

22. During a turn the lift force may be resolved into two forces, these are:

    a) a force opposite to thrust and a force equal and opposite to weight.
    b) centripetal force and a force equal and opposite drag.
    c) centripetal force and a force equal and opposite weight.
    d) centrifugal force and a force equal and opposite thrust.

23. In a turn at a constant IAS, compared to straight and level flight at the same IAS:

    a) the same power is required because the IAS is the same.
    b) more power is required because the drag is greater.
    c) more power is required because some thrust is required to give the centripetal force.
    d) less power is required because the lift required is less.

PRINCIPLES OF FLIGHT   **FLIGHT MECHANICS**

24. In a turn at a given TAS and bank angle:

    a) only one radius of turn is possible.
    b) the radius can be varied by varying the pitch.
    c) the radius can be varied by varying the yaw.
    d) two different radii are possible, one to the right and one to the left.

25. As bank angle is increased in a turn at a constant IAS, the load factor will:

    a) increase in direct proportion to bank angle.
    b) increase at an increasing rate.
    c) decrease.
    d) remain the same.

26. Skidding outward in a turn is caused by:

    a) insufficient rate of yaw.
    b) too much bank.
    c) too much nose up pitch.
    d) insufficient bank

27. For a turn at a constant IAS if the radius of turn is decreased the load factor will:

    a) increase.
    b) decrease but bank angle will increase.
    c) decrease but bank angle will decrease.
    d) remain the same.

28. An aircraft has a stalling speed in level flight of 70 kt IAS. In a 60° balanced turn the stalling speed would be:

    a) 76 kt.
    b) 84 kt.
    c) 99 kt.
    d) 140 kt..

29. An increase in airspeed while maintaining a constant load factor during a level, coordinated turn would result in:

    a) an increase in centrifugal force
    b) the same radius of turn
    c) a decrease in the radius of turn
    d) an increase in the radius of turn

PRINCIPLES OF FLIGHT   FLIGHT MECHANICS

30. How can the pilot increase the rate of turn and decrease the radius at the same time?

   a) shallow the bank and increase airspeed
   b) steepen the bank and increase airspeed
   c) steepen the bank and decrease airspeed

31. If an aircraft with a gross weight of 2,000 kg were subjected to a total load of 6,000 kg in flight, the load factor would be:

   a) 9 G's
   b) 2 G's
   c) 6 G's
   d) 3 G's

32. Why must the angle of attack be increased during a turn to maintain altitude?

   a) Compensate for increase in induced drag.
   b) Increase the horizontal component of lift equal to the vertical component.
   c) Compensate for loss of vertical component of lift.
   d) To stop the nose from dropping below the horizon and the airspeed increasing.

33. Two aircraft of different weight are in a steady turn at the same bank angle:

   a) the heavier aircraft would have a higher "g" load
   b) the lighter aircraft would have a higher "g" load
   c) they would both have the same "g" load

34. For a multi-engined aircraft, V_{MCG} is defined as the minimum control speed on the ground with one engine inoperative. The aircraft must be able to:

   a) abandon the take off.
   b) continue the take off or abandon it.
   c) continue the take off using primary controls only.
   d) continue the take off using primary controls and nosewheel steering.

35. What criteria determines which engine is the "critical" engine of a twin-engine aeroplane?

   a) the one with the centre of thrust farthest from the centerline of the fuselage
   b) the one with the centre of thrust closest to the centerline of the fuselage
   c) the one designated by the manufacturer which develops most usable thrust
   d) the failure of which causes the least yawing moment

36. Following failure of the critical engine, what performance should the pilot of a light, twin-engine aeroplane be able to maintain at V_{MCA}?

   a) Heading, altitude, and ability to climb 50 ft/min
   b) Heading only
   c) Heading and altitude

INTENTIONALLY

LEFT

BLANK

No	A	B	C	D	REF	No	A	B	C	D	REF
1		B				22			C		
2		B				23		B			
3	A					24	A				
4		B				25		B			
5		B				26				D	
6				D		27	A				
7		B				28			C		
8		B				29				D	
9			C			30			C		
10				D		31				D	
11			C			32			C		
12	A					33			C		
13			C			34			C		
14		B				35		B			
15		B				36		B			
16				D		37	/	/	/	/	/
17				D		38	/	/	/	/	/
18	A					39	/	/	/	/	/
19			C			40	/	/	/	/	/
20	A					41	/	/	/	/	/
21		B				42	/	/	/	/	/

INTENTIONALLY LEFT BLANK

CHAPTER 13 - HIGH SPEED FLIGHT

Contents

	Page
INTRODUCTION	13 - 1
SPEED OF SOUND	
MACH NUMBER	13 - 2
EFFECT ON MACH NUMBER OF CLIMBING AT A CONSTANT IAS	
VARIATION OF TAS WITH ALTITUDE AT A CONSTANT MACH NUMBER	13 - 4
TEMPERATURE ON MACH NUMBER AT A CONSTANT FL & IAS	
SUBDIVISION OF AERODYNAMIC FLOW	13 - 5
PROPAGATION OF PRESSURE WAVES	13 - 6
NORMAL SHOCK WAVES	13 - 8
CRITICAL MACH NUMBER	
PRESSURE DISTRIBUTION AT TRANSONIC MACH NUMBERS	13 - 10
PROPERTIES OF A NORMAL SHOCK WAVE	13 - 12
OBLIQUE SHOCK WAVES	13 - 13
EFFECTS OF SHOCKWAVE FORMATION	13 - 14
LIFT	
LIFT CURVE SLOPE AND C_{LMAX}	13 - 16
DRAG	13 - 17
C_L / C_D DRAG POLAR CURVE	13 - 18
CENTRE OF PRESSURE	
CP MOVEMENT	13 - 20
FLYING CONTROLS	
CONTROL BUZZ	13 - 21
BUFFET	
FACTORS WHICH AFFECT THE BUFFET BOUNDARIES	13 - 22
STALL SPEED	
LOAD FACTOR	13 - 23
MACH NUMBER	13 - 24
ANGLE OF ATTACK	
PRESSURE ALTITUDE	13 - 25
WEIGHT	
CG POSITION	

THE BUFFET MARGIN .... 13 - 26
USE OF THE BUFFET ONSET CHART
     1·3 G ALTITUDE
     BUFFET RESTRICTED SPEED LIMITS
     AERODYNAMIC CEILING
     LOAD FACTOR AND BANK ANGLE AT WHICH BUFFET OCCURS
DELAYING THE EFFECTS OF COMPRESSIBILITY .... 13 - 28
     THIN WING SECTIONS
     SWEEPBACK
          DISADVANTAGES OF SWEEP .... 13 - 30
     VORTEX GENERATORS .... 13 - 31
     AREA RULE .... 13 - 32
     MACH TRIM .... 13 - 33
     SUPERCRITICAL AEROFOIL .... 13 - 34
          ADVANTAGES .... 13 - 35
          DISADVANTAGES
AERODYNAMIC HEATING .... 13 - 36
MACH ANGLE .... 13 - 37
MACH CONE .... 13 - 38
AREA (ZONE) OF INFLUENCE
BOW WAVE
EXPANSION WAVES .... 13 - 39
SONIC BANG .... 13 - 41
METHODS OF IMPROVING CONTROL AT TRANSONIC SPEEDS
     SUPERSONIC WAVE CHARACTERISTICS SUMMARY .... 13 - 42
     SWEEPBACK - FACT SHEET .... 13 - 43
SELF ASSESSMENT QUESTIONS .... 13 - 45
     ANSWERS .... 13 - 51

PRINCIPLES OF FLIGHT   **HIGH SPEED FLIGHT**

13.1 INTRODUCTION

During the preceding study of low speed aerodynamics it was assumed that air is incompressible, that is, there is no change in air density resulting from changes of pressure.

At any speed there are changes in air density due to 'compressibility', but if the speed is low the changes are sufficiently small to be ignored. As speed increases however, the changes in air density start to become significant.

When an aircraft moves through the air infinitesimally small pressure disturbances, or waves, are propagated outward from the aircraft in all directions, but only the waves travelling ahead of the aircraft are significant for the study of high speed flight. These pressure waves 'signal' the approach of the aircraft and make the air change direction (upwash) and divide to allow passage of the aircraft.

13.2 SPEED OF SOUND

For the study of high speed flight we are interested in the speed at which the infinitesimally small pressure disturbances (waves) travel through the atmosphere. Pressure waves 'propagate' from their source, that is, each air molecule is rapidly vibrated in turn and passes-on the disturbance to its neighbour. **The speed of propagation of small pressure waves depends upon the temperature of the air ONLY.** The lower the temperature, the lower the speed of propagation. Sound is pressure waves and the speed of any pressure wave through the atmosphere, whether audible or not, has become known as 'the speed of sound'.

The speed of sound at 15°C is 340 metres per second, or approximately 661 kt.

It can be shown that: $a = \sqrt{\gamma R T}$ (Eq 13.1)

Where a = speed of sound R = the gas constant
         γ = a constant (1·4 for air) T = absolute temperature

Since γ and R are constants, **the speed of sound is proportional only to the square root of the absolute temperature.** For example, at 15° C (288 K):

$$a = \sqrt{1.4 \times 287 \times 288} \qquad (R = 287 \text{ J/kg K})$$

$$= 340 \text{ m/s}$$

$a \propto \sqrt{T}$

The speed of sound changes with Temperature ONLY

13 - 1   © Oxford Aviation Services Limited

13.3 MACH NUMBER

As the speed of an aircraft increases, **there is a decrease in the distance between the aircraft and the influence of the advancing pressure waves**. The aircraft begins to catch up the pressure waves, so the air has less time to move from the aircraft's path and upwash has a more acute angle.

At higher speeds there is also a **change in the flow and pressure patterns around the aircraft**. Ultimately lift and drag, manoeuvrability and the stability and control characteristics will all be changed.

These effects are due to the compressibility of air, where density can change along a streamline, and the associated conditions and the characteristics which arise are due to 'compressibility'.

It is vitally important that the flight crew know the speed of the aircraft in relation to the potential effects of 'compressibility'. If the aircraft speed through the air (TAS) and the speed of sound in the air through which it is flying (the local speed of sound) is known, this will give an indication of the degree off compressibility. This relationship is known as the Mach number and **Mach number is a measure of compressibility.** (e.g. M 0·5 is half the local speed of sound).

Mach number (M) is the ratio of the true airspeed (V) to the local speed of sound (a)

$$M = \frac{V}{a}$$ (Eq 13.2)

Equation 13.2 is a good formula to remember because it allows several important relationships to be easily understood.

13.4 EFFECT ON MACH NUMBER OF CLIMBING AT A CONSTANT IAS

- It is known that temperature decreases with increasing altitude, so the speed of sound will decrease as altitude is increased.

- It is also known that if altitude is increased at a constant IAS, the TAS increases.

- Therefore, the **Mach number will increase if altitude is increased at a constant IAS**. This is because (V) gets bigger and (a) gets smaller.

From a practical point of view: climbing at a constant IAS makes the distance between the aircraft and the influence of the advancing pressure waves decrease, which begins to change the flow and pressure patterns around the aircraft.

> The lower the temperature the lower the speed of sound

PRINCIPLES OF FLIGHT   **HIGH SPEED FLIGHT**

The International Standard Atmosphere assumes that temperature decreases from 15°C at sea level to −56·5°C at 36,089 ft (11,000 m), then remains constant. The speed of sound will therefore decrease with altitude up to the tropopause, and then remain constant, Fig. 13.1.

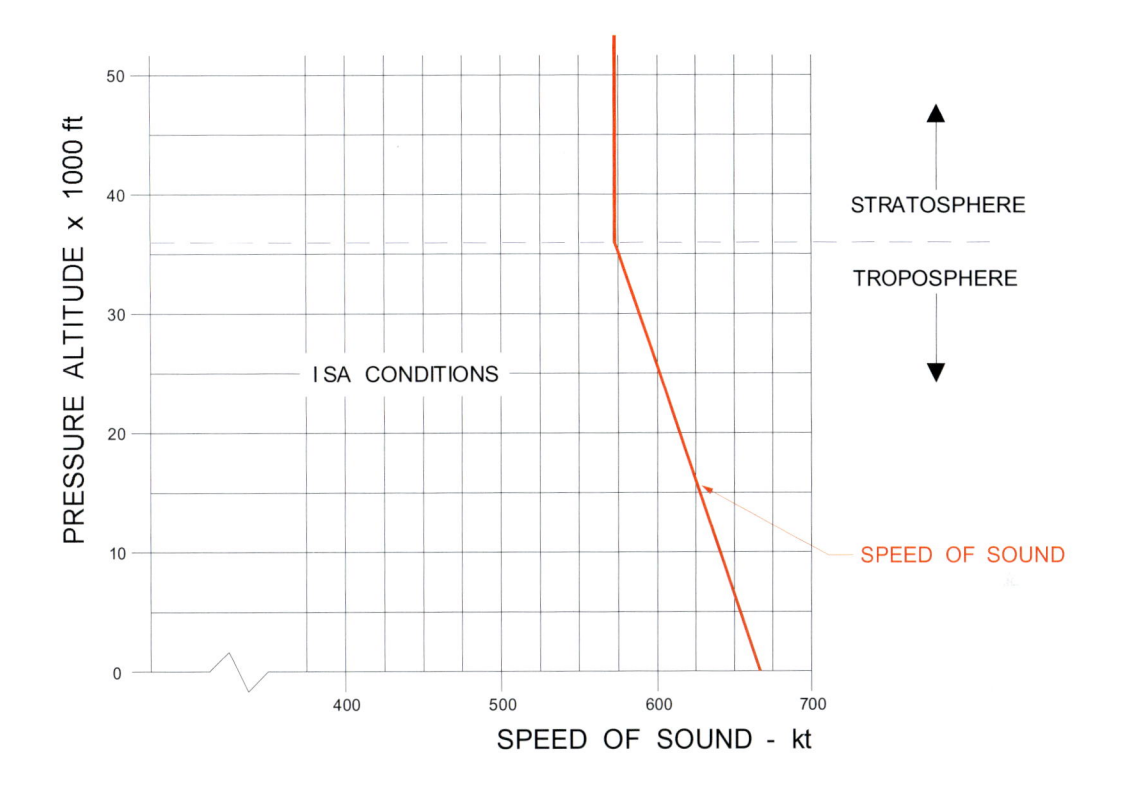

Figure 13.1 Variation of speed of sound with altitude

Chapter 14 will fully describe V_{MO} and M_{MO}, the high speed (generally speaking) operational limit speeds. It has been stated that as an aircraft climbs at a constant IAS its Mach number will be increasing. It is clear that it is possible to exceed the maximum operating Mach number (M_{MO}) in a climb at a constant IAS.

As the climb continues an altitude will be reached at which the flight crew must stop flying at a constant IAS and fly at a constant Mach number, to avoid accidentally exceeding M_{MO}. The altitude at which this changeover takes place will depend on the outside air temperature.

The lower the outside air temperature, the lower the changeover altitude.

PRINCIPLES OF FLIGHT **HIGH SPEED FLIGHT**

13.5 VARIATION OF TAS WITH ALTITUDE AT A CONSTANT MACH NUMBER

$$\text{If } M = \frac{TAS}{a}$$

$$\text{then } TAS = M \times a$$

> When descending at a constant Mach number IAS will be increasing

It can be seen from the equation that if an aircraft is flown at a constant Mach number:

a) as altitude decreases the temperature will rise, local speed of sound will increase and TAS will increase.

b) as altitude increases the temperature will drop, local speed of sound will decrease and TAS will decrease (up to the tropopause and then remain constant).

> When climbing at a constant TAS Mach number will be increasing, up to the tropopause, and then remain constant

13.6 INFLUENCE OF TEMPERATURE ON MACH NUMBER AT A CONSTANT FLIGHT LEVEL AND IAS

An aircraft normally operates at Indicated Air Speeds and the Mach number can be expressed in terms of IAS:

$$M = \frac{IAS}{\text{constant} \sqrt{\frac{p}{p_o}}} \qquad \text{(Eq 13.3)}$$

$$\text{for IAS in knots: } M = \frac{IAS}{661 \sqrt{\frac{p}{p_o}}} \qquad \text{(Eq 13.4)}$$

where, p = pressure at altitude

p_o = pressure at Sea Level

This shows that at a constant pressure altitude (Flight Level), the Mach number is independent of temperature for a constant IAS.

This is because the speed of sound and the TAS for a given IAS, both change as $\sqrt{T}$

PRINCIPLES OF FLIGHT   **HIGH SPEED FLIGHT**

13.7 SUBDIVISIONS OF AERODYNAMIC FLOW

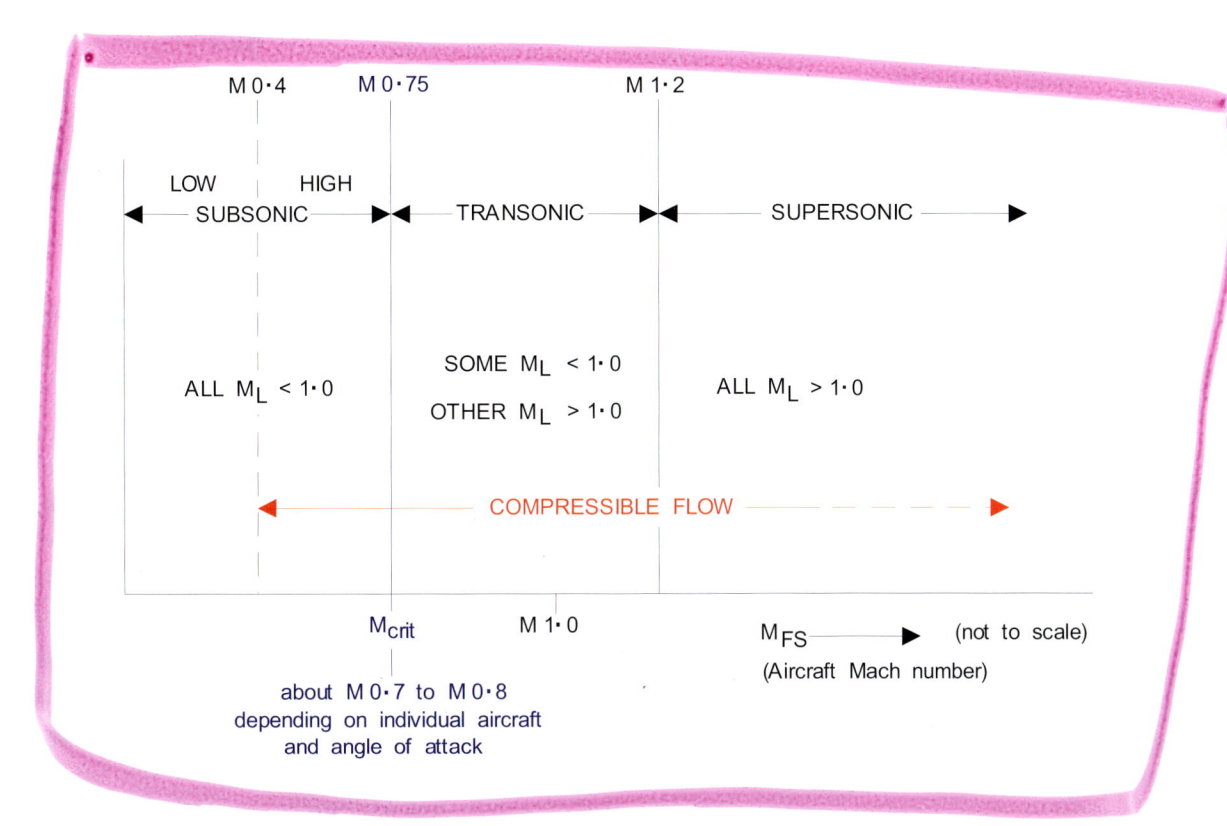

Figure 13.2   Classification of airspeed

Fig. 13.2 shows the flow speed ranges with their approximate Mach number values, where:

M_{FS} = **Free Stream Mach number:** The Mach number of the flow sufficiently remote from an aircraft to be unaffected by it. (In effect, the Mach number of the aircraft through the air). This is the Mach number shown on the aircraft Mach meter.

M_L = **Local Mach number:** When an aircraft flies at a certain M_{FS}, the flow over it is accelerated in some places and slowed down in others.

$M_L > M_{FS}$

Local Mach number (M_L), the boundary layer flow speed relative to the surface of the aircraft, is subdivided as follows:-

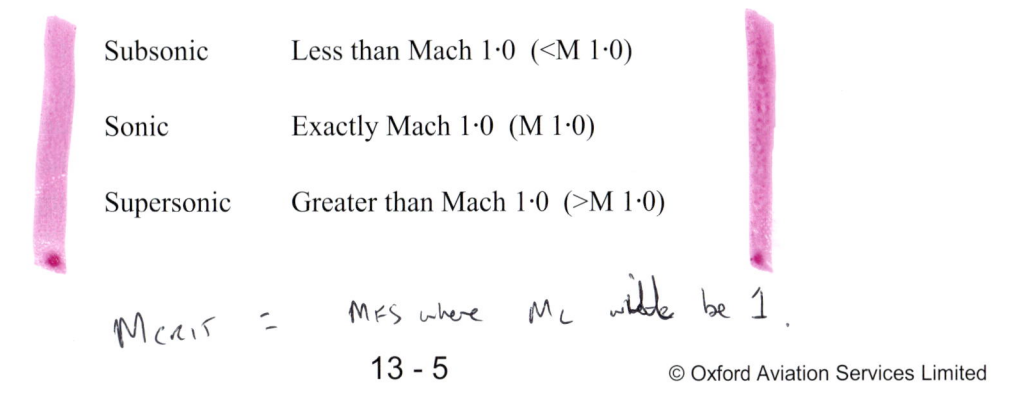

    Subsonic   Less than Mach 1·0 (<M 1·0)

    Sonic   Exactly Mach 1·0 (M 1·0)

    Supersonic   Greater than Mach 1·0 (>M 1·0)

M_{crit} = M_{FS} where M_L will be 1.

PRINCIPLES OF FLIGHT

HIGH SPEED FLIGHT

13.8 PROPAGATION OF PRESSURE WAVES

KEY

○ = POSITION OF OBJECT WHEN PRESSURE WAVE GENERATED

● = POSITION OF OBJECT WHEN PRESSURE WAVE REACHES RADIUS r

M = MACH NUMBER OF OBJECT

(= PRESSURE WAVE EXPANDING FROM SOURCE AT LOCAL SPEED OF SOUND

AIRFLOW   PRESSURE WAVE

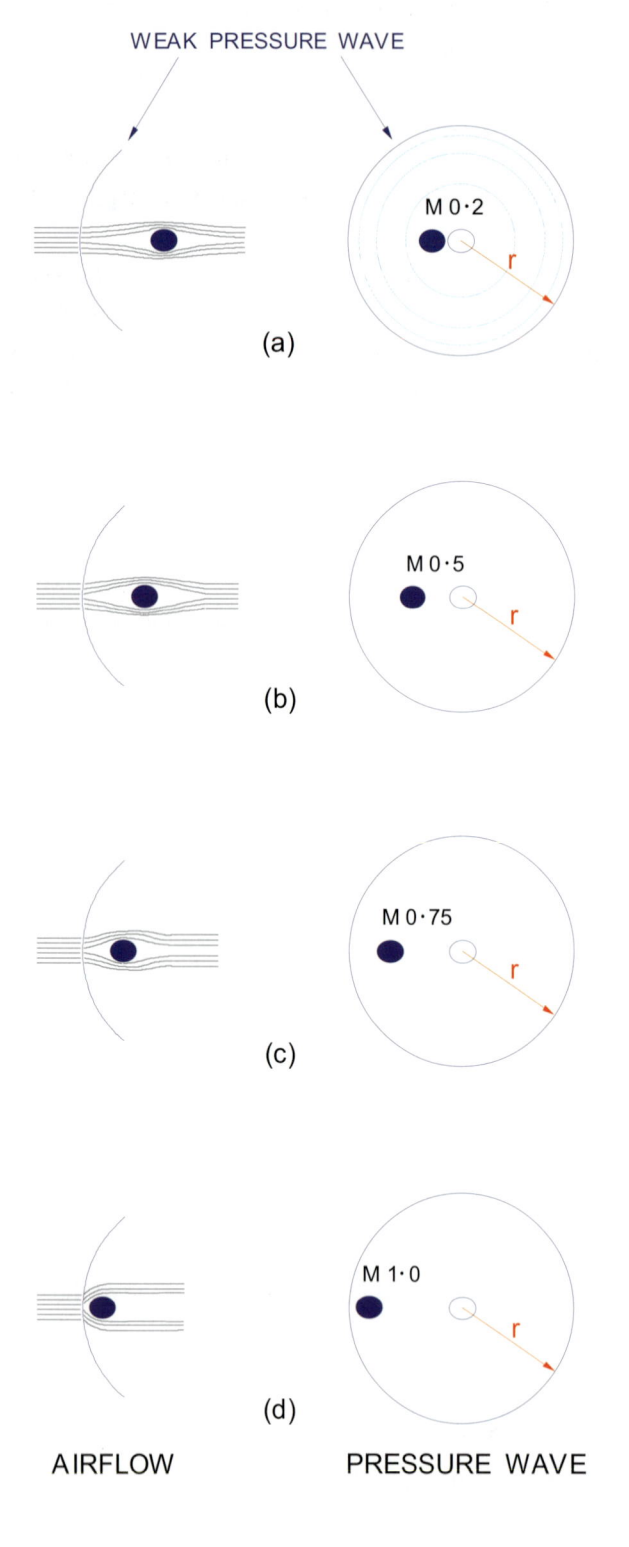

(a) M 0.2

(b) M 0.5

(c) M 0.75

(d) M 1.0

WEAK PRESSURE WAVE

Figure 13.3

Fig. 13.3 shows a series of sketches which illustrate the basic idea of pressure wave formation ahead of an object moving at various Mach numbers and of the airflow as it approached the object. Pressure waves are propagated continuously, but for clarity just one is considered.

If we assume a constant local speed of sound; as the object's Mach number increases, the object gets closer to the 'leading edge' of the pressure wave and the air receives less and less warning of the approach of the object.

The greater the Mach number of the object, the more acute the upwash angle and the fewer the number of air particles that can move out of the path of the object. **Air will begin to build up in front of the object and the density of the air will increase.**

When the object's speed has reached the local speed of sound (d), the pressure wave can no longer warn the air particles ahead of the object because the object is travelling forward at the same speed as the wave.

PRINCIPLES OF FLIGHT
HIGH SPEED FLIGHT

Therefore, the free stream air particles are not aware of anything until the particles that are piled up right in front of the object collide with them. As a result of these collisions, the air pressure and density increase accordingly.

As the object's speed increases to just above M 1·0, the pressure and density of the air just ahead of it are also increased. The region of compressed air extends some distance ahead of the object, the actual distance depends on the speed and size of the object and the temperature of the air.

At one point the free air stream particles are completely undisturbed, having received no advance warning of the approach of a fast moving object, and then are suddenly made to undergo drastic changes in velocity, pressure, temperature and density. Because of the **sudden** nature of these changes, the boundary line between the undisturbed air and the region of compressed air is called a "shock wave", a stylised sketch of which is shown in Fig. 13.3a.

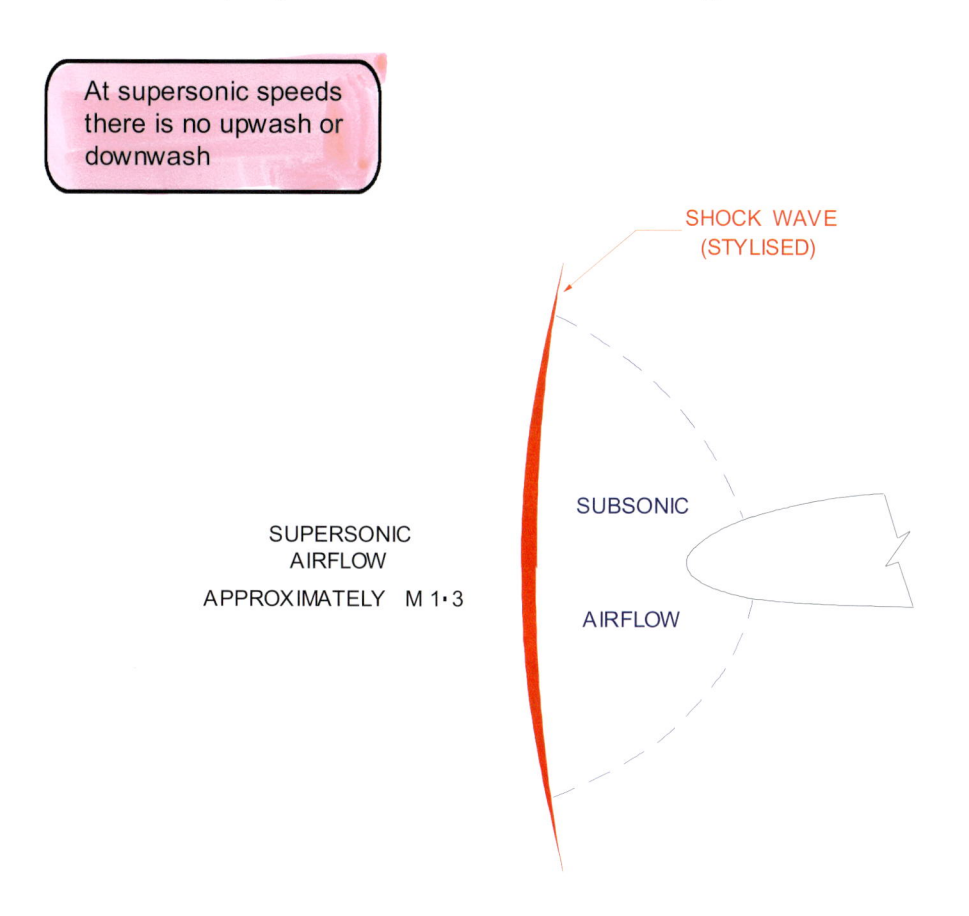

> At supersonic speeds there is no upwash or downwash

Figure 13.3a Stylised shock wave

PRINCIPLES OF FLIGHT　　　　　　　　　　　　　　　　　　HIGH SPEED FLIGHT

13.9 NORMAL SHOCK WAVES

(Normal meaning perpendicular to the upstream flow). In addition to the formation of a shock wave described overleaf, a shock wave can be generated in an entirely different manner when there is no object in the supersonic airflow. (We have now returned to the wind tunnel analogy of a stationary aircraft and moving air). **Whenever supersonic airflow is slowed to subsonic speed without a change in direction, a "normal" shock wave will form as a boundary between the supersonic and subsonic region.** This means that some 'compressibility effects' will occur before the aircraft as a whole reaches Mach 1·0.

*[Diagram: Figure 13.4 showing airflow over an aerofoil with labels:
- AIR BEING ACCELERATED TO SUPERSONIC SPEED
- NORMAL SHOCK WAVE
- LOCAL MACH NUMBER > 1
- LOCAL MACH NUMBER < 1 (PRESSURE WAVES ABLE TO TRAVEL FORWARD)]*

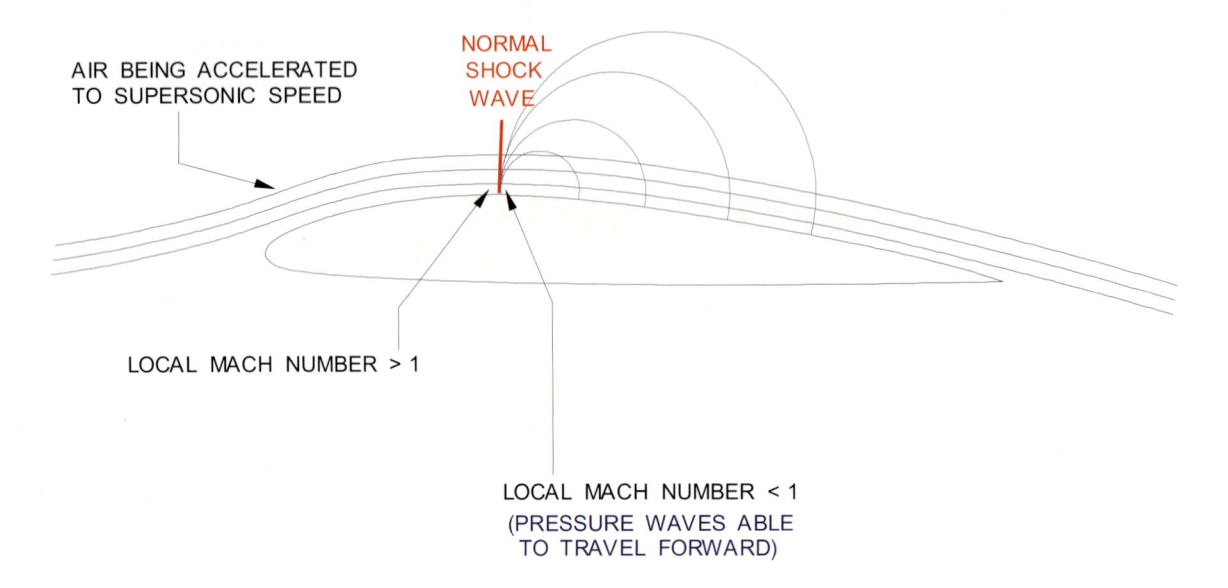

Figure 13.4   Shock wave at subsonic free stream Mach number

13.10 CRITICAL MACH NUMBER

An aerofoil generates lift by accelerating air over the top surface. At small angles of attack the highest local velocity on an aircraft will usually be located at the point of maximum thickness on the wing. For example, at a free stream speed of M0·84, maximum local velocity on the wing might be as high as M1·05 in cruising level flight. At increased angles of attack the local velocity will be greater and further forward, also if the thickness/chord ratio were greater the local speed will be higher.

As the free stream speed increases the maximum speed on the aerofoil will reach the local speed of sound first. **The Free Stream Mach number at which the local velocity first reaches Mach 1·0 (sonic) is called the Critical Mach number (M_{CRIT}).**

> Critical Mach number is the highest speed at which no parts of the aircraft are supersonic

Increased thickness/chord and increased angle of attack cause greater accelerations over the top surface of the wing, so the **critical Mach number will decrease with increasing thickness/chord ratio or angle of attack.**

PRINCIPLES OF FLIGHT   **HIGH SPEED FLIGHT**

13.10.1 ACCELERATING BEYOND M_{CRIT}

At speeds just above the critical Mach number there will be a small region of supersonic airflow on the upper surface, terminated by a shock wave, Fig. 13.5.

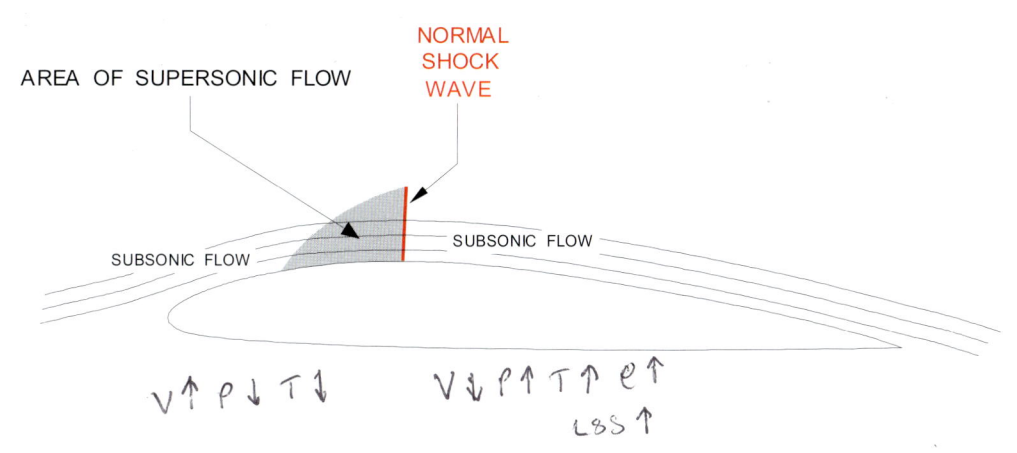

[Diagram: aerofoil showing AREA OF SUPERSONIC FLOW, NORMAL SHOCK WAVE, and SUBSONIC FLOW regions. Handwritten annotations: V↑ P↓ T↓ ; V↓ P↑ T↑ e↑ ; L8S↑]

Figure 13.5 Mixed supersonic and subsonic airflow at transonic speed

As the aircraft speed is further increased the region of supersonic flow on the upper surface extends and the shockwave marking the end of the supersonic region, moves rearwards. A similar sequence of events will occur on the lower surface although the shockwave will usually form at a higher aircraft speed because the lower surface usually has less curvature so the air is not accelerated so much.

When the aircraft speed reaches Mach 1·0 the airflow is supersonic over the whole of both upper and lower surfaces, and both the upper and lower shock waves will have reached the trailing edge. At a speed just above Mach 1·0 the other shockwave previously described and illustrated in Fig 13.3a, the bow wave, forms ahead of the leading edge.

The bow shock wave is initially separated (detached) from the leading edge by the build up of compressed air at the leading edge, but as speed increases it moves closer to the leading edge. For a sharp leading edge the shock eventually becomes attached to the leading edge. The Mach number at which this occurs depends upon the leading edge angle. For a sharp leading edge with a small leading edge angle the bow wave will attach at a lower Mach number than one with a larger leading edge angle.

Fig. 13.7 overleaf, shows the development of shockwaves on an aerofoil section at a small constant angle of attack as the airspeed is increased from subsonic to supersonic.

> A shockwave forms at the rear of an area of supersonic flow

> At M_{CRIT} there is no shockwave because there is no supersonic flow

13.11 PRESSURE DISTRIBUTION AT TRANSONIC MACH NUMBERS

Refer to Fig 13.7. The solid blue line represents upper surface pressure and the dashed blue line the lower surface. Decreased pressure is indicated upwards. The difference between the full line and the dashed line shows the effectiveness of lift production; if the dashed line is above the full line the lift is negative in that area. Lift is represented by the area between the lines, and the Centre of Pressure (CP) by the centre of the area.

During acceleration to supersonic flight, the pressure distribution is irregular.

M 0·75 the subsonic picture. Separation has started near the trailing edge and there is practically no net lift over the rear third of the aerofoil section; the CP is well forward. Fig. 13.6 shows that C_L is quite good and is rising steadily; C_D, on the other hand, is beginning to rise.

M 0·81 A shock wave has appeared on the top surface; notice the sudden increase of pressure (shown by the falling line) caused by decreasing flow speed at the shock wave. The CP has moved back a little, but the area is still large. Fig. 13.6 shows that lift is good, but drag is now rising rapidly.

M 0·89 The pressure distribution shows very clearly why there is a sudden drop in lift coefficient before the aerofoil as a whole reaches the speed of sound; on the rear portion of the aerofoil the lift is negative because the suction on the top surface has been spoilt by the shock wave, while there is still quite good suction and high-speed flow on the lower surface. On the front portion there is nearly as much suction on the lower surface as on the upper. The CP has now moved well forward again. Fig. 13.6 shows that drag is still increasing rapidly.

M 0·98 This shows the important results of the shock waves moving to the trailing edge, and no longer spoiling the suction or causing separation. The speed of the flow over the surfaces is nearly all supersonic, the CP has moved aft again, and owing to the good suction over nearly all the top surface, with rather less on the bottom, the lift coefficient has actually increased. The drag coefficient is just about at its maximum, as shown Fig. 13.6.

M 1·4 The aerofoil is through the transonic region. The bow wave has appeared. The lift coefficient has fallen again because the pressure on both surfaces are nearly the same; and for the first time since the critical Mach number, the drag coefficient has fallen considerably.

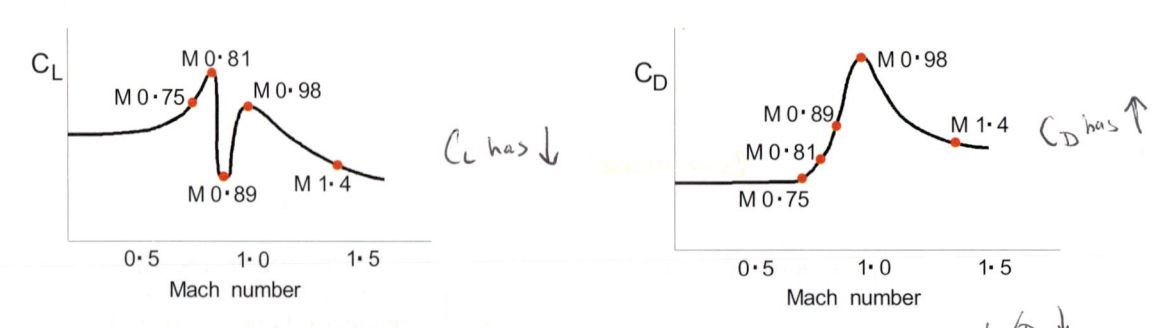

Figure 13.6 Changes in Lift and Drag in the transonic region

PRINCIPLES OF FLIGHT   **HIGH SPEED FLIGHT**

Top surface pressure (solid line)
bottom surface (dashed line)

M 0.75 — CP

M 0.81 — CP — Normal SW

M_N (speed)

M 0.89 — CP — Normal SW's

M 0.98 — CP — Oblique Shockwaves

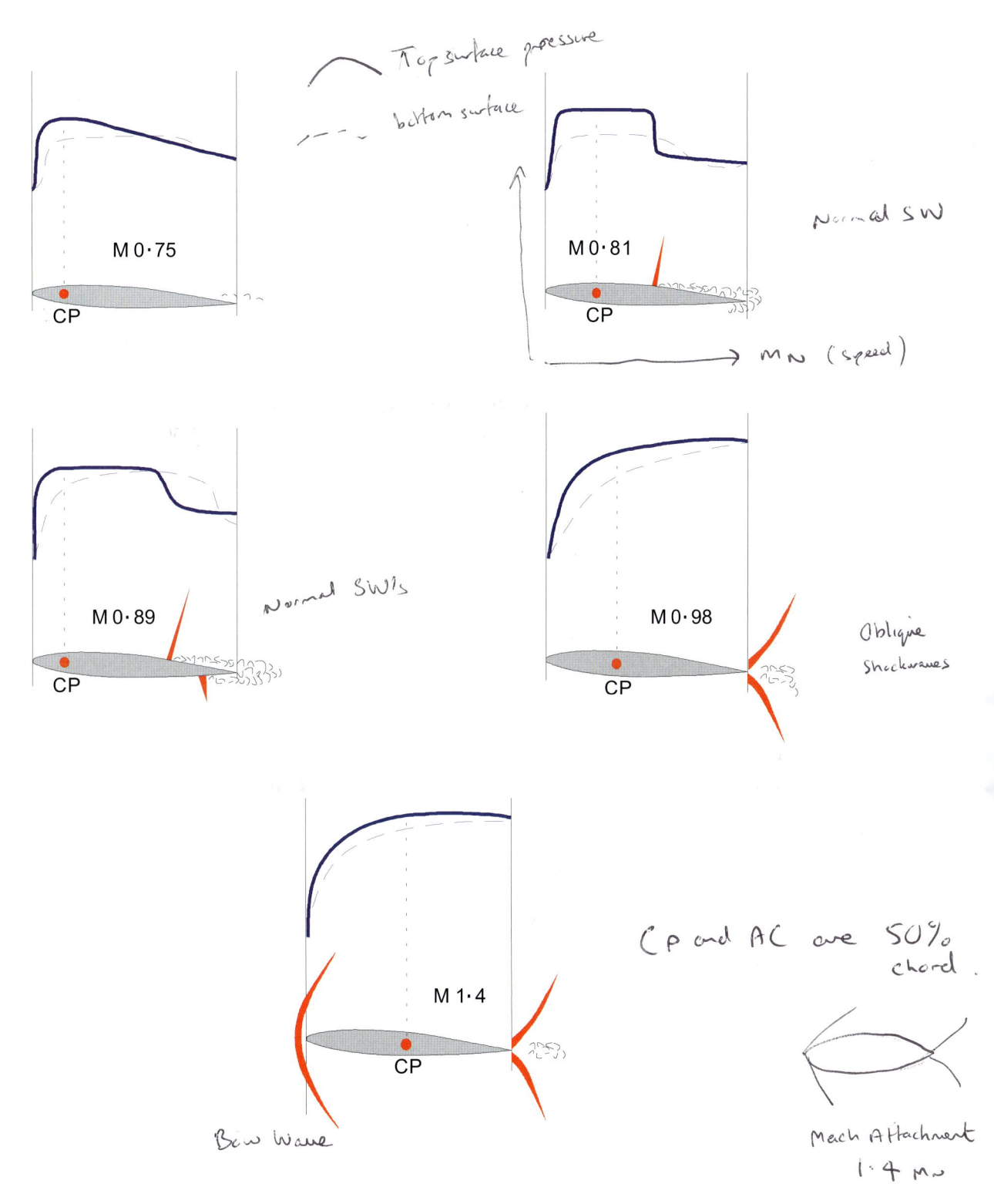

M 1.4 — CP — Bow Wave

CP and AC are 50% chord.

Mach Attachment 1.4 Mn

Figure 13.7 Pressure distribution in the transonic region

Rectangular distribution of pressure.

Oblique shockwave has most total energy. Normal shockwave has most strength.

PRINCIPLES OF FLIGHT   **HIGH SPEED FLIGHT**

13.12 PROPERTIES OF A NORMAL SHOCKWAVE

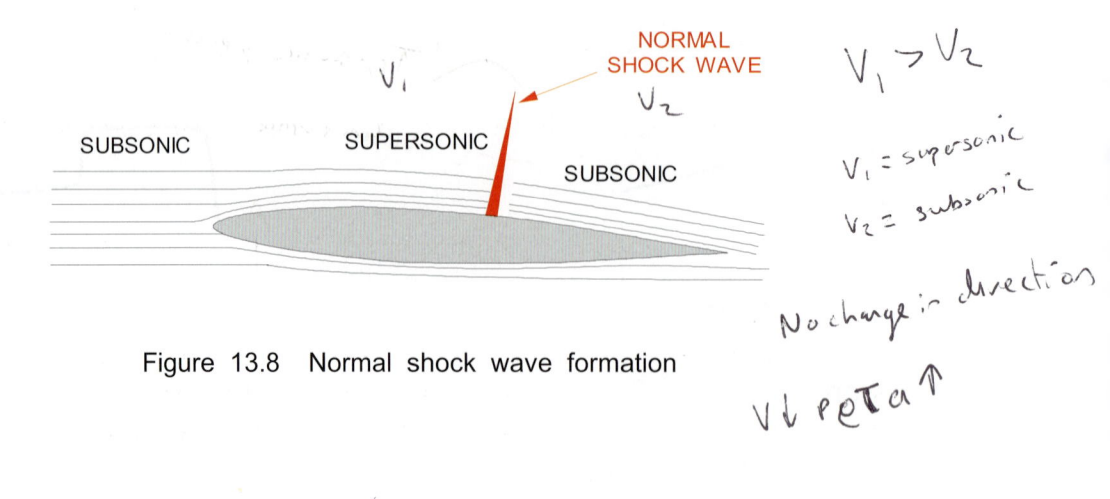

Figure 13.8 Normal shock wave formation

Figure 13.9 Normal and oblique shock waves

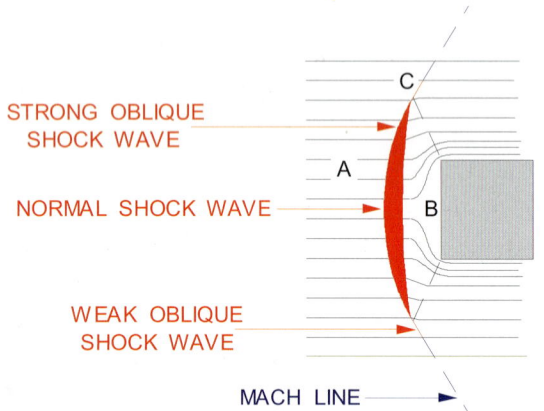

When a shock wave is perpendicular (normal) to the upstream flow, streamlines pass through the shock wave with no change of direction. A supersonic airstream passing through a normal shock wave will also experience the following changes:-

1. The airstream is slowed to subsonic; the local Mach number behind the wave is approximately equal to the reciprocal of the Mach number ahead of the wave e.g., if the Mach number ahead of the wave is 1·25, the Mach number of the flow behind the wave will be approximately 0·80. (The greater the Mach number above M 1·0 ahead of the wave, the greater the reduction in velocity).

2. static pressure increases

3. temperature increases

4. density increases

5. The energy of the airstream [total pressure (dynamic plus static)] is greatly reduced.

Minimum energy loss through a normal shock wave will occur when the Mach number of the airflow in front of the shock wave is small, but supersonic.

PRINCIPLES OF FLIGHT   **HIGH SPEED FLIGHT**

13.13 OBLIQUE SHOCK WAVES

An oblique shock wave is a slightly different type of shock wave.

Referring to Fig. 13.9, at 'A' the air is travelling at supersonic speed, completely unaware of the approaching object.

The air at 'B' has piled up and is subsonic, trying to slip around the front of the object and merge with the airflow.

Through the shock wave supersonic air from 'A' slows immediately, increasing in pressure and density as it does so. As previously pointed out, a rise in temperature also occurs. The centre part of the shock wave, lying perpendicular or normal to the direction of the airstream, is the strong normal shock wave.

Notice that 'above' and 'below' the normal shock wave, the shock wave is no longer perpendicular to the upstream flow, but is at an oblique angle; the airstream strikes the oblique shock wave and is deflected.

Like the normal shock wave, the oblique shock wave in this region is strong. The airflow will be slowed down; the velocity and Mach number of the airflow behind the wave are reduced, but the flow is still supersonic. The primary difference is that the airstream passing though the oblique shock wave changes direction. (The component of airstream velocity normal to the shockwave will always be subsonic downstream, otherwise no shock wave).

The black dashed lines in Fig. 13.9 outline the area of subsonic flow created behind the strong shock wave.

Particles passing through the wave at 'C' do not slow to subsonic speed. They decrease somewhat in speed and emerge at a slower but still supersonic velocity. At 'C' the shock wave is a weak oblique shock wave. Further out from this point the effects of the shock wave decrease until the air is able to pass the object without being affected. Thus the effects of the shock wave disappears, and the line cannot be properly called a shock wave at all; it is called a 'Mach line'.

SHOCK WAVE SUMMARY

1. The change from supersonic to subsonic flow is always sudden and accompanied by rapid and large increases in pressure, temperature and density across the shock wave that is formed. A normal shock wave marks the change from supersonic to subsonic flow.

2. If the shockwave is oblique, that is, at an angle to the upstream flow, the airflow is deflected as it passes through the shock, and may remain supersonic downstream of the shock wave. However the component of velocity normal to the shockwave will always be subsonic downstream of the shock.

13.14 EFFECTS OF SHOCKWAVE FORMATION

The formation and development of shockwaves on the wing have effects on lift, drag, stability and control. Many of these effects are caused by shock induced separation. As the air flows through the shock wave the sudden rise in pressure causes the boundary layer to thicken and often to separate. This increases the depth of the turbulent wake behind the wing.

EFFECT OF SHOCK WAVES ON LIFT

At low subsonic speeds the lift coefficient C_L is assumed to be constant at a given angle of attack. With increasing Mach number however, it will vary as shown in Figure 13.10.

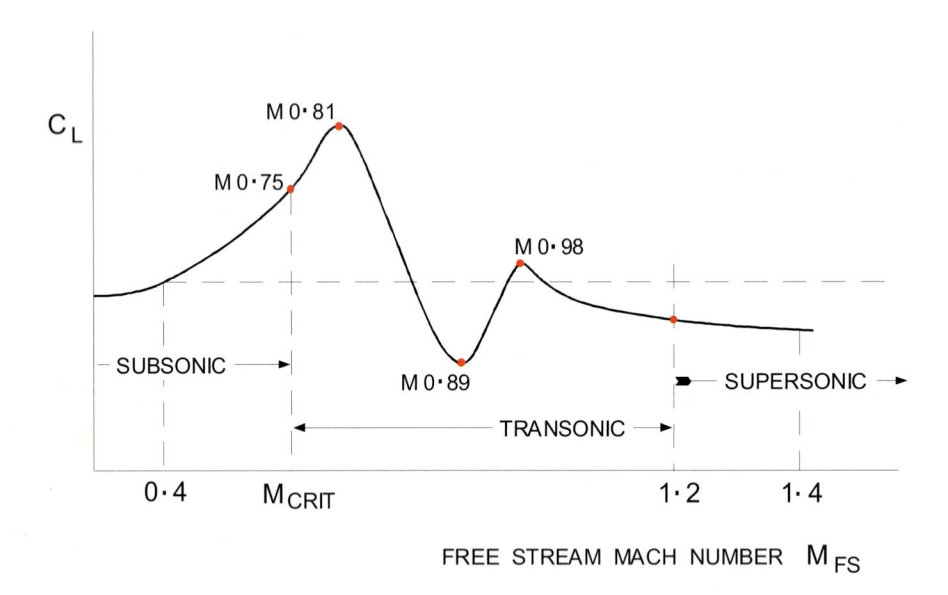

Figure 13.10   Variation of CL with Mach number at constant α

At high subsonic speed C_L increases. This is the result of the changing pattern of streamlines. At low speeds the streamlines begin to diverge well ahead of the aerofoil, Fig. 13.3 and 13.11. At high subsonic speeds they do not begin to deflect until closer to the leading edge, **causing greater acceleration** and pressure drop around the leading edge. It will be remembered from Chapter 7 that this phenomena causes the stall speed to increase at high altitudes. See also paragraph 13.16.

PRINCIPLES OF FLIGHT   **HIGH SPEED FLIGHT**

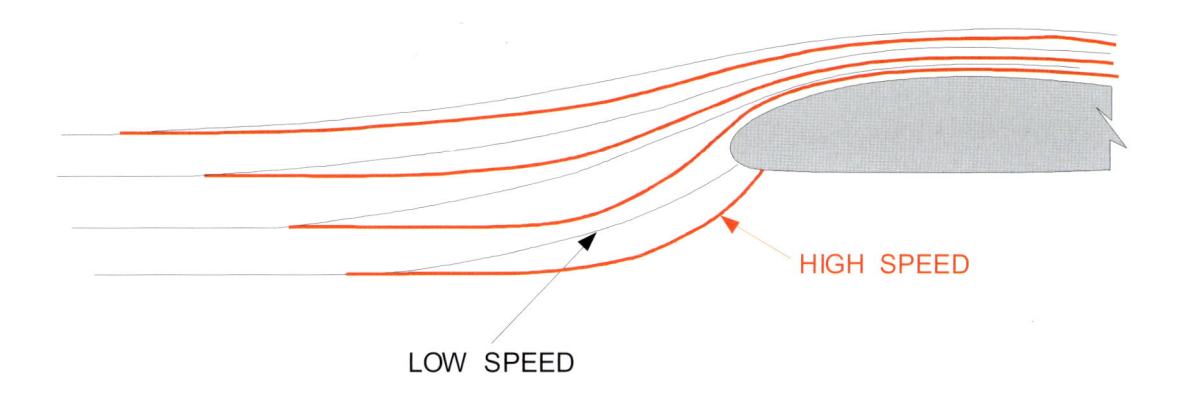

Figure 13.11   Streamlines at low and high subsonic speeds

At speeds above M_{CRIT} a shockwave will have formed on the upper surface. This may cause boundary layer separation aft of the shock wave, causing loss of lift (above M 0·81, as shown in Figs. 13.7 and 13.10).

Figure 13.12   Shock stall

SHOCK INDUCED SEPARATION

HIGH SPEED BUFFET

This is known as the **shock stall** because it results from a separated boundary layer just as the low speed stall does. The severity of the loss of lift depends on the shape of the wing sections. Wings not designed for high speeds may have a severe loss of lift at speeds above M_{CRIT} (Fig. 13.10), but wings designed specifically for high speed flight, with sweep back, thinner sections and less camber will have much less variation of lift through the transonic region.

Separated airflow caused by a shock stall can cause severe damage to the airframe, particularly the empennage. This will be fully discussed in paragraph 13.15.

The lower end of the transonic region is where most modern high speed jet transport aircraft operate and a small shock wave will exist on the top surface of the wing in the cruise.

PRINCIPLES OF FLIGHT HIGH SPEED FLIGHT

EFFECT OF SHOCK WAVES ON LIFT CURVE SLOPE AND $C_{L\,MAX}$

At a constant angle of attack, the increase of C_L as speed increases from about M 0·4 into the low end of the transonic region gives a steeper lift curve slope, i.e. the change of C_L per degree angle of attack will increase. However, because of earlier separation resulting from the formation of the shock wave, C_{LMAX} and the stalling angle will be reduced. Figures.13.13 and 13.14 illustrate these changes.

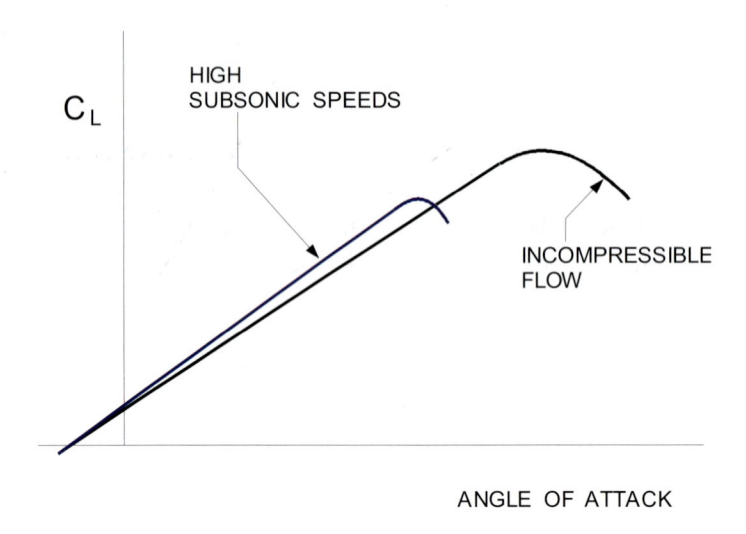

Figure 13.13 Effect of Mach number on Lift curve

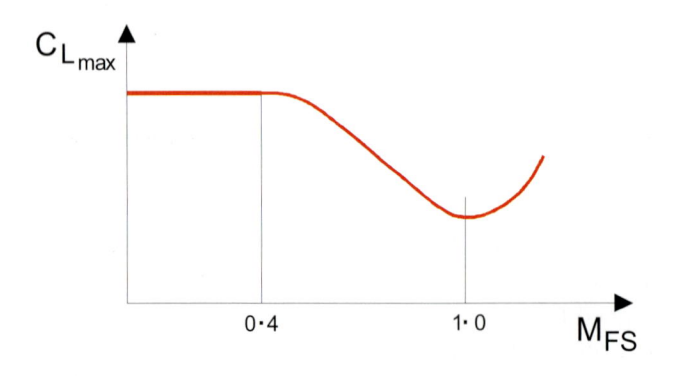

Figure 13.14 Effect of Mach number on $C_{L\,MAX}$

PRINCIPLES OF FLIGHT **HIGH SPEED FLIGHT**

EFFECT OF SHOCK WAVES ON DRAG

As speed increases above M_{CRIT} shock waves begin to form and drag increases more rapidly than it would have done without the shock waves. The additional drag is called wave drag, and is due to energy drag and boundary layer separation.

Energy Drag: Energy drag stems from the irreversible nature of the changes which occur as an airflow crosses a shock wave. Energy has to be used to provide the temperature rise across the shock wave and this energy loss is drag on the aircraft. The more oblique the shock waves are, the less energy they absorb, but because they become more extensive laterally and affect more air, the energy drag rises progressively as M_{FS} increases.

Boundary Layer Separation: In certain stages of shock wave movement there is a considerable flow separation, as shown in Figs. 13.7 and 13.12. This turbulence represents energy lost to the flow and contributes to the drag. As M_{FS} increases through the transonic range the shock waves move to the trailing edge and the separation decreases; hence the drag coefficient decreases.

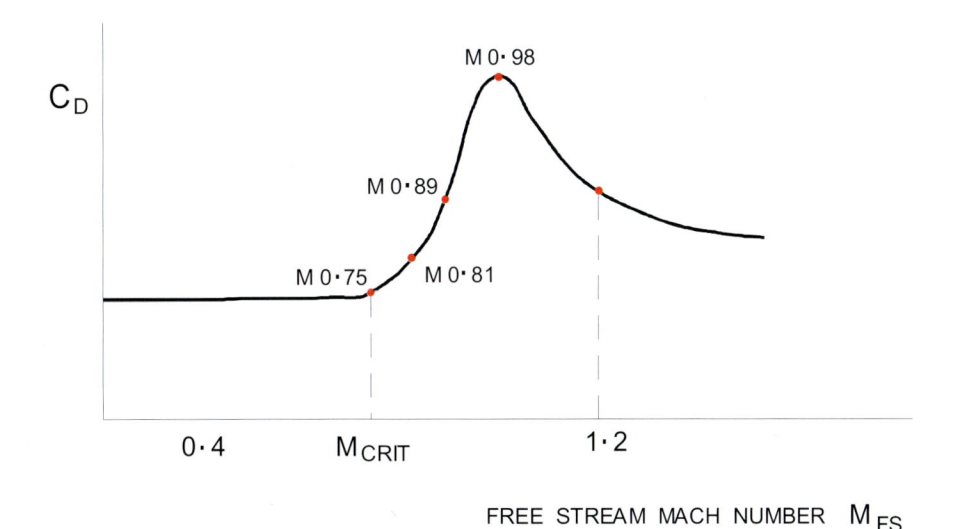

Figure 13.15 Variation of CD with Mach number

The change in drag characteristics is shown by the C_D curve for a basic section at a constant angle of attack in Fig. 13.15. The 'hump' in the curve from M 0·89 to M 1·2 is caused by:

a) The drag directly associated with the trailing edge shock waves (energy loss).

b) Separation of the boundary layer.

c) The formation of the bow shock wave above M 1·0.

PRINCIPLES OF FLIGHT **HIGH SPEED FLIGHT**

EFFECT OF SHOCK WAVES ON THE C_L / C_D DRAG POLAR CURVE

Although the curve of C_L / C_D is unique at low speeds, at transonic speeds when compressibility becomes significant, the curve will change. Figure 13.16 shows the variation of C_L / C_D with Mach number. The point at which the tangent from the origin touches the curve corresponds to the maximum C_L / C_D or maximum L / D. In the transonic region, the L/D ratio is reduced.

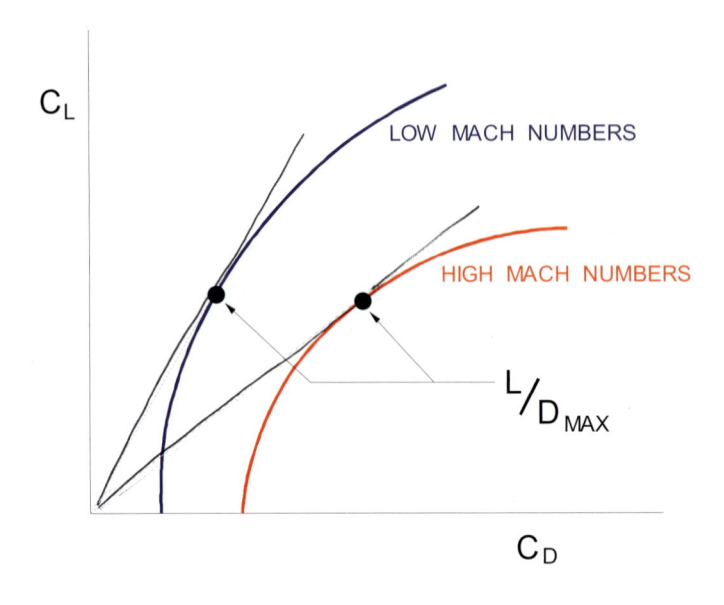

Figure 13.16   Effect of Mach number on C_L/C_D polar

EFFECT OF SHOCK WAVES ON THE CENTRE OF PRESSURE

The centre of pressure of an aerofoil is determined by the pressure distribution around it. As the speed increases through the transonic region, the pressure distribution changes and the centre of pressure will move. It was shown in Fig 13.7 that above M_{CRIT} the upper surface pressure continues to drop on the wing until the shock wave is reached. This means that a greater proportion of the "suction" pressure will comes from the rear of the wing, and the centre of pressure is further aft. The rearward movement of the CP however is irregular, as the pressure distribution on the lower surface also changes. The shockwave on the lower surface usually forms at a higher free stream Mach number than the upper surface shock, but reaches the trailing edge first. The overall effect on the CP is shown in Figure 13.17. **As the aircraft accelerates to supersonic speed the overall movement of the CP is aft to the 50% chord position.**

PRINCIPLES OF FLIGHT — HIGH SPEED FLIGHT

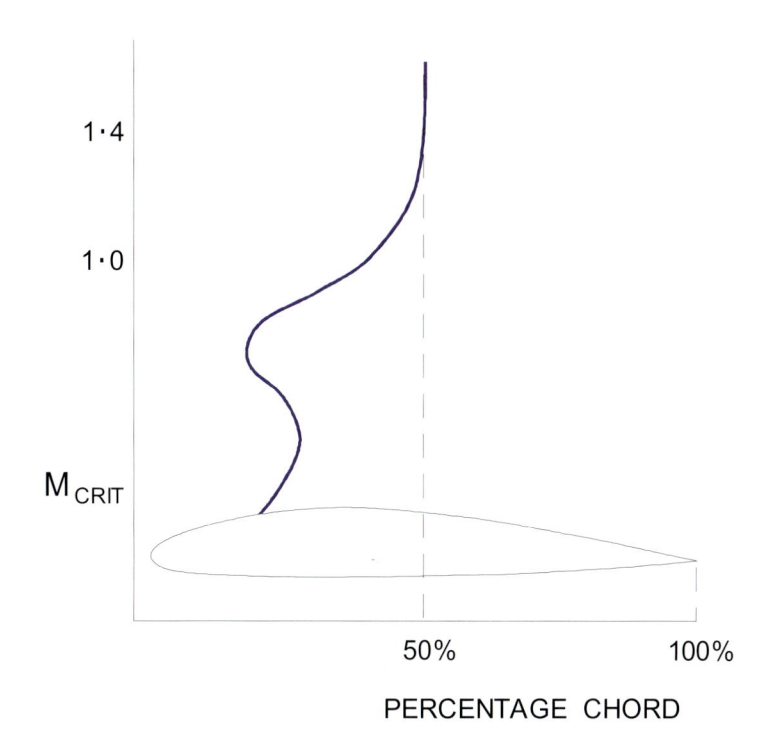

Figure 13.17   CP movement in the transonic region

The wing root usually has a thicker section than the wing tip so will have a lower M_{CRIT} and shock induced separation will occur at the root first. The CP will move towards the tip, and if the wing is swept, this CP movement will also be rearward. This effect will be discussed in detail later.

Official US Navy Photograph

Low pressure area in front of shock wave

PRINCIPLES OF FLIGHT — HIGH SPEED FLIGHT

EFFECT OF SHOCK WAVES ON CP MOVEMENT

Rearward CP movement with increasing Mach number in the transonic region produces a nose down pitching moment. This is known as "Mach Tuck", "High Speed Tuck" or "Tuck under".

A further factor contributing to the nose down pitching moment is decreased downwash at the tail resulting from reduced lift at the wing root. If the tailplane is situated in the downwash, its effective angle of attack is increased, giving an increase in the nose down pitching moment.

For a stable aircraft a push force is required on the stick to produce an increase in speed, but as a result of Mach tuck the push force required may decease with speed above M_{CRIT} giving an unstable stick force gradient, Fig. 13.18.

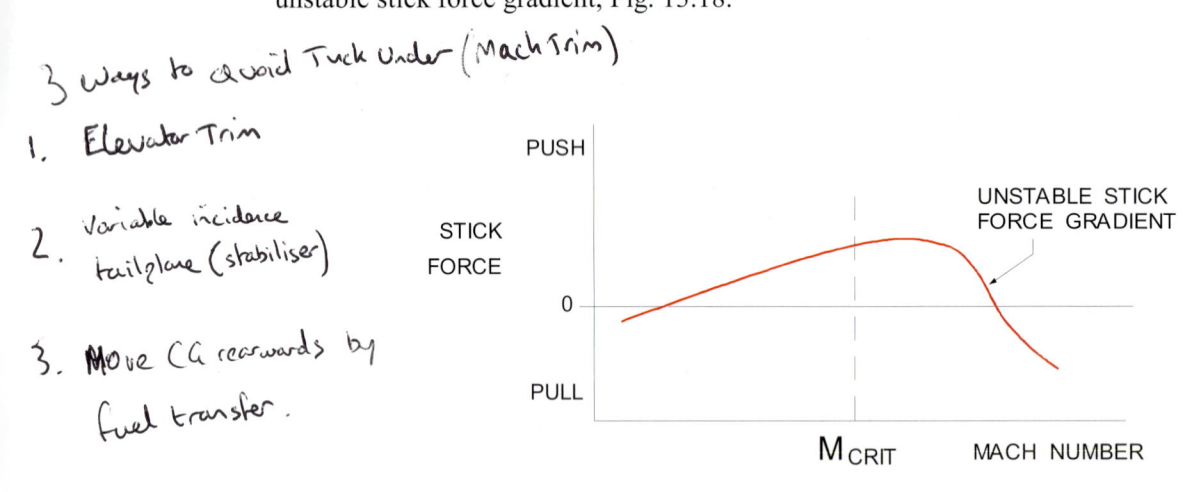

[Handwritten notes: 3 Ways to avoid Tuck Under (Mach Trim)
1. Elevator Trim
2. Variable incidence tailplane (stabiliser)
3. Move CG rearwards by fuel transfer.]

Figure 13.18 Reduction in stick force with increasing Mach number

THE EFFECT OF SHOCK WAVES ON FLYING CONTROLS

A conventional trailing edge control surface works by changing the camber of the aerofoil to increase or decrease its lift. **Deflecting a control surface down will reduce M_{CRIT}.** If the control is moved down at high subsonic speed and a shock wave forms on the aerofoil ahead of the control surface, shock induced separation could occur ahead of the control, reducing its effectiveness. At low speed, movement of a control surface modifies the pressure distribution over the whole aerofoil. If there is a shock wave ahead of the control surface, **movement of the control cannot affect any part of the aerofoil ahead of the shock wave**, and this will also reduce control effectiveness.

Conventional trailing edge control surfaces may suffer from greatly reduced effectiveness in the transonic speed region and may not be adequate to control the changes of moment affecting the aircraft at these speeds. This can be overcome by incorporating some or all of the following into the design: an all moving (slab) tailplane (Fig. 11.2), roll control spoilers (Para. 11.17(c)), making the artificial feel unit in a powered flying control system sensitive to Mach number or by fitting vortex generators (Page 13-31).

PRINCIPLES OF FLIGHT — HIGH SPEED FLIGHT

CONTROL BUZZ

If a shock wave is situated near to a control hinge a control movement may cause the shock wave to move over the hinge, resulting in rapid changes of hinge moment which can set up an oscillation of the control surface called control buzz.

Returning flutter at higher frequency.

13.15 BUFFET

In the same way that separated airflow prior to a low speed stall can cause airframe buffet, shock induced separation (shock stall) at high speed can also cause buffeting.

Aerodynamic buffet is a valuable stall warning, but can damage the aircraft structure. Because of the higher dynamic pressure when an aircraft is operating in the transonic speed region, any shock induced buffet will have a greater potential for severe airframe damage. High speed buffet must be completely avoided.

The aircraft must therefore be operated in such a manner that a (safety) margin exists before aerodynamic buffet will occur.

If the variables which affect both high speed and low speed stall are considered it will be possible to identify the conditions under which buffeting will occur and a chart can be drawn to show all the factors involved. This is called a "Buffet Onset" chart (illustrated in Fig. 13.24) which is used by flight crews to ensure their aircraft is operated at all times with a specified minimum buffet margin.

In Chapter 7 it was shown that stall speed is affected by **several factors**. In this study of low speed stall combined with high speed buffet, the factors to be considered are:-

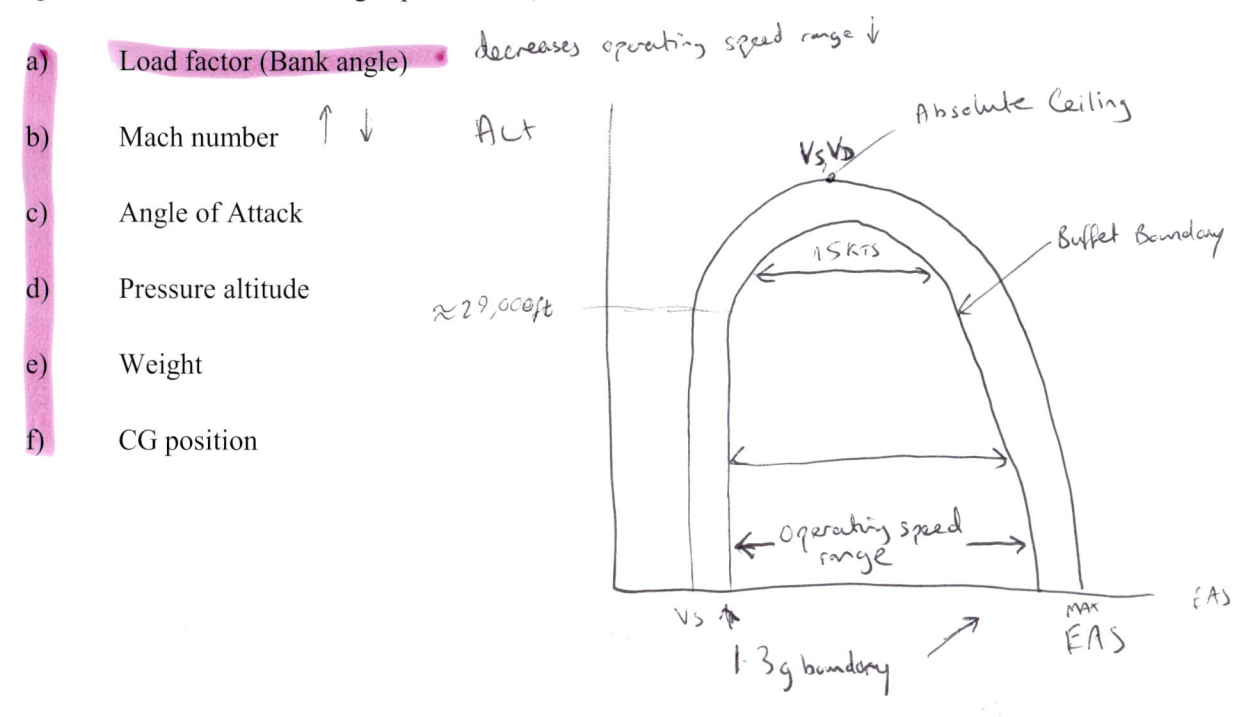

a) **Load factor (Bank angle)** — *decreases operating speed range ↓*
b) Mach number ↑↓   *Alt*
c) Angle of Attack
d) Pressure altitude   *≈ 29,000 ft*
e) Weight
f) CG position

Absolute Ceiling
V_S, V_D
15 KTS
Buffet Boundary
Operating speed range
V_S ↑
1.3g boundary
MAX EAS
EAS

13 - 21

PRINCIPLES OF FLIGHT — HIGH SPEED FLIGHT

13.16 FACTORS WHICH AFFECT THE BUFFET BOUNDARIES

STALL SPEED

As altitude is increased at a constant EAS, TAS will increase and outside air temperature will decrease, causing the local speed of sound to decrease. Mach number is proportional to TAS and inversely proportional to the local speed of sound (a):

$$M = \frac{TAS}{a}$$

Therefore, if altitude is increased at a constant EAS, Mach number will increase. At low speed C_{Lmax} is fairly constant, but above M 0·4 C_{Lmax} decreases as shown in Fig. 13.19. Refer also to Fig. 13.11 for the reason why $C_{L\,MAX}$ starts to decreases at speeds above M 04.

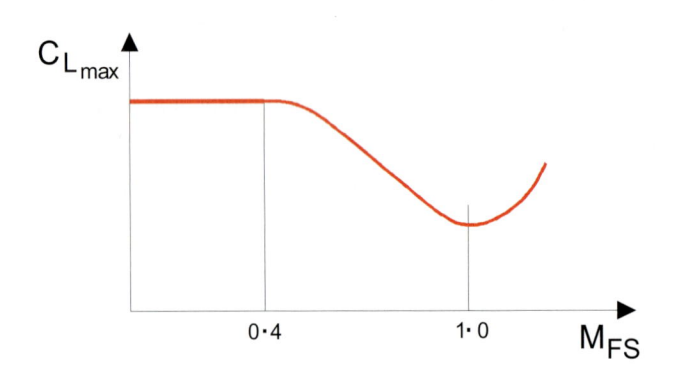

Figure 13.19

From the 1g stall speed formula:

$$V_{S1g} = \sqrt{\frac{L}{\frac{1}{2}\rho\, C_{LMAX}\, S}}$$

It can be seen that as C_{Lmax} decreases with increasing altitude, the 1g stall speed will increase.

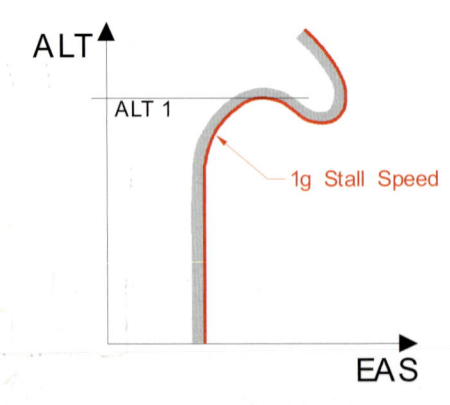

Figure 13.20

PRINCIPLES OF FLIGHT
HIGH SPEED FLIGHT

Fig. 13.20 shows the variation with altitude of stalling speed at constant load factor (n). Such a curve is called the stall boundary for the given load factor, in which altitude is plotted against equivalent airspeed. At this load factor (1g), the aircraft cannot fly at speeds to the left of this boundary. It is clear that over the lower range of altitude, stall speed does not vary with altitude. This is because at these low altitudes, V_S is too low for compressibility effects to be present. Eventually, V_S has increased with altitude to such an extent that these effects are important, and the rise in stalling speed with altitude is apparent.

As altitude increases, stall speed is initially constant then increases.

An altitude (Alt_1 in Fig. 13.20) is eventually reached when there is only one speed at which the aircraft can fly, since increasing or decreasing speed or banking the aircraft will result in a stall. In the case of a 1 g manoeuvre, this altitude is called the 'Aerodynamic Ceiling'. If the aircraft were allowed to 'drift up' to this altitude, the aircraft will stall. Not a pleasant prospect for a modern high speed jet transport aircraft. **This state of difficulty is also called 'coffin corner'.** Refer also to Fig. 13.23.

NB: The recovery in $C_{L\,MAX}$ at supersonic speeds is such that it may still be possible to operate above this ceiling if enough thrust is available to accelerate the aircraft to supersonic speeds at this altitude.

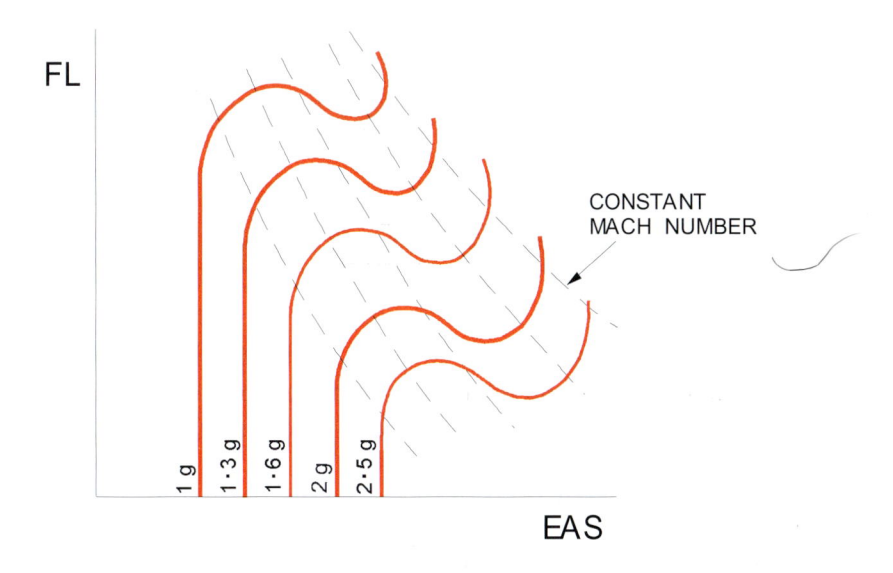

Figure 13.21

LOAD FACTOR

Because load factor increases the stall speed, curves like the one sketched in Fig. 13.20 can be drawn for all values of load factor up to the maximum permissible 'g', and together they constitute the set of stalling boundaries for the given aircraft. Such a set of curves is shown in Fig. 13.21. Superimposed on these curves are dashed lines representing lines of constant Mach number, showing how high Mach number is achieved even at relatively low EAS at high altitudes.

Stall boundaries set a lower limit to the operating speed, according to the load factor. In the case of a high-speed aircraft, there is also an upper limit which is due to the approach of shock stall and the associated buffet which occurs if the aircraft enters the transonic speed range. The limits associated with these effects give the buffet boundaries.

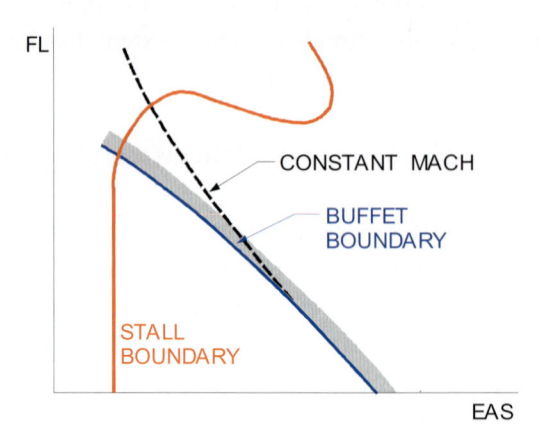

Figure 13.22

MACH NUMBER

For a given aircraft there is a Mach number which, even at low angle of attack, cannot be exceeded because of the onset of shock stall. Fig. 13.21 shows the EAS corresponding to this Mach number falling as altitude increases, so the range of operating speeds is reduced at both ends.

ANGLE OF ATTACK

However, there is a further effect which makes the buffet boundary a more severe limit than that suggested by a curve of constant Mach number. As the EAS associated with a given Mach number falls with increased altitude, so the required C_L, and hence angle of attack increases. This results in a reduction in the Mach number at which buffeting occurs, which results in a further reduction in the permissible airspeed. This effect is made worse as the high angle of attack stall is approached, and by the time the buffet boundary intersects the stall boundary the limiting Mach number may be well below its value at a lower angle of attack, as Fig. 13.22 illustrates.

Also an increase in load factor (bank angle) requires an increase in lift at a given EAS, hence an increase in angle of attack and a further reduction in limiting Mach number.

Thus the greater the load factor (bank angle or gust), the more severe the limitation due to buffeting.

There is a set of buffet boundaries for various load factors (bank angles), just as there is a set of stall boundaries.

The restrictions on speed and 'g' can be summarised in the form of a single diagram in which load factor is plotted against EAS, shown in Fig. 13.23.

PRINCIPLES OF FLIGHT   **HIGH SPEED FLIGHT**

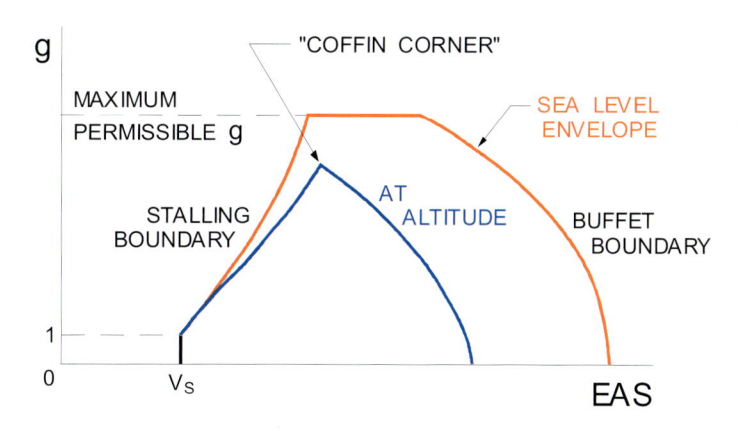

Figure 13.23

PRESSURE ALTITUDE

At sea level there is a stall speed below which the aircraft cannot fly. As load factor increases, so does the stall speed (proportional to the square root of the load factor). The curve of 'g' against EAS modifies the low speed stall boundary. It will continue to rise until the 'limit load factor' is reached (Chapt. 14). The 'limit load factor' must never be exceeded. At the high speed end, when g = 1, there is a limiting speed which must not be exceeded because of shock induced buffet. As the load factor increases, so does the C_L at given speed, and the limiting Mach number falls, slowly at first and then more rapidly. This defines a buffet boundary, which eventually intersects the boundary of maximum permissible 'g', to constitute an overall envelope like the outer curve depicted in Fig. 13.23. Thus the aircraft may operate at any combination of speed and load factor within this envelope, but not outside it.

At altitude the situation is similar. However, at altitude the equivalent stalling speed increases with 'g' rather more rapidly than at sea level, because of the Mach number effect on $C_{L\,MAX}$. Also, the buffet boundary becomes much more severe.

Above a certain altitude the buffet boundary may intersect the stall boundary at a value of 'g' lower than the structural limit, as shown in Fig. 13.23. This 'point' is another representation of "coffin corner".

WEIGHT

The weight of the aircraft also affects the envelope. An increase in weight results in an increase in stall speed, and the stall boundary is moved to the right. It also results in an increase in angle of attack at any given speed, so that the Mach number at which buffeting occurs is reduced, and the buffet boundary is moved to the left. Finally, increase in weight implies a reduction in the maximum permissible 'g'. Thus all the boundaries are made more restrictive by an increase in weight.

CG POSITION

Forward movement of the CG increases stall speed so the buffet boundaries will be affected in a similar way to that due to weight increase.

PRINCIPLES OF FLIGHT   HIGH SPEED FLIGHT

13.17 THE BUFFET MARGIN

It has been stated that an altitude can eventually be reached where there is only one speed at which the aircraft can fly. In the case of a 1 g manoeuvre, this altitude is called the 'Aerodynamic Ceiling'. Operating an aircraft at its aerodynamic ceiling would leave no safety margin. In 1 g flight the aircraft would be constantly on the point of stall. It could not be manoeuvred nor experience the smallest gust without stalling. Regulations require an aircraft to be operated with a minimum buffet margin of 0·3 g.

13.18 USE OF THE BUFFET ONSET CHART (Fig. 13.24)

1·3 g Altitude (1 g + 0·3 g = 1·3 g): At this altitude a 'g' increment of 0·3 can be sustained without buffet occurring. Using the data supplied:-

Follow the vertical solid red line upwards from 1·3 g to the 110 tons line, then horizontally to the 30% CG vertical line, then parallel to the CG reference line, again horizontally to the M 0·8 vertical line. The altitude curve must now be 'parallelled' to read-off the Flight Level of 405. The 1·3 g altitude is 40,500 ft.

If the aircraft is operated above FL 405 at this mass and CG a gust, or bank angle of less than 40°, could cause the aircraft to buffet. (40° of bank at high altitude is excessive, a normal operational maximum at high altitude would be 10° to 15°).

Buffet restricted speed limits: Using the data supplied:-

Follow the vertical dashed red line upwards from 1 g to the 110 tons line, then horizontally to the 30% CG vertical line, then parallel to the CG reference line. Observe the FL 350 curve. The curve does not reach the horizontal dashed red line at the high speed end because M 0·84 (M_{MO}) is the maximum operating speed limit. At the low speed end of the dashed red line, the FL 350 curve is intersected at M 0·555. Thus under the stated conditions, the low speed buffet restriction is M 0·555 and there is no high speed buffet restriction because M_{MO} is the maximum operating Mach number which may not be exceeded under any circumstances.

Aerodynamic ceiling: at 150 tons can be determined by:-

Following the vertical dashed red line from 1 g to the 150 tons line, then following the solid red line horizontally to M 0·8 (via the CG correction). The altitude curve gives an aerodynamic ceiling of FL 390.

Load factor and bank angle at which buffet occurs: Using the data supplied:-

From M 0·8, follow the dashed blue line to obtain 54° bank angle or 1·7 g.

PRINCIPLES OF FLIGHT **HIGH SPEED FLIGHT**

BUFFET ONSET
clean configuration

Aerodynamic Ceiling

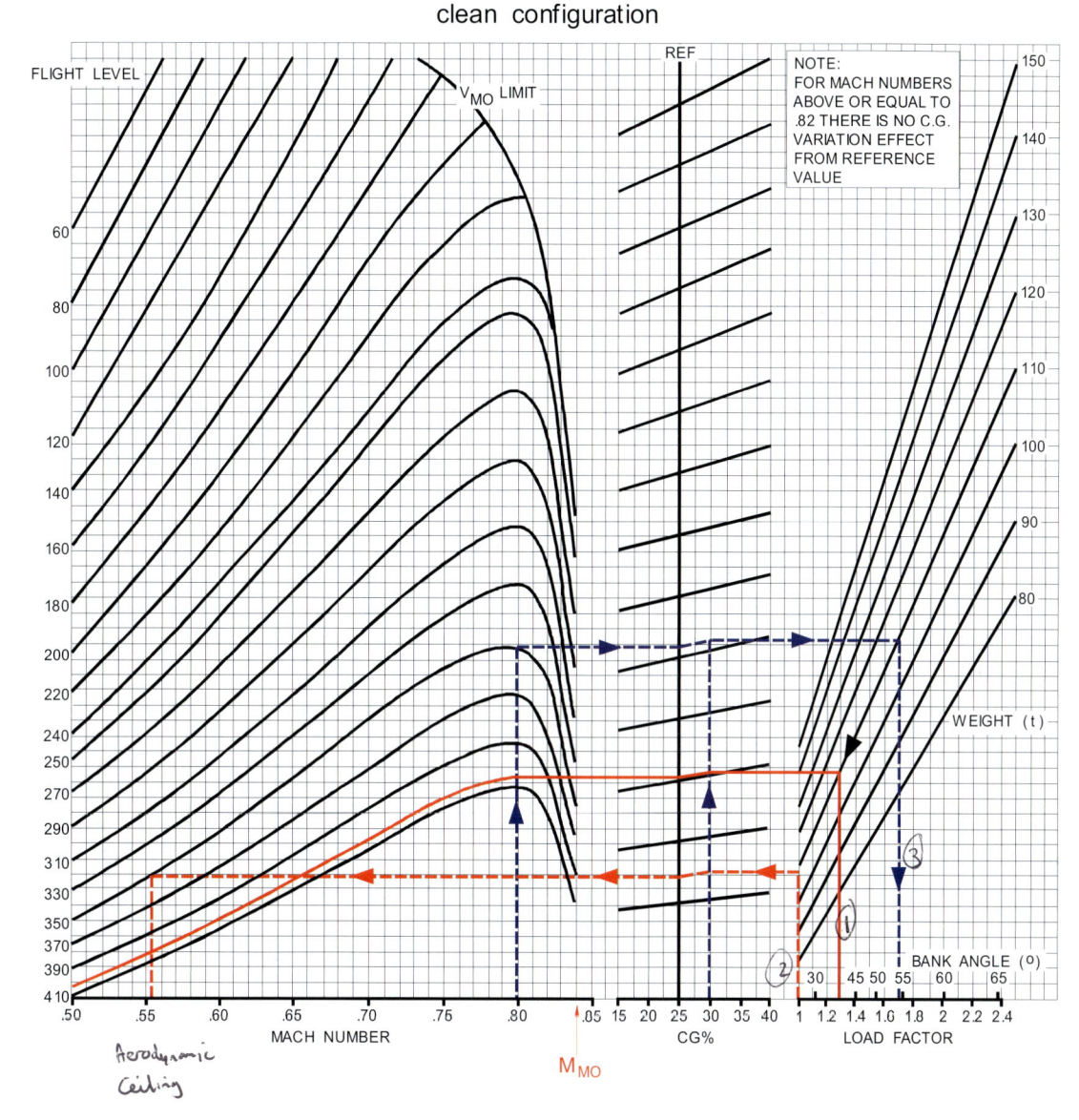

DATA : M = .80
FL = 350
WEIGHT = 110 tons
CG = 30 %

RESULTS : BUFFET ONSET AT :

M = 0.80 WITH 54° BANK ANGLE, OR AT 1.7 g
LOW SPEED (1 g) : M = 0.555
HIGH SPEED : ABOVE M 0.84 (M_{MO})

1.3 g ALTITUDE = FL 405

Figure 13.24 Example of a buffet onset chart

2) Low speed buffet occurs at M 0.555 and below

3) Buffet will occur if AofB exceeds 54° or if you exceed 1.7g.

PRINCIPLES OF FLIGHT   **HIGH SPEED FLIGHT**

13.19 DELAYING OR REDUCING THE EFFECTS OF COMPRESSIBILITY

To maximise revenue, airlines require their aircraft to fly as fast and as efficiently as possible. It has been shown that the formation of shock waves on the wing results in many undesirable characteristics and a massive increase in drag. Up to speeds in the region of M_{CRIT} the effects of compressibility are not too serious. It is therefore necessary to increase M_{CRIT} as much as possible. Many methods have been adopted to delay or reduce the effects of compressibility to a higher Mach number, as detailed below.

THIN WING SECTIONS

On a low t/c ratio wing, the flow acceleration is reduced, thus raising the value of M_{CRIT}. For example if M_{CRIT} for a 15% t/c wing is M 0·75, then M_{CRIT} for a 5% t/c wing will be approximately M 0·85.

The use of a low t/c ratio wing section has some disadvantages:

a)   The lift produced by a thin wing will be less, giving higher take-off and landing speeds and increased distances.

b)   A thin wing requires disproportionally wider main spars for the same strength and stiffness. This increases structural weight.

c)   Limited stowage space is available in a thin wing for:

         i)   fuel

         ii)   high lift devices and their actuating mechanism and

         iii)   the main undercarriage and its actuating mechanism.

SWEEPBACK (see Page 13-43 for Sweepback Fact Sheet)

One of the most commonly used methods of increasing M_{CRIT} is to sweep the wing back. Forward sweep gives a similarly effect but wing bending and twisting creates such a problem that sweep back is more practical for ordinary applications.

A simplified method of visualising the effect of sweepback is shown in Fig. 13.25. The swept wing shown has the free stream velocity broken down to a component of velocity perpendicular to the leading edge and a component parallel to the leading edge.

The component of velocity perpendicular to the leading edge is less than the free stream velocity (by the cosine of the sweep angle) and it is this velocity component which determines the magnitude of the pressure distribution. M_{CRIT} will increase since the velocity component affecting the pressure distribution is less than the free stream velocity.

PRINCIPLES OF FLIGHT HIGH SPEED FLIGHT

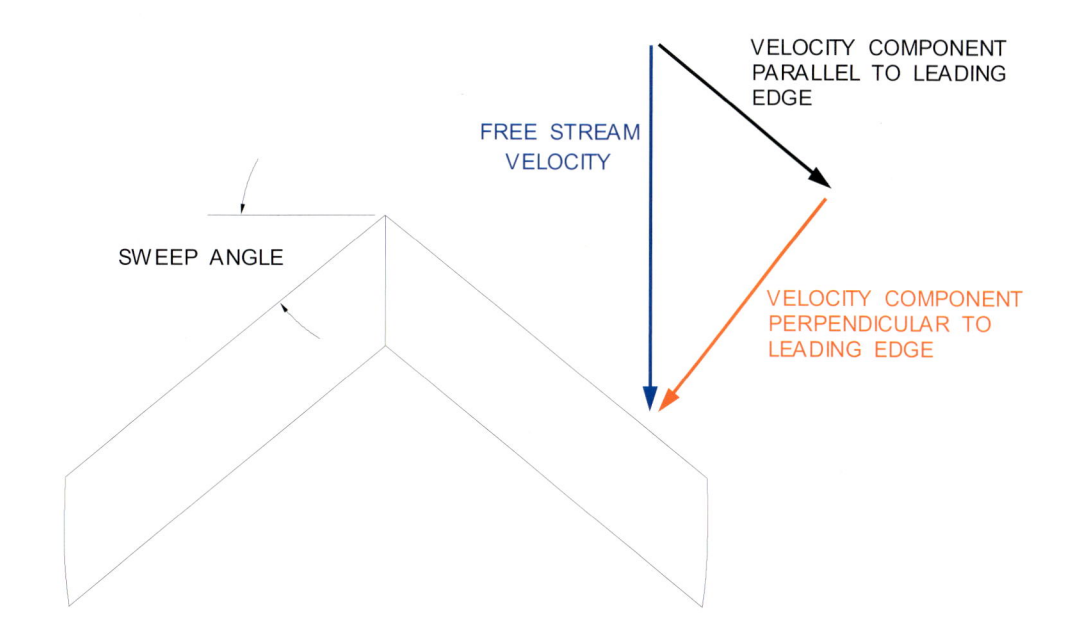

Figure 13.25   Effect of sweepback

Alternatively, it can be considered that compared to a straight wing, a swept back wing of the same aerofoil section has a smaller effective thickness chord ratio. Sweeping the wing back increases the effective aerodynamic chord for the same dimensional thickness, Fig. 13.26.

The local velocity will be lower for a given free stream velocity. In this way, the M_{CRIT} of a swept wing will be higher than a straight wing.

Sweeping the wing back has nearly the same aerodynamic advantages as a thin wing, without suffering reduced strength and fuel capacity. Unfortunately, there are some disadvantages. It was explained in Chapter 7 that swept back wings tend to tip stall, leading to pitch-up and possibly super stall. Swept back wings also increase the magnitude of high speed tuck.

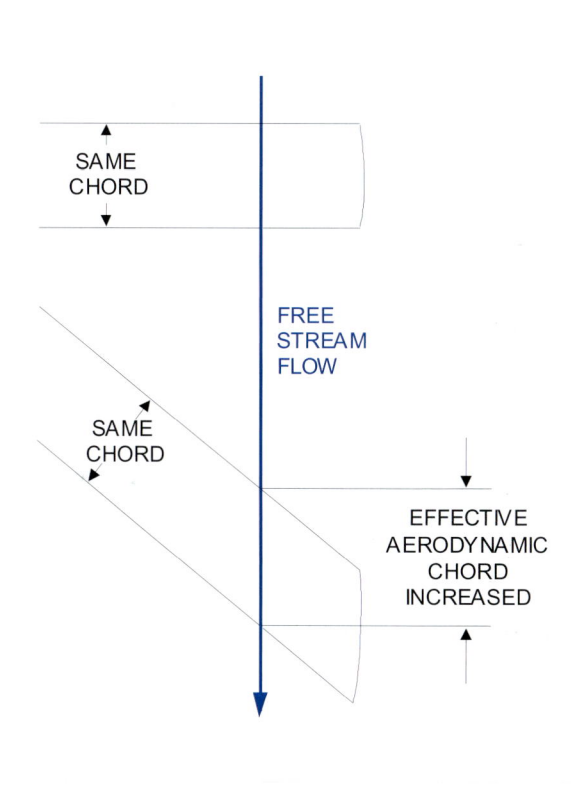

Figure 13.26

PRINCIPLES OF FLIGHT — HIGH SPEED FLIGHT

Another advantage of sweepback is the reduced lift curve slope. This is illustrated by the lift curve comparison in Fig. 13.27 for the straight and swept wing.

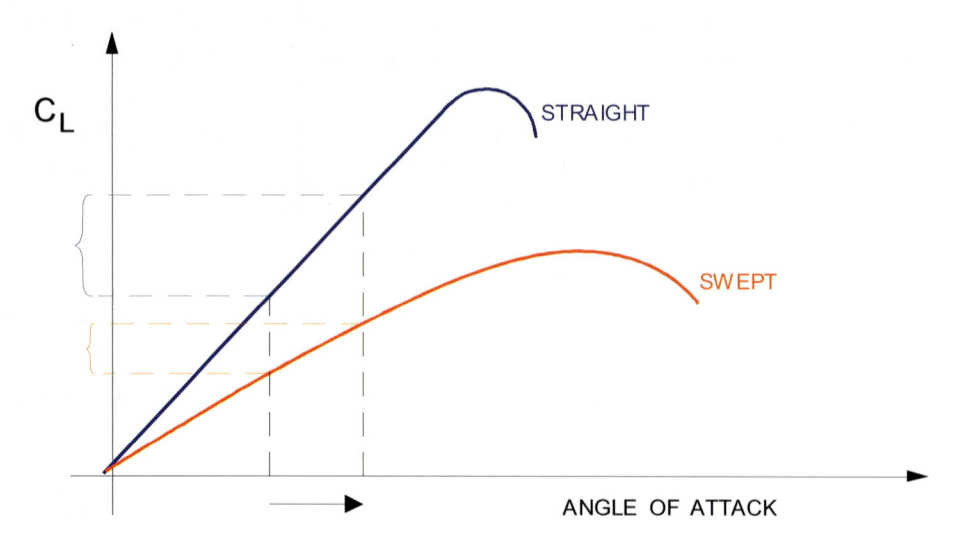

Figure 10.27 Effect of sweepback on sensitivity to gusts

Any reduction of lift curve slope makes the wing less sensitive to changes in angle of attack due to a gust or turbulence. Since the swept wing has the lower lift curve slope, a given vertical gust will increase the C_L, and hence the load factor, by a smaller amount than would occur if the wing were straight. (It is mentioned on Page 10 - 61 that sweeping the fin back reduces the tendency for fin stall at high sideslip angles).

DISADVANTAGES OF SWEEP

a) Reduced C_{LMAX}

   i) gives a higher stall speed and increased take-off and landing distances.

   ii) Maximum lift angle of attack is increased, which complicates the problem of landing gear design (possibility of tail-strike) and reduced visibility from the flight deck during take-off and landing. The contribution to stability of a given tail surface area is also reduced (see Page 10 - 65 for a detailed description).

b) A sweptback wing has an increased tendency to tip stall resulting in pitch-up at the stall and possible deep stall problems (see Page 7 - 15 for a detailed description).

c) Reduced effectiveness of trailing edge control surfaces and high lift devices because their hinge line is swept. To produce a reasonable C_{LMAX} on a swept wing the hinge line of the inboard flaps may be made straight. Leading edge high lift devices are also used to improve the low speed characteristics.

PRINCIPLES OF FLIGHT **HIGH SPEED FLIGHT**

VORTEX GENERATORS

It has been shown that most of the unfavourable characteristics associated with compressibility are due to boundary layer separation behind the shock wave (shock stall).

Flow separation occurs because the boundary layer loses kinetic energy as it flows against the adverse pressure gradient. Shock wave formation increases the adverse pressure gradient so the loss of kinetic energy in the boundary layer will be greater.

Increasing the kinetic energy of the boundary layer will reduce flow separation. A very simple device called vortex generators are used to re-energises the boundary layer.

Vortex generators are small plates, vanes, blades or wedges mounted in spanwise rows along the wing surface, as illustrated in Fig. 13.28. (see also page 7 - 14)

Each vortex generator produces a vortex at its tip which will **induce high energy air from the free stream flow to mix with the boundary layer,** thus increasing its kinetic energy and helping it flow through the shock wave with much less separation.

Vortex generators are usually located on the upper wing surface, particularly ahead of control surfaces, but may be used anywhere where separation is causing high drag, or reduced control effectiveness. It should be noted that vortex generators may also be used on subsonic aircraft, to prevent separation caused by high adverse pressure gradients due to the contours of the surface.

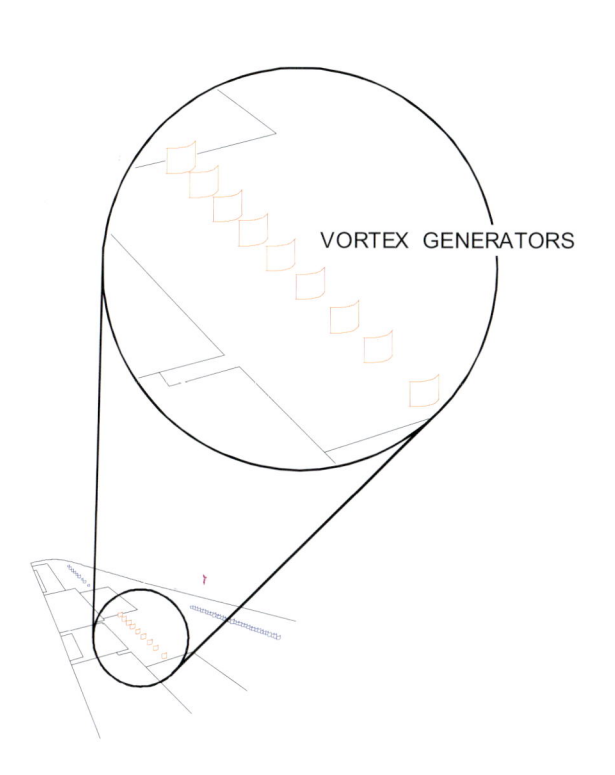

Figure 13.28 Vortex generators (blade type)

PRINCIPLES OF FLIGHT HIGH SPEED FLIGHT

AREA RULE

On Page 6 - 4 it was stated that in addition to the drag of individual components there is an extra drag due to interference between these components, principally between wing and fuselage. This is especially important at high speed. Experiments have shown that a large part of the transonic drag rise for a complete aircraft is due to interference. Interference drag at transonic speeds may be minimised by ensuring that the cross-sectional area distribution along the aircraft's longitudinal axis follows a certain smooth pattern.

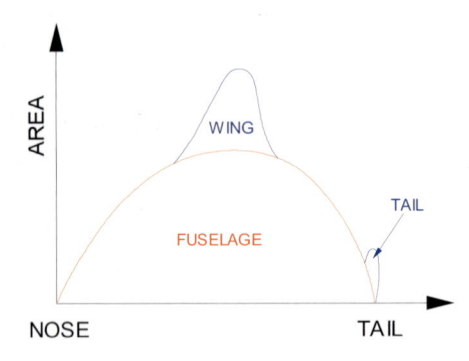

Figure 13.29 Without Area Rule

With some early high speed aircraft designs this was not the case. The area increased rapidly in the region of the wing, again in the vicinity of the tail and decreased elsewhere, giving an area distribution like the one illustrated in Fig. 13.29.

On later aircraft, the fuselage was waisted, i.e., the area was reduced in the region of the wing attachment, and again near the tail, so that there was no "hump" in the area distribution, giving a distribution like the one illustrated in Fig. 13.30. There is an optimum area distribution, and the minimisation of transonic interference drag requires that the aircraft should be designed to fit this distribution as closely as possible. This requirement is known as the 'transonic area rule'. In practice, no aircraft has this optimum distribution, but any reasonably smooth area distribution helps to reduce the transonic drag rise.

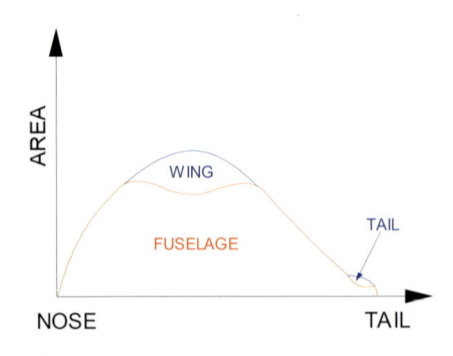

Figure 13.30 Area Rule

PRINCIPLES OF FLIGHT — HIGH SPEED FLIGHT

MACH TRIM

It was stated on page 13 - 20 that as speed increases beyond M_{CRIT}, shock wave formation at the root of a swept back wing will generate a nose down pitching moment because lift forward of the CG is reduced and downwash at the tailplane is reduced.

At high Mach numbers an aircraft will tend to become speed unstable. Instead of an increasing push force being required as speed increases, a pull force becomes necessary to prevent the aircraft accelerating further. This is potentially very dangerous. A small increase in Mach number will give a nose down pitching moment which will tend to further increase the Mach number. This in turn leads to a further increase in the nose down pitching moment. This unfavourable high speed characteristic, known as **"Mach Tuck", "High Speed Tuck"** or **"Tuck Under"** would restrict the maximum operating speed of a modern high speed jet transport aircraft.

Some improvement can be made by mounting the tailplane on top of the fin, where it is clear of the downwash, but it has been shown that this can produce a deep stall problem.

To maintain the required stick force gradient at high Mach numbers, a Mach trim system must be fitted. This device, sensitive to Mach number, may:

a) deflect the elevator up

b) decrease the incidence of the variable incidence trimming tailplane or

c) move the CG rearwards by transferring fuel from the wings to a rear trim tank

by an amount greater than that required merely to compensate for the trim change. This ensures the required stick force gradient is maintained in the cruise at high Mach numbers.

Whichever method of trim is used by a particular manufacturer, **a Mach trim system will adjust longitudinal trim and operates only at high Mach numbers**.

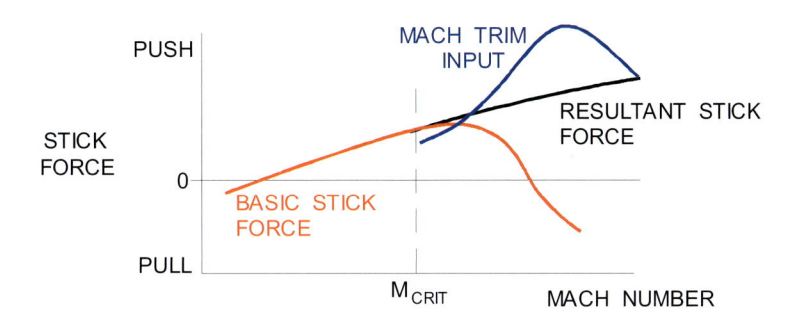

Figure 13.31 Effect of Mach Trim

PRINCIPLES OF FLIGHT   HIGH SPEED FLIGHT

SUPERCRITICAL AEROFOIL

A fairly recent design development, used to increase efficiency when operating in the transonic speed region, is the 'supercritical aerofoil'.

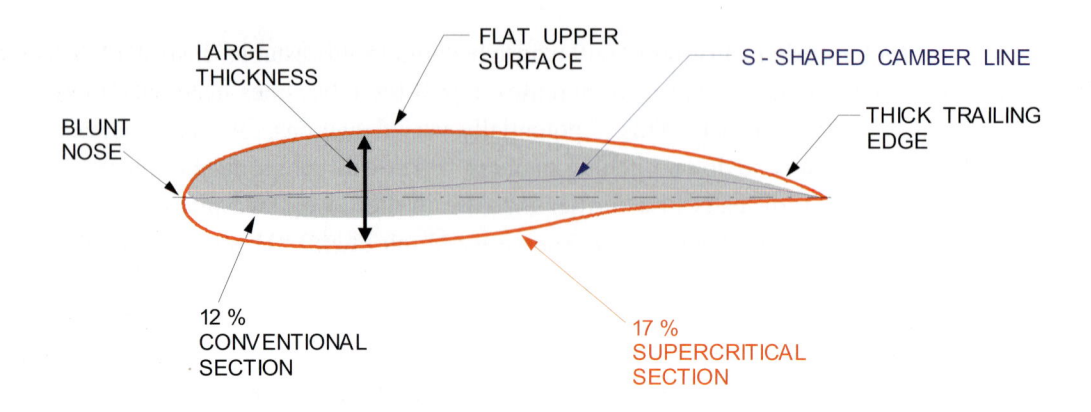

Figure 13.32   Supercritical aerofoil shape

A supercritical aerofoil shape, illustrated in Fig. 13.32, differs from a conventional section by having:

a)   a blunt nose,

b)   large thickness,

c)   an S - shaped camber line,

d)   a relatively flat upper surface and

e)   a thick trailing edge.

Because the airflow does not achieve the same increase of speed over the flattened upper surface compared to a conventional section, the formation of shock waves is delayed to a higher M_{FS} and are much smaller and weaker when they do form.

Because the shock waves are smaller and weaker there is not such a sharp pressure rise on the rear of the section and this gives a much more even 'loading' on the wing.

THE ADVANTAGES OF A SUPERCRITICAL AEROFOIL

a) Because of the delayed formation of shock waves and their weaker nature, less sweep angle is required for a given cruising Mach number, thus reducing some of the problems associated with sweepback.

b) The greater thickness gives increased stiffness and strength for a given structural weight. This also allows a higher aspect ratio to be used which reduces induced drag.

c) The increased section depth gives more storage space for fuel.

This type of wing section can be used to increase performance in one of two ways:

    i) **Increased Payload:** By using existing cruise speeds, the fuel consumption would be reduced, thus allowing an increase in payload with little or no drag increase over a conventional wing at the same speed.

    ii) **Increased Cruising Speed:** By retaining existing payloads, the cruise Mach number could be increased with little or no increase in drag.

THE DISADVANTAGES OF A SUPERCRITICAL AEROFOIL

a) The aerofoil front section has a negative camber to give optimum performance at cruise Mach numbers, but this is less than ideal for low speed flight. C_{LMAX} will be reduced, requiring extensive and complex high lift devices at the leading edge, which may include Krueger flaps, variable camber flaps, slats and slots.

b) The trailing edge of the aerofoil has large positive camber to produce the 'aft loading' required, but which also gives large negative (nose down) pitching moments.

    i) This must be balanced by the tailplane, causing trim drag and

    ii) Shock induced buffet may cause severe oscillations.

PRINCIPLES OF FLIGHT HIGH SPEED FLIGHT

13.20 AERODYNAMIC HEATING

Air is heated when it is compressed or when it is subjected to friction. An aircraft will have compression at the stagnation point, compression through a shock wave, and friction in the boundary layer.

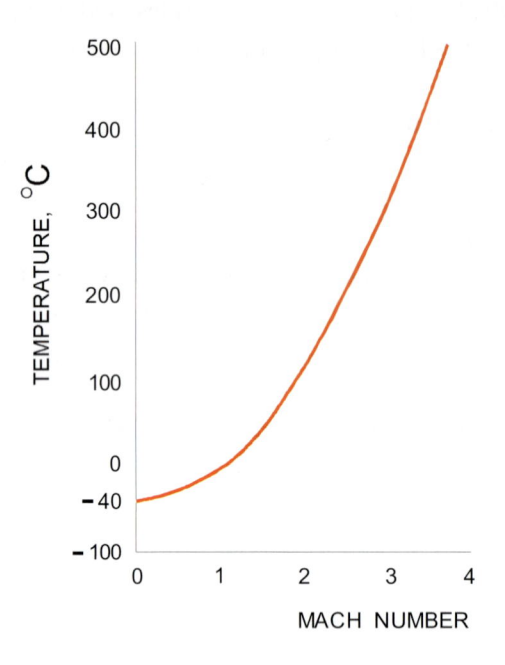

Figure 13.33 Surface temperature rise with Mach number

So when an aeroplane moves through the air it's skin temperature will increase. This occurs at all speeds, but only becomes significant from a skin temperature point of view at higher Mach numbers.

It can be seen from Fig. 13.33 that the temperature rise at M 1·0 is approximately 40°C. Again from a skin temperature point of view, this rise in temperature does not become significant until speeds in the region of M 2·0 are reached, which is the approximate limit speed for aircraft manufactured from conventional aluminium alloys. Above this speed the heat treatment of the structure would be changed and the fatigue life shortened. For speeds above Mach 2·0, Titanium or "stainless steel" must be used.

PRINCIPLES OF FLIGHT HIGH SPEED FLIGHT

13.21 MACH ANGLE

Reference to Fig. 13.7 will show that as the Mach number increases the shock waves become more acute. To illustrate why the angle of the shock waves change it is necessary to consider the meaning and significance of the Mach angle 'μ' (mu).

If the TAS of the aircraft is greater than the local speed of sound, the source of pressure waves is moving faster than the disturbance it creates.

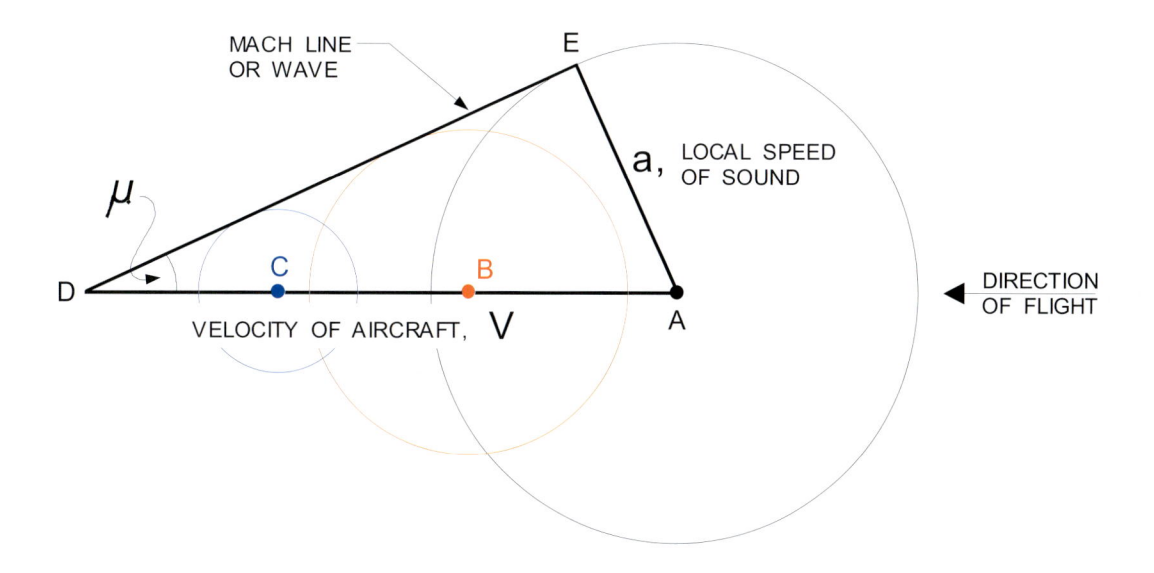

Figure 13.34 Mach angle

Consider a point moving at velocity 'V' in the direction 'A' to 'D', as in Fig. 13.34. A pressure wave propagated when the point is at 'A' will travel spherically outwards at the local speed of sound; but the point is moving faster, and by the time it has reached 'D', the wave from 'A' and other pressure waves sent out when the point was at 'B' and 'C' will have formed circles as shown, and it will be possible to draw a common tangent 'DE' to these pressure waves. The tangent represents the limit to which all the pressure waves have reached when the point has reached 'D'.

'AE' represents the local speed of sound (a) and 'AD' represents the TAS (V)

$$M = \frac{TAS}{a} \quad \text{as illustrated, } M = 2.6$$

The angle 'ADE', or μ is called the **Mach angle** and by simple trigonometry:

$$\sin \mu = \frac{a}{TAS} = \frac{1}{M}$$

The greater the Mach number, the more acute the Mach angle μ. At M 1·0, μ is 90°.

PRINCIPLES OF FLIGHT　　　　　　　　　　　HIGH SPEED FLIGHT

13.22 MACH CONE

In three dimensions, the disturbances propagating from a moving point source expand outward as spheres, not circles. If the speed of the source (V) is greater than the local speed of sound (a), these spheres are enclosed within a Mach cone, whose semi vertical angle is µ.

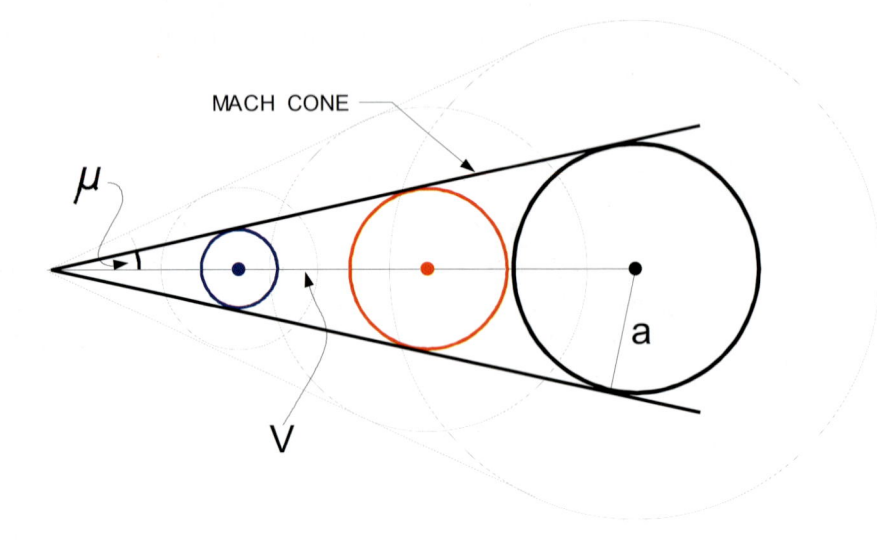

Figure 13.35   Mach cone at approximately M 5·0

It can be seen from Fig. 13.35 that the Mach angle (µ) continues to decrease with increasing Mach number. The Mach angle is inversely proportional to the Mach number.

13.23 AREA (ZONE) OF INFLUENCE

When travelling at supersonic speeds the Mach cone represents the limit of travel of the pressure disturbances created by an aircraft, **anything forward of the Mach cone cannot be influenced by the disturbances**. The space inside the Mach cone is called the area or zone of influence.

A finite body such as an aircraft will produce a similar pattern of waves but the front will be an oblique shock wave and the wave angle will be greater than the Mach angle because the initial speed of propagation of the shock waves will be greater than the free stream speed of sound.

13.24 BOW WAVE   > Mach 1   Attach 1.3

Consider a supersonic stream approaching the leading edge of an aerofoil. In order to flow around the leading edge the air would suddenly have to turn through a right angle (see Fig. 13.3). At supersonic speeds this is not possible in the distance available. The free stream velocity will suddenly decelerate to below supersonic speed and a normal shock wave will form ahead of the wing at the junction of supersonic and subsonic airflow. Behind the shock wave the airflow is subsonic and is able to flow around the leading edge. Within a short distance the flow again accelerates to supersonic speed, as illustrated in Fig. 13.36.

PRINCIPLES OF FLIGHT   **HIGH SPEED FLIGHT**

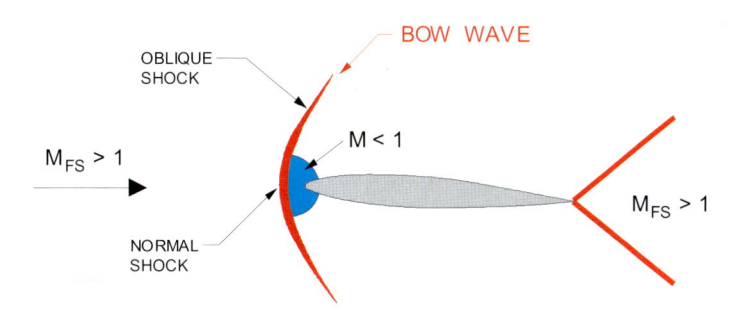

Figure 13.36 Bow wave

The shock wave ahead of the leading edge is called a bow wave and is normal only in the vicinity of the leading edge. Further away from the leading edge ("above" and "below") it becomes oblique. It can be seen in Fig. 13.36 that the trailing edge shock waves are no longer normal because the free stream mach number is greater than 1·0; they are also now oblique.

13.25 EXPANSION WAVES

In the preceding paragraphs it has been shown that supersonic flow is able to turn a corner by decelerating to subsonic speed when it meets an object. A shock wave forms at the junction of the supersonic and subsonic flow, the generation of which is wasteful of energy (wave drag).

There is another way a supersonic flow is able to turn a corner. Consider first a convex corner with a subsonic flow, as illustrated in Fig. 13.37.

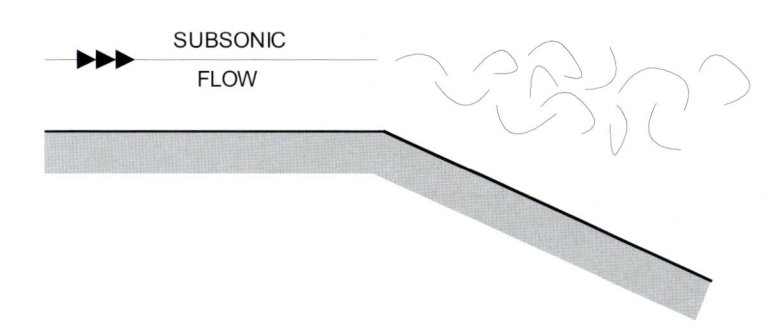

Figure 13.37 Subsonic flow at a convex corner

With subsonic airflow the adverse pressure gradient would be so steep that the airflow would instantly separate at the "corner".

PRINCIPLES OF FLIGHT HIGH SPEED FLIGHT

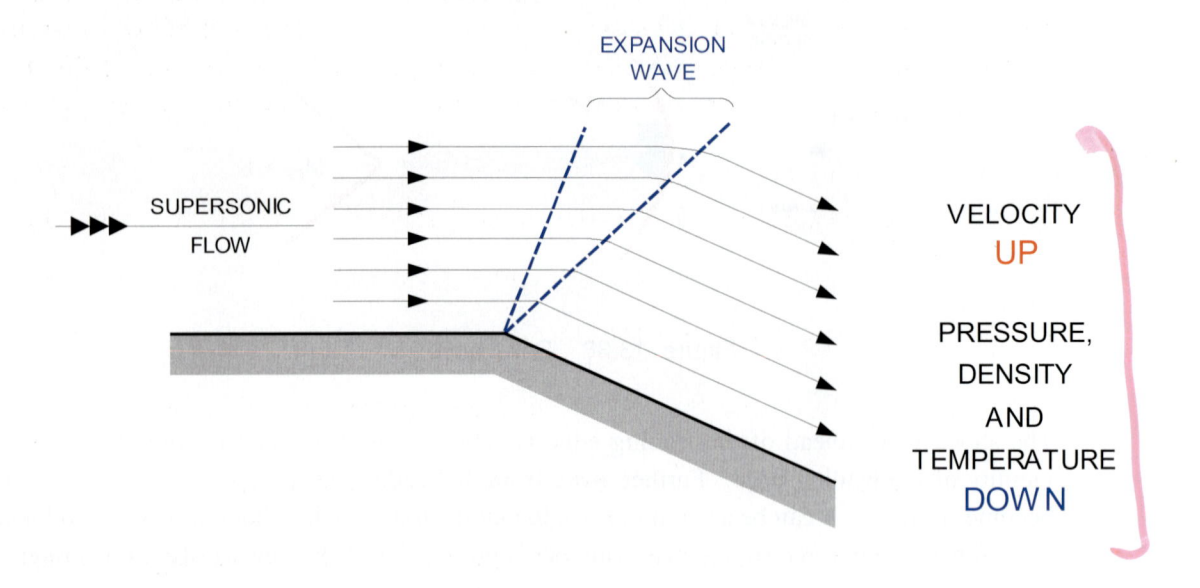

Figure 13.38 Supersonic flow at a convex corner with expansion wave

Fig. 13.38 shows that a supersonic airflow can follow a convex corner because it expands upon reaching the corner. The velocity INCREASES and the other parameters, pressure, density and temperature DECREASE. Supersonic airflow behaviour through an expansion wave is exactly opposite to that through a shock wave.

M_{FS} ABOVE 1·2

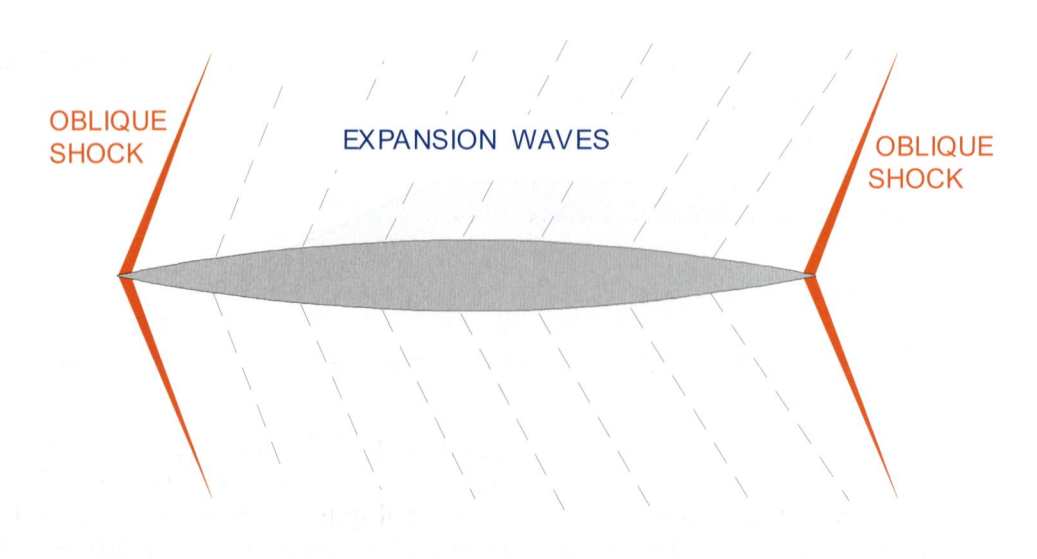

Figure 13.39 Expansion waves in a supersonic flow

Bi-convex

PRINCIPLES OF FLIGHT — HIGH SPEED FLIGHT

Fig. 13.39 shows a series of expansion waves in a supersonic airflow. After passing through the bow shock wave, the compressed supersonic flow is free to expand and follow the surface contour. As there are no sudden changes to the airflow, the expansion waves are NOT shock waves. A supersonic airflow passing through an expansion wave will experience the following changes:-

a) The airflow is accelerated; the velocity and Mach number behind the expansion wave are greater.

b) The flow direction is changed to follow the surface.

c) The static pressure of the airflow behind the expansion wave is decreased.

d) The density of the airflow behind the expansion wave is decreased.

e) Since the flow change is gradual there is no "shock" and no loss of energy in the airflow. An expansion wave does not dissipate airflow energy.

13.26 SONIC BANG

The intensity of shock waves reduces with distance from the aircraft, but the pressure waves can be of sufficient magnitude to create a disturbance on the ground. Thus, "sonic bangs" are a consequence of supersonic flight. **The pressure waves move with aircraft groundspeed over the earth surface.**

13.27 METHODS OF IMPROVING CONTROL AT TRANSONIC SPEEDS

It has been seen that control effectiveness may decrease in the transonic region if conventional control surfaces are used. Some improvement in control effectiveness may be obtained by placing vortex generators ahead of control surfaces.

However, alternative forms of control such as:

a) an all moving (slab) tailplane

b) or roll control spoilers give better control in the transonic speed region.

These types of control are explained in Flying Controls Chapter 11. Control surface buzz is sometimes remedied by fitting narrow strips along the trailing edge of the control surface, or may be prevented by including dampers in the control system or by increasing the stiffness of the control circuit.

Because of the high control loads involved at high speeds and the variation in loads through the transonic region, the controls will normally be fully power operated with artificial feel.

The table in Fig. 13.40 is provided to summarise the characteristics of the three principal wave forms encountered with supersonic flow.

Supersonic Wave Characteristics

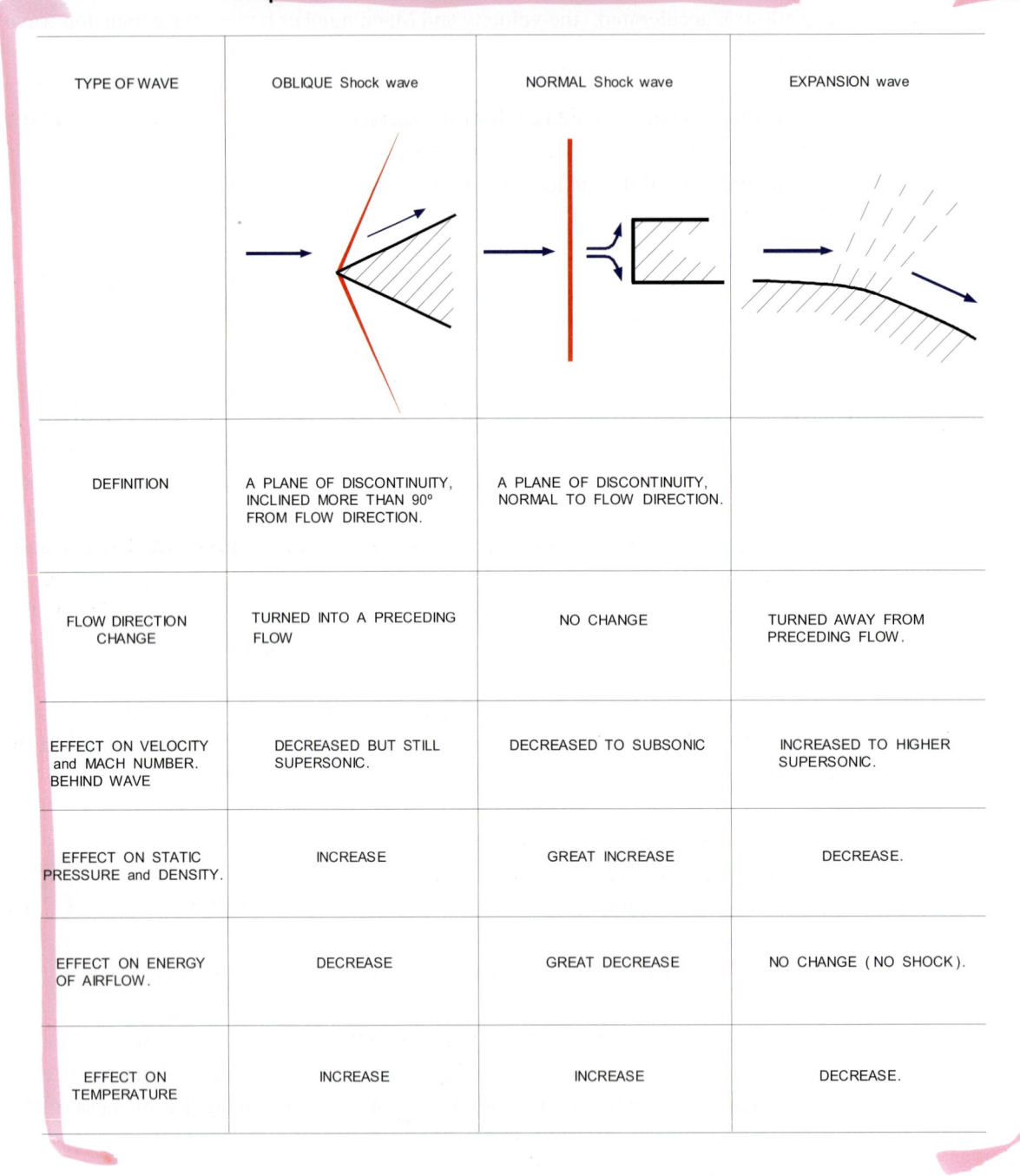

TYPE OF WAVE	OBLIQUE Shock wave	NORMAL Shock wave	EXPANSION wave
DEFINITION	A PLANE OF DISCONTINUITY, INCLINED MORE THAN 90° FROM FLOW DIRECTION.	A PLANE OF DISCONTINUITY, NORMAL TO FLOW DIRECTION.	
FLOW DIRECTION CHANGE	TURNED INTO A PRECEDING FLOW	NO CHANGE	TURNED AWAY FROM PRECEDING FLOW.
EFFECT ON VELOCITY and MACH NUMBER. BEHIND WAVE	DECREASED BUT STILL SUPERSONIC.	DECREASED TO SUBSONIC	INCREASED TO HIGHER SUPERSONIC.
EFFECT ON STATIC PRESSURE and DENSITY.	INCREASE	GREAT INCREASE	DECREASE.
EFFECT ON ENERGY OF AIRFLOW.	DECREASE	GREAT DECREASE	NO CHANGE (NO SHOCK).
EFFECT ON TEMPERATURE	INCREASE	INCREASE	DECREASE.

Figure 13.40 Characteristics of the three principal wave forms

PRINCIPLES OF FLIGHT **HIGH SPEED FLIGHT**

SWEEPBACK - FACT SHEET

Sweep Angle: The angle between the line of 25% chords and a perpendicular to the root chord

Purpose of Sweepback: To increase M_{CRIT}.

A SWEPT WING INCREASES THE CRITICAL MACH NUMBER (M_{CRIT}). All other effects from a swept wing are by-products, most of them disadvantages. However, the benefits from a higher M_{CRIT} outweigh the associated disadvantages.

BY - PRODUCTS OF SWEEPBACK

1. Increased tendency to stall at the tip first - minimised by fitting wing fences, vortilons or saw tooth leading edge.

    a) Tip stall can lead to pitch - up, a major disadvantage.
    b) Pitch - up can give the tendency for a swept wing aircraft to Super Stall.
    c) Aircraft that show a significant tendency to Pitch - up at the stall MUST be fitted with a stall prevention device; a stick Pusher.

    Close to the stall, ailerons and coordinated use of rudder should be used to maintain wings level because the use of rudder alone would give excessive rolling moments. (V_{SR} is adjusted so that adequate roll control exists from the use of ailerons close to the stall).

2. When compared to a straight wing of the same section, a swept wing is less aerodynamically efficient.

    (i) At a given angle of attack C_L is less.
    (ii) C_{LMAX} is less and occurs at a higher angle of attack.
    (iii) The lift curve has a smaller gradient (change in C_L per degree change in alpha is less).

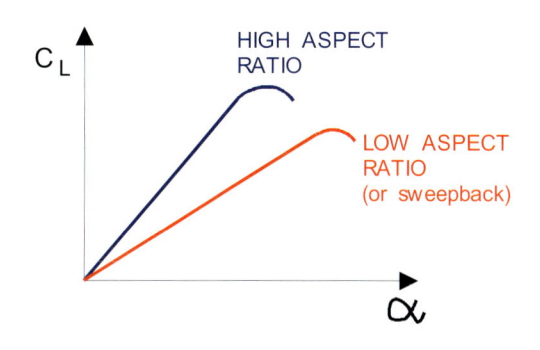

PRINCIPLES OF FLIGHT   HIGH SPEED FLIGHT

        a)   Swept wings must be fitted with complex high lift devices, both leading and trailing edge, to give a reasonable take - off and landing distance.

               (i)   The least efficient type of leading edge device is used on the inboard part of the swept wing to help promote root stall.

        b)   Because of the higher stalling angle of attack, the fin or vertical stabiliser is swept to delay fin stall to a greater sideslip angle.

        c)   A swept wing must be flown at a higher angle of attack than a straight wing to give the required lift coefficient, this is most noticeable at low speeds.

        d)   One of the few advantages of a swept wing is that it is less sensitive to changes in angle of attack due to gust or turbulence; a smaller change in Load Factor for a given gust will result.

3.   A swept wing makes a small positive contribution to static directional stability.

4.   A swept wing makes a significant positive contribution to static lateral stability.

5.   At speeds in excess of M_{CRIT} a swept wing generates a nose down pitching moment; a phenomena known as Mach Tuck, High Speed Tuck or Tuck Under. This must be counteracted by a Mach Trim System which adjusts the aircraft's longitudinal trim.

6.   The hinge line of trailing edge 'flap' type control surfaces are not at right angles to the airflow, which reduces the efficiency of the controls.

PRINCIPLES OF FLIGHT   **HIGH SPEED FLIGHT**

SELF ASSESSMENT QUESTIONS

1. Identify which of the following is the correct formula for Mach number:

   a) $\dfrac{TAS}{M\ a} = $ constant

   b) $M = \dfrac{IAS}{a}$

   c) $TAS = \dfrac{M}{a}$

   d) $M = TAS \times a$

2. What is the result of a shock-induced separation of airflow occurring symmetrically near the wing root of a sweptwing aircraft?

   a) a severe nose-down pitching moment or "tuck under"
   b) a high-speed stall and sudden pitch up
   c) severe porpoising
   d) pitch-up

3. Mach number is:

   a) the ratio of the aircraft's TAS to the speed of sound at sea level.
   b) the ratio of the aircraft's TAS to the speed of sound at the same atmospheric conditions.
   c) the ratio of the aircraft's IAS to the speed of sound at the same atmospheric conditions.
   d) the speed of sound.

4. For an aircraft climbing at a constant IAS the Mach number will:

   a) increase.
   b) decrease.
   c) remain constant.
   d) initially show an increase, then decrease.

5. The term 'transonic speed' for an aircraft means:

   a) speeds where the airflow is completely subsonic.
   b) speeds where the airflow is completely supersonic.
   c) speeds where the airflow is partly subsonic and partly supersonic.
   d) speeds between M 0.4 and M 1.0

6. At M 0·8 a wing has supersonic flow between 20% chord and 60% chord. There will be a shockwave:

   a) at 20% chord only.
   b) at 20% chord and 60% chord.
   c) at 60% chord only.
   d) forward of 20% chord.

7. As air flows through a shockwave:

   a) static pressure increases, density decreases, temperature increases.
   b) static pressure increases, density increases, temperature increases.
   c) static pressure decreases, density increases, temperature decreases.
   d) static pressure decreases, density decreases, temperature decreases.

8. For a wing section of given thickness, the critical Mach number:

   a) will decrease if angle of attack is increased.
   b) will increase if angle of attack is increased.
   c) will not change with changes of angle of attack.
   d) is only influenced by changes in temperature.

9. At speeds just above the critical Mach number, the lift coefficient:

   a) will start to increase.
   b) will start to decrease.
   c) will remain constant.
   d) is directly proportional to the Mach number.

10. As air flows through a shockwave:

    a) its speed increases.
    b) its speed decreases.
    c) its speed remains the same.
    d) it changes direction to flow parallel with the Mach cone.

11. If an aeroplane accelerates above the Critical Mach number, the first high Mach number characteristic it will usually experience is:

    a) a nose up pitch or "Shock Stall".
    b) a violent and sustained oscillation in pitch (porpoising).
    c) Dutch roll and/or spiral instability.
    d) a nose down pitching moment (Mach, or high speed tuck).

12. High speed buffet is caused by:

    a) the shock waves striking the tail.
    b) the high speed airflow striking the leading edge of the wing.
    c) wing flutter caused by the interaction of the bottom and top surface shock waves.
    d) the airflow being detached by the shock wave and the turbulent flow striking the tail.

13. The "area rule" applied to high speed aircraft requires:

    a) that the cross sectional area shall be as small as possible.
    b) that the variation of cross sectional area along the length of the aircraft follows a smooth pattern.
    c) that the maximum cross sectional area of the fuselage should occur at the wing root.
    d) that the fuselage and the wing area be of a ratio of 3 : 1.

14. An all-moving tailplane is used in preference to elevators on high speed aircraft:

    a) because the effect of the elevator is reversed above the critical Mach number.
    b) because shock wave formation on the elevator causes excessive stick forces.
    c) because shock wave formation ahead of the elevator causes separation and loss of elevator effectiveness.
    d) because it would be physically impossible for a pilot to control the aircraft in pitch with a conventional tailplane and elevator configuration.

15. Mach Trim is a device which:

    a) moves the centre of gravity to maintain stable lateral stick forces in the transonic region.
    b) automatically compensates for pitch changes while flying in the transonic speed region.
    c) prevents the aircraft from exceeding its critical Mach number.
    d) switches out the trim control to prevent damage in the transonic region.

16. What is the movement of the centre of pressure when the wingtips of a sweptwing aeroplane are shock-stalled first?

    a) outward and forward
    b) inward and aft
    c) outward and aft
    d) inward and forward

17. The airflow behind a normal shock wave will:

    a) always be subsonic and in the same direction as the original airflow.
    b) always be supersonic and in the same direction as the original airflow.
    c) may be subsonic or supersonic.
    d) always be subsonic and will be deflected from the direction of the original airflow.

PRINCIPLES OF FLIGHT — HIGH SPEED FLIGHT

18. As airflow passes through a normal shock wave, which of the following changes in static pressure (i), density (ii), and Mach number (iii) will occur:

	(i)	(ii)	(iii)
a)	decrease	increase	< 1.0
b)	increase	decrease	< 1.0
c)	increase	decrease	> 1.0 or < 1.0
d)	increase	increase	< 1.0

19. An aerofoil travelling at supersonic speed will:

   a) have its centre of pressure at 50 % chord.
   b) have its centre of pressure at 25% chord.
   c) give a larger proportion of lift from the lower surface than from the upper surface, and have its centre of pressure at 50 % chord.
   d) give approximately equal lift from the upper and lower surfaces, and have its aerodynamic centre at 50% chord.

20. A bow wave is:

   a) a shock wave which forms on the nose of the aircraft at M_{CRIT}.
   b) the shape formed when the shock waves on the upper and lower wing surface meet at the trailing edge.
   c) a shock wave that forms immediately ahead of an aircraft which is travelling faster than the speed of sound.
   d) the shape of a shock wave when viewed vertically.

21. When an aircraft is flying at supersonic speed, where will the area of influence of any pressure disturbance due to the presence of the aircraft be located?

   a) Within the Mach Cone.
   b) In front of the Mach Cone.
   c) In front of the bow wave.
   d) In front of the Mach Cone only when the speed exceeds M 1.0

22. The temperature of the airflow as it passes through an expansion wave:

   a) increases.
   b) decreases.
   c) is inversely proportional to the square root of the Mch number.
   d) remains the same.

23. The influence of weight (wing loading) on the formation of shockwaves is:

    a) a higher wing loading will increase M_{CRIT}
    b) low wing loading will give a higher M_{CRIT}
    c) wing loading does not influence M_{CRIT}
    d) wing loading and M_{CRIT} are directly proportional

24. What influence does an oblique shock wave have on the streamline pattern (i), variation of pressure (ii), temperature (iii), density (iv) and velocity (v)?

	(i)	(ii)	(iii)	(iv)	(v)
a)	parallel to surface	increase	increase	increase	decrease
b)	normal to wave	decrease	decrease	decrease	increase
c)	parallel to wave	decrease	decrease	decrease	increase
d)	parallel to chord	increase	decrease	increase	decrease

25. Wave drag is caused by:

    a) shock waves interfering with the smooth airflow into the engine intakes.
    b) flying faster than M_{MO}.
    c) the conversion of mechanical energy into thermal energy by the shock wave.
    d) flying faster than V_{MO}

26. What is the effect of a shock wave on control surface efficiency?

    a) Increase in efficiency, due to increased velocity.
    b) Increase in efficiency, due to the extra leverage caused by the shock wave.
    c) Decrease in efficiency, due to the bow wave.
    d) loss of efficiency, due to control deflection no longer modifying the total flow over the wing.

27. At what speed does an oblique shock wave move over the earth surface?

    a) Aircraft ground speed
    b) The TAS of the aircraft plus the wind speed
    c) The TAS of the aircraft less the wind speed
    d) The TAS relative to the speed of sound at sea level

INTENTIONALLY LEFT BLANK

ANSWERS

No	A	B	C	D	REF
1	A				
2	A				
3		B			
4	A				
5			C		
6			C		
7		B			
8	A				
9		B			
10		B			
11				D	
12				D	
13		B			
14			C		
15		B			
16				D	
17	A				
18				D	
19	A				
20			C		
21	A				
22		B			
23		B			
24	A				
25			C		
26				D	
27	A				

CHAPTER 14 - LIMITATIONS

Contents

Page

OPERATING LIMIT SPEEDS . . . . 14 - 1
LOADS AND SAFETY FACTORS
LOADS ON THE STRUCTURE
LOAD FACTOR . . . . 14 - 2
THE MANOEUVRE ENVELOPE . . . . 14 - 3
THE $C_{L\,MAX}$ BOUNDARY
DESIGN MANOEUVRING SPEED V_A . . . . 14 - 5
EFFECT OF AIRCRAFT WEIGHT ON V_A
DESIGN CRUISING SPEED V_C . . . . 14 - 6
DESIGN DIVE SPEED V_D
NEGATIVE LOAD FACTORS
THE NEGATIVE STALL . . . . 14 - 7
MANOEUVRE BOUNDARIES
OPERATIONAL SPEED LIMITS . . . . 14 - 8
    V_{MO} / M_{MO}
    V_{NE}
    V_{NO}
GUST LOADS . . . . 14 - 9
EFFECT OF A VERTICAL GUST ON THE LOAD FACTOR . . . . 14 - 10
EFFECT OF THE GUST ON STALLING . . . . 14 - 11
OPERATIONAL ROUGH AIR SPEED . . . . 14 - 12
LANDING GEAR SPEED LIMITATIONS . . . . 14 - 14
    V_{LO}
    V_{LE}
FLAP SPEED LIMIT . . . . 14 - 15
    V_{FE}
AEROELASTICITY (AERO - ELASTIC COUPLING) . . . . 14 - 16
FLUTTER . . . . 14 - 19
        CONTROL SURFACE FLUTTER . . . . 14 - 20
            TORSIONAL AILERON FLUTTER
            FLEXURAL AILERON FLUTTER
AILERON REVERSAL . . . . 14 - 22
    LOW SPEED
    HIGH SPEED
SELF ASSESSMENT QUESTIONS . . . . 14 - 25

PRINCIPLES OF FLIGHT   **LIMITATIONS**

14.1 OPERATING LIMIT SPEEDS

In service an aircraft must observe certain speed limitations. These may be maximum speeds or minimum speeds, but in each case they are set to give safe operation in the prevailing conditions. The limits may be set by various considerations, the main ones being:-

a)   strength of the aircraft structure

b)   stiffness of the aircraft structure

c)   adequate control of the aircraft

Strength is the ability of the structure to withstand a load, and stiffness is the ability to withstand deformation.

14.2 LOADS AND SAFETY FACTORS

Limit load: The maximum load to be expected in service

Ultimate load: The failing load of the structure

Factor of safety: The ratio of ultimate load to limit load

For aircraft structures the factor of safety is 1·5

The safety factor on aircraft structures is much lower than the safety factors used in other forms of engineering because of the extreme importance of minimum weight in aircraft structures. To keep the weight as low as possible the safety factor must be kept to a minimum. Because of this it is extremely important not to exceed the limitations set on the operation of the aircraft, as the safety margin can easily be exceeded and structural damage occur.

14.3 LOADS ON THE STRUCTURE

The airframe structure must obviously be strong enough to take the loads acting upon it in normal level flight, that is the forces due to lift, drag, thrust and weight. However the aircraft is also required to manoeuvre and to fly in turbulent air. Under these conditions the loads on the aircraft will be increased so it must also be strong enough to withstand whatever manoeuvres are specified for the aircraft and by the gusts which are required to be considered.

The structure should also have sufficient stiffness to ensure that phenomena such as aileron reversal, flutter, and divergence do not occur within the permitted speed range of the aircraft.

PRINCIPLES OF FLIGHT — LIMITATIONS

14.4 LOAD FACTOR

The loads which must be considered are given in the design requirements of an aircraft. They are given in terms of load factor (n), colloquially known as 'g'.

$$\text{Load factor (n)} = \frac{\text{Lift}}{\text{Weight}}$$

In level flight, since lift equals weight, the load factor is 1·0 (1g). If the aircraft is performing a manoeuvre such that, for example the lift is twice the weight, the load factor is 2·0 (2g).

The limit load is given in terms of load factor to make the requirement general to all aircraft. However, it should be appreciated that failure of the structure will occur at some particular applied load. For example, if the structure fails at 10,000 lb load, an aircraft weighing 4,000 lb will reach this load at a load factor of 2·5. However, if the aircraft weighs 5,000 lb the failing load is reached at a load factor of 2·0, i.e. it takes less 'g' to overstress a heavy aircraft than a light one.

Limit load factors are based on the maximum weight of the aircraft.

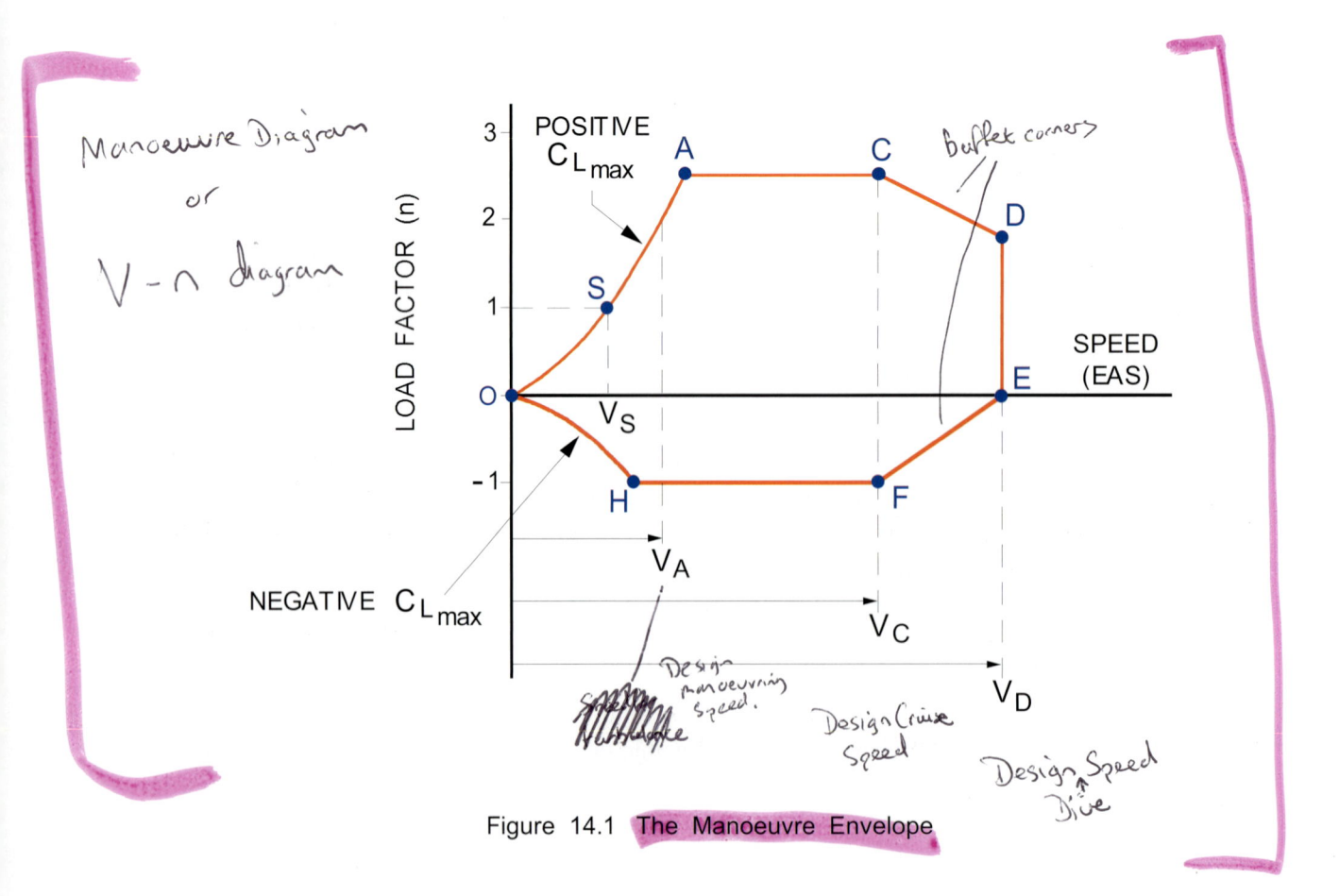

[Handwritten annotations: Manoeuvre Diagram or V-n diagram; Buffet corners; Design manoeuvring Speed; Design Cruise Speed; Design Speed Dive]

Figure 14.1 The Manoeuvre Envelope

PRINCIPLES OF FLIGHT — LIMITATIONS

14.5 THE MANOEUVRE ENVELOPE (V - n Diagram)

The maximum load factors which must be allowed for during manoeuvres are shown in an envelope of load factor against speed (EAS). Fig.14.1 shows a typical manoeuvre envelope or V-n diagram.

The limit load factors will depend on the design category of the aircraft.

The JAR regulations state that:

a) For normal category aircraft, the positive limit load factor may not be less than 2·5 and need not be more than 3·8.

(So that structural weight can be kept to an absolute minimum a manufacturer will not design an aircraft to be any stronger than the minimum required by the regulations).

The positive limit load factor for modern high speed jet transport aircraft is 2·5.

b) For utility category aircraft the positive limit load factor is 4·4

c) For aerobatic category aircraft the positive limit load factor is 6·0

The negative limit load factor may not be less than:

d) −1·0 for normal category aircraft

e) −1·76 for utility category aircraft

f) −3·0 for aerobatic category aircraft

14.6 THE $C_{L\,MAX}$ BOUNDARY

The line OA in Fig.14.1 is determined by the $C_{L\,MAX}$ of the aircraft. In theory, the lift, and hence the load factor for a given weight, depends on the angle of attack of the wing and the airspeed. The maximum possible lift will occur at the angle of attack where C_L is a maximum. At this angle of attack the lift will increase with speed as shown by the line OA.

For level (1g) flight the speed at $C_{L\,MAX}$ will be the stalling speed (V_S), represented by point S in Fig. 14.1.

At Point A, the load factor reaches its positive limit.

PRINCIPLES OF FLIGHT   **LIMITATIONS**

It can be seen from Fig.14.2 that at speeds below point A the wing cannot produce a lift force equal to the limit load factor, whereas at speeds above point A the limit load factor can be exceeded. Manoeuvres at speeds above point A therefore have the **potential** to cause permanent deformation to the structure or structural failure if the ultimate load is exceeded.

This does not mean that any manoeuvre at a speed greater than point A will always cause structural damage; manoeuvres may be performed safely provided that the limit load factor is not exceeded.

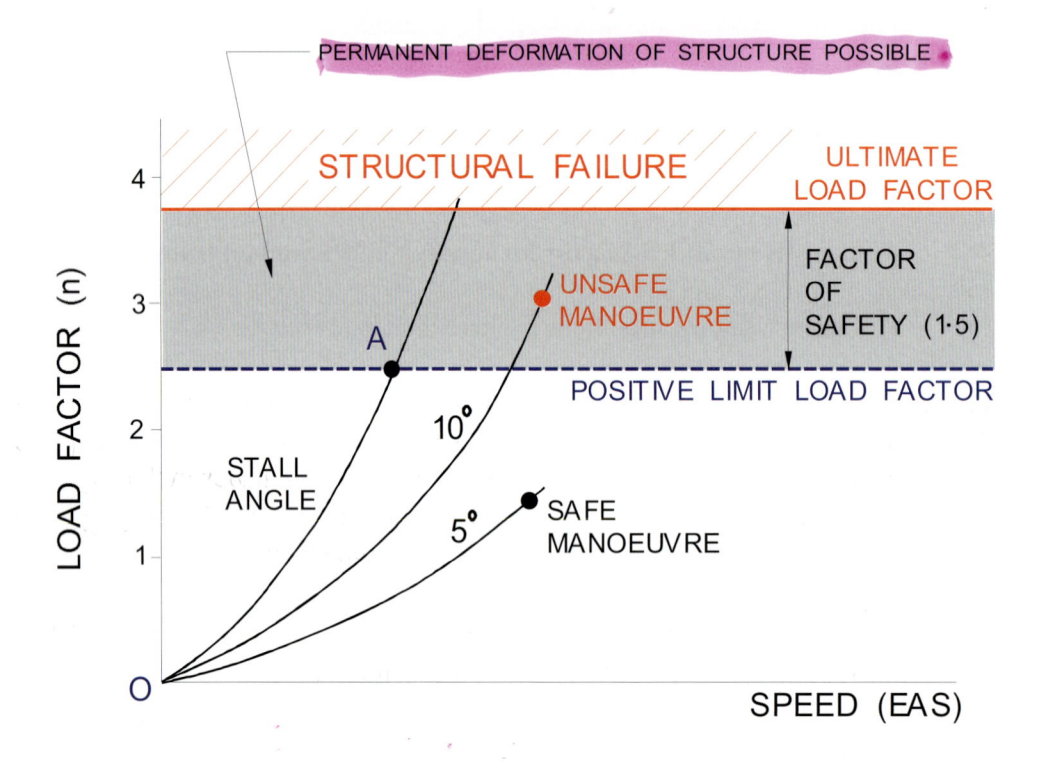

Figure 14.2 Loads Imposed During Manoeuvres

There is of course a safety factor on the airframe of 1·5 so complete failure of the structure will not occur at the load factor of 2·5 but at 2·5 x 1·5 = 3·75.

However, permanent deformation of the structure may occur at load factors between 2·5 and 3·75, so it is not safe to assume that the load factor may be increased above the limiting value just because there is a safety factor.

PRINCIPLES OF FLIGHT — LIMITATIONS

14.7 DESIGN MANOEUVRING SPEED, V_A

The highest speed at which sudden, full elevator deflection (nose up) can be made without exceeding the design limit load factor.

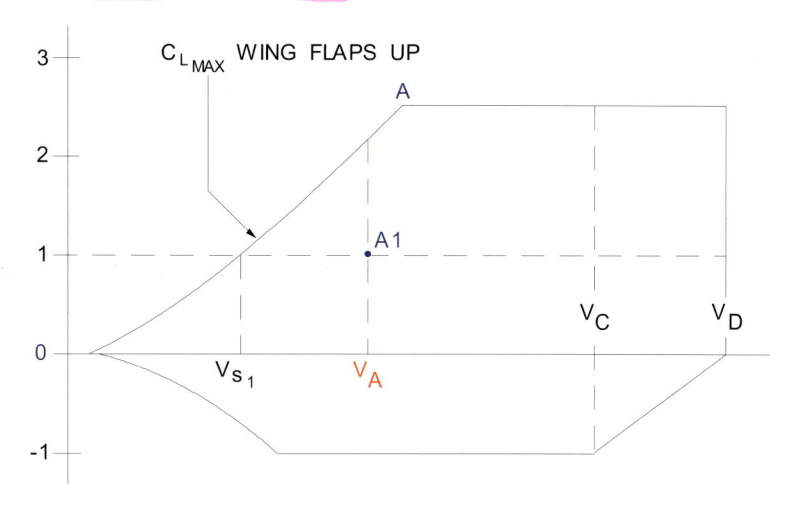

Figure 14.2a Design Manoeuvring Speed VA

When establishing V_A the aeroplane is assumed to be flying in steady level flight, at point A1 in Fig. 14.2a, and the pitch control is suddenly moved to obtain extreme positive pitch acceleration (nose up). V_A is slower than the speed at the intersection of the C_{LMAX} line and the positive limit load factor line (point A) to safeguard the tail structure because of the higher load on the tailplane during the pitch manoeuvre (Ref. paragraph 10.15).

Line OA in Fig. 14.2a represents the variation of stalling speed with load factor. Stalling speed increases with the square root of the load factor, therefore;

$$V_A = V_{S_{1g}} \sqrt{n}$$

For example an aircraft with a 1g stalling speed of 60kt and limit load factor of 2·5 would have a V_A of:

$$60 \sqrt{2.5} = 95 \text{ kt}$$

14.8 EFFECT OF AIRCRAFT WEIGHT ON V_A

The 1g stalling speed depends on the weight of the aircraft. The line OA is drawn for the maximum design weight, so for lower weights the stalling speed will be less.

For the same limit load factor V_A will therefore decrease. For the example considered above, if V_A is 95 kt at 2500 lb weight, then at 2000 lb weight it will be:

$$95 \sqrt{\frac{2000}{2500}} = 85 \text{ kt}$$

NB: 20% decrease in weight has given approximately 10% decrease in V_A.

PRINCIPLES OF FLIGHT　　　　　　　　　　　　　　　　　　　　　　　　　LIMITATIONS

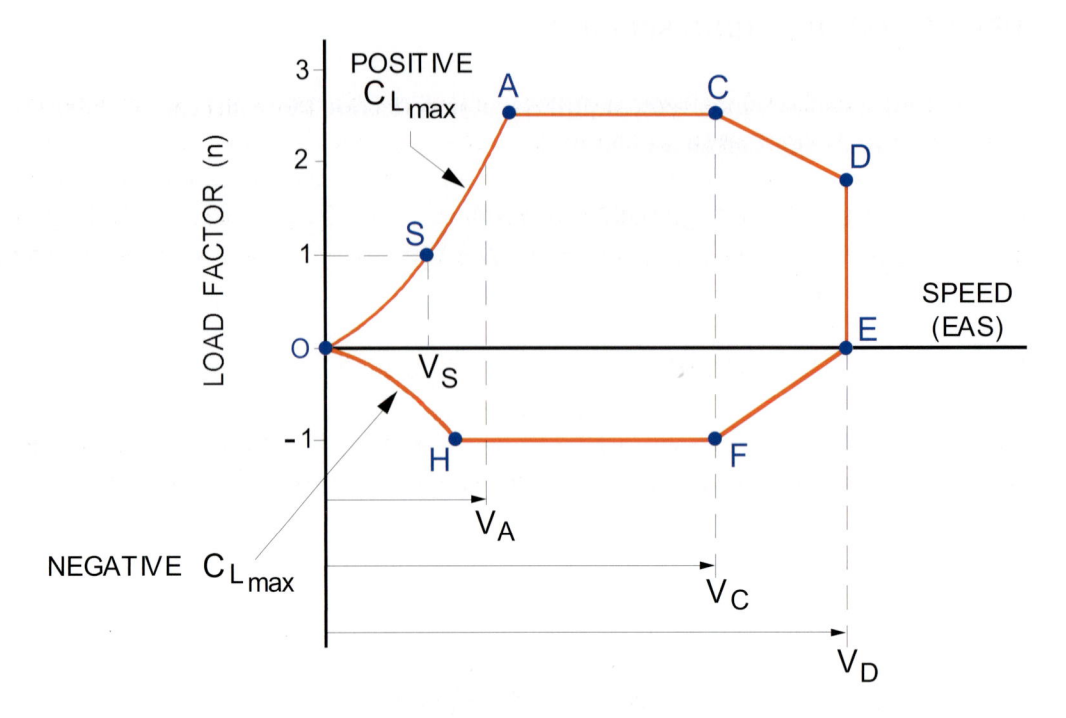

Figure 14.1 (Repeat)

14.9　DESIGN CRUISING SPEED V_C

Point 'C' in Figure 14.1 (repeated above) is the design cruise speed V_C. This is a speed selected by the designer and used to assess the strength requirements in the cruise. Its value is determined by the requirements JAR 25.335 and JAR 23.335. It must give adequate spacing from V_B (Ref. paragraph 14.15) and V_D to allow for speed upsets. For example JAR 25 requires V_C to be at least 43 kt above V_B, and not greater than 0.8 V_D. JAR 23 has similar requirements. V_C need not exceed the maximum speed in level flight at maximum continuous power (V_H) or in JAR 23, 0.9 V_H at sea level

14.10　DESIGN DIVE SPEED V_D

Point 'D' in figure 14.1 is the design dive speed V_D. This is the maximum speed which has to be considered when assessing the strength of the aircraft. It is based on the principle of an upset occurring when the aircraft is flying V_C, resulting in a shallow dive, during which the speed increases, until recovery is effected. If the resulting speed is not suitable because of buffet or other high speed effects, a demonstrated speed may be used. This is called V_{DF} the flight demonstrated design dive speed.

14.11　NEGATIVE LOAD FACTORS.

In normal flying and manoeuvres it is not likely that very large negative 'g' forces will be produced, however some negative 'g' forces may occur during manoeuvres and the aircraft must be made strong enough to withstand them.

PRINCIPLES OF FLIGHT — LIMITATIONS

14.12 THE NEGATIVE STALL.

If the angle of attack of the wing is 'increased' in the negative direction, it will eventually reach an angle at which it will stall. (If the wing section is symmetrical this angle will be the same as the positive stall angle, but for a cambered wing, the angle and the negative C_{LMAX} will usually be lower). The line OH in Fig. 14.1 represents the negative C_{LMAX} boundary. For large aircraft a limit load factor of -1 must be considered up to V_C. From V_C to V_D the negative load factor varies linearly from -1 to 0.

14.13 MANOEUVRE BOUNDARIES.

Taking into account the limiting values of positive and negative load factor, and the maximum speed to be considered, the aircraft is therefore safe to operate within the boundaries shown in Figure 14.3.

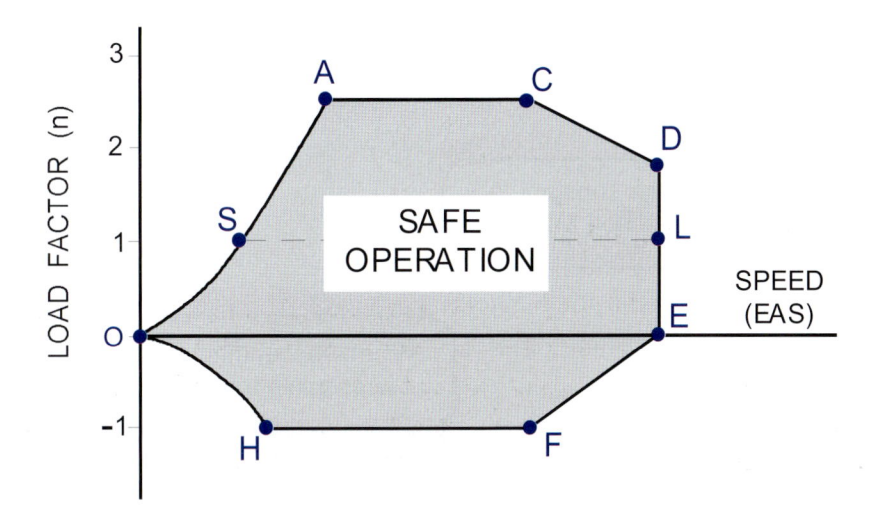

Figure 14.3   Manoeuvre boundaries

Line SL represents level 1g flight. Line SA shows the load factors that could be produced by pitching the wing to its stalling angle. Line ACD is the limit set by the maximum positive 'g' which the airframe is required to withstand. Line OH shows the negative load factors that could be produced with the wing at its negative stalling angle, and line HFE is the negative 'g' limit.

The design speeds (V_C and V_D), already defined, are used for the purpose of assessing the strength requirements of the aircraft in various flight conditions. These speeds are not scheduled in the aircraft's Flight Manual, but the operational speed limits which are scheduled, are related to them.

PRINCIPLES OF FLIGHT — LIMITATIONS

14.14 OPERATIONAL SPEED LIMITS.

The maximum airspeed at which an aircraft is permitted to fly is V_{MO} for 'large aircraft' (JAR 25) or V_{NE} for other aircraft (JAR 23) other than turbine engined aircraft. (For certification, a large aircraft is defined as one of more then 5,700 kg Maximum Certificated Take-off Mass).

Maximum Operating Speed (Large Aircraft) V_{MO} / M_{MO}: V_{MO} is a speed that may not be deliberately exceeded in any regime of flight (climb, cruise or descent). V_{MO} must not be greater than V_C and must be sufficiently below V_D to make it highly improbable that V_D will be inadvertently exceeded in operations.

[Handwritten note: EAS]

[Handwritten note: $V_{MO} \leq V_C$]

Because V_{MO} is an Indicated Air Speed, as altitude increases the Mach number corresponding to V_{MO} will increase. There will be additional limitations on the aircraft because of compressibility effects. In a climb V_{MO} will be superceded by M_{MO} (maximum operating Mach number) at about 24,000 to 29,000 ft, depending on atmospheric conditions.

Mach/Airspeed Warning System (Large Aircraft): Two independant Mach/Airspeed warning systems provide a distinct aural warning (Clacker) any time the maximum speed of Vmo/Mmo is exceeded. The warning clackers can be silenced only by reducing airspeed below Vmo/Mmo.

> When climbing at a constant IAS it is possible to exceed M_{MO}

> When descending at a constant Mach number it is possible to exceed V_{MO}

Never Exceed Speed (Small Aircraft) V_{NE}: V_{NE} is set below V_D to allow for speed upsets to be recovered. ($V_{NE} = 0.9\ V_D$). V_{NE} will be shown by a radial red line on the airspeed indicator at the high speed end of the yellow arc.

Maximum Structural Cruise Speed (Small Aircraft) V_{NO}: V_{NO} is the normal operating cruise speed limit and must be not greater than the lesser of V_C or $0.89\ V_{NE}$.

- On the airspeed indicator V_{NO} is the upper limit of the green arc.

- From V_{NO} to V_{NE} there will be a yellow arc, which is the caution range. You may fly at speeds within the yellow arc only in smooth air, and then only with caution.

14.15 GUST LOADS

The structural weight of an aircraft must be kept to a minimum while maintaining the required strength. The following gust strengths were first formulated in the late 1940's and their continued effectiveness has been verified by regular examination of actual flight data recorder traces.

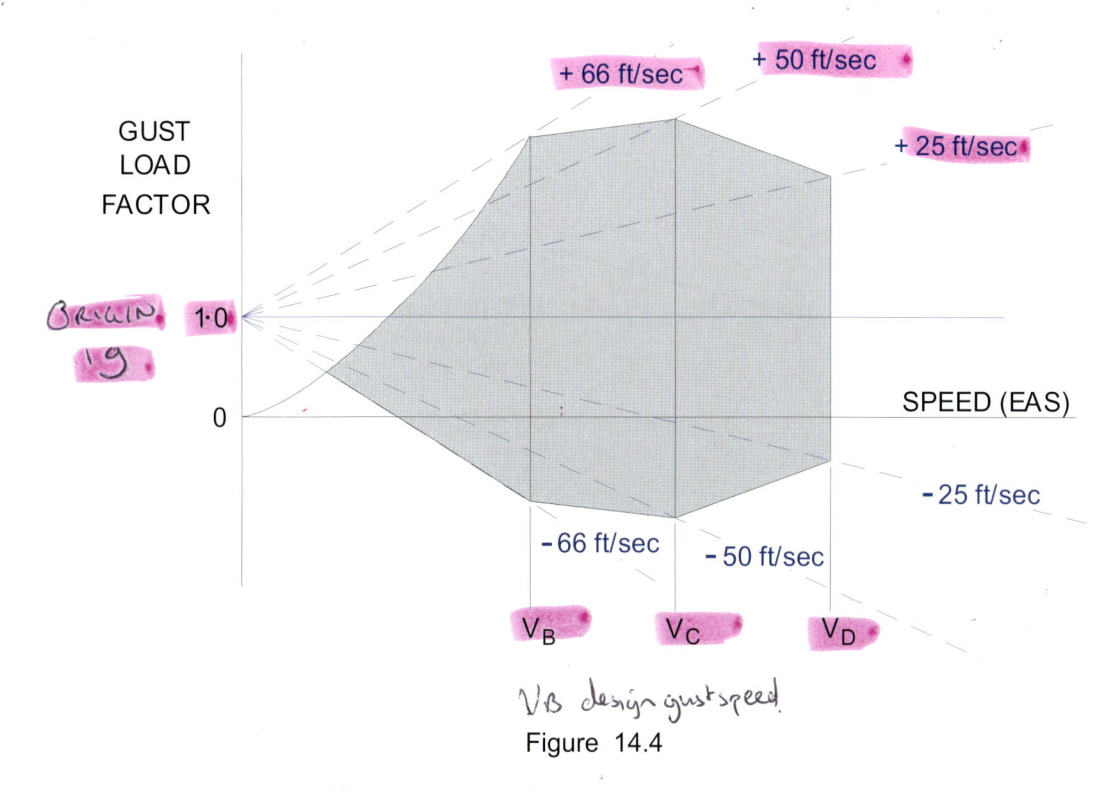

Figure 14.4

Aircraft are designed to be strong enough to withstand a **66 ft/sec vertical gust at V_B** (the design speed for maximum gust intensity). If an aircraft experienced a 66 ft/sec vertical gust while flying at V_B, it would stall before exceeding the limit load factor. In turbulence an aircraft would receive maximum protection from damage by flying at V_B.

V_B is quite a low airspeed and it would take some time for an aircraft to slow from V_C (the design cruising speed) to V_B if it flew into turbulence. Therefore, another design strength requirement is for the aircraft also to be strong enough to withstand a vertical gust of **50 ft/sec (EAS) at V_C**.

Protection is also provided for the remote possibility of a vertical gust during a momentary upset to a speed of V_D (the design diving speed). The aircraft must also be strong enough to withstand a vertical gust of **25 ft/sec at V_D**. (V_B, V_C and V_D are design speeds and are not quoted in an aircraft's flight manual).

In practice, a slightly higher speed than V_B is used for turbulence is penetration. This speed is V_{RA}/M_{RA} (the rough-air speed). **V_{RA} / M_{RA} will give adequate protection from over-stressing the aircraft plus give maximum protection from an inadvertent stall.**

PRINCIPLES OF FLIGHT   LIMITATIONS

14.16 EFFECT OF A VERTICAL GUST ON THE LOAD FACTOR

Vertical gusts will affect the load factor (n) by changing the angle of attack of the wing, Fig. 14.5.

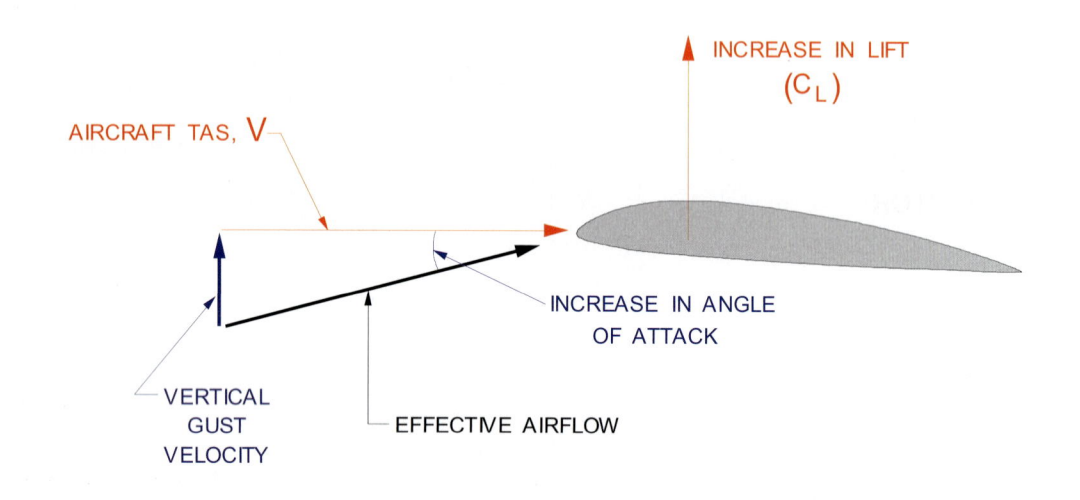

Figure 14.5

The following example illustrates the effect of a vertical gust on the load factor (n).

An aircraft is flying straight and level at a C_L of 0·42. A 1° change in angle of attack will change the C_L by 0·1. If the aircraft is subject to a vertical gust which increases the angle of attack by 3°, what load factor will the aircraft experience?

$$\text{Load factor} = \frac{\text{LIFT}}{\text{WEIGHT}}$$

In straight and level flight: $n = 1$ or $\dfrac{0.42}{0.42}$

a 3° increase in angle of attack will give: $3 \times 0.1 = 0.3$

the C_L will increase by 0.3: $0.42 + 0.3 = 0.72$

$$n = \frac{0.72}{0.42} = 1.7$$

a gust which increases the angle of attack by 3° will increase the load factor to 1.7

PRINCIPLES OF FLIGHT — LIMITATIONS

For a given gust speed and aircraft TAS, the increment in the load factor depends on the increase in C_L per change in angle of attack due to the gust (the slope of the lift curve). If the lift curve has a steep slope, the 'g' increment will be greater. Factors which affect the lift curve are aspect ratio and wing sweep.

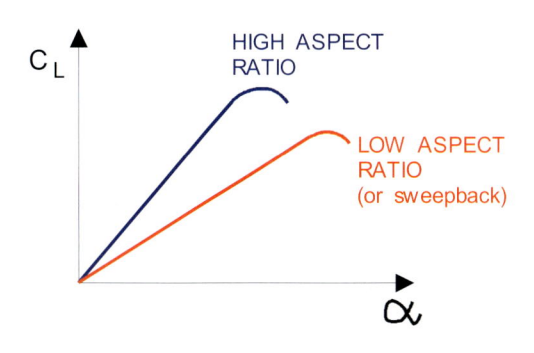

Figure 14.6

Wings having a low aspect ratio, or sweep, will have a lower lift curve slope, and so will give a smaller increase in 'g' when meeting a given gust at a given TAS.

High wing loading reduces the 'g' increment in a gust. This is because the lift increment produced is a smaller proportion of the original lift force for the more heavily loaded aircraft.

For a given aircraft the only variables for load factor increment in a gust are the aircraft TAS and the gust speed.

14.17 EFFECT OF THE GUST ON STALLING

If an aerofoil encounters an upgust, it will experience an increase in angle of attack. For a given gust velocity the increment in angle increases as the aircraft TAS decreases. If the angle of attack is already large (low speed) the increment due to the gust could cause the wing to stall. There is thus a minimum speed at which it is safe to fly if a gust is likely to be met, so as not to stall in the gust.

[Handwritten notes:] WING LOADING = WEIGHT / WING AREA   High wing load reduces susceptability to gusts

PRINCIPLES OF FLIGHT — LIMITATIONS

14.18 OPERATIONAL ROUGH-AIR SPEED (V_{RA} / M_{RA})

For flight in turbulence an air speed must chosen to give protection against two possibilities: stalling and overstressing the aircraft structure. Turbulence is defined by a gust of a defined value. If this defined gust is encountered the aircraft speed must be:

a) high enough to avoid stalling and

b) low enough to avoid damage to the structure.

These requirements are fulfilled by calculating the stall speed in the gust and then building in sufficient strength for this speed.

The key is the chosen value of the gust, as this will dictate the strength required and therefore the aircraft weight. The gust velocity is associated with the design speed, VB, and the vertical value of the gust is 66 ft. per second. Encountering a gust before the pilot is able to slow the aircraft, plus the possibility of hitting a gust if the aircraft is 'upset' at high speed must also be taken into consideration. Because these probabilities are lower however, progressively lower values of gust velocity are chosen at the higher speeds. These values are 50 ft. per second at the design cruise speed V_C and 25 ft. per second at the design dive speed V_D.

The design gust values of 66, 50 and 25 ft. per second for gusts at the design speeds of V_B, V_C and V_D have existed since the early 1940's. In the UK they were established as a result of the earliest "Flight Data Recorder" results. Modern flight recorder results and sophisticated design analyses continue to support the original boundaries of the design gust envelope.

Generally, design for strength is based on calculating the increase in load on the aircraft as a function of an instantaneous increase in angle of attack on the wing (page 14 - 11).

On large aircraft, additional allowances have to be made for several reasons:-

a) The greater dynamic response due to increased structural flexibility.

b) The possible implications of the smaller margin between actual cruise speed and design cruise speed.

c) The significance, in the more advanced designs, of the effects of build-up of gusts and unsteady flow generally.

d) The frequency of storm penetrations.

e) The implications of the limited slow-down capabilities.

PRINCIPLES OF FLIGHT — LIMITATIONS

All design speeds, and design gust values, are EAS. But, remember: the increase in angle of attack due to a gust is a function of the TAS of the aircraft and the TAS of the gust.

The choice of rough-air speed to be used operationally must be consistent with the strength of the aircraft. At the same time the aircraft must comply with both minimum stability and control criteria. There is also the important consideration of what maximum speed reduction can be achieved in a slow-down technique. A typical chart of the speeds to which the rough air speed is related, is shown below in Fig. 14.7. The illustration is drawn for a single (mid) weight. Line AB is the 1g stall speed.

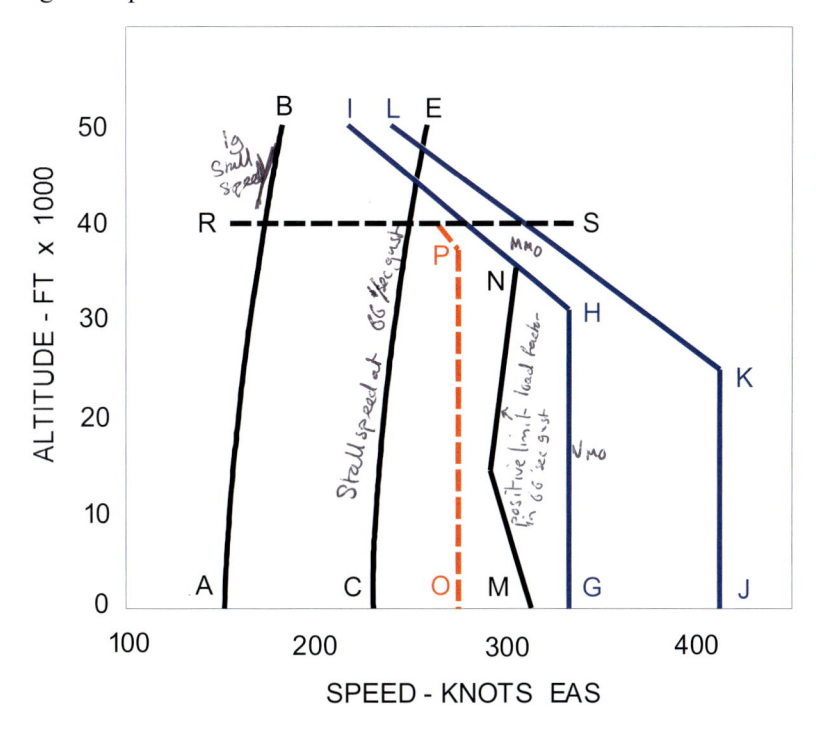

Figure 14.7

Line CE is the stall speed in a 66 ft. per sec. gust.

(This assumes the 66 ft. per sec. gust up to maximum altitude. Note that point E would represent an extremely high true air speed gust value).

Line GHI is the Vmo/Mmo line.

Line JKL is the VDF/MDF line.

Line MN is an example of a maximum strength speed line for a 66 ft. per sec. gust.

Line RS is the maximum altitude at which the aeroplane can sustain 1·5 g without too much buffet.

At all speeds above the line CE the aeroplane will sustain a 66 fps gust without stalling and at all speeds below the line MN the aeroplane is strong enough to withstand a 66 fps gust. The rough-air speed therefore should lie somewhere between these two speeds, and the line OP gives equal protection between accidentally stalling and overstressing the aircraft.

The line MN is a curious shape because different parts of the structure become critical at different altitudes. This line is actually the lowest speed boundary of a collection of curves at the higher speed end of the chart.

Because of the obvious attraction of a single speed at all altitudes up to that at which the rough-air speed becomes a rough-air Mach number, the line could be adjusted slightly so as to avoid any variations with altitude. As turbulence is generally completely random, this halfway speed would give equal protection against the 50-50 probability of being forced too fast or too slow.

It has been stated that the diagram is drawn for a mid weight. The effect of weight change in terms of the lower and upper limits to rough-air speed is, of course, significant, but self-cancelling. At low weights the stall line for a 66 ft. per sec. gust falls to lower speeds and the maximum strength speed line increases to higher speeds. There is therefore no point in attempting a sophisticated variation of V_{RA} with weight.

The maximum altitude limit does, however, vary significantly with weight, and also varies for the level of manoeuvre capability chosen. A 0·5 g increment to buffet is not too much protection in severe turbulence. A lower altitude will therefore be required for a higher level of protection, and, for a given level of protection, a lower altitude will be required for higher weights.

14.19 LANDING GEAR SPEED LIMITATIONS

The landing gear will normally be retracted as soon as possible after take-off, to reduce drag and increase the climb gradient. There is no normal requirement for the gear to be operated at high IAS so the retract and extend mechanism together with the attachment points to the structure are sized for the required task. To design the gear for operation at high IAS would unnecessarily increase structural weight.

V_{LO}: the landing gear operating speed is the speed at which it is safe both to extend and to retract the landing gear. If the extension speed is not the same as the retraction speed, the two speeds must be designated as $V_{LO\,(EXT)}$ and $V_{LO\,(RET)}$.

When the gear is retracted or extended the doors must open first. The doors merely streamline the undercarriage bay and are not designed to take the aerodynamic loads which would be placed on them at high IAS. Consequently V_{LO} is usually lower than V_{LE}.

V_{LE}: the landing gear extended speed. There may be occasions when it is necessary to ferry the aircraft with the gear down, and to do this a higher permissible speed would be convenient. V_{LE} is the speed at which it is safe to fly the aircraft with the landing gear secured in the fully extended position. Because the undercarriage doors are closed, V_{LE} is normally higher than V_{LO}.

PRINCIPLES OF FLIGHT — LIMITATIONS

14.20 FLAP SPEED LIMIT

Flaps are designed to reduce take-off and landing distances and are used when airspeed is relatively low. The flaps, operating mechanism and attachment points to the structure are not designed to withstand the loads which would be applied at high airspeeds (dynamic pressure).

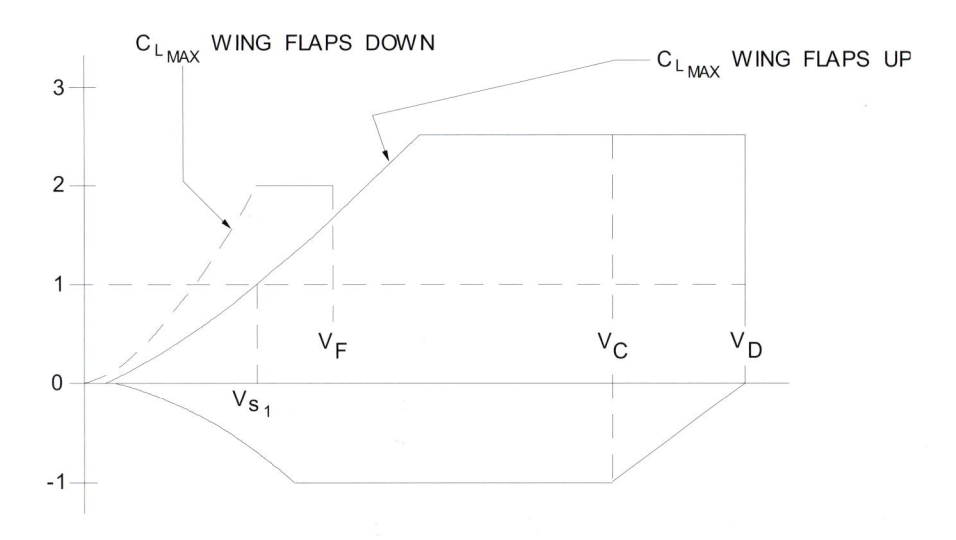

Figure 14.8

Flaps increase $C_{L\,MAX}$ and decrease stall speed, so when flaps are deployed it is necessary to provide additional protection to avoid exceeding the structural limit load. It can be seen from the V-n diagram in Fig. 14.8 that it is possible for a greater load to be applied to the structure at quite moderate airspeeds with flaps down. The limit load factor with flaps deployed is reduced from 2·5 to 2 to give additional protection to the flaps and also the wing structure. If flaps are deployed in turbulence a given vertical gust can generate a much larger lift force, which will subject the structure to a larger load, possibly exceeding the ability of the structure to withstand it and the structure could fail.

V_{FE}: the Wing Flaps Extended Speed is the maximum airspeed at which the aircraft should be flown with the flaps in a prescribed extended position. (Top of the white arc on the ASI).

Extending flaps for turbulence penetration in the cruise would reduce the stall speed and increases the margin to stall, but the margin to structural limitations will be reduced by a greater amount. Flaps must only be used as laid down in the aircraft Flight Manual.

PRINCIPLES OF FLIGHT — LIMITATIONS

14.21 AEROELASTICITY (AERO - ELASTIC COUPLING)

Aerodynamic forces acting on the aircraft produce distortion of the structure, and this distortion produces corresponding elastic forces in the structure ("winding up the spring"). Structural distortion produces additional aerodynamic loading and this process is continued until either an equilibrium condition is reached, or structural failure occurs.

This interaction between the aerodynamic loads and the elastic deformation of the airframe is known as **aeroelasticity, or aero-elastic coupling.**

At low airspeeds, the aerodynamic forces are relatively small, and the resultant distortion of the structure produces only negligible effects. At higher speeds, aerodynamic loads and the consequent distortion are correspondingly greater. Aerodynamic force is proportional to V^2, but **structural torsional stiffness remains constant**. This relationship implies that at some high speed, the aerodynamic force buildup may overpower the resisting torsional stiffness and 'divergence' will occur. The aircraft must be designed so the speed at which divergence occurs is higher than the design speeds V_D/M_D.

Definitions:

> **Elasticity:** No structure is perfectly rigid. The structure of an aircraft is designed to be as light as possible. This results in the aircraft being a fairly flexible structure, the amount of flexibility depending on the design configuration of the aircraft. e.g. aspect ratio, sweepback, taper ratio. etc.
>
> **Backlash:** The possibility of movement of the control surface without any movement of the pilot's controls.
>
> **Mass distribution:** The position of the CG of a surface in relation to its torsional axis.
>
> **Mass balance:** A mass located to change the position of the CG of a surface in relation to its torsional axis.
>
> **Divergence:** The structure will continue to distort until it breaks.
>
> **Flutter:** The rapid and uncontrolled oscillation of a surface resulting from imbalance. Flutter normally leads to a catastrophic failure of the structure.

PRINCIPLES OF FLIGHT   **LIMITATIONS**

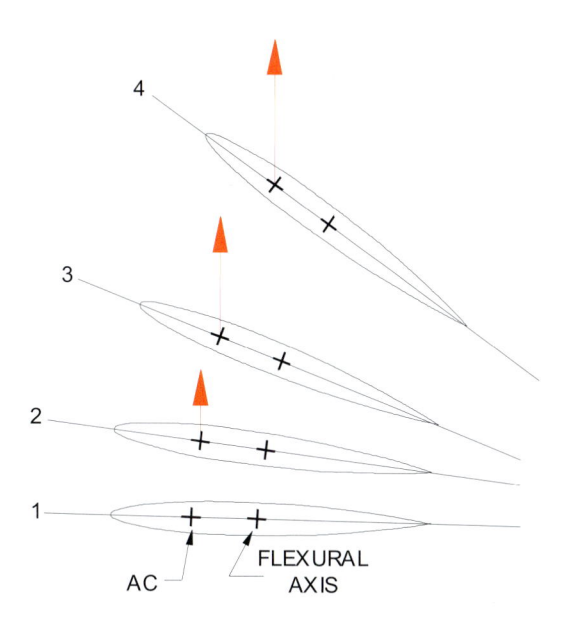

Figure 14.9

Refer to Fig. 14.9 which represents the view of a wingtip, and consider a vertical gust increasing the angle of attack of the wing. The additional lift force will bend the wing tip upwards from position 1 to 2 and the increase in lift acting through the AC, which is forward of the flexural axis, will twist the wing tip nose up; this increases the angle of attack further. The wing tip will rapidly progress to position 3 and 4. The wing is being wound up like a spring and can break if distorted too much.

How far the structure is distorted depends on:

a) the flexibility of the structure

b) the distance between the AC and the flexural axis and

c) the dynamic pressure (IAS).

Methods of delaying divergence to a higher speed:

a) The structure can be made stiffer, but this will increase weight.

b) A better solution is to move the flexural axis closer to the AC. This can easily be accomplished by mounting a mass forward of the AC. Instead of using a large piece of lead, as in control surface mass balance, the engines can be mounted forward of the leading edge and this will move the flexural axis closer to the AC. (also see flutter, paragraph 14.23).

PRINCIPLES OF FLIGHT   LIMITATIONS

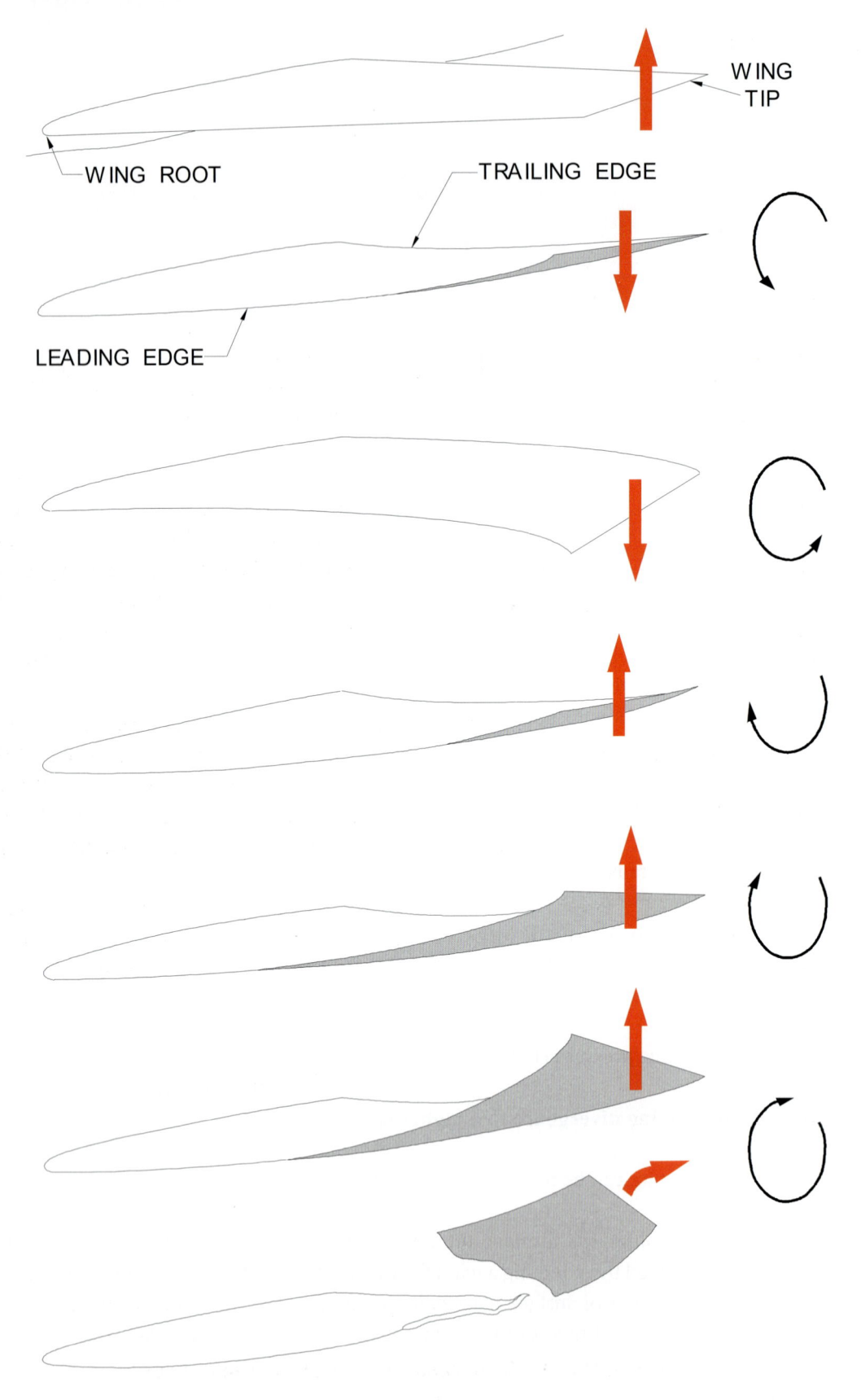

WING TIP
WING ROOT
TRAILING EDGE
LEADING EDGE

Figure 14.10   Typical flutter mode

14.22 FLUTTER.

Flutter involves:

a) aerodynamic forces

b) inertia forces and

c) the elastic properties of a surface.

The distribution of mass and stiffness in a structure determine certain natural frequencies and modes of vibration. If the structure is subject to a 'forcing' frequency near these natural frequencies, a resonant condition can result giving an unstable oscillation which can rapidly lead to destruction.

An aircraft is subject to many aerodynamic excitations (gusts, control inputs, etc.) and the aerodynamic forces at various speeds have characteristic properties for rate of change of force and moment. The aerodynamic forces may interact with the structure and may excite (or negatively damp) the natural modes of the structure and allow flutter. Flutter must not occur within the normal flight operating envelope and the natural modes must be damped if possible or designed to occur beyond V_D/M_D. A typical flutter mode is illustrated in Fig. 14.10.

Since the problem is one of high speed flight, it is generally desirable to have very high natural frequencies and flutter speeds well above the normal operating speeds. Any change of stiffness or mass distribution will alter the modes and frequencies and thus allow a change in the flutter speeds. If the aircraft is not properly maintained and excessive play and flexibility (backlash) exist, flutter could occur at flight speeds well below the operational limit speed (V_{MO}/M_{MO}).

Wing flutter can be delayed to a higher speed, for a given structural stiffness (weight), by mounting the engines on pylons beneath the wing forward of the leading edge, Fig. 14.11. The engines act as 'mass balance' for the wing by moving the flexural axis forward, closer to the AC.

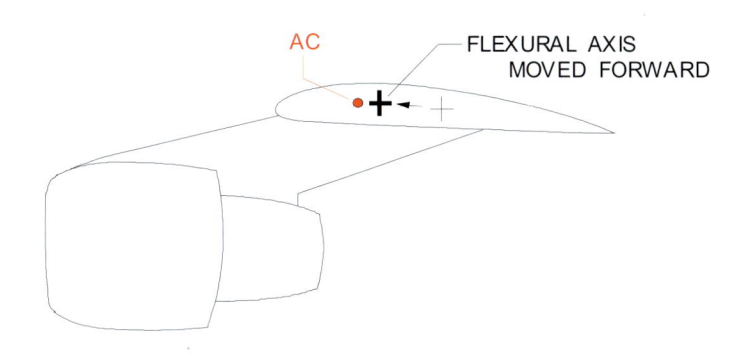

Figure 14.11 Wing mass balanced by podded engines

PRINCIPLES OF FLIGHT LIMITATIONS

14.23 CONTROL SURFACE FLUTTER

Control surface flutter can develop as a result of an oscillation of the control surface coupled with an oscillation in bending or twisting of the wing, tailplane or fin. A control surface oscillation can result from backlash (free play) in the control system, or from a disturbance (gust). Flutter can develop if the CG of the control surface is behind the hinge line, so that the inertia of the control surface causes a moment around the hinge.

Torsional Aileron Flutter: Figure 14.12 illustrates the sequence for a half cycle, which is described below.

1. The aileron is displaced downwards, exerting an upwards force on the aileron hinge.

2. The wing twists about the torsional axis, the trailing edge rising, taking the aileron hinge up with it, but the aileron surface lags behind due to the CG being aft of the hinge line.

3. The inherent stiffness of the wing has arrested the twisting motion (the spring is now wound up), but the air loads on the aileron, the stretch of the control circuit, and its upwards momentum, cause the aileron to 'flick' upwards, placing a down load on the trailing edge of the wing.

4. The energy stored in the twisted wing and the reversed aerodynamic load of the aileron cause the wing to twist in the opposite direction. The cycle is then repeated.

Torsional aileron flutter can be prevented either by mass balancing the ailerons with attachment of a mass ahead of the hinge line to bring the CG onto, or slightly ahead of the hinge line, or by making the controls irreversible (fully powered controls with no manual reversion).

Flexural Aileron Flutter: is generally similar, but is caused by the movement of the aileron lagging behind the rise and fall of the outer portion of the wing as it flexes (wing tips up and down), thus tending to increase the oscillation. This type of flutter can also be prevented by mass balancing the ailerons. The positioning of the mass balance 'weight' is important, the nearer the wing tip the smaller the mass required. On many aircraft the mass is distributed along the whole length of the aileron in the form of a leading edge 'spar', thus increasing the stiffness of the aileron and preventing a concentrated mass starting torsional vibrations in the aileron itself.

Mass balancing must also be applied to elevators and rudders to prevent their inertia and the 'springiness' of the fuselage starting similar motions. Mass balancing may even be applied to tabs.

The danger of all forms of flutter is that the speed and amplitude of each cycle is greater than its predecessor, so that in a second or two the structure may be bent beyond its elastic limit and fail. Decreasing speed if flutter is detected is theoretically the only means of preventing structural failure, but the rate of divergence is so rapid that slowing down is not really a practical solution.

PRINCIPLES OF FLIGHT   **LIMITATIONS**

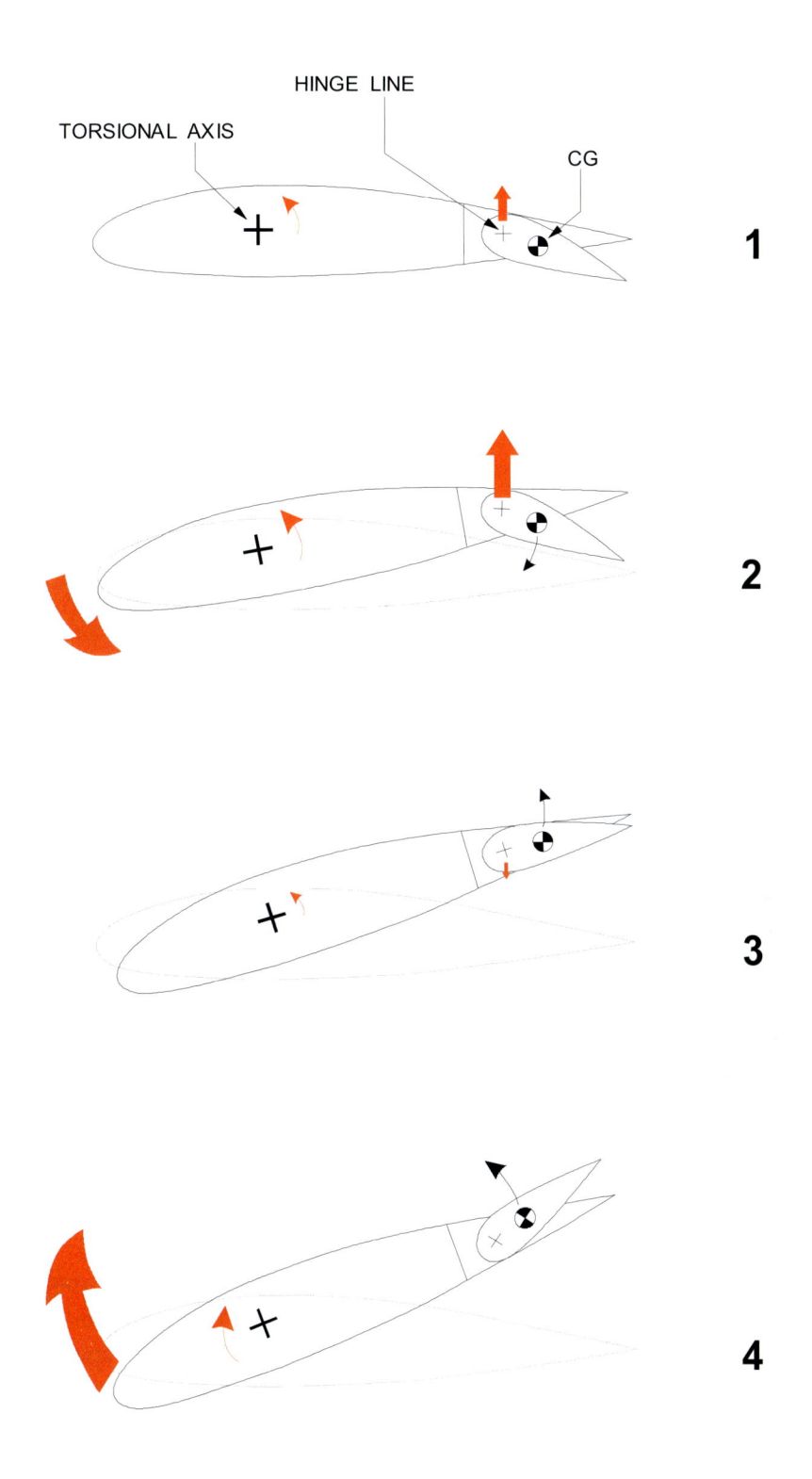

Figure 14.12   Torsional aileron flutter

PRINCIPLES OF FLIGHT   LIMITATIONS

14.24 AILERON REVERSAL

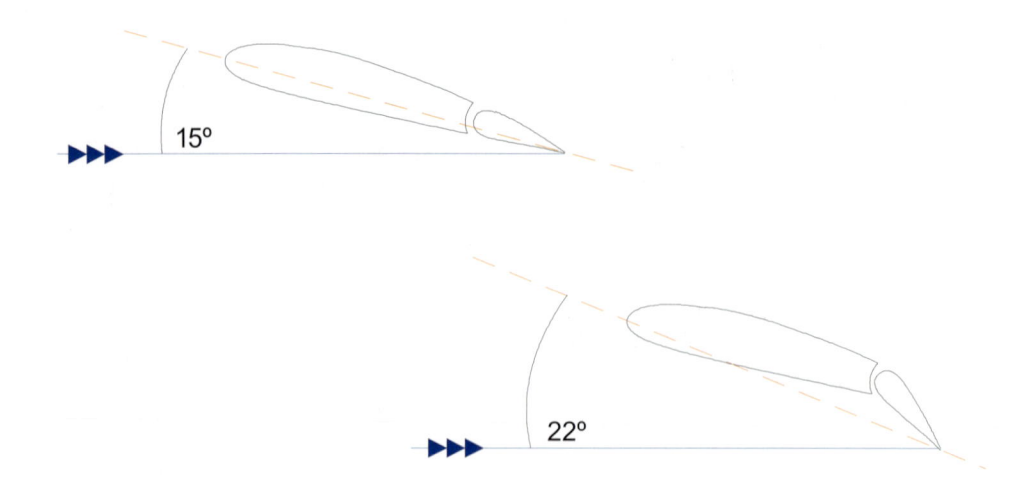

Figure 14.13   Low speed aileron reversal

LOW SPEED: It was described in paragraph 7.6 that if an aileron is lowered when flying at high angles of attack, that wing could possibly stall, Fig. 14.13. In that case the wing will drop instead of rising as intended. Hence the term low speed aileron reversal.

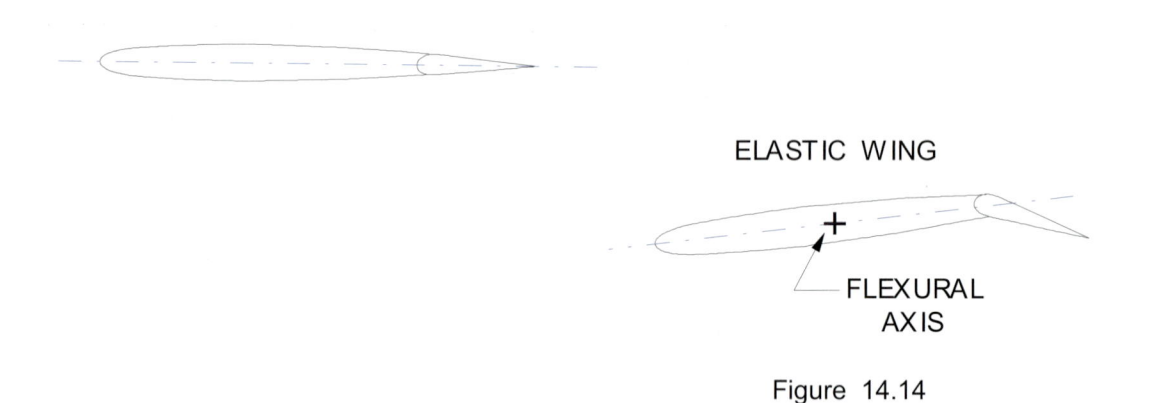

Figure 14.14

HIGH SPEED: Aileron reversal can also occur at high speed when the wing twists as a result of the loads caused by operating the ailerons. In Figure 14.14 the aileron has been deflected downwards to increase lift and raise the wing. Aerodynamic forces act upwards on the aileron, and as this is behind the flexural axis of the wing, it will cause a nose down twisting moment on the wing structure. This will reduce the angle of attack of the wing which will reduce its lift. If the twisting is sufficient, the loss of lift due to decreased angle of attack will exceed the gain of lift due to increased camber, and the wing will drop instead of lifting.

PRINCIPLES OF FLIGHT   **LIMITATIONS**

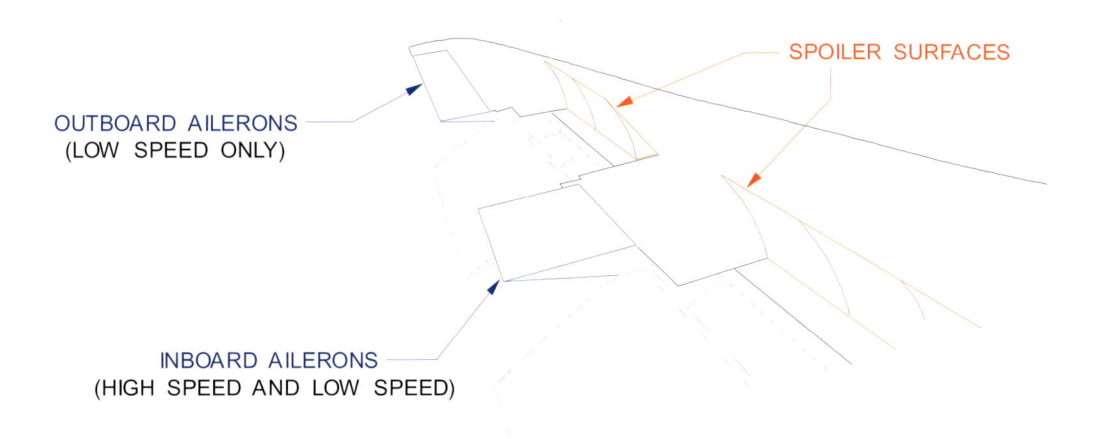

Figure 14.15 Inboard and outboard ailerons and roll control spoilers

High speed aileron reversal can be delayed to a speed higher than V_D / M_D by having inboard and outboard ailerons and/or roll control spoilers. The inboard ailerons, Fig. 14.15, are mounted where the wing structure is naturally stiffer, and work at all speeds. The outboard ailerons work only at low speed, being deactivated when the flaps are retracted.

On most high speed jet transport aircraft roll control spoilers assist the ailerons. Because they are mounted further forward and on a stiffer part of the wing, roll control spoilers do not distort the wing structure to the same degree as ailerons.

INTENTIONALLY

LEFT

BLANK

PRINCIPLES OF FLIGHT   LIMITATIONS

SELF ASSESSMENT QUESTIONS

1. If an aircraft is flown at its design manoeuvring speed V_A :

    a) it is possible to subject the aircraft to a load greater than its limit load during high 'g' manoeuvres.
    b) it is only possible to subject the aircraft to a load greater than its limit load during violent increases in incidence, i.e. when using excessive stick force to pull-out of a dive.
    c) it is not possible to exceed the limit load.
    d) it is possible to subject the aircraft to a load greater than its limit load at high TAS.

2. The speed V_{NE} is:

    a) the airspeed which must not be exceeded except in a dive
    b) the maximum airspeed at which manoeuvres approaching the stall may be carried out
    c) the maximum airspeed at which an aircraft may be flown
    d) the maximum speed, above which flaps should not be extended

3. Maximum structural cruising speed V_{NO} is the maximum speed at which an aeroplane can be operated during:

    a) normal operations.
    b) abrupt manoeuvres.
    c) flight in smooth air.
    d) flight in rough air.

4. The maximum allowable airspeed with flaps extended (V_{FE}) is lower than cruising speed because:

    a) they are used only when preparing to land
    b) the additional lift and drag created would overload the wing and flap structure at higher speeds
    c) flaps will stall if they are deployed at too high an airspeed
    d) too much drag is induced

5. Why is V_{LE} greater than V_{LO} on the majority of large jet transport aircraft?

    a) V_{LO} is used when the aircraft is taking off and landing when the IAS is low.
    b) extending the gear at too high an airspeed would cause excessive parasite drag.
    c) flying at too high an airspeed with the gear down would prevent retraction of the forward retracting nose gear.
    d) V_{LO} is a lower IAS because the undercarriage doors are vulnerable to aerodynamic loads when the gear is in transit, up or down.

6. The phenomenon of flutter is described as:

    a) rapid oscillatory motion involving only rotation of the control surfaces, associated with the shock waves produced around the control surfaces.
    b) oscillatory motion of part or parts of the aircraft relative to the remainder of the structure.
    c) rapid movement of the airframe caused by vibration from the engines.
    d) reversal of the ailerons caused by wing torsional flexibility.

7. What is the purpose of fitting the engines to an aircraft using wing mounted pylons?

    a) They give increased ground clearance in roll.
    b) They give improved longitudinal mass distribution.
    c) The wing structure can be lighter because the engine acts as a mass balance and also relieves wing bending stress.
    d) They enable a longer undercarriage to be used which gives an optimum pitch attitude for take-off and landing.

8. Aileron reversal at high dynamic pressures is caused by:

    a) the down-going aileron increasing the semi-span angle of attack beyond the critical.
    b) flow separation ahead of the aileron leading edge.
    c) uneven shock wave formation on the top and bottom surface of the aileron, with the attendant movement in control surface CP, causing the resultant force to act in the opposite direction from that intended.
    d) dynamic pressure acting on the aileron twisting the wing in the opposite direction, possibly causing the aircraft to bank in a direction opposite to that intended.

9. Controls are mass balanced in order to:

    a) eliminate control flutter.
    b) aerodynamically assist the pilot in moving the controls.
    c) provide equal control forces on all three controls.
    d) return the control surface to neutral when the controls are released.

10. If an aircraft weight is reduced by 15%, V_A will:

    a) Not change.
    b) Increase by 15%.
    c) Increase by 7.5%.
    d) Decrease by 7.5%.

PRINCIPLES OF FLIGHT   **LIMITATIONS**

11. Which of the following statements is correct?

    1 - It is a design requirement that control reversal speeds must be higher than any speed to be achieved in flight.

    2 - The airframe must be made strong and stiff enough to ensure that the wing torsional divergence speed is higher, by a substantial safety margin, than any speed which will ever be achieved in any condition in flight.

    3 - Flying control surfaces are aerodynamically balanced to prevent flutter.

    4 - An aircraft is not a rigid structure.

    5 - Aeroelasticity affects are inversely proportional to IAS.

    6 - Control reversal speed is higher if the aircraft is fitted with outboard ailerons which are locked-out as the aircraft accelerates; the inboard ailerons alone controlling the aircraft in roll at higher speeds.

    a) All the above statements are correct.
    b) 1, 2, 3 and 6.
    c) 1, 2, 4 and 6.
    d) 1, 3, 5 and 6.

12. V_{LO} is defined as:

    a) maximum landing gear operating speed.
    b) maximum landing gear extended speed.
    c) maximum leading edge flaps extended speed.
    d) maximum flap speed.

13. If flutter is experienced during flight, the preferable action would be:

    a) immediately increase speed beyond V_{MO} / M_{MO}, by sacrificing altitude if necessary.
    b) immediately close the throttles, deploy the speed brakes and bank the aircraft.
    c) rapidly pitch-up to slow the aircraft as quickly as possible.
    d) reduce speed immediately by closing the throttles, but avoid rapid changes in attitude and/or configuration.

INTENTIONALLY LEFT BLANK

PRINCIPLES OF FLIGHT — LIMITATIONS

ANSWERS

No	A	B	C	D	REF
1			C		
2			C		
3	A				
4		B			
5				D	
6		B			
7			C		
8				D	
9	A				
10				D	
11			C		
12	A				
13				D	

INTENTIONALLY LEFT BLANK

CHAPTER 15 - WINDSHEAR

Contents

	Page
INTRODUCTION	15 - 1
MICROBURST	
WINDSHEAR ENCOUNTER DURING APPROACH	15 - 3
EFFECTS OF WINDSHEAR	15 - 4
"ENERGY GAIN" DUE TO INCREASE IN HEADWIND	
"ENERGY LOSS" DUE TO DOWNDRAUGHT	15 - 5
"ENERGY LOSS" DUE TO LOSS OF HEADWIND	
"TYPICAL" RECOVERY FROM WINDSHEAR	15 - 6
WINDSHEAR REPORTING	15 - 7
VISUAL CLUES	
CONCLUSIONS	15 - 8
SELF ASSESSMENT QUESTIONS	15 - 9
ANSWERS	15 - 15

PRINCIPLES OF FLIGHT   **WINDSHEAR**

15.1 INTRODUCTION (Ref: AIC 33/1997)

Windshear is a sudden drastic shift in wind speed and/or direction that occurs over a short distance at any altitude in a vertical and/or horizontal plane. It can subject an aircraft to sudden updraughts, downdraughts, or extreme horizontal wind components, causing sudden loss of lift or violent changes in vertical speeds or altitudes. Windshear will cause abrupt displacement from the flight path and require substantial control action to counteract it.

A windshear encounter is a very dynamic event which can strike suddenly and with devastating effect which has been beyond the recovery powers of experienced pilots flying modern and powerful aircraft. An encounter may cause alarm, a damaged undercarriage, or a total catastrophe. **The first and most vital defence is avoidance.**

The most powerful examples of windshear are associated with thunderstorms (cumulonimbus clouds), but windshear can also be experienced in association with other meteorological features such as the passage of a front, or a marked low-level temperature inversion. The meteorological features of windshear will be dealt with fully elsewhere.

15.2 MICROBURST

Microbursts are associated with thunderstorms and are one of the most dangerous sources of windshear. Microbursts are small-scale intense downdraughts which, on reaching the surface, spread outward in all directions from the downdraught centre. This causes the presence of both vertical and horizontal wind shear that can be **extremely hazardous to all types and sizes of aircraft**, especially when within 1,000 feet of the ground.

A microburst downdraught is typically less than 1 mile in diameter as it descends from the cloud base to about 1,000 to 3,000 feet above the ground. In the transition zone near the ground, the downdraught changes to a horizontal outflow that can extend to approximately 2½ miles (4 km) in diameter.

a) **Downdraughts can be as strong as 6,000 feet per minute.**

b) **Horizontal winds near the surface can be as strong as 45 knots resulting in a 90 knot shear as the wind changes to or from a headwind across the microburst.**

c) These strong horizontal winds occur within a few hundred feet of the ground. **An individual microburst seldom lasts longer than 15 minutes from the time it strikes the ground until dissipation.**

These are maximum values but they do indicate how it is possible for large and powerful aircraft to become uncontrollable when they meet such examples of the microburst.

PRINCIPLES OF FLIGHT   **WINDSHEAR**

A microburst intensifies for about 5 minutes after it first strikes the ground, with the maximum intensity winds lasting approximately 2 to 4 minutes. Sometimes microbursts are concentrated into a line structure and, under these conditions, activity may continue for as long as an hour. Once microburst activity starts, multiple microbursts in the same general area are not uncommon and should be expected.

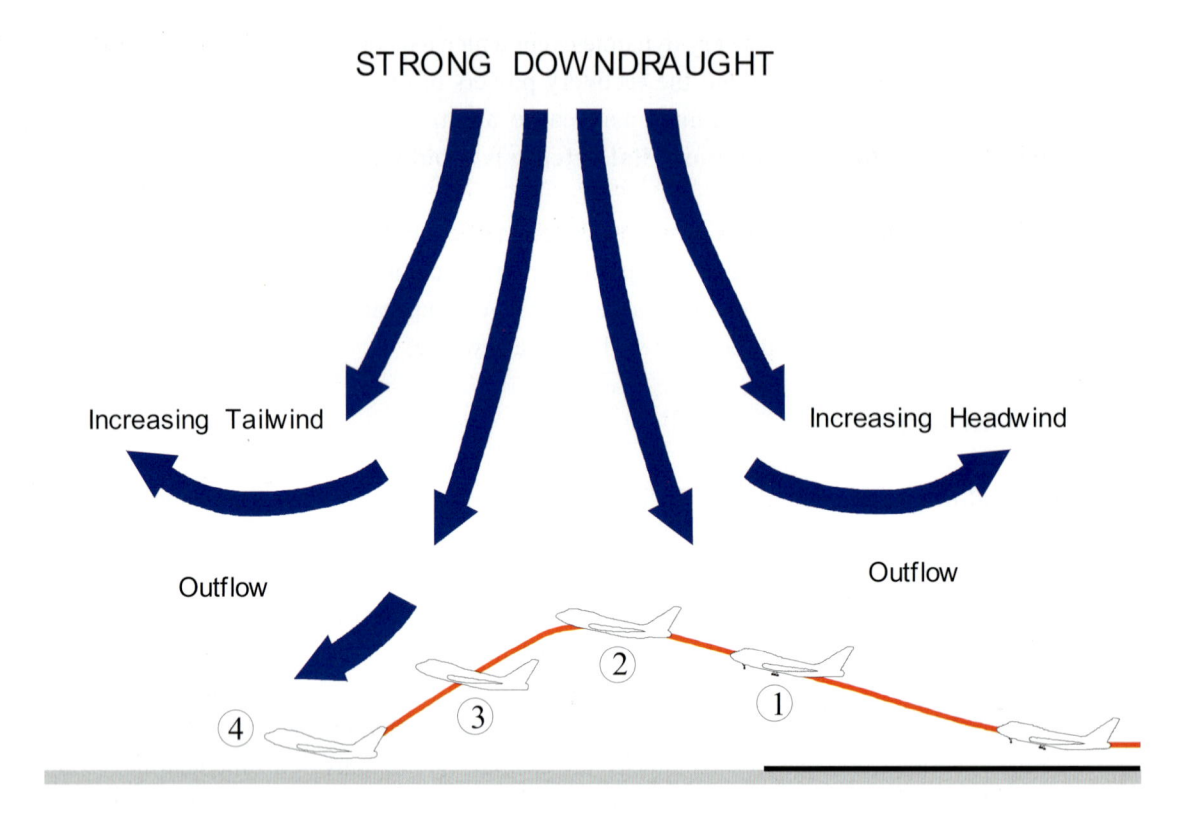

Figure 15.1   A microburst encounter during take-off

During takeoff into a microburst, shown in Fig. 15.1, an aircraft first experiences a headwind which increases performance without a change in pitch and power (1).

This is followed by a decreasing headwind and performance, and a strong downdraft (2).

Performance continues to deteriorate as the wind shears to a tailwind in the downdraft (3).

The most severe downdraft will be encountered between positions 2 and 3, which may result in an uncontrollable descent and impact with the ground (4).

PRINCIPLES OF FLIGHT   **WINDSHEAR**

15.3 WINDSHEAR ENCOUNTER DURING APPROACH

The Power setting and vertical velocity required to maintain the glide slope should be closely monitored. If any windshear is encountered, it may be difficult to stay on the glide path at normal power and descent rates. **If there is ever any doubt that you can regain a reasonable rate of descent, and land without abnormal manoeuvres, you should apply full power and go-around or make a missed approach.**

Windshear can vary enormously in its impact and effect. Clearly some shears will be more severe and consequently more dangerous than others.

When countering the effects of windshear, it is best to assume 'worse case'. **It is impossible to predict at the first stages of a windshear encounter how severe it will be, and it is good advice to suggest that recovery action should anticipate the worst.**

	WIND SHEAR			
	From	To	From	To
	Headwind	Calm or Tailwind	Tailwind	Calm or Headwind
INDICATIONS				
Indicated Airspeed	Decrease		Increase	
Pitch Attitude	Decrease		Increase	
Aircraft	Tends to Sink		Balloons	
Groundspeed	Increases		Decreases	
ACTIONS				
Power	Increase		Decrease	
Fly	Up to Glideslope		Down to Glideslope	
Be prepared to	Reduce Power		Increase Power	
To Stay on Glide Path	Increase Rate of Descent (Due to faster groundspeed)		Decrease Rate of Descent (Due to slower groundspeed)	

Figure 15.2   Indications and recovery actions for windshear encounter during approach

Referring to Fig. 15.2, this table gives guidance should you encounter wind shear during a stabilized landing approach. **Approaches should never be attempted into known wind shear conditions.**

PRINCIPLES OF FLIGHT   WINDSHEAR

15.4 EFFECTS OF WINDSHEAR

The relationship of an aeroplane in a moving air mass to its two reference points must be fully understood. One reference is the air mass itself and the other is the ground.

On passing through a shear line, the change of airspeed will be sudden, but the inertia of the aircraft will at first keep it at its original ground speed. The wind is a form of energy and when it shears, an equivalent amount of energy is lost or gained.

a) A rapid increase in headwind (or loss of tailwind) are both 'energy gains', and will temporarily improve performance, Fig. 15.3.

b) Down-draughts or a sudden drop of headwind (or increase in tailwind) are the main danger at low altitude because they give an 'energy loss', Fig. 15.4 and 15.5.

'ENERGY GAIN' - Rapid increase in headwind.

60 kt

Vertical Speed: 200 ft/min R.O.C.
Ground Speed: 130 kt
IAS: 190 kt

GLIDE SLOPE

10 kt

Vertical Speed: 700 ft/min R.O.D.
Ground Speed: 130 kt
IAS: 140 kt

SHEAR LINE

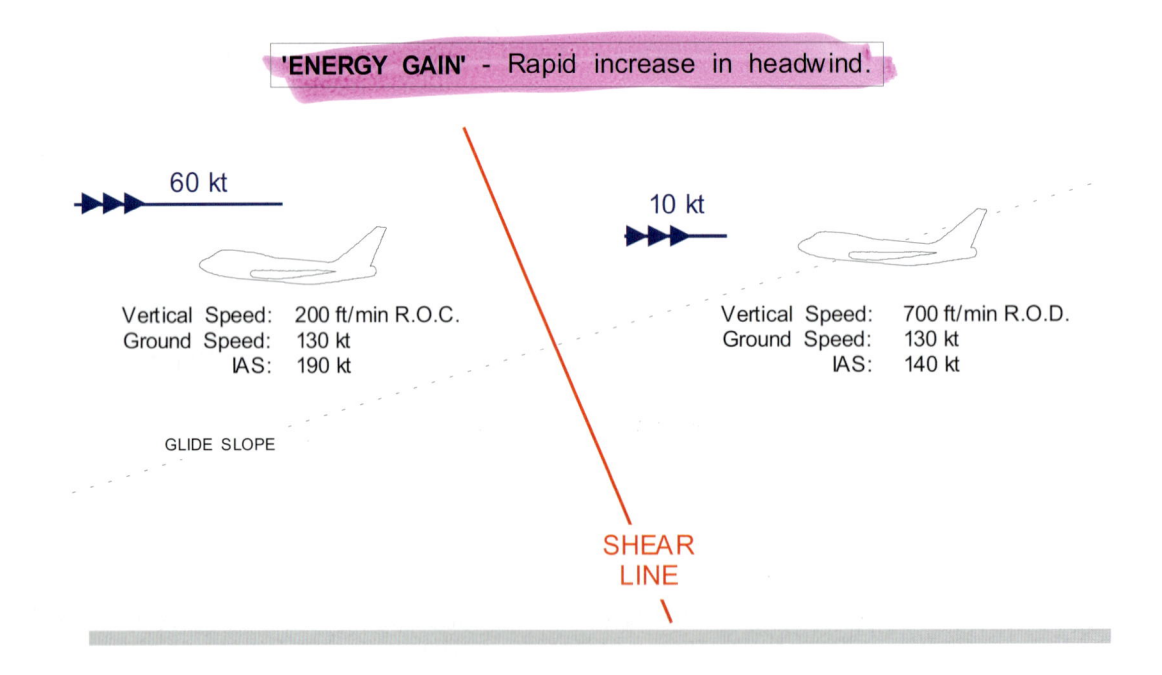

Figure 15.3 "Energy Gain" due to increase in headwind

PRINCIPLES OF FLIGHT   **WINDSHEAR**

'ENERGY LOSS' - Effect of downdraught.

Vertical Speed: 1500 ft/min R.O.D.	Vertical Speed: 700 ft/min R.O.D.
Ground Speed: 130 kt	Ground Speed: 130 kt
IAS: 110 kt	IAS: 140 kt

10 kt

GLIDE SLOPE

SHEAR LINE

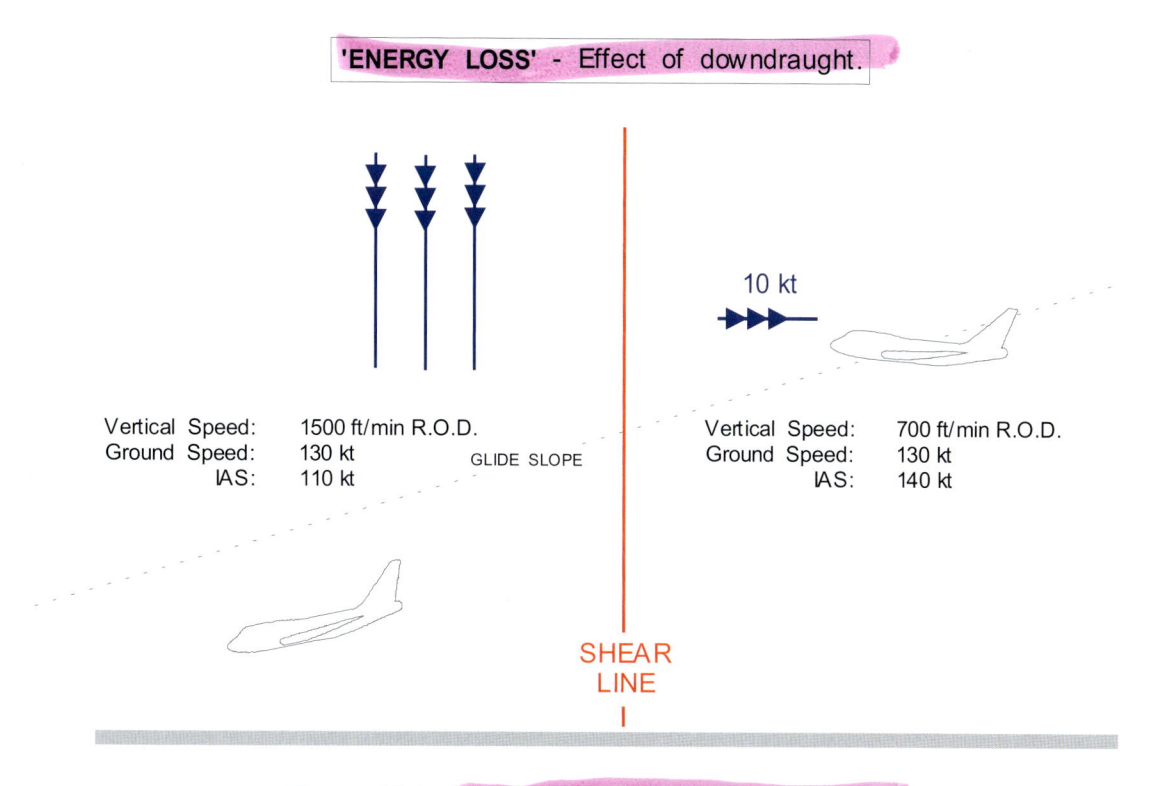

Figure 15.4 "Energy Loss" due to downdraught

'ENERGY LOSS' - Loss of headwind.

10 kt

Vertical Speed: 1000 ft/min R.O.D.	Vertical Speed: 700 ft/min R.O.D.
Ground Speed: 130 kt	Ground Speed: 130 kt
IAS: 110 kt	IAS: 140 kt

GLIDE SLOPE

20 kt

SHEAR LINE

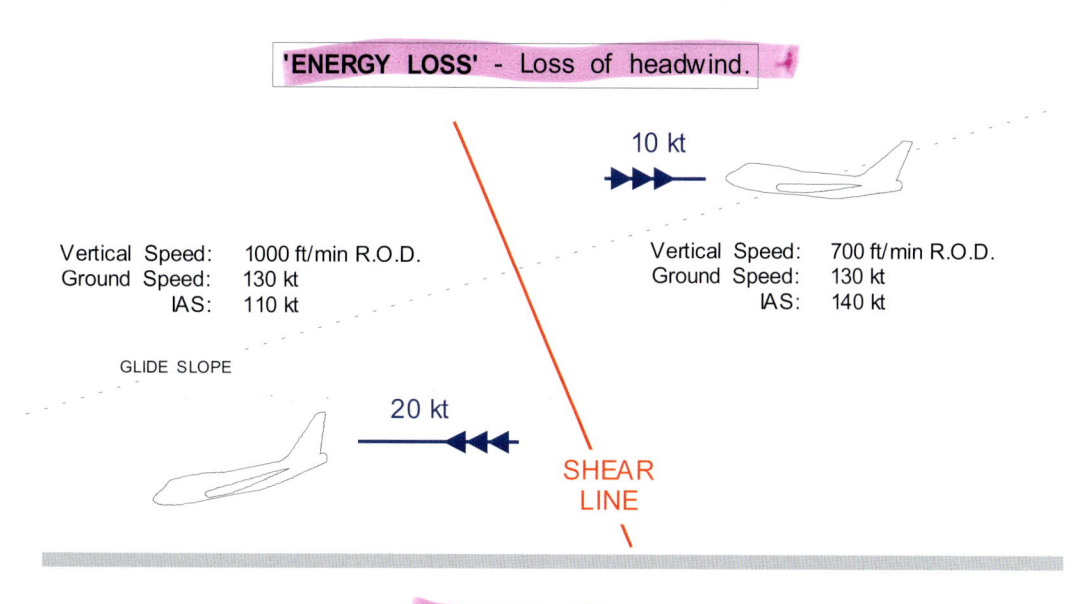

Figure 15.5 "Energy Loss" due to loss of headwind

PRINCIPLES OF FLIGHT   WINDSHEAR

15.5 "TYPICAL" RECOVERY FROM WINDSHEAR

The combination of increasing headwind, followed by down-draught, followed by increasing tailwind should be considered, as this is the sequence which might be encountered in a microburst on the approach, or following take-off.

a) The presence of thunderstorms should be known and obvious, so the increase in speed caused by the rising headwind should be seen as the forerunner of a down-burst or microburst; **any hope of a stabilised approach should be abandoned and a missed approach carried out as the only safe course of action.**

b) The initial rise in airspeed and rise above the approach path (balloon) should be seen as a bonus and capitalised. Without hesitation, increase to go-around power, **being prepared to go to maximum power if necessary**, select a pitch angle consistent with a missed approach, typically about 15° and hold it against turbulence and buffeting.

c) The next phase may well see the initial advantages of increased airspeed and rate of climb being rapidly eroded. The down-draught now strikes, airspeed may be lost and the aircraft may start to descend, despite the high power and pitch angle. It will be impossible to gauge the true angle of attack, so there is a possibility that the stick shaker (if fitted) may be triggered; only then should the attempt to hold the pitch angle normally be relaxed.

d) the point at which a down-draught begins to change to increasing tailwind may well be the most critical period. The rate of descent may lessen, but the airspeed may still continue to fall; the height loss may have cut seriously into ground obstacle clearance margins. **Given that maximum thrust is already applied, as an extreme measure if the risk of striking the ground or an obstacle still exists, it may be necessary to increase the pitch angle further and deliberately raise the nose until stick shaker is felt, decrease back-pressure on the pitch control to try and hold this higher pitch angle**, until the situation eases with the aircraft beginning to escape from the effects of the microburst.

When there is an indefinite risk of shear, it may be possible to use a longer runway, or one that points away from an area of potential threat. It may also be an option to rotate at a slightly higher speed, provided this does not cause undue tyre stress or any handling problems. The high power setting and high pitch angle after rotate, already put the aircraft into a good configuration should a microburst then be encountered. The aircraft is however very low, there is little safety margin and the ride can be rough. **If there is still extra power available, it should be used without hesitation. Ignore noise abatement procedures and maintain the high pitch angle, watching out for stick shaker indications as a signal to decrease back-pressure on the pitch control.**

In both approach and take-off cases, Vital Actions are:

a) Use the maximum power available as soon as possible.

b) Adopt a pitch angle of around 15° and try and hold that attitude. Do not chase airspeed.

c) Be guided by stick shaker indications when holding or increasing pitch attitude, easing the back pressure as required to attain and hold a slightly lower attitude.

15.6 WINDSHEAR REPORTING

If you encounter a wind shear on an approach or departure, you are urged to promptly report it to the controller. An advanced warning of this information can assist other pilots in avoiding or coping with a wind shear on approach or departure. The recommended method for wind shear reporting is to state the loss or gain of airspeed and the altitudes at which it was encountered. If you are unable to report wind shear in specific terms, you are encouraged to make reports in terms of the effect upon your aircraft.

15.7 VISUAL CLUES

You can see thunderstorms and hence receive a mental trigger to 'think windshear'. Once alerted, lookout for tell-tale signs such as:

a) Divergent wind sleeves or smoke;

b) Strong shafts of rain or hail, also 'virga'; (intense precipitation which falls in shafts below a cumulonimbus cloud and evaporates in the dry air beneath);

c) Divergent wind patterns indicated by grass, crops or trees being beaten down or lashed;

d) Rising dust or sand.

To observe and recognise any of the above will suggest that windshear danger is very close, if not imminent; nevertheless a few seconds of advance warning may make all the difference, if the warning is heeded and those seconds put to good use.

PRINCIPLES OF FLIGHT — WINDSHEAR

15.8 CONCLUSIONS

Most pilots will experience windshear in some form or other; for most it may be no more than a very firm landing or a swing on take-off or landing requiring momentary use of, perhaps, full rudder for correction; they will probably put it down to 'gusts'. Some few pilots will experience more authentic examples of windshear which will stretch their skills to the limit. A very small number may find their skills inadequate. There is no sure way of knowing in advance the severity of windshear which will be encountered, so it is better not to put one's skills to the test, rather than find them inadequate. Windshear, particularly when linked with thunderstorms, has caused disaster in the past and may well cause disaster again, but it will not harm those who understand its power and have the good sense to avoid it. **An inadvertent encounter on the approach is most likely to de-stabilise it to such an extent that a missed approach is the only safe course and the sooner that decision is made, the safer it is likely to be.** Other encounters must be treated on their merits, but any hint of 'energy loss' should be met with a firm and positive response in line with the guidance put forward.

Recognise - that windshear is a hazard.

and

Recognise - the signs which may indicate its presence.

Avoid - windshear by delay or diversion.

Prepare - for the inadvertent encounter by a speed 'margin' if 'energy loss' windshear is suspected.

Recover - know the techniques recommended for your aircraft and use them without hesitation if windshear is encountered.

PRINCIPLES OF FLIGHT   WINDSHEAR

SELF ASSESSMENT QUESTIONS

1. Take-off EPR is being delivered by all engines and the take-off is proceeding normally, the undercarriage has just retracted. Which initial indications may be observed when a headwind shears to a downdraught?

    a) Indicated Air Speed: constant. Vertical Speed: decreases. Pitch Attitude: decreases.
    b) Indicated Air Speed: increases. Vertical Speed: decreases. Pitch Attitude: constant.
    c) Indicated Air Speed: decreases. Vertical Speed: constant. Pitch Attitude: constant.
    d) Indicated Air Speed: decreases. Vertical Speed: decreases. Pitch Attitude: decreases.

2. Maximum downdrafts in a microburst encounter may be as strong as

    a) 6,000 ft/min.
    b) 7,000 ft/min.
    c) 8,000 ft/min.
    d) 10,000 ft/min.

3. An aircraft that encounters a headwind of 45 knots, within a microburst, may expect a total shear across the micro burst of

    a) 80 knots.
    b) 40 knots.
    c) 90 knots.
    d) 45 knots.

4. What is the expected duration of an individual micro burst?

    a) Two minutes with maximum winds lasting approximately 1 minute.
    b) Seldom longer than 15 minutes from the time the burst strikes the ground until dissipation.
    c) One micro burst may continue for as long as 2 to 4 hours.
    d) For as long as 1 hour.

5. Which wind-shear condition results in a loss of airspeed?

    a) Decreasing headwind or tailwind.
    b) Increasing headwind and decreasing tailwind.
    c) Decreasing headwind and increasing tailwind.
    d) Increasing headwind or tailwind.

6. Which performance characteristics should be recognized during takeoff when encountering a tailwind shear that increases in intensity?

    a) Loss of, or diminished climb ability.
    b) Increased climb performance immediately after takeoff.
    c) Decreased takeoff distance.
    d) Improved ability to climb.

7. Which condition would INITIALLY cause the indicated airspeed and pitch to increase and the sink rate to decrease?

    a) Tailwind which suddenly increases in velocity.
    b) Sudden decrease in a headwind component.
    c) Sudden increase in a headwind component.
    d) Calm wind which suddenly shears to a tailwind.

8. Which INITIAL cockpit indications should a pilot be aware of when a constant tailwind shears to a calm wind?

    a) Altitude increases; pitch and indicated airspeed decrease.
    b) Altitude, pitch, and indicated airspeed increase.
    c) Altitude, pitch, and indicated airspeed decrease.
    d) Altitude decreases; pitch and indicated airspeed increase.

9. What is the recommended technique to counter the loss of airspeed and resultant lift from wind shear?

    a) Maintain, or increase, pitch attitude and accept the lower-than-normal airspeed indications.
    b) Lower the pitch attitude and regain lost airspeed.
    c) Avoid overstressing the aircraft, pitch to stick shaker, and apply maximum power.
    d) Accelerate the aircraft to prevent a stall by sacrificing altitude.

PRINCIPLES OF FLIGHT   WINDSHEAR

10. Which of the following would be acceptable techniques to minimise the effects of a windshear encounter?

   1 - To prevent damage to the engines, avoid the use of maximum available thrust.
   2 - Increase the pitch angle until the stick shaker activates, then decrease back pressure to maintain that angle of pitch.
   3 - maintain a constant airspeed.
   4 - Use maximum power available as soon as possible.
   5 - Keep to noise abatement procedures.
   6 - Wait until the situation resolves itself before taking any action.

   a)   1, 3, 5 and 6
   b)   2, 3 and 5
   c)   2, 3, 4, 5 and 6
   d)   2 and 4

11. Which of the following statements about windshear is true?

   1 - Windshear can subject your aircraft to sudden up-draughts, down draughts, or extreme horizontal wind components.
   2 - Windshear will cause abrupt displacement from the flight path and require substantial control action to counteract it.
   3 - Windshear only affects small single and twin engine aircraft. Large, modern, powerful, fast gas turbine engine powered aircraft will not suffer from the worst affects of a microburst.
   4 - Microbursts are associated with cumulonimbus clouds.
   5 - Windshear can strike suddenly and with devastating effect which has been beyond the recovery powers of experienced pilots flying modern and powerful aircraft.

   a)   1, 2, 3, 4 and 5
   b)   1, 2 and 4
   c)   1, 2, 4 and 5
   d)   2, 3, 4 and 5

PRINCIPLES OF FLIGHT　　　　　　　　　　　　　　　　　　　　　　　　WINDSHEAR

12. A microburst is one of the most dangerous sources of windshear associated with thunderstorms. They are:

    a) small-scale intense up-draughts, which suck warm moist air into the cumulonimbus cloud.
    b) small-scale shafts of violent rain, which can cause severe problems to gas turbine engines.
    c) large-scale, violent air, associated with air descending from the 'anvil' of a thunder cloud.
    d) small-scale (typically less than 1 mile in diameter) intense down-draughts which, on reaching the surface, spread outward in all directions from the down-draught centre.

13. Thrust is being managed to maintain desired indicated airspeed and the glide slope is being flown. Which of the following is the recommended procedure when you observe a 30 kt loss of airspeed and the descent rate increases from 750 ft/min to 2,000 ft/min?

    a) Increase power to regain lost airspeed and pitch-up to regain the glide slope - continue the approach and continue to monitor your flight instruments.
    b) Decrease the pitch attitude to regain airspeed and then fly-up to regain the glide slope.
    c) Apply full power and execute a go-around; report windshear to ATC as soon as practicable.
    d) Wait until the airspeed stabilises and the rate of descent decreases, because microbursts are quite small and you will soon fly out of it.

14. Which of the following statements are correct?

    1 - A rapid increase in headwind is an 'energy gain'.
    2 - A rapid loss of tailwind is an 'energy gain'.
    3 - A shear from a tailwind to calm is an 'energy gain'.
    4 - A shear from calm to a headwind is an 'energy gain'.
    5 - A shear from headwind to calm is an 'energy loss'.

    a) 1, 2 and 4
    b) 1, 2, 3, 4 and 5
    c) 1, 4 and 5
    d) 4 and 5 only

15. Which of the following statements are correct?

    1 - A downdraught is an 'energy gain'.
    2 - A rapid loss of tailwind is an 'energy loss'.
    3 - A shear from a tailwind to calm is an 'energy loss'.
    4 - A shear from calm to a headwind is an 'energy gain'.
    5 - A downdraught is an 'energy loss'.

    a) 1, 3 and 4
    b) 1, 2, 3 and 5
    c) 1, 4 and 5
    d) 4 and 5 only

16. Which of the following sequences might be encountered when flying into a microburst?

    a) Increased headwind, followed by down-draught, followed by increased tailwind on the approach, or following take-off.
    b) Increased headwind, followed by down-draught, followed by increased tailwind on the approach. Increased tailwind, followed by down-draught, followed by increased headwind following take-off.
    c) Increased headwind, followed by down-draught, followed by increased tailwind on take-off. Increased tailwind, followed by down-draught, followed by increased headwind on the approach.
    d) Increased tailwind, followed by down-draught, followed by increased headwind on take-off. Increased headwind, followed by down-draught, followed by increased tailwind on the approach.

17. Which of the following statements is correct when considering windshear?

    1 - Recognise that windshear is a hazard to all sizes and types of aircraft.
    2 - Recognise the signs which may indicate its presence.
    3 - Avoid windshear by delaying departure or by diverting if airborne.
    4 - Prepare for the inadvertent encounter by a speed 'margin' if 'energy loss' windshear is suspected.
    5 - Know the techniques for recovery recommended for your aircraft and use them without any hesitation if windshear is encountered.

    a) 2, 4 and 5
    b) 3, 4 and 5
    c) 1, 2, and 5
    d) 1, 2, 3, 4 and 5

INTENTIONALLY LEFT BLANK

ANSWERS

No	A	B	C	D	REF
1				D	
2	A				
3			C		
4		B			
5			C		
6	A				
7			C		
8		B			
9			C		
10				D	
11			C		
12				D	
13			C		
14		B			
15				D	
16	A				
17				D	

INTENTIONALLY LEFT BLANK

CHAPTER 16 - PROPELLERS

Contents

	Page
INTRODUCTION	16 - 1
PROPELLER DEFINITIONS	
BLADE ANGLE	
GEOMETRIC PITCH	
BLADE TWIST	16 - 2
EFFECTIVE PITCH	
PROPELLER SLIP	
THE HELIX ANGLE	
ANGLE OF ATTACK	
FIXED PITCH PROPELLER	
AERODYNAMIC FORCES ON THE PROPELLER	16 - 4
THRUST	
TORQUE	
PROPELLER TWISTING MOMENTS	16 - 5
CENTRIFUGAL TWISTING MOMENT (CTM)	
AERODYNAMIC TWISTING MOMENT (ATM)	
PROPELLER EFFICIENCY	16 - 6
VARIATION OF PROPELLER EFFICIENCY WITH SPEED	
VARIABLE PITCH PROPELLERS	16 - 7
ADJUSTABLE PITCH	
TWO PITCH	
CONSTANT SPEED PROPELLER	
WINDMILLING	16 - 9
FEATHERING	16 - 10
POWER ABSORPTION	16 - 11
SOLIDITY	
MOMENTS AND FORCES GENERATED	16 - 12
TORQUE REACTION	
GYROSCOPIC EFFECT	16 - 13
SPIRAL SLIPSTREAM EFFECT	16 - 14
ASYMMETRIC BLADE EFFECT	16 - 15
EFFECT OF ATMOSPHERIC CONDITIONS	
SELF ASSESSMENT QUESTIONS	16 - 17
ANSWERS	16 - 21

PRINCIPLES OF FLIGHT   **PROPELLERS**

16.1 INTRODUCTION

A propeller converts shaft power from the engine into thrust. It does this by accelerating a mass of air rearwards. Thrust from the propeller is equal to the mass of air accelerated rearwards multiplied by the acceleration given to it. A mass is accelerated rearwards and the equal and opposite reaction drives the aircraft forwards.

16.2 DEFINITIONS

The propeller blade is an aerofoil and the definitions for chord, camber, thickness/chord ratio and aspect ratio are the same as those given previously for the wing. Additionally the following must be considered.

BLADE ANGLE or PITCH

The angle between the blade chord and the plane of rotation. Blade angle decreases from the root to the tip of the blade (twist) because rotational velocity of the blade increases from root to tip. For reference purposes, the blade angle is measured at a point 75% of the blade length from the root.

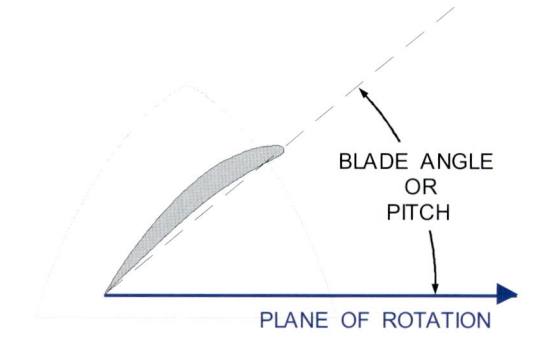

Figure 16.1 Blade angle

GEOMETRIC PITCH

The geometric pitch is the distance the propeller **would** travel forward in one complete revolution if it were moving through the air at the blade angle. (It might help to imagine the geometric pitch as a screw thread, but do not take this "screw" analogy any further).

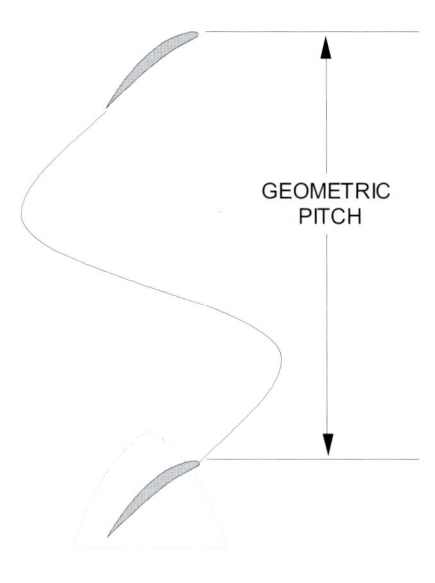

Figure 16.2 Geometric pitch

BLADE TWIST

Sections near the tip of the propeller are at a greater distance from the propeller shaft and travel through a greater distance. Tip speed is therefore greater. The blade angle must be decreased towards the tip to give a constant geometric pitch along the length of the blade.

The blade angle determines the geometric pitch of the propeller. A small blade angle is called "fine pitch", a large blade angle is called "coarse pitch".

EFFECTIVE PITCH

In flight the propeller does not move through the air at the geometric pitch, the distance it travels forward in each revolution depends on the aircraft's forward speed. The distance which it actually moves forward in each revolution is called the "effective pitch" or "advance per revolution".

PROPELLER SLIP

The difference between the Geometric and the Effective Pitch is called the Slip.

THE HELIX ANGLE

The angle that the actual path of the propeller makes to the plane of rotation.

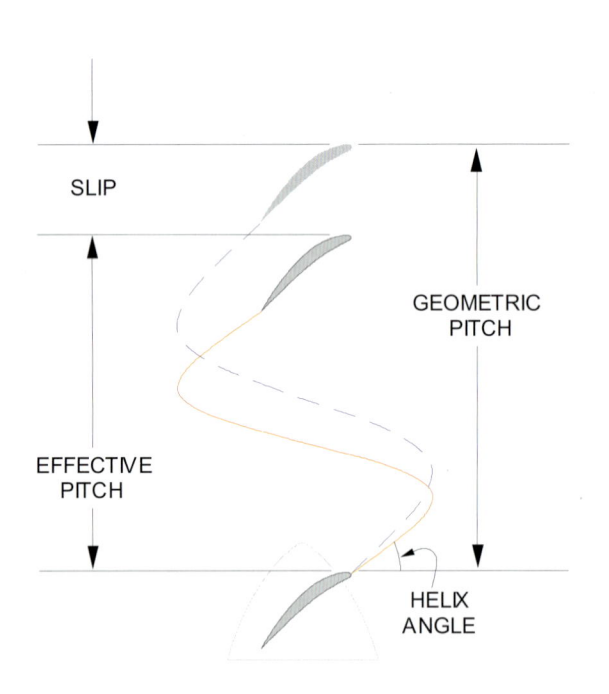

Figure 16.3   Effective pitch & Slip

ANGLE OF ATTACK

The path of the propeller through the air determines the direction of the relative airflow. The angle between the blade chord and the relative airflow is the angle of attack (α), Fig. 16.4. The angle of attack (α) is the result of propeller rotational velocity (RPM) and aircraft forward velocity (TAS).

FIXED PITCH PROPELLER

Fig. 16.5 shows a "fixed pitch" propeller at constant RPM. Increasing TAS decreases the angle of attack of the propeller. Fig. 16.6 shows a "fixed pitch" propeller at a constant TAS. Increasing RPM increases the angle of attack of the propeller.

PRINCIPLES OF FLIGHT   **PROPELLERS**

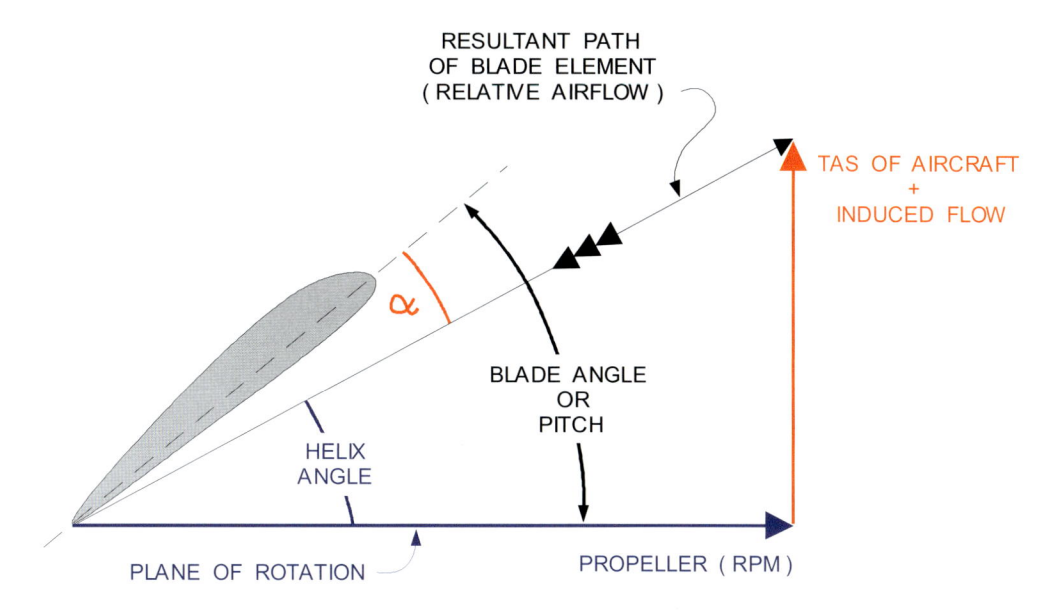

Figure 16.4 Angle of attack

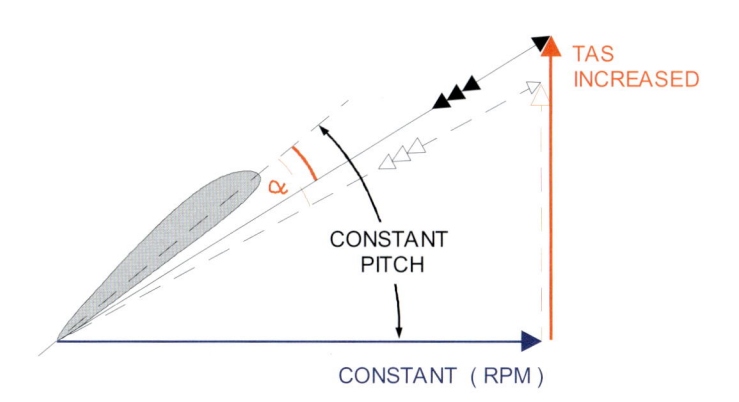

Figure 16.5 Angle of attack decreased by higher TAS

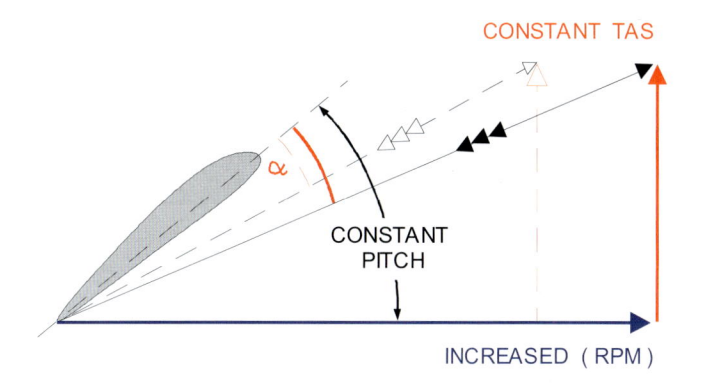

Figure 16.6 Angle of attack increased by higher RPM

PRINCIPLES OF FLIGHT — PROPELLERS

16.3 AERODYNAMIC FORCES ON THE PROPELLER

A propeller blade has an aerofoil section, and when moving through the air at an angle of attack will generate aerodynamic forces in the same way as a wing. The shape of the section will generate a pressure differential between the two surfaces. The surface which has the greater pressure is called the "pressure face" or "thrust face". When the propeller is giving forward thrust, the thrust face is the rear, (flat) surface. The pressure differential will generate an aerodynamic force, the total reaction, which may be resolved into two components, thrust and propeller torque.

16.3.1 THRUST

A component at right angles to the plane of rotation. The thrust force will vary along the length of each blade, reducing at the tip where the pressures equalise and towards the root where the rotational velocity is low. Thrust will cause a bending moment on each blade, tending to bend the tip forward. (Equal and opposite reaction to "throwing" air backwards).

16.3.2 TORQUE (Propeller)

The equal and opposite reaction to being rotated, which generates a turning moment about the aircraft longitudinal axis. Propeller torque also gives a bending moment to the blades in, but in the opposite direction to, the plane of rotation.

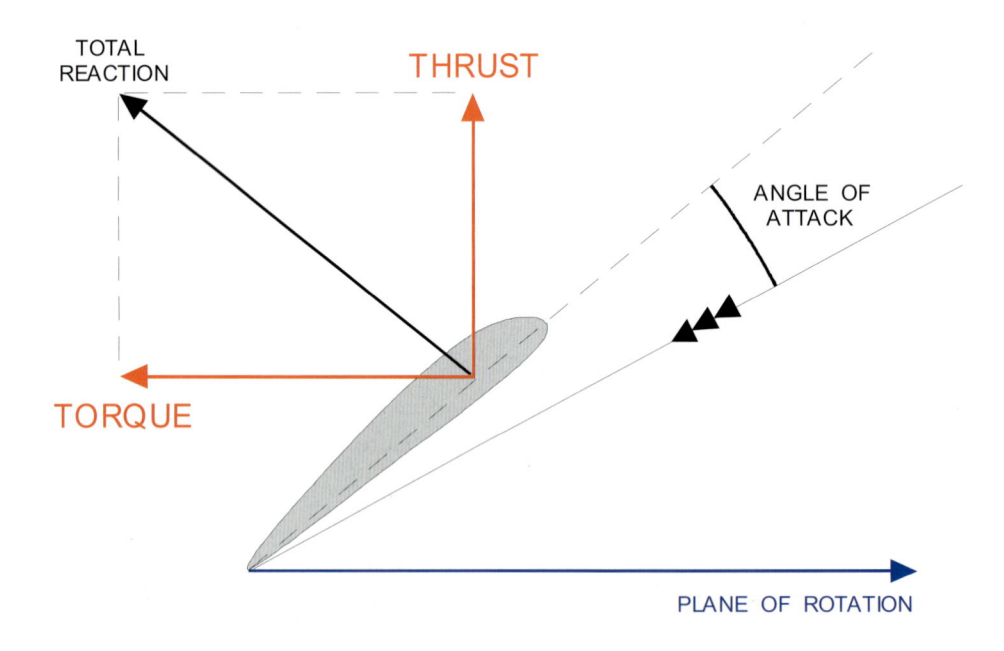

Figure 16.7 Thrust and Torque

PRINCIPLES OF FLIGHT — PROPELLERS

16.4 CENTRIFUGAL TWISTING MOMENT (CTM)

Components 'A' and 'B', of the centrifugal force acting on the blade, produce a moment around the pitch change axis which tends to 'fine' the blade off.

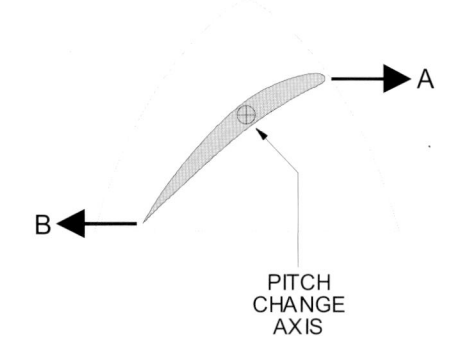

Figure 16.8 Centrifugal Turning Moment (CTM)

16.4.1 AERODYNAMIC TWISTING MOMENT (ATM)

Because the blade CP is in front of the pitch change axis, aerodynamic force generates a moment around the pitch change axis acting in the direction of coarse pitch.

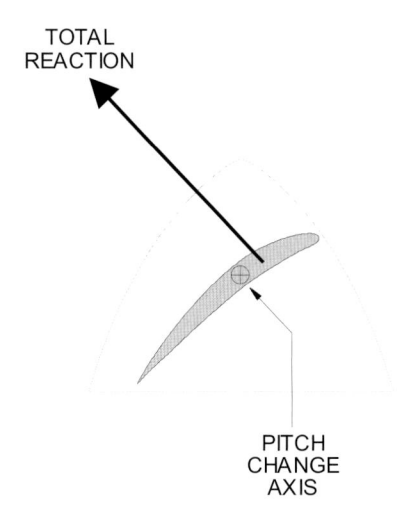

Figure 16.9 Aerodynamic Twisting Moment (ATM)

The ATM partially offsets the CTM during normal engine operations, but the CTM is dominant. However, when the propeller is windmilling the ATM acts in the same direction as the CTM (See Fig. 16.15), and will reinforce it.

PRINCIPLES OF FLIGHT PROPELLERS

16.5 PROPELLER EFFICIENCY

The efficiency of the propeller can be measured from the ratio, Power out / Power in. The power extracted (out) from a propeller "Thrust Power" is the product of Force (Thrust) x Velocity (TAS). The power into the propeller "Shaft Power" is engine torque (Force) x Rotational Velocity (RPM). The efficiency of the propeller can be expressed as:

$$\text{Propeller Efficiency} = \frac{\text{Thrust Power}}{\text{Shaft Power}}$$

16.5.1 VARIATION OF PROPELLER EFFICIENCY WITH SPEED

Fig. 16.5 illustrated that for **a fixed pitch propeller**, increasing TAS at a constant RPM reduces the blade angle of attack. This will decrease thrust. The effect of this on propeller efficiency is as follows:

a) At some high forward speed the blade will be close to zero lift angle of attack and thrust, and therefore Thrust Power, will be zero. From the above 'equation' it can be seen that propeller efficiency will also be zero.

b) There will be only one speed at which a fixed pitch propeller is operating at its most efficient angle of attack and where the propeller efficiency will be maximum, Fig. 16.10.

c) As TAS is decreased, thrust will increase because blade angle of attack is increased. Thrust is very large, but the TAS is low so propeller efficiency will be low. Thus no **useful** work is being done when the aircraft is, for instance, held against the brakes at full power prior to take-off. **The efficiency of a fixed pitch prop' varies with forward speed**

If blade angle can be varied as TAS and/or RPM is changed, the propeller will remain efficient over a much wider range of aircraft operating conditions, as illustrated in Fig. 16.10.

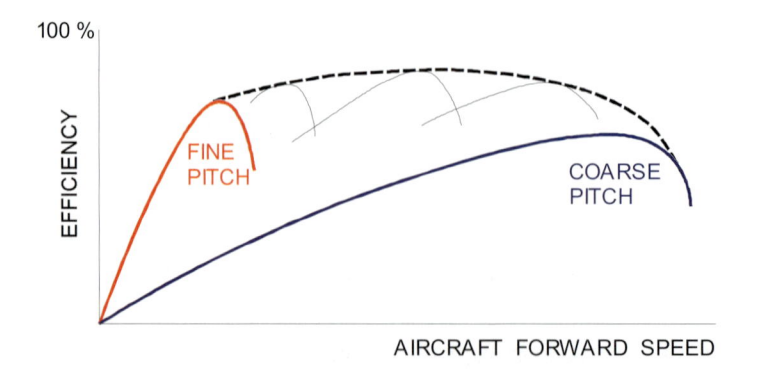

Figure 16.10 Efficiency improved by varying blade angle

16.6 VARIABLE PITCH PROPELLERS

Adjustable pitch propellers: These are propellers which can have their pitch adjusted on the ground by mechanically re-setting the blades in the hub. In flight they act as fixed pitch propellers.

Two pitch propellers: These are propellers which have a fine and coarse pitch setting which can be selected in flight. Fine pitch can be selected for take off, climb and landing and coarse pitch for cruise. They will usually also have a feathered position.

(Variable pitch) Constant speed propellers: Modern aircraft have propellers which are controlled automatically to vary their pitch (blade angle) so as to maintain a selected RPM. A variable pitch propeller permits high efficiency to be obtained over a wider range of TAS, giving improved take-off and climb performance and cruising fuel consumption.

CONSTANT SPEED PROPELLER

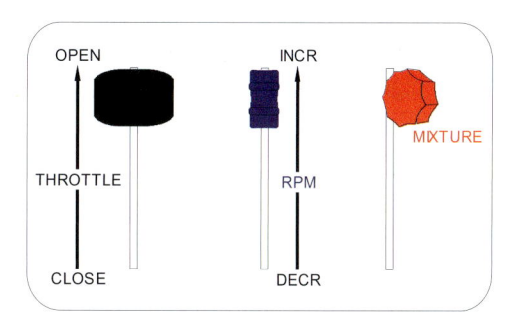

Figure 16.11

Fig. 16.11 illustrates a 'typical' set of engine and propeller controls for a small piston engine aircraft with a variable pitch propeller. Throttle, prop' and mixture are shown in the take-off. (all forward) position.

"Pulling back" on the prop' control will decrease RPM.

"Pushing forward" on the prop' control will increase RPM.

NB: A reasonable analogy is to think of the prop' control as an infinitely variable "gear change".

       Forward (increase RPM) is first gear.

       Back (decrease RPM) is fifth gear.

PRINCIPLES OF FLIGHT PROPELLERS

FINE PITCH
("small" blade angle)

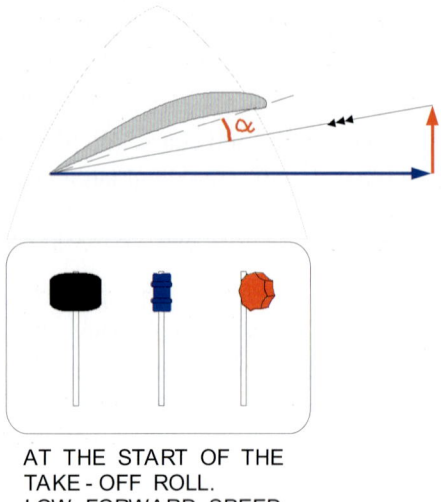

AT THE START OF THE
TAKE - OFF ROLL.
LOW FORWARD SPEED,
HIGH RPM

Fig. 16.12 shows conditions during the early stages of take-off roll. The RPM is set to maximum and the TAS is low. The angle of attack is optimum and maximum available efficiency is obtained. As the aircraft continues to accelerate the TAS will increase, which decreases the angle of attack of the blades. Less thrust will be generated and less propeller torque. This gives less resistance for the engine to overcome and RPM would tend to increase. The constant speed unit (CSU) senses the RPM increase and increases pitch to maintain the blade angle of attack constant.

Figure 16.12 Low TAS, high RPM

Fig. 16.13 shows the conditions at high forward speed in level flight. As the TAS increased, the CSU continually increased the blade angle (coarsened the pitch) to maintain a constant blade angle of attack.

COARSE PITCH
("large" blade angle)

HIGH FORWARD SPEED,
HIGH RPM

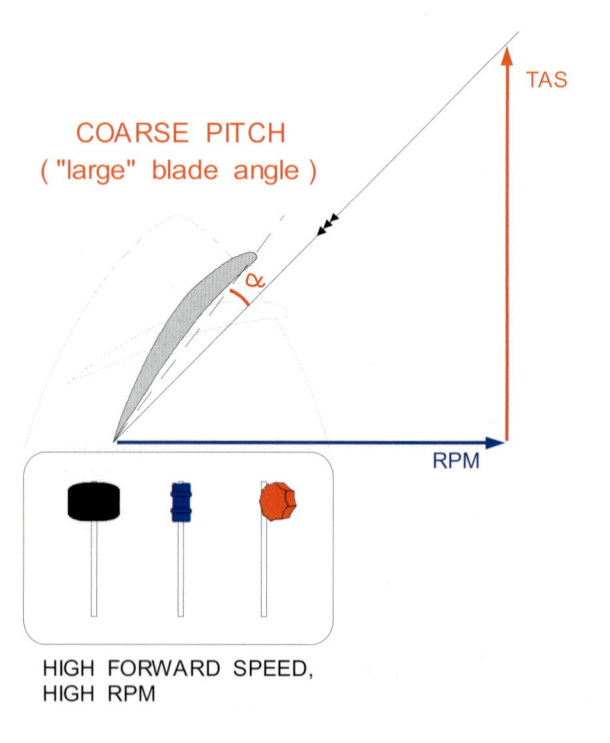

Figure 16.13 High TAS, high RPM

PRINCIPLES OF FLIGHT **PROPELLERS**

Fig. 16.14 shows conditions when the engine and prop' have been set for cruise conditions. Optimum throttle and RPM setting are listed in the aircraft Flight Manual. The recommended procedure is to reduce the throttle first, then RPM.

Whatever configuration into which the aircraft is placed, climb, descent or bank, the CSU will adjust the blade angle (prop' pitch) to maintain the RPM which has been set. At least it will try to maintain constant RPM. There are exceptions, which will be discussed.

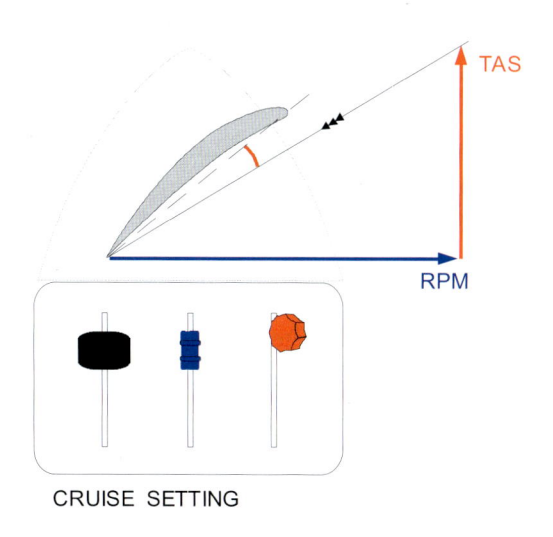

Figure 16.14

WINDMILLING

If a loss of engine torque occurs (the throttle is closed or the engine fails), the prop' will "fine off" in an attempt to maintain the set RPM.

The relative airflow will impinge on the front surface of the blade and generate drag and "negative propeller torque". The propeller will now drive the engine, as shown in Fig. 16.15.

The drag generated by a windmilling propeller is very high.

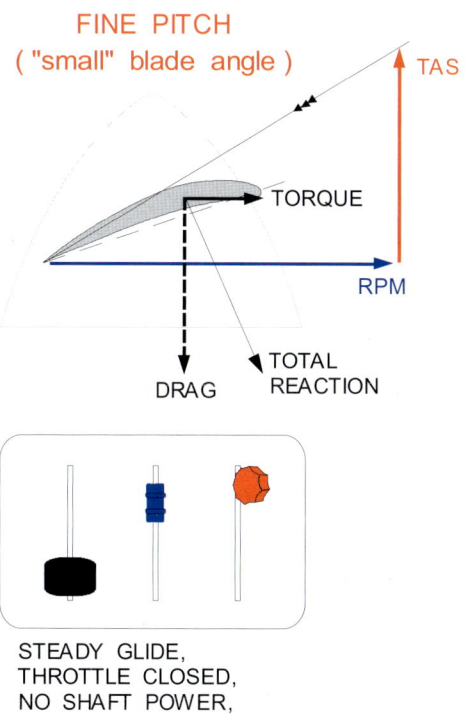

STEADY GLIDE,
THROTTLE CLOSED,
NO SHAFT POWER,
PROPELLER WINDMILLING.

Figure 16.15 Windmilling

16 - 9

FEATHERING

Following an engine failure on a twin engine aeroplane the increased drag from the windmilling propeller will seriously degrade climb performance, limit range and add to the yawing moment caused by the failed engine which will affect controllability. (Please review Paragraphs 12.24 to 12.39 for detailed information). Also, by continuing to turn a badly damaged engine, eventual seizure of the engine or an engine fire might result.

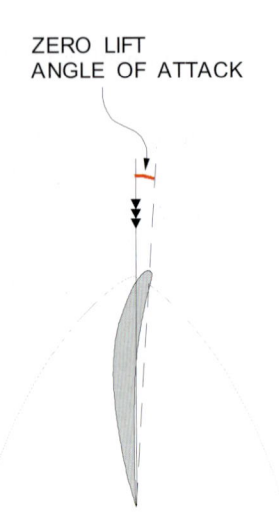

By turning the blades to their zero lift angle of attack, no propeller torque is generated and the propeller will stop, reducing drag to a minimum, as shown in Fig. 16.16. This will improve climb performance because the ability to climb is dependent on excess thrust after balancing aerodynamic drag.

Windmilling drag is one of the "ingredients" of the yawing moment from a failed engine. Feathering the propeller of a failed engine will also reduce the yawing moment and consequently, V_{MC}.

Figure 16.16   Feathered

A single engine aeroplane fitted with a constant speed propeller does not have a "feathering" capability, as such. However, following engine failure, drag can be reduced to a minimum by "pulling" the RPM (prop') control to the fully coarse position, as shown in Fig. 16.17.

In a steady glide with no shaft power from the engine (throttle closed), if the propeller pitch is increased by pulling back the prop' lever, the aircraft Lift/Drag ratio will increase. This will decrease the rate of descent. The RPM would decrease because of the reduction in negative propeller torque.

The opposite will be true if the propeller pitch is decreased.

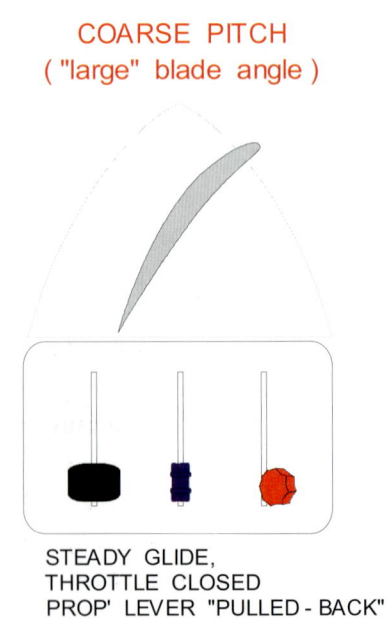

COARSE PITCH
("large" blade angle)

STEADY GLIDE,
THROTTLE CLOSED
PROP' LEVER "PULLED - BACK"

Figure 16.17

PRINCIPLES OF FLIGHT — PROPELLERS

16.7 POWER ABSORPTION

A propeller must be able to absorb all the shaft power developed by the engine and also operate with maximum efficiency throughout the required performance envelope of the aircraft. The critical factor is tip velocity. If tip velocity is too high the blade tips will approach the local speed of sound and compressibility effects will decrease thrust and increase rotational drag. **Supersonic tip speed will considerably reduce the efficiency of a propeller and greatly increase the noise it generates.**

This imposes a limit on propeller diameter and RPM, and the TAS at which it can be used.

Other limitations on propeller diameter are the need to maintain adequate ground clearance and the need to mount the engines of a multi-engine aircraft as close to the fuselage as possible to minimise the thrust arm. Increasing the propeller diameter requires the engine to be mounted further out on the wing to maintain adequate fuselage clearance. To keep V_{MC} within acceptable limits the available rudder moment would have to be increased. Clearly, increasing the propeller diameter to increase power absorption is not the preferred option.

SOLIDITY

To increase power absorption several characteristics of the propeller can be adjusted. The usual method is to increase the 'solidity' of the propeller. Propeller solidity is the ratio of the total frontal area of the blades to the area of the propeller disc. It can be seen from Fig. 16.18 that an increase in solidity can be achieved by:

a) **Increasing the chord of each blade.** This increases the solidity, but blade aspect ratio is reduced, making the propeller less efficient.

b) **Increasing the number of blades.** Power absorption is increased without increasing tip speed or reducing the aspect ratio. **Increasing the number of blades beyond a certain number (five or six) will reduce overall efficiency.**

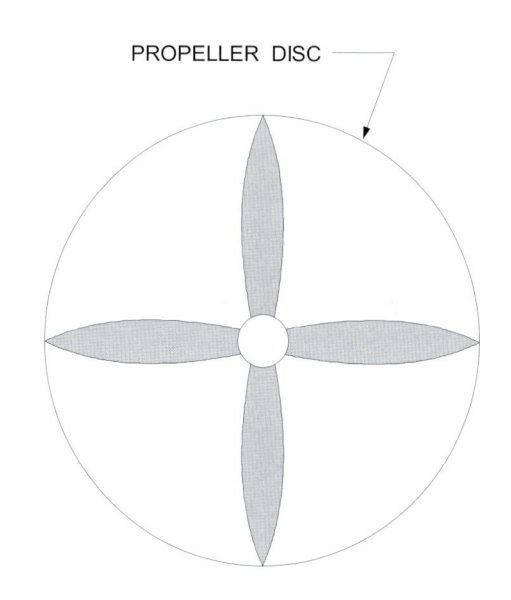

Figure 16.18 Solidity of a propeller

Thrust is generated by accelerating air rearwards. Making the disk too solid will reduce the mass of air that can be drawn through the propeller and accelerated. To increase the number of blades efficiently, two propellers rotating in opposite directions on the same shaft are used. These are called: **contra-rotating propellers.**

PRINCIPLES OF FLIGHT — PROPELLERS

16.8 MOMENTS AND FORCES GENERATED BY A PROPELLER

Due to its rotation a propeller generates yawing, rolling and pitching moments. These are due to several different causes:

a) Torque reaction

b) Gyroscopic precession

c) Spiral (asymmetric) slipstream effect

d) Asymmetric blade effect

NB: **The majority of modern engines are fitted with propellers which rotate clockwise when viewed from the rear**, so called "right-hand" propellers. The exceptions are small twin piston engine aircraft which often have the propeller of the right engine rotating anti-clockwise to eliminate the disadvantage of having a "critical engine" (see Paragraph 12.26) plus some older aircraft.

16.8.1 TORQUE REACTION

Because the propeller rotates clockwise, the equal and opposite reaction (torque) will give the aircraft an anti-clockwise rolling moment about the longitudinal axis. During take-off this will apply a greater down load to the left wheel, Fig. 16.19, causing more rolling resistance on the left wheel making the aircraft want to yaw to the left. In flight, torque reaction will also make the aircraft want to roll to the left. **Torque reaction will be greatest during high power, low airspeed (IAS) flight conditions.** Low IAS will reduce the power of the controls to counter the "turning" moment due to torque.

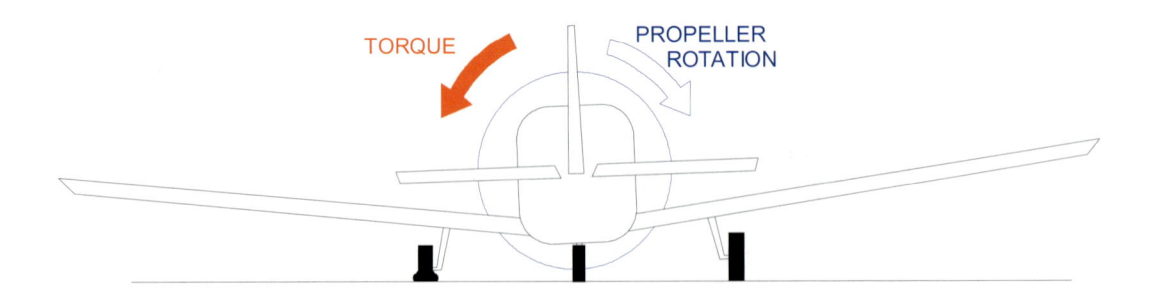

Figure 16.19 Torque reaction giving left turn during take-off

PRINCIPLES OF FLIGHT PROPELLERS

Torque reaction can be eliminated by fitting contra-rotating propellers. Torque from the two propellers, rotating in opposite directions on the same shaft, will cancel each other out. Co-rotating propellers on a small twin will not normally give a torque reaction until one engine fails. A left "turning" tendency would then occur. Counter-rotating propellers on a small twin will reduce the torque reaction following an engine failure. (Review Paragraph 12.28(f)).

16.8.2 GYROSCOPIC EFFECT

A rotating propeller has the properties of a gyroscope - rigidity in space and precession. The characteristic which produces "gyroscopic effect" is precession. Gyroscopic precession is the reaction that occurs when a force is applied to the rim of a rotating disc. When a force is applied to the rim of a propeller the reaction occurs 90° ahead in the direction of rotation, and in the same direction as the applied force. As the aircraft is pitched up or down or yawed left or right, a force is applied to the rim of the spinning propeller disc.

NB: **Gyroscopic effect only occurs when the aircraft pitches and/or yaws.**

For example, if an aircraft with a **clockwise rotating propeller** is pitched nose up, imagine that a forward force has been applied to the bottom of the propeller disc. The force will "emerge" at 90° in the direction of rotation, i.e. a right yawing moment. Gyroscopic effect can be easily determined when the point of application of the imagined forward force on the propeller disc is considered.

Pitch down - forward force on the top, force emerges 90° clockwise, left yaw.

Left yaw - forward force on the right, force emerges 90° clockwise, pitch up.

Right yaw - forward force on the left, force emerges 90° clockwise, pitch down.

Gyroscopic effect will be cancelled if the propellers are contra rotating.

PRINCIPLES OF FLIGHT **PROPELLERS**

16.8.3 SPIRAL SLIPSTREAM EFFECT

As the propeller rotates it produces a backward flow of air, or slipstream, which rotates around the aircraft, as illustrated in Fig. 16.18. This spiral slipstream causes a change in airflow around the fin (vertical stabiliser). Due to the direction of propeller rotation (**clockwise**) the spiral slipstream meets the fin at an angle from the left, producing a sideways force on the fin to the right.

Spiral slipstream effect gives the aircraft a yawing moment to the left.

The amount of rotation given to the air will depend on the throttle and RPM setting. Spiral slipstream effect can be reduced by:

a) the use of contra or counter rotating propellers,

b) a small fixed tab on the rudder,

c) the engine thrust line inclined slightly to the right,

d) or offsetting the fin slightly.

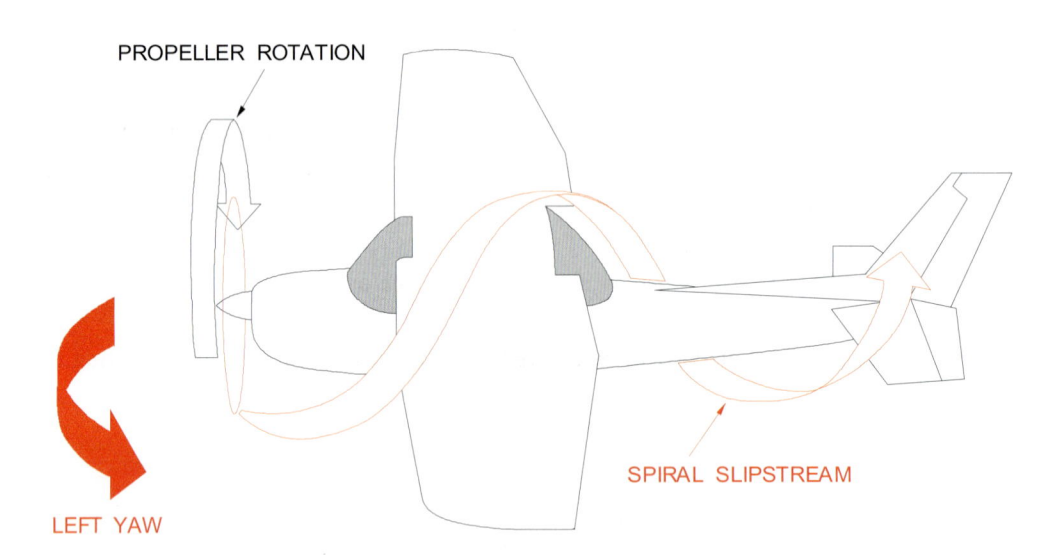

Figure 16.18 Spiral slipstream effect

High Power low Speed Worst Case

16.8.4 ASYMMETRIC BLADE EFFECT

In general the propeller shaft will be inclined upwards from the direction of flight due to the angle of attack of the aircraft. This gives the down going propeller blade a greater effective angle of attack than the up going blade. The down going (right) blade will generate more thrust. **The difference in thrust on the two sides of the propeller disc will give a yawing moment to the left with a clockwise rotating propeller in a nose-up attitude.**

Asymmetric blade effect will be greatest at full power and low airspeed (high angle of attack).

16.9 EFFECT OF ATMOSPHERIC CONDITIONS

Changes of atmospheric pressure or temperature will cause a change of air density. This will affect:

a) the power produced by the engine at a given throttle position and

b) the resistance to rotation of the propeller (its drag).

An increase in air density will increase both the engine power and the propeller drag. **The change in engine power is more significant than the change in propeller drag.**

16.9.1 ENGINE AND PROPELLER COMBINED

If the combined effect of an engine and propeller is being considered, it is the engine power change which will determine the result. For an engine driving a fixed pitch propeller:

a) if density increases, RPM will increase.

b) if density decreases, RPM will decrease.

16.9.2 ENGINE ALONE

If the shaft power required to drive the propeller is being considered, then it is only the propeller torque which needs to be taken into account. To maintain the RPM of a fixed pitch propeller:

a) if density increases, power required will increase,

b) if density decreases, power required will decrease.

PRINCIPLES OF FLIGHT PROPELLERS

SELF ASSESSMENT QUESTIONS

1. As a result of gyroscopic precession, it can be said that:

    a) any pitching around the longitudinal axis results in a yawing moment
    b) any yawing around the normal axis results in a pitching moment
    c) any pitching around the lateral axis results in a rolling moment
    d) any rolling around the longitudinal axis results in a pitching moment

2. A propeller rotating clockwise as seen from the rear, creates a spiralling slipstream that tends to rotate the aeroplane to the:

    a) right around the normal axis, and to the left around the longitudinal axis
    b) right around the normal axis, and to the right around the longitudinal axis
    c) left around the normal axis, and to the left around the longitudinal axis
    d) left around the normal axis, and to the right around the longitudinal axis

3. The reason for variations in geometric pitch (twisting) along a propeller blade is that it:

    a) prevents the portion of the blade near the hub from stalling during cruising flight.
    b) permits a relatively constant angle of attack along its length when in cruising flight.
    c) permits a relatively constant angle of incidence along its length when in cruising flight.
    d) minimises the gyroscopic effect.

4. The Geometric Pitch of a propeller is:

    a) the distance it would move forward in one revolution if there were no slip.
    b) the angle the propeller shaft makes to the plane of rotation.
    c) the distance the propeller actually moves forward in one revolution.
    d) the angle the propeller chord makes to the relative airflow.

5. Propeller 'slip' is:

    a) the air stream in the wake of the propeller.
    b) the amount by which the distance covered in one revolution falls short of the geometric pitch.
    c) the increase in rpm which occurs during take-off.
    d) the change of blade angle from root to tip.

6. The distance a propeller actually advances in one revolution is:

    a) twisting.
    b) effective pitch.
    c) geometric pitch.
    d) blade pitch.

7. Blade angle of a propeller is defined as the angle between the:

    a) angle of attack and chord line.
    b) angle of attack and line of thrust.
    c) chord line and plane of rotation.
    d) thrust line and propeller torque.

8. Propeller efficiency is the:

    a) actual distance a propeller advances in one revolution.
    b) ratio of thrust horsepower to shaft horsepower.
    c) ratio of geometric pitch to effective pitch.
    d) ratio of TAS to rpm.

9. A fixed-pitch propeller is designed for best efficiency only at a given combination of:

    a) airspeed and RPM.
    b) airspeed and altitude.
    c) altitude and RPM.
    d) torque and blade angle.

10. Which statement is true regarding propeller efficiency? Propeller efficiency is the:

    a) difference between the geometric pitch of the propeller and its effective pitch.
    b) actual distance a propeller advances in one revolution.
    c) ratio of thrust horsepower to shaft horsepower.
    d) ratio between the rpm and number of blade elements.

11. Which statement best describes the operating principle of a constant-speed propeller?

    a) As throttle setting is changed by the pilot, the prop governor causes pitch angle of the propeller blades to remain unchanged.
    b) The propeller control regulates the engine RPM and in turn the propeller RPM.
    c) A high blade angle, or increased pitch, reduces the propeller drag and allows more engine power for takeoffs.
    d) As the propeller control setting is changed by the pilot, the RPM of the engines remains constant as the pitch angle of the propeller changes.

12. When does asymmetric blade effect cause the aeroplane to yaw to the left?

    a) When at high angles of attack.
    b) When at high airspeeds.
    c) When at low angles of attack.
    d) In the cruise at low altitude.

13. The left turning tendency of an aeroplane caused by asymmetric blade effect is the result of the:

    a) gyroscopic forces applied to the rotating propeller blades acting 90° in advance of the point the force was applied.
    b) clockwise rotation of the engine and the propeller turning the aeroplane counter-clockwise.
    c) propeller blade descending on the right, producing more thrust than the ascending blade on the left.
    d) the rotation of the slipstream striking the tail on the left.

14. With regard to gyroscopic precession, when a force is applied at a point on the rim of a spinning disc, the resultant force acts in which direction and at what point?

    a) In the same direction as the applied force, 90° ahead in the plane of rotation.
    b) In the opposite direction of the applied force, 90° ahead in the plane of rotation.
    c) In the opposite direction of the applied force, at the point of the applied force.
    d) In the same direction as the applied force, 90° ahead of the plane of rotation when the propeller rotates clockwise, 90° retarded when the propeller rotates counter-clockwise.

15. The angle of attack of a fixed pitch propeller:

    a) depends on forward speed only.
    b) depends on forward speed and engine rotational speed.
    c) depends on engine rotational speed only.
    d) is constant for a fixed pitch propeller.

16. Counter-rotating propellers are:

    a) propellers which rotate counter clockwise.
    b) propellers which are geared to rotate in the opposite direction to the engine.
    c) two propellers driven by separate engines, rotating in opposite directions.
    d) two propellers driven by the same engine, rotating in opposite directions.

17. If engine rpm is to remain constant on an engine fitted with a variable pitch propeller, an increase in engine power requires:

    a) a decrease in blade angle.
    b) a constant angle of attack to be maintained to stop the engine from overspeeding.
    c) an increase in blade angle.
    d) the prop control lever to be advanced.

ANSWERS

No	A	B	C	D	REF
1		B			
2				D	
3		B			
4	A				
5		B			
6		B			
7			C		
8		B			
9	A				
10			C		
11		B			
12	A				
13			C		
14	A				
15		B			
16			C		
17			C		

INTENTIONALLY LEFT BLANK

PRINCIPLES OF FLIGHT SPECIMEN QUESTIONS

CHAPTER SEVENTEEN – SPECIMEN QUESTIONS

Contents

                                                                                               Page

SPECIMEN QUESTIONS………………...…….…………..……………….…..17 – 1

ANSWERS TO SPECIMEN QUESTIONS...……………………….…………17 – 33

EXPLANATIONS TO SPECIMEN QUESTIONS..…………………….………17 – 35

SPECIMEN EXAM PAPER..………………….……………...………………..17 – 61

ANSWERS TO SPECIMEN EXAM PAPER..………….……………..……… …17 – 71

EXPLANATIONS TO ANSWERS…………...……..……………….……… …17 – 73

SPECIMEN QUESTIONS

1. A unit of measurement of pressure is:

    a. kg/square dm
    b. kg/cubic metre
    c. Newtons
    d. psi

2. Which of the following are the correct SI units ?

    a. Density is kilogram's per cubic metre, Force is Newtons
    b. Density is Newton's per cubic metre, Force is kilogram's
    c. Density is kilogram's per Newton, Force is Newton-metre squared
    d. Density is kilogram's per square metre, Force is kilogram's

3. What is the SI unit of density?

    a. m V squared
    b. kg/square cm
    c. kg - metres
    d. kg/cubic metre

4. What is the SI unit which results from multiplying kg and m/s squared?

    a. Newton
    b. Psi
    c. Joule
    d. Watt

5. Which of the following expressions is correct:

    a. A = F x M
    b. F = M x A
    c. M = F x A
    d. A = M / F

6. Which of the following is the equation for power?

    a. N/m
    b. Nm/s
    c. Pa/s squared
    d. Kg/m/s squared

7. At a constant CAS when flying below sea level an aircraft will have:

    a. a higher TAS than at sea level
    b. a lower TAS than at sea level at ISA conditions
    c. the same TAS as at sea level
    d. the same TAS, but an increased IAS

PRINCIPLES OF FLIGHT   SPECIMEN QUESTIONS

8   Static pressure acts:

        a.   parallel to airflow
        b.   parallel to dynamic pressure
        c.   in all directions
        d.   downwards

9   TAS is:

        a.   higher than speed of the undisturbed airstream around the aircraft
        b.   lower than speed of the undisturbed airstream around the aircraft
        c.   lower than IAS at ISA altitudes below sea level
        d.   equal to IAS, multiplied by air density at sea level

10   The difference between IAS and TAS will:

        a.   increase with decreasing temperature
        b.   increase with increasing density
        c.   remain constant at all times
        d.   decrease with decreasing altitude

11   As a smooth flow of subsonic air at a velocity less than M0.4 flows through a divergent duct:
        (i) static pressure (ii) velocity

        a.   (i) increases and (ii) decreases
        b.   (i) increases and (ii) increases
        c.   (i) decreases and (ii) decreases
        d.   (i) decreases and (ii) increases

12   As subsonic air flows through a convergent duct:
        (i) static pressure (ii) velocity

        a.   (i) increases and (ii) decreases
        b.   (i) increases and (ii) increases
        c.   (i) decreases and (ii) decreases
        d.   (i) decreases and (ii) increases

13   Bernoulli's Theorem states:

        a.   dynamic pressure increase and static pressure increase
        b.   dynamic pressure increase and static pressure decrease
        c.   dynamic pressure is maximum at stagnation point
        d.   zero pressure at zero dynamic pressure

14   Consider a uniform flow of air at velocity V in a Streamtube. If the temperature of the air in the tube is raised:

        a.   the mass flow remains constant and velocity V decreases
        b.   the mass flow will increase and velocity V remain constant
        c.   the mass flow will decrease and velocity V will remain constant
        d.   the mass flow remains constant and the velocity V will increase

PRINCIPLES OF FLIGHT   SPECIMEN QUESTIONS

15   In a subsonic flow venturi, the relationship between the total pressure, static pressure and dynamic pressure of undisturbed air and air in the throat will be:

     (i) Dynamic pressure will be constant, static pressure will decrease.
     (ii) Total pressure will be constant, dynamic pressure will increase.

     a.   both (i) and (ii) are correct
     b.   (i) is correct and (ii) is incorrect
     c.   (i) is incorrect and (ii) is correct
     d.   both (i) and (ii) are incorrect

16   In accordance with Bernoulli's Theorem, where PT = Total Pressure, PS = Static pressure and q = Dynamic pressure:

     a.   PT + PS = q
     b.   PT = PS - q
     c.   PT - PS = q
     d.   PS + PT = q

17   The Principle of Continuity states that in a Streamtube of decreasing cross-sectional area, the speed of a subsonic and incompressible airflow will:

     a.   remain the same
     b.   decrease
     c.   increase
     d.   sonic

18   The Principle of Continuity states that in a tube of increasing cross-sectional area, the speed of a subsonic and incompressible airflow will:

     a.   remain the same
     b.   decrease
     c.   sonic
     d.   increase

19   What are the units for wing loading and dynamic pressure?

     a.   N/square metre and N/square metre
     b.   Nm and Nm
     c.   N and N/square metre
     d.   N/square metre and joules

20   When considering the Principle of Continuity for incompressible subsonic flow, what happens in a Streamtube with a change in cross-sectional area?

     a.   The density at the throat will be the same as the density at the mouth
     b.   The density at the throat will be the less than the density at the mouth
     c.   The density at the throat will be greater than the density at the mouth
     d.   Cannot say without knowing the change in cross-sectional area of the Streamtube

21   When considering the Principle of Continuity for subsonic flow, what happens in a streamtube for a change in cross-sectional area?

   a.   RHO 1 = RHO 2
   b.   RHO 1 > RHO 2
   c.   RHO 2 > RHO 1
   d.   Cannot say without knowing the change in cross-sectional area of the streamtube.

22   Which of the following creates Lift?

   a.   An accelerated air mass.
   b.   A retarded air mass.
   c.   A change in direction of mass flow.
   d.   A symmetrical aerofoil at zero angle of attack in a high speed flow.

23   Which of the following statements about a venturi in a subsonic air flow is correct?

   (i) The dynamic pressure in the undisturbed flow and in the throat are equal.
   (ii) The total pressure in the undisturbed flow and in the throat are equal.

   a.   (i) is correct and (ii) is incorrect.
   b.   (i) is incorrect and (ii) is correct.
   c.   (i) and (ii) are correct.
   d.   (i) and (ii) are incorrect.

24   A line from the centre of curvature of the leading edge to the trailing edge, equidistant from the top and bottom wing surface is the:

   a.   camber line
   b.   upper camber line
   c.   mean chord
   d.   mean aerodynamic chord

25   A symmetrical aerofoil section at CL = 0 will produce?

   a.   A negative (nose down) pitching moment
   b.   A positive (nose up) pitching moment
   c.   Zero pitching moment
   d.   No aerodynamic force

26   Angle of attack is the angle between:

   a.   undisturbed airflow and chord line
   b.   undisturbed airflow and mean camber line
   c.   local airflow and chord line
   d.   local airflow and mean camber line

PRINCIPLES OF FLIGHT — SPECIMEN QUESTIONS

27   How is the thickness of an aerofoil section measured?

   a.   As the ratio of wing angle
   b.   Related to camber
   c.   As the percentage of chord
   d.   In metres

28   Lift and drag respectively are normal and parallel to:

   a.   the chord line
   b.   the longitudinal axis
   c.   the horizon
   d.   the relative airflow

29   The angle between the aeroplane longitudinal axis and the chord line is:

   a.   angle of incidence.
   b.   glide path angle.
   c.   angle of attack.
   d.   climb path angle.

30   The term angle of attack is defined as:

   a.   the angle between the relative airflow and the horizontal axis
   b.   the angle between the wing chord line and the relative wind
   c.   the angle that determines the magnitude of the lift force
   d.   the angle between the wing and tailplane incidence

31   What is the angle of attack (Aerodynamic angle of incidence)?

   a.   Angle of the chord line to the relative free stream flow
   b.   Angle of the chord line to the fuselage datum
   c.   Angle of the tailplane chord to the wing chord
   d.   Angle of the tailplane chord to the fuselage datum

32   When considering the coefficient of lift and angle of attack of aerofoil sections:

   a.   a symmetrical section at zero angle of attack will produce a small positive coefficient of lift
   b.   an asymmetrical section at zero angle of attack will produce zero coefficient of lift
   c.   a symmetrical section at zero angle of attack will produce zero coefficient of lift
   d.   aerofoil section symmetry has no effect on lift coefficient

33   When considering the Lift and Drag forces on an aerofoil section:

   a.   they are only Normal to each other at one angle of attack
   b.   they both depend on the pressure distribution on the aerofoil section
   c.   they vary linearly
   d.   Lift is proportional to Drag

34   Where does the lift act on the wing?

   a.   Suction
   b.   Always forward of the CG
   c.   Centre of Gravity
   d.   Centre of Pressure

35   Which of the following creates lift?

   a.   A slightly cambered aerofoil
   b.   An aerofoil in a high speed flow
   c.   Air accelerated upwards
   d.   Air accelerated downwards

36   Which of the following is the greatest factor causing lift?

   a.   suction above the wing
   b.   increased pressure below wing
   c.   increased airflow velocity below the wing
   d.   decreased airflow velocity above the wing

37   Which of the following statements is correct?

   a.   Lift acts perpendicular to the horizontal and drag parallel in a rearwards direction
   b.   Drag acts parallel to the chord and opposite to the direction of motion of the aircraft and lift acts perpendicular to the chord
   c.   Lift acts at right angles to the top surface of the wing and drag acts at right angles to lift
   d.   Drag acts in the same direction as the relative wind and lift perpendicular to the relative wind.

38   With reference to Annex 'E', how do the speeds relate to relative wind/airflow (V)?

   a.   V1 < V2 and V2 < V
   b.   V1 = 0 and V2 = V
   c.   V1 > V2 and V2 < V
   d.   V1 = 0 and V2 > V

39   If IAS is doubled, by which of the following factors should the original CL be multiplied to maintain level flight?

   a.   0·25
   b.   0·5
   c.   2·0
   d.   4·0

PRINCIPLES OF FLIGHT   SPECIMEN QUESTIONS

40   On entering ground effect:

     a.   more power is required
     b.   less power is required
     c.   ground effect has no effect on power required
     d.   lift decreases

41   On the approach to land, ground effect will begin to be felt at:

     a.   twice the wingspan above the ground
     b.   half the wingspan above the ground
     c.   when the angle of attack is increased
     d.   upon elevator deflection

42   The formula for lift is:

     a.   L = W
     b.   L = 2 rho V squared S CL
     c.   L = 1/2 rho V squared S CL
     d.   L = rho V S CL

43   The influence of ground affect on landing distance will:

     a.   increase landing distance
     b.   decrease landing distance
     c.   have no affect on landing distance
     d.   depend on flap position

44   Two identical aircraft of the same weight fly at different altitudes. All other important factors remaining constant, assuming no compressibility and ISA conditions, what is the TAS of each aircraft?

     a.   The same
     b.   Greater in the higher aircraft
     c.   Greater in the lower aircraft
     d.   Less in the higher aircraft

45   What do 'S' and 'q' represent in the lift equation?

     a.   Static pressure and chord
     b.   Wing span and dynamic pressure
     c.   Wing area and dynamic pressure
     d.   Wing area and static pressure

46   What effect on induced drag does entering ground effect have?

     a.   Increase
     b.   Decrease
     c.   Remain the same
     d.   Induced drag will increase, but profile drag will decrease

47   What is the CL and CD ratio at normal angles of attack

   a.   CL higher
   b.   CD higher
   c.   the same
   d.   CL much higher

48   What is the MAC of a wing?

   a.   Area of wing divided by the span
   b.   The same as the mean chord of a rectangular wing of the same span
   c.   The mean chord of the whole aeroplane
   d.   The 25% chord of a swept wing

49   When an aircraft enters ground effect:

   a.   the lift vector is inclined rearwards which increases the thrust required
   b.   the lift vector is inclined forwards which reduces the thrust required
   c.   the lift vector is unaffected, the cushion of air increases
   d.   the lift vector is inclined forward which increases the thrust required

50   When an aircraft enters ground effect:

   a.   the induced angle of attack increases
   b.   lift decreases and drag increases
   c.   lift increases and drag decreases
   d.   the aircraft will be partially supported on a cushion of air

51   When considering an angle of attack versus coefficient of lift graph for a cambered aerofoil, where does the lift curve intersect the vertical CL axis?

   a.   above the origin
   b.   below the origin
   c.   at the point of origin
   d.   to the left of the origin

52   When in level flight at 1·3 VS, what is the CL as a percentage of CL MAX?

   a.   59%
   b.   77%
   c.   130%
   d.   169%

53   Which of the following is the cause of wing tip vortices?

   a.   Air spilling from the top surface to the bottom surface at the wing tip
   b.   Air spilling from the bottom surface to the top surface at the wing tip
   c.   Air spilling from the bottom surface to the top surface at the left wing tip and from the top surface to the bottom surface at the right wing tip
   d.   Spanwise flow vector from the tip to the root on the bottom surface of the wing

54   Which of the following is the correct definition of aspect ratio?

   a.   Span divided by tip chord
   b.   Chord divided by span
   c.   Span divided by mean chord
   d.   Chord divided by span, measured at the 25% chord position

55   Which of the following most accurately describes the airflow which causes wing tip vortices?

   a.   From the root to the tip on the top surface and from the tip to the root on the bottom surface over the wing tip
   b.   From the root to the tip on the top surface and from the tip to the root on the bottom surface over the trailing edge
   c.   From the tip to the root on the top surface and from the root to the tip on the bottom surface over the trailing edge
   d.   From the tip to the root on the top surface and from the root to the tip on the bottom surface over the wing tip

56   Which point on the curve in Annex 'H' represents minimum level flight speed?

   a.   C
   b.   A
   c.   D
   d.   B

57   Wing tip vortices are caused by unequal pressure distribution on the wing which results in airflow from:

   a.   bottom to top round the trailing edge
   b.   top to bottom round the trailing edge
   c.   bottom to top round wingtip
   d.   top to bottom round wingtip

58   With flaps deployed, at a constant IAS in straight and level flight, the magnitude of tip vortices:

   a.   increases or decreases depending upon the initial angle of attack
   b.   increases
   c.   decreases
   d.   remains the same

59   A high aspect ratio wing:

   a.   increases induced drag
   b.   decreases induced drag
   c.   is structurally stiffer than a low aspect ratio
   d.   has a higher stall angle than a low aspect ratio

60 An aircraft flying straight and level; if density halves, aerodynamic drag will:

   a. increase by a factor of four
   b. increase by a factor of two
   c. decrease by a factor of two
   d. decrease by a factor of four

61 At a constant IAS, induced drag is affected by:

   a. aircraft weight
   b. changes in thrust
   c. angle between chord line and longitudinal axis
   d. wing location

62 CDI is proportional to which of the following?

   a. CLmax
   b. CL squared
   c. the square root of the CL
   d. CL

63 Considering the lift to drag ratio, in straight and level flight which of the following is correct?

   a. L/D is maximum at the speed for minimum total drag
   b. L/D maximum decreases with increasing lift
   c. L/D is maximum when lift equals weight
   d. L/D is maximum when lift equals zero

64 High aspect ratio:

   a. reduces parasite drag
   b. reduces induced drag
   c. increases stalling speed
   d. increases manoeuverability

65 How does aerodynamic drag vary when airspeed is doubled?

   a. 4
   b. 16
   c. 1
   d. 2

66 If dynamic (kinetic) pressure increases, what is the effect on total drag (if all important factors remain constant)?

   a. Drag decreases
   b. Drag increases
   c. It has no effect on drag
   d. Drag only changes with changing ground speed

67 If IAS is increased from 80 kt to 160 kt at a constant air density TAS will double. What would be the effect on (i) CDI and (ii) DI?

   a. (i) 2; (ii) 2
   b. (i) 4; (ii) 2
   c. (i) 1/4; (ii) 4
   d. (i) 1/16; (ii) ¼

68 If pressure increases, with OAT and TAS constant, what happens to drag?

   a. Increase
   b. Decrease
   c. Remain constant
   d.

69 If the frontal area of an object in an airstream is increased by a factor of three, by what factor does drag increase?

   a. 9
   b. 3
   c. 6
   d. 1·5

70 If the IAS is increased by a factor of 4, by what factor would the drag increase?

   a. 4
   b. 8
   c. 12
   d. 16

71 In a stream tube, if density is halved, drag will be reduced by a factor of:

   a. 3
   b. 4
   c. 6
   d. 2

PRINCIPLES OF FLIGHT — SPECIMEN QUESTIONS

72 In straight and level flight, which of the following would cause induced drag to vary linearly if weight is constant?

   a. 1/V
   b. V
   c. 1/V squared
   d. V squared

73 In subsonic flight, which is correct for VMD?

   a. Parasite drag greater than induced drag
   b. CL and CD are minimum
   c. Parasite and Induced Drag are equal
   d. Induced Drag is greater than Parasite Drag

74 Induced drag can be reduced by:

   a. increased taper ratio
   b. decreased aspect ratio
   c. use of a wing tip with a thinner aerofoil section
   d. increased aspect ratio

75 Refer to ANNEX 'B', which of the following is represented by vertical axis (x)?

   a. Total drag
   b. Induced drag
   c. Parasite drag
   d. Form drag

76 The advantage of a turbulent boundary layer over a laminar boundary layer is:

   a. decreases energy
   b. thinner
   c. increased skin friction
   d. less tendency to separate

77 The effect of Winglets is:

   a. elliptical pressure distribution increases
   b. reduction in induced drag
   c. decrease in stall speed
   d. longitudinal static stability increases

78 What does parasite drag vary with?

   a. Square of the speed
   b. CLmax
   c. Speed
   d. Surface area

79 What effect does aspect ratio have on induced drag?

  a. Increased aspect ratio increases induced drag
  b. Increased aspect ratio reduces induced drag
  c. Changing aspect ratio has no effect
  d. Induced drag will equal 1·3 x aspect ratio/chord ratio

80 What happens to total drag when accelerating from CL MAX to maximum speed?

  a. Increases
  b. Increases then decreases
  c. Decreases
  d. Decreases then increases

81 What is interference drag?

  a. Airflow retardation over the aircraft structure due to surface irregularities
  b. Drag caused by high total pressure at the leading edges when compared to the lower pressure present at the trailing edge
  c. Drag caused by the generation of lift
  d. Drag due to the interaction of individual boundary layers at the junction of aircraft major components

82 What is the cause of induced angle of attack?

  a. Downwash from trailing edge in the vicinity of the wing tips
  b. Change in flow from effective angle of attack
  c. The upward inclination of the free stream flow around the wing tips
  d. Wing downwash altering the angle at which the airflow meets the tailplane

83 What is the ratio of CDi ?

  a. (CL) squared to S
  b. (CL) squared to AR
  c. ½ rho V squared
  d. ½ rho V squared S

84 What phenomena causes induced drag?

  a. Wing tip vortices
  b. Wing tanks
  c. The increased pressure at the leading edge
  d. The spanwise flow, inward below the wing and outward above

85 When compared to a laminar boundary layer:

  a. a turbulent boundary layer has more kinetic energy
  b. a turbulent boundary layer is thinner
  c. less skin friction is generated by a turbulent layer
  d. a turbulent boundary layer is more likely to separate

86 When considering the aerodynamic forces acting on an aerofoil section:

- a. lift and drag increase linearly with an increase in angle of attack
- b. lift and drag act normal to each other only at one angle of attack
- c. lift and drag increase exponentially with an increase in angle of attack
- d. lift increases linearly and drag increases exponentially with an increase in angle of attack

87 When considering the properties of a laminar and turbulent boundary layer, which of the following statements is correct?

- a. Friction drag is the same
- b. Friction drag higher in laminar
- c. Friction drag higher in turbulent
- d. Separation point is most forward with a turbulent layer

88 When the undercarriage is lowered in flight:

- a. form drag will increase and the aircraft's nose down pitching moment will be unchanged
- b. induced drag will increase and the aircraft's nose down pitching moment will increase
- c. form drag will increase and the aircraft's nose down pitching moment will increase
- d. induced drag will decrease and the aircraft's nose down pitching moment will increase

89 Which of the following decreases induced drag?

- a. Wing fences
- b. Anhedral
- c. Winglets
- d. Low aspect ratio plan form

90 Which of the following is a characteristic of laminar flow boundary layer?

- a. Constant velocity
- b. Constant temperature
- c. No flow normal to the surface
- d. No vortices

91 Which of the following is the correct formula for drag?

- a. ½ rho V squared CL S
- b. ½ rho V (CL)squared S
- c. ½ rho V squared AR CD S
- d. ½ rho V squared CD S

92. Which statement about induced drag and tip vortices is correct?

    a. Vortex generators diminish tip vortices
    b. Flow on upper and lower wing surfaces is towards the tip
    c. They both decrease at high angle of attack
    d. On the upper surface there is a component of flow towards the root, whilst on the lower surface it is towards the tip

93. With reference to Annex 'F', which curve represents drag versus true airspeed?

    a. (c)
    b. (b)
    c. (a)
    d. (d)

94. A jet aircraft flying at high altitude encounters severe turbulence without encountering high speed buffet. If the aircraft decelerates, what type of stall could occur first?

    a. Low speed stall
    b. Accelerated stall
    c. Deep stall
    d. Shock stall

95. A swept wing aircraft stalls and the wake contacts the horizontal tail. What would be the stall behaviour?

    a. nose down
    b. nose up and/or elevator ineffectiveness
    c. tendency to increase speed after stall
    d. nose up

96. An aircraft at a weight of 237402N stalls at 132 kt. At a weight of 356103N it would stall at:

    a. 88 kt
    b. 162 kt
    c. 108 kt
    d. 172 kt

97. An aircraft at low subsonic speed will never stall:

    a. as long as the CAS is kept above the power-on stall speed
    b. as long as the IAS is kept above the power-on stall speed
    c. as long as the maximum angle of attack is not exceeded
    d. as long as the pitch angle is negative

98   At high angle of attack, where does airflow separation begin?

   a.   Upper surface, towards the leading edge
   b.   Lower surface, towards the trailing edge
   c.   Upper surface, towards the trailing edge
   d.   Lower surface, towards the leading edge

99   At the point of stall:

   a.   lift decreases, drag decreases
   b.   lift constant, drag increases
   c.   lift decreases, drag increases
   d.   lift decreases, drag constant

100   During erect spin recovery the correct recovery actions are:

   a.   control stick pulled aft
   b.   ailerons held neutral
   c.   control stick sideways against bank
   d.   control stick sideways towards bank

101   Force on the tail and its effect on VS due to CG movement:

   a.   if rearward movement of the CG gives a reduced down-force on the tail, VS will be higher
   b.   if forward movement of the CG gives a reduced down-force on the tail, VS will be higher
   c.   if rearward movement of the CG gives a reduced down-force on the tail, VS will be reduced
   d.   if rearward movement of the CG gives an increased down-force on the tail, VS will be reduced

102   How do vortex generators work?

   a.   Re-direct spanwise flow
   b.   Take energy from free stream and introduce it into the boundary layer
   c.   Reduce kinetic energy to delay separation
   d.   Reduce the adverse pressure gradient

103   If a jet aircraft is at 60 degrees bank angle during a constant altitude turn, the stall speed will be:

   a.   1·60 greater
   b.   1·19 greater
   c.   1·41 greater
   d.   2·00 greater

PRINCIPLES OF FLIGHT   SPECIMEN QUESTIONS

104 If the stalling speed in a 15 degree bank turn is 60 kt, what would the stall speed be in a 45 degree bank?

   a.   83 kt
   b.   70 kt
   c.   85 kt
   d.   60 kt

105 If the straight and level stall speed is 100 kt, what will be the stall speed in a 1·5g turn?

   a.   122 kt
   b.   150 kt
   c.   81 kt
   d.   100 kt

106 If VS is 100 kt in straight and level flight, during a 45 bank turn VS will be:

   a.   100 kt
   b.   140 kt
   c.   80 kt
   d.   119 kt

107 In level flight at 1.4Vs what is the approximate bank angle at which stall will occur?

   a.   44 degrees
   b.   30 degrees
   c.   60 degrees
   d.   32 degrees

108 In recovery from a spin:

   a.   ailerons should be kept neutral
   b.   airspeed increases
   c.   ailerons used to stop the spin
   d.   rudder and ailerons used against the direction of spin rotation

109 Stall speed in a turn is proportional to:

   a.   Lift
   b.   Weight
   c.   the square root of the load factor
   d.   TAS squared

110 Stalling speed increases when:

   a.   recovering from a steep dive
   b.   the aircraft is subjected to minor altitude changes, i.e. 0 to 10,000 ft
   c.   the aircraft weight decreases
   d.   flaps are deployed

PRINCIPLES OF FLIGHT   SPECIMEN QUESTIONS

111 The angle of attack at the stall:

   a. increases with forward CG
   b. increases with aft CG
   c. decreases with decrease in weight
   d. is not affected by changes in weight

112 The CP on a swept wing aircraft will move forward due to:

   a. boundary layer fences and spanwise flow
   b. tip stall of the wing
   c. flow separation at the root due to spanwise flow
   d. change in wing angle of incidence

113 The effect of tropical rain on drag and stall speed would be to:

   a. increase drag and increase stall speed
   b. increase drag and decrease stall speed
   c. decrease drag and increase stall speed
   d. decrease drag and decrease stall speed

114 The IAS of a stall:

   a. increases with high altitude; more flaps; slats
   b. may increase with increasing altitude, especially high altitude; forward CG and icing
   c. decreases with forward CG and increasing altitude
   d. altitude never affects stall speed IAS

115 Vortex generators:

   a. take energy from the laminar flow to induce boundary layer separation
   b. use free stream flow to induce laminar flow
   c. prevent spanwise flow
   d. use free stream flow to increase energy in the turbulent boundary layer

116 VS is 100 kt at n = 1, what will the stall speed be at n = 2?

   a. 200 kt
   b. 119 kt
   c. 141 kt
   d. 100 kt

117 What are the effects of tropical rain on: (i) CLMAX (ii) Drag

   a. (i) increase (ii) decrease
   b. (i) decrease (ii) increase
   c. (i) increase (ii) increase
   d. (i) decrease (ii) decrease

118   What causes a swept wing aircraft to pitch-up at the stall:

   a. Negative camber at the root
   b. Separated airflow at the root
   c. Spanwise flow
   d. Rearward movement of the CP

119   What causes deep stall in a swept back wing?

   a. CP moves aft
   b. CP moves forward
   c. Root stall
   d. Spanwise flow from tip to root on wing upper surface

120   What does a stick pusher do?

   a. Activate at a certain angle of attack and pull the control column backwards.
   b. Activate at a certain angle of attack and push the stick forward.
   c. Activate at a certain IAS and vibrate the stick.
   d. Activate at a certain IAS and push the stick forward.

121   What effect on stall speed do the following have?

   a. Increased anhedral increases stall speed
   b. Fitting a 'T' tail will reduce stall speed
   c. Increasing sweepback decreases stall speed
   d. Decreasing sweep angle decreases stall speed

122   What happens to the stall speed with flaps down, when compared to flaps up?

   a. Increase
   b. Decrease
   c. Remain the same

123   What influence does the CG being on the forward limit have on Vs and the stall angle?

   a. Vs increases, stall angle remains constant
   b. Vs increases, stall angle increases
   c. Vs decreases, stall angle remains constant
   d. Vs decreases, stall angle decreases

124   What is a high speed stall?

   a. Separation of the airflow due to shockwave formation
   b. A stall caused by increasing the load factor (g) during a manoeuvre
   c. A stall due to decreasing CLmax at speeds above M0.4
   d. Excessive dynamic pressure causing airflow separation

PRINCIPLES OF FLIGHT   SPECIMEN QUESTIONS

125   What is load factor?

    a.   1 / Bank Angle
    b.   Weight / Lift
    c.   Lift / Weight
    d.   Weight / Wing area

126   What is the percentage increase in stall speed in a 45 bank turn?

    a.   45%
    b.   41%
    c.   19%
    d.   10%

127   What is the standard stall recovery for a light aircraft?

    a.   Pitch down, stick neutral roll, correct for bank with rudder
    b.   Pitch down, stick neutral roll, correct for bank with aileron
    c.   Pitch down, stick neutral, wait for neutral tendency
    d.   Pitch down, stick neutral roll, do not correct for bank

128   What percentage increase in lift is required to maintain altitude while in a 45 degree bank turn?

    a.   19%
    b.   41%
    c.   50%
    d.   10%

129   When an aircraft wing stalls:

    a.   A swept back wing will stall from the root and the CP will move aft
    b.   A non-swept rectangular wing will stall from the root and the CP will move forwards
    c.   A non-swept rectangular wing will tend to stall from the tip and the CP will move backwards
    d.   A swept back wing will stall from the tip and the CP will move forward

130   When entering a stall, the CP of a straight rectangular wing (i) and a strongly swept wing (ii) will:

    a.   (i) move aft (ii) move forward
    b.   (i) move aft (ii) move aft
    c.   (i) move aft (ii) not move
    d.   (i) not move (ii) not move

PRINCIPLES OF FLIGHT — SPECIMEN QUESTIONS

131. Which is the most critical phase regarding ice on a wing leading edge?

    a. During the take off run
    b. The last part of rotation
    c. Climb with all engines operating
    d. All phases are equally important

132. Which kind of stall occurs at the lowest angle of attack?

    a. Deep stall.
    b. Accelerated stall.
    c. Low speed stall.
    d. Shock stall.

133. Which of the following aircraft designs would be most prone to super stall?

    a. 'T' tail
    b. swept forward wing
    c. swept back wing
    d. pod mounted engines beneath the wing

134. Which of the following combination of characteristics would be most likely make an aircraft susceptible to deep stall?

    a. Swept wing and wing mounted engines
    b. Swept wing and 'T' tail
    c. Straight wing and wing mounted engines
    d. Straight wing and 'T' tail

135. Which of the following is the correct designation of stall speed in the landing configuration?

    a. Vs1g
    b. Vs1
    c. Vso
    d. VsL

136. Which of the following is the most important result/problem caused by ice formation?

    a. Increased drag
    b. Increased weight
    c. Blockage of the controls
    d. Reduction in CLMAX

137. Which of the following is the speed that would activate the stick shaker?

    a. 1.5 VS
    b. 1.15 VS
    c. 1.2 VS
    d. Above VS

138 Which of the following is used to activate a stall warning device?

   a. Movement of the CP
   b. Movement of the CG
   c. Movement of the stagnation point
   d. A reduction in dynamic pressure

139 Which of the following would indicate an impending stall?

   a. Stall strip and stick shaker
   b. Stall strip and angle of attack indicator
   c. Airspeed indicator and stick shaker
   d. Stick shaker and angle of attack indicator

140 Which stall has the greatest angle of attack?

   a. Low speed stall
   b. High speed stall (shock stall)
   c. Deep stall
   d. Accelerated stall

141 With a swept wing the nose up phenomena is caused by:

   a. deploying lift augmentation devices
   b. wing fences
   c. wing sweep prevents the nose up phenomena
   d. tip stall

142 When flying straight and level in 1g flight, slightly below max' all up weight, a basic stall warning system (flapper switch) activates at 75 kt IAS and the aircraft stalls at 68 kt IAS. Under the same conditions at maximum all up weight the margin between stall warning and stall will:

   a. increase because increasing weight increases the 1g stall speed.
   b. decrease because the 1g stall speed is an IAS.
   c. decrease because increasing weight increases the 1g stall speed.
   d. remain the same because increased weight increases the IAS that corresponds to a particular angle of attack.

143 A slat on an aerofoil:

   a. increases the energy of the boundary layer and decreases the critical angle of attack
   b. increases the wing leading edge radius by rotating forward and down from its stowed position on the bottom side of the wing leading edge
   c. deploys automatically under the influence of increased stagnation pressure at high angles of attack / low IAS
   d. increases the energy of the boundary layer and increases the maximum angle of attack

144	After takeoff why are the slats (if installed) always retracted later than the trailing edge flaps?

	a.	Because VMCA with slats extended is more favourable compared to the flaps extended position.
	b.	Because flaps extended gives a large decrease in stall speed with relatively less drag.
	c.	Because slats extended provides a better view from the cockpit than flaps extended.
	d.	Because slats extended gives a large decrease in stall speed with relatively less drag.

145	An aircraft has trailing edge flap positions of 0, 15, 30 and 45 degrees plus slats can be deployed. What will have the greatest negative influence on CL / CD?

	a.	Deploying slats
	b.	0 - 15 flaps
	c.	15 - 30 flaps
	d.	30 - 45 flaps

146	Extending the flaps while maintaining a constant angle of attack (all other factors constant):

	a.	the aircraft will sink suddenly
	b.	the aircraft will yaw
	c.	the aircraft will climb
	d.	the aircraft will roll

147	For an aircraft flying straight and level at constant IAS, when flaps are deployed the induced drag:

	a.	increases
	b.	decreases
	c.	increases or decreases depending on the aircraft
	d.	stays the same

148	How does a plain flap increase CL?

	a.	Increases camber
	b.	Increases angle of attack
	c.	Changes position of CP
	d.	Decreases the Aspect Ratio

149	How is the pitching moment affected if flaps are deployed in straight and level flight?

	a.	Pitch up
	b.	Pitch down
	c.	Depends on CG position
	d.

PRINCIPLES OF FLIGHT   SPECIMEN QUESTIONS

150   If flaps are extended in level flight

   a.   Lift and Drag increase
   b.   CL max increases
   c.   CL and Drag increase
   d.   CL increases

151   If the angle of attack is maintained constant, what happens to the coefficient of lift when flaps are deployed?

   a.   Increased
   b.   Decreased
   c.   Changes with the square of IAS
   d.   Remains constant because angle of attack remains the same

152   In order to maintain straight and level flight when trailing edge flaps are retracted, the angle of attack must:

   a.   be increased or decreased depending on type of flap
   b.   be decreased
   c.   be increased
   d.   stay the same because the lift requirement will be the same

153   On a highly swept back wing with leading edge flaps and leading edge slats, which device would be fitted in the following possible locations?

   a.   Slats inboard, leading edge flaps outboard.
   b.   Slats outboard, leading edge flaps inboard.
   c.   Alternate leading edge flaps and slats along the wing leading edge
   d.   There is no preferred position for these two devices

154   On a swept back wing, in which of the following locations would Krueger Flaps be fitted?

   a.   Inboard leading edge
   b.   Outboard leading edge
   c.   The leading edge
   d.   The trailing edge

155   The effects of leading edge slats:

   a.   increase boundary layer energy, move suction peak on to slat and increase CLMAX angle of attack
   b.   increase camber, increase suction peak on main wing, increase effective angle of attack and move CLMAX to higher angle of attack
   c.   increase boundary layer energy, increase suction peak on main wing section, move CLMAX to a higher angle of attack
   d.   decrease boundary layer energy, move suction peak onto slat, move CLMAX to a lower angle of attack

156 The illustration of ANNEX 'C' shows a:

   a.   plain flap
   b.   slotted flap
   c.   fowler flap
   d.   split flap

157 The maximum angle of attack for the flaps down configuration, compared to flaps up is:

   a.   greater
   b.   smaller
   c.   unchanged
   d.   smaller or greater, depending on CG position

158 What is the effect of deploying leading edge flaps?

   a.   Decrease CLMAX
   b.   Decrease the critical angle of attack
   c.   Not affect the critical angle of attack
   d.   Increase the critical angle of attack

159 What is the effect of deploying trailing edge flaps?

   a.   Increased minimum glide angle
   b.   Decreased minimum glide angle
   c.   Increased glide range
   d.   Decreased sink rate

160 What is the purpose of a slat on the leading edge?

   a.   decelerate the air over the top surface
   b.   thicken the laminar boundary layer over the top surface
   c.   increase the camber of the wing
   d.   allow greater angle of attack

161 What is true regarding deployment of Slats / Krueger flaps?

   a.   Slats increase the critical angle of attack, Krueger flaps do not
   b.   Krueger flaps increase the critical angle of attack, Slats do not
   c.   Krueger flaps form a slot, Slats do not
   d.   Slats form a slot, Krueger flaps do not

162 What must happen to the CL when flaps are deployed while maintaining a constant IAS in straight and level flight?

   a.   increase then decrease
   b.   remain constant
   c.   decrease
   d.   increase

163 What pitching moment will be generated when Fowler flaps are deployed on an aircraft with a high mounted ('T' tail) tailplane?

   a. An aircraft nose up pitching moment
   b. An aircraft nose down pitching moment
   c. The nose up pitching moment will be balanced by the nose down pitching moment
   d. The resultant aircraft pitching moment will depend upon the relative position of the CP and CG

164 When trailing edge flaps are deployed:

   a. a higher angle of attack is required for maximum lift.
   b. glide distance is degraded.
   c. CLmax decreases.
   d. VS1g increases.

165 Which of the following increases the stall angle?

   a. Slats
   b. Flaps
   c. Spoilers
   d. Ailerons

166 A low wing jet aircraft is flaring to land. The greatest stick force will be experienced with:

   a. flaps up and CG at the aft limit.
   b. flaps fully down and Cg at the aft limit.
   c. flaps fully down and CG at the forward limit.
   d. flaps fully up and Cg at the forward limit.

167 Positive static lateral stability is the tendency of an aeroplane to:

   a. roll to the right in the case of a positive sideslip angle (aeroplane nose to the right).
   b. roll to the left in the case of a positive sideslip angle (aeroplane nose to the left).
   c. roll to the left in a right turn.
   d. roll to the right in a right turn.

168 Positive static longitudinal stability means:

   a. nose down pitching moment when encountering an up gust.
   b. nose up pitching moment with a speed change at a constant angle of attack.
   c. nose down pitching moment with a speed change at a constant angle of attack.
   d. nose up moment when encountering an up gust.

PRINCIPLES OF FLIGHT   SPECIMEN QUESTIONS

169 The CG of an aeroplane is in a fixed position forward of the neutral point. Speed changes cause a departure from the trimmed position. Which of the following statements about the stick force stability is correct?

   a. An increase of 10 kt from the trimmed position at low speed has more affect on the stick force than an increase in 10 kt from the trimmed position at high speed.
   b. Increase of speed generates pull forces.
   c. Aeroplane nose up trim decreases the stick force stability.
   d. Stick force stability is not affected by trim.

170 Too much lateral static stability is undesirable because:

   a. too much aileron needed in a cross-wind landing.
   b. too much rudder needed in a cross-wind landing.
   c. constant aileron in cruise in a cross-wind.
   d.

171 What is the effect of an aft shift of the CG on (1) static longitudinal stability and (2) the required control deflection for a given pitch change?

   a. (1) reduces, (2) increases.
   b. (1) increases, (2) increases.
   c. (1) increases, (2) reduces.
   d. (1) reduces, (2) reduces.

172 Which statement is correct?

   a. The stick force per 'g' increases when the CG is moved aft.
   b. The stick force per 'g' must have both upper and lower limits in order to assure acceptable control characteristics.
   c. If the slope of the fe-n line becomes negative, generally speaking this is not a problem for control of an aeroplane.
   d. The stick force per 'g' can only be corrected by means of electronic devices (stability augmentation) in the case of an unacceptable value.

173 What is pitch angle?

   a. The angle between the chord line and the horizontal plane.
   b. The angle between the longitudinal axis and the horizontal plane.
   c. The angle between the chord line and the longitudinal axis.
   d. The angle between the relative airflow and the longitudinal axis.

174 An aircraft of 50 tonnes mass, with two engines each of 60,000 N Thrust and with an L/D ratio of 12:1 is in a straight steady climb. Taking 'g' to be 10 m/s/s, what is the climb gradient?

   a. 12%
   b. 24%
   c. 15.7%
   d. 3.7%

PRINCIPLES OF FLIGHT   SPECIMEN QUESTIONS

175   In a straight steady descent:

   a.   Lift is less than weight, load factor is equal to one
   b.   Lift is less than weight, load factor is less than one
   c.   Lift is equal to weight, load factor is equal to one
   d.   Lift is equal to weight, load factor is less than one

176   Two aircraft of the same weight and under identical atmospheric conditions are flying level 20 degree bank turns. Aircraft 'A' is at 130 kt, aircraft 'B' is at 200 kt.

   a.   The turn radius of 'A' will be greater than 'B'.
   b.   The coefficient of lift of 'A' will be less than 'B'.
   c.   The load factor of 'A' is greater than 'B'.
   d.   Rate of turn of 'A' is greater than 'B'.

177   VMCL can be limited by: (i) engine failure during takeoff, (ii) maximum rudder deflection.

   a.   Both (i) and (ii) are incorrect.
   b.   (i) is incorrect and (ii) is correct.
   c.   (i) is correct and (ii) is incorrect.
   d.   Both (i) and (ii) are correct.

178   Assuming ISA conditions, which statement with respect to the climb is correct?

   a.   At constant TAS the Mach number decreases.
   b.   At constant Mach number the IAS increases.
   c.   At constant IAS the TAS decreases.
   d.   At constant IAS the Mach number increases.

179   The regime of flight from the critical Mach number (Mcrit) to approximately M1.3 is called?

   a.   Transonic.
   b.   Hypersonic.
   c.   Subsonic.
   d.   Supersonic.

180   The speed range between high and low speed buffet:

   a.   decreases during a descent at a constant Mach number.
   b.   is always positive at Mach numbers below MMO.
   c.   increases during a descent at a constant IAS.
   d.   increases during climb.

PRINCIPLES OF FLIGHT   SPECIMEN QUESTIONS

181 When does the bow wave first appear?

  a. At Mcrit.
  b. At Mach 1.
  c. Just above Mach 1.
  d. Just below Mach 1,

182 What can happen to the aeroplane structure flying at a speed just exceeding VA?

  a. It may suffer permanent deformation if the elevator is fully deflected upwards.
  b. It may break if the elevator is fully deflected upwards.
  c. It may suffer permanent deformation because the flight is performed at to large a dynamic pressure.
  d. It will collapse if a turn is made.

183 Which of the following can effect VA?

  a. Mass and pressure altitude.
  b. Mass only.
  c. Pressure altitude only.
  d. It remains a constant IAS.

184 With a vertical gust, what is the point called where the change in the vertical component of lift acts?

  a. Neutral point.
  b. Aerodynamic Centre.
  c. Centre of Gravity.
  d. Centre of Thrust.

185 A single engine aircraft with a constant speed propeller is in a gliding descent with the engine idling, what would be the effect of decreasing the propeller pitch?

  a. Increased L/Dmax, increased rate of descent.
  b. Decreased L/Dmax, increased rate of descent.
  c. Increased L/Dmax, decreased rate of descent.
  d. Decreased L/Dmax, decreased rate of descent.

186 The advantage of a constant speed propeller over a fixed pitch propeller is:

  a. higher maximum thrust available
  b. higher maximum efficiency
  c. more blade surface area available
  d. nearly maximum efficiency over wide speed range

187 You are about to take-off in an aircraft with a variable pitch propeller. At brake release:
(i) Blade pitch and (ii) Propeller RPM lever:

   a.   (i) reduced, (ii) increase.
   b.   (i) reduced, (ii) decrease.
   c.   (i) increased, (ii) decrease.
   d.   (i) increased, (ii) increase.

PRINCIPLES OF FLIGHT

SPECIMEN QUESTIONS

ANSWERS

1	D	52	A	103	C	154	A
2	A	53	B	104	B	155	C
3	D	54	C	105	A	156	D
4	A	55	D	106	D	157	B
5	B	56	C	107	C	158	D
6	B	57	C	108	A	159	A
7	B	58	C	109	C	160	D
8	C	59	B	110	A	161	D
9	C	60	C	111	D	162	B
10	D	61	A	112	B	163	B
11	A	62	B	113	A	164	B
12	D	63	A	114	B	165	A
13	B	64	B	115	D	166	C
14	D	65	A	116	C	167	B
15	C	66	B	117	B	168	A
16	C	67	D	118	C	169	D
17	C	68	A	119	B	170	A
18	B	69	B	120	B	171	D
19	A	70	D	121	D	172	B
20	A	71	D	122	B	173	B
21	A	72	C	123	A	174	C
22	A	73	C	124	C	175	B
23	B	74	D	125	C	176	D
24	A	75	B	126	C	177	A
25	C	76	D	127	A	178	D
26	A	77	B	128	B	179	A
27	C	78	A	129	D	180	C
28	D	79	B	130	A	181	C
29	A	80	D	131	B	182	A
30	B	81	D	132	D	183	A
31	A	82	A	133	C	184	B
32	C	83	B	134	B	185	B
33	B	84	A	135	C	186	D
34	D	85	A	136	D	187	A
35	B	86	D	137	D		
36	A	87	C	138	C		
37	D	88	C	139	D		
38	D	89	C	140	C		
39	A	90	C	141	D		
40	B	91	D	142	D		
41	B	92	D	143	D		
42	C	93	C	144	D		
43	A	94	B	145	D		
44	B	95	B	146	C		
45	C	96	B	147	D		
46	B	97	C	148	A		
47	D	98	C	149	C		
48	B	99	C	150	B		
49	B	100	B	151	A		
50	C	101	C	152	C		
51	A	102	B	153	B		

PRINCIPLES OF FLIGHT SPECIMEN QUESTIONS

EXPLNATIONS TO SPECIMEN QUESTIONS

Q 1
(d) psi is the "imperial" unit of pressure (pounds per square inch). Although not an SI unit it is still widely used in the aircraft industry for hydraulic pressure and air pressure – answer (d) is not only a unit of pressure, it is also the only possibly correct answer among those offered.

The SI unit of pressure [force per unit area] is Newtons per square metre. This unit however is not on offer, but knowing this fact helps eliminate some of the possible answers. Answer (a) is kilograms per square decimetre – the kilogram is the SI unit of mass, so straightaway this answer can be eliminated and answer (b) can be eliminated for the same reason. Answer (c) is incorrect because the Newton is the SI unit of force.

Q 2
(a) Density is mass per unit volume and the SI unit is kilograms per cubic metre. A force is a push or a pull and the SI unit is the Newton. (Page 1-5 & 2-1)

Q 3
(d) Density is mass (kg) per unit volume (cubic metre). (Page 2-1)

Q 4
(a) If a mass is accelerated a force must have been applied. The kg is the SI unit for mass and m/s squared is the SI unit for acceleration. The applied force can be determined by multiplying the mass by the acceleration and the answer must use the SI unit for force - the Newton. (Page 1-5)

Answer (b) is incorrect because psi is not an SI unit. Answer (c) is incorrect because the Joule is the SI unit for work. Answer (d) is incorrect because the Watt is the SI unit for power.

Q 5
(b)   Refer to Page 1-7.
Acceleration (A) is proportional to force (F) and inversely proportional to mass (M).

Q 6
(b) Power is the rate of doing work - force (N) x distance (m) divided by time (s). (Page 1-6)

Q 7
(b) The Air Speed Indicator is calibrated at Sea Level ISA density. To maintain a constant dynamic pressure (CAS) when below sea level (density higher) the TAS will have to be lower. [Q = density x TAS squared] (Pages 2-5 & 6).

Q 8
(c) Static pressure is due to the weight of the atmosphere pressing down on the air beneath, so a body immersed in the atmosphere will experience an equal pressure in all directions due to Static pressure. Static pressure will exert the same force per square metre on all surfaces of an aeroplane. (Page 2-1).

Q 9
(c) True Air Speed (TAS) is the relative velocity between the aircraft and undisturbed air which is close to, but unaffected by the presence of the aircraft. Changing the TAS (the speed of the aircraft through the air; the only speed there is) compensates for changes in air density and ensures a constant mass flow of air over the wing. If an altitude below ISA sea level is considered, the air density would be higher and therefore the TAS would have to be lower than IAS to compensate and keep Lift constant.

PRINCIPLES OF FLIGHT   SPECIMEN QUESTIONS

Q 10
(d) IAS is a measure of dynamic pressure, whereas TAS is the speed of the aircraft through the air. Changes in TAS are used to compensate for changes in air density to maintain a constant dynamic pressure. The lower the density, the higher the TAS must be to maintain a constant IAS. (Pages 2-4 to 2-9).

Answer (a) is incorrect because decreasing temperature increases air density, which decreases the difference between IAS and TAS. Answer (b) is incorrect because increasing air density decreases the difference between IAS and TAS. Answer (c) is incorrect because density changes with altitude.

Q 11
(a) The Principle of Continuity states: "The product of the cross sectional-area, the density and velocity is constant" and Bernoulli's theorem states: "Pressure plus kinetic energy is constant. Subsonic airflow at speeds less than M0.4 will not change the density significantly so density need not be considered. Through a divergent duct (increasing cross sectional-area in the direction of flow) velocity will decrease and static pressure will increase. (Pages 3-1 &
3-2).

Q 12
(d) The Principle of Continuity states: "The product of the cross sectional-area, the density and velocity is constant" and Bernoulli's theorem states: "Pressure plus kinetic energy is constant. Subsonic airflow at speeds less than M0.4 will not change the density significantly so density need not be considered. Through a convergent duct (decreasing cross sectional-area in the direction of flow) velocity will increase and static pressure will decrease. (Pages 3-1 &
3-2).

Q 13
(b) Bernoulli's theorem states: "In the steady flow of an ideal fluid the sum of the pressure and kinetic energy per unit volume remains constant". Put another way: Pressure + Kinetic energy = Constant. (Page 3-2).

Answer (a) is incorrect because it contradicts Bernoulli's theorem. Answer (c) is not a true statement. Answer (d) is incorrect because there will be Static pressure.

Q 14
(d) Raising the temperature of the air in the streamtube will decrease its density. The Principle of Continuity states: "The product of the cross sectional-area, the density and velocity is constant". Therefore, if the density of the air decreases the mass flow must remain constant and the velocity will increase. (Page 3-1).

Q 15
(c) Bernoulli's theorem states: "Pressure plus kinetic energy is constant.
Subsonic airflow at speeds less than M0.4 will not change the density significantly so density need not be considered.
Through a venturi, Total pressure will remain constant. In the throat, dynamic pressure will increase and static pressure will decrease. (Page 3-2).

Q 16
(c) Bernoulli's theorem states: "In the steady flow of an ideal fluid the sum of the pressure and kinetic energy per unit volume remains constant".
Put another way: Pressure + Kinetic energy = Constant. (Page 3-2). Therefore, Total Pressure minus Static Pressure equals Dynamic Pressure. (Page 3-2).

PRINCIPLES OF FLIGHT   SPECIMEN QUESTIONS

Q 17
(c) The Principle of Continuity states: "The product of the cross sectional-area, the density and velocity is constant". The question stipulates "subsonic and incompressible flow", so the affects of density need not be considered. So if the cross sectional-area decreases the velocity will increase. (Page 3-1).

Q 18
(b) The Principle of Continuity states: "The product of the cross sectional-area, the density and velocity is constant". If the cross sectional-area increases the velocity of a subsonic and incompressible flow will decrease. (Page 3-1).

Q 19
(a) Wing loading is the ratio of aircraft weight (a force) to the wing area - Newton's per square metre. Dynamic pressure is force per unit area - also Newton's per square metre.
(Pages 1-13 & 2-4).

Q 20
(a) For incompressible subsonic flow it is assumed that the density of the air remains constant. (Page 3-1).

Q 21
(a) See question 13. The answers merely use a different method of saying the same thing. The Greek letter RHO is the symbol for density.

Q 22
(a) Reference Paragraph 3.1 and 3.2: the Principle of Continuity and Bernoulli's Theorem. In accordance with Bernoulli's Theorem, it is the acceleration of the mass of air over the upper surface of the wing that creates Lift.
None of the other available answers are even remotely correct.

Q 23
(b) Bernoulli's Theorem states: In the steady flow of an "ideal" fluid the sum of the pressure and kinetic energy per unit volume remains constant.
Statement (i) is incorrect because the dynamic pressure in the throat of the venturi is higher than the free stream flow.
Statement (ii) is correct.

Q 24
(a) A line from the centre of the leading edge to the centre of the trailing edge, equidistant from the top and bottom surface is called the camber line, mean line or mean camber line.
(Page 4-3).

Q 25
(c) One of the advantages of a symmetrical aerofoil section is that the pitching moment is zero. (Page 4-11).

Answer (a) is incorrect because it is a positive camber aerofoil section that gives a negative (nose down) pitching moment. Answer (b) is incorrect because it is a negative camber aerofoil section that will give a positive (nose up) pitching moment. Answer (d) is incorrect because a symmetrical section at zero coefficient of lift will generate drag.

PRINCIPLES OF FLIGHT   SPECIMEN QUESTIONS

Q 26
(a) The angle of attack is the angle between the relative airflow and the chord line. Undisturbed airflow is one of the conditions of relative airflow and is an acceptable alternative name for relative airflow. (Page 4-3).

Answers (b) and (d) are obviously incorrect, but answer (c) is incorrect because the angle between local airflow and chord line is the Effective angle of attack.

Q 27
(c) The (maximum) thickness of an aerofoil section is measured as a percentage of the chord. (Page 4-3).

Q 28
(d) Paragraph 4.1. Lift is the aerodynamic force that acts at right angles to the relative airflow and drag is the aerodynamic force that acts parallel and in the same direction as the relative airflow.

Q 29
(a) Reference Para 4.1. The angle between the chord line and longitudinal axis is called the angle of incidence - which is fixed for a wing, but may be variable for the tailplane (horizontal stabiliser).

Q 30
(b) Angle of attack is the angle between the chord line and the relative airflow. (Page 4-3). Relative wind is the American term for relative airflow and is an acceptable alternative.

Q 31
(a) Angle of Attack is the angle between the chord line and the relative airflow. (Page 4-3). Relative free stream flow is an acceptable alternative name for relative airflow. Aerodynamic angle of incidence is an out of date alternative name for angle of attack, which has gone out of general use to prevent confusion with the ANGLE OF INCIDENCE (the angle between the chord line and the longitudinal axis - fixed for a wing, but possibly variable for a tailplane).

Q 32
(c) A symmetrical aerofoil section at zero angle of attack will produce no lift, only drag. (Page 4-11).
An "asymmetrical" section is what we refer to as cambered.

Q 33
(b) Both Lift and Drag forces depend on the pressure disribution on the aerofoil.
1. Total Reaction is split into two vectors: Lift, which acts at 90 degrees to the Relative Airflow and Drag, which is parallel to and in the same direction as the Relative Airflow - this is true for all "normal" angles of attack. 2. Lift varies linearly with angle of attack, but Drag varies exponentially. 3. The lift drag ratio at "normal" angles of attack is between approximately 10:1 and 20:1.

Q 34
(d) Both top and bottom surfaces of the aerofoil contribute to lift, but the point along the chord where the distributed lift is effectively concentrated is termed the Centre of Pressure. (Fig. 4.8).

PRINCIPLES OF FLIGHT   SPECIMEN QUESTIONS

Q 35
(b) This is a strange set of possible answers. The definition of an aerofoil from Page 4-2 is: "A shape capable of producing lift with relatively high efficiency".
To work successfully an aerofoil does not need to be cambered, many symmetrical section aerofoils are used on aircraft. To generate lift it is considered necessary to have an aerofoil set at a suitable angle of attack and an airflow of reasonably high velocity, in the region between 65 kt and 180 kt, depending on the weight of the aircraft.

Answer (a) is considered to be incorrect because a slightly cambered aerofoil with no airflow won't create anything. Answer (c) is incorrect because accelerating air upwards will not create a lift force. Answer (d) is considered to be incorrect because there is no NET acceleration of air downwards. Air upwashes in front of an aerofoil and downwashes behind - back to its original position. The Newton's third law of motion explanation of lift generation is considered a fallacy. There may be a very small amount of lift created in this way, but it is insignificant.

Q 36
(a) The greatest contribution to overall lift comes from the upper surface. (Page 4-7). Answer (b) is incorrect. Although a small amount of lift is generated by the increase in pressure beneath the wing, particularly at higher angles of attack, it always remains a small percentage of the total lift. Answer (c) is incorrect because the velocity below the wing is always lower. Answer (d) is incorrect because a decreased velocity on the top surface would increase the static pressure and lift would decrease.

Q 37
(d) Drag acts parallel to and in the same direction as the relative wind (airflow). Lift acts at right angles (90 degrees or normal) to the relative wind. (Page 4-3).

Q 38
(d)   V1 is the stagnation point where the relative velocity is zero. V2 is the point of boundary layer minimum cross sectional-area where the relative velocity is greater than the free stream flow (TAS). (Pages 4-3 and 4-6).

Q 39
(a) If IAS is doubled, dynamic pressure will be four times greater and lift will be four times greater. To maintain Lift constant the angle of attack should be reduced to a quarter of its previous value. (Page 5-2 et seq).

Q 40
b)   Power required is an alternative name for drag multiplied by TAS.   On entering ground effect induced drag is decreased so power required is decreased. Answer (b) states less power is required. This means that to maintain the same IAS the throttle(s) should be closed further. As the engine(s) are probably already at idle, the aircraft will accelerate. (Page 5-26).

Q 41
(b) Ground effect becomes significant within half the wingspan above the ground. (Page 5-22).

Q 42
(c) L = 1/2 rho x V squared x CL x S (Page 5-2).

PRINCIPLES OF FLIGHT   SPECIMEN QUESTIONS

Q43
(a) As an aircraft flies into ground effect (within half the wingspan of the ground), its proximity to the ground will weaken the tip vortices. Downwash is decreased which decreases the induced angle of attack and increases effective angle of attack. Lift is increased and induced drag is decreased. It will take a greater distance from the screen height for the aircraft to touch down. Because lift is increased there will be less weight on the wheels, making the brakes less effective. Because drag is decreased there is more work for the brakes to do. Therefore, landing distance will be increased by ground effect. (Pages 5-17 and 5-22 et seq).

Q44
(b) The only difference caused by the different altitudes will be the air density. To compensate for the decreased density at the higher altitude and maintain a constant Lift force, the TAS of the higher aircraft will need to be greater. (Page 5-2 et seq).

Q45
(c) Lift = half rho (Density) x Velocity (V) squared x Coefficient of Lift (CL) x The wing area (S). Half rho (Density) x Velocity (V) squared = Dynamic pressure (Q). (Pages 5-1 and 5-2).

Q46
(b) As an aircraft flies into ground effect (within half the wingspan of the ground), its proximity to the ground will weaken the tip vortices. Downwash is decreased which decreases the induced angle of attack and increases effective angle of attack. Lift is increased and induced drag is decreased. (Pages 5-17 and 5-22 et seq).

Q47
(d) For maximum aerodynamic efficiency it is necessary to generate enough lift to balance the weight, while at the same time generate as little drag as possible. The higher the Lift/Drag ratio the greater the aerodynamic efficiency. Therefore, at normal angles of attack CL is much higher than CD - between 10 and 20 times greater. (Pages 5-10, 11 & 12).

Q48
(b) A rectangular wing of this chord and the same span would have broadly similar pitching moment characteristics. The MAC is a primary reference for longitudinal stability considerations. (Page 5-14 & 15).

Q49
(b) As an aircraft enters ground effect downwash is decreased which decreases the induced angle of attack and increases effective angle of attack. The lift vector, being at right angles to the effective airflow, will be inclined forwards and it is this forward inclination which reduces the induced drag (thrust required). (Page 5-17 et seq).

Q50
(c) Lift increases and induced drag decreases. (Page 5-22 et seq)
When an aircraft enters ground effect the induced angle of attack decreases, which increases lift and reduces induced drag - making answers (a) and (b) incorrect. Answer (d) is obviously incorrect.

Q51
(a) The zero lift angle of attack for a positively cambered aerofoil section is about minus 4 degrees. (Fig. 4.6). As the angle of attack is increased the CL will increase, at zero angle of attack the CL will be a small positive value - the lift curve will intersect the vertical CL axis above its point of origin. (Fig. 5.2).

PRINCIPLES OF FLIGHT   SPECIMEN QUESTIONS

Q 52
(a) (CL MAX is regarded as Vs, making 1.3 Vs 30% faster than CL MAX). The lift formula (L = half rho x V squared x CL x S) can be transposed to give: (CL = L / half rho x V squared x S). As density (half rho), Lift (L) and wing area (S) are constant, this can be written: (CL is proportional to 1 / V squared). 1.3 Vs gives: 1 / 1.3 squared, which = 1 / 1.69, which = 0.59 x 100 = 59%. (Page 5-5).

Q 53
(b) Air will flow from areas of higher pressure towards areas of lowerer pressure. When a wing is generating lift, the air pressure on the top surface is lower than that outside the wing tip and generally, air on the bottom surface is slightly higher than that outside the wing tip. This causes air to flow inwards from the tip towards the root on the top surface and outwards from the root towards the tip on the bottom surface. The pressure difference at the wing tip will cause air to flow from the bottom surface to the top surface around the wing tip and this rotating airflow generates the tip vortices. (Page 5-16).

Q 54
(c) Aspect ratio is the ratio of the wing span to the average or mean chord (AR = Span/Chord or Span squared/ Wing area). A high aspect ratio wing is one with a long span and a narrow chord, a low aspect ratio wing is one with a short span and a wide chord. (Page 5-15).

Q 55
(d) Air will flow from areas of higher pressure towards areas of lowerer pressure. When a wing is generating lift, the air pressure on the top surface is lower than that outside the wing tip and generally, air on the bottom surface is slightly higher than that outside the wing tip. This causes air to flow inwards from the tip towards the root on the top surface and outwards from the root towards the tip on the bottom surface. The pressure difference at the wing tip will cause air to flow from the bottom surface to the top surface around the wing tip and this rotating airflow generates the tip vortices. (Page 5-16).

Q 56
(c) Point 'D' represents CL MAX, which equates to the minimum level flight speed. See Paragraph 5.3.1.

Q 57
(c) Air will flow from areas of higher pressure towards areas of lowerer pressure. When a wing is generating lift, the air pressure on the top surface is lower than that outside the wing tip and generally, air on the bottom surface is slightly higher than that outside the wing tip. This causes air to flow inwards from the tip towards the root on the top surface and outwards from the root towards the tip on the bottom surface. The pressure difference at the wing tip will cause air to flow from the bottom surface to the top surface around the wing tip and this rotating airflow generates the tip vortices. (Page 5-16).

Q 58
(c) Wing tip vortices are strongest with the aircraft in the clean configuration. With flaps down, the flaps generate their own vortices which interfere with and weaken the main, tip vortices. (Pages 5-18 to 21 and AIC 17/1999).

Q 59
(b) Increasing the aspect ratio, the ratio of the span to the mean chord, decreases the proportion of wing area affected by the tip vortices. (Only approximately one and a half chord lengths in from the tip are affected by tip vortices). This can best be remembered by referring to the Induced Drag coefficient formula: CDi is proportional to CL squared and inversely proportional to Aspect Ratio - See pages 6-8 and 6-9.

PRINCIPLES OF FLIGHT　　　　　　　　　SPECIMEN QUESTIONS

Q 60
(c) If density halves, drag will halve (decrease by a factor of 2). (Page 6-5).

Q 61
(a) Generally speaking, induced drag is the result of lift production. If aircraft weight increases, more lift is required which will increase induced drag. (Page 6-8).

Answer (b) is incorrect because thrust has no influence on induced drag. Answer (c) is incorrect because this is a definition of 'angle of incidence' which has no influence on induced drag. Answer (d) is incorrect because wing location has no influence on induced drag.

Q 62
(b) Cdi is proportional to CL squared and inversely proportional to the Aspect Ratio. (Page 6-9).

Q 63
(a) Since flying at VMD incurs the least total drag for 1g flight, the aeroplane will also be at L/D max angle of attack (approximately 4 degrees). (Page 6-14).

L/D max is a measure of aerodynamic efficiency and is a constant value for a given configuration. Answer (b) is incorrect because L/D max doesn't change with increasing lift, but the L/D ratio will change. Answer (c) is incorrect because lift can equal weight at any combination of angle of attack and IAS. Answer (d) is incorrect because with lift zero, there would still be drag which would decrease the L/D ratio.

Q 64
(b) Increasing aspect ratio is the designers chief means of reducing induced drag. (Pages 6-8 to 10).

Answer (a) is incorrect because aspect ratio has no significant influence on Parasite drag. Answer (c) is incorrect because increasing aspect ratio tends to increase CL max which reduces stall speed. Answer (d) is incorrect because increasing aspect ration decreases rate of roll.

Q 65
(a) It has to be assumed that airspeed is increasing beyond VMD, when Parasite drag will be dominant. Refer to the drag formula. If airspeed is doubled, dynamic pressure will be four times greater due to the square function of Velocity. If dynamic pressure is four times greater, drag will be four times greater.

Q 66
(b) With questions like this it is a good idea to refer to the appropriate formula, in this case the Drag formula: 1/2 rho x V squared x CD x S. If dynamic pressure (1/2 rho x V squared) increases and the other factors remain the same, Drag will increase.

Q 67
(d) CDi is directly proportional to CL squared and inversely proportional to Aspect Ratio (Page 6-9). Induced Drag (Di) = 1/2 rho x V squared x CDi x S (Page 6-11). If IAS is doubled, Dynamic Pressure will be four times greater and CL will need to be reduced to 1/4 of its previous value to maintain constant Lift. 1/4 squared = 1/16, making CDi 1/16 of its previous value. 'Plugging' all these new values into the Di formula gives: Di = 1/2 rho x 4 x 1/16 x S, making Di 1/4 of its previous value. (Page 6-11).

PRINCIPLES OF FLIGHT   SPECIMEN QUESTIONS

Q 68
(a) The Drag formula shows that: D = 1/2 rho x V squared x CD x S. If pressure increases with outside air temperature (OAT) and True Air Speed (TAS) or (V) constant, density will increase. If density (1/2 rho) increases, Drag will increase. (Page 6-5).

Q 69
(b) Once again, using the Drag formula is an easy way to remember the key facts. If the area 'S' is increased by a factor of 3, drag will also increase by a factor of 3. (Page 6-5).

Q 70
(d) Due to the V squared function, if IAS is increased by a factor of 4, four squared being sixteen times greater, drag will increase by a factor of 16. (Page 6-5).

Q 71
(d) A stream tube is used to illustrate Bernoulli's theorem. A stream tube is a streamlined flow of air with no losses. Drag is proportional to density, so if density is halved drag will be halved.

Q 72
(c) Induced Drag is inversely proportional to V squared (Induced drag is proportional to 1/V squared). (Page 6-8).

Q 73
(c) Induced drag is dominant at low speed and Parasite drag is dominant at high speed. Because Induced drag decreases with an increase in speed and Parasite increases with an increase in speed - as speed is increased from a low value, a speed will be reached at which Induced and Parasite drag are equal. This speed gives minimum Total drag and is known as VMD. (Pages 6-14 and 15).

Answer (a) is incorrect because at VMD Parasite drag and Induced drag are equal. Answer (b) is incorrect because CL is a minimum when no lift is produced and CD is a minimum when the aircraft is not moving, neither of which are practical propositions. Answer (d) is also incorrect because at VMD Parasite drag and Induced drag are equal.

Q 74
(d) Increasing the aspect ratio, the ratio of the span to the mean chord, decreases the proportion of wing area affected by the tip vortices. (Only approximately one and a half chord lengths in from the tip are affected by tip vortices). This can best be remembered by referring to the Induced Drag coefficient formula: CDi is proportional to CL squared and inversely proportional to Aspect Ratio - See pages 6-8 and 6-9.

Q 75
(b) This graph shows an exponential curve indicating a value which decreases with the square of the speed (inversely proportional to the square of the speed). From Figure 6.15 it can be seen that the appropriate characteristic is Induced Drag.

Answer (a) is incorrect because with increasing speed from the minimum level flight value, Total drag decreases, reaches a minimum value and then begins to increase. Answer (c) and (d) are incorrect because Parasite Drag and form drag are both directly proportional to the square of the speed.

PRINCIPLES OF FLIGHT   SPECIMEN QUESTIONS

Q 76
(d) A turbulent boundary layer is thicker and gives more skin friction, but has more resistance to separation due to its higher Kinetic Energy. A laminar boundary layer is thinner and gives less skin friction, but has a greater tendency to separate. (pages 6-2 to 4).

Answer (a) is incorrect because a turbulent layer contains more kinetic energy. Answer (b) is incorrect because a turbulent layer is thicker. Answer (c) is incorrect because, though a true statement, increased skin friction is not an advantage.

Q 77
(b) Winglets are small vertical aerofoils which form part of the wing tip; they reduce tip vortex intensity, thus reduce induced drag - this is their only function. (Page 6-12).

Answer (a) is incorrect because the statement is not difinitive. Answers (c) and (d) are incorrect because the only function of winglets is to reduce tip vortex strength, thereby reducing induced drag.

Q 78
(a) Parasite Drag (Dp) varies with air density, velocity squared, coefficient of drag and area. [Dp = 1/2 rho x V squared x CD x S]. (Page 6-5).

Answer (b) and (d) are incorrect because any increase in Parasite area (drag) caused by increasing the angle of attack beyond the zero lift angle of attack is included-in with induced drag. Answer (c) is less correct than (a) because although parasite drag does increase with speed it is the square of the speed to which parasite drag is proportional.

Q 79
(b) Increasing aspect ratio decreases the proportion of the wing area effected by the tip vortices, thus reducing induced drag. (Page 6-8)

Q 80
(d) Total Drag is made up of Parasite Drag and Induced Drag. Parasite Drag is directly proportional to the square of the IAS and Induced Drag is inversely proportional to the square of the IAS.

At low speed, Total Drag is predominantly Induced Drag and at high speed, predominantly Parasite Drag. As speed is increased from CL MAX, Induced Drag will be decreasing and Parasite Drag will be increasing. Eventually a speed will be reached when Parasite Drag will be the same as Induced Drag, this speed is the minimum (Total) drag speed (VMD). At speeds greater than VMD, Induced Drag will continue to decrease and Parasite Drag will continue to increase.
From CL MAX Total Drag will decrease to a minimum at VMD the start to increase again (Page 6-14)

Q 81
(d) Interference drag is the result of boundary layer 'interference' at wing/fusealge, wing/
engine nacelle and other such junctions. (Page 6-5).

Answer (a) is incorrect because this is a description of skin friction. Answer (b) is incorrect because this is a description of Form (pressure) drag. Answer (c) is incorrect because this is a description of Induced drag.

PRINCIPLES OF FLIGHT — SPECIMEN QUESTIONS

Q 82
(a) Induced angle of attack is the angle between the relative airflow and the Effective airflow - a result of tip vortices increasing the downwash from the wing trailing edge in the vicinity of the wing tips. Increasing vortex strength will increase downwash and increase the induced angle of attack (Page 6-6 and Fig 6.9).

Q 83
(b) Cdi is the induced drag coefficient and is proportional to CL squared and inversely proportional to aspect ratio. (Page 6-11).

Q 84
(a) Induced drag is due to the formation of wing tip vortices. (Pages 6-6 to 8).

Answer (b) is incorrect because tip tanks reduce the strength of tip vortices, thereby reducing induced drag. Answer (c) is incorrect because increased pressure at the leading edge is the cause of Form (pressure) drag. Answer (d) is incorrect because this statement is wrong, in that spanwise flow is the opposite.

Q 85
(a) A Laminar boundary layer has less kinetic energy than a turbulent layer, is thinner and gives less skin friction but separates more easily, whereas a turbulent boundary layer contains more kinetic energy making it separate less easily, but will give more skin friction. (Pages 6-2 to 4).

Q 86
(d) With reference to the lift curve on Page 5-7 it can be seen that as angle of attack increases lift will increase linearly. With reference to the drag 'curve' on page 5-11 it can be seen that as angle of attack increases drag will increase exponentially (increase at an increasing rate).

Q 87
(c) A Laminar boundary layer has less kinetic energy than a turbulent layer, is thinner and gives less skin friction but separates more easily, whereas a turbulent boundary layer contains more kinetic energy making it separate less easily, but will give more skin friction. (Pages 6-2 to 4).

Answers (a) and (b) are incorrect because a turbulent boundary layer gives more skin friction than a laminar boundary layer. Answer (d) is incorrect: the turbulent boundary layer seperates further aft because it contains more kinetic energy.

Q 88
(c) Form drag is generated by the fore and aft pressure differential on a body in an airflow, whereas Induced Drag is caused by the generation of lift (Wing tip vortices). If the undercarriage is lowered the frontal area of the aircraft will increase which will increase form drag. The undercarriage is below the aircraft CG, hopefully, giving a backwards force below the aircraft CG, generating a nose down pitching moment. (Page 6-13 & 17). Lowering the undercarriage will not affect induced drag.

Q 89
(c) Winglets reduce the intensity of tip vortices, thus reducing induced drag. (Page 6-12).
Answer (a) is incorrect because wing fences reduce spanwise flow and help minimise tip stalling. Answer (b) is incorrect because anhedral reduces lateral static stability. Answer (d) is incorrect because a low aspect ratio will increase the proportion of the wing area affected by the tip vortices and increase induced drag.

PRINCIPLES OF FLIGHT　　　　　　　　　　　　　　　　SPECIMEN QUESTIONS

Q 90
(c) The "key" characteristic of a laminar boundary layer is that there is no flow normal to the surface.

Velocity is not constant because the relative velocity at the surface is zero and full stream velocity at its outer limit. Neither is the temperature constant in a laminar flow boundary layer due to skin friction variations from the surface to its outer limit. Just because a boundary layer contains no vortices does not make it laminar – a turbulent boundary layer may contain no vortices, but it has flow normal to the surface.

Q 91
(d) Drag = 1/2 rho x V squared x CD x S (Page 6-5).

Q 92
(d) Air will flow from areas of higher pressure towards areas of lower pressure. When a wing is generating lift, the air pressure on the top surface is lower than that outside the wing tip and generally, air on the bottom surface is slightly higher than that outside the wing tip. This causes air to flow inwards from the tip towards the root on the top surface and outwards from the root towards the tip on the bottom surface. The pressure difference at the wing tip will cause air to flow from the bottom surface to the top surface around the wing tip and this rotating airflow generates the tip vortices. (Page 5-16). Induced Drag is a result of the tip vortices inclining the effective airflow so as to decrease the effective angle of attack. To maintain the required lift force, the whole wing must be flown at a higher angle of attack. This increase in angle of attack is called the induced angle of attack   Because Lift acts at right angles to the effective airflow the lift vector is Answer (a) is incorrect because vortex generators are used to re-energise the boundary layer in order to delay boundary layer separation. Vortex generators have no influence on either Induced Drag or tip vortices. (Page 7-15). Answer (b) is incorrect because flow on the upper surface of a wing is towards the root. Answer (c) is incorrect because both tip vortices and induced drag increase at high angles of attack (low IAS). This is due to the reduced chordwise vector at low IAS (high angles of attack) and the same pressure differential making the tip vortices stronger.

Q 93
(c) Curve 'a' is that for Total Drag at various TAS's (Fig 6.15)
Curve 'b' is Lift coefficient at various angles of attack.
Curve 'c' is a whole aeroplane CL / CD
polar curve and curve (d) is nothing identifiable.

Q 94
(b) An accelerated stall is a stall that occurs at a load factor greater than '1' , in other words, at more than 1g.
A stall can occur at any speed, but an accelerated stall, by definition, will occur at a speed higher than a 1g stall. The speed at which a deep stall occurs is difficult to define, but if the accepted indications of a stall are considered, a deep stall could be said to occur at a speed higher than the 1g stall speed, but at a speed less than that of an accelerated stall. As the question stipulates that the aircraft is decelerating a shock stall should not occur.

Q 95
(b) By the time the separated airflow (wake) from a stalled swept wing contacts the tailplane the aircraft would already be pitching-up due to tip stall. If the tailplane is immersed in separated airflow the elevator will be ineffective. (Page 7-22 & 23).

PRINCIPLES OF FLIGHT   SPECIMEN QUESTIONS

Q 96
(b) The formula to calculate the effect of weight change on stall speed is: New stall speed equals the old stall speed multiplied by the square root of the new weight divided by the old weight. (Page 7-25).

Q 97
(c) Stalling is due to airflow separation and airflow separation depends upon the relationship between the boundary layer kinetic energy and the adverse pressure gradient. Generally speaking, the adverse pressure gradient is a function of angle of attack; the adverse pressure gradient will increase with an increase in angle of attack. Therefore, stalling is due to exceeding the critical angle of attack and has nothing to do with IAS, in and of itself.

Answers (a) and (b) are incorrect for the reasons given above. Answer (d) is incorrect because pitch angle is the angle between the aircraft's longitudinal axis and the horizon, which has nothing whatsoever to do with angle of attack - the angle between the relative qairflow and the chord line. The relative airflow direction is parallel to and in the opposite direction to the flightpath, so an aircraft whose nose was below the horizon could still easily be at an angle of attack greater than the critical angle of attack.

Q 98
(c) As angle of attack increases the increasing adverse pressure gradient in the presence of a constant boundary layer kinetic energy causes the boundary layer to start to separate first at the trailing edge. Increasing angle of attack/adverse pressure gradient moves the separation point forward.

Q 99
(c) At the point of stall lift decreases and drag continues to increase. (Fig. 7.29).

Q 100
(b) Please refer to Paragraphs 7.35 to 7.39. The ailerons should either be held neutral or returned to neutral.

Answer (a) is incorrect because the angle of attack must be decreased to unstall the wing. Answers (c) and (d) are incorrect for general spin recovery because rudder should be used agnist the direction of spin to equalise the angle of attack on both halves of the wing, thus preventing further autorotation.

Q 101
(c) For the vast majority of aircraft the CP is aft of the CG and as the aircraft rotates around the CG this will generate a nose down pitching moment. A tail down force is required to generate the equal and opposite nose up pitching moment required for equilibrium. The tail down force gives an 'effective' increase in weight which requires a slight increase in Lift to maintain the balance of up and down forces. This increase in lift increases the stall speed. The further forward the CG, the greater the increase in stall speed. (Page 7-30).

Q 102
(b) Vortex generators are rows of small thin blades which project vertically about 2.5 cm into the airstream. They each generate a small vortex which causes the free stream flow of high energy air to mix with and add kinetic energy to the boundary layer. This re-energises the boundary layer and delays separation.

Answer (a) is incorrect because vortex generators only have an effect immediately downstream of their location, so will not significantly influence spanwise flow. Answer (c) is incorrect because vortex generators re-energise the boundary layer.
Answer (d) is incorrect because vortex generators to not directly influence air pressure.

PRINCIPLES OF FLIGHT — SPECIMEN QUESTIONS

Q 103
(c) Refer to Paragraphs 7.20 to 7.24. Increase in stall speed in a level banked turn is proportional to the 1g stall speed multiplied by the square root of the load factor or 1/cos phi.

Q 104
(b) It is always necessary to use the 1g stall speed to determine the increased stall speed in a bank. In this case it is necessary to transpose the formula in order to determine the 1g stall speed. (Please refer to Page 7-29).

Q 105
(a) 'g' is the colloquial symbol for load factor. Load factor is the relationship between Lift and Weight. When an aircraft is banked in level flight, Lift must be greater than Weight and the relationship can be calculated by using the formula: L = 1/cos phi (where phi = bank angle). To calculated the stall speed in a 1.5 g turn, multiply the 1g stall speed by the square root of 1.5, in this case 1.22. 100 x 1.22 = 122 kt. [It can be said that 'g' is the same as 1/cos phi]. (Page 7-26 to 28).

Q 106
(d) Stall speed in a turn equals the 1g stall speed multiplied by the square root of the Load Factor and the Load Factor in a turn equals 1 divided by the cosine of the bank angle. (Page 7-26 to 29). The cosine of 45 degrees is 0.707. 1 divided by 0.707 equals 1.41 (this is a 41 percent increase in lift). The square root of 1.41 equals 1.19. 100 kt multiplied by 1.19 equals 119 kt (a 19 percent increase in stall speed).

Q 107
(c) (Ref: Para 7.23 & 24) The effect of bank angle on stall speed can be visualised by reference to the geometry of a vector diagram of Weight, Lift and bank angle – Ref: Fig 7.20.

The trigonometry formula (Ref: Para 7.24): Vs1g multiplied by the square root of 1 divided by the cosine of the bank angle (phi) is used to calculate the actual change in stall speed at various bank angles.

To answer this question it is necessary to transpose the trig' formula mentioned above to:
cos phi = 1/1 4 squared (1 4 being the margin above stall speed at which the aircraft is

Q 108
(a) The recommended, but general spin recovery technique is full opposite rudder (against spin direction), reduce throttle(s) to idle, neutralise the ailerons and gently but progressively apply forward pitch control.
All four actions can be accomplished simultaneously. (Para 7.39).

Q 109
(c) Refer to Paragraphs 7.20 to 7.24. Increase in stall speed in a level banked turn is proportional to the 1g stall speed multiplied by the square root of the load factor or 1/cos phi.

Q 110
(a) Stall speed varies with wing contamination, configuration (flaps & gear), thrust and prop slipstream, weight, load factor, mach number and CG position. Load factor varies with manoeuvring and turbulence. When recovering from a steep dive load factor will increase and stall speed will increase. (Page 7-24 et seq).

Answer (b) is incorrect because lower level altitude changes will not effect stall speed; it is only at very high altitude that stall speed increases with altitude (approx. 29000ft). Answer (c) is incorrect because a decrease in weight will decrease stall speed. (Answer (d) is incorrect because deploying flaps decreases stall speed.

PRINCIPLES OF FLIGHT   SPECIMEN QUESTIONS

Q111
(d) Stall angle is affected by flaps and wing contamination. CG movement and changes in Weight will only affect stall speed. (Page 7-24 et seq).

Q112
(b) The increased tendency of a swept wing to stall from the tips (over and above the tendency of a tapered wing to stall from the tips) is due to the root to tip spanwise flow on the top surface. Because the tips stall before the root, the CP moves forward, giving the tendency to 'pitch-up'.

Answer (a) is incorrect because boundary layer fences are fitted to reduce spanwise flow and therefore reduce the tendency of a swept wing to tip stall; their function does not directly affect CP movement. Answer (c) is incorrect because the spanwise flow on the top surface of a swept wing is from root to tip, which increases the tendency for airflow separation at the tip - the cause of CP forward movement. Answer (d) is incorrect because wing incidence is a fixed value - the angle between the chord line and the longitudinal axis.

Q113
(a) Tropical rain increases Weight and distorts the aerodynamic shape, thus decreasing lift and increasing drag. The weight increase and the lift decrease will increase the stall speed.

Q114
(b) Stall speed varies: at very high altitude due to Mach number, with flap and slat position, with CG position, with wing contamination, with load factor, with engine thrust and propeller slipstream and with weight.

Answer (a) is incorrect because though stall speed does increase at high altitude, more flaps or slats will decrease stall speed. Answer (c) is incorrect because stall speed increases with forward CG and unless high altitude is mentioned, moderate altitudes do not affect stall speed. Answer (d) is incorrect because very high altitude does affect stall speed because of increasing Mach number.

Q115
(d) Vortex generators are rows of small thin blades which project vertically about 2.5 cm into the airstream. They each generate a small vortex which causes the free stream flow of high energy air to mix with and add kinetic energy to the boundary layer. This re-energises the boundary layer and delays separation.

Q116
(c) 'g' is the colloquial symbol for load factor. Load factor is the relationship between Lift and Weight. When an aircraft is banked in level flight, Lift must be greater than Weight and the relationship can be calculated by using the formula: $L = 1/\cos \phi$ (where phi = bank angle). To calculated the stall speed in a 2g turn, multiply the 1g stall speed by the square root of 2, in this case 1.41. $100 \times 1.41 = 141$ kt. [It can be said that 'g' is the same as $1/\cos \phi$]. (Page 7-26 to 28).

Q117
(b) Tropical rain increases Weight and distorts the aerodynamic shape, thus decreasing lift (CLMAX) and increasing drag.

Q118
(c) Pitch-up of an aircraft fitted with a swept wing is caused by tip stall. The increased tendency of a swept wing to tip stall is due to an induced spanwise flow of the boundary layer from root to tip on the top surface. (Page 7-16 & 17).

PRINCIPLES OF FLIGHT　　　　　　　　　　SPECIMEN QUESTIONS

Q 119
(b) 'Deep stall' or 'Super stall' is the possible final result of 'pitch-up'. 'Pitch-up' is caused by forward movement of the CP on a swept back wing. (Page 7-22 & 23).

Q 120
(b) Reference Para 7.16. A stick pusher is an automatic device which activates at a certain angle of attack and physically pushes the stick forward to prevent the angle of attack increasing beyond a certain maximum value. This device is fitted to aircraft that exhibit excessive pitch-up at the stall to prevent super stall.

Q 121
(d) A swept wing has a smaller lift curve gradient and a reduced CLmax. The reduced CLmax gives an increased stall speed. Reducing sweep angle will therefore reduce stall speed. (Page 13-30).

Answer (a) is incorrect because the function of anhedral is to reduce static lateral stability and has no influence on stalling. Answer (b) is incorrect because a 'T' tail is generally incorporated in an aircraft design to remove the tailplane from the influence of downwash from the wing and its location on the top of the fin has no influence on stall speed. Answer (c) is incorrect because increasing the sweep angle decreases CLmax which increases stall speed.

Q 122
(b) Reference Paragraph 7.25. The purpose of high lift devices is to reduce the take-off and landing run. This is generally achieved by increasing the wing camber, resulting in an increased CLmax.
Incraesing CLmax will decrease the stall speed and hence the minimum operational speed.

Q 123
(a) The CG on the forward limit gives a large nose down pitching moment. This must be balanced by a tail down force. The tail down force is an effective increase in weight which requires more lift. The increase in lift required increases the stall speed, but the angle at which the wing stalls remains constant at approximately 16 degrees. (Page 7-30).

Q 124
(c) At speeds higher than M0.4 the proximity of the aircraft to its leading pressure wave increases upwash. This decreases CLmax which gives a higher stall speed. (Paragraph 7.29).

Answer (a) is incorrect because the separation of airflow due to shockwave formation is known as "Shock Stall". Answer (b) is incorrect because a stall that occurs due to load factors greater than 1 is known as an "Accelerated Stall". Answer (d) is incorrect because dynamic pressure itself has no influence on airflow separation.

Q 125
(c) Load factor ('n' or 'g') is the ratio of Lift to Weight or Lift / Weight.

Q 126
(c) To calculate the increase in Lift in a 45 degree bank: L = 1 / cos 45 or 1.41. The increase in stall speed is the square root of 1 / cos 45 or 1.19. This is a 19 percent increase in stall speed. (Page 7-28).

PRINCIPLES OF FLIGHT   SPECIMEN QUESTIONS

Q 127
(a) Stalling is caused by airflow separation, which generally is due to exceeding the critical angle of attack. The standard procedure to prevent a full stall or to recover from a stall is to decrease the angle of attack. It is recommended that the nose be lowered to or slightly below the horizon to reduce the angle of attack and at the same time apply maximum power to minimise height lost during stall recovery. For small aircraft it is recommended that wings level be maintained by use of the rudder. If ailerons are used, the downgoing aileron may fully stall the lower wing and make it drop faster. (Para. 7.4).

Answer (b) is incorrect because this is the recommended stall recovery for a swept wing aircraft - whose stall warning margin to CLmax is sufficient for roll control still to be effective. Answer (c) is incorrect because all stall recovery techniques require positive pilot action to regain full control of the aircraft. Answer (d) is incorrect because rudder is recommended to lift a dropping wing on small aircraft; not correcting for a dropped wing could leave the aircraft in a 90 degree bank!!

Q 128
(b) Paragraph 7.23. The extra lift required when the aircraft is banked is dependant upon the bank angle. The lift required to maintain a constant vertical force to oppose the weight is proportional to the length of the hypotenuse of a right angled triangle. In this case, Lift = 1 / cos 45 = 1.41 which is a 41% increase in Lift.

Q 129
(d) A swept back wing stalls from the tip and the CP moves forward, giving the tendency to pitch-up.
Answer (a) is incorrect because a swept wing stalls from the tip and the CP moves forward. Answer (b) is incorrect because a rectangular wing will stall from the root, but the CP moves rearwards. Answer (c) is incorrect because a rectangular wing will stall from the root and the CP moves rearwards.

Q 130
(a) When approaching the critical angle of attack with a rectangular wing the upper suction peak flattens and begins to collapse due to airflow separation. The lower surface pressure distribution is not immediatly affected, resulting in the CP moving aft.

Because the swept wing stalls from the tip and the tip is located behind the aircraft CG, at the stall the CP of a swept back wing moves forwards. (Fig 7.7 & 7.12).

Q 131
(b) Ice on a wing leading edge will produce large changes in the local contour (of the aerofoil section), leading to severe local advese pressure gradients. This will cause the wing to stall at a much smaller angle of attack than would occur with an aerodynamically clean wing. Angle of attack during the last part of rotation may well exceed the lower, icing induced critical angle of attack, thus preventing the aircraft from becoming airborne. Speed will be greater than V1, so it may not be possible to stop within the remaining take-off distance available.

Answer (a) is incorrect because during the take-off run only the extra drag from the ice would be a factor and while increasing the take-off run this would not be the most critical phase. Answer (c) is incorrect because during a steady climb with all engines operating the angle of attack should be that which gives L/Dmax (4 degrees), this should be far enough below the lower icing induced critical angle of attack that it will not to be a factor.

Answer (d) is incorrect because at the majority of phases of flight the angle of attack will be much below the icing induced critical angle of attack.

PRINCIPLES OF FLIGHT   SPECIMEN QUESTIONS

Q 132
(d) Ref. 4.1: Angle of Attack is the angle between the Relative Airflow and the chord line. Ref. 7.2: A stall is caused by airflow separation and separation can occur when either the boundary layer has insufficient kinetic energy or the adverse pressure gradient is too great. Generally speaking: adverse pressure gradient is increased by increasing the angle of attack. Answer (d) is correct because shock stall is caused by the presence of the shock wave on the wing top surface. It is the shock wave that causes a marked increase in adverse pressure gradient; the angle of attack remains small.

Answer (a) is incorrect because a deep stall is the "automatic" progression of tip stall on a swept wing leading to pitch-up, and would occur at a relatively large angle of attack. Answer (b) is incorrect because an accelerated stall is one that occurs at greater than 1g, but at the "normal" high angle of attack of 16 degrees. Answer (c) is incorrect because the low speed stall also occurs at 16 degrees angle of attack.

Q 133
(c) A swept back wing tends to stall first near the tips which moves the CP forward causing a phenomena known as 'pitch-up'. This tends to further increase the angle of attack, reducing lift and the aircraft can start to sink rapidly, further increasing the angle of attack. Separated airflow from the fully stalled swept wing can then immerse a 'T' tail and reduce elevator effectiveness and prevent recovery. It is the tip stalling of the swept back wing which causes super stall. (Page 7-16 to 23).

Answer (a) is incorrect because the contribution of the 'T' tail is to make super stall recovery more difficult, it doesn't cause deep stall. Answer (b) is incorrect because a swept forward wing would experience a rearward movement of the CP following tip stall, which would give an aircraft nose down pitching moment. Answer (d) is incorrect. The pylons of Pod mounted engines below the wing act as vortilons and reduce span-wise flow which can lead to tip stall.

Q 134
(b) The primary cause of 'deep stall' is 'pitch-up' whicht is the result of tip stalling of a swept wing. A contributory factor is a 'T' tail, which may place the tailplane and elevator in the path of the separated airflow from the wing once 'pitch-up' has ocurred - this reduces the effectiveness of the elevator and may prevent prompt recovery from the 'deep stall'. It must be emphasised that 'pitch-up' is the primary cause of deep stall and a 'T' tail is a contributory factor. (Page 7-22 & 23).

Answer (a) is incorrect because wing mounted engines do not contribute to deep stall.
Answer (c) is incorrect because neither an unswept wing nor wing mounted engines contribute to deep stall.
Answer (d) is incorrect because an unswept wing does not 'pitch-up' at the stall and a 'T' tail is only a contributory factor if the aircraft suffers 'pitch-up'. (Page 7-22 & 23).

Q 135
(c) Vso means "The stall speed or the minimum steady flight speed in the landing configuration".

Answer (a) is incorrect because Vs1g means "The stall speed at which the aeroplane can develop a lift force (normal to the flight path) equal to its weight".
Answer (b) is incorrect because Vs1 means "The stall speed or the minimum steady flight speed obtained in a specified configuration". Answer (d) is incorrect because there is no such designation.

PRINCIPLES OF FLIGHT SPECIMEN QUESTIONS

Q 136

(d) Reference Paragraph 7.30. There will be a significant decrease in CLmax due to ice formation on the wing. This is due to a radical change in aerofoil section contour. This effect could cause the aircraft to stall in the cruise and is of greater consequence than any of the other possible answers.

Answer (a) is not the preferred answer; although drag will be increased by ice formation and will be a contibutory factor.
Answer (b) is not the preferred answer, although increased weight will increase the stall speed.
Answer (c) is a significant effect, but is still less significant than the reduction in CLmax.

Q 137
(d) Reference Paragraph 7.9. JAR 25 specifies that the stall warning must begin at 5 kt or 5% before the stall, whichever is the greater. This equates to 1.05 Vs.
Answers (a), (b) and (c) are incorrect because they all exceed 1.05 Vs.

Q 138
(c) Any stall warning device must be sensitive to changes in angle of attack. As angle of attack increases the stagnation point will move downwards and backwards from the leading edge to a position slightly below. A small sensitive electric switch attached to a vane can be positioned at the leading edge so that downwards and backwards movement of the stagnation point moves the vane up and closing a circuit, activates the stall warning device. (Page 7-8).

Answer (a) is incorrect. Although the CP does move with changes in angle of attack, its movement cannot be detected. Answer (b) is incorrect because the CG does not move with changing angle of attack. Answer (d) is incorrect because stalling is due to increasing angle of attack causing airflow separation. The critical angle of attack can be exceeded at any dynamic pressure.

Q 139
(d) Stalling is the result of airflow separation. Airflow separation is due to the combined effect of adverse pressure gradient and boundary layer kinetic energy. Adverse pressure gradient increases with increasing angle of attack. A stall warning device must therefore be sensitive to angle of attack. A stick shaker is signalled by a device sensitive to changes in angle of attack - a flapper switch (leading edge stall warning vane), an angle of attack vane or an angle of attack probe. An angle of attack indicator, if fitted, will indicate to the flight crew the angle of attack at any moment.

Answer (a) & (b) are incorrect because a stall strip is a device used to encourage a stall to occur by locally decreasing the leading edge radius. Answer (c) is incorrect because Indicated Air Speed (IAS) is not a reliable indicator of an impending stall because the critical angle of attack can be exceeded at any IAS.

Q 140
(c) As an aircraft enters a deep stall the 'pitch-up' tendency increases the angle of attack to a very high value and the aircraft also starts to sink, which further increases the angle of attack. (Page 7-22 & 23).

Answer (a) is incorrect because low speed (1g) stall ocurrs at aproximately 16 degrees. Answer (d) is incorrect because an accelerated stall also ocurrs at about 16 degrees. Answer (b) is incorrect because a high speed (shock) stall ocurrs at a small angle of attack, being due to shock induced airflow separation above Mcrit.

PRINCIPLES OF FLIGHT   SPECIMEN QUESTIONS

Q 141
(d) A swept wing stalls from the tip which is behind the aircraft CG. As the portion of the swept wing in front of the CG is still producing lift an aircraft nose up pitching moment is generated - this phenomena is known as 'pitch-up'. (Page 7-16).

Answer (a) is incorrect because, generally speaking, deploying flaps will give a modern high speed jet transport aircraft a nose down pitching moment. Answer (b) is incorrect because wing fences are fitted to minimise spanwise airflow and will not themselves cause a reaction from the aircraft. Answer (c) is incorrect because one of the major disadvantages of sweep back is the pitch-up phenomena.

Q 142
(d) Refer to Paragraph 5.3.1 and Page 7-8. Stalling is caused by airflow separation. The amount of airflow separation is due to the relationship between the adverse pressure gradient and boundary layer kinetic energy. The adverse pressure gradient will increase if angle of attack is increased. A 1g stall occurs at the critical angle of attack (CLmax). A stall warning must begin with sufficient margin to prevent inadvertent stalling, so a stall warning device must also be sensitive to angle of attack. Therefore, a 1g stall will occur at the critical angle of attack and the stall warning will activate at an angle of attack which is slightly less. In 1g flight each angle of attack requires a particular IAS (dynamic pressure). An increase in weight will not alter the respective angles of attack, but will increase both the IAS at which the stall warning activates and the IAS at which the 1g stall occurs but the margin between them will remain essentially the same

Q 143
(d) Reference Paragraph 8.22 et seq. Slats increase boundary layer kinetic energy which delays separation to a higher angle of attack (adverse pressure gradient). In and of themselves, deploying slats do nothing, but they enable a higher angle of attack to be used, thus decreasing the minimum operational speed. Slats also increase the critical angle of attack (Ref: Fig 8.15).

Answer (a) is incorrect because slats increase the critical angle of attack. Answer (b) is incorrect because this is a description of a Krueger flap. Answer (c) is incorrect on all counts.

Q 144
(d) Extended slats do not change CL or CD significantly, they do however increase CLmax and therefore give greater margin to the stall speed.

Answering this question correctly requires a full understanding of the properties of slats. Consider answer (a): Vmca is the minimum IAS at which directional control can be maintained following failure of the critical engine. Paragraph 12.11.7 discusses the indirect effect of trailing edge flap position on Vmca, but the "intent" of the question is very precise, in that all types of aircraft (both turbo jet and propeller) are implied by the wording "...... why are the slats always retracted ..... ". Also, propeller driven aircraft are unlikely to be fitted with slats - there is no need with their relatively unsophisticated wing design. Answer (b) can be shown to be incorrect by referring to Paragraph 8.26. Answer (c) is incorrect because with trailing edge flaps extended there is a requirement for a greater aircraft nose down pitch angle to maintain a given CL, this gives a better view over the nose from the flight deck, with slats extended however, this is not the case.

PRINCIPLES OF FLIGHT   SPECIMEN QUESTIONS

Q 145
(d) Reference Figs 8.18 and 19. Deploying trailing edge flaps increases both CL and CD. At small flap angles there is a greater percentage increase in CL than CD. However, further flap deployment gives a smaller percentage increase in CL and a larger percentage incraese in CD. Any amount of flap deployment will decraese the maximum L / D ratio; the graeter the flap angle used, the greater will be the decrease in L / D max.

Q 146
(c) Refer to Fig 8.22. It can be seen that moving from position 'A' to position 'C' fulfils the information provided in the question. CL would increase, Lift would be greater than Weight and the aircraft would gain altitude.

Q 147
(d) Reference Fig 8.22. For an aircraft to maintain level flight when flaps are deployed the angle of attack must be decreased to maintain a constant CL. CDi is proportional to CL squared and inversely proportional to Aspect Ratio. Therefore, induced drag will remain the same.

Q 148
(a) Reference Paragraph 8.4 et seq. Trailing edge high lift devices function by increasing the camber of the wing, thus increasing CLmax and CL for a given angle of attack.

Answer (b) is incorrect because angle of attack is the angle between the chord line and the relative airflow. Lift curves for flaps are drawn with reference to the original chord line. A plain flap has a decreased stall angle, so a smaller maximum angle of attack is possible. Answers (c) is incorrect because though the statement is correct changing the position of the CP does not alter the CL. Answer (d) is incorrect because a plain flap has no significant influence on either wing chord or span.

Q 149
(c) Reference Paragraph 8.14 et seq. Centre of Pressure movement will generate a nose down pitching moment, whereas the change in downwash generates a nose up pitching moment. The resultant aircraft pitching moment will depend upon which of these two moments is dominant. From the information given in the question it is not possible to say what aircraft pitching moment will result, so the only answer that can be given is: "It depends".

Q 150
(b) For level flight Lift must remain the same as the weight, so as flaps are extended the angle of attack must be decreased. Flaps, generally speaking, increase the camber which increases CLmax.

Answers (a), (b) and (c) are incorrect because CL and Lift remains constant and drag increases.

Q 151
(a) Refer to Fig 8.22. It can be seen that moving from position 'A' to position 'C' fulfils the information provided in the question. CL would increase.

Q 152
(c) Reference Fig. 8.20. Moving from Point 'B' to Point 'C' fulfils the requirements of the question and illustrates the need to increase the angle of attack as flaps are retracted in order to maintain CL constant.

Q 153
(b) Reference Paragraph 8.20.1. To preserve the tendency for root stall first on a swept wing, the least efficient leading edge high lift device is fitted inboard. The following list shows leading edge devices in order of increasing efficiency: Krueger, Variable Camber, Slat.

PRINCIPLES OF FLIGHT — SPECIMEN QUESTIONS

Q 154
(a) Reference Paragraph 8.20.1. To preserve the tendency for root stall first on a swept wing, the least efficient leading edge high lift device is fitted inboard. The following list shows leading edge devices in order of increasing efficiency: Krueger, Variable Camber, Slat.

Answer (d) is incorrect because a Krueger Flap is a leading edge device.

Q 155
(c) Reference Paragraph 8.22 et seq and Fig 8.16. Slats increase boundary layer kinetic energy and enable a higher angle of attack to be used. It can be seen that the "suction" peak does not move forward onto the slat and has no significant effect on the pitching moment.

Q 156
(d) Reference Fig. 8.2

Q 157
(b) Reference Fig 8.5 and Paragraph 8.11.
Angle of attack is the angle between the Relative Airflow and the ORIGINAL chord line - with no flap deployed. Trailing edge flaps decrease the critical angle of attack.

Q 158
(d) Reference Fig 8.13 and Paragraph 8.21. Angle of attack is the angle between the Relative Airflow and the ORIGINAL chord line - with no flap deployed. Leading edge devices increase the critical angle of attack.

Q 159
(a) Reference Paragraph 8.13 ANY deployment of flap decreases the L/D ratio. Reference Paragraph 12.8 et seq. Glide angle is a function ONLY of the L/D ratio. Therefore, deploying flaps will decrease L/D ratio which will increase glide angle, decrease glide distance and increase sink rate.

Q 160
(d) Reference Paragraph 8.22 et seq and in particular Fig 8.15. At a given angle of attack, deploying slats does nothing, but enables a higher angle of attack (adverse pressure gradient) to be used without airflow separation, thus decreasing the minimum operational IAS.

Answer (a) is incorrect because slats increase boundary layer kinetic energy. Answer (b) is not the preferred answer, but is a true statement. Because slats increase boundary layer kinetic energy the boundary layer will have a slightly increased thickness, but this is not the purpose of slats.

Answer (c) is not the correct answer because slats do not significantly increase wing camber.

Q 161
(d) Reference Figs 8.11 and 8.14.

Answers (a) and (b) are incorrect because both slats and Krueger flaps increase the critical angle of attack (Figs 8.13 and 8.15). Answer (c) is incorrect because Krueger flaps do not form a slot, but slats do form a slot (Figs 8.11 and 8.14).

Q 162
(b) Reference Fig 8.22. Point 'A' to Point 'B' illustrates the wording of the question and it can be seen that CL must remain constant if IAS is constant and level flight is to be maintained as flaps are deployed, in order that the Lift remains the same as the Weight. Answers (a), (c) and (d) are incorrect because any change in CL at a constant IAS will change the Lift generated and will not allow the aircraft to maintain level flight.

PRINCIPLES OF FLIGHT SPECIMEN QUESTIONS

Q 163
(b) Reference Paragraph 8.14 et seq.

Q 164
(b) Ref. Paragraph 8.13: Lowering ANY amount of flap decreases L/Dmax and referring to Paragraph 12.8.1 will remind you that glide angle is a function ONLY of L/D ratio. Therefore, when trailing edge flaps are deployed glide distance is degraded, making answer (b) correct.

With reference to Figure 8.5 it can be seen that with deployment of trailing edge flaps a lower angle of attack is required for maximum lift (CLmax), making answer (a) incorrect. Answer (c) is incorrect because flap deployment increases C/Lmax, the whole object of deploying flaps – to reduce the take-off and landing distance. Answer (d) is incorrect because increasing C / Lmax decreases stall speed.

Q 165
(a) Refer to Fig. 8.15. It can be seen that slats increase the stall angle. They do this by increasing the boundary layer kinetic energy - enabling a higher adverse pressure gradient/angle of attack before reaching CLmax.

Answer (b) is incorrect because flaps decrease the stall angle, Fig. 8.5. Answer (c) is incorrect because spoilers would tend to decrease the stall angle slightly and answer (d) is incorrect because ailerons would not significantly affect stall angle.

Q 166
(c) Reference paragraph 10.21: When landing, the most critical requirement for sufficient control power in pitch will exist when the CG is at the most forward position, flaps are fully extended, power is set to idle and the aircraft is being flared to land in ground effect.

Q 167
(b) Paragraph 10.31 states: "When an aircraft is subject to a positive sideslip angle, lateral stability will be evident if a negative rolling moment coefficient results". It can be seen from Figure 10.57 that a positive sideslip angle is aeroplane nose left – right sideslip. Answer (b) is correct because the tendency of an aeroplane to roll to the left in a right sideslip is static lateral stability.

Answer (a) the tendency of an aeroplane to – "roll to the right in the case of a positive sideslip angle (aeroplane nose to the right)" is incorrect on two counts; a roll to the right in the case of a positive sideslip angle is an example of negative static lateral stability, plus the fact that a positive sideslip angle is nose left. Answers (c) and (d) are both incorrect because static lateral stability is a function of sideslipping (uncoordinated flight) and turns are coordinated, such that no sideslipping takes place.

Q 168
(a) For positive static longitudinal stability any change in angle of attack must generate an opposing pitching moment so that the aircraft tends to return towards its trim angle of attack. Answer (a) is the right answer because a nose down moment when encountering an up gust is an example of positive static longitudinal stability.

Answer (b) and (c) are incorrect because no change in angle of attack takes place – which is a stated requirement for static stability. Answer (d) is incorrect because a nose up pitching moment when encountering an up gust is an example of negative static longitudinal stability.

PRINCIPLES OF FLIGHT   SPECIMEN QUESTIONS

Q 169
(d) In and of itself, stick force stability is not affected by trim, making (d) the correct answer.

It can be seen from Figure 10.31 that the slope of the curve is much smaller at low speed than at high speed, indicating that answer (a) is incorrect. An increase in speed MUST generate a pull force, making answer (b) incorrect.

Answer (c) is incorrect because aeroplane nose up trim decreases stick force stability.

Q 170
Reference Page 10-64.

Q 171
(d) Reference Para. 10.11 and 10.14: Moving the CG aft reduces static longitudinal stability and increases manoeuvrability. Increased manoeuvrability gives a smaller control deflection requirement for a given pitch change.

Q 172
(b) This question concerns stick force per 'g' – reference Paragraph 10.16. Tthere must be both an acceptable upper and lower limit to stick force. The illustrations of Figure 10.36 show the factors which affect the gradient of stick force per 'g' and the text highlights the requirements for any transport aircraft.

Answer (a) is incorrect – it can be seen from Figure 10.36 that stick force gradient decreases with rearward CG position. Answer (c) is incorrect because the stick force gradient must always be positive. (The term "fe-n line" is assumed to mean the stick force gradient line). Answer (d) is incorrect because it can be seen from Paragraph 10.17 that there are various methods of modifying stick forces which are not electronic in nature.

Q 173
(b) In this context, pitch angle is defined as: "the angle between the longitudinal axis and the horizontal plane". Pitch angle can also be referred to as "Body Angle" or as "The Pitch Attitude".

Q 174
(c) Paragraph 12.5 shows the forces and climb angle (gamma) in a steady climb. Climb gradient is the ratio of vertical height gained to horizontal distance travelled, expressed as a percentage. Trigonometrically, the tangent of the climb angle (gamma) will give climb gradient (tan = opp/adj), where 'opp' is the vertical height gained and 'adj' is the horizontal distance covered. Unfortunately these values are not provided in the question, or indeed in real life - so other values must be substituted and certain assumptions made in order to "calculate" the answer. Climb angle is the same as the angle between the Weight vector and W cos gamma. The 'adjacent' is W cos gamma or Lift and the 'opposite' is the backward component of Weight or W sin gamma. From the question Weight (50,000kg x 10 = 500,000N), Thrust (60,000N x 2 = 120,000N) and Drag (1/12 of Lift) are known or can be estimated. The value of Lift is not given but we do know the Weight, so it has to be assumed that Lift and Weight are equal (at small climb angles [<20 degrees], although we know Lift is in fact less than Weight, for practical purposes the difference is insignificant). Therefore, the value of Lift is assumed to be 500,000N and the Drag to be 500,000N / 12 = 41667N. The formula for climb gradient is: Percentage Gradient = (T - D / W) x 100. i.e. Thrust minus Drag is the backward component of Weight or 'opp' and Weight is the 'hyp'. For small angles [<20 degrees] of climb or descent the length of the hypotenuse and adjacent are, for all practical purposes, the same; so the sine formula can be used and will give an answer which is accurate enough. We now have Thrust (120,000N) minus Drag (41667N) divided by Weight (500,000N) = 0.157 x 100 = 15.7% Climb Gradient.

PRINCIPLES OF FLIGHT   SPECIMEN QUESTIONS

Q 175
(b) Paragraph 12.6 shows Lift is less than Weight in a steady descent. Load factor is Lift Divided by Weight, but when the aircraft is in equilibrium in a steady descent the vertical force opposing the Weight is the Total Reaction. However, JAR 25.321 states: "Flight load factors represent the ratio of the aerodynamic force component (acting normal to the assumed longitudinal axis of the aeroplane) to the weight of the aeroplane". This clarifies the issue completely; such that in a steady descent Lift is less than Weight and the load factor is less than one. Load factor is useful when considering the loads applied to the aeroplane in flight. While the load factor will not be altered significantly in a steady descent, the concept holds true.

Q 176
(d) Refer to Paragraph 12.10. When considering turning, remind yourself first of the appropriate formulae – these help consolidate the variables.

1. L = 1 / cos phi reminds us that the only variable for Lift and hence load factor in a turn is bank angle.

2. The next two formulae must be considered together:
(a) Radius = V squared / g tan phi
(b) Rate = V / Radius
Formula 1 shows that answers (b) and (c) are incorrect because the bank angle for both aircraft is the same.
Aircraft 'A' is slower than aircraft 'B', so Formula 2a shows that answer (a) is incorrect because the turn radius of 'A' will in fact be smaller than 'B'.

Q 177
(a) Reference Para 12.11.10: VMCL is the minimum IAS at which directional control can be maintained with the aircraft in the landing configuration, BUT with the added ability of being able to roll the aircraft from an initial condition of steady flight, through an angle of 20 degrees in the direction necessary to initiate a turn away from the inoperative engine(s), in not more than 5 seconds. VMCL is the "odd one out" among the VMC speeds for this reason. It can clearly be seen that neither statement is correct, making (a) the correct answer.

Q 178
(d) Reference Para 13.3 to 13.5.

Q 179
(a) Reference to Figure 13.2 will show that the speed region between Mcit and approximately M1.3 is called "Transonic".

Q 180
(c) Reference Para. 13.5 and 13.16: it can be seen that the speed range between high and low speed buffet decreases with increasing altitude.

Q 181
(c) Reference Para 13.8.

Q 182
(a) Reference Para 14.6.

PRINCIPLES OF FLIGHT	SPECIMEN QUESTIONS

Q 183
(a)	Reference Paragraph 14.7 and 10.15. For SMALL aircraft VA is the speed at the intersection of CLmax and the positive limit load factor and is dependant upon mass (which will affect the speed at which CLmax is achieved).

As this is the examination is for ATPL, LARGE aeroplanes (JAR 25) must be considered. VA is defined as:- The highest speed at which sudden, full elevator deflection (nose up) can be made without exceeding the design limit load factor - making VA slower than the speed intersection of CLmax and the positive limit load factor. This is due to the effect of the tailplane moving downward when the aircraft is being pitched nose up increasing the effective angle of attack of the tailplane and increasing the load imposed on the whole

Q 184
(b)	Reference Fig 14.9: Changes in lift force due to a gust are considered to act through the Aerodynamic Centre.

Q 185
(b)	Ref. Paragraph 16.2. The key to answering this question successfully is an understanding of what is meant by "......decreasing the propeller pitch." Decreasing the propeller pitch is reducing the blade angle. This would increase the aircraft's Parasite area and Total Drag, which would decrease L/Dmax. Because of decreased L/Dmax the aircraft would have an increased rate of descent.

Q 186
(d)	IAS is a measure of dynamic pressure, whereas TAS is the speed of the aircraft through the air. Changes in TAS are used to compensate for changes in air density to maintain a constant dynamic pressure. The lower the density, the higher the TAS must be to maintain a constant IAS. (Pages 2-4 to 2-9).

Answer (a) is incorrect because decreasing temperature increases air density, which decreases the difference between IAS and TAS. Answer (b) is incorrect because increasing air density decreases the difference between IAS and TAS. Answer (c) is incorrect because density changes with altitude.

Q 187
(a) Reference Fig 16.12.

PRINCIPLES OF FLIGHT

SPECIMEN QUESTIONS

SPECIMEN EXAMINATION PAPER

1. What is the SI unit which results from multiplying kg and m/s squared?

    a. Newton
    b. Psi
    c. Joule
    d. Watt

2. TAS is:

    a. higher than speed of the undisturbed airstream around the aircraft
    b. lower than speed of the undisturbed airstream around the aircraft
    c. lower than IAS at ISA altitudes below sea level
    d. equal to IAS, multiplied by air density at sea level

3. Which of the following statements about a venturi in a subsonic air flow is correct?

    (i) The dynamic pressure in the undisturbed flow and in the throat are equal.
    (ii) The total pressure in the undisturbed flow and in the throat are equal.

    a. (i) is correct and (ii) is incorrect.
    b. (i) is incorrect and (ii) is correct.
    c. (i) and (ii) are correct.
    d. (i) and (ii) are incorrect.

4. The angle between the aeroplane longitudinal axis and the chord line is:

    a. angle of incidence.
    b. glide path angle.
    c. angle of attack.
    d. climb path angle.

5. What is the MAC of a wing?

    a. Area of wing divided by the span
    b. The same as the mean chord of a rectangular wing of the same span
    c. The mean chord of the whole aeroplane
    d. The 25% chord of a swept wing

PRINCIPLES OF FLIGHT   SPECIMEN QUESTIONS

6   With flaps deployed, at a constant IAS in straight and level flight, the magnitude of tip vortices:

   a. increases or decreases depending upon the initial angle of attack
   b. increases
   c. decreases
   d. remains the same

7   Which of the following is a characteristic of laminar flow boundary layer?

   a. Constant velocity
   b. Constant temperature
   c. No flow normal to the surface
   d. No vortices

8   Which of the following is the correct formula for drag?

   a. ½ rho V squared CL S
   b. ½ rho V (CL)squared S
   c. ½ rho V squared AR CD S
   d. ½ rho V squared CD S

9   VS is 100 kt at n = 1, what will the stall speed be at n = 2?

   a. 200 kt
   b. 119 kt
   c. 141 kt
   d. 100 kt

10 When flying straight and level in 1g flight, slightly below max' all up weight, a basic stall warning system (flapper switch) activates at 75 kt IAS and the aircraft stalls at 68 kt IAS. Under the same conditions at maximum all up weight the margin between stall warning and stall will:

   a. increase because increasing weight increases the 1g stall speed.

   b. decrease because the 1g stall speed is an IAS.

   c. decrease because increasing weight increases the 1g stall speed.

   d. remain the same because increased weight increases the IAS that corresponds to a particular angle of attack.

11 After takeoff why are the slats (if installed) always retracted later than the trailing edge flaps?

   a. Because VMCA with slats extended is more favourable compared to the flaps extended position.

   b. Because flaps extended gives a large decrease in stall speed with relatively less drag.

   c. Because slats extended provides a better view from the cockpit than flaps extended.

   d. Because slats extended gives a large decrease in stall speed with relatively less drag.

12 What must happen to the CL when flaps are deployed while maintaining a constant IAS in straight and level flight?

   a. increase then decrease

   b. remain constant

   c. decrease

   d. increase

13 If an aircraft is longitudinally statically unstable, at the same time it will be:

   a. dynamically unstable

   b. dynamically neutral

   c. dynamically stable

   d. dynamically positively stable

14 Positive static lateral stability is the tendency of an aeroplane to:

   a. roll to the right in the case of a positive sideslip angle (aeroplane nose to the
   b. roll to the left in the case of a positive sideslip angle (aeroplane nose to the left).
   c. roll to the left in a right turn.
   d. roll to the right in a right turn.

15 To provide the required manoeuvre stability an aircraft in straight and level flight (n = 1) requires a stick force of 150 lb/g. If n = 2.5 what is the increase in stick force required?

   a. 225 lb
   b. 375 lb
   c. 150 lb
   d. No increase

16 What effect does a positive swept wing have on static directional stability?

   a. Destabilising dihedral effect
   b. Stabilising
   c. Negative dihedral effect
   d. No effect

17 What type of wing arrangement decreases static lateral stability?

   a. Anhedral
   b. Dihedral
   c. High wing
   d. Large wing span

18 When considering the relationship between lateral static stability and directional stability:

   a. dominant lateral static stability gives an increased tendency for dutch roll
   b. dominant lateral static stability gives an increased tendency for spiral instability
   c. dominant directional static stability gives an increased tendency for dutch roll
   d. no effect because they are mutually independent

19 Which statement is correct?

   a. The stick force per 'g' increases when the CG is moved aft.

   b. The stick force per 'g' must have both upper and lower limits in order to assure acceptable control characteristics.

   c. If the slope of the fe-n line becomes negative, generally speaking this is not a problem for control of an aeroplane.

   d. The stick force per 'g' can only be corrected by means of electronic devices (stability augmentation) in the case of an unacceptable value.

20 At cruising speed an aircraft fitted with spoilers, inboard ailerons and outboard ailerons will use which of the following combinations?

   a. Inboard ailerons and spoilers.

   b. Inboard and outboard ailerons.

   c. Outboard ailerons only.

   d. Spoilers and outboard ailerons.

21 How does the exterior view of an aircraft change when trim is adjusted to maintain straight and level flight with speed decrease?

   a. No change

   b. Elevator up, trim tab down

   c. Elevator down, trim tab up

   d. Elevator changes due to horizontal stabiliser changing

22 What is pitch angle?

   a. The angle between the chord line and the horizontal plane.

   b. The angle between the longitudinal axis and the horizontal plane.

   c. The angle between the chord line and the longitudinal axis.

   d. The angle between the relative airflow and the longitudinal axis.

23 What is the location of mass balance weights?

   a. Always on the hinge line, irrespective of the type of aerodynamic balance

   b. On the hinge line if the control surface doe not have an inset hinge

   c. On the hinge line if the control surface has an inset hinge

   d. In front of the hinge line

24 Which of the following is the correct example of differential aileron deflection to initiate a left turn?

   a. Left aileron up 5 degrees, right aileron down 2 degrees

   b. Right aileron up 5 degrees, left aileron down 2 degrees

   c. Left aileron up 2 degrees, right aileron down 5 degrees

   d. Right aileron up 2 degrees, left aileron down 5 degrees

25 Which statement in respect to trim settings of a stabiliser is correct?

   a. With a nose heavy aeroplane, the stabiliser leading edge should be higher than for a tail heavy aeroplane.

   b. With a nose heavy aeroplane, the stabiliser leading edge should be lower than for a tail heavy aeroplane.

   c. With CG on the forward limit, the stabiliser should be fully adjusted nose down to obtain maximum elevator deflection at rotation during take-off.

   d. Since typical take-off speeds are independent of CG position, stabiliser settings are dependent only on flap setting.

26 Why does a transport aircraft with powered controls use a horizontal stabiliser trim?

   a. Pilot input is not subject to aerodynamic control forces

   b. Trim tabs are not effective enough

   c. Overly complex mechanism

   d. Trim tabs would increased Mcrit

27 An aircraft of 50 tonnes mass, with two engines each of 60,000 N Thrust and with an L/D ratio of 12:1 is in a straight steady climb. Taking 'g' to be 10 m/s/s, what is the climb gradient?

   a. 12%

   b. 24%

   c. 15.7%

   d. 3.7%

28 If lift in straight and level flight is 50,000 N, the lift of an aircraft in a constant altitude 45 degree bank would increase to?

   a. 50,000 N

   b. 60,000 N

   c. 70,000 N

   d. 80,000 N

29 In a straight steady descent:

   a. Lift is less than weight, load factor is equal to one

   b. Lift is less than weight, load factor is less than one

   c. Lift is equal to weight, load factor is equal to one

   d. Lift is equal to weight, load factor is less than one

30 Two aircraft of the same weight and under identical atmospheric conditions are flying level 20 degree bank turns. Aircraft 'A' is at 130 kt, aircraft 'B' is at 200 kt.

   a. The turn radius of 'A' will be greater than 'B'.

   b. The coefficient of lift of 'A' will be less than 'B'.

   c. The load factor of 'A' is greater than 'B'.

   d. Rate of turn of 'A' is greater than 'B'.

31 VMCL can be limited by: (i) engine failure during takeoff, (ii) maximum rudder deflection.

   a. Both (i) and (ii) are incorrect.

   b. (i) is incorrect and (ii) is correct.

   c. (i) is correct and (ii) is incorrect.

   d. Both (i) and (ii) are correct.

32 As Mach number increases at transonic speed, tuck under is caused by the CP moving (i) and downwash at the tail (ii):

   a. (i) aft, (ii) increasing

   b. (i) aft, (ii) decreasing

   c. (i) fwd, (ii) increasing

   d. (i) fwd, (ii) decreasing

33 The regime of flight from the critical Mach number (Mcrit) to approximately M1.3 is called?

   a. Transonic.

   b. Hypersonic.

   c. Subsonic.

   d. Supersonic.

34 The speed range between high and low speed buffet:

   a. decreases during a descent at a constant Mach number.

   b. is always positive at Mach numbers below MMO.

   c. increases during a descent at a constant IAS.

   d. increases during climb.

35 What happens to the local speed of sound of air passing through an expansion wave?

   a. Increase.

   b. Decrease.

   c. Remain the same.

   d. Decrease up to a certain Mach number and then increase.

36   What happens to the Mach number of the airflow as it passes through an expansion wave?

   a. Increase

   b. Constant

   c. Decrease

   d. Decreases then above a certain Mach number it will increase

37   Which of the following is required so the flight crew can determine the effects of compressibility?

   a. IAS

   b. TAS

   c. Mach number

   d. EAS

38   An aircraft is descending at a constant Mach number, which of the following operational speed limitations may be exceeded?

   a. VMO

   b. VNE

   c. MMO

   d. VD

39   An aircraft is in straight and level flight has a CL of 0.42 and a 1 degree increase in angle of attack would increase the CL by 0.1. Following a gust which increases the angle of attack by 3 degrees, what load factor would the aircraft be subject to?

   a. 1·7

   b. 0·7

   c. 1·4

   d. 1·0

PRINCIPLES OF FLIGHT — SPECIMEN QUESTIONS

40 Which of the following can effect VA?

    a. Mass and pressure altitude.

    b. Mass only.

    c. Pressure altitude only.

    d. It remains a constant IAS.

41 A single engine aircraft with a constant speed propeller is in a gliding descent with the engine idling, what would be the effect of increasing the propeller pitch?

    a. Increased L/Dmax, increased rate of descent

    b. Decreased L/Dmax, increased rate of descent

    c. Increased L/Dmax, decreased rate of descent

    d. Decreased L/Dmax, decreased rate of descent

42 A single engine aircraft with a constant speed propeller is in a gliding descent with the engine idling, what would be the effect of decreasing the propeller pitch?

    a. Increased L/Dmax, increased rate of descent.

    b. Decreased L/Dmax, increased rate of descent.

    c. Increased L/Dmax, decreased rate of descent.

    d. Decreased L/Dmax, decreased rate of descent.

43 The advantage of a constant speed propeller over a fixed pitch propeller is:

    a. higher maximum thrust available

    b. higher maximum efficiency

    c. more blade surface area available

    d. nearly maximum efficiency over wide speed range

44 With a clockwise rotating propeller (when viewed from the rear) at low forward speed, the propeller asymmetric blade effect will cause:

    a. roll to the left

    b. yaw to the left

    c. roll to the right

    d. yaw to the right

PRINCIPLES OF FLIGHT — SPECIMEN QUESTIONS

ANSWERS TO SPECIMEN EXAM PAPER

1.	A	27.	C
2.	C	28.	C
3.	B	29.	B
4.	A	30.	D
5.	B	31.	A
6.	C	32.	B
7.	C	33.	A
8.	D	34.	C
9.	C	35.	B
10.	D	36.	A
11.	D	37.	C
12.	B	38.	A
13.	A	39.	A
14.	B	40.	A
15.	A	41.	C
16.	B	42.	B
17.	A	43.	D
18.	A	44.	B
19.	B		
20.	A		
21.	B		
22.	B		
23.	D		
24.	A		
25.	B		
26.	B		

PRINCIPLES OF FLIGHT   SPECIMEN QUESTIONS

EXPLANATIONS TO SPECIMEN EXAM PAPER

Q 1
(a) If a mass is accelerated a force must have been applied. The kg is the SI unit for mass and m/s squared is the SI unit for acceleration. The applied force can be determined by multiplying the mass by the acceleration and the answer must use the SI unit for force - the Newton. (Page 1-5)

Q 2
(c) True Air Speed (TAS) is the relative velocity between the aircraft and undisturbed air which is close to, but unaffected by the presence of the aircraft. Changing the TAS (the speed of the aircraft through the air; the only speed there is) compensates for changes in air density and ensures a constant mass flow of air over the wing. If an altitude below ISA sea level is considered, the air density would be higher and therefore the TAS would have to be lower than IAS to compensate and keep Lift constant.

Q3
(b) Bernoulli's Theorem states: In the steady flow of an "ideal" fluid the sum of the pressure and kinetic energy per unit volume remains constant. Statement (i) is incorrect because the dynamic pressure in the throat of the venturi is higher than the free stream flow. Statement (ii) is correct.

Q 4
(a) Reference Para 4.1. The angle between the chord line and longitudinal axis is called the angle of incidence - which is fixed for a wing, but may be variable for the tailplane (horizontal stabiliser).

Q 5
(b) A rectangular wing of this chord and the same span would have broadly similar pitching moment characteristics. The MAC is a primary reference for longitudinal stability considerations. (Page 5-14 & 15).

Q 6
(c) Wing tip vortices are strongest with the aircraft in the clean configuration. With flaps down, the flaps generate their own vortices which interfere with and weaken the main, tip vortices. (Pages 5-18 to 21 and AIC 17/1999).

Q 7
(c) The "key" characteristic of a laminar boundary layer is that there is no flow normal to the surface.

Q 8
(d) Drag = 1/2 rho x V squared x CD x S (Page 6-5).

Q 9

(c) 'g' is the colloquial symbol for load factor. Load factor is the relationship between Lift and Weight. When an aircraft is banked in level flight, Lift must be greater than Weight and the relationship can be calculated by using the formula: L = 1/cos phi (where phi = bank angle). To calculated the stall speed in a 2g turn, multiply the 1g stall speed by the square root of 2, in this case 1.41. 100 x 1.41 = 141 kt. [It can be said that 'g' is the same as 1/cos phi]. (Page 7-26 to 28).

PRINCIPLES OF FLIGHT   SPECIMEN QUESTIONS

Q 10
(d) Refer to Paragraph 5.3.1 and Page 7-8. Stalling is caused by airflow separation. The amount of airflow separation is due to the relationship between the adverse pressure gradient and boundary layer kinetic energy. The adverse pressure gradient will increase if angle of attack is increased. A 1g stall occurs at the critical angle of attack (CLmax). A stall warning must begin with sufficient margin to prevent inadvertent stalling, so a stall warning device must also be sensitive to angle of attack. Therefore, a 1g stall will occur at the critical angle of attack and the stall warning will activate at an angle of attack which is slightly less. In 1g flight each angle of attack requires a particular IAS (dynamic pressure). An increase in weight will not alter the respective angles of attack, but will increase both the IAS at which the stall warning activates and the IAS at which the 1g stall occurs but the margin between them will remain essentially the same

Q 11
(d) Extended slats do not change CL or CD significantly, they do however increase CLmax and therefore give greater margin to the stall speed.

Q 12
(b) Reference Fig 8.22. Point 'A' to Point 'B' illustrates the wording of the question and it can be seen that CL must remain constant if IAS is constant and level flight is to be maintained as flaps are deployed, in order that the Lift remains the same as the Weight

Q 13
Negative Longitudinal static stability means the aircraft will be further displaced from equilibrium following removal of the original disturbing force. Therefore, over a period of time (Dynamic Stability) it can NEVER be Dynamically stable.

Q 14
(b) Paragraph 10.31 states: "When an aircraft is subject to a positive sideslip angle, lateral stability will be evident if a negative rolling moment coefficient results". It can be seen from Figure 10.57 that a positive sideslip angle is aeroplane nose left – right sideslip. Answer (b) is correct because the tendency of an aeroplane to roll to the left in a right sideslip is static lateral stability.

Q 15
To calculate stick force per 'g' it must be remembered that in straight and level flight the aircraft as at 1g. Therefore the increment is only 1.5g. 150 lb/g x 1.5 = 225 lb.

Q 16
Reference Page 10 - 58. Sideslip angle decreases the effective sweep on the wing 'into wind' and increases the effective sweep on the wing 'out of wind'.
Decreasing effective sweep angle increases Lift and therefore Induced Drag. This will give a positive contribution to Directional Static Stability - making (b) the only correct answer.

Q 17
Reference paragraph 10.32. Dihedral (Geometric) makes a powerful contribution to Lateral static stability. A wing mounted high on the fuselage gives a positive contribution the Lateral static dtability. Large wing span makes no contribution to Lateral static stability. A reduction in Dihedral will reduce Lateral static stability - as the definition of Geometric Dihedral is "The upward inclination of the plane of the wing from the horizontal. If the plane of the wing is angled below the horizontal, this will further decrease Lateral static stability and is known as Anhedral - making answer (a) correct.

PRINCIPLES OF FLIGHT   SPECIMEN QUESTIONS

Q 18
Reference paragraph 10.33 et seq. The relationship between Lateral Static and Directional Static Stability will determine which type of Dynamic instabilty the aircraft is most likely to exhibit.

If Static Lateral Stability is dominant, the extreme incrase in Lift on the wing into wind will also give a significant increase in Induced Drag. Thus, as the wing 'into wind' is accelerating upwards it will also be accelerating rearwards. By the time the aircraft has reached 'wings level' the other wing tip will be moving forward about the CG, which will increase its Lift and the aircraft will tend to roll back in the opposite direction and this process will continue and maybe diverge - this is Dutch Roll. Because the Lateral Static Stability is much 'stronger' than the Directional Static Stability, the fin is not able to prevent the yawing motion.

It is the DOMINANCE of Lateral over Directional that determines the likelyhood of Dutch Roll - therefore, decreased Directional Static Stability AND increased Lateral Static Stability will make Lateral Static Stability dominant and the aircraft susceptable to Dutch Roll.

If Static Lateral Stability is dominant, the aircraft will be susceptable to Spiral instability. This is because the fin will give a larger yawing and consequent rolling moment with the aircraft in a sideslip than the Lateral Static Stability is able to counter.
Similarly to the case of Dutch Roll - the aircraft can be more susceptable to Spiral Instability due to a decrease in Lateral Static Stability AND and increase in Directional Static Stability - it's the dominance that should be considered.

Q 19
(b) This question concerns stick force per 'g' – reference Paragraph 10.16. Tthere must be both an acceptable upper and lower limit to stick force. The illustrations of Figure 10.36 show the factors which affect the gradient of stick force per 'g' and the text highlights the requirements for any transport aircraft.

Q 20
Reference paragraphs 11.6.5, 7 and 8: At cruise speed the flaps will be up, which de-activates (locks-out) the outboard ailerons. Therefore, the inboard ailerons and the roll spoilers will operate, making (a) the only correct answer.

Q 21
There is only one tab that moves in the same direction as the control surface - the anti-balance tab, so a good general rule is that all tabs (except one) move in the opposite direction to the control surface.
The best approach to questions about controls and / or tabs is to first consider what you want the aeroplane to do. In this case, a speed decrease will generate a nose down pitching moment. To oppose this, the pilot need to increase back pressure on the pitch control. This moves the elevator up. To hold the elevator in this new position, the trim tab is moved down. Thus (b) is the only correct answer.

Q 22
(b) In this context, pitch angle is defined as: "the angle between the longitudinal axis and the horizontal plane". Pitch angle can also be referred to as "Body Angle" or as "The Pitch Attitude".

Q 23
Mass balance weights are used to prevent control surface flutter. Flutter is prevented by re-distributing the mass of the control surface to move its CG forward onto its hinge line. To accomplish the forward movement of control surface CG a mass balance weight is attached in front of the hinge line. This makes (d) the only possible answer.

PRINCIPLES OF FLIGHT				SPECIMEN QUESTIONS

Q 24
Differential ailerons are used to decrease adverse aileron yaw. Adverse aileron yaw is the result of increased Induced drag from the down-going aileron. A mechanism makes the down-going aileron move through a smaller angle than the up-going aileron.

Q 25
A nose heavy aeroplane is one in which a backward force on the pitch control is required to maintain level flight. To trim-out the backward stick force a down force on the tailplane is required. A trimming tailplane must have its incidence decreased (leading edge lowered) to generate the required tail downforce - making (b) the only correct answer.
Answer (c) is incorrect because one of the advantages of a trimming tailplane is that the effective pitch control is not influence by the amount of pitch trim used.
Answer (d) is incorrect because its statement is complete rubbish.

Q 26
Reference paragraph 11.10.4: Compared to a trim tab, the advantages of using a Variable Incidence Trimming Tailplane are that it is very powerful and gives an increased ability to trim for a larger speed and CG range, it reduces trim drag, and it does not reduce the 'effective' range of the pitch control. Answer (a) is incorrect because pilot input moves the elevator, not the trimming tailplane. Answer (c) is incorrect because its relative complexity is a disadvantage. Answer (d) is incorrect because Mcrit is not affected by trim tabs. Answer (b) is the only possible correct answer.

Q 27
(c) Paragraph 12.5 shows the forces and climb angle (gamma) in a steady climb. Climb gradient is the ratio of vertical height gained to horizontal distance travelled, expressed as a percentage. Trigonometrically, the tangent of the climb angle (gamma) will give climb gradient (tan = opp/adj), where 'opp' is the vertical height gained and 'adj' is the horizontal distance covered. Unfortunately these values are not provided in the question, or indeed in real life - so other values must be substituted and certain assumptions made in order to "calculate" the answer. Climb angle is the same as the angle between the Weight vector and W cos gamma. The 'adjacent' is W cos gamma or Lift and the 'opposite' is the backward component of Weight or W sin gamma. From the question Weight (50,000kg x 10 = 500,000N), Thrust (60,000N x 2 = 120,000N) and Drag (1/12 of Lift) are known or can be estimated. The value of Lift is not given, but we do know the Weight, so it has to be assumed that Lift and Weight are equal (at small climb angles [<20 degrees], although we know Lift is in fact less than Weight, for practical purposes the difference is insignificant). Therefore, the value of Lift is assumed to be 500,000N and the Drag to be 500,000N / 12 = 41667N. The formula for climb gradient is: Percentage Gradient = (T - D / W) x 100. i.e. Thrust minus Drag is the backward component of Weight or 'opp' and Weight is the 'hyp'. For small angles [<20 degrees] of climb or descent the length of the hypotenuse and adjacent are, for all practical purposes, the same; so the sine formula can be used and will give an answer which is accurate enough. We now have Thrust (120,000N) minus Drag (41667N) divided by Weight (500,000N) = 0.157 x 100 = 15.7% Climb Gradient.

Q 28
In level flight, Lift is a function of the bank angle. The formula is L = 1 / cos phi
In a 45 dgree bank the lift is increased by 1.41 (41%)
50,000N x 1.41 = 70500N, making (c) the correct answer.

PRINCIPLES OF FLIGHT   SPECIMEN QUESTIONS

Q 29
(b) Paragraph 12.6 shows Lift is less than Weight in a steady descent. Load factor is Lift Divided by Weight, but when the aircraft is in equilibrium in a steady descent the vertical force opposing the Weight is the Total Reaction. However, JAR 25.321 states: "Flight load factors represent the ratio of the aerodynamic force component (acting normal to the assumed longitudinal axis of the aeroplane) to the weight of the aeroplane". This clarifies the issue completely; such that in a steady descent Lift is less than Weight and the load factor is less than one. Load factor is useful when considering the loads applied to the aeroplane in flight. While the load factor will not be altered significantly in a steady descent, the concept holds true.

Q 30
(d) Refer to Paragraph 12.10. When considering turning, remind yourself first of the appropriate formulae – these help consolidate the variables.
1. L = 1 / cos phi reminds us that the only variable for Lift and hence load factor in a turn is bank angle.
2. The next two formulae must be considered together:
(a) Radius = V squared / g tan phi
(b) Rate = V / Radius

Q 31
(a) Reference Para 12.11.10: VMCL is the minimum IAS at which directional control can be maintained with the aircraft in the landing configuration, BUT with the added ability of being able to roll the aircraft from an initial condition of steady flight, through an angle of 20 degrees in the direction necessary to initiate a turn away from the inoperative engine(s), in not more than 5 seconds. VMCL is the "odd one out" among the VMC speeds for this reason. It can clearly be seen that neither statement is correct, making (a) the correct answer.

Q 32
The initial formation of a shockwave is on the top surface of the wing at the point of maximum local velocity - this is usually the thickest part of the wing, at the wing root. Shockwaves cause a localised reduction in CL. On a swept wing this gives a reduction in Lift forward of the CG and the CP will move aft. In addition, shockwave formation at the wing root reduces downwash at the tailplane. These factors together cause Mach Tuck, Tuck Under or High Speed Tuck (three names for the same phenomina).

Q 33
(a) Reference to Figure 13.2 will show that the speed region between Mcit and approximately M1.3 is called "Transonic".

Q 34
(c) Reference Para. 13.5 and 13.16: it can be seen that the speed range between high and low speed buffet decreases with increasing altitude.

Q 35
Speed of sound is proportional to temperature. The temperature decreases as it passes through an expansion wave, therefore the local speed of sound decreases.

Q 36
Mach number is proportional to TAS and inversely proportional to Local Speed of Sound. Through an expansion wave, velocity increases and temperature decreases. Therefore the Mach number of the airflow will increase.

PRINCIPLES OF FLIGHT — SPECIMEN QUESTIONS

Q 37
Compressibility, in this context, is the general term which refers to the effects on the aircraft when flying faster than approximately Mach 0.4. To determine the effects of compressibility the flight crew need to know the aircraft Mach number.

Q 38

Q 39

Q 40
(a) Reference Paragraph 14.7 and 10.15. For SMALL aircraft VA is the speed at the intersection of CLmax and the positive limit load factor and is dependant upon mass (which will affect the speed at which CLmax is achieved).
As this is the examination is for ATPL, LARGE aeroplanes (JAR 25) must be considered.
VA is defined as:- The highest speed at which sudden, full elevator deflection (nose up) can be made without exceeding the design limit load factor - making VA slower than the speed intersection of CLmax and the positive limit load factor. This is due to the effect of the tailplane moving downward when the aircraft is being pitched nose up increasing the effective angle of attack of the tailplane and increasing the load imposed on the whole aircraft. This is aerodynamic damping, which is a function of the tailplane vertical velocity and TAS. Therefore VA varies with both aircraft mass and pressure altitude.

Q 41
Reference Page 16 - 9 and 16 - 10: Increasing the propeller pitch, by pulling the propeller RPM control lever backwards to "Decrease RPM" will drive the blades towards the coarse pitch stop. This decreases the Parasite drag of the aeroplane, thus increasing L/Dmax and allowing a decreased rate od descent.

Q 42
(b) Ref. Paragraph 16.2. The key to answering this question successfully is an understanding of what is meant by "......decreasing the propeller pitch." Decreasing the propeller pitch is reducing the blade angle. This would increase the aircraft's Parasite area and Total Drag, which would decrease L/Dmax. Because of decreased L/Dmax the aircraft would have an increased rate of descent.

Q 43
(d) IAS is a measure of dynamic pressure, whereas TAS is the speed of the aircraft through the air. Changes in TAS are used to compensate for changes in air density to maintain a constant dynamic pressure. The lower the density, the higher the TAS must be to maintain a constant IAS. (Pages 2-4 to 2-9).

Q 44
Reference Paragraph 16.8.4: Asymmetric blade effect gives more thrust on the side with the down-going blade. With a clockwise rotating propeller, this gives a left turning moment.